Scott Foresman-Addison Wesley
enVisionMATH® Common Core

Authors

Randall I. Charles
Professor Emeritus
Department of Mathematics
San Jose State University
San Jose, California

Janet H. Caldwell
Professor of Mathematics
Rowan University
Glassboro, New Jersey

Mary Cavanagh
Executive Director of Center for Practice,
Research, and Innovation in Mathematics
Education (PRIME)
Arizona State University
Mesa, Arizona

Juanita Copley
Professor Emerita, College of Education
University of Houston
Houston, Texas

Warren Crown
Professor Emeritus of Mathematics Education
Graduate School of Education
Rutgers University
New Brunswick, New Jersey

Francis (Skip) Fennell
L. Stanley Bowlsbey Professor of Education and
Graduate and Professional Studies
McDaniel College
Westminster, Maryland

Stuart J. Murphy
Visual Learning Specialist
Boston, Massachusetts

Kay B. Sammons
Coordinator of Elementary Mathematics
Howard County Public Schools
Ellicott City, Maryland

Jane F. Schielack
Professor of Mathematics
Associate Dean for Assessment and
Pre K-12 Education, College of Science
Texas A&M University
College Station, Texas

William Tate
Edward Mallinckrodt Distinguished University
Professor in Arts & Sciences
Washington University
St. Louis, Missouri

Mathematicians

David M. Bressoud
DeWitt Wallace Professor of Mathematics
Macalester College
St. Paul, Minnesota

Roger Howe
Professor of Mathematics
Yale University
New Haven, Connecticut

Gary Lippman
Professor of Mathematics and Computer Science
California State University East Bay
Hayward, California

PEARSON

Glenview, Illinois • Boston, Massachusetts • Chandler, Arizona • Upper Saddle River, New Jersey

Consulting Author

Grant Wiggins
Researcher and Educational Consultant
Hopewell, New Jersey

ELL Consultant

Jim Cummins
Professor
The University of Toronto
Toronto, Canada

Common Core State Standards Reviewers

Elizabeth Baker
Mathematics Coordinator
Gilbert Public Schools
Gilbert, Arizona

Amy Barber
K-12 Math Coach
Peninsula School District ESC
Gig Harbor, Washington

Laura Cua
Teacher
Columbus City Schools
Columbus, Ohio

Wafa Deeb-Westervelt
Assistant Superintendent for
Curriculum, Instruction, and
Professional Development
Freeport Public Schools
Freeport, New York

Lynn Gullette
Title 1 Math Intervention
Mobile County Public Schools
Gilliard Elementary
Mobile, Alabama

Beverly K. Kimes
Director of Mathematics
Birmingham City Schools
Birmingham, Alabama

Kelly O'Rourke
Elementary School Assistant Principal
Clark County School District
Las Vegas, Nevada

Piper L. Riddle
Evidence-Based Learning Specialist
Canyons School District
Sandy, Utah

Debra L. Vitale
Math Coach
Bristol Public Schools
Bristol, Connecticut

Diane T. Wehby
Math Support Teacher
Birmingham City Schools
Birmingham, Alabama

Scott Foresman·Addison Wesley
enVisionMATH®
Common Core

ISBN-13: 978-0-328-67264-6
ISBN-10: 0-328-67264-5

10 V057 15 14

Grade 6 Topic Titles

Grade 6 Contents

Common Core

Standards for Mathematical Practice

- ☑ Make sense of problems and persevere in solving them.
- ☑ Reason abstractly and quantitatively.
- ☑ Construct viable arguments and critique the reasoning of others.
- ☑ Model with mathematics.
- ☑ Use appropriate tools strategically.
- ☑ Attend to precision.
- ☑ Look for and make use of structure.
- ☑ Look for and express regularity in repeated reasoning.

Grade 6 Domain Colors

● **Domain: The Number System**
  Topics: 1, 3, 5, 6, 7, 8, 9, and 10

● **Domain: Expressions and Equations**
  Topics: 2, 4, and 15

● **Domain: Geometry**
  Topics: 11, 17, and 18

● **Domain: Ratios and Proportional Relationships**
  Topics: 12, 13, 14, and 16

● **Domain: Statistics and Probability**
  Topic: 19

Standards for Mathematical Content

Domain
The Number System

Cluster
• Compute fluently with multi-digit numbers and find common factors and multiples.

Standards
6.NS.3, 6.EE.1

Lessons in this topic reinforce concepts and skills required for Topic 3.

Topic 1 Numeration

Topic 6 Decimals, Fractions, and Mixed Numbers

Standards for Mathematical Content

Domain

The Number System

Cluster

- Compute fluently with multi-digit numbers and find common factors and multiples.

Standard

6.NS.3

Lessons in this topic reinforce concepts and skills required for Topic 9.

Topic 7 Adding and Subtracting Fractions and Mixed Numbers

Standards for Mathematical Content

Domain

The Number System

Cluster

- Compute fluently with multi-digit numbers and find common factors and multiples.

Standards

6.NS.4, 6.RP.1

Lessons in this topic reinforce concepts and skills required for Topic 9.

Step-Up lessons preview forthcoming standards.

Step-Up lessons preview forthcoming standards.

Step-Up lessons preview forthcoming standards.

Problem-Solving Handbook

Use this Problem-Solving Handbook throughout the year to help you solve problems.

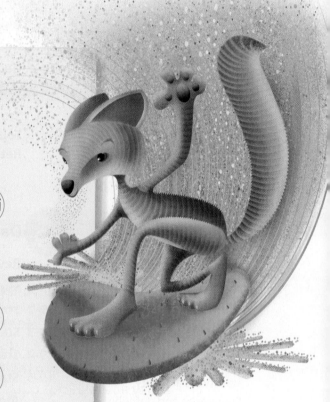

Don't give up!

Everybody can be a good problem solver!

There's almost always more than one way to solve a problem!

Don't trust key words.

Pictures help me understand!

Explaining helps me understand!

Problem-Solving Process

MATHEMATICAL PRACTICES

Read and Understand

© Answer these questions to make sense of problems.

❓ **What am I trying to find?**
- Tell what the question is asking.

❓ **What do I know?**
- Tell the problem in my own words.
- Identify key facts and details.

Plan and Solve

© Choose an appropriate tool.

❓ **What strategy or strategies should I try?**

❓ **Can I show the problem?**
- Try drawing a picture.
- Try making a list, table, or graph.
- Try acting it out or using objects.

❓ **How will I solve the problem?**

❓ **What is the answer?**
- Tell the answer in a complete sentence.

Strategies
- Show What You Know
- Draw a Picture
- Make an Organized List
- Make a Table
- Make a Graph
- Act It Out/ Use Objects
- Look for a Pattern
- Try, Check, Revise
- Write an Equation
- Use Reasoning
- Work Backward
- Solve a Simpler Problem

Look Back and Check

© Give precise answers.

❓ **Did I check my work?**
- Compare my work to the information in the problem.
- Be sure all calculations are correct.

❓ **Is my answer reasonable?**
- Estimate to see if my answer makes sense.
- Make sure the question was answered.

Using Bar Diagrams

Ⓒ Bar diagrams are tools that will help you understand and solve word problems. Bar diagrams show how the quantities in a problem are related.

Problem 1

The Sports Club has $167.75 from advanced sales of tickets to a basketball game. The sales at the door were $228.75. What is the total ticket sales for the game?

Bar Diagram

TOTAL: →
Total amount of ticket sales for the game

?

| $167.75 | $228.75 |

PART:
Amount of advanced ticket sales

PART:
Amount of ticket sales at the door

$167.75 + $228.75 = ▩

 Think I can add to find the total.

Problem 2

Lourdes ran 15.25 miles in the first week of practice. She ran 20.75 miles the second week. How much farther did she run the second week than the first week?

15.25 mi

20.75 mi

Bar Diagram

TOTAL: →
The greater distance that Lourdes ran

20.75 mi

| 15.25 mi | ? |

PART:
The lesser distance that she ran

PART:
The difference between the two distances

20.75 − 15.25 = ▩

 Think I can subtract to find the missing part.

Pictures help me
understand!

Don't trust
key words!

Problem 3

Each stack in a warehouse has 4 boxes piled on top of one another. Each box is 2.5 feet high. How tall is each stack?

Problem 4

Juan, Luke, and Jordan have $4\frac{1}{2}$ sandwiches to share. How much sandwich should each boy get?

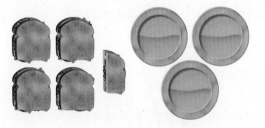

Bar Diagram

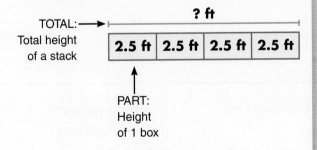

TOTAL: →
Total height
of a stack

? ft

| 2.5 ft | 2.5 ft | 2.5 ft | 2.5 ft |

PART:
Height
of 1 box

$$2.5 \times 4 = \blacksquare$$

 Think I can multiply because the parts are equal.

Bar Diagram

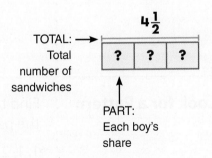

$4\frac{1}{2}$

TOTAL: →
Total
number of
sandwiches

| ? | ? | ? |

PART:
Each boy's
share

$$4\frac{1}{2} \div 3 = \blacksquare$$

 Think I can divide to find how many are in each part.

Problem-Solving Strategies

© These are tools for understanding and solving problems.

Strategy	Example	When I Use It
Draw a Picture	How many lines of symmetry does the hexagon below have?	Try drawing a picture when it helps you visualize the problem or when the relationships such as joining or separating are involved.
Make a Table	What is the least common multiple of 5 and 6? 	Try making a table when: • there are 2 or more quantities, • amounts change using a pattern.
Look for a Pattern	Find the next three numbers in the pattern. 1, 1, 2, 3, 5, 8, ?, ?, ? $1 + 1 = 2$ The sum of the first two numbers $1 + 2 = 3$ The sum of the second and third number $2 + 3 = 5$ The sum of the third and fourth number	Look for a pattern when something repeats in a predictable way.

Table for Make a Table example:

Multiples of 5	5	10	15	20	25	**30**
Multiples of 6	6	12	18	24	**30**	36

Strategy	Example	When I Use It
Make an Organized List	Jimmy is designing a sweatshirt for his club's sports team. The club voted to have 4 horizontal stripes that are red, blue, white, and green. How many ways can he arrange the stripes?	Make an organized list when asked to find combinations of two or more items.
Try, Check, Revise	Madison glued 3 boards end-to-end to make an 11-foot board. What boards did she use? **Board Lengths** $5\frac{1}{4}$ ft, $4\frac{1}{4}$ ft, $3\frac{3}{4}$ ft, $2\frac{1}{2}$ ft, $1\frac{1}{2}$ ft $$5\frac{1}{4} \text{ ft} + 2\frac{1}{2} \text{ ft} + 4\frac{1}{4} \text{ ft} = 12 \text{ ft}$$ $$5\frac{1}{4} \text{ ft} + 1\frac{1}{2} \text{ ft} + 4\frac{1}{4} \text{ ft} = 11 \text{ ft}$$	Use Try, Check, Revise when quantities are being combined to find a total, but you don't know which quantities.
Write an Equation	Tyler sold 3 old video games online for $5.19 each. He wants to buy a new game for $39.99. Not including shipping or tax, how much more money does he need? Find $39.99 - (3 \times 5.19) = n$.	Write an equation when the story describes a situation that uses an operation or operations.

Even More Strategies

© These are more tools for understanding and solving problems.

Strategy	Example	When I Use It
Act It Out	Ari is using centimeter cubes to make a structure. How many cubes will Ari need to make the 8 rows of the structure? $1 + 3 + 5 + \ldots$	Think about acting out a problem when the numbers are small and there is action in the problem you can do.
Use Reasoning	In May, 4 out of every 10 animals in the animal shelter were adopted. What fraction of the animals were not adopted?	Use reasoning when you can use known information to reason out unknown information.
Work Backward	Finn went to the festival and paid $3.50 for admission. At the festival he bought a hat and a T-shirt for $11.00. He had $15.00 when he left the festival. How much did he have when he arrived? $? when he arrived ←$3.50— $? after he paid for admission ←$11.00— **$15.00** when he left	Try working backward when: • you know the end result of a series of steps, • you want to know what happened at the beginning.

MATHEMATICAL **PRACTICES**

Strategy	Example	When I Use It
Solve a Simpler Problem	A soccer tournament involves 12 teams. In the first round, each team plays one game against each other team. How many games were played in the first round? Look at the games played by smaller numbers of teams. **2 teams** A–B, 1 game **3 teams** A–B, A–C, B–C 3 games **4 teams** A–B, A–C, A–D, B–C, B–D, C–D 6 games	Try solving a simpler problem when you can create a simpler case that is easier to solve.
Make a Graph	Miguel and his class travel to school by walking, taking the school bus, riding bikes, or getting driven by car. How do the modes of transportation change depending on the month of the year? **Travel to School** *bar graph showing Number of Students (0–60) vs Mode of Transportation (Bus, Walk, Bike, Car) with May and Jan data*	Make a graph when: • data for a survey are given, • the question can be answered by reading the graph.

Writing to Explain

© Good written explanations communicate your reasoning to others. Here is a good math explanation.

Writing to Explain Find the next three numbers in this pattern: 1.21, 1.32, 1.43, 1.54.

I see that the first digit is always 1 followed by a decimal point. So, I'll write 1 followed by a decimal point as the first digit in my numbers.

1.　　1.　　1.

The second digit starts with 2 and goes up by 1 each time. So, I'll start with 6 and go up by one each time.

1.6　　1.7　　1.8

The third digit starts with 1 and goes up by 1 each time. So, I'll start with 5 and go up by 1 each time.

1.65　　1.76　　1.87

So 1.65, 1.76, and 1.87 are the next three numbers in the pattern.

Tips for Writing Good Math Explanations ...

A good explanation should be:
- correct
- simple
- complete
- easy to understand

Math explanations can use:
- words
- pictures
- numbers
- symbols

Explaining helps me understand!

Problem-Solving Recording Sheet

© This helps you organize your work and make sense of problems.

Name _Lin_   Teaching Tool
                                                                    1

Problem-Solving Recording Sheet

Problem:
What are the dimensions of a rectangle whose perimeter is 24 inches and whose area is 32 square inches?

Find?
Dimensions of a rectangle

Know?
Perimeter is 24 in.
Area is 32 sq. in.

Strategies?
Show the Problem
- ☑ Draw a Picture
- ☐ Make an Organized List
- ☐ Make a Table
- ☐ Make a Graph
- ☐ Act It Out/Use Objects

- ☐ Look for a Pattern
- ☑ Try, Check, Revise
- ☐ Write an Equation
- ☑ Use Reasoning
- ☐ Work Backwards
- ☐ Solve a Simpler Problem

Show the Problem?

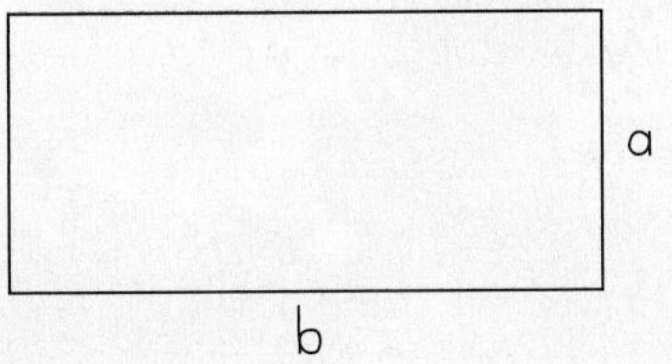

[rectangle diagram with side labels a and b]

$P = 2(a + b) = 24$ in.
$A = a \times b = 32$ sq. in.

Solution?
If $P = 2(a + b) = 24$, then I know that $a + b = 12$. I'll try pairs of numbers that add to 12 and then multiply them to find the products. When I see 32, I am done.

1 + 11 = 12	1 × 11 = 11
2 + 10 = 12	2 × 10 = 20
3 + 9 = 12	3 × 9 = 27
4 + 8 = 12	4 × 8 = 32 correct!

Answer?
The dimensions are 4 in. and 8 in.

Check? Reasonable?
Perimeter: $2(4 + 8) = 2 \times 12 = 24$. $P = 24$ in.
Area: $4 \times 8 = 32$. $A = 32$ sq. in.
So my answer is correct.

Problem-Solving Recording Sheet **1**

Topic 1

Numeration

1 How high can the Helios Prototype airplane fly in comparison to other aircraft? You will find out in Lesson 1-2.

2 Coral Reefs are formed by tiny marine animals, known as coral polyps, that live in colonies. About how many coral polyps could form 1 square foot of coral reef? You will find out in Lesson 1-5.

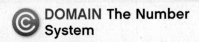

3 The Milky Way Galaxy may have about 200 billion stars. How do you write very large numbers such as this? You will find out in Lesson 1-1.

Review What You Know!

Vocabulary

Choose the best term from the box.

- place
- decimal point
- digits

1. A period placed in a number to separate whole number values from values less than one is called a __?__.

2. The value of the position of any digit in a number is called its __?__.

3. The symbols used to write numbers 0, 1, 2, 3, 4, 5, 6, 7, 8, and 9 are __?__.

Writing Numbers

Write each word form in standard form.

4. nineteen   5. thirty-seven

6. three hundred   7. two thousand
   five   twelve

8. forty thousand   9. one hundred
                        thousand

Write the word form of each number.

10. 49   11. 112   12. 10,465

Decimals

© **Writing to Explain** Write an answer for the question.

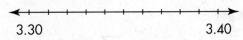

3.30   3.40

13. How would you locate 3.33 on the number line? Explain.

Lesson
1-1

Common Core

This lesson reinforces concepts and skills required for Topic 3.

Place Value

How can you read very large numbers?

In astronomy, a light-year is the distance that light can travel in one year. One light-year is equal to about 9,500,000,000,000 kilometers. Use a place-value chart to help you find the value of the digit 9 and read the number.

> Earth is this far from the Sun.

Another Example **What are different ways to write very large numbers?**

A place-value chart can help you write a very large number, such as 44,600,000,000, in different forms.

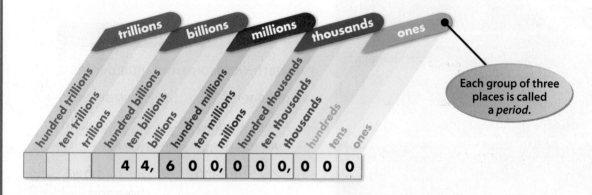

> Each group of three places is called a *period*.

Standard form: 44,600,000,000

Word form: forty-four billion, six hundred million

Short word form: 44 billion, 600 million

Expanded form: 40,000,000,000 + 4,000,000,000 + 600,000,000 **or**
(4 × 10,000,000,000) + (4 × 1,000,000,000) + (6 × 100,000,000)

Explain It

1. What is the relationship between the commas in a number and the periods in a place-value chart?

2. In the example above, how do you know what the addends are for a number written in expanded form?

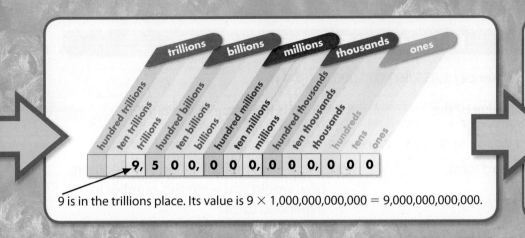

trillions | billions | millions | thousands | ones

hundred trillions · ten trillions · trillions · hundred billions · ten billions · billions · hundred millions · ten millions · millions · hundred thousands · ten thousands · thousands · hundreds · tens · ones

9, 5 0 0, 0 0 0, 0 0 0, 0 0 0

9 is in the trillions place. Its value is $9 \times 1,000,000,000,000 = 9,000,000,000,000$.

You can use the word form to read the number.

Word form: nine trillion, five hundred billion

Guided Practice*

 MATHEMATICAL PRACTICES

Do you know **HOW?**

In **1** through **4**, write the place and value of the underlined digit.

1. 1,2<u>3</u>4,567

2. <u>9</u>,870,563,142,000

3. 36,1<u>9</u>2,748

4. <u>8</u>2,765,432,109,497

In **5** and **6**, write each number in the form indicated.

5. 57,000,000,009 in expanded form

6. 321 trillion, 705 thousand in standard form

Do you **UNDERSTAND?**

7. How do you use periods to read and write very large numbers?

8. In the example at the top, how would you write the number in expanded form?

© **9.** **Reason** When writing 136,000,000 in expanded form, why would you skip the hundred thousands, ten thousands, thousands, hundreds, tens, and ones?

Independent Practice

In **10** through **12**, write the place and value of the digit 3 in each number?

10. 3,476

11. 384,400

12. 5,437,200,184,400

In **13** through **15**, write each number in short-word form.

13. 18,429,000,050,000

14. 10,007,000,000,000

15. 8,507,004,041

DIGITAL · Animated Glossary · www.pearsonsuccessnet.com

*For another example, see Set A on page 28.

For **16** through **19**, use the number 1,435,600,000,000.

16. What is the place and value of the digit 5?

17. What is the value of the digit 3?

18. Write the number in word form.

19. Using both multiplication and addition, how would you write this number in expanded form?

Problem Solving

MATHEMATICAL **PRACTICES**

© **20. Reason** How do you write the number of stars in the Milky Way Galaxy in standard form?

The Milky Way galaxy is thought to have about 200 billion stars.

© **21. Writing to Explain** Describe how you would use the standard form of a number to write the short-word form.

In a recent year, the country of Ecuador used an estimated 15,850,000,000 kilowatt hours of electricity. Use this information to answer **22** through **24**.

22. What is the value of each non-zero digit in the number?

23. From left to right, what is the place of the second 5 in this number?

  A trillions

  B hundred millions

  C ten millions

  D hundred thousands

24. At this rate, about how many kilowatt hours of electricity might Ecuador use over a 10-year period?

  A 160 million

  B 160 billion

  C 16 trillion

  D 160 trillion

25. Which of these numbers represents seventy-six trillion, two hundred seven thousand?

  A 76,000,000,207,000

  B 76,000,000,007,200

  C 76,000,207,000,000

  D 76,000,207,000

26. Which of these numbers is ten million more than three billion, four hundred twenty-nine million?

  A 3,419,000,000,000

  B 3,439,000,000,000

  C 3,419,000,000

  D 3,439,000,000

Mixed Problem Solving

Ancient Civilizations in Today's World

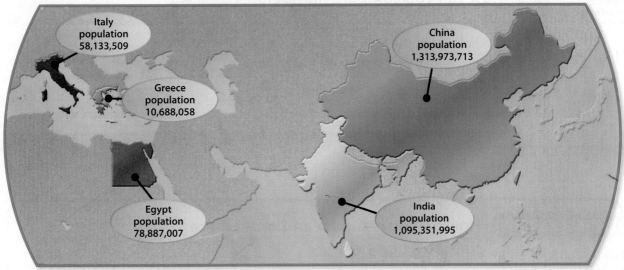

Italy
population
58,133,509

Greece
population
10,688,058

China
population
1,313,973,713

Egypt
population
78,887,007

India
population
1,095,351,995

Use the estimated populations shown on the map above to answer **1** through **10**.

1. Which countries have a population in the billions?

2. Which value does the digit 1 have in Greece's population?

3. Which places does the digit 3 occupy in China's population?

4. Which country has a population close to 80 million?

5. Which countries have a population between ten million and one hundred million?

6. Draw a place-value chart to show the place and value of each of the digits in India's population.

Tip *You might want to use a calculator to do calculations with very large numbers.*

7. Which country has the least population? How much less is its population than the greatest population shown?

8. How many people would India need to gain for its population to equal that of China?

9. In a recent year, the population of Italy's capital, Rome, was about 2,553,873. About how many times larger was Italy's population than the population of Rome?

10. It is projected that China's population will increase approximately 20% by 2025. Approximately how many more people will China have?

    A 130,000,000   **C** 260,000,000

    B 89,000,000   **D** 3,190,000,000

Common
Core

This lesson reinforces
concepts and skills required
for Topic 3.

Comparing and Ordering Whole Numbers

How can you compare numbers?

Use the data in the table to compare the heights of the buildings. Which is taller, the Petronas Towers or the Willis Tower?

Tall Buildings	Height (ft)
Jin Mao Tower	1,380
Taipei 101	1,670
Petronas Towers	1,483
Willis Tower	1,450

Another Example How do you compare and order more than two numbers?

Order the heights of the buildings in the above table from least to greatest.

Step 1

Write the numbers, lining up the places. Compare the digits.

1,483

1,380 → least

1,670 → greatest

1,450

Step 2

Write the remaining numbers, lining up the places. Compare.

1,483 → greater

1,450

Step 3

Order the numbers and the heights of the buildings from least to greatest.

1,380; 1,450; 1,483; 1,670

Jin Mao Tower, Willis Tower, Petronas Towers, Taipei 101

Guided Practice*

MATHEMATICAL PRACTICES

Do you know HOW?

In **1** and **2**, use < or > to compare.

1. 27,318 ◯ 28,001

2. 1,000,001 ◯ 1,000,010

In **3**, order the numbers from least to greatest.

3. 3,964   4,160   3,395   4,000

Do you UNDERSTAND?

© **4. Persevere** In the example at the top, where do you begin comparing digits?

5. Two International Finance Centre is 1,362 feet tall. Use the table above to find which is taller, Two International Finance Centre or the Jin Mao Tower?

Step 1

Write the numbers in a column to line up the places.

1,483
1,450

Compare the digits from left to right.

Step 2

Find the first place where the digits are different.

1,483
1,450

Use > or < to compare.

8 > 5

So, 1,483 > 1,450.

Step 3

Write your answer.

1,483 > 1,450

or

1,450 < 1,483

The Petronas Towers are taller than the Willis Tower.

Independent Practice

For **6** through **8**, use < or > to compare.

6. 8,867 ◯ 8,896   **7.** 102,086 ◯ 100,266   **8.** 5,743,834 ◯ 5,745,618

For **9** and **10**, order the numbers from least to greatest.

Tip *Compare each place from left to right.*

9. 85,634; 86,364; 86,446; 68,989   **10.** 4,088,777; 4,221,000; 4,202,006

For **11** and **12**, order the numbers from greatest to least.

11. 400 billion; 857 thousand; 3 trillion   **12.** 5,743,834; 5,754,618; 5,900,962

Problem Solving

MATHEMATICAL PRACTICES

© 13. Writing to Explain The SR-71 spy plane can fly at an altitude of 85,000 feet. Explain how you would compare this altitude with the altitude of the Helios shown below. Tell which plane could fly higher.

14. When comparing 1,290 km and 1,130 km, which place do you use to determine which number is greater?

© 15. Reason Which measurement of this rectangular vegetable garden has the greatest value?

A length

B width

C perimeter

D length + width

40 ft

30 ft

SR-71 spy plane

The Helios Prototype flew to an altitude of 96,863 ft.

Common
Core

6.EE.1 Write and evaluate
numerical expressions
involving whole-number
exponents.

Exponents and Place Value

How can you write a number using exponents?

Each place in a place-value chart has a value that is 10 times as great as the place to its right. Use this pattern to write 1,000,000 as repeated multiplication.

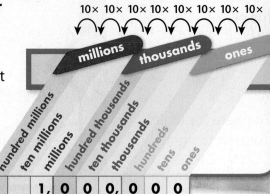

Another Example How do you write the expanded form of a number using exponents?

Standard form: 562,384

Expanded form: $(5 \times 100{,}000) + (6 \times 10{,}000) + (2 \times 1{,}000) + (3 \times 100) +$
$(8 \times 10) + (4 \times 1)$

Expanded form using exponents: $(5 \times 10^5) + (6 \times 10^4) + (2 \times 10^3) + (3 \times 10^2) + (8 \times 10^1) + (4 \times 10^0)$

Any number raised to the first power always equals that number. $10^1 = 10$

Explain It

1. How many times is 9 used as a factor in the exponent 9^8?

2. Why does $3 \times 10^0 = 3$?

Other Examples

Write each in exponential form.

$36 = 6 \times 6 = 6^2$ 6^2 is read as six squared.

$10 \times 10 \times 10 = 10^3$ 10^3 is read as ten cubed.

Evaluate numbers in exponential form.

$5^3 = 5 \times 5 \times 5 = 125$ $3^4 = 3 \times 3 \times 3 \times 3 = 81$

10 is used as a factor six times.

$1{,}000{,}000 = 10 \times 10 \times 10 \times 10 \times 10 \times 10$

You can write <u>the repeated multiplication of a number</u> in exponential form.

$1{,}000{,}000 = 10^6$

The base is the <u>number that is repeatedly multiplied</u>.

The exponent or power is the <u>number of times the base is used as a factor</u>.

Each place in the place-value chart can be written using an exponent.

Value	Exponential Form
100,000	10^5
10,000	10^4
1,000	10^3
100	10^2
10	10^1
1	10^0

Guided Practice*

 MATHEMATICAL PRACTICES

Do you know HOW?

1. Write 10,000 as repeated multiplication of 10s.

2. Write $7 \times 7 \times 7 \times 7$ in exponential form.

3. Write 37,169 in expanded form using exponents.

4. Write 5^3 in standard form.

Do you UNDERSTAND?

5. In the example at the top, why was the number 10 used as the base to write 1,000,000 in exponential form?

 6. **Reasonableness** How many times would 10 be used as a factor to equal 100,000?

7. How many zeros are in 10^7 when it is written in standard form?

Independent Practice

Leveled Practice What number is the base?

8. 4^9

9. 17^6

What number is the exponent?

10. 31^9

11. 2^{100}

Write each as a power of 10.   **Tip** *Count the number of zeros in each number.*

12. 1,000

13. 1,000,000,000

14. $10 \times 10 \times 10 \times 10 \times 10$

Write each number in expanded form using exponents.

15. 841

16. 5,832

17. 1,874,161

18. 22,600,000

Evaluate **19** through **22**.

19. $6^2 =$ ▨

20. $10^8 =$ ▨

21. $4^3 =$ ▨

22. $2^7 =$ ▨

Animated Glossary
www.pearsonsuccessnet.com

*For another example, see Set B on page 28.

23. The population of one U.S. state is approximately 33,871,648. What is this number in expanded form using exponents?

24. Reason What number raised to both the first power and the second power equals 1?

25. Writing to Explain Explain how to compare 2^5 and 5^2.

26. In Exercise 23, what is the place of the digit 7?

   A hundreds

   B thousands

   C ten thousands

   D millions

27. Critique Reasoning Kalesha was asked to write 80,808 in expanded form using exponents. Her response was $(8 \times 10^2) + (8 \times 10^1) + (8 \times 10^0)$. Explain where she made mistakes and write the correct response.

28. Think About the Structure You invest $1 in a mutual fund. Every 8 years, your money doubles. If you don't add more money, which expression shows how much your investment is worth after 48 years?

   A 1^{48}

   B $1 \times 2 \times 2 \times 2 \times 2 \times 2$

   C $1 + 2 + 2 + 2 + 2 + 2 + 2$

   D $1 \times 2 \times 2 \times 2 \times 2 \times 2 \times 2$

29. Using the map, write the population of the United States in expanded form using exponents.

30. Model In 1900, there were 76,803,887 people in the United States. How many more people were there in the United States 100 years after 1900?

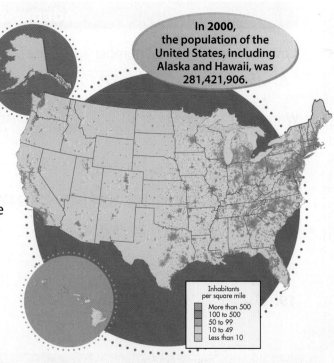

In 2000, the population of the United States, including Alaska and Hawaii, was 281,421,906.

Inhabitants per square mile
More than 500
100 to 500
50 to 99
10 to 49
Less than 10

Algebra Connections

Solution Pairs

An equation is a mathematical sentence that uses an equals sign to show that two expressions are equal. Any values that make an equation true are solutions to the equation.

An inequality is a mathematical sentence that contains $<$, $>$, $\leq$, or $\geq$. Any value that makes the inequality true is a solution. You can graph the solutions of an inequality on a number line.

 Tip *Read $\geq$ as "is greater than or equal to."*
Read $\leq$ as "is less than or equal to."

Example: Find two values for each variable that make the equation, $y = x + 3$, true.

If $x = 1$, then $y = 1 + 3 = 4$ is true.
If $x = 5$, then $y = 5 + 3 = 8$ is true.
(1, 4) and (5, 8) are solution pairs.

Example: Graph three values that make the inequality, $x > 3$, true.

$x = 3.1$, $x = 4$, $x = 5$

Draw a number line. Plot three points that are greater than 3.

For **1** through **4**, copy the table and find two values for each variable that make the equation true.

1. $y = 4 + x$

x		
y		

2. $b = a - 2$

a		
b		

3. $t = 3w$

w		
t		

4. $y = x \div 2$

x		
y		

5. Copy the number line and graph three values that make the inequality, $d \geq 9$, true.

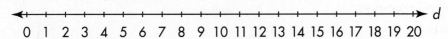

6. Copy the number line and graph three values that make the inequality, $\frac{x}{3} < 4$, true.

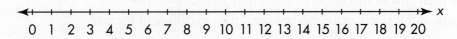

Decimal Place Value

How can you read very small decimal numbers?

One gallon equals 3.7854 liters. How do you read this number?

A decimal is <u>a number that uses a decimal point and has one or more digits to the right of the decimal point.</u>

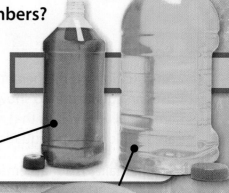

One bottle is filled with exactly 1 liter.

The other bottle is filled with exactly 1 gallon.

Another Example **What are different ways to write decimals?**

The atomic mass of the chemical chromium is 51.9961.
Use a place-value chart to write the decimal in different forms.

tens	ones		tenths	hundredths	thousandths	ten thousandths
5	1	.	9	9	6	1

Standard form: 51.9961

Short-word form: 51 and 9,961 ten thousandths

Word form: fifty-one and nine thousand nine hundred sixty-one ten thousandths

Expanded form: $(5 \times 10) + (1 \times 1) + (9 \times 0.1) + (9 \times 0.01) + (6 \times 0.001) + (1 \times 0.0001) =$
$50 + 1 + 0.9 + 0.09 + 0.006 + 0.0001$

Explain It

1. What is the purpose of the decimal point in a decimal number?

2. If the first digit to the right of the decimal was changed to "0" in the number above, how would you write the new number in different forms?

Use a place-value chart to help you read a decimal.

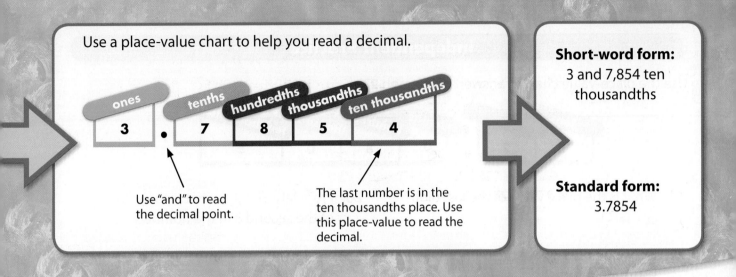

ones		tenths	hundredths	thousandths	ten thousandths
3	.	7	8	5	4

Use "and" to read the decimal point.

The last number is in the ten thousandths place. Use this place-value to read the decimal.

Short-word form:
3 and 7,854 ten thousandths

Standard form:
3.7854

Guided Practice*

MATHEMATICAL
PRACTICES

Do you know HOW?

In **1** through **4**, write the place and value of the underlined digit.

1. 17.00<u>1</u>

2. 987.654<u>2</u>

3. 14.9<u>2</u>84

4. 7.291<u>6</u>

In **5** through **7**, write the number in the form indicated.

5. 1.5629 in word form

6. 568.0101 in short-word form

7. 27.6003 in expanded form

Do you UNDERSTAND?

© **8. Communicate** How do you use a decimal point to read and write very small numbers?

9. In the example at the top of the page, how do you know that 0.005 is the value of the digit 5?

© **10. Be Precise** What is the decimal portion of 63.029? What is the whole number portion?

Independent Practice

 All digits to the left of the decimal point are whole numbers, and all digits to the right of the decimal point are decimals.

Write the place and value of the underlined digit.

11. 1,957.0<u>1</u>

12. 647.47<u>6</u>

13. 84.<u>4</u>8

14. 327.0<u>0</u>94

15. 0.05<u>2</u>1

16. 78.<u>6</u>67

17. <u>3</u>.016

18. 8.591<u>4</u>

DIGITAL Animated Glossary
www.pearsonsuccessnet.com

Use the place-value chart to answer **19** through **23**.

tens	ones		tenths	hundredths	thousandths	ten thousandths
2	2	.	9	8	0	8

19. What is the place value of the last digit?

20. From left to right, what is the value of the second 8 in the number?

21. How would you write the number in short-word form?

22. How would you write the number in word form?

23. How would you write the number in expanded form?

MATHEMATICAL
PRACTICES

ⓒ **24.** **Persevere** Write a decimal that has the digit 9 in the tenths place and the ten thousandths place.

ⓒ **25.** **Writing to Explain** What would happen if you removed the decimal point from a number?

Use this data table to answer items **26** through **29**.

Downhill Skiing Records	
Old Record	New Record
154.165 mph	154.25 mph

26. Which place do you use to tell that the new record is faster?

   A tens   **B** tenths   **C** hundreds   **D** thousandths

27 Which is the word form of the new record?

   A one hundred fifty-four and one hundred sixty-five thousandths

   B one hundred fifty-four and twenty-five thousandths

   C one hundred fifty-four and twenty-five hundredths

   D one hundred fifty-four

ⓒ **28.** **Think About the Structure** Which expression tells how to find how much faster the new record was?

   A 154.165 + 154.25   **C** 154.165 × 154.25

   B 154.25 − 154.165   **D** 154.25 ÷ 154.165

ⓒ **29.** **Construct Arguments** Explain why writing the new record as 154.250 mph does not change its value.

Mixed Problem Solving

Some Facts About the Grizzly Bear

Mass (adult)	381.82 kg
Height (adult)	2.1 m
Claw Length (adult)	10.16 cm

2.1 m

Use the table above to answer **1** through **3**.

1. Write the height of an adult grizzly bear in short-word form.

2. Write the length of an adult grizzly bear's claw in expanded form.

3. If newborn grizzlies weigh about 0.45 kg, how many kilograms do grizzly bears gain from the time they are newborns until they are adults?

4. If a bear ran at a speed of 54.078 km/h, then increased its speed two-hundredths of a kilometer per hour, how fast would it be running?

5. A male grizzly can weigh twice as much as a female grizzly. How much would a female weigh if the male weighed 381.82 kg?

6. The female grizzly has one to four cubs every other year. If a female has four cubs every other year for 12 years, how many cubs would she have given birth to?

7. If one cub weighed 0.45 kg and another cub weighed 1.23 kg, how much more would the heavier cub weigh than the lighter one?

Lesson
1-5

Common Core

6.NS.3 Fluently add, subtract, multiply, and divide multi-digit decimals using the standard algorithm for each operation.

Multiplying and Dividing by 10, 100, and 1,000

How can you multiply by powers of 10?

The sailfish has been recorded swimming at speeds greater than 100 kilometers per hour. About how many miles per hour is this? Use 1 km ≈ 0.62 mi.

Choose an Operation Multiply 0.62×100 to convert 100 kilometers to miles.

Another Example **How can you divide by powers of 10?**

Find $5.7 \div 1,000$ or $5.7 \div 10^3$.

A relationship exists between divisors that are powers of 10, their exponential forms, and the number of places the decimal point is moved to the left to find the quotient.

Divisor	Exponential Form	Decimal Point Moves Left
10	10^1	1 place
100	10^2	2 places
1,000	10^3	3 places

$5.7 \div 1,000 = 0.005.7$

Move the decimal point 3 places to the left. Annex zeros in the tenths and hundredths places.

$5.7 \div 10^3 = 0.005.7$

$5.7 \div 1,000 = 0.0057$ or $5.7 \div 10^3 = 0.0057$

Explain It

1. Use the pattern in the table above. How many places to the left would you move the decimal point in the dividend to divide by 10,000?

2. If the dividend is 641.2 and the quotient is 6.412, what is the divisor in standard form and in exponential form?

The table shows the relationship between the number of zeros in factors that are powers of 10, their exponential forms, and the number of places the decimal point of another factor is moved to the right to find the product.

Factor	Exponential Form	Decimal Point Moves Right
10	10^1	1 place
100	10^2	2 places
1,000	10^3	3 places

Find 0.62×100.

To multiply by 100, or 10^2, move the decimal point 2 places to the right. Annex zeros if needed.

$$0.62 \times 100 = .62\underset{\curvearrowright}{}$$

The decimal point moves 2 places to the right.

$$0.62 \times 100 = 62$$

100 kilometers is about 62 miles. Sailfish can swim faster than 62 miles per hour.

Guided Practice*

 MATHEMATICAL **PRACTICES**

Do you know HOW?

In **1** through **4**, find each missing number.

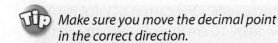 *Make sure you move the decimal point in the correct direction.*

1. $3.98 \times 10 = $ ▢

2. $95.2 \times $ ▢ $ = 9,520$

3. $1,342.9 \div $ ▢ $ = 1.3429$

4. $2.601 \div 10^2 = $ ▢

Do you UNDERSTAND?

5. Communicate Explain how to move the decimal point when you are multiplying by a power of 10.

6. Suppose a jet is flying 1,000 kilometers per hour. How many zeros would you need to annex to multiply $0.62 \times 1,000$? What is the product?

Independent Practice

In **7** through **18**, find each missing number.

7. $60.014 \times $ ▢ $ = 600.14$

8. $34.12 \times 100 = $ ▢

9. $80.9 \times 100 = $ ▢

10. $127.3 \times 1,000 = $ ▢

11. $5,100 \div $ ▢ $ = 51$

12. $8,231 \div 10,000 = $ ▢

13. $41.2 \div 10^1 = $ ▢

14. $1,304.25 \div 10^3 = $ ▢

15. $8 \div $ ▢ $ = 0.008$

16. $0.0603 \times $ ▢ $ = 603$

17. $905.01 \div $ ▢ $ = 9.0501$

18. $459.532 \times $ ▢ $ = 459,532$

---

*For another example, see Set D on page 29.

19. What number do you get when you divide 504 by 1,000?

20. Critique Reasoning Jimmy says that if you multiply any whole number or decimal by 100, all you have to do is move the decimal point to the hundreds place. Is he right?

21. Which 5 in 32,535,832,708 has the greater value? How do you know?

22. A coral polyp is a tubular saclike animal with a central mouth surrounded by a ring of tentacles. The size of polyps varies. If each polyp is 0.12 inch in diameter, how many polyps would fit in a row 12 inches long?

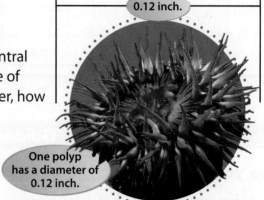

0.12 inch.

One polyp has a diameter of 0.12 inch.

23. If each polyp is 0.12 inch in diameter, how many polyps would fit in an area of coral reef that is 1 foot long by 1 foot wide?

24. After 6 weeks, Scott had collected $42 for charity. If he collected the same amount each week, how much did he collect each week?

25. Persevere One carton of juice is 10 cm wide by 10 cm long. How many cartons of juice will fit on a refrigerator shelf that is 80 cm wide by 100 cm long? Find $(80 \times 100) \div (10 \times 10)$.

26. In 2005, the estimated population of Jacksonville, FL, was 782,623; of Indianapolis, IN, was 784,118; and of Columbus, OH, was 730,657. Order the populations of the three cities from greatest to least.

27. Writing to Explain Why can you just move the decimal point to find a solution when you multiply or divide by 10, 100, or 1,000, but not when you multiply or divide by a number that is not a power of 10?

28. A *googol* is described as 10^{100}. How many zeros are in a googol written in standard form?

29. A megabyte of computer memory can be estimated as 10^6 bytes. Write 10^6 in standard form.

30. Think About the Structure A bottle contains 1,500 milliliters of water. Which expression can be used to find the number of 100-milliliter glasses that can be filled with water?

    A 1.5×100 **C** $1.5 \div 100$

    B $1,500 \div 100$ **D** $150 \div 100$

31. Think About the Structure Suppose that one bacterial cell divides every 30 minutes to make 2 cells. Which expression will find how many cells there will be after 3 hours?

    A $1 \times 2 \times 2 \times 2 \times 2 \times 2$

    B 2×30

    C $1 \times 2 \times 2 \times 2 \times 2 \times 2 \times 2$

    D $2 \times 2 \times 30$

Roman Numerals

The numbers we use every day are part of the decimal number system. In ancient Rome, a system of letters, called *Roman numerals*, was used to represent numbers. Roman numerals are based on adding and subtracting.

The seven Roman numerals are shown in the table below. These letters can be combined.

Data

Roman Numeral	Value
I	1
V	5
X	10
L	50
C	100
D	500
M	1,000

Rules for Roman Numerals

1. If the value of a letter is greater than or equal to the value of the letter to its right, add. Write the values of VI and CCC.

   $$V \quad I \qquad\qquad C \quad C \quad C$$
   $$5 + 1 = 6 \qquad 100 + 100 + 100 = 300$$

2. If the value of a letter is less than the value of the letter to its right, subtract. Write the values of IV and XL.

   $$I \quad V \qquad\qquad X \quad L$$
   $$5 - 1 = 4 \qquad\qquad 50 - 10 = 40$$

3. A letter cannot be repeated more than three times in a row. There is no such numeral as CCCC; 400 is written as CD (500 − 100).

   Example: Write the value of CMXXIX.

   Think CM XX IX

   $$= (1,000 - 100) + (10 + 10) + (10 - 1)$$
   $$= \quad 900 \quad + \quad 20 \quad + \quad 9 \quad = 929$$

Practice

1. Write each missing Roman numeral in the table at the right.

For **2** through **9**, use the rules for reading and writing Roman numerals to write the value of each.

2. XIV   3. MLX   4. CCLIV   5. MXVII

6. XLV   7. XXIX   8. XCVII   9. LXXXIV

For **10** through **12**, tell whether each statement is true or false.

10. 33 = XXXIII   11. DCCXXI = 721   12. 102 = IIC

Data

Number	Roman Numeral
3	▪
8	
13	▪
29	
105	▪
2,009	

Lesson
1-6

Common Core

This lesson reinforces concepts and skills required for Topic 3.

Comparing and Ordering Decimals

How can you compare decimals?

Batting averages for a single season are shown for some baseball players. Which of the two batting averages circled is greater?

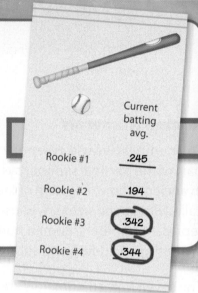

	Current batting avg.
Rookie #1	.245
Rookie #2	.194
Rookie #3	.342
Rookie #4	.344

Another Example How do you order decimals using place value?

One Way Use a number line to order 4.002, 3.985, and 4.01 from least to greatest.

```
        3.985      4.002 4.01
  ←—+——+——+——+——+——+——+——+→
  3.97  3.98  3.99  4.0  4.01  4.02
```

3.985 is left of 4.002 and 4.002 is left of 4.01. So, 3.985 < 4.002 < 4.01.

Another Way Order 4.002, 3.985, and 4.01 from least to greatest by lining up the numbers so their decimal points align. Then compare digits from left to right and order the digits of each place value.

Order ones.	**The tenths digits are the same.**	**Order hundredths.**
4.002	3.985	3.985
3.985 ← Least	4.002	4.002
4.010	4.010	4.010 ← Greatest

Write your answer: 3.985, 4.002, 4.01

Guided Practice*

 MATHEMATICAL PRACTICES

Do you know HOW?

In **1** through **4**, use >, <, or =.

1. 1.09 ◯ 1.9   **2.** 18.001 ◯ 18.01

3. 7.25 ◯ 7.3   **4.** 0.1 ◯ 0.1000

5. Order 7.08, 6.257, 7.6, 6.1, 6.29 from least to greatest.

Do you UNDERSTAND?

© 6. Construct Arguments Explain why 46.69 is less than 46.7.

7. In the example at the top of the page, what place value determines which batting average is greater?

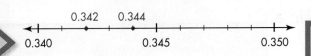

One Way

Compare 0.342 and 0.344 by locating them on a number line.

0.344 is right of 0.342 on the number line.

So, 0.344 > 0.342.

Another Way

Line the numbers up so their decimal points align.

0.342
0.344
↑

Compare the digits from left to right.

0.342
0.344   4 > 2

So, 0.344 > 0.342.

Independent Practice

In **8** through **15**, use >, <, or = to compare each pair of numbers.

8. 5.084 ◯ 5.84   **9.** 52.01 ◯ 51.99   **10.** 0.721 ◯ 0.7021   **11.** 1.22 ◯ 1.222

12. 2.99 ◯ 2.9900   **13.** 438.783 ◯ 438.738   **14.** 3.1428 ◯ 3.1420   **15.** 3.35 ◯ 2.44

Order these numbers from least to greatest.

16. 12.23, 12.223, 12.322   **17.** 1.01, 1.0, 1.011, 1.001

18. 35.43, 35.435, 35.44, 35.451   **19.** 0.7841, 0.834, 0.705, 0.81

Problem Solving

MATHEMATICAL
PRACTICES

ⓒ **20. Writing to Explain** A redwood tree has a diameter of 30.2 ft. Lyndell says this tree has a smaller diameter than a tree with a diameter of 30.20 because 2 is less than 20. Is Lyndell correct? Explain.

ⓒ **21. Reasonableness** Arliss ran the fitness run in 9.65 seconds. Bonita ran it in 9.9 seconds. Cory ran it in 9.625 seconds, and Darla ran it in 10 seconds. Who ran it in the least amount of time?

A Arliss   **C** Cory

B Bonita   **D** Darla

ⓒ **22. Reason** Is a decimal with 4 digits always greater than a decimal with 3 digits? Give an example to explain.

23. Name three decimals between 0.55 and 0.56.

Lesson
1-7

Common Core

This lesson reinforces concepts and skills required for Topic 3.

Problem Solving

Make an Organized List

Suppose you throw three darts at the target pictured on the right. All of the darts hit the target. How can you find all of the different total points that you could score?

1,000 points

50,000 points

100,000 points

Guided Practice*

MATHEMATICAL
PRACTICES

Do you know HOW?

Suppose two darts hit a target that has two rings. The outer ring is worth 50 points, and the inner ring is worth 150 points. Use this information to answer **1** and **2**.

1. Make an organized list to show all of the possible scores.

2. How many possible totals are there?

Do you UNDERSTAND?

3. In the example at the top, how is the list organized?

© 4. **Write a Problem** Write a problem that you can solve by making an organized list.

Independent Practice

MATHEMATICAL
PRACTICES

Solve **5** by making an organized list. The list has been started for you.

5. Yolanda needs a 3-digit code for her locker. She wants to use the first three digits of her phone number, 763. How many different combinations using each of these digits does Yolanda have to choose from?

7	6	3
763	673	376

Applying Math Practices

- What am I asked to find?
- What else can I try?
- How are quantities related?
- How can I explain my work?
- How can I use math to model the problem?
- Can I use tools to help?
- Is my work precise?
- Why does this work?
- How can I generalize?

What do you know? There are 3 different point values on the target. All 3 darts hit the target.

Make an organized list to find all the possible scores.

There are ten different totals possible.

1,000	50,000	100,000	Total
✓✓✓			3,000
✓✓	✓		52,000
✓✓		✓	102,000
✓	✓✓		101,000
✓		✓✓	201,000
✓	✓	✓	151,000
	✓✓✓		150,000
	✓✓	✓	200,000
	✓	✓✓	250,000
		✓✓✓	300,000

What are you trying to find? What are the different total points that you could score?

Solve **6** using the art on the right.

6. Randy went to the school fun fair and played the beanbag toss. He tossed 3 beanbags, and each went into a hole on the board. What are the possible total points he could have scored?

1.1 points

2.2 points

4.4 points

7. Ariana, Mia, Ethan, and Nick are planning a one-on-one basketball tournament. In the tournament, each player will play the other three just once. How many games will be played?

8. **Estimation** About how many eggs would be laid by 7 chickens if each chicken lays 36 eggs?

9. Is your estimate of the number of eggs 7 chickens could lay more or less than the actual answer? Explain.

ⓒ 10. **Reason** Look for a pattern in the table of values at the right. Find a rule for the table.

Input	1	3	9	17
Output	6	8	14	22

ⓒ 11. **Writing to Explain** How could you find the number of different ways to arrange 4 students in a row for a photo?

ⓒ 12. **Use Tools** Dani has only quarters, dimes, and nickels in her bank. She needs $0.60 for the bus. She wants to use at least one quarter. How many different ways can Dani combine the coins to pay for the bus?

WXYZ

WXZY

WYXZ

WYZX

WZXY

ⓒ 13. **Think About the Structure** Cassie is making an organized list of all the different ways to arrange the letters WXYZ. Following Cassie's organization, which arrangement of letters will she place on the list next?

A WZYX   **B** XWYZ   **C** YWXZ   **D** ZWYZ

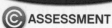
1. The table gives the number of members in some Native American tribes. Which lists the tribes from the least to the greatest membership? (1-2)

Tribe	Membership
Crow	13,394
Ottawa	10,677
Ute	10,385
Yakama	10,851

Data

A Ute, Ottawa, Yakama, Crow

B Ottawa, Ute, Yakama, Crow

C Yakama, Ottawa, Ute, Crow

D Ute, Crow, Ottawa, Yakama

2. Pluto's mean distance from the Sun is about 5 billion 900 million kilometers. What is the number written in expanded form? (1-3)

A $(5 \times 10^9) + (9 \times 10^8)$

B $(5 \times 10^6) + (9 \times 10^5)$

C $(5 \times 10^9) + (9 \times 10^7)$

D $(5 \times 10^{12}) + (9 \times 10^8)$

3. Mario has 320 new plants to landscape 10 flowerbeds of a new office complex. If each flowerbed has the same number of plants, how many plants go in each flowerbed? (1-5)

A 3,200 plants

B 310 plants

C 32 plants

D 3 plants

4. What is the value of the 6 in 196,937,000? (1-1)

A 6 billion

B 6 million

C 6 hundred million

D 6 hundred thousand

5. Which of the following is equal to 5^4? (1-3)

A $4 \times 4 \times 4 \times 4 \times 4$

B 5×4

C $(4 \times 5)^4$

D $5 \times 5 \times 5 \times 5$

6. Which of the following is between 0.007 and 0.016? (1-6)

A 0.0008

B 0.070

C 0.0015

D 0.010

7. Which of the following is a way to write four and eight hundred two ten thousandths? (1-4)

A 4.802

B 4.082

C 4.0802

D 4.0082

8. Which of the following lists the numbers in order from greatest to least? (1-6)

A 2.1027, 2.1127, 2.0127

B 2.1027, 2.0127, 2.1127

C 2.1127, 2.0127, 2.1027

D 2.1127, 2.1027, 2.0127

9. The record for the fastest car belongs to a British jet car that traveled at 763.035 miles per hour. What is this number written in expanded form? (1-4)

A 700 + 60 + 3 + 0.03 + 0.05

B 700 + 60 + 3 + 0.3 + 0.5

C 700 + 60 + 3 + 0.3 + 0.05

D 700 + 60 + 3 + 0.03 + 0.005

10. The maximum climbing speed of a three-toed sloth is 0.15 miles per hour. Which speed is less than 0.15 mph? (1-6)

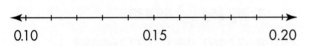

0.10   0.15   0.20

A 0.146 mph

B 0.162 mph

C 0.157 mph

D 0.153 mph

11. Which country listed in the table has a population greater than 188,078,227? (1-2)

Country	Population
Bangladesh	147,365,352
Indonesia	245,452,739
Pakistan	165,803,560
Russia	142,893,540

Data

A Bangladesh

B Indonesia

C Pakistan

D Russia

12. What is 0.043×100? (1-5)

A 43

B 4.3

C 0.43

D 0.0043

13. Which is 10,000,000 written in exponential form? (1-3)

A 7^{10}

B 10^7

C 10^8

D 8^{10}

14. In a recent year, the United States had about two trillion, two hundred two billion, six hundred million dollars in outstanding consumer credit. What is this number in standard form? (1-1)

A $2,202,600,000

B $2,000,202,600,000

C $2,202,600,000,000

D $200,202,600,000,000

15. Make a list to determine all the possible combinations of pennies, nickels, dimes, and quarters that total 25 cents. How many combinations are possible? (1-7)

A 13

B 11

C 9

D 4

Set A, pages 4–6, 8–9

Write different forms of the number 82,700,360,000,000.

Word form: eighty-two trillion, seven hundred billion, three hundred sixty million

Expanded form: $(8 \times 10,000,000,000,000) +$ $(2 \times 1,000,000,000,000) +$ $(7 \times 100,000,000,000) +$ $(3 \times 100,000,000) +$ $(6 \times 10,000,000)$

Use > or < to compare the numbers.

728,316 ◯ 728,361

Compare the digits in each place. The digits are the same until we get to the tens place.

728,316 ⊗ 728,361

Remember to start at the right and work your way left through each period when finding the place and value of a whole number digit.

In **1** through **6**, what is the place and value of the underlined digit?

1. 32<u>7</u>,018
2. 19,3<u>4</u>5
3. 71,<u>3</u>29,684
4. <u>6</u>,291,378
5. 6<u>3</u>2,109,874
6. 7,26<u>3</u>

Remember to compare digits of numbers from left to right.

7. 69,354 ◯ 69,435
8. 27,461,398 ◯ 27,164,398
9. eighteen trillion ◯ 18,000,001
10. 638,127 ◯ 637,217

Set B, pages 10–12

Evaluate 6^3.

6 is the base and 3 is the exponent.

6 is used as a factor 3 times.

$6 \times 6 \times 6 = 216$

Remember that any base number, except zero, with an exponent of 0 has a value of 1.

Evaluate **1** through **3**.

1. 9^2
2. 99^1
3. $3,105^0$

Set C, pages 14–16

ones	tenths	hundredths	thousandths	ten thousandths
2 .	0	7	9	5

Write the place and value of the underlined digit in 2.0<u>7</u>95.

The 7 is in the hundredths place. Its value is $7 \times 0.01 = 0.07$.

Remember to pay attention to the decimal point and zeros when determining the place and value of a decimal digit.

What is the place of the underlined digit?

1. 17.90<u>3</u>
2. 28.<u>1</u>
3. 68.000<u>9</u>
4. 9<u>4</u>.002

When multiplying by 10, 100, or 1,000, move the decimal point one place to the right for each power of 10 or for each zero.

$5.459 \times 10 = 54.59$

When dividing by 10, 100, or 1,000, move the decimal point one place to the left for each power of 10 or for each zero. Annex zeros if needed.

$0.0214 \div 1,000 = 0.0000214$

Remember to move the decimal point one place for each power of ten or for each zero.

Solve.

1. $0.25 \times \boxed{} = 250$
2. $15.23 \times 10 = \boxed{}$
3. $2.39 \times 100 = \boxed{}$
4. $0.29 \div \boxed{} = 0.00029$
5. $14.21 \div 10 = \boxed{}$
6. $1.31 \div 100 = \boxed{}$

Use $<$, $>$, or $=$ to compare the two decimals.

$37.106 \bigcirc 37.110$

Compare the digits in each place. The digits are the same until the hundredths place.

37.106

37.110
$\qquad 0 < 1$, so $37.106 < 37.110$.

Remember when you compare decimals, line up their decimal points and then compare their digits from left to right.

Use $<$, $>$, or $=$ to compare the two decimals.

1. $95.17 \bigcirc 95.71$ 2. $0.74 \bigcirc 0.7400$
3. $37 \bigcirc 0.37$ 4. $224.9 \bigcirc 224.92$

Elise, Jasmine, Fatima, and Nola want to jump rope at recess. In how many different ways can the girls be paired to twirl the rope?

Make an organized list. Find the possible pairs for each girl. Then cross out any repeated pairs.

Elise	Jasmine	Fatima	Nola
EJ	J̶E̶	F̶E̶	N̶E̶
EF	JF	F̶J̶	N̶J̶
EN	JN	FN	N̶F̶

6 different pairs of girls can twirl the rope.

Remember to keep each item fixed and find all the possible outcomes for that item.

1. Heyden's mom bought peaches, pears, bananas, apples, and grapes. How many ways can Heyden combine the fruit so he has two different pieces of fruit in his lunch, without repeating any combinations?

2. How many three-letter arrangements can be made from the letters in the word "MATH"?

Variables, Expressions, and Properties

1 How many flowers can decorate one float for the Tournament of Roses Parade®? You will find out in Lesson 2-1.

2 One of the world's tallest fountains is located in Fountain Hills, Arizona. How high does the fountain spray water into the air? You will find out in Lesson 2-5.

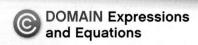

3

There have been 12 astronauts who have walked on the surface of the Moon. How many pounds of lunar rock and soil did these astronauts bring back to Earth? You will find out in Lesson 2-6.

4

This superflag hung over Hoover Dam during the 1996 Olympic Torch relay. How many grommets does it take to hang the flag over the dam? You will find out in Lesson 2-3.

Review What You Know!

Vocabulary

Choose the best term from the box.

- algebraic expression
- variable
- exponential form
- compatible

1. A(n) __?__ is a mathematical phrase that includes at least one variable and one operation.

2. The __?__ of a number uses exponents to write the repeated multiplication of the number called the base.

3. Numbers that are easy to compute mentally are called __?__ numbers.

4. A(n) __?__ is a symbol, such as n, that takes the place of a number or value.

Evaluating Expressions

Evaluate each expression for $x = 4$ and $x = 7$.

5. $3x + 8$
6. $24 - 3x$

7. $5 + 5 + x$
8. $84 \div x$

9. $2x + 5 - x$
10. $9x$

11. $2x + 4$
12. $28 \div x$

Answer Terms

©**Writing to Explain** Write an answer for each question.

13. How are these terms alike: differences, sums, quotients, and products?

14. What does it mean to evaluate an algebraic expression?

© Common Core

6.EE.2.a Write expressions that record operations with numbers and with letters standing for numbers.... Also 6.EE.2, 6.EE.2.b, 6.EE.6

Using Variables to Write Expressions

How can you write an algebraic expression?

Donnie bought CDs for $10 each. How can you represent the total cost of the CDs?

A variable is <u>a quantity that can change or vary and is often represented with a letter</u>. Variables help you translate word phrases into algebraic expressions.

$10 each

Other Examples

The table shows algebraic expressions for given situations.

Word Phrase	Operation	Algebraic Expression
five minutes more than time t	addition	$t + 5$
ten erasers decreased by a number n	subtraction	$10 - n$
six times a width w	multiplication	$6 \times w$ or $6w$
n nectarines divided by three	division	$n \div 3$ or $\frac{n}{3}$
eight more than four times an amount x	multiplication and addition	$4x + 8$

A coefficient is <u>the number that is multiplied by a variable</u>. For the expression $4x + 8$, the coefficient is 4.

Guided Practice*

 MATHEMATICAL PRACTICES

Do you know HOW?

Write an algebraic expression for each situation.

1. 12 times a number g

2. the difference of a number m and 18

3. p pennies added to 22 pennies

4. 5 less than 3 times a number z

Do you UNDERSTAND?

© 5. **Be Precise** Identify the variable and the operation in the algebraic expression $\frac{6}{x}$.

6. What is the coefficient of the variable n in the expression $15 + 2n$?

7. Write an algebraic expression for this situation: f more flowers than the 9 flowers planted in each of the 2 rows.

DIGITAL   Animated Glossary
www.pearsonsuccessnet.com

*For another example, see Set A on page 56.

CDs cost $10 each. The operation is multiplication.

Number of CDs	Total Cost
1	$10 × 1
2	$10 × 2
3	$10 × 3
4	$10 × 4

Use the variable n to represent the number of CDs and write an algebraic expression.

$$\$10 \times n$$

An algebraic expression is <u>a mathematical phrase that has at least one variable and one operation</u>. The total cost of the CDs is represented by

$$10 \times n$$
$$\text{or } 10n.$$

The operation is multiplication. The variable is n.

Independent Practice

For **8** through **13**, write an algebraic expression for each situation.

8. 22 divided by a number s

9. A number r increased by 15

10. 12 less than 7 times a number x

11. 6 more players than a number 8 times p

12. 4 more than the product of x and 12

13. 9 times the difference of y and 5

Problem Solving

MATHEMATICAL PRACTICES

14. One float for the Tournament of Roses parade uses as many flowers as a florist usually uses in 6 years. If y is the number of flowers a florist uses in 1 year, write an algebraic expression for the number of flowers used to make a float.

15. Persevere A group of cows produced the same number of gallons of milk each day for a week. Sara collected the milk for six days. Write an expression to show the number of gallons Sara did NOT collect.

16. Yuri walked p poodles and b bull dogs. Write an algebraic expression to represent how many dogs were walked.

17. The distance around a closed shape can be expressed as 8 times side s, or $8s$. Draw an example of this geometric shape.

18. Writing to Explain Trevor's CD tower has 4 rows of slots, and 6 slots are empty. If x equals the number of slots in a row, explain how the expression $4x - 6$ relates to Trevor's CD tower.

19. Think About the Structure Which expression shows a quantity of pears, p, added to 16 grapes?

   A $16 - p$ **C** $16 + p$

   B $16p$ **D** $p \div 16$

Common
Core

6.EE.3 Apply the properties
of operations to generate
equivalent expressions....

Properties of Operations

How can you use properties of operations to rewrite expressions?

The Commutative Property of Addition states <u>the order in which numbers are added does not change the sum of the numbers</u>. The Commutative Property of Multiplication states <u>the order in which numbers are multiplied does not change the product of the numbers.</u>

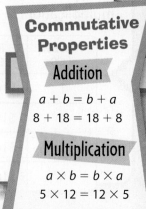

Commutative Properties

Addition

$a + b = b + a$
$8 + 18 = 18 + 8$

Multiplication

$a \times b = b \times a$
$5 \times 12 = 12 \times 5$

Guided Practice*

 MATHEMATICAL PRACTICES

Do you know HOW?

Find each missing number. Tell what property is shown.

1. $19 + (42 + 8) = (\boxed{} + 42) + 8$

2. $12 + 8 = \boxed{} + 12$

3. $42 \times 8 \times 3 = 42 \times 8 \times \boxed{} \times 3$

4. $32 \times 85 = 85 \times \boxed{}$

Do you UNDERSTAND?

5. Reason For the Identity Property, why does addition involve a zero and multiplication involve a one? Why don't they both use one or both use zero?

6. Use Structure Yuen Lee put 3 cartons of markers in the closet. Each carton contains 3 rows of 7 boxes. Use one of the Associative Properties to show two different ways of finding the number of marker boxes.

Independent Practice

Find each missing number. Tell what property or properties are shown.

7. $\boxed{} \times (14 \times 32) = (5 \times 14) \times 32$

8. $5 + 23 + 4 = 23 + 4 + \boxed{}$

9. $25 + 0 + (3 + 16) = (25 + \boxed{}) + 3$

10. $(7 + 12) + 4 = (7 + \boxed{}) + 12$

11. $(5 \times 7) \times (3 \times 8) = (5 \times 3) \times (8 \times \boxed{})$

12. $(43 \times 1) \times 4 = \boxed{} \times 43$

13. $(6 + 3) + 4 = 6 + (3 + \boxed{})$

14. $(8 \times 9) \times \boxed{} = 8 \times (9 \times 10)$

15. $7 \times \boxed{} = 6 \times 7$

16. $15 + 48 = \boxed{} + 15$

17. $8 + \boxed{} = 4 + 8$

18. $(1 \times 2) \times 3 = \boxed{} \times (2 \times 3)$

DIGITAL
Animated Glossary
www.pearsonsuccessnet.com

For another example, see Set B on page 56.

The Associative Property of Addition states that <u>the way numbers are grouped does not affect the sum</u>.

$$a + (b + c) = (a + b) + c$$
$$2 + (8 + 10) = (2 + 8) + 10$$

The Identity Property of Addition states that <u>the sum of any number and zero is that number</u>.

$$a + 0 = a$$
$$24 + 0 = 24$$

The Associative Property of Multiplication states that <u>the way numbers are grouped does not affect the product</u>.

$$a \times (b \times c) = (a \times b) \times c$$
$$2 \times (4 \times 5) = (2 \times 4) \times 5$$

The Identity Property of Multiplication states that <u>the product of a number and one is that number</u>.

$$a \times 1 = a$$
$$36 \times 1 = 36$$

Find each missing number. Tell what property or properties are shown.

19. $(41 \times 43) \times (3 \times 19) = (41 \times \quad) \times (19 \times 43)$

20. $(5 \times 3) \times \quad = 5 \times (8 \times 3)$

21. $328 \times 1 = \quad$

22. $(12 + 0) \times (1 \times 12) = \quad \times \quad$

Problem Solving

MATHEMATICAL PRACTICES

For **23** and **24**, use the table to the right.

23. Donnie and Pete live in Bluewater. They rode their bikes to Zink and then to Riverton. Then they rode back home, using the same route. Write a number sentence using the Commutative Property of Addition to show the distances each way.

ⓒ **24. Model** Once they rode from Riverton to Red Rock, from Red Rock to Curry, and then rode back to Riverton. How many miles did they ride that time?

Where Donnie and Pete Rode	Distance
Bluewater to Zink	13 miles
Zink to Riverton	9 miles
Riverton to Red Rock	12 miles
Red Rock to Curry	11 miles

ⓒ **25. Think About the Structure** Stage 15 of the Tour de France bicycle race includes legs from Gap to Embrun, Embrun to Guillestre, and Guillestre to Arvieux. One way to express the distance of these legs is $33.5 + (20.5 + 21.5)$. Which expression below is another way to express these legs?

A $(23 + 33.5) + (20.5 - 21.5)$

C $33.5 + (20.5 \times 21.5)$

B $(33.5 + 20.5) + 21.5$

D $(33.5 \times 21.5) + 20.5$

26. Write the standard form for 6.45 billion.

ⓒ **27. Writing to Explain** Can you use the Associative Properties with subtraction and division? Use $(14 - 8) - 2$ and $24 \div (4 \div 2)$ to explain.

Common Core

6.EE.3 Apply the properties of operations to generate equivalent expressions....

Order of Operations

How do you know which operation to perform first?

Evaluate $14 + 8 \times 6$.

Adding first gives:

$$14 + 8 \times 6$$
$$22 \times 6$$
$$132$$

Multiplying first gives:

$$14 + 8 \times 6$$
$$14 + 48$$
$$62$$

Other Examples

Evaluate $20 + (30 - 10) \div 5$.

Using order of operations:

$20 + (30 - 10) \div 5$ ← Compute inside the parentheses first.

$20 + 20 \div 5$ ← Next, divide.

$20 + 4$ ← Finally, add.

24

Using a scientific calculator:

Press:

20   30 − 10 ÷ 5 ENTER =

Display will read: 24

Evaluate $4^2 - (4 + 6) \div 2$.

Using order of operations:

$4^2 - (4 + 6) \div 2$ ← Compute inside the parentheses first.

$4^2 - 10 \div 2$ ← Evaluate exponents.

$16 - 10 \div 2$ ← Then divide.

$16 - 5$ ← Finally, subtract.

11

Using a scientific calculator:

Press:

4 2 − (4 + 6) + 2 ENTER =

Display will read: 11

Explain It

1. To evaluate $3 \times (7 + 5)$, what should you do first and why?

2. In the second example using the scientific calculator, what is the purpose of the key?

Mathematicians use a set of rules known as order of operations 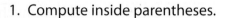, the order in which to perform operations in calculations.

1. Compute inside parentheses.
2. Evaluate terms with exponents.
3. Multiply and divide from left to right.
4. Add and subtract from left to right.

Using the correct order of operations, $14 + 8 \times 6 = 62$.
A scientific calculator uses order of operations.

Press: 14

Display will read: 62

Guided Practice*

MATHEMATICAL PRACTICES

Do you know HOW?

Evaluate each expression.

1. $36 \div 6 + 6$

2. $36 \div (6 + 6)$

3. $24 \div (4 + 8) + 2$

4. $48 \div (4 + 8) + 2^2$

5. $24 \div 4 + 8 + 2$

6. $48 \div 4 + 8 + 2^2$

Do you UNDERSTAND?

7. Persevere Where could you insert parentheses to make this number sentence true? $80 \div 8 \times 5 + 4 = 90$

8. Donavan entered $12 + 4 \times 3 - 6$ into Lidia's scientific calculator. The display showed 18. In what order did the calculator complete the operations?

Independent Practice

Evaluate each expression.

9. $3^3 - 8 \times 3$

10. $(5^2 + 7) \div 4$

11. $6 \times 4 - 4 + 2$

12. $18 - 3 \times 5 + 2$

13. $49 - 4 \times (49 \div 7)$

14. $(64 \div 8) \times 3 + 6$

15. $72 \div (4 + 4) \times 5$

16. $(3 \times 3) \times (2 \times 2) \div 36$

Use parentheses to make each number sentence true.

17. $5 + 4 \times 3 \times 3 = 41$

18. $9 \times 0 + 4 = 36$

19. $5^2 - 6 \times 0 = 25$

20. $8 \times 9 - 2 - 3 = 32$

21. $5 + 4 \times 3 \times 3 = 81$

22. $9 \times 0 + 4 = 4$

23. $5^2 - 6 \times 0 = 0$

24. $8 \times 9 - 2 - 3 = 53$

25. $1 + 2 \times 3 + 4 = 21$

26. $2^2 + 4 \times 6 = 48$

27. $5 \times 6 \times 8 - 7 = 30$

28. $6^2 + 7 + 9 \times 10 = 133$

DIGITAL

Animated Glossary
www.pearsonsuccessnet.com

© **29. Reason** Use the symbols +, −, ×, and ÷ to make the number sentence true.

(3 ☐ 5) ☐ 4 ☐ (14 ☐ 2) = 12

© **30. Persevere** Meredith bought 3 T-shirts for $12.00 each. Her grandmother paid for half the total cost. To find how much Meredith paid, evaluate the expression: $(3 \times 12) \div 2$.

31. Luke needs a new fence around his garden, but the gate across the narrow end of the garden will not be replaced. To find how many feet of fencing Luke needs, evaluate the expression: $12 + (2 \times 14)$.

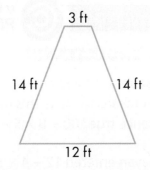

3 ft

14 ft   14 ft

12 ft

© **32. Writing to Explain** If p is greater than zero, tell which of these expressions will result in the higher value: $(2 \times p) + 5$ or $2 \times (p + 5)$. Explain how you know.

© **33. Model** Jaron walked 15 blocks north and then 3 blocks west to school. Marisol walked 3 blocks east and then 15 blocks south to school. Write an equation to show that each traveled the same distance.

34. On Saturday, every seat in Mazen Theater was full. The balcony has 10 rows with 22 seats in each. The main floor has 25 rows with 30 seats each. To find the number of people at the theater, evaluate the following expression: $(10 \times 22) + (25 \times 30)$.

A 16   **C** 970

B 87   **D** 14,100

35. On her math test, Bianca scored 5 points on each of 5 questions, 2 points on each of 2 questions, and 3 points on each of 4 questions. To find the number of points she scored, evaluate the expression: $5^2 + 2^2 + (3 \times 4)$.

A 26   **C** 41

B 40   **D** 84

36. The world's largest flag measures 505 ft by 225 ft. The flag hangs by a cable through grommets on one of the shorter sides. There is a grommet every 30 in. If there is a grommet at each end, evaluate the expression $1 + (225 \times 12) \div 30$ to find out how many grommets are used to hang the flag.

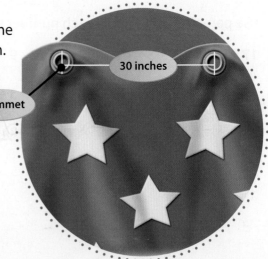

30 inches

grommet

Exponents and Order of Operations

Evaluate 5^6 on a calculator two ways.

Step 1 Use the exponent key $\boxed{\wedge}$.

Press: 5 $\boxed{\wedge}$ 6 $\boxed{\text{ENTER} =}$

Display: 15625

Step 2 Use repeated multiplication.

5 $\boxed{\times}$ 5 $\boxed{\times}$ 5 $\boxed{\times}$ 5 $\boxed{\times}$ 5 $\boxed{\times}$ 5 $\boxed{\text{ENTER} =}$

Display: 15625

Evaluate $9^3 + (27 \div 3 + 47)$ on a calculator two ways.

Step 1 Use the calculator's order of operations.

9 $\boxed{\wedge}$ 3 $\boxed{+}$ $\boxed{(}$ 27 $\boxed{\div}$ 3 $\boxed{+}$ 47 $\boxed{)}$ $\boxed{\text{ENTER} =}$

Display: 785

Step 2 Follow order of operations to verify that the calculator used the correct order of operations.

27 $\boxed{\div}$ 3 $\boxed{\text{ENTER} =}$ $\boxed{+}$ 47 $\boxed{\text{ENTER} =}$

Display: 9 56

9 $\boxed{\wedge}$ 3 $\boxed{\text{ENTER} =}$ $\boxed{+}$ 56 $\boxed{\text{ENTER} =}$

Display: 729 785

Practice

Evaluate each expression two ways.

1. 8^5　　　　　　**2.** 7^4　　　　　　**3.** $8 \times 19 - 36 + 12^5$

4. $(72 \div 9) + 6 \times 3^5$　　**5.** 3^7　　　　　　**6.** $1204 \div 14 - 2^5 + 178$

ⓒ
**Common
Core**

6.EE.3 Apply the properties
of operations to generate
equivalent expressions....

The Distributive Property

How can you use the Distributive Property to evaluate expressions?

The Distributive Property states that multiplying a sum (or difference) by a number gives the same result as multiplying each number in the sum (or difference) by the number and adding (or subtracting) the products.

Distributive Property

$a(b+c) = a(b) + a(c)$ $a(b-c) = a(b) - a(c)$

Guided Practice*

ⓒ **MATHEMATICAL PRACTICES**

Do you know HOW?

In **1** through **4**, find each missing number.

1. $8(7 + 23) = 8(7) + 8(\ \ )$

2. $4(28) = 4(20) + 4\ (\ \ )$

3. $8(57) - 8(7) = 8(\ \ )$

4. $5(26 - 3) = 5\ (\ \ ) - 5(3)$

Do you UNDERSTAND?

ⓒ **5. Construct Arguments** Why is it easier to evaluate 7×60 than to evaluate $7 \times 55 + 7 \times 5$?

6. Tony read 22 pages in the morning and 28 pages in the afternoon for 5 days. Lois read 47 pages each day for 5 days. Explain how to use the Distributive Property to find how many pages each of them read.

Independent Practice

Leveled Practice In **7** through **16**, use the Distributive Property to find each missing number.

7. $6(32) = 6(\ \ ) + 6(2)$

8. $20(5) - 20(2) = 20(\ \ )$

9. $3(28) + (3)2 = \ \ (30)$

10. $9(23) = 9(\ \ ) + 9(3)$

11. $6(46) - 6(6) = 6(\ \ )$

12. $4(33) = 4(30) + 4(\ \ )$

13. $30(22 - 10) = 30(22) - 30(\ \ )$

14. $8(99) = 8(100) - 8(\ \ )$

15. $20(33 - 5) = 20(\ \ )$
$= 20(\ \ ) + 20(8)$

16. $5(42) + 5(5) = 5(\ \ )$
$= 5(\ \ ) + 5(7)$

For another example, see Set D on page 57.

Use the Distributive Property to break apart a number to find the product for 5 × 27.

5 × 27   ← Break 27 apart.

5(20 + 7)   ← 27 = 20   7

5(20) + 5(7)   ← Multiply each addend.

100 + 35   ← Add.

135

5 × 27 = 135

Use the Distributive Property to join numbers together to find 8(32) − 8(2).

8(32) − 8(2)

8(32 − 2)   ← Join factors.

8(30)   ← Subtract.

240   ← Multiply.

8(32) − 8(2) = 240

Independent Practice

Use the Distributive Property and mental math to evaluate.

Tip *When doing mental math, choose to join or break apart based on which is easier.*

17. 7(29)

18. 6(21) + 6(31)

19. 5(22) + 5(8)

20. 8(47)

21. 6(41) + 6(9)

22. 30(3) + 30(5)

23. 4(21) − 4(11)

24. 5(25 − 3)

Problem Solving

25. Writing to Explain The 6th graders ordered lunch from the Big Group Menu. They ordered 22 organic chilis and 8 veggie plates. Their order can be expressed as 6(22) + 6(8). Explain what mental math steps you would use to find the total cost of the order.

26. Using the Big Group Menu, write and solve a problem where you can use the Distributive Property.

27. Critique Reasoning LeAnn says that $x + x + x + x = 4x$. Use the Distributive Property to explain why you agree or disagree with LeAnn's statement.

28. Hiroko put money in a savings account each week. After 9 weeks, there was $49.50 in the account. If Hiroko put the same amount in each week, how much did she save each week?

29. Think About the Structure Which choice shows a problem with common factors that could be used for mental math?

A 3(45) + 3(5)

B 4(18) − 7(8)

C 2(22) + 3(33)

D 8(39) + 4(40)

Big Group Menu (Data)

Organic Chili	$6.00
Chicken Tacos	$4.00
Fruit Salad	$5.00
Organic Salad	$5.00
Veggie Plate	$6.00

$49.50

?								

↑

Amount saved each week

Lesson
2-5

Common
Core

This lesson reinforces
concepts and skills required
for Topic 3.

Mental Math

How can you break apart numbers to compute mentally?

Jo has to read 45 history pages and 46 science pages by the end of next week.

How many total pages must Jo read?

46 pages

45 pages

Another Example **What other strategies can you use to compute mentally?**

Look for compatible numbers and use properties of operations to compute mentally.

$5 \times 28 \times 20$

$(5 \times 20) \times 28$

100×28

$2,800$

$42 + 39 + 8$

$(42 + 8) + 39$

$50 + 39$

89

Tip *Use the Commutative and Associative Properties when multiplying or adding.*

Use compensation to create compatible numbers that are easy to compute mentally.

$57 + 698$

$(57 - 2) + (698 + 2)$

$55 + 700$

755

$355 - 297$

$355 - (297 + 3)$

$355 - 300$

$55 + 3$

58

$5(89)$

$5(90 - 1)$

$5(90) - 5(1)$

$450 - 5$

445

Explain It

1. When you use compensation to subtract 297 from 355, why must you add to the difference you find?

2. When you use compensation to multiply, which property are you using?

Use mental math.

Break apart the numbers into tens and ones.

$$45 = 40 + 5$$
$$\underline{+\ 46 = 40 + 6}$$

Do simpler calculations: Add the tens and add the ones.

$$40 + 5$$
$$\underline{+\ 40 + 6}$$
$$80 + 11$$

Combine the sums.

$$80 + 11 = 91$$

So, $45 + 46 = 91$.

Explain why breaking apart the numbers works.

$(40 + 5) + (40 + 6)$ ← Break apart numbers.

$(40 + 40) + (5 + 6)$ ← Use Commutative and Associative Properties.

$80 + 11$ ← Add.

91 ← Add.

Jo has 91 pages to read.

Guided Practice*

Do you know HOW?

Compute mentally.

1. $89 + 32 + 8$

2. $76 + 59 + 6$

3. $2 \times 9 \times 20$

4. $5 \times 31 \times 2$

5. 8×39

6. $48 + 52$

7. $453 - 397$

8. $6(42)$

Do you UNDERSTAND?

© **9. Construct Arguments** When you use the Compensation Strategy in a problem such as 5×698, you turn one multiplication problem into two and then combine them. Why does this idea make sense?

10. Jo has to read 2 science chapters for each of the next 5 weeks. Each chapter is 45 pages long. How many pages does she have to read?

Independent Practice

Compute mentally.

11. $10 + 23 + 130$

12. $721 - 395$

13. $2 \times 38 \times 5$

14. $28 + 26 + 32 + 14$

15. $5 \times 3 \times 40$

16. $(856 - 400) - 3$

17. $6(69)$

18. $80 \times 10 \times 5$

19. $44 + 56$

20. $840 + 260 + 72$

21. $495 + 75 + 14$

22. $397 + 255$

23. $8(82)$

24. $4 \times 5 \times 25$

For another example, see Set E on page 58.

Use the data table for **25** and **26**. Find the answers mentally.

25. How much did Jacob make during the first three weeks?

ⓒ **26. Reasonableness** Jamal earned $5 for every dollar Jacob earned during week 4 on his paper route. How much money did Jamal earn?

Jacob's earnings on his paper route this month	
Week 1	$45
Week 2	$32
Week 3	$55
Week 4	$64

ⓒ **27. Communicate** Avis swam her first lap in 32 seconds and her second lap in 45 seconds. Explain the steps you can use to mentally calculate her total time.

28. Use the break-apart strategy to mentally solve 81 + 43 + 2.

ⓒ **29. Use Tools** Copy and complete the bar diagram to show how to use the Distributive Property to mentally compute the problem below.

Four friends are having a snack. They each have 8 strawberries and 22 blueberries. How many berries do they have altogether?

? Berries

↑
Berries to
each friend

30. What kind of numbers would make 3-factor multiplication problems easy to do mentally?

ⓒ **31. Writing to Explain** Explain how you can use the Distributive Property to multiply 6 and 82.

One of the world's tallest fountains shoots water 171 m into the air once per hour. Use this information for **32** and **33**.

ⓒ **32. Think About the Structure** Which expression shows a break-apart strategy to mentally calculate the total of the heights of the water this fountain shoots in the air in 5 hours?

A 171×5 **B** $5(100 \times 71)$ **C** $170 \times 5 + 1$ **D** $5(100 + 70 + 1)$

33. The fountain sprays water for 15 minutes during every hour between 10:00 A.M. and 9:00 P.M. If the fountain sprayed water 10 times higher than it does, how high would the water shoot up? Solve mentally, and then check your answer.

171 m high spray
each hour

Mixed Problem Solving

Counting Calories

Calories come from the food you eat. Your body converts those calories into the energy you need every day.

After class, the sixth grade had the snack foods shown in the chart. For **1** through **5**, write an expression to show how many calories the person ate. Then, evaluate each expression.

Tip *Make sure to watch the units on the chart compared to the units in the problems.*

Calories in Snack Foods			
Snack Food	**Calories**	**Snack Food**	**Calories**
Dried Fruit (oz)		**Fruit (med)**	
raisins	115	apple	80
apricots	40	banana	105
dates	70	orange	60
Other (cup)		peach	35
pretzels	60	**Veggies (cup)**	
plain popcorn	25	carrots	70
Cheese (oz)		celery	20
cheddar	105	**Nuts (tbsp)**	
low fat cottage cheese	25	almonds	55
		Brazil nuts	60
Swiss	105	cashews	50
		peanuts	50

1. Wen-Wei ate a peach and an apple for lunch. After class, he ate 2 cups of celery and 8 tablespoons of peanuts. How many calories did he eat after class?

2. Andrea ate 3 tablespoons of Brazil nuts. Then she ate 2 more tablespoons. Later, she ate another 4 tablespoons.

3. Gloria ate 2 ounces of low fat cottage cheese, a cup of carrots, and 6 tablespoons of cashews. Then, she went back and got 4 more tablespoons of cashews and an orange. She ate everything but half of the orange.

4. Ayesha ate 4 cups of celery, 3 oranges, and 2 ounces of Swiss cheese.

5. Daryl took 2 oz dried apricots, 4 tbsp almonds, and 2 cups of pretzels. He ate all of it, except for 1 oz of apricots.

For **6** and **7**, write an expression that describes the situation, and then evaluate the expression.

6. Paulo took 4 bananas, 6 ounces of dates, 4 ounces of cheddar cheese, and 2 ounces of Swiss cheese. He split it all evenly with Alex. How many calories did Paulo eat?

7. Kyle filled a basket with 10 cups of plain popcorn. He shared it equally with 4 other people. Then, he got an apple and shared it equally with 1 other person. On his last trip to the snack table, he took 3 ounces of raisins, but he tripped and dropped 1 ounce of them. How many calories did Kyle eat?

Lesson
2-6

Common
Core

6.EE.2 Write, read, and
evaluate expressions in
which letters stand for
numbers. Also 6.EE.2.a,
6.EE.2.b, 6.EE.2.c, 6.EE.3,
6.NS.2

Evaluating Expressions

How can you evaluate an algebraic expression?

Willie has one large case that holds 20 miniature racecars.
He also has 3 smaller cases with miniature racecars.

The number of miniature cars Willie has
can be expressed as $20 + 3x$. How many
miniature cars does he have if each
smaller case holds 14 cars?

Guided Practice*

 MATHEMATICAL
PRACTICES

Do you know HOW?

Use substitution to evaluate.

Tip *Remember that substituting means to
replace the variable with a value.*

1. $t - 8$; $t = 18$ **2.** $6(w) + 9$; $w = 3$

3. $2x \div 4$; $x = 12$ **4.** $3z + 4 - 2z$; $z = 5$

5. $p + (8p - 4)$; $p = 9$

Do you UNDERSTAND?

6. Communicate Why is it important
to use order of operations to evaluate
algebraic expressions?

7. Suppose that Willie's large case holds
36 cars, and the 3 small cases each hold
18 cars. Write an algebraic expression
to represent the number of cars. Then,
evaluate the expression for $x = 18$.

Independent Practice

For **8** through **22**, evaluate each expression
for 3, 4, and 10.

 Tip *Remember to keep the order
of operations in mind.*

8. $9x$ **9.** $3x + 6$ **10.** $48 \div x$ **11.** $x(0)$ **12.** $1x$

13. $x(4) \div 2$ **14.** $x - 3$ **15.** $x^2 + 1$ **16.** $x \div x$ **17.** $100 - x^2$

18. $3x + 4x$ **19.** $2x + 7$ **20.** $3x + 9$ **21.** $5x + 6x$ **22.** $x^2 - 1$

23. Evaluate the expression for the values
of n.

n	3	5	8	12	25
$2 + 3n$					

24. Evaluate the expression for the values
of k.

k	6	9	12
$2(k - 4)$			

Animated Glossary
www.pearsonsuccessnet.com

DIGITAL

For another example, see Set F on page 58.

Evaluate 20 + 3*x*.

Evaluate means to <u>find a value of an expression</u>. To evaluate an algebraic expression, use substitution to <u>replace the variable with a number</u>.

If *x* equals the number of miniature cars in each smaller case, then evaluate for *x* = 14.

$$20 + 3(14)$$
$$20 + 42$$
$$62$$

Willie has 62 miniature racecars.

Suppose that the smaller cases each hold 10 miniature cars. How many cars would he have then?

$$20 + 3x$$
$$20 + 3(10)$$
$$50$$

Willie would have 50 cars.

x	20 + 3*x*
14	62
10	50

Problem Solving

MATHEMATICAL
PRACTICES

Use the table at right for **25** and **26**.

Ⓒ **25. Model** Corinne wants to rent a small white car. It will cost the weekly fee plus 30¢ per mile. Write an expression that shows the amount Corinne will owe for her car. Then solve for 100 miles.

Ⓒ **26. Be Precise** Trey is renting a luxury car for a week and a few days. He does not have to pay a per-mile fee. Write an expression that shows the amount Trey will owe for his car. Then solve for an 11-day rental.

Vehicle	Week	Day
Small car	$250	$100
Medium car	$290	$110
Luxury car	$325	$120
Small van	$350	$150
Large van	$390	$170

Ⓒ **27. Writing to Explain** What operations are involved in the expressions 2*x* + 7 and 3*x* + 6?

Ⓒ **28. Persevere** There have been more than 30 spacecraft landings on the Moon and 12 astronauts have walked on the Moon's surface. They have brought 842 pounds of lunar rock and soil back to Earth. If *x* equals the average number of pounds of lunar rock and soil brought back by each astronaut, evaluate 12*x* = 842 to find the value of *x*.

29. The Moon is about 238,900 miles from Earth. Which expression best shows the distance, *d*, to the Moon from a spacecraft that is directly between the Earth and the Moon and is 50,000 miles from Earth?

A 50,000 + *d* = 238,900   **C** *d* + 238,900 = 50,000

B 50,000 − *d* = 238,900   **D** 50,000*d* = 238,900

Lesson
2-7

Common
Core

6.EE.2 Write, read, and
evaluate expressions in
which letters stand for
numbers.

Using Expressions to Describe Patterns

How can you write expressions to describe patterns?

Delvin saves a part of everything he earns. The table
at the right shows Delvin's savings pattern.

The INPUT column shows the money he has earned.
The OUTPUT column shows the money he has saved.

Write an expression to describe the pattern.

INPUT	OUTPUT
$84	$42
$66	$33
$50	$25
$22	▢
$30	▢

Guided Practice*

MATHEMATICAL
PRACTICES

Do you know HOW?

Use the input/output table for **1** and **2**.

INPUT	0	1	2	3	4
OUTPUT	3	4	5	6	7

1. If the input number is 8, what is the
output number?

2. Write an algebraic expression that
describes the output pattern.

Do you UNDERSTAND?

3. Suppose that Delvin earned $36
mowing lawns. What input and output
entries would you add to his table?

4. Reasonableness Is it reasonable for
an output to be greater than the input
in the table above? Explain.

5. What algebraic expression using division
also describes the output pattern for the
table above?

Independent Practice

Use this table for **6** and **7**.

6. What is the cost of 4 lb, 5 lb, and 10 lb
of apples?

Apple Weight	1 lb	2 lb	3 lb	4 lb	5 lb	10 lb
Apple Price	$2	$4	$6	▢	▢	▢

7. Write an algebraic expression that describes the output
pattern if the input is a variable a.

Use this table for **8** and **9**.

8. Copy and complete the table.

9. Write an algebraic expression that describes
the relationship between the input and
output values.

Total Students	12	18	24	27	36	39
Number of Study Groups	▢	6	8	▢	12	▢

Animated Glossary
www.pearsonsuccessnet.com

An input/output table is a <u>table of related values</u>. Identify the pattern.

What is the relationship between the values?

$\frac{1}{2}$ (84) = 42 ➙ 42 is half of 84.

$\frac{1}{2}$ (66) = 33 ➙ 33 is half of 66.

$\frac{1}{2}$ (50) = 25 ➙ 25 is half of 50.

The pattern is: $\frac{1}{2}$ (INPUT) = OUTPUT

Let x = INPUT.

So, the pattern is $\frac{1}{2}$ x.

Use the pattern to find the missing values.

$\frac{1}{2}$ (22) = 11

$\frac{1}{2}$ (30) = 15

INPUT	OUTPUT
$84	$42
$66	$33
$50	$25
$22	$11
$30	$15

Problem Solving

MATHEMATICAL PRACTICES

Use the input/output table at right for **10** and **11**.

© **10. Model** Hazem keeps $\frac{1}{3}$ of the tips he earns. Also, he gets $1 each night to reimburse his parking fee. This information is shown in the input/output table. Write an algebraic expression that describes the output pattern if the input is the variable *k*.

11. How much money would Hazem keep in a night if he takes in $36 in tips?

INPUT	OUTPUT
$12	$5
$27	$10
$36	
$48	$17

Use the input/output table at right for **12** and **13**.

12. Ms. Windsor's classroom has a tile floor. The students are making stars to put in the center of 4-tile groups. This input/output chart shows the pattern. Write an algebraic expression that describes the output pattern if the input is the variable *t*.

© **13. Writing to Explain** There are 30 rows with 24 tiles in each row on a floor. Explain how to find the number of stars needed to complete the pattern for the floor.

INPUT (tiles)	OUTPUT (stars)
4	1
8	2
12	3

Use the table at right for **14**.

© **14. Think About the Structure** Which algebraic expression shows the cost of a chosen number of books *b*?

A b + $2.50

B $2.50b

C $b − $2.50

D b ÷ $2.50

Number of Books	Total Cost
1	$2.50
2	$5.00
3	$7.50

Data

Common Core

6.EE.6 Use variables to represent numbers and write expressions when solving a real-world or mathematical problem; understand that a variable can represent an unknown number, or, depending on the purpose at hand any number in a specified set. **Also 6.EE.2**

Make a Table

The Douglas family had $700 in their road-trip fund. They spent $75 each day on their trip. If *x* equals the number of days, write an expression that describes the amount of money left in the fund after *x* days.

Make a table to show the values of the expression for *x* = 3 days, *x* = 5 days, and *x* = 9 days.

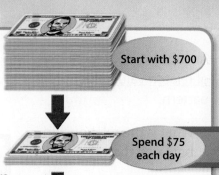

Start with $700

Spend $75 each day

Amount left

Guided Practice*

 MATHEMATICAL PRACTICES

Do you know HOW?

1. The sixth-grade chess club is washing cars for a fund-raiser. They started with $150 in their fund and are charging $5 per car. Use the expression $150 + 5x$ to copy and complete the table, to find how much money the chess club will have after washing 25, 31, and 54 cars.

x	25		

Do you UNDERSTAND?

2. Be Precise How do you know what labels to use in a table?

3. Use Tools Use the table to write a word problem that could be solved using the table below.

x	5	6	7
$6.25x - 3.45$	27.80	34.05	40.30

Independent Practice

MATHEMATICAL PRACTICES

4. For every A Josh earns on his report card, he is given 2 movie passes. He still has 2 movie passes left from his last report card. If *x* equals the number of A's Josh earns, use the expression $2x + 2$ to copy and complete the table to find how many movie passes Josh will have for 1, 2, or 3 A's.

x	
1	
2	
3	

Applying Math Practices

- What am I asked to find?
- What else can I try?
- How are quantities related?
- How can I explain my work?
- How can I use math to model the problem?
- Can I use tools to help?
- Is my work precise?
- Why does this work?
- How can I generalize?

Write an expression that describes the amount of money left in the fund after x days.

700

| 75 | x days ⟶ | |

↑
amount left

Total in fund − $75(number of days)

$700 − 75x$

Make a table to solve for different values of x. Include labels for the variable and the expression.

Enter the values of x you want to find. Then evaluate the expression for each value.

x	$700 − 75x$
3	475
5	325
9	25

© **5. Reason** Kat is playing a game called "500." Each player starts with 500 points and loses 10 points for each question answered correctly. The first player to reach 0 points wins. Which expression represents how many points Kat will have if she answers x questions correctly?

A $500x$ 　　　 **C** $500 + 10x$

B $500 − 10x$ 　 **D** $10x − 500$

© **6. Use Tools** Copy and complete the table for Exercise 5 to find how many points Kat will have if she answers 9, 13, and 24 questions correctly.

x	
9	
13	
24	

7. Jordan is playing in a charity basketball game. The local barber pledged to pay $2 for every point he scores. The local grocery store will give a one-time donation of $75. Which expression represents how much money Jordan will raise if he scores x points?

A $75 + 2x$ 　　 **C** $75 + 4x$

B $77x$ 　　　　 **D** $75 − 2x$

© **8. Generalize** Jeremy started a club to help senior citizens use computers. On the first day, he was the only member. On the second day, two friends joined. Each day after that, two more members joined. If x equals the number of days, evaluate the expression $1 + 2(x − 1)$ to find the membership of the club on the 10th day.

9. The camp chef is making waffles for breakfast. The recipe calls for 3 cups of milk for every batch. If x equals the number of batches, copy and complete the table to show how much milk the chef needs for 3, 7, and 10 batches.

x	
3	
7	
10	

Use the information at right for **10** through **14**.

Ⓒ **10.** **Reason** Carver bought some plants at the Garden Center sale. On his bill, he saw that he had paid $20 for 5 plants. What size did Carver buy?

Garden Center Sale	
Small Plants	$2
Medium Plants	$3
Large Plants	$4

Ⓒ **11.** **Model** Sally and her mother went to the sale at the Garden Center. Sally bought x large plants and y small plants. She paid with a twenty-dollar bill. Make a table using the expression $20 - (4x + 2y)$ to show how much change she received if she bought 2 large plants and 4 small plants; 4 large plants and 2 small plants; or 1 large plant and 7 small plants.

Tip *Make a separate column for each variable.*

12. Elyse has a small flower garden in her backyard. She wants to plant seven rows of flowers. She drew a plan of her garden.

   a If each row can hold 3 large plants, 4 medium plants, or 8 small plants, how many of each should Elyse buy?

   b What will the total cost be for all of Elyse's plants?

Ⓒ **13.** **Communicate** Maggie wants to plant a 10 ft row of large plants. A large plant needs 1.5 ft between plants. Maggie will put her first plant 0.5 ft from the end. How much money will Maggie need to fill the row? Explain how you found your answer.

14. Art has $32. How many large plants could he buy? medium plants? small plants?

Ⓒ **Think About the Structure**

15. William and Anne are selling magazines. For each magazine sold, their soccer team raises $2.25. Which value completes this table?

x	$2.25x$
17	▩

   A 19.25   **C** 382.5

   B 3825   **D** 38.25

16. Tanya has a job delivering newspapers. Every week, each of her customers pay her $1.50. She also receives an allowance of $5 a week. If Tanya has x newspaper customers, which expression best describes how much money Tanya receives each week?

   A $5x - 1.5$ **C** $5 + 1.5x$

   B $5x + 1.5$ **D** $5 - 1.5x$

Skills Review Write each phrase as an algebraic expression.

1. 7 less than a number x

2. 5 times a number p

3. 4 times a number m, minus 3 times a number k

4. 8, plus two times a number j

Use the properties of operations to fill in the blanks in each expression.

5. $28 \times 5 = 5 \times \rule{1em}{0.8em}$

6. $12 \times 25 \times 32 = 12 \times \rule{1em}{0.8em} \times 25 \times 32$

7. $7 + (30 + 15) = (7 + 30) + \rule{1em}{0.8em}$

8. $23 + 8 = 23 + 8 + \rule{1em}{0.8em}$

Evaluate each expression for $x = 3$ and $y = 5$.

9. $5x + 8$

10. $(10 - y)(10)$

11. $10y + 23$

12. Write an algebraic expression for the value of y that explains the relationship between x and y. Then finish the table.

x	7	8	9	10	11
y	17	19	21		

Error Search Find each answer that is not correct. Write it correctly and explain the error.

13. $8 + 2 \times 6 = 60$

14. $8 \times 0 + (4 \times 1) = 4$

15. $4(24) = 4(6) + 4(4)$

16. $32 + 73 = (30 + 70) + (2 + 3)$

17. $58(40) = 50(40) \times 8(40)$

18. $4(51 + 32) = 4(80) + 4(3)$

Number Sense

Insert parentheses to make each sentence true.

19. $3 \times 8 + 3 \times 2 = 66$

20. $2 \times 5 + 4 - 8 = 10$

21. $15 - 2 \times 3 + 5^2 = 64$

22. $4x - 5 = 4x - 20$

23. $6 + 8 - 3 \times 7 = 41$

24. $4 + 4 \times 3 + 5 = 29$

25. $3^2 - 8 \times 0 = 9$

26. $80 \div 2 \times 2 + 2 \times 3 = 26$

27. $25 - 10 + 3 \div 2 + 4 = 3$

1. Tickets cost $30 each plus a one-time $2 postage fee. Which expression shows the cost for *n* tickets? (2-1)

   A $30n + 2$

   B $30n - 2$

   C $30(n + 2)$

   D $30 + 2n$

2. Luis bought 5 boxes of ceramic tiles with 20 tiles in each. Each tile covers 36 square inches. Use mental math to evaluate $20 \times 36 \times 5$ and find the total square inches. (2-5)

   A $1,360 \text{ in}^2$

   B $3,600 \text{ in}^2$

   C $7,200 \text{ in}^2$

   D $9,000 \text{ in}^2$

3. What number makes the number sentence true? (2-5)

   $4 \times 8 \times 25 = 100 \times$ ▨

   A 200

   B 32

   C 25

   D 8

4. At the Jacovic family reunion, 42 tables each had 6 people. To find the number of people, Ivan did the computation shown below. What number makes the number sentence true? (2-4)

   $6(40 + 2) = 240 +$ ▨

   A 62

   B 42

   C 14

   D 12

5. What is the value of the expression in the table when $m = 6$? (2-6)

m	$50 - 4m$
2	42
4	34
6	

   A 24

   B 26

   C 44

   D 52

6. Large balloons are sold in packages of 12. Which expression can represent the total number of balloons in *a* packages of large balloons? (2-1)

   A $12a$

   B $12 \div a$

   C $a \div 12$

   D $12 + a$

7. Which algebraic expression can be used to describe the output pattern in the table if the input is a variable *p*? (2-7)

Boxes of Pens and Total Number of Pens			
Input	4	6	8	10
Output	32	48	64	80

   A $p + 14$

   B $2p$

   C $8p$

   D $p \div 9$

8. Use the expression shown to find how many people attended the field trip. (2-3)

$15 \times 4 + 10 \times 5$

A 110 people

B 350 people

C 810 people

D 1,050 people

9. Which of the following shows a way to find $127 + 396$ using compensation? (2-5)

A $127 + 400 + 4$

B $127 - 400 + 4$

C $127 - 400 - 4$

D $127 + 400 - 4$

10. Alita sells necklaces for $3 each. She spent $14 on supplies. The expression $3x - 14$ can be used to find the amount Alita earns for selling x necklaces. How much will Alita earn if she sells 12 necklaces? (2-6)

A $36

B $24

C $22

D $6

11. The expression shown below can be used to find the total cost of violin lessons for a year. What is the first step to evaluate the expression? (2-3)

$25 + 14 \times (52 - 6)$

A Add $25 + 14$.

B Multiply 14×52.

C Subtract $52 - 6$.

D Multiply 14×6.

12. Which property is shown below? (2-2)

$2 \times 32 \times 5 = 2 \times 5 \times 32$

A Associative Property of Multiplication

B Commutative Property of Multiplication

C Identity Property of Multiplication

D Multiplication Property of Zero

13. If the input number is 20 in the table shown, what is the output number? (2-7)

Input	Output
6	12
8	14
10	16

A 26

B 24

C 22

D 18

14. A machine can make 375 bales of hay in 3 hours. At this rate, how long does it take the machine to make 875 bales of hay? (2-8)

Time, h	1	3	
Bales, $125 \times h$	125	375	875

A 9 hours

B 8 hours

C 7 hours

D 6 hours

Set A, pages 32–33

Variables represent values that can change.

The expression 24 + *n* means "the sum of 24 and a number." The unknown number is a variable that is expressed by a letter, *n*.

Operation Terms

Addition	→ Sum
Subtraction	→ Difference
Multiplication	→ Product
Division	→ Quotient

Remember that you can use any letter as a variable that stands for an unknown value.

Write the phrases as algebraic expressions.

1. 22 less forks than a number, *f*
2. 48 times a number of game markers, *g*
3. a number of eggs, *e*, divided by 12
4. 3 times the number of milk cartons, *m*, used by the 6th grade class

Set B, pages 34–35

The properties of operations help you evaluate expressions.

Properties of Operations	
Commutative Property of Addition	7 + 5 = 12 So, 5 + 7 = 12.
Commutative Property of Multiplication	3 × 8 = 24 So, 8 × 3 = 24.
Associative Property of Addition	2 + (3 + 5) = 10 So, (2 + 3) + 5 = 10.
Associative Property of Multiplication	4 × (3 × 5) = 60 So, (4 × 3) × 5 = 60.
Identity Property of Addition	Adding zero does not change a number. So, 435 + 0 = 435.
Identity Property of Multiplication	Multiplying by one does not change a number. So, 84 × 1 = 84.

Evaluate the expression: 4 + 8 + 3 + 2

Following properties of operations:

$$\begin{aligned} 4 + 8 + 3 + 2 &= 4 + 3 + 8 + 2 \\ &= 7 + 10 \\ &= 17 \end{aligned}$$

Remember that when the properties of operations are not followed, numerical expressions are computed incorrectly.

Tell what properties are shown.

1. 3(4 × 32) = (3 × 4)32
2. 21 × 1 = 21
3. 9 + 8 + 4 = 8 + 4 + 9
4. 9 + 0 = 9
5. 6 × 8 = 8 × 6
6. 5 + 4 = 4 + 5
7. 6 × (4 × 3) = (6 × 4) × 3
8. 8 + (2 + 4) = (8 + 2) + 4
9. 9 × 5 × 4 = 9 × 4 × 5
10. 12 + 0 = 12
11. 425 × 1 = 425
12. (8 × 5) × 4 = 4 × (5 × 8)

The order of operations helps you get the correct answer. The order of operations rules are:

Step 1 Compute inside parentheses.

Step 2 Evaluate terms with exponents.

Step 3 Multiply and divide from left to right.

Step 4 Add and subtract from left to right.

Evaluate $8 + 6 \times 9 - 4 \div 2$.

First, multiply and divide. $8 + 54 - 2$

Then, add and subtract. 60

Remember that when the order of operations rules are followed, it helps you get the correct answer.

Use parentheses to make each sentence true.

1. $9 + 8 - 2 \times 7 + 1 = 1$

2. $40 - 4 \times 4^2 \div 2 = 8$

3. $5 \times 5 - 3 - 2 = 0$

4. $8 + 12 \div 4 + 6 = 11$

5. $9 + 8 \div 2 \times 4 + 3^2 = 19$

6. $6 \times 2 - 1 + 5^2 = 31$

7. $8 \times 3 + 8 - 2^2 = 84$

8. $50 - 3 \times 6 + 2 + 4^2 = 42$

Use the Distributive Property to evaluate mentally.

$8(42)$

Break the numbers apart to find numbers that are easier to multiply mentally.

$8(40 + 2)$

Apply the Distributive Property.

$8(40) + 8(2)$

Multiply the separate terms. Add the products.

$320 + 16 = 336$

Remember that the Distributive Property says that multiplying a sum by a number is the same as multiplying each addend by the number and adding the products.

Use the Distributive Property to evaluate mentally.

1. $5(41) + 5(9)$

2. $3(45)$

3. $4(23)$

4. $9(32) + 9(8)$

5. $3(27)$

6. $6(7) + 6(23)$

Set E, pages 42–44

Ⓒ **INTERVENTION**

Find 4 × 18 × 25 using compatible numbers to compute mentally.

Look for compatible numbers that are easy to compute.

$4 \times 18 \times 25$

$4 \times 25 \times 18$

Then do the remaining calculation.

$100 \times 18 = 1{,}800$

So, $4 \times 18 \times 25 = 1{,}800$.

Remember to find compatible numbers to make your mental math easier.

Compute mentally.

1. $15 + 67 + 25$

2. $463 - 333$

3. $6 \times 23 \times 5$

4. $250 \times 6 \times 4$

5. $921 + 529$

6. $297 - 100$

7. $2 \times 8 \times 5$

8. $20 \times 16 \times 5$

Set F, pages 46–47

Evaluate each expression for $x = 2$.

1. $7x - 3$

$7(2) - 3$ ⟵ Use substitution.

$14 - 3 = 11$ ⟵ Compute.

2. $4x + 2$

$4(2) + 2$ ⟵ Use substitution.

$8 + 2 = 10$ ⟵ Compute.

3. $9x \div 3$

$9(2) \div 3$ ⟵ Use substitution.

$18 \div 3 = 6$ ⟵ Compute.

Remember that using *substitution* means to replace the variables with the chosen values.

Evaluate each expression for $x = 4$.

1. $12x - 7$

2. $3x + 18$

3. $11x + 4$

4. $8x + 2$

5. $6x \div 2$

6. $8x - 5$

7. $7x \div 4$

8. $4x - 9$

9. $22x + 6$

10. $9x - 3$

11. $4x \div (x - 2)$

12. $10x - 8$

You can write an algebraic expression that explains an input/output relationship. If x is 4, how can you express 9?

Try: $2x + 1 = 9$

See if that works for the other input values.

$2 \times 8 + 1 = 17$

$2 \times 11 + 1 = 23$

Yes, it works!

INPUT	OUTPUT
4	9
8	17
11	23

Remember that input/output tables can help you see patterns in expressions.

Use this input/output table for **1** and **2**.

Dollars Sold	Prize Points
$20	4
$40	8
$60	12
$115	■

1. Students earn prize points for selling fundraising items. Write an algebraic expression that explains the relationship between input dollars sold, d, and output prize points.

2. How many prize points would a student earn for selling $115 worth of items?

Making a table to organize your data helps to identify patterns and quickly find solutions. When making a table, include labels for the variable and the expression. Enter the values of x you want to find. Then solve the expression for each value.

Ginny is paid $12 a week for doing chores. She puts the money in her savings account. If she started out with $112, find out how much money she has in her account after 3 weeks and after 8 weeks.

Step 1 Identify the expression.
$112 + 12x$

Step 2 Make a table.

x	$112 + 12x$
3	$148
8	$208

Remember to choose labels based on the information to be found.

Write an expression for each problem. Then make a table to solve it.

1. Anna walks her dog 2 miles a day, 5 days a week. Write an expression describing how far Anna and her dog walked after x weeks.

2. Todd earns $500 a week, plus $50 every time he sells a computer. Write an expression to show how much money Todd earns per week when he sells x computers. Then make a table to show how much Todd earns in a week if he sells 2, 4, or 5 computers.

Operations with Decimals

1 The wings of a ruby-throated hummingbird beat an average of 52 times per second. How many times would its wings beat in a minute? You will find out in Lesson 3-4.

2 What is the world record for jumping the farthest distance on a pogo stick? You will find out in Lesson 3-3.

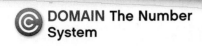

DOMAIN The Number System

3 In 1927, Charles Lindbergh flew across the Atlantic Ocean in about 33 hours. About how many miles per hour did he fly? You will find out in Lesson 3-7.

4 The longest spin of a basketball on one finger is 255 minutes. How many hours is this? You will find out in Lesson 3-6.

Review What You Know!

Vocabulary

Choose the best term from the box.

- dividend
- base
- decimal
- variable

1. A(n) __?__ is a quantity that can vary and is often represented by a letter.

2. A number that is being divided by another number is called the __?__ .

3. A number that uses a decimal point and has one or more digits to the right of the decimal point is a(n) __?__ .

4. The repeated factor raised to a power in exponential form is called the __?__ .

Whole Number Operations

Calculate each value.

5. $9{,}007 - 3{,}128$ **6.** $7{,}964 + 3{,}872$

7. 35×17 **8.** 181×42

9. $768 \div 6$ **10.** $506 \div 22$

Order of Operations

Evaluate each expression.

11. $6 \times 2 + 4$ **12.** $45 - 24 \div 6$

13. $(20 + 19) \div 3$ **14.** $25 - 5 \times 2$

Decimals

15. Writing to Explain What decimal does this model represent? Explain.

Lesson
3-1

Common
Core

6.NS.3 Fluently add,
subtract, multiply, and
divide multi-digit decimals
using the standard
algorithm for each
operation.

Estimating Sums and Differences

How can you estimate with decimals?

To estimate means <u>to find an approximate answer or solution</u>.

The 10-second barrier in the 100-meter dash was broken
in the 1968 Olympics, when the winning time was
9.95 seconds. Mrs. Johnson, the gym teacher, ran the
100 meters in 14.7 seconds. About how
much faster was the 1968 Olympic
time than Mrs. Johnson's time?

14.7
seconds

9.95
seconds

Guided Practice*

MATHEMATICAL
PRACTICES

Do you know HOW?

In **1** and **2**, complete each estimate by
rounding to the nearest tenth.

1. 1.769 + 0.686

    1.▢ + 0.▢ = ▢.5

2. 20.45 − 13.15

    ▢ − 13.2 = ▢

Round each number to the nearest whole
number to estimate the answer.

3. 1.456 + 5.4 + 14.08 =

4. 72.43 − 59.8 =

Do you UNDERSTAND?

5. Communicate When might you want
to estimate an answer?

6. In the problem above, how does
comparing the remaining digits in
the original numbers tell you whether
the estimate is an overestimate or an
underestimate?

7. Model Write your own real-world
problem that would be appropriate for
estimating the sum or difference
of decimals.

Independent Practice

In **8** through **10**, round each number to the nearest whole
number to estimate each answer.

8. 20.791 + 5.25 + 3.84   **9.** $10.10 − $3.69   **10.** 376.52 − 9.14

In **11** through **13**, use front-end estimation to estimate
each answer.

11. 7.12 + 2.501 + 9.2   **12.** 91.26 − 30.463   **13.** $3.79 − $1.22

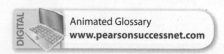

Animated Glossary
www.pearsonsuccessnet.com

One Way

Use rounding to quickly estimate sums and differences. Round each number to the same place value.

Round each number to the nearest whole number.

$$14.7 \rightarrow 15$$
$$-\ 9.95 \rightarrow -10$$
$$5$$

The difference is about 5 seconds.

Another Way

Use the front-end digits to make a front-end estimate, and then adjust the estimate using the remaining digits.

$$14.7 \rightarrow 14$$
$$-\ 9.95 \rightarrow -9$$
$$5$$

Since $0.7 < 0.95$, the difference is less than 5.

The 1968 Olympic time is less than 5 seconds faster than Mrs. Johnson's time.

Problem Solving

MATHEMATICAL
PRACTICES

14. Rachel is shopping and needs to buy bread, lunchmeat, and pretzels to make lunch. She has a ten-dollar bill. Will she have enough money for her purchases? Use estimation to find whether she will have enough money. Explain your reasoning.

Grocery List
☑ Bread $1.82
☐ Lunchmeat $4.93
☐ Pretzels $2.03

© 15. **Writing to Explain** Kira and Jerome want to go to a movie and have popcorn and a drink. A movie ticket costs $7.75, and the snack and drink combo costs $2.85. Kira says if they each bring $10, it will be enough. Jerome says they each need more than $10. Who is correct and why?

© 16. **Reason** Which of the following is the best estimate for $0.375 + 2.46$?

   A 2.5   **B** 3   **C** 3.5   **D** 4

© 17. **Be Precise** In baseball, an earned run average (ERA) is the average of earned runs given up by a pitcher per nine innings pitched.

   a Order the ERAs in the table from greatest to least.

   b About how many tenths difference is there between the lowest and highest ERAs in the table?

Player	Earned Run Average (ERA)
Eddie	1.82
John	2.10
Mario	2.06
Scott	2.04
Josh	1.89

© 18. **Think About the Structure** Which expression will give an answer of 10?

   A $(5 + 3) \times 9 - 2 \div 5$

   B $5 + (3 \times 9 - 2) \div 5$

   C $2 \times (9 - 5) + 3 \div 5$

   D $2 + 9 \times (5 - 3) \div 5$

Lesson
3-2

©
Common
Core

6.NS.3 Fluently add, subtract, multiply, and divide multi-digit decimals using the standard algorithm for each operation.

Adding and Subtracting

How can you add whole numbers and decimals?

Kim and Martin swam 50 meters. Martin took 0.26 seconds longer than Kim. What was Martin's time in the race?

Choose an Operation Add to find Martin's time.

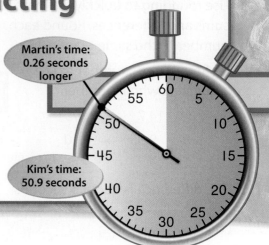

Martin's time: 0.26 seconds longer

Kim's time: 50.9 seconds

Another Example How can you subtract whole numbers and decimals?

Asha ran a race in 20.7 seconds. Katie ran the same race 0.25 seconds faster. How fast did Katie run the race?

Subtract to find Katie's time.
Find 20.7 − 0.25. Estimate the difference by rounding.

$$20.7 - 0.3 = 20.4$$

To find the difference, line up the decimal points.

$$\begin{array}{r} 20.70 \\ -0.25 \\ \hline \end{array}$$ ← Annex a zero as a placeholder.

Subtract each place.
Regroup the seven tenths to subtract the hundredths.

$$\begin{array}{r} \overset{6\ 10}{20.\cancel{7}0} \\ -0.25 \\ \hline 20.45 \end{array}$$

Katie ran the race in 20.45 seconds. 20.45 is close to the estimate 20.4.

Guided Practice*

MATHEMATICAL
PRACTICES

Do you know HOW?

In **1** through **6**, find each sum or difference.

1. 5.9 + 2.7   **2.** 4.01 − 2.95

3. 2.57 + 7.706   **4.** 1.5 − 1.056

5. 10 + 3.284   **6.** 15 − 6.108

Do you UNDERSTAND?

© **7. Construct Arguments** How is adding and subtracting decimals similar to and different from adding and subtracting whole numbers?

8. In Another Example, how does the estimate help you determine if the answer is reasonable?

Find 50.9 + 0.26. Estimate first by rounding each addend.

$$51 + 0.3 = 51.3$$

To find the sum, line up the decimal points.

$$\begin{array}{r} 50.90 \\ +\ \ 0.26 \\ \hline \end{array}$$ ← Annex a zero to 50.9 so that each place has a digit.

Add each place. You can regroup the sum of nine tenths and two tenths.

$$\begin{array}{r} \overset{1}{} \\ 50.90 \\ +\ \ 0.26 \\ \hline 51.16 \end{array}$$

Martin swam the race in 51.16 seconds. The sum 51.16 is close to the estimate, 51.3.

Independent Practice

Find each sum or difference.

9. 2.17 − 0.8   **10.** 4.3 + 4.16   **11.** 7.62 − 3.867   **12.** 4.815 + 2.17

13. 5.187 − 0.48   **14.** 5.78 + 16.597   **15.** 9.501 − 9.45   **16.** 14 + 9.8

17. 46.91 − 28.7   **18.** 5.61 + 2.4   **19.** 27 + 0.185   **20.** 0.46 − 0.333

Problem Solving

MATHEMATICAL PRACTICES

Ⓒ **21. Be Precise** The U.S. Census Bureau tracks the time it takes people to travel to work.

Location	Average Travel Time to Work (minutes)
United States	25.5
Los Angeles, CA	29.6
Chicago, IL	35.2
New York, NY	40.0

How does the average travel time for New Yorkers compare to the United States?

   A 14.5 minutes longer

   B 14.5 minutes shorter

   C 4.8 minutes longer

   D 10.4 minutes longer

Ⓒ **22. Writing to Explain** Mr. Smith gave a cashier a $50 bill for a purchase of $38.70. The cashier gave him a $10 bill, two $1 bills, and three dimes back. Did Mr. Smith get the correct change? Why or why not?

Ⓒ **23. Reason** Minh wrote the following number sentence: 2.6 + 0.33 = 5.9. Use estimation to show that Minh's answer is incorrect.

Ⓒ **24. Look for Patterns** Copy and complete the sequence of numbers.

   7.5, 6.25, 5, ▢ , ▢

Common Core

6.NS.3 Fluently add, subtract, multiply, and divide multi-digit decimals using the standard algorithm for each operation.

Estimating Products and Quotients

How can you use estimation to find a product?

The students at Waldron Middle School are selling tins of popcorn to raise money for new uniforms. They sold 42 tins in the first week. Estimate how much money the students have raised selling popcorn in the first week.

POPCORN

$9.25
each

Another Example How can you use estimation to find a quotient?

One Way

Estimate 7.83 ÷ 3.8 by rounding each factor.

$$7.83 \div 3.8$$
$$\downarrow \qquad \downarrow$$
$$8.0 \div 4.0$$

$$8.0 \div 4.0 = 2$$

So, 7.83 ÷ 3.8 ≈ 2.

Another Way

Estimate 44.3 ÷ 6.7 using compatible numbers.

$$44.3 \div 6.7$$ **44.3 is close to 42 and 6.7 is close to 7.**
$$\downarrow \qquad \downarrow$$
$$42 \div 7 = 6$$

So, 44.3 ÷ 6.7 ≈ 6.

Tip *The symbol ≈ is read "is approximately equal to."*

Explain It

1. Explain when you would use rounding or compatible numbers to estimate a product or quotient.

 2. **Reasonableness** Would it be reasonable to use 60 and 6 as compatible numbers in the Another Way problem above? Explain.

3. When estimating a quotient such as 44.3 ÷ 6.7, why is using compatible numbers easier than rounding each factor?

One Way

Estimate by rounding each factor.

$$42 \times \$9.25$$
$$\downarrow \qquad \downarrow$$
$$40 \times \$9 = \$360$$

So, $42 \times \$9.25 \approx \$360$.

The students raised about $360 the first week.

Another Way

Estimate by using compatible numbers. Compatible numbers <u>are close to the actual numbers</u>, but they are <u>easier to compute mentally</u>.

$$42 \times \$9.25$$
$$\downarrow \qquad \downarrow$$
$$42 \times \$10 = \$420$$

$9.25 is close to 10 and it is easy to multiply by 10.

So, $42 \times \$9.25 \approx \$420$.

The students raised about $420 the first week.

Guided Practice*

MATHEMATICAL PRACTICES

Do you know HOW?

Estimate each answer using rounding.

1. 6.8×53

2. $3,520 \div 6.82$

3. 65.13×2.89

4. $2,386.25 \div 40.1$

Estimate each answer by using compatible numbers.

5. 9.34×0.68

6. $35.7 \div 8.9$

7. 20.6×3.7

8. $52.3 \div 9.7$

Do you UNDERSTAND?

© 9. Communicate Which method is easier to use to estimate the amount of money the students will raise if they sell 112 tins of popcorn?

© 10. Writing to Explain In the examples at the top of the page, are the estimates overestimates or underestimates? Explain.

Independent Practice

For **11** through **26**, estimate each product or quotient.

11. $615 \div 5.3$

12. $12.10 \div 3.69$

13. 376.52×9.94

14. 20.2×1.96

15. 412×2.421

16. 98.2×33.46

17. $73.6 \div 7.16$

18. $\$73.09 \div 0.88$

19. 11.3×0.8

20. $\$26.15 \div \$3.29$

21. $973 \div 4.8$

22. 2.06×15.5

23. $240 \div 3.5$

24. 9.3×52.7

25. $\$29.95 \div 4$

26. 2.875×12.5

27. Which compatible numbers could you use to estimate $636.2 \div 91.702$?

Animated Glossary
www.pearsonsuccessnet.com

DIGITAL

28. Construct Arguments Javier used compatible numbers to estimate that 328 ÷ 49 is about 10. Do you think this is a good estimate? Explain.

29. Be Precise In the number 24.543, why is the value of each 4 different?

30. Julie estimates that she can produce 28 puzzles in one week. She sells each puzzle for $12.25. Estimate the amount of money Julie can earn in a month.

31. Use the Distributive Property to rewrite the following expression: $22 \times 3 + 11 \times 3 = 99$.

32. Estimation Use rounding to estimate 32.782×99.898. Will the estimate be greater or less than the exact product?

33. Estimation The sixth grade ordered 19 medium veggie pizzas. Each cost $8.49. Estimate the cost of the pizzas.

34. Persevere The diagram at the right shows the distance and time records set in 1997 for pogo-stick jumping. Estimate the number of miles jumped each hour.

35. Use your estimate of the number of miles jumped per hour from Exercise 34 to estimate how many miles were jumped after 5 hours.

36. Look for Patterns Copy and complete the pattern.

6.5, 5.25, 4, ▢, ▢

37. Think About the Structure Latrell is buying clothes for school. He has $150. He wants to buy two pairs of jeans for $38 each and 2 shirts for $25 each. Which expression shows how to find whether he has enough money?

A $(150 \times 2) - 38 + (2 + 25)$

B $150 - (2 \times 38) - (2 \times 25)$

C $150 + (2 \times 38) \div (2 \times 25)$

D $150 \div (2 + 38) \times (2 \times 25)$

38. Reason Charlie practiced his clarinet for 1.5 hours on Monday and 2.25 hours on Tuesday. If he promised his teacher that he would practice 6 hours a week, about how much more time does he need to practice this week?

A About 1 hour

B About 2 hours

C About 3 hours

D About 4 hours

Mixed Problem Solving

Lafayette dollar weighs 26.73 g.

Diameter is 38.1 mm.

Washington dollar weighs 8.1g.

Diameter is 26.5 mm.

The United States Mint makes coins called commemorative coins. Commemorative coins honor people, places, or events. The Lafayette dollar, issued in 1900, was the first commemorative dollar coin. One side shows an image of both George Washington and General Lafayette, the French nobleman who served with George Washington in the Revolutionary War. In 2007, the United States Mint issued a George Washington dollar coin, the first in a series of Presidential dollar coins.

Coins are minted to exact specifications. Use the information in the pictures for **1** through **5**.

1. The Lafayette dollar was $\frac{9}{10}$ silver. Estimate the weight of 12 Lafayette dollars.

2. Estimate how many Washington dollars, laid side by side, it would take to equal the length of a meter stick. Explain.

3. How much heavier is a Lafayette dollar than a Washington dollar?

4. The Washington dollar has a thickness of about 0.0787 inches. Round 0.0787 to the nearest hundredth.

5. Patti used rounding to estimate the length of six Lafayette dollars laid side by side. Is her estimate an overestimate or an underestimate? Explain.

$$38.1 \times 6 \approx 40 \times 6$$
$$\approx 240 \text{ mm}$$

6. The United States Mint has been producing and distributing coins since 1792. How many years passed between 1792 and 1900, when it issued the first commemorative dollar coin?

7. Presidents are elected for 4-year terms. George Washington served as President from 1789 to 1797. How many terms did George Washington serve as President?

8. When George Washington was elected President, the population of the United States was about 4 million. Write 4 million in standard form.

9. Which expression shows the total weight of W Washington dollars and L Lafayette dollars?

   A $8.1(W + L)$ **C** $8.1W + 26.73L$

   B $26.73(W + L)$ **D** $26.73W + 8.1L$

10. George Washington was one of the tallest Presidents. He was about 6 feet 2 inches tall. How many inches is 6 feet 2 inches?

Lesson
3-4

Common
Core

6.NS.3 Fluently add,
subtract, multiply, and
divide multi-digit decimals
using the standard
algorithm for each
operation.

Multiplying Decimals

Hands-On
grid paper

How can you multiply whole numbers and decimals?

Bari displayed four paintings side-by-side in one row.
Each painting has the same width. What is the total
width of the 4 paintings?

Choose an Operation Multiply to find the total
width of the four paintings.

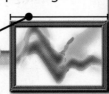
Each is 0.36
meters wide.

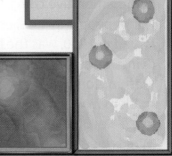

Another Example **How can you multiply a decimal
by a decimal?**

Find 0.5 × 0.3. Use what you know about multiplying whole
numbers to multiply decimals.

What You Think

Think of 0.5 as shading the first five
columns of a decimal model. Think of
0.3 as shading the first 3 rows of the
decimal model.

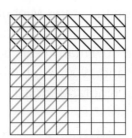

The product is the area where the
shading overlaps.

$$0.5 \times 0.3 = 0.15$$

What You Write

Multiply. Count the number of
decimal places in each factor to place
the decimal in the product.

$$
\begin{array}{r}
\overset{1}{}0.5 \\
\times\ 0.3 \\
\hline
0.15
\end{array}
$$

0.5 ← 1 decimal place
× 0.3 ← +1 decimal place
0.15 ← 2 decimal places

You can multiply using a calculator.

Press: 0.5 × 0.3 ENTER =

Display: 0.15

Explain It

1. When multiplying two decimals, how do you determine
   where to place the decimal point in the product?

Find 0.36 × 4. Multiplying 0.36 × 4 is like adding 0.36 four times on a decimal model.

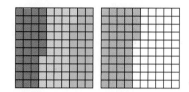

The product is the total area shaded.

0.36 × 4 = 1.44

Multiply. Add the number of decimal places to place the decimals.

```
      1 2
   0.36  ←——  2 decimal places
 ×    4  ←——  + 0 decimal places
   1.44  ←——  2 decimal places
```

The total width is 1.44 meters. You can also multiply using a calculator.

Press: 0.36 × 4 **ENTER =**

Display: *1.44*

Other Examples

Place the decimal in a product.

Find 48.2 × 3.9.

Estimate: 50 × 4 = 200

```
    48.2   ←——  1 decimal place
 ×   3.9   ←——  + 1 decimal place
    4338
   14460
  187.98   ←——  2 decimal places
```

The answer is reasonable because 187.98 is close to 200.

Annex zeros to the left of a product.

Sometimes you need to insert zeros to the left of a product in order to place the decimal point correctly.

Find 0.43 × 0.2.

```
    0.43   ←——  2 decimal places
 ×   0.2   ←——  + 1 decimal place
   0.086   ←——  3 decimal places
```

You can multiply using a calculator.

Press: 0.43 × 0.2 **ENTER =**

Display: *0.086*

Guided Practice*

 MATHEMATICAL
PRACTICES

Do you know HOW?

In **1** through **4**, place the decimal point in the product. You may use grids to help.

1. 4 × 0.94 = 376   **2.** 5 × 0.487 = 2435

3. 3.4 × 6.8 = 2312   **4.** 3.9 × 0.08 = 312

In **5** and **6**, find the product.

5. 0.06 × 5   **6.** 0.9 × 36

Do you UNDERSTAND?

7. What can you do if a decimal product has two final zeros to the right of the decimal point?

© **8. Communicate** When multiplying 0.51 × 9, is it easier to use a calculator or paper and pencil to find the product? Explain.

 eTools
www.pearsonsuccessnet.com

Independent Practice

Leveled Practice In **9** through **14**, place the decimal point in each product.

9. $0.9 \times 1.8 = 162$ **10.** $5 \times 0.35 = 175$ **11.** $0.21 \times 0.4 = 084$

12. $0.214 \times 3 = 642$ **13.** $0.487 \times 7 = 3409$ **14.** $9 \times 3.54 = 3186$

In **15** through **25,** find the product. You may use grids to help.

15. 10×0.52 **16.** 4×0.397 **17.** 0.9×0.5 **18.** 33.4×2.8

19. 100×0.219 **20.** 17×4.765 **21.** 22.9×0.7 **22.** 2.123×3.9

23. $1.2 \times 5.3 \times 7.1$ **24.** $4.2 \times 0.6 \times 100$ **25.** $83.2 \times 1.3 \times 0.1$

Problem Solving

MATHEMATICAL
PRACTICES

© **26. Writing to Explain** Why does multiplying numbers by 10 move the decimal point to the right, but multiplying by 0.10 move the decimal point to the left?

© **27. Critique Reasoning** Kim multiplied 8×0.952 and got 76.16. How can you use estimation to show that Kim's answer is wrong? What mistake did Kim make?

28. The wings of a ruby-throated hummingbird beat an average of 52 times per second.

  a If a ruby-throated hummingbird hovers for 35.5 seconds, on average how many times does its wings beat?

  b Estimate about how many times its wings would beat in a minute.

© **29. Think About the Structure** Which expression does this decimal model show?

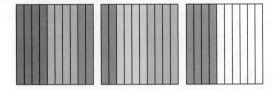

  A 0.4×6 **C** $0.4 \div 6$

  B $0.4 + 6$ **D** $0.4 - 6$

© **30. Think About the Structure** Which expression does this decimal model show?

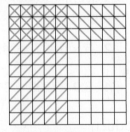

  A $0.5 \div 0.3$ **C** $0.5 - 0.3$

  B 0.5×0.3 **D** $0.5 + 0.3$

Algebra Connections

True or False?

Remember that a variable is a value that can change and is often represented by a letter. If you are given the value of the variable, you can substitute the value for the letter to evaluate an expression or equation.

Example: Evaluate $x - 0.5 = 0.8$ for $x = 1.3$.

Substitute 1.3 for the variable.

$1.3 - 0.5 = 0.8$

$0.8 = 0.8$

The equation is **true** when $x = 1.3$.

In **1** through **8**, evaluate for the variable. Write **true** or **false** for each equation.

1. $x + 7 = 8.3; x = 1.3$

2. $x - 2.88 = 7.11; x = 4$

3. $6x = 12.6; x = 21$

4. $0.5 + x = 1.2; x = 0.7$

5. $x \div 3 = 4.8; x = 14.4$

6. $x - 4.5 = 5.9; x = 9.4$

7. $7x = 21.35; x = 3.5$

8. $27.6 \div x = 9.2; x = 3$

. . . .

In **9** through **12**, evaluate the equations to find the answers.

9. If $b = 5.7$, which equation is true?

   A $3 + b = 6$

   B $b - 2 = 5.5$

   C $b + 4.4 = 9.1$

   D $6 - b = 0.3$

10. If $s = 8.9$, which equation is true?

   A $0.1 + s = 8.8$

   B $s - 0.01 = 8.807$

   C $s + 1.1 = 10$

   D $11.1 - s = 3.2$

11. If $g = 0.29$, which equation is true?

   A $g - 0.02 = 0.27$

   B $g - 0.22 = 0.7$

   C $g + 0.2 = 0.31$

   D $g + 2 = 0.49$

12. If $n = 1.78$, which equation is true?

   A $n - 0.3 = 2.08$

   B $2.3 + n = 4.08$

   C $n + 0.3 = 1.48$

   D $5 - n = 4.22$

Lesson
3-5
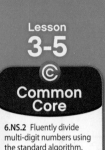

Common
Core

6.NS.2 Fluently divide
multi-digit numbers using
the standard algorithm.

Dividing Whole Numbers

432
candles

Why use division?

Six students sold 432 candles. Each student
sold the same number of candles. How many
candles did each student sell?

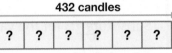

432 candles

?	?	?	?	?	?

← Number of candles
  sold by each student

Another Example   **How do you find a quotient with a remainder?**

2-digit quotient with remainder Find 380 ÷ 6.
Estimate to place the first digit in the quotient.
360 ÷ 6 = 60, so the first digit goes in the tens place.

```
     6
6)380
  -36
    2
```

```
    63 R2
6)380
  -36 ↓
    20
   -18
     2
```

To check a division problem
with a remainder, multiply
the divisor and the quotient.
Then add the remainder.

```
    63
  ×  6
   378
  +  2
   380
```

3-digit quotient with remainder Find 547 ÷ 4.

```
    1
4)547
 -4
  1
```

```
   13
4)547
 -4 ↓
  14
 -12
   2
```

```
   136 R3
4)547
 -4 ↓
  14 ↓
 -12 ↓
   27
  -24
    3
```

Check:

```
   136
 ×  4
  544
 +  3
  547
```

Guided Practice*

MATHEMATICAL
PRACTICES

Do you know HOW?

In **1** through **6**, find each quotient.

1. 9)360   **2.** 3)342

3. 6)75   **4.** 5)339

5. 7)785   **6.** 4)732

Do you UNDERSTAND?

© **7. Communicate** How can estimating
with compatible numbers help you
find the quotient?

8. In the first example, find the quotient if
the total number of candles is 726.

Step 1

Find 432 ÷ 6.

Estimate. Decide where to place the first digit in the quotient.

Use compatible numbers.
420 ÷ 6 = 70
The first digit is in the tens place.

Step 2

Divide the tens. Multiply and subtract.

$$6)\overline{432}$$
$$\underline{-\ 42}$$
$$1$$
(quotient 7)

Divide. 43 ÷ 6 ≈ 7
Multiply. 7 × 6 = 42
Subtract. 43 − 42 = 1
Compare. 1 < 6

Step 3

Bring down the ones. Divide the ones. Multiply and subtract.

$$6)\overline{432}$$
$$\underline{-\ 42}\downarrow$$
$$1\ 2$$
$$\underline{-\ 1\ 2}$$
$$0$$
(quotient 72)

Divide. 12 ÷ 6 = 2
Multiply. 2 × 6 = 12
Subtract. 12 − 12 = 0
Compare. 0 < 6

Each student sold 72 candles.

Independent Practice

In **9** through **16**, use compatible numbers to estimate. Then decide where to place the first digit of the quotient.

9. 5)421 **10.** 8)239 **11.** 6)543 **12.** 3)595

13. 9)723 **14.** 7)689 **15.** 5)156 **16.** 6)175

In **17** through **28**, copy and complete the calculation. Check your answers.

17. 5)385 **18.** 7)637 **19.** 4)564 **20.** 6)828

21. 8)131 **22.** 2)187 **23.** 7)416 **24.** 5)469

25. 7)644 **26.** 3)845 **27.** 4)139 **28.** 6)798

Problem Solving

MATHEMATICAL PRACTICES

ⓒ **29. Reason** How can you tell before you divide 468 by 3 that the first digit of the quotient is in the hundreds place?

ⓒ **30. Writing to Explain** Why is the following incorrect?
296 ÷ 6 = 48 R8

31. Will biked for 6 hours to raise money for his favorite charity. He raised $210. How much money did he raise for each hour he biked?

　A $25　　**C** $35

　B $28　　**D** $36

ⓒ **32. Reasonableness** Suppose 9 cowboys herded 414 cattle. If each cowboy herded the same number of cattle, how many animals was each cowboy responsible for?

Common
Core

6.NS.3 Fluently add,
subtract, multiply, and
divide multi-digit decimals
using the standard
algorithm for each
operation.

Dividing by a Whole Number

How can you write a quotient for a decimal dividend?

Three friends received $2.58 for aluminum cans they recycled.
They decided to share the money equally. How much
will each friend get?

Choose an Operation Divide
to find how much each friend
will get.

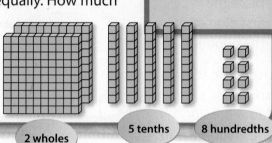

2 wholes   5 tenths   8 hundredths

Another Example **How can you write a decimal quotient
when dividing whole numbers?**

Find 180 ÷ 8.

Step 1

Estimate.
Since 180 ÷ 10 = 18,
start dividing in the
tens place.

$$\begin{array}{r} 2 \\ 8\overline{)180} \\ -16 \\ \hline 2 \end{array}$$

Compare: 2 < 8

Step 2

Divide the ones.

$$\begin{array}{r} 22 \\ 8\overline{)180} \\ -16\downarrow \\ \hline 20 \\ -16 \\ \hline 4 \end{array}$$ Bring down.

Compare: 4 < 8

Step 3

Divide the tenths.

$$\begin{array}{r} 22.5 \\ 8\overline{)180.0} \\ -16\downarrow \\ \hline 20 \\ -16\downarrow \\ \hline 40 \\ -40 \\ \hline 0 \end{array}$$ Place the decimal.
Annex a zero.

Bring down.

Guided Practice*

**MATHEMATICAL
PRACTICES**

Do you know HOW?

Copy and complete.

1.
$$\begin{array}{r} .7 \\ 53\overline{)304.75} \\ -6 \\ \hline 3 \\ -371 \\ \hline \\ -265 \end{array}$$

2.
$$\begin{array}{r} 0. \\ 18\overline{)15.3} \\ - \\ \hline 9 \\ -0 \end{array}$$

Do you UNDERSTAND?

3. How do you know where to place
   the decimal point in long division with
   decimals?

4. **Reason** How would you estimate the
   quotient of $722 ÷ 89 and in which
   place would you start dividing?

DIGITAL   eTools
www.pearsonsuccessnet.com

*For another example, see Set F on page 91.

What You Think

Find 2.58 ÷ 3. Estimate using compatible numbers. Since 3 ÷ 3 = 1, then 2.58 ÷ 3 < 1.

Divide the models into 24 tenths and 18 ones to share equally.

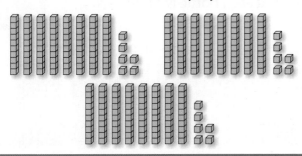

What You Write

Use the estimate to start dividing in the tenths place.

```
     0.86
  3)2.58
  - 24
    18
```

Place the decimal point in the quotient above the decimal point in the dividend. Divide as usual.

Each of the three friends will get $0.86.

Independent Practice

In **5** through **20**, find each quotient.

5. $54.18 ÷ 6

6. 86.1 ÷ 6

7. 64.8 ÷ 9

8. 187.2 ÷ 8

9. 22.34 ÷ 10

10. 6.3 ÷ 7

11. $2.75 ÷ 25

12. 232 ÷ 40

13. 34.64 ÷ 8

14. 4 ÷ 4,000

15. $44.90 ÷ 5

16. 76.4 ÷ 8

17. $21.56 ÷ 22

18. 396 ÷ 88

19. 10 ÷ 1,000

20. 3.87 ÷ 15

Problem Solving

MATHEMATICAL PRACTICES

21. Admission to an amusement park cost $107.25 for three friends. If the price was the same for each friend, what was the cost of each admission?

22. Generalize If Brand A fruit snacks cost $16.20 for 15 pounds and Brand B fruit snacks cost $22.25 for 25 pounds, which cost less per pound?

23. Writing to Explain Is the work below correct? If not, explain why and give a correct response.

Find 0.8 ÷ 20.

```
      0.40
  20)0.80
   - 80
      0
```

24. Think About the Structure How might you best estimate the quotient of 479.25 ÷ 24?

A Round 479.25 to 479.

B Round 479.25 to 479 and 24 to 20.

C Round 479.25 to 480 and 24 to 30.

D Use compatible numbers 500 and 25.

25. The longest spin of a basketball on one finger is 255 minutes. How many hours is this?

Common
Core

6.NS.3 Fluently add, subtract, multiply, and divide multi-digit decimals using the standard algorithm for each operation.

Dividing Decimals

How can you divide using a decimal divisor?

Michelle purchases several bottles of water. Before tax is added, the total cost is $3.60 and the cost of each bottle is $1.20. How many bottles did she buy?

Choose an Operation
Divide 3.60 by 1.20.

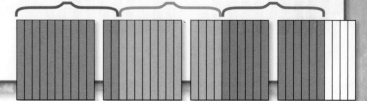

Another Example **How can you divide a decimal by a decimal?**

Find $0.021 \div 0.35$.

Step 1

Use multiplication to estimate.

$\boxed{} \times 0.35 = 0.021$.

You know:

$1 \times 0.35 = 0.35$ and
$0.1 \times 0.35 = 0.035$.

So, the quotient is < 0.1.

Step 2

Multiply the divisor and dividend by the same power of 10 to make the divisor a whole number, and place the decimal in quotient.

$$0.35\overline{)0.021} = 35\overline{)2.1}$$

Step 3

Divide. Annex zeros as needed.

$$\begin{array}{r} 0.06 \\ 35\overline{)2.10} \\ -210 \\ \hline 0 \end{array}$$

Since $0.06 < 0.1$, the answer is reasonable.

Guided Practice*

MATHEMATICAL
PRACTICES

Do you know HOW?

Find each quotient.

> **Tip** *Use estimation to check answers for reasonableness.*

1. $3 \div 0.6$ **2.** $2.50 \div 0.50$

3. $3.6 \div 0.9$ **4.** $8.8 \div 0.4$

Do you UNDERSTAND?

© **5. Look for Patterns** When dividing by a decimal, why do you move the decimal point in both the divisor and the dividend?

6. Why is a zero annexed to the dividend in Step 3 of the example above?

Step 1	Step 2	Step 3

Step 1

Estimate.

$4 \div 1 = 4$

Think of a power of 10 that will make the divisor a whole number.

$$1.20\overline{)3.60}$$

Multiply 1.20 by 100.

Step 2

Multiply the divisor and dividend by the same power of 10 and place the decimal in the quotient.

$$1.20\overline{)3.60}$$

Find: $120\overline{)360}$.

Step 3

Divide.

$$120\overline{)360} \quad \begin{array}{r} 3 \\ -360 \\ \hline 0 \end{array}$$

3 is close to 4. The answer is reasonable.

Michelle purchased 3 bottles of water.

Independent Practice

Leveled Practice In **7** through **10**, estimate each quotient.

7. $4.2 \div 0.8$

8. $10.1 \div 0.2$

9. $18.3 \div 2.9$

10. $93.8 \div 5.2$

In **11** through **22,** find each quotient.

11. $64 \div 0.8$

12. $33.9 \div 0.03$

13. $0.04 \div 0.005$

14. $624 \div 0.6$

15. $52.6 \div 0.08$

16. $127.5 \div 0.03$

17. $287 \div 0.7$

18. $19.8 \div 0.3$

19. $36.4 \div 52$

20. $0.4462 \div 9.7$

21. $4.8 \div 6$

22. $6.588 \div 0.54$

Problem Solving

MATHEMATICAL PRACTICES

© **23. Use Tools** Heather solves $1.4 \div 0.2$ using the diagram below. Is her reasoning correct? Explain her thinking.

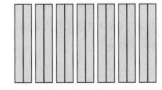

© **26. Think About the Structure** What value can you multiply the divisor and dividend by to begin dividing this problem?

$93 \div 0.007$

A 1

B 10

C 100

D 1,000

24. In 1927, Charles Lindbergh made the first solo, non-stop flight of approximately 3,610.2 miles across the Atlantic. The flight lasted about 33 hours. About how many miles per hour did he fly?

© **25. Reasonableness** Alec estimates that $34,627 \div 0.94$ is about 35,000. Is his estimate reasonable? Why or why not?

© **27. Reason** Kristin estimates that $70 \div 7.2$ is about 10. Will the actual quotient be greater than or less than 10? Explain.

© Common Core

6.EE.2.c Evaluate expressions at specific values of their variables. Include expressions that arise from formulas used in real-world problems. Perform arithmetic operations, including those involving whole number exponents, in the conventional order when there are no parentheses to specify a particular order (Order of Operations)....

Evaluating Expressions

How can you evaluate with brackets?

Evaluate $3.2 \times 12 - [2 + (3.6 \div 0.6)]$

Some expressions look difficult because they include parentheses and brackets. You can think of brackets as "outside" parentheses.

You evaluate inside parentheses first.

Order of Operations

❶ Evaluate inside parentheses and brackets.

❷ Evaluate terms with exponents.

❸ Multiply and divide from left to right.

❹ Add and subtract from left to right.

Another Example How can you evaluate expressions with brackets and variables?

Evaluate $[6(x - 3.5)] \div 12 + 4.2$ for $x = 9.5$.

Step 1

Substitute a number for the variable; $x = 9.5$.

$[6(x - 3.5)] \div 12 + 4.2$
$[6 \times (9.5 - 3.5)] \div 12 + 4.2$

Step 2

Evaluate inside parentheses and brackets.

$[6 \times (9.5 - 3.5)] \div 12 + 4.2$
$[6 \times 6] \div 12 + 4.2$
$36 \div 12 + 4.2$

Step 3

Continue to follow order of operations.

$36 \div 12 + 4.2$
$3 + 4.2$
7.2

Guided Practice*

MATHEMATICAL PRACTICES

Do you know HOW?

Evaluate each expression.

1. $5.5 + (6.7 - 3.1)$

2. $(8.2 + x) \times 3.2; x = 5.3$

3. $[(7.3 + 3.6) - 4.7] + 1.8$

4. $[(11.2 + 8.9) - (y + 9.6)]; y = 7.3$

Do you UNDERSTAND?

5. Explain why brackets are sometimes used in an expression. What purpose do they serve?

© 6. **Writing to Explain** In the expression $(21 - 3) \times (7 + 2) \div (12 - 4)$, what operation should you perform last? Why?

Step 1

Evaluate inside parentheses and brackets.

$3.2 \times 12 - [2 + (3.6 \div 0.6)]$

$3.2 \times 12 - [2 + 6]$

$3.2 \times 12 - 8$

Step 2

There are no exponents, so you can multiply next.

$3.2 \times 12 - 8$

$38.4 - 8$

Remember to work from left to right.

Step 3

Lastly, subtract.

$38.4 - 8 = 30.4$

When you evaluate expressions, follow the rules of the order of operations.

Independent Practice

Evaluate each expression.

7. $4.3 + (8.4 - 5.1)$

8. $(8.7 + x) \div 0.5; x = 2.3$

9. $157.8 - (4.5 \div 0.3) \times 3$

10. $[(3.2 + 8.1) - 3.1] + 5.8$

11. $[3.5 \times (152 \div 8)] - 7.2$

12. $[(12 \times 4.8) \div 0.75] + 6 - 8^2$

13. $12.8 + [(25 - 14.5) \times 7.2]$

14. $53.7 - [(79.8 \div 13.3) \times 8]$

15. $5 \times [(24 \times 3.5) \div y]; y = 1.5$

Problem Solving

MATHEMATICAL PRACTICES

© 16. Communicate How do you know which part of the expression to evaluate first? Explain.

$(26 + 2.5) - [(8.3 \times 3) + (1 - 0.25)]$

© 17. Reason Explain how you could use estimation to get an approximate answer for the expression below.

$(24.5 + 8.5) - (7.5 \times 4.1)$

© 18. Model Lillian bought four hair brushes at $3.99 each. She had a coupon for $1 off. Her mom paid for half of the remaining cost. Evaluate the expression $[(4 \times 3.99) - 1] \div 2$.

19. Fredrick solves the problem below and thinks that the answer is 69.5. Lana solves the same problem, but thinks that the answer is 76.9. Who is correct?

$[(53.7 + 37.2) - (9.1 + 3.7)] - 8.6$

© 20. Think About the Structure Using order of operations, which is the last operation you should perform to evaluate this expression?

$(1 \times 2.5) + (98 - 8) + (5 + 6.7) \times (52 \div 13)$

A Addition

B Subtraction

C Multiplication

D Division

21. How long of a piece of tape would be needed to go around the perimeter of the triangle below?

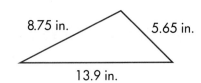

8.75 in.   5.65 in.

13.9 in.

6.EE.5 Understand solving an equation or inequality as a process of answering a question: which values from a specified set, if any, make the equation or inequality true? Use substitution to determine whether a given number in a specified set makes an equation or inequality true. **Also 6.EE.6**

Solutions for Equations and Inequalities

How can you determine whether a given number makes an equation true?

Jordan received a $15.00 gift card for cell phone apps. He has used $4.50 of the value and wants to buy one more app to use up the balance. Which app could he buy?

Cell Phone Apps	
All Recipes	$ 9.50
Headliners Sports	$10.50
Remote Desktop	$12.00

$15.00

$4.50	x

Another Example **How can you determine whether a given number makes an inequality true?**

An inequality is <u>a mathematical sentence that contains > (greater than), < (less than), ≥ (greater than or equal to), or ≤ (less than or equal to)</u>. Any value for the variable that makes an inequality true is a solution.

Which apps could Jordan buy with all or part of the balance on his gift card? Use the costs of the apps above. Which values of *x* are solutions to the inequality $4.50 + x ≤ $15.00?

Try x = $9.50: $4.50 + $9.50 ≤ $15.00   Solution
Try x = $10.50: $4.50 + $10.50 = $15.00   Solution
Try x = $12.00: $4.50 + $12.00 > $15.00   Not a solution

From the set of values there are two solutions to the inequality. Jordan could buy *All Recipes* or *Headliners Sports*.

Guided Practice*

MATHEMATICAL
PRACTICES

Do you know HOW?

Tell which value(s) of the variable are solutions to the equation or inequality.

1. $p + 2.7 > 4$ $p = 1, 2, 3, 4$

2. $c = 17 - 3.4$ $c = 13.4, 14.6, 15.6, 16.6$

Do you UNDERSTAND?

© **3. Critique Reasoning** Carlos says 6, 7, 8, and 9 are not solutions to $x + 6 > 11$ because the value of $x + 6$ does not equal 11 for any of the numbers he substitutes for *x*. What mistake did Carlos make?

Animated Glossary
www.pearsonsuccessnet.com

An equation is true when both sides of the equation are equal.

A solution to an equation is the value for the variable that makes the equation true.

To find the solution of $\$4.50 + x = \$15$, substitute the different costs of the apps for x.

Try $x = \$9.50$: $\$4.50 + \$9.50 = \$14.00$ Not a solution
Try $x = \$10.50$: $\$4.50 + \$10.50 = \$15.00$ Solution
Try $x = \$12.00$: $\$4.50 + \$12.00 = \$16.50$ Not a solution

Since the solution is $\$10.50$, Jordan should buy *Headliners Sports*.

Independent Practice

In **4** through **10**, tell which value(s) of the variable are solutions to the equation or inequality.

4. $t - 2.1 = 0$ $t = 2.1, 2.4, 2.6, 2.8$

5. $6 + v > 19$ $v = 13, 14, 15, 16$

6. $8.9 + a = 9.7$ $a = 0.7, 0.8, 0.9, 1.2$

7. $x - 5 < 67$ $x = 75, 72, 70, 65$

8. $4.4 - y \leq 4.4$ $y = 3.3, 3.6, 4.4, 0$

9. $n + 10 \geq 38.2$ $n = 23, 24, 28, 28.1$

10. $\$6.76 + b = \$13.00$ $b = \$7.00, \$6.24, \$5.24, \$4.54$

Problem Solving

MATHEMATICAL
PRACTICES

© **11. Generalize** The values 2, 7, 9, and 11 are solutions to the inequality $x + 2 \leq 13$, but the values 12, 15, 29, and 32 are not. Give a rule for the value of x that will be a solution to the inequality.

© **12. Reason** Meagan has spent $\$6.65$ of a $\$20.00$ music gift card. Will she be able to purchase another $\$12.35$ worth of music from the card? If $x = \$12.35$, use $\$6.65 + x \leq \$20.00$ to decide.

© **13. Writing to Explain** Write an inequality using addition and the variable t so that solutions to the inequality will include 0, 1, 2, and 3.

© **14. Model** Michael is 5 years older than his sister. Write an algebraic expression to show Michael's age when his sister is s years old.

15. Anton walked 8.9 miles of his 13.5-mile goal for this week. He drew the diagram to the right to show how much he had left to walk. What is the solution to the equation?

13.5	
y	8.9

A 3.6 mi   **C** 4.6 mi

B 4.4 mi   **D** 5.6 mi

Lesson
3-10

Common
Core

6.NS.3 Fluently add,
subtract, multiply, and
divide multi-digit decimals
using the standard
algorithm for each
operation.

Problem Solving

Multiple-Step Problems

Lucy is 13 years old. Her parents are treating Lucy and her friends to a movie. Six of her friends are 12 years old. Two other friends are 13 years old. How much will it cost for Lucy and her friends to see a movie?

Break the problem into simpler parts to find the total cost of the movie tickets.

12 years and under

Movie theater $4.50
12 YEARS AND UNDER

Movie theater $7.25
13 YEARS AND OLDER

13 years and older

Another Example

Mr. Lee needs to calculate how much he will pay for his cell phone bill. He talked 326 minutes during the daytime on weekdays and 286 minutes during the evening on weekdays. How much will Mr. Lee's total bill be?

Call Time	Cost per Minute
Weekday–Day	$0.10
Weekday–Evening	$0.07
Weekend	Free

Read and Understand

What do I know? Mr. Lee used 326 minutes during the daytime on weekdays.

He used 286 minutes during the evening on weekdays.

What am I asked to find? What is the total cost of his cell phone bill?

Plan and Solve

Hidden Question 1: How much do Mr. Lee's weekday daytime phone calls cost?

326 minutes × $0.10 = $32.60

Hidden Question 2: How much do Mr. Lee's weekday evening phone calls cost?

286 minutes × $0.07 = $20.02

$32.60 + $20.02 = $52.62

Mr. Lee's total cell phone bill is $52.62.

Explain It

1. Explain how the hidden questions were found in the problem above.

2. When can you break a problem into simpler parts?

What do I know? Tickets cost $4.50 for 12 years and under and $7.25 for 13 years and older.

Lucy and 2 friends are 13 years old. 6 other friends are 12 years old.

What am I asked to find? What is the total cost of the movie tickets?

Find the hidden questions in the problem. Use the answers from the hidden questions to solve the problem.

Hidden Question 1: How much are movie tickets for 6 friends who are 12 years old?

$6 \times \$4.50 = \$27.00$

Hidden Question 2: How much are movie tickets for 3 friends who are 13 years old?

$3 \times \$7.25 = \$21.75$

$$\$27.00 \quad + \quad \$21.75 \quad = \quad \$48.75$$

The total cost is $48.75 for all 9 tickets.

Guided Practice*

MATHEMATICAL PRACTICES

Do you know HOW?

1. Pat is traveling from Seattle to Los Angeles. The trip is 1,000 miles. For the first 250 miles, it costs $0.29 per mile. After that, it costs $0.16 per mile. How much will the whole trip cost?

1,000 miles	
250 miles	*m* miles

Do you UNDERSTAND?

2. What are the hidden questions in Exercise 1?

3. **Persevere** Use a real-life situation to create a problem in which there is a hidden question or hidden questions.

Independent Practice

MATHEMATICAL PRACTICES

Use the table for **4** and **5**.

School Supplies	Cost
Pencil	$0.24
Notebook	$3.73
Pen	$1.29

4. Rose buys three pencils, two pens, and a notebook. How much money does she spend on school supplies?

5. Neil needs a pencil and five notebooks. How much will this cost?

Applying Math Practices

- What am I asked to find?
- What else can I try?
- How are quantities related?
- How can I explain my work?
- How can I use math to model the problem?
- Can I use tools to help?
- Is my work precise?
- Why does this work?
- How can I generalize?

MATHEMATICAL
PRACTICES

ⓒ **Look for Patterns** Use the pattern to the right for **6** and **7**.

6. Describe the pattern in words.

7. Predict how many dots the fifth image will have.

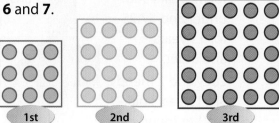

1st   2nd   3rd

8. It takes 523 gallons of water to fill Bill's pool. It takes 983 gallons to fill Jamie's pool. How many more gallons does it take to fill Jamie's pool than Bill's?

ⓒ 9. **Persevere** Tyler reads 25 pages of his book on Monday and 31 pages on Tuesday. On Wednesday, he reads half of the sum of the pages read on both Monday and Tuesday. How many pages does he read on Monday through Wednesday?

ⓒ 10. **Look for Patterns** Jon takes a break at 9:15 A.M., 11:45 A.M., and 2:15 P.M. If this pattern continues, when will his next break be?

11. Christy needs to buy three shirts. At Mia's Outlet, she can buy three shirts for $28.25. At Suzy's Store, shirts cost $9.05 each. At which store will Christy pay the cheaper price?

12. Laila is older than Bob and Juan. Nelson is younger than Juan but older than Bob. Who is the youngest?

ⓒ **Think About the Structure**

13. Kurt has four cats. Maria has half as many cats as Kurt. How many cats do they have together? What is the hidden question?

    A How many cats does Kurt have?

    B How many cats does Maria have?

    C How many cats do Maria and Kurt have together?

    D How many more cats does Kurt have than Maria?

14. Leslie's ceramics class meets for 1.5 hours twice a week, and she must work with clay for another 3 hours a week. To find how much time Leslie spends doing ceramics each week, identify the hidden question.

    A How much time does she spend in ceramics class each week?

    B How much time must she practice ceramics per week?

    C How long is a ceramics class?

    D How many hours are in a day?

Skills Review Estimate the value. Then find the answer.

1. $6.07 - 3.96$
2. $2.93 + 8.9$
3. 5×0.19

4. $322 \div 16$
5. $298.34 + 9.104$
6. 12.3×2.85

7. $52.02 \div 5.1$
8. $89.3 - 21.88$
9. $29.3 + 9.8$

10. $45.012 - 4.98$
11. $2.22 + 0.88$
12. 9.35×0.88

13. $45.63 \div 7.02$
14. 129.31×2.89
15. $189.9 - 88.9$
16. $839.52 \div 79.2$

Error Search Find each product that is not correct. Write it correctly and explain the error.

17.
$$\begin{array}{r} 10 \\ \times\ \ 4.3 \\ \hline 0.043 \end{array}$$

18.
$$\begin{array}{r} 3.20 \\ \times\ \ 89 \\ \hline 284.8 \end{array}$$

19.
$$\begin{array}{r} 132.8 \\ \times\ \ 4.32 \\ \hline 5{,}736.96 \end{array}$$

20.
$$\begin{array}{r} 934.2 \\ \times\ \ 12.3 \\ \hline 11{,}490.66 \end{array}$$

Number Sense

Determine whether each statement is true or false. Explain your answer.

21. The product of 29.7 and 2.87 is greater than 90.

22. The sum of 38.7 and 149.89 is less than 200.

23. The difference between 98.01 and 23.0003 is less than 75.

24. The quotient of 25.8 and 5.1 is less than 5.

25. The product of 239 and 9.8 is greater than 2,400.

26. The difference between 432,093 and 131,081 is greater than 300,000.

1. The table gives the size of some park areas. Which is the best estimate of the difference between the sizes of Shady Heights and Pine Island? (3-1)

	Park Area	Size in Acres
Data	Shady Heights	58.38
	Pine Island	27.5
	Oak Woods	792.84

A 30 acres

B 35 acres

C 38 acres

D 40 acres

2. If eight ounces of canned pumpkin have 82 calories, how many calories are in one ounce? (3-6)

A 16.25 calories

B 12.5 calories

C 10.25 calories

D 10.025 calories

3. What is the sum of 23.7 and 6.912? (3-2)

A 7.149

B 16.778

C 30.919

D 30.612

4. Which of the following is equal to 4.2? (3-8)

A $2.4 + 3 \times 4 - 2 \div 2$

B $2.4 + [3 \times (4 - 2)] \div 2$

C $[(2.4 + 3) \times 4 - 2] \div 2$

D $[2.4 + 3 \times (4 - 2)] \div 2$

5. One day, 2,149 people visited an amusement park. If the cost of admission for each person is $28.95, which is the best estimate of the total cost of admissions for the day? (3-3)

A $60,000   C $600,000

B $55,000   D $6,000

6. Kimberly scored a total of 35.104 points in four events for her gymnastic competition. If she scored the same amount on each event, how many points did she score on each? (3-6)

A 0.8776 points

B 8.0776 points

C 8.776 points

D 87.76 points

7. The average annual rainfall in Tucson, Arizona, is 12.17 inches. If Tucson receives 14.1 inches in one year, how many inches above average is that amount? (3-2)

A 12.03 inches

B 2.93 inches

C 1.93 inches

D 1.07 inches

8. There are 108 campers at a summer camp that are divided evenly into 9 cabins. How many campers are in each cabin? (3-5)

A 120 campers

B 13 campers

C 12 campers

D 11 campers

9. What is $1.61 \div 2.3$? (3-7)

  A 0.8

  B 0.7

  C 0.08

  D 0.07

10. The unit used to measure the height of a horse is called a hand. One hand is equal to 10.16 centimeters. If a horse is 15 hands tall, how many centimeters tall is it? (3-4)

  A 60.96 centimeters

  B 151.14 centimeters

  C 152.04 centimeters

  D 152.4 centimeters

11. Which set of numbers, when substituted for p, are solutions to the following inequality? (3-9)

  $5.6 + p \geq 9.8$

  A 1, 2, 3, 4

  B 3, 4.2, 4.4, 6

  C 4.1, 4.2, 4.3, 5

  D 4.2, 4.3, 4.4, 5

12. Russ has a car that averages 9.8 miles per gallon while Mike's car averages 39.2 miles per gallon. How many times more miles per gallon does Mike's car get than Russ's car? (3-7)

  A 4.1

  B 4

  C 3.5

  D 3

13. To ship a package, a shipping company charges $1.68 for each pound. How much would it cost to ship a 5.5 pound package? (3-4)

  A $8.40

  B $9.24

  C $16.80

  D $92.40

14. The table shows the entrance prices at a museum. The Rodriguez family has 2 adults and 5 children. If they have a coupon for $10 off, what is the total cost of admission for the family? (3-10)

Type of Ticket	Cost
Adult	$12.50
Child	$4.00
Senior	$5.00

  A $35

  B $45

  C $50

  D $58

15. What is the first step in evaluating the expression shown below? (3-8)

  $[3 \times (12.4 + 2.1)] - 14 + 7.9$

  A Multiply 3 and 12.4.

  B Add 14 and 7.9.

  C Add 12.4 and 2.1.

  D Multiply 3 and 2.1.

Set A, pages 62–63

Jesse has $20 to buy school supplies. The items he wants to buy cost $5.49, $4.39, $6.99, and $4.96. Does he have enough money?

Use rounding to estimate the sum. Round each number to the same place value.

5.49 + 4.39 + 6.99 + 4.96

   ↓   ↓   ↓   ↓

  5   +   4   +   7   +   5   = 21

Jesse does not have enough money.

Remember that you can estimate sums and differences of decimals by rounding or using front-end estimation.

Estimate each answer.

1. 91.2 + 89.9   **2.** 902.3 − 8.8

3. 62.99 − 10.83   **4.** 423.22 + 98.30

5. 24.52 − 9.6   **6.** 369.45 + 32.42

7. 16 + 19.234   **8.** 62.54 − 32.92

Set B, pages 64–65

Lucy bought 3 pounds of pears and 9.12 pounds of apples. Find the number of pounds of pears and apples Lucy bought.

Write the numbers. Add a decimal to the whole number and annex zeros as placeholders. Then add.

$$\begin{array}{r} 3.00 \\ +\ 9.12 \\ \hline 12.12 \end{array}$$

Lucy bought 12.12 pounds of pears and apples.

Remember to line up the decimal points and to annex zeros as placeholders before calculating sums and differences.

1. 523.2 + 25.2

2. 902.3 − 7.8

3. 98.23 − 42.33

4. 178.23 + 220.34

5. 2.93 + 7.24

Set C, pages 66–68

Estimate 27.183 ÷ 3.2.

Use compatible numbers to estimate a product or quotient.

27.183 ÷ 3.2   27.183 and 3.2 are
   ↓   ↓   close to the compatible
                       numbers 27 and 3.
  27 ÷ 3 = 9

So, 27.183 ÷ 3.2 ≈ 9.

Remember that you can estimate products and quotients using rounding or compatible numbers.

Estimate each answer. Tell which method you used.

1. 6.42 ÷ 2.96   **2.** 15.23 × 9.15

3. 495.12 ÷ 74.5   **4.** 12.421 × 3.17

5. 132 × 820   **6.** 998 ÷ 12

7. 9,032 ÷ 289   **8.** 68 × 31

Find 52.5×1.9. Estimate: $50 \times 2 = 100$.

$$
\begin{array}{r}
52.5 \quad \leftarrow \text{1 decimal place} \\
\times \quad 1.9 \quad \leftarrow \underline{+ \text{ 1 decimal place}} \\
\hline
4725 \\
5250 \\
\hline
99.75 \quad \leftarrow \text{2 decimal places}
\end{array}
$$

The answer is reasonable because 99.75 is close to 100.

Remember to count the number of decimal places in both factors in order to place the decimal correctly in the product.

Find each product.

1. 5×98.2
2. 4×0.21
3. 4.4×6
4. 7×21.6
5. 12.5×163.2
6. 16×52.3
7. 0.8×0.11
8. 0.07×0.44
9. 6.4×3.2
10. 31.5×0.01

Find $549 \div 6$. Estimate: $540 \div 6 = 90$.

$$
\begin{array}{r}
91 \text{ R3} \\
6\overline{)549} \\
-54 \\
\hline
09 \\
-6 \\
\hline
3
\end{array}
$$

Check:
$$
\begin{array}{r}
91 \\
\times \quad 6 \\
\hline
546 \\
+ \quad 3 \\
\hline
549
\end{array}
$$

The quotient 91 R3 is close to the estimate, 90.

Remember that you can use your estimate to check that your answer is reasonable.

Divide.

1. $74 \div 5$
2. $89 \div 9$
3. $232 \div 4$
4. $488 \div 8$
5. $682 \div 7$
6. $492 \div 6$

Divide $333.37 \div 53$. Estimate: $300 \div 50 = 6$.

$$
\begin{array}{r}
6.29 \\
53\overline{)333.37} \\
-318 \quad \downarrow \\
\hline
153 \quad \text{Bring down 3.} \\
-106 \quad \downarrow \\
\hline
477 \quad \text{Bring down 7.} \\
-477 \\
\hline
0
\end{array}
$$

The answer is reasonable because 6.29 is close to 6.

Remember to place the decimal point in the quotient above the decimal point in the dividend.

Find each quotient. Round to the nearest hundredth if necessary.

1. $\$1.89 \div 3$
2. $638.4 \div 7$
3. $116 \div 8$
4. $110.7 \div 9$
5. $511.2 \div 6$
6. $\$24.60 \div 8$
7. $35.75 \div 55$
8. $120.4 \div 602$

Set G, pages 78–79

Find 2.75 ÷ 0.05.

Step 1 Use multiplication to estimate.
You know 100 × 0.05 = 5.
So 2.75 ÷ 0.05 < 100.

Step 2 Multiply the divisor and dividend by the same power of 10 and place the decimal in the quotient.

$$0.05\overline{)2.75} \rightarrow 5\overline{)275.}$$

Step 3 Divide.

$$
\begin{array}{r}
55. \\
5\overline{)275.} \\
-25 \\
\hline
25 \\
-25 \\
\hline
0
\end{array}
$$

Since 55 < 100, the answer is reasonable.
2.75 ÷ 0.05 = 55

Remember to think of a power of 10 that will make the divisor a whole number.

Find the power of 10 that will make the divisor a whole number.

1. 9.6 ÷ 1.6

2. 48.4 ÷ 0.4

3. 13.2 ÷ 0.006

4. 10.8 ÷ 0.09

Find each quotient.

5. 80.1 ÷ 0.9   **6.** 12.8 ÷ 0.4

7. 1.26 ÷ 0.2   **8.** 1.68 ÷ 0.8

9. 2.24 ÷ 3.2   **10.** 3.78 ÷ 4.2

11. 42.5 ÷ 0.05   **12.** 75.5 ÷ 0.5

13. 117.3 ÷ 2.3   **14.** 132.68 ÷ 2.14

Set H, pages 80–81

Use the order of operations to evaluate expressions with brackets.

Order of Operations

1. Compute inside parentheses and brackets.

2. Evaluate terms with exponents.

3. Multiply and divide from left to right.

4. Add and subtract from left to right.

Remember that you can think of brackets as outside parentheses and evaluate the inside parentheses first.

Evaluate each expression.

1. $(7.8 + 4.7) ÷ 0.25$

2. $92.3 - (3.2 ÷ 0.4) × 2^3$

3. $[(8 × 2.5) ÷ 0.5] + 120$

4. $31.2(40 + 60) ÷ 0.6$

5. $(8.7 - 3.2) ÷ 0.5$

Use the values given for variables to evaluate each expression.

6. $4.2 + 5 × x ÷ 0.10; x = 4$

7. $2^2 × (4.2 - y); y = 1.2$

8. $12 + (4^2 ÷ z); z = 0.04$

An equation is true when both sides of the equation are equal. A solution to an equation is the value that makes the equation true.

Which of the value(s) is a solution to $3.4 + b = 5$?

$b = 1, 1.6, 2$

Try $b = 1$:	$3.4 + 1 = 4.4$	Not a solution
Try $b = 1.6$:	$3.4 + 1.6 = 5$	Solution
Try $b = 2$:	$3.4 + 2 = 5.4$	Not a solution

Any value that makes an inequality true is a solution. Which value(s) for y make the inequality true?

$y - 1.5 \geq 4 \qquad y = 1.5, 6, 7$

Try $y = 1.5$:	$1.5 - 1.5 < 4$	Not a solution
Try $y = 6$:	$6 - 1.5 \geq 4$	Solution
Try $y = 7$:	$7 - 1.5 \geq 4$	Solution

Remember variables are used to represent numbers in mathematical expressions, so numbers can be substituted for the variables to make an equation or inequality true.

Tell which value(s) are solutions to the equations or inequalities.

1. $t - 3.4 = 5$

   $t = 9.4, 8.5, 8.4, 8$

2. $43 + y = 81$

   $y = 48, 38, 36, 28$

3. $\$13.01 + x \geq \$21.56$

   $x = \$9.02, \$8.55, \$8.00, \$7.98$

4. $t - 134 \leq 19$

   $t = 154, 156, 158, 160$

5. $5.7 + b < 8.2$

   $b = 0.9, 1.5, 1.9, 2.6$

Find and answer the hidden questions to solve multiple-step word problems.

Each layer of a box will hold 16 toys. If a box has 4 layers, will 3 boxes be enough to hold 180 toys?

Hidden Question 1: How many toys does one box hold?

You know each layer holds 16 toys and each box has 4 layers.

So, 16 toys × 4 layers = 64 toys per box.

Hidden Question 2: How many toys are in 3 boxes?

64 toys per box × 3 boxes = 192 toys

Yes, 3 boxes will hold 180 toys.

Remember to find and answer the hidden questions to solve the problem.

1. Melina is in charge of buying 30 snack packs of dried fruit for the picnic. Where should she buy the dried fruit for the lowest cost?

Dried Fruit Snack Pack Prices	
Fresh Foods Market	5/$4
Karmel's Fruit Stand	3/$2.50

2. One weekend, Franco hiked 3 miles on Saturday and twice as many miles on Sunday. How many total miles did Franco hike?

Solving Equations

1 How high do hot-air balloons fly? The world record is about 65,000 feet. How much higher is this than a normal flight? You will find out in Lesson 4-2.

The world's largest fish is a whale shark. How many times longer is this fish than you? You will find out in Lesson 4-4.

2

3

How do scientists measure the mass of objects when doing experiments? You will find out in Lesson 4-1.

Review What You Know!

Vocabulary

Choose the best terms from the box.

- equal   - variable
- algebraic expression

1. In 6x, x is a(n) __?__.

2. x + 5 is an example of a(n) __?__.

3. An equation is a math statement that shows that two parts are __?__.

Equality

Tell whether the equation is true.

4. $6 + 2 = 2 + 6$

5. $4 + 5 = 3 + 6$

6. $10 - 8 = 2 + 0$

Expressions

Evaluate each expression.

7. $x - 2$ when $x = 8$

8. $2b$ when $b = 9$

9. $\frac{15}{x}$ when $x = 3$

Order of Operations

© **10. Writing to Explain** Explain in which order you should compute the operations in the expression. Then evaluate the expression.

$(\frac{33}{3}) + 1$

Lesson

4-1

Common Core

6.EE.4 Identify when two expressions are equivalent (i.e., when the two expressions name the same number regardless of which value is substituted into them).... Also **6.EE.3**

Properties of Equality

How can you keep an equation balanced?

An equation is <u>a sentence that uses an equals sign to show that two expressions have the same value</u>.

$$5 + 3 = 8$$

Think of an equation as a pan balance. To keep the pans balanced, you do the same thing to both sides. Use the Addition Property of Equality to <u>add the same amount to both sides of an equation</u>.

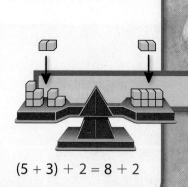

$$(5 + 3) + 2 = 8 + 2$$

Other Examples

Addition Property of Equality

If $12 + 18 = 30$, does $12 + 18 + 5 = 30 + 5$? Why or why not?

Yes; the same number, 5, was added to both sides of the equation.

Division Property of Equality

If $4x = 20$, does $4x \div 4 = 20 \div 5$? Why or why not?

No; both sides of the equation are divided by different numbers, not by the same amount.

Guided Practice*

 **MATHEMATICAL PRACTICES**

Do you know HOW?

In **1** through **4**, analyze each set of equations.

1. If $23 + 37 = 60$, does $23 + 37 + 9 = 60 + 9$? Why or why not?

2. If $7m = 63$, does $7m - 9 = 63 - 9$? Why or why not?

3. If $35 - 7 = 28$, does $(35 - 7) \div 7 = 28 \div 28$? Why or why not?

4. If $8x - 2 = 34$, does $(8x - 2) \times 8 = 34 \times 2$? Why or why not?

Do you UNDERSTAND?

5. **Reason** A pan balance shows $7 + 5 = 12$. If 4 units are removed from one side, what needs to be done to the other side to keep the pans balanced?

6. **Reason** For the equation $23 + 43 = 66$, if one side is multiplied by 3, what needs to be done to the other side of the equation to keep them equal?

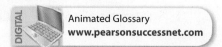

Animated Glossary
www.pearsonsuccessnet.com

DIGITAL

For another example, see Set A on page 116.

The Subtraction Property of Equality lets you subtract the same amount from both sides of the equation.

$$5 + 3 = 8$$
$$(5 + 3) - 2 = 8 - 2$$

The Multiplication Property of Equality lets you multiply both sides of the equation by the same non-zero amount.

$$5 + 3 = 8$$
$$(5 + 3) \times 2 = 8 \times 2$$

The Division Property of Equality lets you divide both sides of the equation by the same non-zero amount.

$$5 + 3 = 8$$
$$(5 + 3) \div 2 = 8 \div 2$$

Independent Practice

In **7** through **12**, analyze each set of equations.

7. If $10 \times 3 = 30$, does $10 \times 3 + 4 = 30 + 5$? Why or why not?

8. If $8n = 180$, does $8n \div 8 = 180 \div 8$? Why or why not?

9. If $78 - 7 = 71$, does $78 - 7 + 23 = 71 + 23$? Why or why not?

10. If $12 - 2 = 10$, does $12 - 2 - 3 = 10 - 2$? Why or why not?

11. If $102 \div 2 = 51$, does $102 \div 2 \times 3 = 51 \times 3$? Why or why not?

12. If $d \div 3 = 10$, does $d \div 3 + 3 = 10 + 3$? Explain.

Problem Solving

© 13. Use Tools Scientists often use a pan balance to measure mass when doing experiments. Draw a picture of a pan balance to show $4 + 3 - 1 = 7 - 1$ if a scientist takes one unit of mass from each side of a pan balance.

14. You use a $20 bill to pay for a purchase of $18.60. The cashier gives you two $1 bills and four dimes back. Were you given the correct change? Why or why not?

© 15. Writing to Explain Jim wrote that $5 + 5 = 10$. Then he wrote that $5 + 5 + n = 10 + n$. Are his equations balanced? Explain.

© 16. Think About the Structure Which property was used below?

If $7m = 49$, then $7m \div 7 = 49 \div 7$

   A Addition Property of Equality

   C Multiplication Property of Equality

   B Subtraction Property of Equality

   D Division Property of Equality

Common
Core

6.EE.7 Solve real-world and mathematical problems by writing and solving equations of the form $x + p = q$ and $px = q$ for cases in which p, q and x are all nonnegative rational numbers. Also **6.EE.5, 6.EE.6**

Solving Addition and Subtraction Equations

How can you get the variable alone in an addition equation?

George had x plastic figures. After he bought 7 more figures, he had 25. How many plastic figures did George have before he bought more?

Solve the equation $x + 7 = 25$ to find the answer.

George bought 7 more figures.

Another Example **How can you get the variable alone in a subtraction equation?**

Solve: $x - 19.1 = 34.4$.

What You Think

How can I get x alone on one side of the equation $x - 19.1 = 34.4$?

Adding 19.1 will undo subtracting 19.1. That will leave the x alone.

 Think Adding 19.1 is the inverse of subtracting 19.1.

What You Write

$$x - 19.1 = 34.4$$
$$x - 19.1 + 19.1 = 34.4 + 19.1$$
$$x = 53.5$$

To check, substitute 53.5 for x.

$$x - 19.1 = 34.4$$
$$53.5 - 19.1 = 34.4$$
$$34.4 = 34.4 \quad \text{It checks.}$$

Explain It

1. Explain how addition and subtraction have an inverse relationship.

2. Explain which Property of Equality was used to solve the subtraction equation above.

Think How can I get *x* alone on one side of the equation *x* + 7 = 25?

<u>Operations that undo each other</u> have an inverse relationship. Subtracting 7 is the inverse of adding 7.

Take 7 away from each side. That will leave the *x* alone.

x is 18.

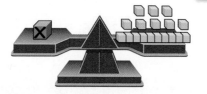

$x + 7 = 25$

$x + 7 - 7 = 25 - 7$

$x = 18$

To check, substitute 18 for *x*.

$x + 7 = 25$

$18 + 7 = 25$

$25 = 25$ It checks.

George started with 18 figures.

Guided Practice*

 MATHEMATICAL PRACTICES

Do you know HOW?

In **1** and **2**, explain how to get the variable alone in each equation.

1. $25 + m = 49$ **2.** $t - 40.5 = 3.7$

In **3** and **4**, solve each equation and check your answer.

3. $12 = x - 11$ **4.** $22.7 = 13.3 + x$

Do you UNDERSTAND?

5. In the example above, which Property of Equality was used to solve the equation?

ⓒ **6. Model** Claire had *x* books. After she bought 8 more books, she had 24 books. How many books did Claire start with?

Solve $x + 8 = 24$.

Independent Practice

Leveled Practice Explain how to get the variable alone in each equation.

7. $y - 12 = 89$

$y - 12 + \boxed{} = 89 + 12$

8. $80.5 + r = 160$

$80.5 + r - \boxed{} = 160 - \boxed{}$

9. $60.6 = x - 16.8$

$60.6 + \boxed{} = x - 16.8 + \boxed{}$

Complete solving each equation and check your answer.

10. $20 = y + 12$

$20 - 12 = y + 12 - 12$

11. $x + 0.2 = 1.9$

$x + 0.2 - 0.2 = 1.9 - 0.2$

12. $z - 31.3 = 17.6$

$z - 31.3 + 31.3 = 17.6 + 31.3$

13. $55 = x - 48$

$55 + 48 = x - 48 + 48$

14. $19.5 = x + 8.8$

$19.5 - 8.8 = x + 8.8 - 8.8$

15. $76 = y - 18$

$76 + 18 = y - 18 + 18$

Animated Glossary
www.pearsonsuccessnet.com

DIGITAL

Solve each equation and check your answer.

16. $y + 13 = 98$ **17.** $r - 80 = 160$ **18.** $t + 2.7 = 3.3$ **19.** $c - 8.9 = 4.6$

20. $r + 2.3 = 40$ **21.** $67.2 = s - 18.6$ **22.** $4.9 = x - 3.8$ **23.** $29 = c + 0.8$

24. $x + 13.9 = 98.9$ **25.** $m - 21.34 = 22.51$ **26.** $s - 90.9 = 43.45$ **27.** $d + 15.5 = 56.03$

Problem Solving

MATHEMATICAL
PRACTICES

Ⓒ **28. Use Structure** Lila would like to take a ceramics class. The class costs $120. She has saved $80 so far. Solve the equation $80 + d = 120$ to find the amount that Lila still needs.

Ⓒ **29. Use Structure** Every 2 weeks, Manny mows a total of 43 lawns in his neighborhood. He has 27 lawns left to mow this time. Solve the equation $43 - n = 27$ to find the number of lawns that Manny has mowed.

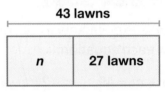

30. Give the standard form for 85 million, 16 thousand, twelve.

31. Alma pays $26.88 each week for gas and $24.95 every three months to change the oil in her car. How much does Alma pay in total for these every year?

32. The world record for a hot-air balloon flight is 65,000 feet high. Most hot-air balloons fly 62,150 feet below this height. At what height do most hot-air balloons fly? Use the equation $h + 62,150 = 65,000$.

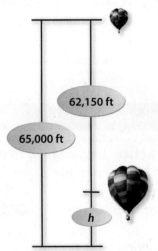

Ⓒ **33. Think About the Structure** How could you find the solution to $c - 35.2 = 40$?

   A Add 35.2 to one side.   **C** Add 35.2 to both sides.

   B Subtract 35.2 from one side.   **D** Subtract 35.2 from both sides.

Ⓒ **34. Reason** Will the solution of the equation $x - 14 = 7$ be greater than or less than 7? Use number sense to decide.

Ⓒ **35. Writing to Explain** Explain how to get n alone in the equation $n + 25 = 233$.

Other Properties of Equality

When you solve equations, you apply the Addition, Subtraction, Multiplication, and Division Properties of Equality. There are three more properties that can help you to solve equations: the Reflexive, Symmetric, and Transitive Properties of Equality.

Property	Mathematical Statement	What It Means
Reflexive Property	$a = a$	A number equals itself.
Symmetric Property	If $a = b$, then $b = a$.	If numbers are equal, they remain equal if their order is changed.
Transitive Property	If $a = b$ and $b = c$, then $a = c$.	If numbers equal the same number, they equal each other.

 When using the Transitive Property of Equality, make sure that both equations have equal values in common.

Examples:

Reflexive Property
$4 = 4$
$9h = 9h$

Symmetric Property
If $4 = y$, then $y = 4$.
If $1 + 2 = 3$, then $3 = 1 + 2$.

Transitive Property
If $3 + 2 = 5$, and $5 = 8 - 3$,
then $3 + 2 = 8 - 3$.

Practice

For **1** through **3**, identify each property.

1. If $\frac{12}{6} = \frac{4}{2}$ and $\frac{4}{2} = 2$, then $\frac{12}{6} = 2$.   **2.** If $12 = 3x$, then $3x = 12$.   **3.** $9 + 3 = 9 + 3$

For **4** through **9**, name the property that describes each situation.

4. Jessica is the same height as Juan, and Juan is the same height as Lina. So, Lina and Jessica are the same height.

5. While doing a science experiment, Ali found that 12 mL + $x = y$ and $y = 16$ mL, so 12 mL + $x = 16$ mL.

6. Twelve thousand dollars equals twelve thousand dollars.

7. Wendy's dog is the same weight as Mike's dog, so Mike's dog is the same weight as Wendy's dog.

8. $d + 25 = 25 + d$

9. A number to the second power equals the same number to the second power.

Lesson
4-3

Common
Core

6.EE.7 Solve real-world and
mathematical problems by
writing and solving
equations of the form
$x + p = q$ and $px = q$ for
cases in which p, q and x
are all nonnegative rational
numbers.

Problem Solving

Draw a Picture and Write an Equation

Jaron and Max sell pens and notebooks for the student council. Their total sales this year are $170. If they sold $48 worth of pens, how many dollars worth of notebooks did they sell?

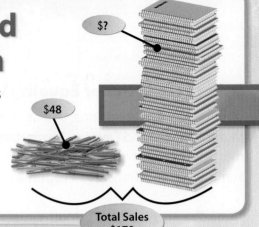

$?

$48

Total Sales
$170

Another Example How can you translate words into subtraction equations?

Nina buys lunch for herself and her sister. She pays $7.50. Nina has $5.25 left over. How much money did she begin with?

Read and Understand

What do I know? Nina pays $7.50 for lunch for herself and her sister. She has $5.25 left.

What am I asked to find? How much money did Nina have before she bought lunch?

Plan and Solve

Use the picture to represent the problem, and write an equation. Let b = the money Nina began with.

b	
$7.50	$5.25

Solve $b - 7.50 = 5.25$.

$b - 7.50 + 7.50 = 5.25 + 7.50$

$b = 12.75$

Nina began with $12.75.

Explain It

1. How can you use estimation to know if the answer is reasonable?

2. Tell how to check the problem.

What do I know? Jaron and Max sold $170 worth of pens and notebooks. They sold $48 worth of pens.

What am I asked to find? How many dollars worth of notebooks did they sell?

Draw a Picture Use a picture to represent the problem, and write an equation.

Let s = the sales of notebooks in dollars.

$170

s	$48

Solve $s + 48 = 170$.

$s + 48 - 48 = 170 - 48$

$s = 122$

They sold $122 worth of notebooks.

Guided Practice*

MATHEMATICAL PRACTICES

Do you know HOW?

Draw a picture and write an equation to solve.

1. Drew sold lemonade and apples at the school fair. She sold a total of $64. If she sold $21 in lemonade, how many dollars worth of apples did she sell?

Do you UNDERSTAND?

© 2. **Generalize** In the example at the top of the page, how can you use estimation to know if the answer is reasonable?

3. In the example at the top of the page, how can you check the answer?

Independent Practice

MATHEMATICAL PRACTICES

Solve.

4. Raquel and Mark want to buy their mom a gift that costs $32.95. Raquel earns $18.20 babysitting. How much does Mark need to earn to pay for the gift? Draw a picture and write an equation to solve.

© 5. **Model** Steven bicycled 126 miles in a month. He bicycled 17 miles less than Jessica. Write and solve an equation to find how far Jessica went.

x

126	17

Applying Math Practices

- What am I asked to find?
- What else can I try?
- How are quantities related?
- How can I explain my work?
- How can I use math to model the problem?
- Can I use tools to help?
- Is my work precise?
- Why does this work?
- How can I generalize?

---

*For another example, see Set C on page 116.

6. The band has sold 184 tickets for their concert. They want to sell 31 more. How many tickets do they want to sell?

x

| 184 | 31 |

7. Mike knows that it will cost $66.34 to get his bike fixed. He has $42.68. How much more money does Mike need?

$66.34

| $42.68 | ? |

Ⓒ **8. Reason** Lake Victoria in Africa is 26,828 square miles. It is 26,635 square miles larger than Lake Tahoe in the United States. How big is Lake Tahoe? Use the equation $x + 26,635 = 26,828$.

Ⓒ **9. Reason** Anya pays the bus fare for herself and her brother. She pays $3.50. Anya is left with $6.25. How much money did she begin with? Use the equation $x - \$3.50 = \$6.25$.

Ⓒ **10. Persevere** Mirabel is thinking of a number. She tells her friend if she subtracts 87 from the number, she will get 37. What is the number?

x

| 87 | 37 |

11. A sequoia known as Tall Tree measures about 368 feet. Another sequoia known as General Grant measures about 267 feet. How much would General Grant have to grow to be as tall as Tall Tree?

368

| 267 | x |

Ⓒ **Think About the Structure**

12. Simon has collected 27 pairs of glasses for charity. He wants to collect a total of 55 pairs. If x equals the number of pairs of glasses Simon still wants to collect, which equation best describes the total number of pairs he wants to collect?

A $27 + x = 55$

B $x - 27 = 55$

C $x - 55 = 27$

D $27 + 55 = x$

13. In a survey of pet owners, 267 people owned only dogs. The remaining 258 people owned only cats. Which equation could you use to find the total number of pet owners, T?

A $T + 258 = 267$

B $T - 267 = 258$

C $267 - T = 258$

D $267 + T = 258$

Going Digital

Solving Addition Equations

Use tools
Place-Value Blocks

Use the Place-Value Blocks eTool to solve $x + 35 = 52$.

Step 1 Go to the Place-Value Blocks eTool. Select the Two-part workspace. Think of the top space as representing the left side of the equation and the bottom space as representing the right side. Click on the long vertical block. Then, click in the top part of the workspace 3 times to show 30. Click on the small cube and click in the top part of the workspace 5 times to show 5. The odometer should read 35. Use blocks to show 52 in the bottom part of the workspace, similarly. Imagine an x in the top part.

Step 2 Use the Erase tool to remove a vertical block from both the top and the bottom part of the workspace. This is like subtracting 10 from both sides of the equation. Remove as many pairs of 10 as you can. Erase two pairs of small cubes, similarly. You should have

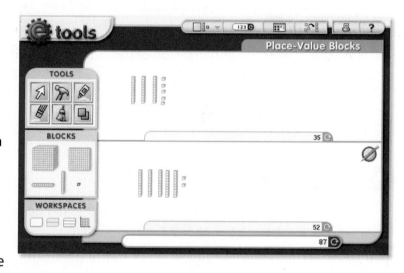

3 ones in the top workspace and 2 tens in the bottom work space. Use the Hammer tool to break apart one of the tens in the bottom part into 10 ones. Then remove 3 more pairs of ones from the top and bottom. The bottom part of the workspace now has 17. Thus, $x = 17$ is the solution to the equation $x + 35 = 52$.

Practice

Solve each equation.

1. $x + 43 = 61$

2. $x + 28 = 74$

3. $x + 29 = 85$

4. $38 + x = 105$

5. $41 + x = 163$

6. $176 + x = 326$

© Common Core

6.EE.7 Solve real-world and mathematical problems by writing and solving equations of the form $x + p = q$ and $px = q$ for cases in which p, q and x are all nonnegative rational numbers. Also 6.EE.5, 6.EE.6, 6.NS.2

Solving Multiplication and Division Equations

How can you get the variable alone in a multiplication equation?

Juan is an artist. He sold 3 paintings for a total of 45 dollars. If all the paintings cost the same amount, how much did he charge for each painting?

Solve the equation $3x = 45$ to find the answer.

3 paintings sold for $45.

Another Example How can you get the variable alone in a division equation?

Solve $x \div 2.5 = 40$.

What You Think

How can I get x alone on one side of the equation $x \div 2.5 = 40$?

Multiplying by 2.5 will undo dividing by 2.5. That will leave x alone.

 Think Multiplying by 2.5 is the inverse of dividing by 2.5.

What You Write

$$x \div 2.5 = 40$$
$$x \div 2.5 \times 2.5 = 40 \times 2.5$$
$$x = 100$$

To check, substitute 100 for x.

$$x \div 2.5 = 40$$
$$100 \div 2.5 = 40$$
$$40 = 40 \text{ It checks.}$$

Explain It

1. Explain why inverse relationships were important in the example above.

2. How can you check your answer after you solve an equation?

Think How can I get *x* alone on one side of the equation $3x = 45$?
Dividing by 3 is the inverse of multiplying by 3.

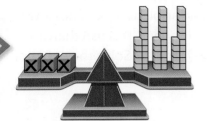

Divide both sides into
3 equal groups.

x is 15.

$3x = 45$

$3x \div 3 = 45 \div 3$

$x = 15$

To check,
substitute 15 for *x*.

$3x = 45$

$3(15) = 45$

$45 = 45$ It checks.

Juan charged $15
for each painting.

Guided Practice*

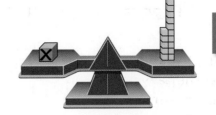 MATHEMATICAL
PRACTICES

Do you know HOW?

In **1** and **2**, explain how to get the variable
alone in each equation.

1. $18x = 36$ **2.** $w \div 3.3 = 10$

In **3** and **4**, solve the equation and check
your answer.

3. $2t = 12.5$ **4.** $r \div 5 = 22$

Do you UNDERSTAND?

5. In Exercise 1, which Property of
Equality did you use to get x alone?

 6. Communicate In Exercise 1, solve the
equation and explain how you would
check your answer.

7. In Exercise 2, which Property of
Equality did you use to get the
variable alone?

Independent Practice

Leveled Practice In **8** through **11**, explain how to get the
variable alone in each equation.

8. $8y = 56$ **9.** $x \div 15.2 = 3$ **10.** $u \div 8.7 = 12$ **11.** $31.4 = 31.4y$

Solve each equation. Check your answers.

12. $d \div 2 = 108$ **13.** $7{,}200s = 800$ **14.** $x \div 3 = 29.4$ **15.** $9.9 = 3x$

16. $m \div 3.5 = 4.2$ **17.** $x \div 2.9 = 1$ **18.** $9.6 = 1.6y$ **19.** $35s = 10.5$

20. $1.6s = 80$ **21.** $30 = x \div 4.5$ **22.** $k \div 0.5 = 29$ **23.** $270 = 2.7x$

© 24. Writing to Explain How can you find the solution to the equation $4x = 20$?

© 26. Persevere Two teams of students earned money by washing cars. Team 1 washed 19 cars at $4.25 each. Team 2 washed 17 cars for a total of $82.50. Which team earned more money? By how much?

27. A supertaster can have about 4.5 times more taste buds than a nontaster. If a supertaster has 425 taste buds per square centimeter, how many taste buds might a nontaster have per square centimeter? Use the equation $4.5t = 425$.

28. Estimation About how much is the value of x in the equation $254 = 75x$?

30. Josh's class is planting a garden. Josh divided seeds so that 20 students had 35 seeds each.

  a How many seeds did Josh start with? Use the equation $y \div 20 = 35$.

  b How many seeds would each student get if there were 25 students to divide the same number of seeds?

© 32. Reason Which algebraic equation best describes total weight (T) of four baskets of strawberries, if w equals the weight of one box of strawberries?

  A $T = 4 + w$ **C** $T = 4 \div w$

  B $T = w \div 4$ **D** $T = 4w$

25. A female whale shark is 35 feet long. An average 12-year-old is 5 feet tall. How many times longer is this fish than an average 12-year-old? Solve the equation $35 = 5x$.

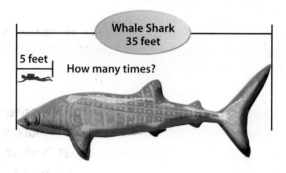

Whale Shark
35 feet

5 feet

How many times?

© 29. Construct Arguments Is 280 the solution of $x \div 4 = 70$? Explain your answer.

© 31. Think About the Structure What is the first step in solving the equation below?

$x \div 30 = 8$

  A Add 30 to both sides.

  B Subtract 30 from both sides.

  C Multiply both sides by 30.

  D Divide both sides by 30.

© 33. Reason Eric paid a library fine (f) for returning a book 4 days late. If the library charges $0.15 per day for late returns, which equation best describes his fine?

  A $f \times 4 = 0.15$ **C** $4 \div f = 0.15$

  B $f \div 4 = 0.15$ **D** $4 - f = 0.15$

Enrichment

Square Roots

A *square number* is any number that can be written as the product of a whole number multiplied by itself. For example, $9 = 3 \times 3$, so 9 is a square number. The square of 3 is 3^2, or 9.

Square numbers can be modeled as the area of square arrays.

$3^2 = 9$

Finding the *square root* of a number is the inverse of squaring a number. To find the square root of a number, ask, "What number times itself equals the given number?" The symbol for a square root is $\sqrt{\ }$. It's called a radical sign.

Find the square root of 16, or $\sqrt{16}$. What number times itself is 16?

$4 \times 4 = 16$

The square root of 16 is 4, or $\sqrt{16} = 4$.

Example: Find the square root of 25, or $\sqrt{25}$.

Ask, "What number times itself is 25?"

$$5 \times 5 = 25$$

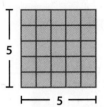

The square root of 25 is 5, or $\sqrt{25} = 5$.

Notice that the length of one of the sides of the array is the same as the square root.

Practice

For **1** through **5**, write the square number for each array. Then find the square root.

1.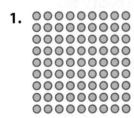

2.

3.

4.

5.

For **6** through **11**, find each square root.

6. $\sqrt{4}$
7. $\sqrt{169}$
8. $\sqrt{1}$
9. $\sqrt{400}$
10. $\sqrt{324}$
11. $\sqrt{484}$

Ⓒ **12. Writing to Explain** Gina says that the square root of 100 is 50. She says that finding a square root of a number is easy; all you need to do is add two of the same number to get the answer. Is she right? Explain.

Common Core

6.EE.7 Solve real-world and mathematical problems by writing and solving equations of the form $x + p = q$ and $px = q$ for cases in which p, q, and x are all nonnegative rational numbers.

Problem Solving

Draw a Picture and Write an Equation

Min and her 4 friends had a garage sale to help pay for their choir trip. They divided their total earnings so that each person had $37. How much was the total earnings from the garage sale?

$37 each

Another Example **How can you translate words into multiplication equations?**

Gary collects minerals. His friend Elli has 5 times as many minerals as he does. If Elli has 125 minerals, how many does Gary have?

Read and Understand

What do I know? — Elli has 5 times more minerals than Gary has. Elli has 125 minerals.

What am I asked to find? — How many minerals Gary has.

Plan and Solve

Use the picture to represent the problem, and write an equation. Let x equal the minerals Gary has.

Solve $5x = 125$.

$5x \div 5 = 125 \div 5$

$x = 25$

125 minerals

x	x	x	x	x

Gary has 25 minerals.

Explain It

1. How can you use estimation to know if the answer is reasonable?

2. Tell how to check the problem.

What do I know? Min and 4 friends had a garage sale and each earned $37.

What am I asked to find? How much was the total earnings from the garage sale?

Draw a Picture Use a picture to represent the problem and write an equation.

Let t = the total earnings in dollars.

t = total earnings

$37	$37	$37	$37	$37

Solve $t \div 5 = 37$.

$t \div 5 \times 5 = 37 \times 5$

$t = 185$

The garage sale raised $185.

Guided Practice*

Do you know HOW?

Draw a picture and write an equation to solve.

1. Ryan made a CD of his favorite songs. There are 42 minutes of time on the CD. He records 14 songs. What is the average length of each song?

Do you UNDERSTAND?

© 2. **Generalize** In the example at the top of the page, how can you use estimation to know if the answer is reasonable?

3. In the example at the top of the page, how can you check the answer?

Independent Practice

Solve.

© 4. **Model** David saves $15 each week that he earns babysitting. After 8 weeks, how much money will he have saved? Draw a picture and write an equation to solve.

© 5. **Persevere** The Technology Club pools their money to buy robot parts. They divide the parts among the 13 members. Each gets 24 parts. Write an equation to find the total number of parts.

t = total number of parts

24	24	24	24	24	24	24	24	24	24	24	24	24

Applying Math Practices

- What am I asked to find?
- What else can I try?
- How are quantities related?
- How can I explain my work?
- How can I use math to model the problem?
- Can I use tools to help?
- Is my work precise?
- Why does this work?
- How can I generalize?

6. **Persevere** In a lunch survey, 3 times as many students preferred soft tacos as preferred pizza. If 324 students preferred soft tacos, how many students preferred pizza?

7. **Reason** A charity group divides donated items among 19 families. Each family receives 14 items. How many items were donated in total? Use the picture to help solve.

i = total items

14	14	14	14	14	14	14	14	14	14	14	14	14	14	14	14	14	14	14

8. Vicki hands out stickers to 23 preschool students. If each child gets 9 stickers, how many stickers were there to begin with? Solve the equation $s \div 23 = 9$.

9. Darby rents in-line skates for 4.5 hours. His total bill is $27. How much did he pay per hour to rent the skates? Solve the equation $4.5x = \$27$.

10. In an orchestra, there are 5 times as many string instruments as percussion instruments. If there are 45 string instruments, how many percussion instruments are there?

11. Raffle tickets are sold to 435 people attending the school fair. If 6 tickets were sold per person, how many tickets were sold? Solve the equation $t \div 435 = 6$.

© **Think About the Structure**

12. Raquel walks dogs for her neighbors. She worked for 11 hours and earned $71.50.

    If x equals how much Raquel charges per hour, which equation best describes how much she earned?

    A $x - 11 = \$71.50$

    B $x \div 11 = \$71.50$

    C $11x = \$71.50$

    D $x + 11 = \$71.50$

13. Among 65 people at a Strawberry Festival, each person eats 13 strawberries. If s equals the total number of strawberries eaten, which equation best shows how the total strawberries were divided among the people?

    A $s - 65 = 13$

    B $65 \div 13 = s$

    C $13s = 65$

    D $s \div 65 = 13$

Skills Review Complete the equations.

1. $12 + 15 = 27$
   $12 + 15 + 6 = 27 +$ ▩
   ▩ $=$ ▩

2. $57 - 9 = 48$
   $57 - 9 - 7 = 48 -$ ▩
   ▩ $=$ ▩

3. $6 \times 6 = 36$
   $6 \times 6 \div 4 = 36 \div$ ▩
   ▩ $=$ ▩

4. $64 \div 8 = 8$
   $64 \div 8 \times 3 = 8 \times$ ▩
   ▩ $=$ ▩

Solve each equation.

5. $15 + x = 34$

6. $s + 1.7 = 30$

7. $u - 12 = 45$

8. $n - 5.7 = 7.5$

9. $40y = 360$

10. $1.5z = 10.5$

11. $g \div 10 = 15$

12. $k \div 7.25 = 8$

13. $6.12 + t = 66$

14. $p \div 5.5 = 11$

15. $0.8z = 48$

16. $m - 9.45 = 2.7$

Error Search Find each solution that is not correct.
Write it correctly and explain the error.

17. $w - 15 = 35$
    $w = 20$

18. $27 + r = 56$
    $r = 29$

19. $7p = 63$
    $p = 56$

20. $v \div 4 = 32$
    $v = 8$

21. $12q = 60$
    $q = 5$

Number Sense

Write whether each statement is true or false.
Explain your answer.

22. In the equation $4 + c = 18$, the value of c will be less than 18.

23. In the equation $18h = 108$, h will be less than 5.

24. The value of x in the equation $12 + x = 30$ will be less than
    the value of p in the equation $15 + p = 30$.

25. In the equation $9.9c = 119$, the value of c will be greater than 10.

26. The value of k will be the same in all of these equations:
    $k + 5 = 62$ $k - 5 = 62$ $5k = 62$

1. If $2x = 12$, which of the following is also true? (4-1)

A $2x - 7 = 12 - 7$

B $2x - 7 = 12 + 7$

C $2x - 7 = 12$

D $2x + 7 = 12 - 7$

2. The local animal shelter has 3 times as many cats as dogs. If there are 27 cats at the shelter, solve the equation $3x = 27$ to find the number of dogs. (4-4)

A $x = 81$

B $x = 24$

C $x = 9$

D $x = 3$

3. The choir had 50 members after 3 students joined. The equation shown can be used to find the membership, x, before the students joined. What step should be taken to get x alone on one side of the equation? (4-2)

$x + 3 = 50$

A Multiply each side of the equation by 3.

B Add 3 to each side of the equation.

C Subtract 3 from each side of the equation.

D Divide each side of the equation by 3.

4. If $3x = 15 + 3$, which of the following is also true? (4-1)

A $3x \div 3 = (15 + 3) \times 3$

B $3x \div 3 = (15 + 3) \div 3$

C $3x - 3 = (15 + 3) \div 3$

D $3x + 3 = 15 + 3$

5. The math club is selling popcorn for a fundraiser. Gina sold 9 boxes for a total of $108 in sales. Which equation can be used to find c, the cost of each box? (4-5)

108
c	c	c	c	c	c	c	c	c

A $c \div 9 = 108$

B $9c = 108$

C $c - 9 = 108$

D $c + 9 = 108$

6. Some animals have different blood types. Dogs have 13 blood types, which is 10 more than cats have. Which picture and equation can be used to find c, the number of blood types cats have? (4-3)

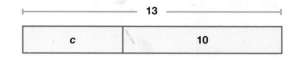

13
c	c	c	c	c	c	c	c	c	c

A $10c = 13$

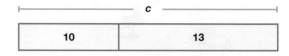

c	
13	10

B $c - 13 = 10$

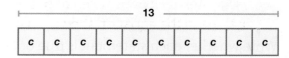

c	
10	13

C $c - 10 = 13$

13
c	10

D $c + 10 = 13$

7. Which value of m makes the following equation true? (4-4)

$m \div 1.5 = 6$

A $m = 9$

B $m = 6$

C $m = 3$

D $m = 1.5$

8. A baseball team won 36 games this season, 6 more games than last season. Solve the equation $n + 6 = 36$ to find n, the number of games they won last season. (4-2)

A $n = 6$

B $n = 30$

C $n = 40$

D $n = 42$

9. What step should be taken to get x alone in the equation shown? (4-4)

$4.2x = 60$

A Add 4.2 to each side of the equation.

B Subtract 4.2 from each side of the equation.

C Multiply each side of the equation by 4.2.

D Divide each side of the equation by 4.2.

10. Which value of t makes the following equation true? (4-2)

$t - 15.5 = 25.5$

A $t = 10$

B $t = 15.5$

C $t = 25.5$

D $t = 41$

11. Amy's horse eats 3 bales of hay each week. Which picture and equation can be used to find w, the number of weeks that 36 bales of hay will feed the horse? (4-5)

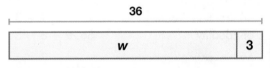

A $w + 3 = 36$

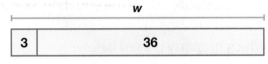

B $w - 3 = 36$

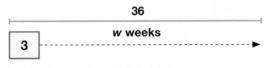

C $3w = 36$

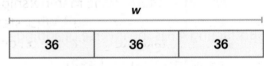

D $w \div 3 = 36$

12. There are 53 countries in Africa, including 6 countries that are islands off the coast of the main continent. Which equation can be used to find c, the number of countries that are on the main continent? (4-3)

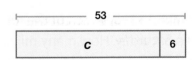

A $c + 6 = 53$

B $c - 6 = 53$

C $6c = 53$

D $c \div 6 = 53$

Set A, pages 96–97

The properties of equality are illustrated in the table.

Properties of Equality	
Addition Property of Equality	$4 + 3 = 7$ So, $4 + 3 + 2 = 7 + 2$
Subtraction Property of Equality	$9 + 8 = 17$ So, $9 + 8 - 5 = 17 - 5$
Multiplication Property of Equality	$3 \times 5 = 15$ So, $3 \times 5 \times 2 = 15 \times 2$
Division Property of Equality	$16 + 2 = 18$ So, $(16 + 2) \div 2 = 18 \div 2$

Which property is used below?

$$2 \times 3 = 6 \qquad (2 \times 3) - 4 = 6 - 4$$

The Subtraction Property of Equality is used.

Remember that the properties of equality allow you to apply the same operation with the same amount to both sides of an equation.

1. If $6 + 2 = 8$, does $6 + 2 + 3 = 8 + 3$? Why or why not?

2. If $8 - 1 = 7$, does $8 - 1 - 2 = 7 - 3$? Why or why not?

3. If $8x = 56$, does $8x \div 8 = 56 \div 56$? Why or why not?

4. If $y - 6 = 13$, does $(y - 6) \times 7 = 13 \times 7$? Why or why not?

Set B, pages 98–100

Solve for x in $x + 4.8 = 19$.

Subtracting 4.8 is the inverse of adding 4.8.

$x + 4.8 = 19$ ← Solve the equation.

$x + 4.8 - 4.8 = 19 - 4.8$ ← Use the Subtraction Property of Equality.

$x = 14.2$ ← Simplify.

Remember that addition and subtraction have an inverse relationship. To check, substitute your answer back into the original equation.

Solve for x.

1. $x + 2 = 11$ 2. $x + 3.4 = 15.2$

3. $x - 2.1 = 4.2$ 4. $x - 17 = 13$

Set C, pages 102–104

Daniel hiked 13 miles on the weekend. He hiked 8 miles on Saturday. How many miles did he hike on Sunday? Draw a picture to represent the problem.

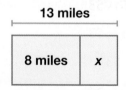

13 miles

8 miles | x

Remember that drawing a picture can help translate words into addition and subtraction equations to solve problems.

1. Use the picture to write an equation for the hiking problem.

2. Solve the equation you wrote.

Solve for x in $9x = 1.8$.

Dividing by 9 is the inverse of multiplying by 9.

$9x = 1.8$ ← Solve the equation.

$9x \div 9 = 1.8 \div 9$ ← Use the Division Property of Equality.

$x = 0.2$ ← Simplify.

Remember that multiplication and division have an inverse relationship. To check, substitute your answer back into the original equation.

Solve for x.

1. $8x = 64$ **2.** $x \div 20 = 120$

3. $x \div 1.2 = 2$ **4.** $7x = 7.7$

5. $2.6 = 1.3x$ **6.** $24.2 = x \div 2.2$

7. $x \div 5 = 110$ **8.** $40x = 1{,}000$

9. $11x = 264$ **10.** $x \div 10 = 70$

Raphael and 3 friends raised money for a band trip. If each person raised $21, what was the total amount that the 4 friends raised?

Let x be the total amount of money the 4 friends raised. Draw a picture to represent the problem.

x			
$21	$21	$21	$21

Use the drawing to write an equation and solve the problem.

$x \div 4 = 21$ ← Write the equation.

$(x \div 4) \times 4 = 21 \times 4$ ← Solve the equation.

$x = 84$ ← Simplify.

The 4 friends raised a total of $84.

Remember that drawing a picture can help translate words into multiplication and division equations to solve problems.

Solve.

1. Tyler buys cinder blocks to build a garden wall. A cinder block weighs 25 pounds. How many blocks should Tyler buy if he wants to buy 500 pounds?

2. Chris buys snacks after school. After 12 weeks, he spent $60. If he spent the same amount each week, how much did he spend each week?

3. Kyle buys 3 erasers and 1 pen. The pen costs $4.50, which is 3 times the cost of 1 eraser. How much does 1 eraser cost?

Topic 5

Number and Fraction Concepts

2

The ostrich is the largest bird that is alive today. How does the length of an ostrich's neck compare to its height? You will find out in Lesson 5-6.

1

A koala spends from 18 to 22 hours a day dozing! What fraction of the day does a koala sleep? You will find out in Lesson 5-4.

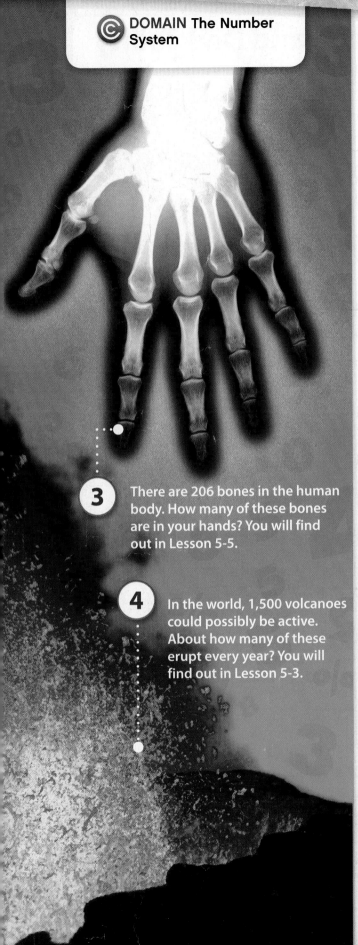

There are 206 bones in the human body. How many of these bones are in your hands? You will find out in Lesson 5-5.

4

In the world, 1,500 volcanoes could possibly be active. About how many of these erupt every year? You will find out in Lesson 5-3.

Review What You Know!

Vocabulary

Choose the best term from the box.

- divisor
- array
- factors
- multiples

1. A (an) __?__ is an arrangement of objects in rows and columns.

2. 2 and 5 are __?__ of 10.

3. The number used to divide another number is the __?__ .

4. 10 and 20 are __?__ of 5.

Finding Factors

List all the factors of each number.

5. 5   6. 6   7. 14

8. 25   9. 32   10. 48

11. 56   12. 67   13. 100

Fractions

Write the fraction shown by the shaded part or region.

14. △ △ ▲
    △ ▲ ▲
    △ ▲ ▲

15.

Exponents

© 16. **Writing to Explain** How can the expression $11 \times 11 \times 11 \times 11$ be written in exponential form? Explain.

Lesson
5-1

Common
Core

This lesson reinforces
concepts and skills
required for Topic 9.

Factors, Multiples, and Divisibility

How are factors and divisibility related?

How many different ways can Raul build a dog pen that has an area of 36 square feet and has sides measured in whole feet?

Choose an Operation Divide to find the possible measurements.

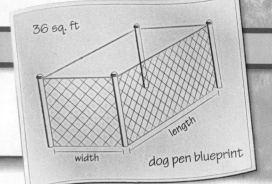

36 sq. ft

length

width

dog pen blueprint

Another Example How can you use divisibility rules?

Is 126 divisible by 2, 3, 4, 6, 9, or 10? You can use divisibility rules to find out.

Divisibility Rules

A whole number is divisible by	Examples:	Is 126 divisible by the number?
2 if the ones digit is an even number.	10; 6; 108	Yes, the ones digit is even.
3 if the sum of the digits is divisible by 3.	3; 627; 891	Yes, 1 + 2 + 6 = 9. 9 is divisible by 3.
4 if the last two digits of the number are divisible by 4.	64; 5,888	No, 26 is not divisible by 4.
5 if the ones digit is 0 or 5.	380; 9,005	No, the ones digit is 6.
6 if the number is divisible by both 2 and 3.	240; 8,982	Yes, 126 is divisible by both 2 and 3.
9 if the sum of the digits is divisible by 9.	189; 1,035	Yes, 1 + 2 + 6 = 9. 9 is divisible by 9.
10 if the ones digit is 0.	170; 1,380	No, the ones digit is not 0.

What is a multiple of a number?

Is 126 a multiple of 7? A multiple of a given number is <u>a product of that number and a whole number greater than 0</u>.

Since 126 ÷ 7 = 18, 126 is the product of 7 and 18.
So, 126 is a multiple of 7. Other multiples of 7 are 7, 14, 21, 28, 35, 42, 49, and so on.

Explain It

1. Is 53,802 a multiple of 9? Explain your answer.

A number is divisible by another number <u>when the quotient is a whole number and the remainder is 0</u>.

The divisors and quotients are factors of 36.

$36 \div 1 = 36$ 1 and 36 are factors.
$36 \div 2 = 18$ 2 and 18 are factors.
$36 \div 3 = 12$ 3 and 12 are factors.
$36 \div 4 = 9$ 4 and 9 are factors.
$36 \div 5 = 7 \text{ R}1$ 5 and 7 are <u>not</u> factors of 36.
$36 \div 6 = 6$ 6 is a factor.

All the factors have been found. The factors of 36 are 1, 2, 3, 4, 6, 9, 12, 18, and 36.

Use each pair of factors to find the possible measurements of the dog pen.

1 and 36	4 and 9	12 and 3
2 and 18	6 and 6	18 and 2
3 and 12	9 and 4	36 and 1

There are 9 different ways Raul can build the dog pen.

Guided Practice*

MATHEMATICAL PRACTICES

Do you know HOW?

In **1** through **4**, tell whether each number is divisible by 2, 3, 4, 5, 6, 9, or 10.

1. 60

2. 228

3. 78

4. 117

In **5** through **8**, tell whether the first number is a multiple of the second.

5. 72; 3

6. 368; 2

7. 2,102; 5

8. 1,780; 10

Do you UNDERSTAND?

9. In the example at the top of the page, how can you tell if 36 is divisible by 2?

© **10. Communicate** How can you tell that 189 is divisible by 3 without doing the division?

© **11. Construct Arguments** If a number is divisible by 10, will it always be divisible by 4? Explain.

Independent Practice

In **12** through **15**, use the divisibility rules to tell if each number is divisible by 2, 3, 4, 5, 6, 9, or 10.

12. 63

13. 225

14. 399

15. 4,090

In **16** through **23**, name at least three factors of each number that are greater than 1.

16. 70

17. 84

18. 98

19. 75

20. 150

21. 333

22. 3,000

23. 1,200

Animated Glossary
www.pearsonsuccessnet.com

In **24** through **31**, tell whether the first number is a multiple of the second.

24. 50; 10

25. 92; 3

26. 123; 9

27. 289; 5

28. 1,099; 3

29. 6,012; 6

30. 10,235; 2

31. 31,233; 6

Problem Solving

MATHEMATICAL
PRACTICES

Use the table for **32** and **33**.

32. One game of Four-Square needs exactly 4 players. Which schools can divide their participants exactly by 4?

33. **Writing to Explain** Can the total number of participants in the Four-Square Tournament be divided evenly by 4? Why? Explain your answer.

Four-Square Tournament	
School	**Number of Participants**
Almont Junior High	244
Sheridan Elementary	189
Kellogg Elementary	437
Dalton Middle School	178

34. **Construct Arguments** Is the number 10,387 divisible by 3? Why or why not?

35. **Reason** Leah is helping her mother paint the exterior of the house. She knows that paint rollers come in packages of 3. If her mother needs 20 rollers, how many packages will she need to buy?

36. A Venn diagram shows groups and how they are related. What does the area of overlap in the Venn diagram below show?

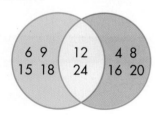

6 9
15 18 12
24 4 8
16 20

A factors of 3

B factors of 4

C multiples of 3 and 4

D multiples of 8

37. **Persevere** Maury notes that 31 and 41 are not divisible by any number except themselves and 1. He concludes that if a number ends in 1, it cannot be divided by any number other than itself and 1. Which number disproves this rule?

A 91   **C** 71

B 61   **D** 81

38. If x is a whole number greater than 0, which is always true?

A $6x$ is divisible by 3.

B $6x$ is divisible by 4.

C $6x$ is divisible by 5.

D $6x$ is divisible by 9.

Venn Diagrams

A Venn diagram uses circles, loops, or other shapes to show relationships between sets. Sets are described by the data or objects they contain. Circles overlap, or intersect, when some data belong to more than one set. The Venn diagram below relates parallelograms. Notice that squares are a subset of both rectangles and rhombuses.

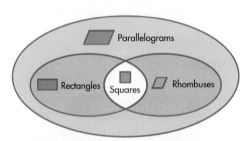

Example: Describe the sets shown in the Venn diagram below.

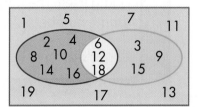

Counting numbers less than 20 are shown in the rectangle. The numbers in the red loop are divisible by 2. The numbers in the green loop are divisible by 3. The numbers divisible by both 2 and 3 are a subset of both loops.

Practice

1. In the Venn diagram of parallelograms above, is the set of rectangles a subset of parallelograms? Explain.

2. In the example above, what other divisibility rule is true of the subset of numbers divisible by both 2 and 3?

For **3** through **5**, describe the sets shown.

3.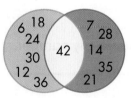

4.

5.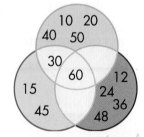

6. Draw a Venn diagram with two sets: one set of numbers divisible by 10 and the other set of numbers divisible by 25. Use at least 10 numbers in the diagram.

7. Draw a Venn diagram with three sets. One set of numbers is divisible by 5. The second set of numbers is divisible by 10. The third set of numbers is divisible by 15. Use at least 10 numbers and tell which sets are subsets of other sets.

Lesson
5-2

Common
Core

This lesson reinforces
concepts and skills
required for Topic 9.

Prime Factorization

How can you write the prime factorization of a number?

Whole numbers greater than 1 are either prime or composite numbers.

A prime number has <u>exactly two factors, 1 and itself</u>. The numbers 2, 3, and 5 are prime numbers.

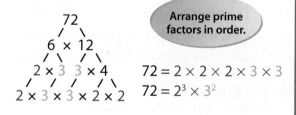

Model	Dimension	Factors
	1×2	1, 2
	1×3	1, 3
	1×4	1, 4
	2×2	2
	1×5	1, 5

Another Example How can you use a factor tree to find the prime factorization of a number?

One Way

To find the prime factorization of 72, begin with the smallest prime factor. Write factors until all the factors are prime numbers.

```
        72
       /  \
     2 × 36          72 = 2 × 2 × 2 × 3 × 3
    / / \
  2 × 2 × 18         72 = 2³ × 3²
 / / / \
2 × 2 × 2 × 9
/ / / / \
2 × 2 × 2 × 3 × 3
```

$72 = 2 \times 2 \times 2 \times 3 \times 3$

$72 = 2^3 \times 3^2$

Another Way

To find the prime factorization of 72, begin with any two factors of 72. Write factors until all the factors are prime numbers.

Arrange prime factors in order.

```
       72
      /  \
     6 × 12
    / \   / \
  2 × 3 3 × 4
 / / / / \
2 × 3 × 3 × 2 × 2
```

$72 = 2 \times 2 \times 2 \times 3 \times 3$

$72 = 2^3 \times 3^2$

There is only one prime factorization for any number.

Guided Practice*

MATHEMATICAL
PRACTICES

Do you know **HOW?**

In **1** through **8**, write the prime factorization of each number. If it is prime, write *prime*.

1. 18   **2.** 23   **3.** 32   **4.** 45

5. 89   **6.** 169   **7.** 216   **8.** 243

Do you **UNDERSTAND?**

9. Construct Arguments How do the two factor trees above show that there is only one prime factorization for 72?

10. Is 1 prime, composite, or neither?

*For another example, see Set B on page 140.

A composite number has more than two factors and can be written as the product of its prime factors. This is called its prime factorization.

4 is a composite number. The factors of 4 are 1, 2, and 4. 2 is its only prime factor. The prime factorization of 4 is 2×2, or 2^2.

To find the prime factorization of 60, write its factors, beginning with the smallest prime factor.

$60 = 2 \times 30$ ← 2 is a factor of 60.

$= 2 \times 2 \times 15$ ← 2 is a factor again.

$= 2 \times 2 \times 3 \times 5$ ← 3 and 5 are factors.

$= 2^2 \times 3 \times 5$ ← Use exponents.

Independent Practice

In **11** through **25**, write the prime factorization of each number. If it is prime, write *prime*.

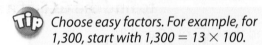 **Tip** *Choose easy factors. For example, for 1,300, start with $1,300 = 13 \times 100$.*

11. 26 **12.** 47 **13.** 68 **14.** 125 **15.** 490

16. 750 **17.** 210 **18.** 2,100 **19.** 120 **20.** 65

21. 300 **22.** 27 **23.** 38 **24.** 99 **25.** 57

Problem Solving

 MATHEMATICAL PRACTICES

26. A triangle has a 60°, a 30°, and a 90° angle. Is the triangle acute, right, or obtuse?

© **27. Be Precise** Which is a prime number?

A 33   **B** 35   **C** 37   **D** 39

© **28. Writing to Explain** Raul makes a conjecture that every odd number greater than 3 can be expressed as the sum of two primes. Use the number 11 to explain that Raul is wrong.

A famous unsolved problem referred to as *Goldbach's conjecture* states that every even number greater than 2 can be written as the sum of two prime numbers. For example, $4 = 2 + 2, 6 = 3 + 3, 8 = 3 + 5$, and so on. Computers have shown that Goldbach's conjecture is true for all even numbers up to 100,000,000,000,000!

In **29** through **33**, use *Goldbach's conjecture*. Show that each number can be written as the sum of two primes.

29. 18   **30.** 30   **31.** 32   **32.** 46   **33.** 66

DIGITAL Animated Glossary www.pearsonsuccessnet.com

Lesson
5-3
©
Common
Core

6.NS.4 Find the greatest common factor of two whole numbers less than or equal to 100 and the least common multiple of two whole numbers less than or equal to 12. Use the distributive property to express a sum of two whole numbers 1–100 with a common factor as a multiple of a sum of two whole numbers with no common factor….

Greatest Common Factor

How can you find the GCF of a set of numbers?

Keesha is putting together bags of supplies. She has 42 craft sticks and 12 glue bottles. If she puts an equal number of craft sticks and an equal number of glue bottles in each bag, what is the greatest number of bags Keesha can make so that nothing is left over?

12 bottles of glue

42 craft sticks

Another Example **How can you use prime factorization to find the GCF of a set of numbers?**

Find the GCF of 60 and 84.

Step 1

Find the prime factorization of each number.

Tip *You can use factor trees to find the prime factorizations.*

$60 = 2 \times 2 \times 3 \times 5 = 2^2 \times 3 \times 5$

$84 = 2 \times 2 \times 3 \times 7 = 2^2 \times 3 \times 7$

Step 2

Multiply the common prime factors.

$2^2 \times 3 = 2 \times 2 \times 3 = 12$

12 is the GCF of 60 and 84.

Guided Practice*

MATHEMATICAL
PRACTICES

Do you know HOW?

Find the GCF for each set of numbers.

1. 18, 36   **2.** 14, 35

3. 22, 55   **4.** 25, 100

5. 15, 44   **6.** 27, 81

7. 39, 69   **8.** 99, 121

Do you UNDERSTAND?

9. Why can the greatest common factor also be called the *greatest common divisor*?

© **10. Communicate** How are the two ways shown to find the GCF for a set of numbers alike and different?

Animated Glossary
www.pearsonsuccessnet.com
DIGITAL

*For another example, see Set C on page 140.

Step 1

List and compare all the factors of each number in the set.

Factors of 12: 1, 2, 3, 4, 6, 12

Factors of 42: 1, 2, 3, 6, 7, 14, 21, 42

1, 2, 3 and 6 are factors of both 12 and 42. These are called common factors.

Step 2

Identify the greatest common factor (GCF). The greatest common factor is <u>the greatest number that is a factor of two or more numbers</u>.

You can see that 6 is the GCF of 12 and 42.

This means that 6 is the greatest number that can be divided evenly into 12 and 42. So, Keesha can make 6 bags.

Independent Practice

In **11** through **22**, find the greatest common factor for each set of numbers.

11. 21, 49

12. 8, 52

13. 20, 35

14. 15, 36

15. 30, 66

16. 52, 78

17. 32, 81

18. 45, 120

19. 34, 51, 85

20. 56, 63, 72

21. 20, 32, 44

22. 46, 92, 138

Problem Solving

MATHEMATICAL **PRACTICES**

The Venn diagram to the right shows the factors of 24 and 40.

23. What is the meaning of each of the three shaded regions? Which factor is the GCF?

© **24. Use Tools** Draw a Venn diagram to show the common factors of 36 and 54. What is the GCF?

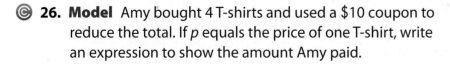

25. About 50 of the 1,500 possibly active volcanoes on Earth erupt every year. What is the GCF of 50 and 1,500?

© **26. Model** Amy bought 4 T-shirts and used a $10 coupon to reduce the total. If p equals the price of one T-shirt, write an expression to show the amount Amy paid.

© **27. Writing to Explain** How does finding the prime factorization of a group of numbers help you to find their GCF?

© **28. Generalize** What is the GCF of 45 and 60?

    A 5   **B** 10   **C** 15   **D** 20

Lesson
5-4

Common
Core

This lesson reinforces
concepts and skills required
for Topic 9.

Understanding Fractions

How can fractions be used?

Fractions are <u>numbers that describe the</u> <u>division of a whole into equal parts</u>. Sometimes the whole is a region. The numerator tells <u>the number of equal parts</u> <u>or objects being considered</u>. The denominator tells <u>the total number of equal</u> <u>parts or objects</u>.

$$\frac{2}{6} \begin{array}{l}\text{numerator}\\\text{denominator}\end{array}$$

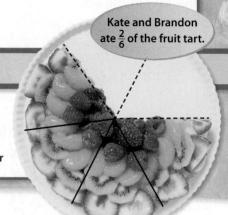

Kate and Brandon ate $\frac{2}{6}$ of the fruit tart.

Other Examples

A fraction is relative to the size of the whole.

In each circle, $\frac{1}{4}$ is shaded. Since the circles are not the same size, the shaded areas are not the same size.

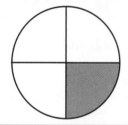

The fraction $\frac{1}{2}$ of each line segment is shaded. Since the line segments are different lengths, the shaded segments are not the same lengths.

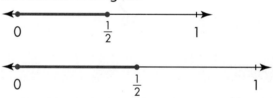

Guided Practice*

 MATHEMATICAL PRACTICES

Do you know HOW?

What fraction represents the shaded portion in each of the following?

1.    **2.**

What fraction represents each point on the number line below?

3.

Do you UNDERSTAND?

4. Reason How are the parts of a region described by a fraction like the segments of a number line described by a fraction?

5. Use Tools Draw pictures to represent the fraction $\frac{2}{5}$ as a region, a set, and a segment of a number line.

6. There are 16 boys and 14 girls in the 6th grade class. What fraction represents the boys?

Sometimes the whole is a set. Fractions can describe part of a set of things.

$\frac{7}{8}$ of the baseball gloves are for right-handed players.

Fractions also can describe a segment of a number line. The number 1 represents a whole unit. This unit on the number line is divided into 7 equal segments.

$\frac{5}{7}$ is shaded.

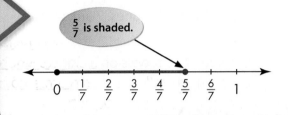

Independent Practice

In **7** through **10**, write the fraction that represents the shaded portion.

7.

8.

9.  **1**

cm

10.

In **11** and **12**, identify the fraction representing each point on the number line.

11.

0   1

12.

0   1

In **13** through **17**, draw models to show the fractions.

13. Draw a number line to represent $\frac{7}{12}$.

14. Draw a number line to represent $\frac{5}{8}$.

15. Draw a set to represent $\frac{2}{3}$.

16. Draw a region to represent $\frac{6}{9}$.

17. Draw a set to represent $\frac{7}{9}$.

DIGITAL

Animated Glossary
www.pearsonsuccessnet.com

Use Tools For **18** through **21**, draw a picture to show how you would represent each of the following fractions.

18. Jay picks up 15 stones. 7 are gray.

19. Shi-An mows $\frac{3}{4}$ of her lawn.

20. In a line of 10 towels on a clothesline, 8 are striped.

21. Joan runs $\frac{2}{5}$ of the distance to the car.

Estimation For **22** through **25**, estimate the fraction of the circle that is shaded.

22.

23.

24.

25.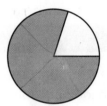

26. A koala often sleeps 18 hours in one day. Write the fraction of the day that a koala often sleeps.

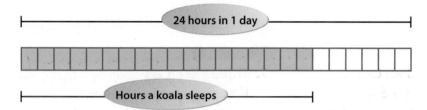

27. Use Tools What fraction represents the point shown on the number line?

A $\frac{3}{9}$ **B** $\frac{4}{9}$ **C** $\frac{3}{8}$ **D** $\frac{4}{8}$

28. Think About the Structure In which picture does the blue shaded portion NOT represent the fraction $\frac{4}{7}$?

A    **B**   **C**   **D**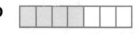

Algebra Connections

Completing Tables

Remember that you can make and use a table to solve a problem that relates one quantity to another.

For **1** through **3**, copy and complete each table.

1. Becca saved $150. Now, she saves $15 more each week. If x equals the number of weeks Becca saves, find her total savings after 3, 4, 6, and 10 weeks.

Weeks Becca saves x	Total savings 15x + 150
3	
4	
6	
10	

Example: At the market, a pound of fruit costs $2. If x equals the number of pounds of fruit, make a table to show the total cost of 1, 2, 3, or 4 pounds of fruit.

Pounds of fruit x	Total cost 2x
1	$2
2	$4
3	$6
4	$8

2. An adult takes some children to the movies. A child's ticket costs $4.25. An adult ticket costs $6.50. If x equals the number of children, find the total cost of the tickets for 1, 2, 3, or 4 children taken.

Children x	Total cost 6.50 + 4.25x
1	
2	
3	
4	

3. Three friends are sharing a pizza equally. If x equals the number of same-size pieces into which the pizza is cut, find the number of pieces each friend will get if the pizza is cut into 3, 6, 9, or 12 pieces.

Total number of pieces x	Pieces per friend $\frac{x}{3}$
3	
6	
9	
12	

Equivalent Fractions

Hands-On fraction strips

$\frac{1}{8}$

How can you find equivalent fractions?

Fractions that have different numerators and denominators but name the same amount are called equivalent fractions.

The fraction strips show equivalent fractions.
$\frac{2}{3} = \frac{4}{6} = \frac{6}{9} = \frac{8}{12}$

1		
$\frac{1}{3}$	$\frac{1}{3}$	$\frac{1}{3}$

$\frac{1}{6}$	$\frac{1}{6}$	$\frac{1}{6}$	$\frac{1}{6}$	$\frac{1}{6}$	$\frac{1}{6}$

$\frac{1}{9}$ $\frac{1}{9}$ $\frac{1}{9}$ $\frac{1}{9}$ $\frac{1}{9}$ $\frac{1}{9}$ $\frac{1}{9}$ $\frac{1}{9}$ $\frac{1}{9}$

$\frac{1}{12}$ $\frac{1}{12}$ $\frac{1}{12}$ $\frac{1}{12}$ $\frac{1}{12}$ $\frac{1}{12}$ $\frac{1}{12}$ $\frac{1}{12}$ $\frac{1}{12}$ $\frac{1}{12}$ $\frac{1}{12}$ $\frac{1}{12}$

Guided Practice*

MATHEMATICAL PRACTICES

Do you know HOW?

In **1** through **5**, write two fractions that are equivalent to the one fraction given. You may use fraction strips to help.

1. $\frac{2}{4}$ $\frac{2 \times 10}{4 \times 10} = \frac{\square}{\square}$ $\frac{2 \div 2}{4 \div 2} = \frac{\square}{\square}$

2. $\frac{12}{36}$

3. $\frac{9}{15}$

4. $\frac{5}{10}$

5. $\frac{12}{27}$

Do you UNDERSTAND?

6. **Reason** Why is multiplying or dividing the numerator and denominator by the same nonzero number the same as multiplying or dividing the fraction by 1?

7. **Construct Arguments** Why wouldn't you use division to find an equivalent fraction for $\frac{9}{14}$?

Independent Practice

Leveled Practice In **8** through **21**, write two fractions that are equivalent to each fraction given. You may use fraction strips to help.

8. $\frac{5}{15}$ $\frac{5 \times 2}{15 \times 2} = \frac{\square}{\square}$ $\frac{5 \div 5}{15 \div 5} = \frac{\square}{\square}$

9. $\frac{25}{100}$ $\frac{25 \div 5}{100 \div 5} = \frac{\square}{\square}$ $\frac{25 \div 25}{100 \div 25} = \frac{\square}{\square}$

10. $\frac{3}{8}$

11. $\frac{12}{21}$

12. $\frac{8}{32}$

13. $\frac{7}{12}$

14. $\frac{27}{30}$

15. $\frac{14}{16}$

16. $\frac{50}{100}$

17. $\frac{6}{24}$

18. $\frac{1}{5}$

19. $\frac{5}{9}$

20. $\frac{20}{48}$

21. $\frac{2}{1,000}$

DIGITAL Animated Glossary, eTools
www.pearsonsuccessnet.com

For another example, see Set E on page 141.

One Way

You can multiply both the numerator and the denominator by the same nonzero number.

$$\frac{10 \times 2}{15 \times 2} = \frac{20}{30}$$

$\frac{10}{15}$ and $\frac{20}{30}$ are equivalent fractions.

Another Way

You can divide the numerator and denominator by the same nonzero number if they can both be divided evenly.

$$\frac{10 \div 5}{15 \div 5} = \frac{2}{3}$$

$\frac{10}{15}$ and $\frac{2}{3}$ are equivalent fractions.

Problem Solving

MATHEMATICAL PRACTICES

22. **Communicate** How can you use equivalent fractions to know that $\frac{43}{200}$ is between $\frac{1}{5}$ and $\frac{1}{4}$?

23. Lonnette says that $\frac{2}{3} = \frac{4}{9}$. Is Lonnette correct? Explain.

24. **Writing to Explain** Brion claims that no matter how many equivalent fractions are found for any fraction, he can always find one more. Is he right? Explain.

25. Find the value of *x* that makes the fractions equivalent.

   a $\frac{5}{7} = \frac{x}{42}$ **b** $\frac{x}{200} = \frac{1}{20}$

26. There are 206 bones in the body. The fraction $\frac{54}{206}$ represents the number of bones in both hands compared to the total number of bones in the body. Write an equivalent fraction.

27. **Persevere** Which of the following is NOT equivalent to the others?

   A $\frac{1}{4}$ **B** $\frac{6}{24}$ **C** $\frac{5}{21}$ **D** $\frac{5}{20}$

28. **Reason** How does this diagram help show that $\frac{2}{6} = \frac{8}{24}$?

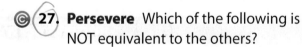

There are 27 bones in each human hand.

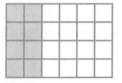

29. **Use Tools** Draw a grid like the one in Exercise 28 to show that $\frac{5}{6} = \frac{15}{18}$.

Lesson
5-6

Common
Core

This lesson reinforces
concepts and skills required
for Topic 9.

Fractions in Simplest Form

How do you write fractions in simplest form?

Thirty-six out of the 48 sixth graders at Lincoln Middle
School are going on a field trip to the Museum
of Art. Write the fraction $\frac{36}{48}$ in simplest form.

A fraction is in simplest form if
the only common factor of the
numerator and denominator is 1.

Guided Practice*

MATHEMATICAL PRACTICES

Do you know HOW?

In **1** and **2**, find the GCF of the numerator
and denominator. Use the GCF to write
each fraction in its simplest form.

1. $\frac{18}{24}$ **2.** $\frac{12}{36}$

Write each fraction in simplest form.

3. $\frac{35}{49}$ **4.** $\frac{4}{24}$

5. $\frac{180}{200}$ **6.** $\frac{24}{27}$

Do you UNDERSTAND?

7. Communicate Which way do you
prefer to use to find the simplest form
of a fraction? Why?

8. Of the 36 students who went to the art
museum, 18 had been there before.
What is the simplest form for the
fraction of students on the trip who
had been there before?

Independent Practice

Leveled Practice In **9** through **15**, find the GCF of the numerator and
denominator. Use the GCF to write each fraction in its simplest form.

9. $\frac{15}{24}$ The GCF is 3. $\frac{15 \div 3}{24 \div 3} = \frac{}{}$

10. $\frac{16}{32}$ The GCF is 16. $\frac{16 \div 16}{32 \div 16} = \frac{}{}$

11. $\frac{14}{63}$ **12.** $\frac{40}{64}$ **13.** $\frac{27}{45}$ **14.** $\frac{24}{72}$ **15.** $\frac{35}{55}$

Write each fraction in simplest form.

16. $\frac{9}{36}$ **17.** $\frac{8}{96}$ **18.** $\frac{12}{78}$ **19.** $\frac{72}{81}$ **20.** $\frac{9}{63}$

21. $\frac{4}{92}$ **22.** $\frac{10}{75}$ **23.** $\frac{75}{165}$ **24.** $\frac{39}{300}$ **25.** $\frac{30}{108}$

Animated Glossary
www.pearsonsuccessnet.com

DIGITAL

*For another example, see Set E on page 141.

One Way

Use common factors to do repeated division of the numerator and denominator until 1 is the only common factor.

$$\frac{36 \div 2}{48 \div 2} = \frac{18 \div 6}{24 \div 6} = \frac{3}{4}$$

I can divide by 2. Next I can divide by 6. Now 1 is the only common factor.

Another Way

Divide the numerator and denominator by the GCF (greatest common factor).

$$\frac{36 \div 12}{48 \div 12} = \frac{3}{4}$$

$36 = 2 \times 2 \times 3 \times 3$
$48 = 2 \times 2 \times 2 \times 2 \times 3$
$GCF = 2 \times 2 \times 3 = 12$

$\frac{3}{4}$ of the students are going on the trip.

Problem Solving

MATHEMATICAL PRACTICES

26. The table shows Aaron's batting averages for four years. How much did Aaron's batting average improve between years 1 and 4?

Year	Batting Average
1	.279
2	.281
3	.287
4	.295

27. Writing to Explain How do you know that a fraction is in simplest form?

28. Place the decimal point in each product.

  a $3 \times 0.476 = 1428$ **b** $5.8 \times 6.32 = 36656$

29. Generalize If $\frac{x}{24}$ is a fraction in simplest form, which could be a value for x?

  A 3   **B** 6   **C** 7   **D** 9

30. Which of the following fractions is in simplest form?

  A $\frac{12}{15}$ **B** $\frac{39}{65}$ **C** $\frac{27}{98}$ **D** $\frac{11}{121}$

31. Persevere Ostriches have very long necks. The ostrich pictured at the right is 91 inches tall. Its neck is 39 inches. Write a fraction in simplest form to compare the length of the ostrich's neck to its height.

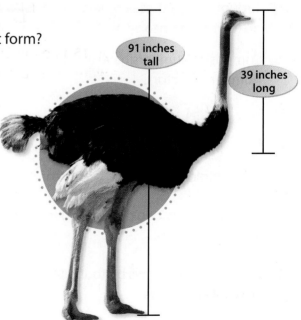

91 inches tall

39 inches long

Problem Solving

Make and Test Conjectures

A conjecture is <u>a generalization that you think is true</u>.
A question can help you make a conjecture.

How many factors do perfect square numbers have?

16 is a perfect square. Other perfect squares are: 4, 9, 25, 36, 49, 64, 81, 100.

Find the factors of some perfect squares.

Guided Practice*

MATHEMATICAL PRACTICES

Do you know HOW?

Test these conjectures. Explain whether they are correct or incorrect.

1. The difference of two odd numbers is always even.

2. The sum of two decimals is always a decimal.

Do you UNDERSTAND?

© **3. Communicate** How can you test or check a conjecture to see if it is correct?

© **4. Generalize** Write a conjecture about the sum of three odd numbers. Then test your conjecture.

Independent Practice

MATHEMATICAL PRACTICES

In **5** through **9**, test these conjectures. Explain whether they are correct or incorrect.

5. Composite numbers have an even number of factors.

6. The product of two prime numbers is never an even number.

7. All multiples of 6 end in 0, 2, 4, 6 or 8.

8. The sum of any two perfect squares is an even number.

9. A GCF cannot always be found for a set of whole numbers.

Applying Math Practices

- What am I asked to find?
- What else can I try?
- How are quantities related?
- How can I explain my work?
- How can I use math to model the problem?
- Can I use tools to help?
- Is my work precise?
- Why does this work?
- How can I generalize?

Try several cases to help you make a conjecture.

Factors of 4: 1, 2, 4
3 factors

Factors of 9: 1, 3, 9
3 factors

Make a Conjecture
All perfect square numbers have exactly 3 factors.

Test Your Conjecture
Find the factors of other perfect squares.

16: 1, 2, 4, 8, 16
5 factors

25: 1, 5, 25
3 factors

36: 1, 2, 3, 4, 6, 9, 12, 18, 36
9 factors

The conjecture is not right. Use reasoning to make another conjecture.

Make a Conjecture
All perfect squares have an odd number of factors.

Test Your Conjecture
100: 1, 2, 4, 5, 10, 20, 25, 50, 100
9 factors

The conjecture works for the numbers tested.

In **10** through **13**, make a conjecture about each of the following. Then test your conjecture.

10. Adding two odd numbers.

11. Multiplying two odd numbers.

12. Adding an even number and an odd number.

13. Multiplying an even number and an odd number.

14. Writing to Explain How can you test the following conjecture: all fractions have an equivalent fraction?

15. Describe the similarities and differences between a square and a rhombus.

16. Model Hector deposits $153.32 into his savings account, raising the balance to $3,126.70. Use an algebraic equation to find how much was in Hector's account before the deposit.

17. Leela is making jumps on her skateboard at the skate park. One ramp is at an 18° angle. Another ramp is at an angle 7° greater. What is the angle of the steeper ramp?

18. Use Tools Sekino is going skiing in the mountains. When he left his home, it was 25° Celsius. When he arrived at the ski lodge, it was −5° Celsius. What was the difference in temperature? Hint: Use the thermometer to help you.

°C
30
25
20
15
10
5
0
−5
−10
−15
−20
−25
−30

19. Which fraction is equivalent to $\frac{3}{4}$?

A $\frac{7}{8}$ **B** $\frac{8}{12}$ **C** $\frac{12}{16}$ **D** $\frac{16}{20}$

DIGITAL
Animated Glossary
www.pearsonsuccessnet.com

1. The 20 students in Ms. Roho's class and the 16 students in Mr. Wann's class are going on a field trip. The teachers want to divide the students in each class into groups that are the same size, and no group has students from both classes. What is the largest size possible for each group? Find the greatest common factor of 20 and 16. (5-3)

   A 2 students

   B 4 students

   C 5 students

   D 10 students

2. At the beginning of the school year, Adrienne's class had 4 new students out of 20 students enrolled. What is $\frac{4}{20}$ written in simplest form? (5-6)

   A $\frac{4}{5}$

   B $\frac{2}{10}$

   C $\frac{1}{5}$

   D $\frac{1}{4}$

3. Todd has run two of the nine laps he needs to run. Which point on the number line represents $\frac{2}{9}$? (5-4)

   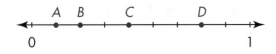

   A Point *A*

   B Point *B*

   C Point *C*

   D Point *D*

4. Three-twelfths of the girls on Jamila's softball team missed practice. Which of the following is equal to $\frac{3}{12}$? (5-5)

   A $\frac{1}{10}$

   B $\frac{1}{4}$

   C $\frac{9}{24}$

   D $\frac{5}{14}$

5. What is the greatest common factor (GCF) of 36 and 54? (5-3)

   A 2

   B 6

   C 9

   D 18

6. Which step can be used to write $\frac{10}{15}$ in simplest form? (5-6)

   A Divide 10 and 15 by their GCF, 5.

   B Divide 10 and 15 by their GCF, 10.

   C Multiply 10 and 15 by their GCF, 5.

   D Multiply 10 and 15 by their GCF, 10.

7. Which of the following numbers is prime? (5-2)

   A 9

   B 15

   C 21

   D 23

8. Which is the prime factorization of 75? (5-2)

A 3×25

B 5×3^2

C 3×5^2

D $3^2 \times 5^2$

9. Aaron made a conjecture that any number ending in zero will be divisible by 4. Which of the following best describes whether or not the conjecture is correct? (5-7)

A No, it is not correct because 10 is not divisible by 4.

B No, it is not correct because 4, 8, 12, and 16 do not end in 0.

C Yes, it is correct because 100 is divisible by 4.

D Yes, it is correct because 20, 160, and 200 are all divisible by 4.

10. What portion of the football field, including the end zones, is shaded blue? (5-4)

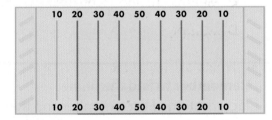

A $\frac{12}{7}$

B $\frac{7}{7}$

C $\frac{7}{10}$

D $\frac{7}{12}$

11. Which step should be taken to find the value of x that makes the fractions equivalent? (5-5)

$$\frac{5}{7} = \frac{x}{21}$$

A Add 3 to 5.

B Add 14 to 5.

C Multiply 5 by 3.

D Multiply 5 by 7.

12. Which divisibility rule would you apply to tell whether a number is divisible by 3? (5-1)

A The last digit is divisible by 3.

B The sum of the digits is divisible by 3.

C The last two digits are divisible by 3.

D The sum of the digits is divisible by 9.

13. Which two fractions can be used to represent point M? (5-5)

A $\frac{6}{8}$ and $\frac{3}{4}$

B $\frac{6}{8}$ and $\frac{3}{5}$

C $\frac{2}{3}$ and $\frac{6}{9}$

D $\frac{2}{6}$ and $\frac{3}{4}$

Set A, pages 120–122

Ⓒ **INTERVENTION**

Tell whether 63 is divisible by 2, 3, 4, 5, 6, 9, or 10.

Use divisibility rules.

2: Is the ones digit even? No

3: Is the sum of the digits divisible by 3? Yes

4: Are the last two digits divisible by 4? No

5: Is the ones digit 0 or 5? No

6: Is the number divisible by both 2 and 3? No

9: Is the sum of the digits divisible by 9? Yes

10: Is the ones digit a 0? No

So, 63 is divisible by 3 and 9.

Remember that you can use divisibility rules to tell whether a number is divisible by another number.

Tell whether each number is divisible by 2, 3, 4, 5, 6, 9, or 10.

1. 40　　　　　　**2.** 33

3. 75　　　　　　**4.** 113

Tell whether the first number is a multiple of the second.

5. 25; 5　　　　　**6.** 81; 9

7. 310; 3　　　　　**8.** 29; 7

Set B, pages 124–125

Find the prime factorization of 140. Use a factor tree to write factors beginning with the smallest factor. Write factors until all the factors are prime numbers.

$$140$$
$$2 \times 70 \qquad 140 = 2 \times 2 \times 5 \times 7$$
$$2 \times 2 \times 35$$
$$\qquad\qquad = 2^2 \times 5 \times 7$$
$$2 \times 2 \times 5 \times 7$$

Remember to order factors from least to greatest and to use exponents.

Find the prime factorization of each number. Write *prime*, if the number is prime.

1. 24　　　　　　**2.** 56

3. 81　　　　　　**4.** 37

5. 83　　　　　　**6.** 48

Set C, pages 126–127

Find the greatest common factor, or GCF, of 24 and 132 by using prime factorization.

24 and 132

Step 1 Find the prime factorization of each number.

$24 = 2 \times 2 \times 2 \times 3$　　　$132 = 2 \times 2 \times 3 \times 11$

Step 2 Multipy the common prime factors. The GCF of 24 and 132 is $2 \times 2 \times 3 = 12$.

Remember to find the prime factorization of each number and then multiply common factors to find the GCF for each set of numbers.

Find the GCF of each pair of numbers.

1. 30, 105　　　　**2.** 8, 52

3. 28, 126　　　　**4.** 35, 63

5. 75, 128　　　　**6.** 120, 168

Write a fraction to describe the shaded part of the whole.

$\frac{5}{12}$ of the circle is shaded.

Remember that a set of objects or a number line can represent a whole. Write each fraction represented.

1.   2.

3.
0   1

Write two equivalent fractions for $\frac{4}{18}$.

One Way

$$\frac{4 \div 2}{18 \div 2} = \frac{2}{9}$$

Another Way

$$\frac{4 \times 2}{18 \times 2} = \frac{8}{36}$$

Remember to divide or multiply the numerator and denominator by the same nonzero number. Write two equivalent fractions for each.

1. $\frac{6}{20}$ 2. $\frac{7}{11}$
3. $\frac{1}{11}$ 4. $\frac{98}{100}$

Write $\frac{28}{70}$ in simplest form.

$\frac{28}{70}$ ← The GCF of 28 and 70 is 14.

$\frac{28 \div 14}{70 \div 14} = \frac{2}{5}$ ← Simplest form

Write each fraction in simplest form.

5. $\frac{13}{39}$ 6. $\frac{12}{63}$ 7. $\frac{18}{49}$
8. $\frac{1}{48}$ 9. $\frac{90}{150}$ 10. $\frac{8}{72}$

A conjecture is a generalization that you think is true.

Make a Conjecture The product of two odd numbers is an odd number.

Test your conjecture.

$3 \times 3 = 9$ $5 \times 7 = 35$

$9 \times 9 = 81$ $11 \times 13 = 143$

The conjecture works for the numbers tested.

Remember to try several cases to test a conjecture. Explain whether these conjectures are correct or incorrect.

1. If a number is divisible by 8, it is divisible by 2 and 4.

2. The difference of two odd numbers is always odd.

3. The product of an even number and a multiple of 3 is always a multiple of 6.

Topic 6

Decimals, Fractions, and Mixed Numbers

1 The capybara is the world's largest rodent. It is related to the guinea pig. How long is a capybara? You will find out in Lesson 6-3.

2 Alaska is the largest state. What part of the total area of the United States does Alaska make up? You will find out in Lesson 6-2.

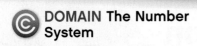

3

The Green Darner dragonfly is an excellent flier. How fast can a Green Darner fly? You will find out in Lesson 6-4.

Review What You Know!

Vocabulary

Choose the best term from the box.

> • denominator   • numerator
> • fraction

1. The top value of a fraction, which names the number of objects or equal parts being considered, is the __?__.

2. The bottom value of a fraction, which tells the number of equal parts in all, is the __?__.

3. A number used to name a part of a whole, such as a region or a set, is a __?__.

Simplifying Fractions

Write each fraction in simplest form.

4. $\dfrac{6}{10}$ 5. $\dfrac{2}{4}$ 6. $\dfrac{10}{12}$

7. $\dfrac{3}{9}$ 8. $\dfrac{18}{24}$ 9. $\dfrac{10}{24}$

Equivalent Fractions

Find an equivalent fraction for each of the following fractions.

10. $\dfrac{2}{3}$ 11. $\dfrac{1}{2}$ 12. $\dfrac{10}{100}$

13. $\dfrac{5}{9}$ 14. $\dfrac{14}{42}$ 15. $\dfrac{4}{5}$

Number Lines

Ⓒ **16. Writing to Explain** How can you draw a number line that shows the point 0.6? Draw an example.

Common Core

This lesson reinforces concepts and skills required for Topic 9.

Fractions and Division

How are fractions related to division?

Eleven members of the 6th grade Science Club stayed after school to help their teacher, Ms. Oliva, set up the laboratory. Afterwards, Ms. Oliva bought two large pizzas. If all twelve people divide the pizza equally, what fraction of a large pizza will each person get?

Two large pizzas to divide

Another Example How can you use a number line to show fractions are related to division?

Use number lines to show $\frac{2}{3} = 2 \div 3$.

One Way

$\frac{2}{3}$

 Think 2 groups of $\frac{1}{3}$

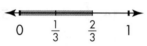

Another Way

$2 \div 3$

 Think $\frac{1}{3}$ of 2 wholes

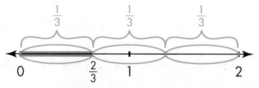

One way to think about a fraction is the division of the numerator by the denominator.

Guided Practice*

 MATHEMATICAL PRACTICES

Do you know HOW?

Write a division expression for the following fractions.

1. $\frac{4}{7}$

2. $\frac{7}{8}$

Write each division expression as a fraction.

3. $2 \div 9$

4. $6 \div 11$

Do you UNDERSTAND?

5. Reason How do the numerator and denominator of a fraction compare with the dividend and divisor of a division expression?

6. Use Tools Copy the number line below and use it to show $3 \div 4$.

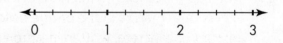

For another example, see Set A on page 158.

One Way

Divide each pizza into 12 equal parts. Then each person would get two slices of one of the pizzas.

$\frac{2}{12} = \frac{1}{6}$

Another Way

Divide the two pizzas into 12 equal parts: $2 \div 12$. Each pizza has six equal parts.

$\frac{1}{6}$

You can think of fractions as division:

$$\frac{2}{12} = 2 \div 12$$

Independent Practice

Write a division expression for the following fractions.

7. $\frac{5}{9}$ **8.** $\frac{1}{6}$ **9.** $\frac{9}{13}$ **10.** $\frac{3}{5}$ **11.** $\frac{2}{3}$

12. $\frac{11}{15}$ **13.** $\frac{6}{8}$ **14.** $\frac{8}{9}$ **15.** $\frac{7}{10}$ **16.** $\frac{5}{12}$

Write each division expression as a fraction.

17. $7 \div 8$ **18.** $4 \div 11$ **19.** $25 \div 50$ **20.** $15 \div 24$ **21.** $1 \div 7$

22. $6 \div 20$ **23.** $13 \div 14$ **24.** $15 \div 60$ **25.** $20 \div 21$ **26.** $9 \div 11$

Problem Solving

ⓒ **MATHEMATICAL PRACTICES**

ⓒ **27. Writing to Explain** Into how many sections would you divide this number line to graph $\frac{4}{5}$? Why?

0   1

The table at the right shows the weights of different materials used to build a bridge. Use the table to answer **28** and **29**.

ⓒ **28. Model** Write a division expression that represents the weight of the concrete compared to the total weight of the bridge's materials.

29. Which of the following fractions equals the amount of glass and granite in the bridge divided by the amount of concrete, written in simplest form?

A $\frac{1}{5}$ **B** $\frac{1}{3}$ **C** $\frac{1}{4}$ **D** $\frac{1}{2}$

Material	Weight
Concrete	1,000 tons
Steel structure	400 tons
Glass and granite	200 tons

Lesson
6-2

Common Core

This lesson reinforces concepts and skills required for Topic 9.

Fractions and Decimals

How can you write equivalent fractions and decimals?

A banana slug moves through forests in northern California at a rate of about $\frac{1}{20}$ of an inch per minute. Which decimal is equivalent to $\frac{1}{20}$?

$\frac{1}{20}$ in.

INCHES 0 1 2 3 4 5 6 7 8 9

Guided Practice*

MATHEMATICAL PRACTICES

Do you know HOW?

In **1** and **2**, write a decimal and a fraction in simplest form for each shaded area.

1.   **2.**

Write each fraction as a decimal.

3. $\frac{3}{4}$ **4.** $\frac{13}{20}$ **5.** $\frac{9}{1000}$

Do you UNDERSTAND?

6. Generalize Describe how you could use mental math to write a decimal as a fraction.

7. Communicate Describe how you would use an equivalent fraction with a denominator that is a multiple of 10 to solve Exercise 3.

Independent Practice

Leveled Practice Write a decimal and a fraction in simplest form for each shaded portion.

8.   **9.**   **10.**

In **11** through **18**, write each decimal as a fraction in simplest form.

11. 0.4 **12.** 0.06 **13.** 0.08 **14.** 0.35

15. 0.75 **16.** 0.43 **17.** 0.025 **18.** 0.999

For another example, see Set B on page 158.

Fractions can be written in equivalent forms. A fraction with a denominator of 10, 100, 1,000, and so on can also be written as a decimal.

You can change $\frac{1}{20}$ to an equivalent fraction in 100ths:

$$\frac{1 \times 5}{20 \times 5} = \frac{5}{100}$$

So, $\frac{1}{20} = 0.05$.

Divide the numerator by the denominator:

$$\frac{1}{20} = 1 \div 20 \qquad \begin{array}{r} 0.05 \\ 20\overline{)1.00} \\ -\ 100 \\ \hline 0 \end{array}$$

You can use division to change any fraction to a decimal.

$$\frac{1}{20} = 0.05$$

Independent Practice

In **19** through **33**, convert each fraction to a decimal.

19. $\frac{3}{8}$ **20.** $\frac{1}{2}$ **21.** $\frac{1}{4}$ **22.** $\frac{6}{15}$ **23.** $\frac{9}{10}$

24. $\frac{3}{5}$ **25.** $\frac{18}{100}$ **26.** $\frac{27}{50}$ **27.** $\frac{15}{20}$ **28.** $\frac{19}{38}$

29. $\frac{9}{25}$ **30.** $\frac{7}{8}$ **31.** $\frac{1}{200}$ **32.** $\frac{4}{125}$ **33.** $\frac{39}{40}$

Problem Solving

MATHEMATICAL PRACTICES

ⓒ **34. Use Tools** How can you show $\frac{1}{4}$ on a hundredths grid? What decimal does the model show?

ⓒ **35. Writing to Explain** Kirsten thinks that $\frac{2}{5}$ and $\frac{10}{25}$ both convert to the same decimal. Is she right? Explain.

ⓒ **36. Reasonableness** Kennedy Space Center, located on Merritt Island, is also a National Wildlife Refuge. Only about 0.04 of the total area is used for space operations. Which fraction best represents the area used for space operations?

    A $\frac{2}{5}$ **C** $\frac{1}{25}$

    B $\frac{1}{4}$ **D** $\frac{1}{200}$

37. Alaska is the largest state, with an area that is about $\frac{163}{1,000}$ of the area of the United States. Write this number as a decimal.

38. Use the information below to classify the triangle.

Lesson
6-3

©
Common
Core

This lesson reinforces concepts and skills required for Topic 9.

Improper Fractions and Mixed Numbers

How can you represent quantities that are greater than or equal to 1?

Jenny and Tyler are baking bread. How do the measurements they make relate to fractions and mixed numbers?

$4\frac{1}{2}$ cups of flour

$\frac{1}{2}$ cup of sugar

$\frac{4}{3}$ cup of milk

Another Example **How can you change between improper fractions and mixed numbers?**

Write $\frac{12}{9}$ as a mixed number.

- Divide the numerator by the denominator.

$$9)\overline{12} \quad \begin{array}{r} 1\ R3 \\ -\ 9 \\ \hline 3 \end{array}$$

- Replace the remainder with a fraction in simplest form.

$$\frac{3}{9} = \frac{1}{3}$$

- So, $\frac{12}{9} = 1\frac{1}{3}$.

Write $3\frac{5}{8}$ as an improper fraction.

$$3\frac{5}{8} = 3 + \frac{5}{8}$$
Write 3 as a fraction using a denominator of 8.

$$= \frac{24}{8} + \frac{5}{8}$$

$$= \frac{29}{8}$$

Shortcut

- Multiply the whole number by the fraction denominator.

$$3 \times 8 = 24$$

- Add the fraction numerator to this product. This is the new numerator.

$$24 + 5 = 29$$

- Keep the same denominator. $\frac{29}{8}$

Guided Practice* MATHEMATICAL PRACTICES

Do you know HOW?

Write each improper fraction as a mixed number in simplest form.

1. $\frac{11}{4}$　　**2.** $\frac{35}{9}$　　**3.** $\frac{10}{3}$

Do you UNDERSTAND?

© **4. Construct Arguments** Why can you divide the numerator of an improper fraction by its denominator?

DIGITAL
Animated Glossary
www.pearsonsuccessnet.com

For another example, see Set C on page 158.

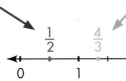

A **proper fraction** is less than 1. <u>Its numerator is less than its denominator.</u>

An **improper fraction** is greater than or equal to 1. <u>Its numerator is greater than or equal to its denominator.</u>

A **mixed number** combines <u>a whole number and a fraction</u>. It is greater than 1.

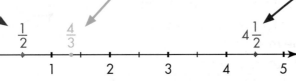

Independent Practice

Write each improper fraction as a whole number or mixed number in simplest form.

5. $\frac{23}{5}$ **6.** $\frac{34}{6}$ **7.** $\frac{12}{4}$ **8.** $\frac{22}{3}$ **9.** $\frac{27}{8}$ **10.** $\frac{30}{9}$

Write each mixed number as an improper fraction.

11. $2\frac{1}{4}$ **12.** $5\frac{6}{7}$ **13.** $3\frac{4}{9}$ **14.** $4\frac{5}{8}$ **15.** $2\frac{3}{5}$ **16.** $7\frac{5}{11}$

For **17** through **21**, which letter on the number line corresponds to each number?

17. $\frac{4}{2}$ **18.** $1\frac{3}{8}$ **19.** $\frac{9}{4}$ **20.** $\frac{1}{2}$ **21.** $3\frac{3}{4}$

Problem Solving

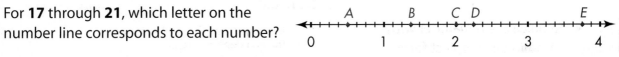

MATHEMATICAL PRACTICES

22. A capybara is the world's largest rodent. It can grow to be $1\frac{3}{10}$ m long. Which improper fraction represents the length of the capybara?

A $\frac{36}{13}$ m

B $\frac{13}{10}$ m

C $\frac{29}{10}$ m

D $\frac{11}{10}$ m

1 3/10 m

© 23. Writing to Explain Kara said that $\frac{9}{4}$ and $1\frac{1}{4}$ are equivalent. Is she right? Explain.

24. Name three different types of triangles based on the lengths of their sides. Draw a picture of each type.

© 25. Reason Should $\frac{15}{15}$ be expressed as a mixed number or a whole number? How do you know?

Lesson
6-4

Common
Core

This lesson reinforces
concepts and skills required
for Topic 9.

Decimal Forms of Fractions and Mixed Numbers

How can you write fractions as decimals?

Recall that a fraction can represent division of the numerator by the denominator. Write $\frac{3}{8}$ and $2\frac{5}{11}$ as decimals.

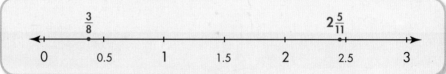

$\frac{3}{8}$ $2\frac{5}{11}$

0   0.5   1   1.5   2   2.5   3

Another Example **How can you write decimals as fractions or mixed numbers?**

Convert decimals to fractions by writing the decimal as a fraction with a denominator of tenths, hundredths, or thousandths. Then write the fraction in simplest form. Use a similar approach to convert a decimal greater than 1 to a mixed number.

Write 0.28 as a fraction.

Think   0.28 = 28 hundredths

$$0.28 = \frac{28}{100}$$

Simplify. $\frac{28}{100} = \frac{7}{25}$

So, $0.28 = \frac{7}{25}$.

Write 4.125 as a mixed number.

Think   4.125 = 4 + 0.125

     4 + 0.125 = 4 and 125 thousandths

$$4 + 0.125 = 4 + \frac{125}{1,000}$$

$$= 4\frac{125}{1,000}$$

Simplify. $4\frac{125}{1,000} = 4\frac{1}{8}$

So, $4.125 = 4\frac{1}{8}$.

Explain It

1. When simplifying $\frac{28}{100}$, why were the numerator and denominator divided by 4?

2. When writing 4.125 as a mixed number, why should you first think of 4.125 as 4 + 0.125?

Divide to write $\frac{3}{8}$ as a decimal.

$$\begin{array}{r} 0.375 \\ 8\overline{)3.000} \end{array}$$

The decimal 0.375 is a terminating decimal because <u>the digits in the quotient end and there is no remainder</u>.

$$\frac{3}{8} = 0.375$$

Think of $2\frac{5}{11}$ as $2 + \frac{5}{11}$.

Divide the numerator and denominator of the fraction to find the decimal portion of the number.

$$\begin{array}{r} 0.4545 \\ 11\overline{)5.0000} \\ -\,44 \\ \hline 60 \\ -\,55 \\ \hline 50 \\ -\,44 \\ \hline 60 \\ -\,55 \\ \hline 5 \end{array}$$

The decimal 0.4545... is a repeating decimal because <u>the digits in the quotient repeat</u>. A bar is written over the repeating digits: $0.\overline{45}$.

So, $2\frac{5}{11} = 2.4545... = 2.\overline{45}$.

Guided Practice*

MATHEMATICAL **PRACTICES**

Do you know HOW?

Write each decimal as a fraction or a mixed number in simplest form.

1. 0.8 **2.** 3.125 **3.** 2.75

Write each fraction or mixed number as a decimal.

4. $\frac{7}{10}$ **5.** $1\frac{5}{8}$ **6.** $4\frac{5}{9}$

Do you UNDERSTAND?

© **7. Be Precise** In the example at the top of the page, why is there a bar over the 45?

© **8. Communicate** How could you check your answer to Exercise 2 in Do you know HOW?

Independent Practice

Write each fraction or mixed number as a decimal.

9. $\frac{2}{3}$ **10.** $1\frac{1}{2}$ **11.** $\frac{1}{11}$ **12.** $\frac{9}{10}$ **13.** $\frac{5}{4}$

14. $3\frac{3}{8}$ **15.** $\frac{1}{16}$ **16.** $\frac{4}{3}$ **17.** $\frac{2}{15}$ **18.** $5\frac{7}{8}$

Write each decimal as a fraction or a mixed number in simplest form.

19. 0.4 **20.** 1.6 **21.** 0.375 **22.** 4.45 **23.** 0.032

24. 0.08 **25.** 0.68 **26.** 2.25 **27.** 12.875 **28.** 0.002

DIGITAL

Animated Glossary
www.pearsonsuccessnet.com

For another example, see Set D on page 159.

Mercury, Venus, Earth, and Mars are the inner planets in our solar system. The table shows the volume of each inner planet as a decimal, compared to the volume of Earth. Use the table for **29** and **30**.

Planet	Volume Compared to Earth
Mercury	0.054
Venus	0.88
Earth	1
Mars	0.15

29. What is the fraction equivalent for the volume of Mars compared to Earth?

30. What is the fraction equivalent for the volume of Venus compared to Earth?

31. Julie found an arrowhead that measured 2.625 in. Write the length of the arrowhead as a mixed number.

32. A radio station broadcasts news 1.75 hours each weekday. On Saturday and Sunday, the news broadcasts are twice as long. How many hours of news are broadcast each week?

ⓒ **33. Writing to Explain** If you know the decimal equivalent of $\frac{1}{8}$, explain how you could use that to find the decimal equivalent of $\frac{3}{8}$.

ⓒ **34. Persevere** The Green Darner dragonfly is one of the largest dragonflies. It has a wingspan of about 4 inches and weighs about 0.04 ounces. Write its weight as a fraction in simplest form.

35. The Green Darner dragonfly is an excellent flier. It can fly at speeds of greater than 50 miles per hour. If a Green Darner is flying at $50\frac{3}{16}$ miles per hour. What is its speed written as a decimal?

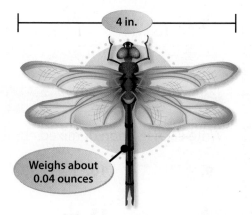

4 in.

Weighs about 0.04 ounces

ⓒ **36. Reason** What do the decimal forms of the fractions $\frac{1}{3}$, $\frac{5}{6}$, and $\frac{7}{11}$ have in common?

ⓒ **37. Be Precise** Which of the following fractions can be changed to a terminating decimal?

A $\frac{1}{5}$ **B** $\frac{5}{11}$ **C** $\frac{1}{3}$ **D** $\frac{7}{9}$

Algebra Connections

What's the Rule?

Remember that you can find a rule for a table of values by looking for a mathematical relationship between the two variables.

Find a rule for each table. Then write a sentence that tells the rule.

Example:

Speed of Car A	Speed of Car B
40 mph	37 mph
72 mph	69 mph
25 mph	22 mph
57 mph	54 mph

Find a rule relating the speeds of the cars.

Subtract 3 mph from the speed of Car A to get the speed of Car B. So, Car A is always 3 mph faster than Car B.

1.

Number of races Jessica ran	Number of miles Jessica ran
4	12
2	6
9	27
5	15

2.

Scotty's allowance	Clint's allowance
$8.50	$17.00
$3.00	$6.00
$6.25	$12.50
$2.20	$4.40

3.

Mya's age	Sabrina's age
4	29
2	27
7	32
11	36

4.

Apples	Plums
24	6
12	3
32	8
16	4

5.

Speed of Car A	Speed of Car B
36 mph	18 mph
42 mph	21 mph
60 mph	30 mph
112 mph	56 mph

6.

Height of bean plant	Height of corn plant
3 in.	5 in.
6 in.	8 in.
12 in.	14 in.
15 in.	17 in.

Common Core

6.NS.3 Fluently add, subtract, multiply, and divide multi-digit decimals using the standard algorithm for each operation.

Problem Solving

Draw a Picture

An engineer is creating a straight two-mile go-cart track to be marked every tenth of a mile. She marked the 0.6 mile mark, but did not finish her drawing. Use a ruler to copy and complete the track, marking every tenth of a mile.

```
◄─┼────────────┼──────────────────────────────►
  0            0.6
```

Guided Practice*

MATHEMATICAL **PRACTICES**

Do you know HOW?

Ⓒ **1. Use Tools** Smithville is 0.9 mile from Jamestown. Use a ruler to copy the line below and then locate Smithville in relation to Jamestown.

```
Jamestown
◄─┼──────┼──────────────────►
  0     0.3
```

Do you UNDERSTAND?

Ⓒ **2. Persevere** What information was needed to label the number line in Exercise 1?

Ⓒ **3. Write a Problem** Write a real-world problem that you can solve by measuring decimal units on a number line.

Independent Practice

MATHEMATICAL **PRACTICES**

Ⓒ **4. Be Precise** Paleontologists often use special tools to dig for fossils beneath the surface of sedimentary rock. Draw a vertical number line showing the locations of fossils dug up at 0.3, 0.7, and 1.4 meters below the surface of the rock. Label locations beneath the surface as negative numbers.

Ⓒ **5. Use Tools** Sharon and Jerome are hiking a trail from the Field Station to the Dinosaur Dig. The hike is 2.25 miles long. Use a ruler to copy the line below and locate the Dinosaur Dig in relation to the Field Station.

```
Field
Station
◄─┼──────┼──────────────────►
        0.75
```

Applying Math Practices

- What am I asked to find?
- What else can I try?
- How are quantities related?
- How can I explain my work?
- How can I use math to model the problem?
- Can I use tools to help?
- Is my work precise?
- Why does this work?
- How can I generalize?

Copy the length of 0.6 mile.

0   0.6

Measure and divide the length into equal segments of 0.1 mile.

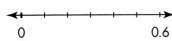

0   0.6

Copy and complete the track. Use the length of 0.1 mile to mark every tenth of a mile on the track. Mark every 0.1 mile on the two-mile track.

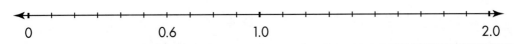

0   0.6   1.0   2.0

6. Reason Who am I? Use these clues to decide. Then draw a picture of me.

Clue 1: My opposite sides are parallel.

Clue 2: I do not have any right angles.

Clue 3: I have 4 equal sides.

7. Reason Who am I? Use these clues to decide. Then draw a picture of me.

Clue 1: I have 4 sides.

Clue 2: Two of my sides are not parallel.

Clue 3: Two of my sides are parallel.

8. Road engineers were surveying and marking every mile on a straight highway. Use a ruler to copy and complete their work, from mile marker 1 to 10.

0   4

9. Persevere To protect her soil from erosion, a farmer wants to plant shrubs along one edge of her garden. The garden measures 7.5 meters, and she wants to plant the shrubs at 1.5 meter intervals. If she also plants a shrub at each end of the garden, how many shrubs will she plant?

0   7.5

10. Use Tools Caitlin is trying to find her house on an aerial photograph. She sees the grocery store and her school in the photo. These locations are 0.2 mile apart. Her house is located on a straight line, 1.0 mile from the grocery store. Use a ruler to trace the line. Then complete the line to show the distance to Caitlin's house.

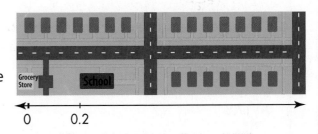

1. Which of the fractions is equal to 4 ÷ 10? (6-1)

   A $\frac{5}{2}$

   B $\frac{6}{4}$

   C $\frac{4}{6}$

   D $\frac{2}{5}$

2. Eduardo has won 5 out of the 8 swim meets in which he has participated. Which decimal is equal to $\frac{5}{8}$? (6-2)

   A 0.5

   B 0.525

   C 0.625

   D 1.6

3. Which point represents $\frac{21}{8}$ on the number line? (6-3)

   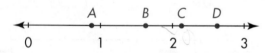

   A Point A

   B Point B

   C Point C

   D Point D

4. The largest hailstone on record had a diameter of $17\frac{4}{5}$ centimeters. What is $17\frac{4}{5}$ written as a decimal? (6-4)

   A 17.8

   B 17.5

   C 17.45

   D 17.4

5. Which number is equivalent to $3\frac{5}{6}$? (6-3)

   A $\frac{33}{6}$

   B $\frac{23}{6}$

   C 18

   D 4

6. The table shows the measures recorded by several groups of students as they did a science experiment. Which of the following shows the Group D measurement as a decimal? (6-4)

Group	Measures
A	$21\frac{3}{4}$ in.
B	$22\frac{1}{8}$ in.
C	$21\frac{15}{16}$ in.
D	$21\frac{5}{8}$ in.

   A 21.625

   B 21.58

   C 21.85

   D 21.8$\overline{3}$

7. What is $3\frac{1}{4}$ written as an improper fraction? (6-3)

   A $\frac{13}{4}$

   B $\frac{12}{4}$

   C $\frac{8}{4}$

   D $\frac{7}{4}$

8. Tracy purchased 5.32 gallons of gasoline. What is 5.32 written as a fraction? (6-4)

A $5\frac{8}{100}$

B $5\frac{8}{25}$

C $5\frac{32}{50}$

D $5\frac{32}{10}$

9. Seventeen of the 34 students in Ms. Randall's class walk to school. Which decimal is equal to $\frac{17}{34}$? (6-2)

A 0.34

B 0.5

C 0.17

D 0.2

10. Five siblings are dividing 2 acres of land evenly between them. Which number sentence can be used to find the amount of land each sibling will receive? (6-1)

A $5 \div 2 = \frac{5}{2}$

B $2 \div 5 = \frac{5}{2}$

C $5 \div 2 = \frac{2}{5}$

D $2 \div 5 = \frac{2}{5}$

11. Which of the following is equal to 0.65? (6-2)

A $\frac{65}{10}$

B $\frac{13}{2}$

C $\frac{13}{20}$

D $\frac{13}{200}$

12. Mrs. Francisco is making a walkway out of steppingstones. The walkway is 7.2 yards long and has stones every 0.9 yard. She has placed the first stone, the middle stone, and the last stone, as shown in the diagram below.

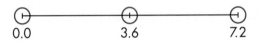

Which picture shows how she should place the other stones? (6-5)

A
0.0   3.6   7.2

B
0.0   3.6   7.2

C
0.0   3.6   7.2

D
0.0   3.6   7.2

13. Which is equivalent to $\frac{93}{4}$? (6-3)

A $20\frac{3}{4}$

B $23\frac{1}{4}$

C $9\frac{3}{4}$

D 89

Set A, pages 144–145

Ⓒ INTERVENTION

You can represent the fraction $\frac{2}{3}$ as division.

Think $\frac{1}{3}$ of 2 wholes

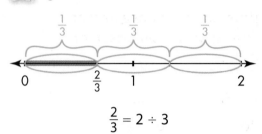

$$\frac{2}{3} = 2 \div 3$$

Remember that any fraction can be represented as division of the numerator by the denominator.

Write a division expression for each.

1. $\frac{7}{9}$ **2.** $\frac{2}{3}$ **3.** $\frac{11}{17}$

Write each expression as a fraction.

4. $7 \div 12$ **5.** $17 \div 20$

Set B, pages 146–147

You can write equivalent decimals for fractions.

Convert $\frac{1}{25}$ to a decimal. Change $\frac{1}{25}$ to an equivalent fraction in 100ths.

$$\frac{1 \times 4}{25 \times 4} = \frac{4}{100} = 0.04$$

Or, divide the numerator by the denominator.

$$\begin{array}{r} 0.04 \\ 25\overline{)1.00} \\ -100 \\ \hline 0 \end{array}$$

So, $\frac{1}{25} = 0.04$.

Remember that any decimal can be written as a fraction by using the place value of the decimal as the denominator of the fraction.

Write each decimal as a fraction in simplest form.

1. 0.7   **2.** 0.125   **3.** 0.69

4. 0.015   **5.** 0.501   **6.** 0.34

Write each fraction as a decimal.

7. $\frac{1}{20}$ **8.** $\frac{7}{10}$ **9.** $\frac{41}{250}$

Set C, pages 148–149

Write $\frac{19}{3}$ as a mixed number.

- Divide the numerator by the denominator.

$$\begin{array}{r} 6\,R1 \\ 3\overline{)19} \end{array}$$

- Replace the remainder with a fraction in simplest form.

$$\frac{19}{3} = 6\frac{1}{3}$$

Write $9\frac{5}{8}$ as an improper fraction.

$$9\frac{5}{8} = 9 + \frac{5}{8} \text{ and } 9 + \frac{5}{8} = \frac{72}{8} + \frac{5}{8}$$

So, $9\frac{5}{8} = \frac{77}{8}$.

Remember to always write the answer in simplest form.

Write each improper fraction as a mixed number or whole number.

1. $\frac{16}{6}$ **2.** $\frac{24}{9}$ **3.** $\frac{9}{2}$

Write each as an improper fraction.

4. $4\frac{5}{9}$ **5.** $2\frac{7}{11}$ **6.** $8\frac{5}{7}$

7. $5\frac{1}{3}$ **8.** $10\frac{4}{5}$ **9.** $8\frac{8}{11}$

Write 0.15 as a fraction in simplest form.

$$0.15 = \frac{15}{100} = \frac{3}{20}$$

Write $1\frac{7}{8}$ as a decimal.

Think $1\frac{7}{8} = 1 + \frac{7}{8}$

So, $1\frac{7}{8} = 1.875$.

```
      0.875
  8)7.000
   - 64
    ____
     60
   - 56
    ____
     40
   - 40
    ____
      0
```

Remember that a repeating decimal has one or more digits that repeat. A bar is written over the repeating digits.

Write each decimal as a fraction or mixed number in simplest form.

1. 0.125　　　**2.** 0.7　　　**3.** 0.08

4. 0.875　　　**5.** 0.99　　　**6.** $6.\overline{6}$

Write each as a decimal.

7. $\frac{3}{8}$　　　**8.** $1\frac{1}{3}$　　　**9.** $2\frac{3}{4}$

10. $3\frac{5}{12}$　　**11.** $\frac{1}{6}$　　　**12.** $21\frac{4}{5}$

Find the finish line for a race that is 0.7 mile long.

Measure and divide the length into equal segments of 0.1 mile.

Use the length of 0.1 mile to mark every tenth of a mile to the finish line.

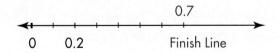

Remember that drawing a picture can help you solve problems.

1. Park planners were designing a straight 2-mile track for dirt bikes. There will be a hill at the 1.75 mile point. Use a ruler to copy their work, find the 2-mile finish, and mark the place of the hill.

Tip　*Use the information in the picture to find equal segments of 0.25 miles.*

Adding and Subtracting Fractions and Mixed Numbers

1 Chilies from plants like these are cut up or ground into powder to add flavor to foods like enchiladas and tacos. How do fractions help you measure chili powder? You will find out in Lesson 7-1.

2 The hiking trail around Mirror Lake in Yosemite National Park is 5 miles long. How can adding and subtracting fractions help when you go hiking? You will find out in Lesson 7-3.

3

Fairy penguins are the smallest kind of penguin. They come ashore in large groups at night. How tall are these penguins? You will find out in Lesson 7-6.

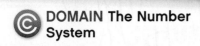

Review What You Know!

Vocabulary

Choose the best term from the box.

- equivalent fractions
- mixed number
- improper fraction

1. A(n) __?__ includes both a whole number and a fraction.

2. A(n) __?__ is a fraction in which the numerator is greater than or equal to the denominator.

3. Two or more different fractions that name the same amount are called __?__ .

Factoring

Find the greatest common factor (GCF) for the numbers in each set.

4. 10, 12   **5.** 10, 25   **6.** 7, 21

7. 2, 6, 8   **8.** 2, 5, 10   **9.** 3, 6, 9, 12

Equivalent Numbers

Find each missing value.

10. $1\frac{1}{6} = \frac{\blacksquare}{6}$ **11.** $\frac{\blacksquare}{10} = \frac{1}{2}$ **12.** $\frac{10}{15} = \frac{\blacksquare}{3}$

13. $\frac{4}{8} = \frac{1}{\blacksquare}$ **14.** $1\frac{1}{2} = \frac{3}{\blacksquare}$ **15.** $\frac{4}{16} = \frac{1}{\blacksquare}$

Fractions

© **Writing to Explain** Write an answer for each question.

16. How can you find equivalent fractions?

17. How do you know when a fraction is in simplest form?

4

Mountains near oceans have a rainy side and a dry side. The side facing the ocean gets much more rain than the other side. How much rain does the ocean side get? You will find out in Lesson 7-5.

Lesson
7-1

Common
Core

This lesson reinforces concepts and skills required for Topic 9.

Adding and Subtracting: Like Denominators

How can you add fractions with like denominators?

Greg ate $\frac{1}{8}$ of a quesadilla with peppers and $\frac{1}{8}$ of a same-size quesadilla with beans. How much of one whole quesadilla did he eat?

Choose an Operation Add the fractional parts.

Another Example How can you subtract fractions with like denominators?

Step 1

Find $\frac{5}{8} - \frac{1}{8}$.

The fractions have like denominators. Subtract the numerators. Write the difference over the like denominator.

$\frac{5}{8} - \frac{1}{8} = \frac{4}{8}$ The difference is $\frac{4}{8}$.

Step 2

Simplify the answer.

The GCF of 4 and 8 is 4.

$$\frac{4 \div 4}{8 \div 4} = \frac{1}{2}$$

So, $\frac{5}{8} - \frac{1}{8} = \frac{4}{8} = \frac{1}{2}$.

Guided Practice*

MATHEMATICAL PRACTICES

Do you know HOW?

Find each sum or difference. Simplify.

1. $\frac{1}{3} + \frac{1}{3}$

2. $\frac{3}{4} - \frac{2}{4}$

3. $\frac{5}{9} + \frac{3}{9}$

4. $\frac{11}{12} - \frac{2}{12}$

Do you UNDERSTAND?

5. When fractions have like denominators, how can you find their sum?

© 6. **Construct Arguments** Why is $\frac{1}{8} + \frac{1}{8} = \frac{2}{16}$ not correct?

Independent Practice

Find each sum or difference. Simplify your answers.

7. $\frac{1}{4} + \frac{1}{4}$

8. $\frac{3}{5} - \frac{2}{5}$

9. $\frac{3}{4} + \frac{3}{4}$

10. $\frac{8}{9} - \frac{5}{9}$

DIGITAL   Animated Glossary   www.pearsonsuccessnet.com

Find $\frac{1}{8} + \frac{1}{8}$. The fractions have the same denominators or like denominators.

Add the numerators. Write the sum over the like denominator.

$$\frac{1}{8} + \frac{1}{8} = \frac{2}{8}$$

Greg ate $\frac{2}{8}$ of one whole quesadilla.

Simplify the answer. The greatest common factor (GCF) of 2 and 8 is 2.

$$\frac{2 \div 2}{8 \div 2} = \frac{1}{4}$$

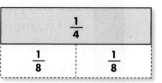

So, $\frac{1}{8} + \frac{1}{8} = \frac{2}{8}$ or $\frac{1}{4}$.

Find each sum or difference. Simplify your answers.

11. $\frac{3}{8} - \frac{1}{8}$

12. $\frac{5}{14} + \frac{6}{14}$

13. $\frac{6}{11} + \frac{5}{11}$

14. $\frac{10}{15} - \frac{6}{15}$

15. $\frac{1}{4} + \frac{1}{4} + \frac{3}{4}$

16. $\frac{3}{16} + \frac{4}{16} + \frac{8}{16}$

17. $\frac{8}{20} + \frac{1}{20} + \frac{3}{20}$

18. $\frac{3}{26} + \frac{3}{26} + \frac{19}{26}$

Evaluate **19** and **20** for $x = \frac{1}{5}$.

19. $\frac{3}{5} - x$

20. $x + \frac{4}{5}$

Evaluate **21** and **22** for $x = \frac{3}{8}$.

21. $\frac{9}{8} - x$

22. $\left(x - \frac{2}{8}\right) + \frac{7}{8}$

Problem Solving

MATHEMATICAL
PRACTICES

23. Many recipes use ingredients that are measured as fractional amounts. Use the recipe to answer the questions.

  a What is the total amount of olive oil, flour, and red chili powder in the sauce?

  b What is the total amount of cumin and garlic powder in the sauce?

Red Enchilada Sauce Recipe

• 1 tablespoon olive oil
• $\frac{1}{2}$ tablespoon flour
• $\frac{1}{2}$ tablespoon red chili powder
• $\frac{1}{2}$ teaspoon cumin
• $\frac{1}{2}$ teaspoon garlic powder
• 3 ounces tomato paste
• 1 cup water

Makes $1-1\frac{1}{2}$ cups

Ⓒ **24. Model** Kari has 8 CDs and Ian has 14 CDs. Write a number sentence that uses the Commutative Property of Addition to show two ways to find how many CDs they have altogether.

26. Lynn had $\frac{7}{8}$ of a set of markers. She gave part of the set to her friend Cheryl. Lynn has $\frac{3}{8}$ of a set left. What fraction of a set did she give to Cheryl?

Ⓒ **25. Think About the Structure** Sarah's book has 100 pages. She read 12 pages on Sunday, 20 pages on Monday, and 13 pages on Tuesday. She wants to know what fraction of the book she has read. Which expression finds the numerator?

A $12 + 20 + 13$ **C** $100 - 10$

B $100 - 45$ **D** $12 + 20 + 13 + 100$

Lesson
7-2

Common Core

This lesson reinforces concepts and skills required for Topic 9.

Least Common Multiple

How can you find the least common multiple of two numbers?

Grant is making picnic lunches. He wants to buy as many juice bottles as applesauce cups, but no more than he really needs to get an equal number of each.

How many packages of each should Grant buy?

8 applesauce cups per pack

6 juice bottles per pack

Guided Practice*

MATHEMATICAL PRACTICES

Do you know HOW?

In **1** and **2**, list multiples of each number to find the LCM of each pair of numbers.

1. 2, 5   **2.** 6, 10

In **3** and **4**, use prime factorization to find the LCM of each set of numbers.

3. 12, 24   **4.** 3, 6, 9

Do you UNDERSTAND?

5. After 48, what is the next common multiple of 6 and 8?

6. Construct Arguments Grant finds juice bottles that come in packages of 3, but can only find applesauce in packages of 8. Will the LCM change? Explain.

Independent Practice

Find the LCM for each set of numbers.

 Tip *You can use a factor tree to find a prime factorization.*

```
    12
   / \
  3 × 4
     / \
3 × 2 × 2
```

7. 4, 10   **8.** 3, 4   **9.** 10, 12   **10.** 15, 20

11. 3, 13   **12.** 8, 10   **13.** 6, 27   **14.** 4, 11

15. 6, 15   **16.** 7, 8   **17.** 5, 7   **18.** 10, 25

19. 4, 5, 12   **20.** 6, 8, 10   **21.** 9, 18, 24   **22.** 5, 12, 30

Animated Glossary
www.pearsonsuccessnet.com

For another example, see Set B on page 182.

One Way

List multiples of each pack size.

6: 6, 12, 18, 24, 30, 36, 42, 48 …

8: 8, 16, 24, 32, 40, 48 …

24 and 48 are common multiples of 6 and 8.

The least common multiple (LCM) is 24, <u>the common multiple with the least value.</u>

6 × 4 = 24   8 × 3 = 24

4 packages of juice bottles   **3 packages of applesauce cups**

Another Way

Use prime factorization. Circle the greater number of times each different factor appears.

6: 2 × ③

8: (2 × 2 × 2)

Then find the product of those circled factors.

3 × 2 × 2 × 2 = 24

To get 24 of each, Grant should buy 4 packages of juice bottles and 3 packages of applesauce cups.

Problem Solving

MATHEMATICAL PRACTICES

© **23. Communicate** Films play continuously at the museum. If the 3 films shown in the table to the right begin to play at the same time at 8 A.M., what time will it be before they begin playing together again? Explain.

Museum Film Schedule

Film Title	Length
Introduction to the Museum	2 minutes
Profiles of Artists	30 minutes
Art and Architecture	45 minutes

© **24. Writing to Explain** Can you use the Associative Property with division or subtraction? Use 30 ÷ (10 ÷ 5) and (16 − 8) − 4 to explain your answer.

25. Linda is sending out cards. If envelopes come in boxes of 25 and stamps come in packs of 10, what is the least number of stamps and envelopes she can buy to get one stamp for each envelope?

26. Blue buttons come in packs of 25, and green buttons come in packs of 40. What is the LCM of 25 and 40?

A 100   C 200

B 1,000   D 400

© **27. Persevere** Granola bars are sold in 12-ounce and 36-ounce packages. What is the least number of ounces you can buy of each package to have equal amounts of each of the different sizes?

A 12   B 36   C 72   D 144

© **28. Critique Reasoning** Ron is working to find the LCM of 6, 9, and 10. Is his work shown below correct?

6: (2 × 3)

9: 3 × 3

10: (2 × 5)

2 × 3 × 2 × 5 = 60, so the LCM of 6, 9, and 10 is 60.

29. The red kangaroo was 2 years old when it came to the zoo in 2003. How old will the kangaroo be in the year 2015?

Common Core

6.NS.1 Interpret and compute quotients of fractions, and solve word problems involving division of fractions by fractions, e.g., by using visual fraction models and equations to represent the problem....

Adding and Subtracting: Unlike Denominators

How can you add fractions with unlike denominators?

Abby and Faith each had cereal for breakfast. Abby ate $\frac{1}{2}$ cup of cereal and Faith ate $\frac{1}{3}$ cup of cereal. How much cereal did they eat all together?

Choose an Operation Add the fractional parts.

Faith ate $\frac{1}{3}$ cup.

Abby ate $\frac{1}{2}$ cup.

Another Example How can you subtract fractions with unlike denominators?

Find $\frac{1}{3} - \frac{1}{4}$.

Step 1

To subtract fractions with unlike denominators, find the least common multiple (LCM) of the denominators to use as the least common denominator (LCD).

Multiples of 3: 3, 6, 9, 12…

Multiples of 4: 4, 8, 12…

Since the LCM of 3 and 4 is 12, the LCD is 12.

Step 2

Write the fractions as equivalent fractions with the LCD of 12.

$\frac{1 \times 4}{3 \times 4} = \frac{4}{12}$ and $\frac{1 \times 3}{4 \times 3} = \frac{3}{12}$

$\frac{1}{3}$				$\frac{1}{4}$		
$\frac{1}{12}$	$\frac{1}{12}$	$\frac{1}{12}$	$\frac{1}{12}$	$\frac{1}{12}$	$\frac{1}{12}$	$\frac{1}{12}$

Step 3

Subtract. Simplify if possible.

$\frac{4}{12} - \frac{3}{12} = \frac{1}{12}$

The difference is $\frac{1}{12}$.

Explain It

1. In Step 1, why do you find the LCM of 3 and 4?

2. In Step 2, why do you multiply the numerators and denominators of the different fractions by 4 and by 3?

3. In Step 3, why should you simplify if possible?

Step 1

Find $\frac{1}{2} + \frac{1}{3}$.

To add fractions with different or unlike denominators, find a common denominator.

The least common multiple (LCM) of the denominators is the least common denominator (LCD).

Multiples of 2: 2, 4, 6 …

Multiples of 3: 3, 6 …

The LCM is 6, so the LCD is 6.

Step 2

Write the addends as equivalent fractions with the LCD of 6.

$$\frac{1 \times 3}{2 \times 3} = \frac{3}{6}$$

and

$$\frac{1 \times 2}{3 \times 2} = \frac{2}{6}$$

| $\frac{1}{2}$ | | $\frac{1}{3}$ | | |
| $\frac{1}{6}$ | $\frac{1}{6}$ | $\frac{1}{6}$ | $\frac{1}{6}$ | $\frac{1}{6}$ |

Step 3

Add. Simplify if possible.

$$\frac{3}{6} + \frac{2}{6} = \frac{5}{6}$$

Abby and Faith ate a total of $\frac{5}{6}$ cup of cereal.

Guided Practice*

 MATHEMATICAL PRACTICES

Do you know HOW?

In **1** and **2**, find the LCD for each pair of fractions.

1. $\frac{3}{4}$, $\frac{2}{5}$ **2.** $\frac{2}{7}$, $\frac{1}{3}$

In **3** through **6**, find each sum or difference. Simplify your answers.

3. $\frac{5}{8} - \frac{1}{2}$ **4.** $\frac{1}{2} + \frac{1}{5}$

5. $\frac{4}{5} - \frac{3}{10}$ **6.** $\frac{11}{15} - \frac{2}{3}$

Do you UNDERSTAND?

© **7. Be Precise** Why do you need to find a common denominator before you can add or subtract fractions with unlike denominators?

8. In Step 1 above, how else could you find the LCM of the denominators?

© **9. Reason** What equivalent fraction would you use for $\frac{2}{3}$ to find $\frac{2}{3} - \frac{1}{4}$?

Independent Practice

Leveled Practice Find the LCD for each pair of fractions.

10. $\frac{3}{5}$, $\frac{1}{2}$ **11.** $\frac{5}{8}$, $\frac{9}{16}$ **12.** $\frac{4}{9}$, $\frac{1}{6}$ **13.** $\frac{3}{4}$, $\frac{1}{3}$ **14.** $\frac{1}{3}$, $\frac{7}{9}$

Find two fractions equivalent to each fraction.

 Multiply or divide the numerator and denominator by the same nonzero number.

15. $\frac{1}{4}$ **16.** $\frac{3}{8}$ **17.** $\frac{6}{9}$ **18.** $\frac{5}{25}$ **19.** $\frac{10}{11}$

Animated Glossary
www.pearsonsuccessnet.com

Independent Practice

In **20** through **28**, find each sum or difference. Simplify your answer.

20. $\frac{3}{4} - \frac{1}{3}$

21. $\frac{5}{12} + \frac{5}{10}$

22. $\frac{2}{5} + \frac{1}{6}$

23. $\frac{2}{5} + \frac{1}{7}$

24. $\frac{5}{12} + \frac{5}{15}$

25. $\frac{5}{12} - \frac{5}{15}$

26. $\frac{1}{4} + \frac{1}{4} + \frac{1}{3}$

27. $\frac{3}{10} + \frac{3}{12} + \frac{3}{15}$

28. $\frac{3}{10} - \frac{3}{12} + \frac{3}{15}$

Problem Solving

MATHEMATICAL
PRACTICES

29. Tom wants to add $\frac{3}{10}$ and $\frac{4}{15}$. Which is the LCM for 10 and 15?

   A 5   **B** 25   **C** 30   **D** 60

© **30. Use Tools** The fractions $\frac{1}{12}$, $\frac{1}{6}$, and $\frac{1}{4}$ have a common denominator of 12. Draw a fraction model to find $\frac{1}{12} + \frac{1}{6} + \frac{1}{4}$. Simplify your answer if possible.

Tip *Draw equivalent fraction strips to make a model.*

31. The lines shown at the right represent two streets that cross at a common point. What type of lines are these?

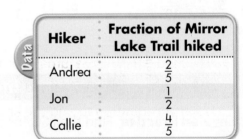

© **32. Writing to Explain** What is the difference between lines that are parallel and lines that are perpendicular?

© **Persevere** Use the table for **33** and **34**.

   33. How much more of the trail did Jon hike than Andrea?

   34. How much more of the trail did Callie hike than Jon?

Hiker	Fraction of Mirror Lake Trail hiked
Andrea	$\frac{2}{5}$
Jon	$\frac{1}{2}$
Callie	$\frac{4}{5}$

© **35. Model** Max needs $\frac{3}{4}$ cup of beans to make chili. He already has $\frac{1}{2}$ cup. Write an equation that Max could use to find how many more cups of beans he needs to make the chili.

© **36. Think About the Structure** Which equivalent fractions would you use to find the sum of $\frac{3}{4}$ and $\frac{1}{3}$?

   A $\frac{3}{12}$ and $\frac{1}{12}$ **B** $\frac{9}{12}$ and $\frac{4}{12}$ **C** $\frac{3}{4}$ and $\frac{3}{9}$ **D** $\frac{3}{4}$ and $\frac{4}{3}$

Algebra Connections

Equations with Fractions

Remember that you can determine whether an equation is true by substituting a value of the variable and simplifying.

Use $v = \frac{1}{4}$ in each equation to determine whether it is true.

1. $\frac{2}{3} + v = \frac{3}{7}$

2. $v + \frac{1}{2} = \frac{3}{4}$

3. $v - \frac{1}{5} = \frac{1}{20}$

4. $\frac{1}{4} + v = \frac{3}{16}$

5. $\frac{4}{5} - v = \frac{2}{3}$

6. $\frac{3}{4} - v = \frac{1}{2}$

7. $\frac{3}{10} + v = \frac{11}{20}$

8. $v + \frac{1}{6} = \frac{5}{12}$

9. $\frac{1}{3} + v = \frac{1}{2}$

10. $v - \frac{1}{4} = 0$

11. $v - \frac{1}{8} = \frac{1}{8}$

12. $v + \frac{2}{5} = \frac{7}{8}$

Example: If $m = \frac{2}{5}$, which of the three equations listed below are true?

$$\frac{1}{2} + m = 1; \quad m + \frac{3}{5} = 1; \quad \frac{4}{9} - m = \frac{1}{2}$$

Think How can I check to see if each equation is true?

Substitute $\frac{2}{5}$ for m in each equation.

$$\frac{1}{2} + \frac{2}{5} = \frac{5}{10} + \frac{4}{10} = \frac{9}{10} \neq 1$$

$$\frac{2}{5} + \frac{3}{5} = 1$$

$$\frac{4}{9} - \frac{2}{5} = \frac{20}{45} - \frac{18}{45} = \frac{2}{45} \neq \frac{1}{2}$$

The only true equation is $m + \frac{3}{5} = 1$.

---

13. It rained $\frac{2}{3}$ inch on Saturday. Find the total amount of rain, t, for the weekend if it rained $\frac{1}{4}$ inch on Sunday. Write and solve an equation to find the answer.

14. Jill walked $\frac{1}{3}$ mile less than Romero walked. If w equals how far Romero walked, which expression describes how far Jill walked?

A $\frac{1}{3} - w$

C $w - \frac{1}{3}$

B $\frac{1}{3} + w$

D $\frac{1}{3} + w$

© **15. Write a Problem** Write a real-world problem using the equation $n = \frac{3}{8} - \frac{1}{6}$.

Lesson
7-4

© Common Core

This lesson reinforces concepts and skills required for Topic 9.

Estimating Sums and Differences of Mixed Numbers

What are some ways to estimate?

Jamila's mom wants to make a size 10 dress and jacket. About how many yards of fabric does she need? Estimate the sum $2\frac{1}{4} + 1\frac{7}{8}$ to find out.

Fabric Required (in yards)

	Size 10	Size 14
Dress	$2\frac{1}{4}$	$2\frac{7}{8}$
Jacket	$1\frac{7}{8}$	$2\frac{1}{4}$

Another Example How can you use benchmark fractions such as $\frac{1}{4}, \frac{1}{3}, \frac{1}{2}, \frac{2}{3}$, and $\frac{3}{4}$ to estimate?

Estimate $\frac{5}{8} - \frac{3}{16}$.

$\frac{5}{8}$ is close to $\frac{6}{8}$, and $\frac{6}{8} = \frac{3}{4}$.

$\frac{3}{16}$ is close to $\frac{4}{16}$, and $\frac{4}{16} = \frac{1}{4}$.

So, $\frac{5}{8} - \frac{3}{16}$ is close to $\frac{3}{4} - \frac{1}{4}$.

$\frac{3}{4} - \frac{1}{4} = \frac{2}{4}$ or $\frac{1}{2}$

So, $\frac{5}{8} - \frac{3}{16} \approx \frac{1}{2}$.

Guided Practice*

© **MATHEMATICAL PRACTICES**

Do you know HOW?

Round to the nearest whole number.

1. $\frac{2}{3}$ **2.** $3\frac{2}{7}$ **3.** $5\frac{7}{9}$

Estimate each sum or difference using benchmark fractions.

4. $4\frac{7}{15} + 2\frac{5}{12}$ **5.** $3\frac{11}{16} - 1\frac{1}{4}$

Do you UNDERSTAND?

© **6. Generalize** To estimate with mixed numbers, when should you round up to the nearest whole number?

7. Suppose Jamila's mom wants to make a size 14 dress and jacket. About how many yards of fabric does she need?

Independent Practice

Leveled Practice Use the number line to round the mixed numbers to the nearest whole number.

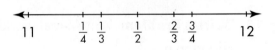

8. $11\frac{6}{8}$ **9.** $11\frac{2}{6}$ **10.** $11\frac{11}{12}$ **11.** $11\frac{3}{10}$

*For another example, see Set C on page 182.

One Way

Use a number line to round fractions and mixed numbers to the nearest whole number.

$1\frac{7}{8}$ rounds to 2 $2\frac{1}{4}$ rounds to 2

1          $\frac{1}{2}$ $\frac{7}{8}$ 2 $\frac{1}{4}$ $\frac{1}{2}$ 3

So, $2\frac{1}{4} + 1\frac{7}{8} \approx 2 + 2$, or 4.

Jamila's mom needs about 4 yards of fabric.

Another Way

Use $\frac{1}{2}$ as a benchmark to round fractions to the nearest whole number.

Round fractions less than $\frac{1}{2}$ down. Since $\frac{1}{4} < \frac{1}{2}$, $2\frac{1}{4}$ rounds to 2.

Round fractions greater than or equal to $\frac{1}{2}$ up. Since $\frac{7}{8} > \frac{1}{2}$, $1\frac{7}{8}$ rounds to 2.

So, $2\frac{1}{4} + 1\frac{7}{8} \approx 2 + 2 = 4$.

Estimate each sum or difference.

12. $3\frac{2}{7} - \frac{7}{8}$

13. $8\frac{1}{2} + 3\frac{8}{9}$

14. $7\frac{2}{5} - 5\frac{1}{3}$

15. $4\frac{3}{4} + 3\frac{14}{25}$

16. $10\frac{7}{9} - \frac{2}{3}$

17. $15\frac{2}{11} + 9\frac{5}{7}$

18. $30\frac{2}{9} - 7\frac{19}{23}$

19. $26\frac{2}{25} + 32\frac{9}{20}$

Problem Solving

MATHEMATICAL PRACTICES

20. Use the recipes to answer the questions.

  a About how many cups of raisins would you need to make both recipes?

  b Estimate how many cups of Fruit Trail Mix this recipe can make.

  c Estimate how much trail mix you would have if you made both recipes.

Fruit Trail Mix
- $1\frac{1}{4}$ cups raisins
- $\frac{5}{8}$ cup sunflower seeds
- $1\frac{1}{2}$ cups unsalted peanuts
- $\frac{3}{4}$ cup coconut

Fun Trail Mix
- $2\frac{2}{3}$ cups raisins
- $1\frac{1}{2}$ cups dried berries
- 1 cup granola
- $\frac{1}{2}$ cup cashews

21. In the equation $3\frac{1}{7} + x = 6\frac{9}{11}$, estimate the value of x.

©22. Writing to Explain Liam uses a pattern to get ready for a race. The table shows how many minutes he trains each day. Use the pattern to find the missing numbers. Explain Liam's pattern.

Number of Minutes by Day

Day	M	Tu	W	Th	F	Sa	Su
Minutes	5	10	20	35	55		

©23. Think About the Structure To round $4\frac{4}{7}$ to the nearest whole number, which two numbers should you compare?

A 4 and $\frac{4}{7}$

B $\frac{4}{7}$ and $\frac{2}{3}$

C $\frac{4}{7}$ and $\frac{1}{2}$

D 4 and $\frac{1}{2}$

Lesson
7-5

Common Core

This lesson reinforces concepts and skills required for Topic 9.

Adding Mixed Numbers
How do you find the sum of mixed numbers?

The students in Mr. Lopez's science class measured the rainfall each day for two weeks. The amounts for each week are listed in the table.

What was the total amount of rainfall for the two weeks?

Choose an Operation Add to find the total amount of rainfall for the two weeks.

Week	Rainfall
1	$2\frac{1}{2}$ in.
2	$1\frac{9}{10}$ in.

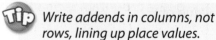

Guided Practice*

MATHEMATICAL PRACTICES

Do you know HOW?

Find each sum. Simplify if possible.

1. $\quad 1\frac{1}{4} = \quad 1\frac{}{20}$

$\quad + 2\frac{2}{5} = \quad + 2\frac{}{20}$

2. $\quad 3\frac{1}{3} = \quad 3\frac{}{21}$

$\quad + 4\frac{3}{7} = + \quad 4\frac{}{21}$

3. $5\frac{1}{2} + 9\frac{2}{3}$

4. $6\frac{4}{5} + 8\frac{6}{7}$

5. $2\frac{3}{5} + 4\frac{1}{2}$

6. $8\frac{3}{4} + 6\frac{7}{9}$

Do you UNDERSTAND?

7. When adding mixed numbers, should you add the whole numbers first or the fractions first?

8. Generalize When adding mixed numbers, when do you need to find an LCD to write equivalent fractions?

9. Rainy City received $3\frac{1}{2}$ inches of rain on Monday and $2\frac{3}{4}$ on Tuesday. How much total rain fell during the two days?

Independent Practice

In **10** through **21**, find each sum. Simplify if possible.

Tip *Write addends in columns, not rows, lining up place values.*

10. $9\frac{1}{4} + 10\frac{3}{5}$

11. $3\frac{1}{8} + 3\frac{3}{8}$

12. $4\frac{2}{13} + 2\frac{7}{13}$

13. $5\frac{1}{10} + 4\frac{3}{10}$

14. $3\frac{2}{3} + 4\frac{2}{5}$

15. $3\frac{7}{16} + 2\frac{8}{16}$

16. $7\frac{7}{24} + 4\frac{2}{3}$

17. $4\frac{5}{7} + 4\frac{2}{5}$

18. $11\frac{5}{13} + 4\frac{7}{11}$

19. $30\frac{10}{39} + 50\frac{45}{78}$

20. $24\frac{32}{45} + 42\frac{9}{10}$

21. $3\frac{1}{7} + 2\frac{1}{8} + 3\frac{3}{7}$

For another example, see Set D on page 183.

Step 1

Estimate.

$$2\frac{1}{2} \approx 3$$
$$+ 1\frac{9}{10} \approx + 2$$
$$\overline{ 5}$$

The total rainfall was about 5 inches.

Step 2

Find the LCD of the fractions and use it to write equivalent fractions.

$$2\frac{1}{2} = 2\frac{5}{10}$$
$$+ 1\frac{9}{10} = + 1\frac{9}{10}$$
$$\overline{ 3\frac{14}{10}}$$

Then add whole numbers and fractions separately.

Step 3

Rename improper fractions as mixed numbers. Simplify.

$$3\frac{14}{10} = 3 + 1\frac{4}{10}$$
$$= 4\frac{4}{10} = 4\frac{2}{5}$$

The total rainfall was $4\frac{2}{5}$ inches.

Problem Solving

MATHEMATICAL PRACTICES

Use the room diagram for **22** and **23**.

22. Brittany wants to hang a "Congratulations" banner around the four walls of the room. The banner is 1 ft wide. Estimate how long the banner will be. Round to the nearest foot.

23. How long should the banner be to fit around the walls exactly? Express your answer in feet.

Room — $20\frac{1}{4}$ ft

$10\frac{2}{3}$ ft

24. Writing to Explain John bought three different salads from the deli. The salads weighed 1.5 lbs, $2\frac{3}{4}$ lbs, and $1\frac{1}{4}$ lbs. Find the total weight using decimals, and explain how you did it.

Use the table to answer **25** and **26**.

25. Reasonableness How much rain does the side of the mountain facing the ocean get from January through June?

A $7\frac{1}{2}$ in. **B** $8\frac{9}{10}$ in. **C** $9\frac{1}{5}$ in. **D** $9\frac{3}{10}$ in.

Average Annual Rainfall (in inches)			
Side of Mountain	Jan. to Mar.	April to June	July to Sept.
Facing ocean	$4\frac{2}{5}$	$4\frac{9}{10}$	$2\frac{3}{10}$
Facing away from ocean	$\frac{3}{10}$	$\frac{7}{10}$	$\frac{2}{5}$

26. How much rain does the side of the mountain facing away from the ocean get from April through September?

A $1\frac{1}{10}$ in. **B** 1 in. **C** $1\frac{3}{10}$ in. **D** $\frac{7}{10}$ in.

27. Reason Put the following numbers in order from least to greatest: 1.1, 1.25, 1.0067, 1.01, 1.0034

28. Jason is 5 feet tall. His baby sister was 20 inches at birth. How much taller in feet is Jason than his sister?

Lesson
7-6

Common
Core

This lesson reinforces
concepts and skills required
for Topic 9.

Subtracting Mixed Numbers

How can you find the difference of mixed numbers?

North Park has two go-cart paths: the Little Indy and the Grand Prix. How much longer is the Grand Prix than the Little Indy?

Choose an Operation Subtract to find how much longer the Grand Prix is.

Grand Prix
$4\frac{1}{3}$ miles

Grand Prix

Little Indy

Little Indy
$1\frac{3}{4}$ miles

Another Example How can you find the difference between a whole number and a mixed number?

Find $15 - 2\frac{1}{3}$.

Step 1

Estimate. $15 - 2 = 13$

$$\begin{array}{r} 15 \\ -\ 2\frac{1}{3} \\ \hline \end{array}$$

There is no fraction from which to subtract $\frac{1}{3}$.

Step 2

To subtract, rename 15 to show thirds.

 Think

$$15 \quad = 14 + 1 = \quad 14\frac{3}{3}$$

$$-\ 2\frac{1}{3} \qquad\qquad -\ 2\frac{1}{3}$$

Step 3

Subtract and simplify.

$$\begin{array}{r} 14\frac{3}{3} \\ -\ 2\frac{1}{3} \\ \hline 12\frac{2}{3} \end{array}$$

Explain It

1. How is renaming mixed numbers for subtraction like regrouping for whole number subtraction?

2. How is the problem $6 - 2\frac{3}{4}$ different from $6\frac{3}{4} - 2$?

© 3. **Reasonableness** Was the answer for Another Example reasonable? Explain.

Estimate: $4 - 2 = 2$.

Then find the LCD to write equivalent fractions.

$$4\frac{1}{3} = 4\frac{4}{12}$$
$$-1\frac{3}{4} = -1\frac{9}{12}$$

To subtract, rename $4\frac{4}{12}$ to show more twelfths.

Think $4\frac{4}{12} = 3 + 1 + \frac{4}{12}$

$$= 3 + \frac{12}{12} + \frac{4}{12}$$
$$= 3\frac{16}{12}$$

Subtract and simplify.

$$4\frac{4}{12} = 3\frac{16}{12}$$
$$-1\frac{9}{12} = -1\frac{9}{12}$$
$$\overline{} \quad \overline{2\frac{7}{12}}$$

Check for reasonableness. The Grand Prix is $2\frac{7}{12}$ miles longer.

Guided Practice*

MATHEMATICAL
PRACTICES

Do you know HOW?

Find each difference. Simplify your answers.

1. $2\frac{3}{4} - 2\frac{1}{4}$ **2.** $4\frac{1}{4} - 3\frac{1}{3}$

3. $9\frac{3}{4} - 7$ **4.** $5\frac{5}{8} - 5\frac{1}{8}$

5. $2\frac{3}{4} - 2\frac{1}{3}$ **6.** $6 - 2\frac{7}{8}$

Do you UNDERSTAND?

 7. Reason In the example above, why was $4\frac{4}{12}$ renamed as $3\frac{16}{12}$?

8. The Grand Prix is $4\frac{1}{3}$ miles long. The road around the park is $6\frac{1}{8}$ miles long. How much longer is the road than the Grand Prix?

Independent Practice

Leveled Practice Find each difference. Simplify if possible.   **TIP** *Write the mixed fractions in columns, lining up place values.*

9. $5\frac{2}{3} - 2\frac{1}{3}$ **10.** $10\frac{4}{5} - 6\frac{3}{5}$ **11.** $4\frac{7}{8} - 2\frac{1}{8}$

12. $7\frac{1}{2} - 4\frac{1}{3}$ **13.** $8\frac{2}{3} - 4\frac{1}{4}$ **14.** $12\frac{3}{4} - 8\frac{1}{3}$

15. $14\frac{1}{3} - 6\frac{2}{3}$ **16.** $5\frac{4}{8} - 2\frac{6}{8}$ **17.** $5\frac{1}{10} - 4\frac{1}{8}$

18. $6\frac{7}{24} - 5\frac{1}{3}$ **19.** $3\frac{1}{3} - 2\frac{3}{4}$ **20.** $2\frac{3}{8} - 1\frac{1}{2}$

21. $6\frac{15}{32} - 2\frac{5}{8}$ **22.** $5\frac{12}{25} + 18\frac{13}{25} - 12\frac{4}{5}$ **23.** $22\frac{5}{13} - 11\frac{12}{13} - 2\frac{1}{13}$

24. Which of the above exercises could you compute mentally?

25. Of 1,400 students in the school, 448 play chess. Solve $448 + x = 1,400$ to find how many do not play chess.

© **26.** **Writing to Explain** How are the steps different for renaming fractions when adding and subtracting mixed numbers with unlike denominators?

27. During half time, the soccer players drank $2\frac{1}{2}$ pitchers of water. After the game, they drank $4\frac{2}{3}$ pitchers of water.

   a How much water did they drink altogether?

   b How many more pitchers of water did the players drink after the game than during half time?

28. A triangular flowerbed in Kimiko's yard has a perimeter of 47 feet. The measure of two of its sides are shown. What is the measure of the third side?

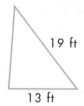
19 ft

13 ft

© **29.** **Think About the Structure** Which expression could you use to find the difference between $6\frac{1}{3}$ and $4\frac{1}{2}$?

   A $5\frac{8}{6} - 4\frac{3}{6}$ **C** $5\frac{2}{6} - 4\frac{3}{6}$

   B $6\frac{1}{6} - 4\frac{1}{6}$ **D** $6\frac{8}{6} - 4\frac{3}{6}$

30. Which shows the Commutative Property of Addition?

   A $6\frac{2}{3} + 4\frac{1}{2} = 11\frac{1}{6}$

   B $6\frac{2}{3} + 4\frac{1}{2} = 4\frac{1}{2} + 6\frac{2}{3}$

   C $6\frac{2}{3} = 11\frac{1}{6} - 4\frac{1}{2}$

   D $4\frac{1}{2} = 11\frac{1}{6} - 6\frac{2}{3}$

31. Write a number story to add or subtract mixed numbers.

© **32.** **Persevere** Fairy penguins are the smallest kind of penguin. Adults are usually 13 inches to 16 inches tall. One mother penguin is $13\frac{1}{2}$ inches tall. Her chick is $7\frac{3}{4}$ inches tall. How much taller is the mother than her chick?

33. There is a fence around 3 sides of Ryan's backyard. Two sides are each 55 feet. The back is 27 ft 8 in. How long is the fence in inches? In feet?

34. Trevor has a piece of wood that is $2\frac{2}{3}$ feet long. How much should he cut off to make it $1\frac{3}{4}$ feet long?

? $13\frac{1}{2}$ $7\frac{3}{4}$

```
  1        1¾  2      2⅔   3
```

   A $\frac{1}{4}$ ft   **B** $\frac{1}{3}$ ft   **C** $1\frac{1}{3}$ ft   **D** $\frac{11}{12}$ ft

Mixed Problem Solving

Mr. Blake's class is having a formal debate. He keeps track of the time each student speaks in a table.

Use the data at right for **1** and **2**.

1. How much longer did Tim speak than Erik?

2. How many total minutes did Julie and Heather speak?

Student Debate Time				
Student	Tim	Erik	Julie	Heather
Time (minutes)	$3\frac{1}{2}$	$1\frac{3}{4}$	$5\frac{1}{3}$	$2\frac{1}{4}$

Use the data at right for **3** and **4**.

3. Micalann presented on Tuesday and Friday. How many minutes did Micalann speak?

4. Lowell was allowed 6 minutes to present his project. How many more minutes could he have spoken?

Presentation Time			
Student	**Tuesday**	**Wednesday**	**Friday**
Micalann	$2\frac{1}{3}$ min.		$2\frac{3}{4}$ min.
Lowell		$4\frac{1}{2}$ min.	

5. Three students gave a group presentation. Roberta spoke for $2\frac{1}{2}$ minutes. Alice spoke for $3\frac{1}{3}$ minutes, and Kai spoke for $4\frac{3}{4}$ minutes. How long was their presentation?

6. The teacher wants the students to give a 10-minute group presentation. If Jamie's group has already prepared $6\frac{1}{3}$ minutes, how much do they still need to prepare?

Use the data at right for **7** and **8**.

7. Who presented longer, Group 1 or Group 2? How many more minutes did they present?

8. Group 5 did not finish their 10-minute group presentation. How much of the presentation was left?

   A $1\frac{4}{5}$ minutes   **C** $\frac{4}{5}$ minute

   B 2 minutes   **D** $1\frac{1}{5}$ minutes

Group Presentation Time	
Group	**Time**
Group 1	$9\frac{1}{3}$ min.
Group 2	$9\frac{3}{5}$ min.
Group 3	$5\frac{1}{2}$ min.
Group 4	$6\frac{1}{4}$ min.
Group 5	$8\frac{1}{5}$ min.

Common Core

6.RP.1 Understand the concept of a ratio and use ratio language to describe a ratio relationship between two quantities....

Problem Solving

Make a Table

Kyle offers to buy 10 of Todd's model airplanes. Kyle offers two plans for payment. Which payment plan should Todd accept?

Plan 1: Pay a single $200 payment for the 10 model airplanes.

Plan 2: Pay $0.50 for one model airplane; then pay enough for each additional model to double the previous total payment.

Plan 1: $200 for 10 model airplanes

Plan 2: $0.50 for 1 model, $1.00 for 2 models, $2.00 for 3 models, and so on

---

Guided Practice*

MATHEMATICAL PRACTICES

Do you know HOW?

1. Look for Patterns Larissa swam $3\frac{1}{2}$ laps the first day. Each day after that she swam $1\frac{1}{2}$ laps more than the previous day. How far will Larissa swim on Day 6? Copy and complete the table.

Day	1	2	3	4	5	6
Laps	$3\frac{1}{2}$					

Do you UNDERSTAND?

2. In the example at the top, how did making a table help answer the question?

3. Write a Problem Write a real-world problem that you can solve by making a table.

Independent Practice

MATHEMATICAL PRACTICES

Solve. Copy and extend the table for Exercise 4.

4. Persevere Skyler wants to buy a pair of inline skates for $75. She earns $10 a week. If she saves $\frac{1}{2}$ of her money each week, how many weeks will she need to save to buy the skates?

Number of Weeks	Total Savings ($)
1	5
2	10
3	
4	

Applying Math Practices

- What am I asked to find?
- What else can I try?
- How are quantities related?
- How can I explain my work?
- How can I use math to model the problem?
- Can I use tools to help?
- Is my work precise?
- Why does this work?
- How can I generalize?

What do I know? Plan 1 would pay $200.

What am I being asked to find? Find how much would be paid under Plan 2.

Make a table to find the total payment for the 10 models under Plan 2.

Models Bought	1	2	3	4	5	6	7	8	9	10
Total Payments ($)	0.5	1	2	4	8	16	32	64	128	256

Todd would receive $200 under Plan 1 and $256 under Plan 2. He should accept Plan 2.

5. Fabian plans to read for $2\frac{1}{2}$ minutes the first day and then double his reading time each day. How many minutes will Fabian read on Day 6?

6. **Reason** Ruth wants to earn a prize for reading for 500 minutes. If she reads for $\frac{1}{4}$ hour every day for 15 days, will she earn the prize she wants? Explain.

7. Trevor bought 3 new pairs of jeans and 2 new sweaters for school. How many different clothing combinations can he make? Make an organized list to help you find the answer.

8. **Model** Every day, Martha and her mother go for a walk around Lake Andrea. The path is $1\frac{3}{5}$ miles long. How many total miles have Martha and her mother walked after 4 days?

9. **Critique Reasoning** Read the problem and Jerome's answer to the problem below. Explain why his answer is incorrect and fix it.

The Grant family is saving for a vacation. They open a savings account with $225 and deposit money each week. The first week, they deposit $15. Each week after that, they deposit $15 more than they deposited the week before. How much money will the Grants have saved after Week 6?

Jerome's answer:

After Week 6, the Grants will have saved $90.

10. **Use Tools** Cody is building towers in the shape of a triangle out of cereal boxes for a display in his dad's store. How many boxes will he need to make 3 towers if each tower has 5 boxes in the bottom row and each higher row has one less box than the previous row? Draw a picture to help you find the answer.

11. National Cellular charges $0.75 for the first minute and $0.07 for each additional minute of a cell phone call. American Cellular charges $0.85 for the first minute, but only $0.05 for each additional minute. Which company charges less for an 8-minute cell phone call? How much less?

1. A buttonhole should be $\frac{1}{16}$-inch wider than the button. How wide should a buttonhole be made to fit a button that is $\frac{14}{16}$ inches wide? (7-1)

A $\frac{15}{32}$

B $\frac{13}{16}$

C $\frac{14}{16}$

D $\frac{15}{16}$

2. What is the least common multiple of 5, 8, and 16? (7-2)

A 40

B 80

C 120

D 640

3. The table lists the North American records for barometric pressure. What is the difference between the highest and the lowest pressure recorded? (7-6)

Record	Inches of Mercury	Location
Highest pressure	$31\frac{17}{20}$	Northway, Alaska
Lowest pressure	$26\frac{7}{20}$	Key West, Florida

A $\frac{10}{20}$ inch

B $\frac{1}{2}$ inch

C $5\frac{1}{2}$ inches

D 5 inches

4. Sabrina tried to tighten a $\frac{1}{8}$-inch bolt with a $\frac{3}{16}$-inch wrench. What is the difference in measure between the bolt and the wrench? (7-3)

A $\frac{1}{16}$ inch

B $\frac{1}{8}$ inch

C $\frac{1}{4}$ inch

D $\frac{5}{16}$ inch

5. What is $7\frac{6}{15} + 4\frac{4}{5}$? (7-5)

A $11\frac{1}{5}$

B $11\frac{2}{3}$

C $12\frac{2}{15}$

D $12\frac{1}{5}$

6. Hotdogs are sold in packages of 10 and hotdog buns are sold in packages of 8. What is the least number of hot dogs and buns that Angel must buy so that she has the same number of each? (7-2)

A 20

B 40

C 80

D 100

7. Which expression is the best estimate for $1\frac{3}{4} + 2\frac{3}{8}$? (7-4)

A 2 + 2

B 1 + 2

C 2 + 3

D 1 + 3

8. The table shows the lengths of some movies. How much longer is the action movie than the comedy movie? (7-6)

Movie	Length (in hours)
Action	$2\frac{3}{4}$
Comedy	$1\frac{5}{6}$
Drama	$2\frac{1}{3}$

A $\frac{1}{6}$ hour

B $\frac{11}{12}$ hour

C $1\frac{1}{12}$ hours

D $1\frac{11}{12}$ hours

9. What is the difference between $\frac{3}{8}$ and $\frac{1}{8}$? (7-1)

A $\frac{1}{2}$

B $\frac{1}{4}$

C $\frac{3}{16}$

D $\frac{1}{8}$

10. Sadie wrote a report for school that was $3\frac{1}{4}$ pages long. Robert's report was $4\frac{9}{10}$ pages long. Which is the best estimate of how much longer Robert's report was than Sadie's? (7-4)

A $\frac{1}{2}$ page

B 1 page

C 2 pages

D 3 pages

11. What is the least common denominator to add $\frac{2}{9} + \frac{4}{15}$? (7-3)

A 45

B 60

C 90

D 135

12. What is $12\frac{11}{18}$ rounded to the nearest whole number? (7-4)

A 11

B 12

C 13

D 18

13. Serafina can choose between two dining halls for a banquet. Hall A charges $200 plus $4 per person. Hall B charges $150 plus $5 per person. How many people would have to attend for the charges to be the same? (7-7)

Dining Hall	Number of People			
	0	10	20	30
A	$200	$240	$280	
B	$150	$200	$250	

A 30

B 40

C 50

D 60

Set A, pages 162–163

Find $\frac{2}{9} + \frac{1}{9}$.   Find $\frac{7}{9} - \frac{1}{9}$.

The fractions have like denominators.
Add or subtract the numerators.

$\frac{2}{9} + \frac{1}{9} = \frac{3}{9}$ $\frac{7}{9} - \frac{1}{9} = \frac{6}{9}$

Use the GCF, 3, to simplify.

$\frac{2}{9} + \frac{1}{9} = \frac{3}{9} = \frac{1}{3}$ $\frac{7}{9} - \frac{1}{9} = \frac{6}{9} = \frac{2}{3}$

Remember that when the denominators are the same, you add or subtract only the numerators.

Find each sum or difference. Simplify.

1. $\frac{2}{5} + \frac{1}{5}$ 2. $\frac{9}{10} - \frac{7}{10}$

3. $\frac{7}{8} + \frac{2}{8}$ 4. $\frac{12}{13} - \frac{8}{13}$

Set B, pages 164–168

Find the least common multiple (LCM) of 5 and 6.

List multiples of each number.

5: 5; 10; 15; 20; 25; 30 . . .   6: 6; 12; 18; 24; 30 . . .

The LCM is 30. Use this LCM as the least common denominator (LCD) to calculate below.

$\begin{array}{r} \frac{3}{5} = \frac{18}{30} \\ + \frac{1}{6} = + \frac{5}{30} \\ \hline \frac{23}{30} \end{array}$ $\begin{array}{r} \frac{3}{5} = \frac{18}{30} \\ - \frac{1}{6} = - \frac{5}{30} \\ \hline \frac{13}{30} \end{array}$

Remember that the LCM of the denominators in a set of fractions is the LCD for that set of fractions.

Find the LCM for each set of numbers.

1. 10, 20   2. 3, 6

3. 8, 10   4. 2, 3, 5

Find each sum or difference. Simplify.

5. $\frac{1}{2} + \frac{1}{7}$ 6. $\frac{1}{3} + \frac{2}{4}$

7. $\frac{3}{4} - \frac{1}{3}$ 8. $\frac{5}{6} - \frac{1}{2}$

Set C, pages 170–171

Estimate $5\frac{1}{3} + 9\frac{9}{11}$.

Compare fractions to $\frac{1}{2}$ to round to the nearest whole number.

Round fractions that are less than $\frac{1}{2}$ down to the nearest whole number. $5\frac{1}{3}$ rounds to 5.

Round fractions greater than or equal to $\frac{1}{2}$ up to the nearest whole number. $9\frac{9}{11}$ rounds to 10.

So, $5\frac{1}{3} + 9\frac{9}{11} \approx 5 + 10 = 15$.

Remember that you can also use benchmark fractions such as $\frac{1}{4}, \frac{1}{3}, \frac{1}{2}, \frac{2}{3}$, and $\frac{3}{4}$ to help you estimate.

Round to the nearest whole number.

1. $2\frac{9}{10}$ 2. $9\frac{19}{20}$ 3. $6\frac{2}{7}$

Estimate each sum or difference.

4. $3\frac{1}{4} - 1\frac{1}{2}$ 5. $5\frac{2}{9} + 4\frac{11}{13}$

6. $2\frac{3}{8} + 5\frac{3}{5}$ 7. $9\frac{3}{7} - 6\frac{2}{5}$

Find $2\frac{5}{8} + 3\frac{1}{2}$.

Rewrite the fractions as equivalent fractions with like denominators.

$$2\frac{5}{8} = \quad 2\frac{5}{8}$$
$$+ \ 3\frac{1}{2} = + \ 3\frac{4}{8}$$

Add.

$$2\frac{5}{8}$$
$$+ \ 3\frac{4}{8}$$
$$\overline{\quad 5\frac{9}{8}}$$

Rename the improper fraction.

$$5\frac{9}{8} = 5 + 1\frac{1}{8}$$
$$= 6\frac{1}{8}$$

Find $3\frac{1}{2} - 2\frac{5}{8}$.

$$3\frac{1}{2} = \quad 3\frac{4}{8}$$
$$- \ 2\frac{5}{8} = - \ 2\frac{5}{8}$$

Rename $3\frac{4}{8}$ to make more eighths.

$$3\frac{4}{8} = \quad 2\frac{12}{8}$$
$$- \ 2\frac{5}{8} = - \ 2\frac{5}{8}$$

Subtract and simplify.

$$2\frac{12}{8}$$
$$- \ 2\frac{5}{8}$$
$$\overline{\quad \frac{7}{8}}$$

Remember to rename improper fractions as mixed numbers in sums.

Also remember to rename the fraction part of a mixed number when necessary to subtract a larger fraction.

Find each sum or difference. Simplify.

1. $3\frac{1}{5} + 2\frac{3}{5}$

2. $3\frac{5}{8} + 3\frac{7}{8}$

3. $5\frac{3}{5} + \frac{2}{3}$

4. $50\frac{3}{4} + 50\frac{4}{5}$

5. $5\frac{11}{12} + \frac{1}{2}$

6. $3\frac{4}{5} + 2\frac{1}{9}$

7. $10\frac{2}{3} - 6\frac{1}{3}$

8. $8\frac{3}{8} - 3\frac{7}{8}$

9. $19\frac{1}{2} - 10\frac{1}{4}$

10. $16\frac{1}{3} - 12\frac{5}{6}$

11. $21\frac{3}{5} - 10\frac{29}{30}$

12. $14\frac{11}{12} - \frac{1}{4}$

For every movie you rent you earn 15 points toward a free movie rental. How many movies would you need to rent in order to earn a free rental worth 90 points? Copy and continue the table to solve the problem.

Movies Rented	1	2	3
Points	15	30	45

For 4 movies rented, you earn 60 points.
For 5 movies rented, you earn 75 points.
For 6 movies rented, you earn 90 points.

Remember when making a table to solve a problem, look for a pattern in the data and extend the table to find the answer.

Make a table to solve. Give the answer in a complete sentence.

1. Ramir makes T-shirts to sell. It costs him $3.25 in materials to make a T-shirt. He sells the T-shirts for $5. How many T-shirts does he need to sell to make a profit of $12.25 ?

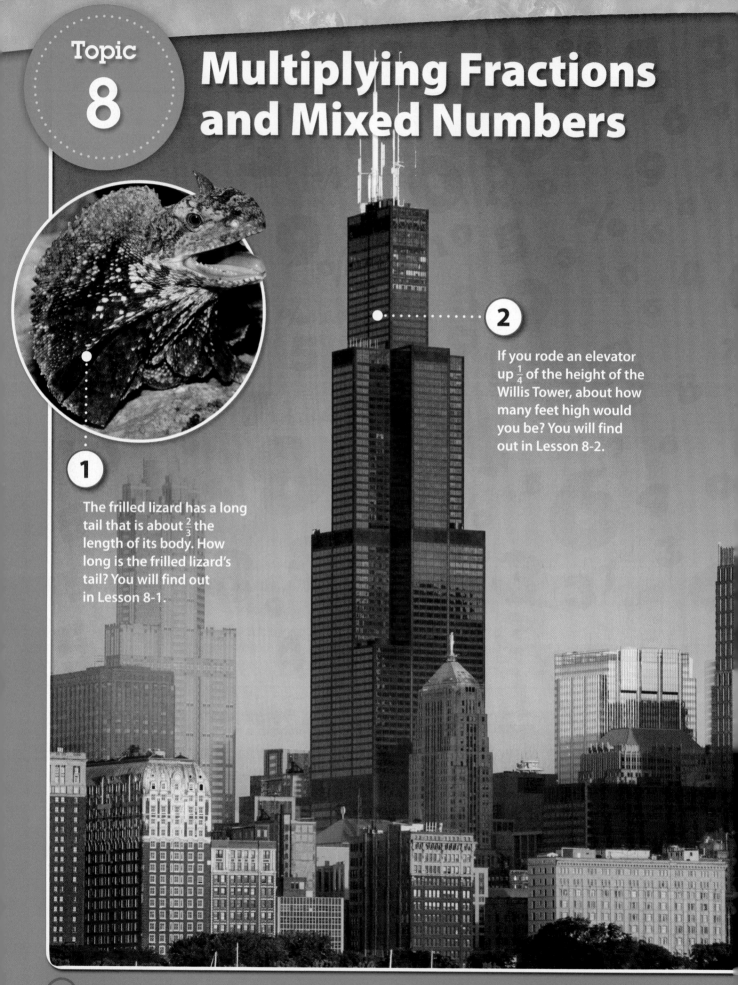

Topic 8

Multiplying Fractions and Mixed Numbers

1

The frilled lizard has a long tail that is about $\frac{2}{3}$ the length of its body. How long is the frilled lizard's tail? You will find out in Lesson 8-1.

2

If you rode an elevator up $\frac{1}{4}$ of the height of the Willis Tower, about how many feet high would you be? You will find out in Lesson 8-2.

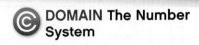
3 Adult horses have 40 permanent teeth. How many permanent teeth do people have? You will find out in Lesson 8-3.

Review What You Know!

Vocabulary

Choose the best term from the box.

> - estimate
> - like denominators
> - greatest common factor

1. The __?__ is the greatest number that is a factor of two or more numbers.

2. To find an approximate answer or solution is to __?__.

3. $\frac{4}{8}$ and $\frac{7}{8}$ have __?__.

Estimation

Estimate each sum, difference, or product.

4. $1,478 + 2,822$ **5.** $305 - 197$

6. $6,490 - 3,510$ **7.** $1,213 + 4,797 + 403$

8. 38×6 **9.** 59×21

Fractions and Decimals

Write the shaded part as a fraction.

10.    **11.**

Express each decimal as a fraction or mixed number. Simplify where possible.

12. 0.80   **13.** 5.25   **14.** 15.95

Divisibility

15. Writing to Explain How can you tell if 78 is divisible by 2, 3, or 6?

Common
Core

This lesson reinforces
concepts and skills required
for Topic 9.

Multiplying a Fraction and a Whole Number

Hands-On
counters

How can you multiply a fraction and whole number?

A recipe makes 12 soft pretzels. If Ilene sprinkles parmesan cheese as a topping over $\frac{2}{3}$ of the baked pretzels, how many cheese pretzels will Ilene make?

Choose an Operation Multiply to find $\frac{2}{3} \times 12$.

Other Examples

Renaming the Whole Number

Find $10 \times \frac{3}{4}$.

To find $10 \times \frac{3}{4}$, you can change 10 to $\frac{10}{1}$ and then multiply.

$\frac{10}{1} \times \frac{3}{4} = \frac{30}{4}$ ← $10 \times 3 = 30$
← $1 \times 4 = 4$

Simplify.

$\frac{30}{4} = 7\frac{2}{4} = 7\frac{1}{2}$

So, $10 \times \frac{3}{4} = 7\frac{1}{2}$.

Using a Calculator

Find $81 \times \frac{4}{9}$.

Press: 81 $\boxed{\times}$ 4 $\boxed{n}$ 9 $\boxed{d}$ $\boxed{\text{ENTER} =}$

Display: $\boxed{81 \times \frac{4}{9} = 36}$

So, $81 \times \frac{4}{9} = 36$.

Guided Practice*

 MATHEMATICAL
PRACTICES

Do you know HOW?

Find each product.

1. $\frac{1}{8} \times 4$

2. $\frac{3}{8} \times 4$

3. $\frac{1}{4} \times 16$

4. $\frac{3}{4} \times 16$

5. $9 \times \frac{1}{6}$

6. $9 \times \frac{5}{6}$

Do you UNDERSTAND?

7. **Reason** In the example at the top of the page, how does finding $\frac{1}{3}$ of 12 help you find $\frac{2}{3}$ of 12?

8. If $\frac{3}{4}$ of the 12 pretzels were sprinkled with cheese, how many pretzels would be sprinkled?

eTools
www.pearsonsuccessnet.com

*For another example, see Set A on page 198.

You can think of a fraction as division, $\frac{2}{3} = 2 \div 3$.

Use this relationship to find $\frac{2}{3} \times 12$.

If the whole number is divisible by the denominator of the fraction, you can divide first and then multiply.

12 is divisible by 3. So, divide 12 by 3.

Dividing 12 by 3 is the same as multiplying $\frac{1}{3}$ and 12.

$12 \div 3 = 4$ and $\frac{1}{3} \times 12 = 4$.

You can think of $\frac{2}{3}$ as 2 times $\frac{1}{3}$. So, multiply by 2:

$$\frac{2}{3} \times 12 = 2(\frac{1}{3} \times 12)$$
$$= 2(4) = 8$$

Ilene makes 8 cheese pretzels.

Independent Practice

In **9** through **20**, find the product. You may use counters to help.

9. $5 \times \frac{2}{3}$ **10.** $\frac{7}{8}$ of 24   **11.** $\frac{9}{10}$ of 20   **12.** $18 \times \frac{2}{3}$

13. $\frac{3}{5} \times 30$ **14.** $\frac{9}{20}$ of 40   **15.** $\frac{7}{100}$ of 700   **16.** $\frac{1}{5}$ of 45

17. $\frac{5}{9}$ of 36   **18.** $\frac{3}{4}$ of 200   **19.** $\frac{7}{8}$ of 32   **20.** $\frac{9}{10}$ of 25

Problem Solving

MATHEMATICAL PRACTICES

During a nature walk, Jill identified 20 species of plants and animals. Use this information for **21** and **22**.

Ⓒ **21. Reasonableness** Jill said that $\frac{1}{3}$ of the species she identified were animals. Can this be correct? Explain.

22. If $\frac{3}{5}$ of the species Jill identified were plants, how many species were plants?

Ⓒ **23. Think About the Structure** The cornbread recipe needs to be tripled for the band dinner. If $\frac{2}{3}$ cup of sugar and $\frac{3}{4}$ cup of cornmeal are needed for 1 recipe, which expression shows the total amount of cornmeal and sugar used for the dinner?

A $3(\frac{3}{4} \times \frac{2}{3})$ **C** $(3 \times \frac{2}{3}) + (3 \times \frac{3}{4})$

B $\frac{2}{3}(3 + \frac{3}{4})$ **D** $(\frac{2}{3} + \frac{3}{4}) \times (\frac{2}{3} + \frac{3}{4})$

24. Some frilled lizards grow to be 90 cm long. If $\frac{2}{3}$ of this length is its tail, how long is the tail?

Ⓒ **25. Writing to Explain** How can you use mental math to find $250 \times \frac{3}{10}$?

Lesson
8-2

Common
Core

This lesson reinforces
concepts and skills required
for Topic 9.

Estimating Products

How can you use compatible numbers to estimate products of fractions?

Sara has 14 postcards that are each $\frac{3}{8}$ foot wide.

Estimate the width of these postcards placed side by side.

Choose an Operation Multiply to find the width of the postcards side by side.

Each postcard is $\frac{3}{8}$ foot wide.

Another Example How can you use rounding to estimate products of fractions and mixed numbers?

Estimate $3\frac{3}{4} \times 14\frac{1}{2}$. Round to the nearest whole numbers.

$$3\frac{3}{4} \times 14\frac{1}{2}$$

$$\downarrow \qquad \downarrow$$

$$4 \times 15 = 60$$

So, $3\frac{3}{4} \times 14\frac{1}{2} \approx 60$.

Estimate $\frac{5}{6} \times 3\frac{7}{8}$. Round to the nearest whole numbers.

$$\frac{5}{6} \times 3\frac{7}{8}$$

$$\downarrow \qquad \downarrow$$

$$1 \times 4 = 4$$

So, $\frac{5}{6} \times 3\frac{7}{8} \approx 4$.

Guided Practice*

MATHEMATICAL
PRACTICES

Do you know HOW?

For **1** through **4**, estimate each product.

1. $\frac{3}{4} \times 13$

2. $24 \times \frac{5}{9}$

3. $19\frac{3}{4} \times \frac{1}{4}$

4. $4 \times 7\frac{4}{5}$

Do you UNDERSTAND?

5. Reason In the example at the top, why can you have two different estimates?

6. How can rounding to the nearest whole number help you estimate products?

Independent Practice

For **7** through **14**, estimate each product.

7. $\frac{1}{3} \times 25$

8. $60 \times \frac{5}{8}$

9. $\frac{5}{6} \times 20$

10. $7\frac{5}{6} \times 12\frac{1}{9}$

11. $15\frac{7}{8} \times 2\frac{1}{3}$

12. $\frac{11}{12} \times 8\frac{9}{10}$

13. $3\frac{1}{16} \times 20\frac{3}{4}$

14. $65\frac{5}{6} \times 3\frac{1}{8}$

*For another example, see Set B on page 198.

Use a compatible whole number to estimate $\frac{3}{8} \times 14$.

Change 14 to the nearest whole number that is compatible with the denominator of the fraction $\frac{3}{8}$.

$$\frac{3}{8} \times 14 \approx \frac{3}{8} \times 16$$

Think $\frac{1}{8} \times 16 = 2$, so $\frac{3}{8} \times 16 = 6$.

The width of 14 postcards would be about 6 feet.

Use a compatible benchmark fraction to estimate $\frac{3}{8} \times 14$.

$\frac{3}{8}$ is close to the benchmark fraction $\frac{1}{2}$, and the denominator of $\frac{1}{2}$ is compatible with 14.

$$\frac{3}{8} \times 14 \approx \frac{1}{2} \times 14, \text{ or } 7$$

The width of 14 postcards would be about 7 feet.

Problem Solving

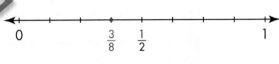 MATHEMATICAL PRACTICES

Emily's brother is returning home. Emily wants to make her brother a banner for a party. The table shows how much space is taken up by different types of letters and numerals. Use the table for **15** and **16**.

Type of lettering	Length (inches)
Capital letter	$\frac{3}{4}$
Lowercase letter	$\frac{5}{9}$

15. Estimate the length needed to spell out "PARTY" in all capital letters.

16. Estimate the length needed to spell out "party" in all lowercase letters.

17. Writing to Explain Mason says the answer to $33 \times \frac{2}{9}$ is $7\frac{1}{3}$. Is Mason's answer reasonable? Use an estimate to explain.

18. The Willis Tower in Chicago is about 1,400 feet tall. If you took an elevator about $\frac{1}{4}$ the way up the tower, how many feet high would you be?

19. Which inverse relationship could you use to get x alone on one side of the equation $x + 6\frac{5}{8} = 8\frac{1}{3}$?

  A Addition   **C** Multiplication

  B Subtraction   **D** Division

20. Reasonableness Use estimation to determine which of the following comparisons is true.

  A $5\frac{1}{5} \times 3\frac{3}{4} < 14$ **C** $7\frac{1}{3} \times 9\frac{7}{8} > 54$

  B $4\frac{4}{7} \times 4\frac{5}{9} < 16$ **D** $44\frac{2}{3} \times 2\frac{5}{7} > 150$

21. Think About the Structure Which of the following would best help you estimate $2\frac{6}{7} \times 4\frac{1}{3}$?

  A Change the mixed numbers to improper fractions.

  B Round the factors to the nearest whole numbers.

  C Draw a picture to show the problem.

  D Change the mixed numbers to decimals.

Lesson
8-3

Common
Core

This lesson reinforces
concepts and skills required
for Topic 9.

Multiplying Fractions

How do you find products of fractions?

Paige is planting $\frac{3}{4}$ of her garden with flowers, and $\frac{2}{3}$ of the flowers she plants will be morning-glories. What fraction of the garden will be planted with morning-glories?

Choose an Operation Multiply to find what fraction of the garden will be planted with morning-glories.

$\frac{3}{4}$ flowers

$\frac{2}{3}$ morning-glories

Another Example **How can you simplify before you multiply?**

Find $16 \times \frac{5}{12}$.

← Simplify before you multiply by finding the GCFs of any numerator and any denominator.

$\frac{^4\cancel{16}}{1} \times \frac{5}{\cancel{12}^3}$

← The GCF of 16 and 12 is 4. Divide 16 and 12 by this GCF. The GCF of 1 and 5 is 1. 1 and 5 are simplified.

$\frac{^4\cancel{16}}{1} \times \frac{5}{\cancel{12}^3} = \frac{20}{3} = 6\frac{2}{3}$ ← Multiply.

Guided Practice*  **MATHEMATICAL PRACTICES**

Do you know HOW?

In **1** through **4**, write a multiplication sentence for each picture.

1.   **2.**

$\frac{1}{2} \times \frac{1}{2} = \blacksquare$ $\frac{1}{4} \times \blacksquare = \blacksquare$

3.   **4.**

Do you UNDERSTAND?

5. Reason In the morning-glory example, look at the model for multiplying fractions that are both less than 1. Compare the size of the product to the size of each factor.

6. In Another Example, how would the answer to $16 \times \frac{5}{12}$ be different if you did not simplify before multiplying?

This model shows the meaning of multiplying $\frac{3}{4} \times \frac{2}{3}$.

Six of the 12 squares have overlapping colors.

$\frac{3}{4} \times \frac{2}{3} = \frac{6}{12}$

To find the product:

Multiply the numerators.

Multiply the denominators.

Simplify if possible.

$\frac{3}{4} \times \frac{2}{3} = \frac{3 \times 2}{4 \times 3}$

$= \frac{6}{12}$

$= \frac{1}{2}$

Use a calculator. Press:

3 [n] 4 [d] [×]

2 [n] 3 [d] [ENTER =]

[Simp] [ENTER =]

[Simp] [ENTER =]

Display:

Paige will plant $\frac{1}{2}$ of her garden in morning-glories.

Independent Practice

In **7** through **21**, find each product. Simplify if possible.

7. $54 \times \frac{5}{6}$

8. $\frac{4}{7} \times 56$

9. $16 \times \frac{3}{8}$

10. $\frac{5}{9} \times \frac{3}{5}$

11. $\frac{1}{2} \times \frac{3}{7}$

12. $\frac{2}{9} \times 72$

13. $\frac{3}{4} \times \frac{1}{4}$

14. $\frac{5}{11} \times \frac{33}{35}$

15. $18 \times \frac{7}{12}$

16. $\frac{5}{8} \times 26$

17. $3\frac{3}{5} \times 15$

18. $2\frac{1}{3} \times 21$

19. $\frac{5}{8} \times \frac{3}{10}$

20. $\frac{10}{12} \times \frac{3}{5}$

21. $18 \times \frac{3}{4}$

Problem Solving

MATHEMATICAL PRACTICES

22. Brianna lives $\frac{1}{3}$ mile from school. If she walks to and from school every day for 5 days, how far will she walk?

Ⓒ **23. Use Tools** Mr. Reed is planting peppers in $\frac{2}{5}$ of his garden, and $\frac{4}{5}$ of the peppers are sweet peppers. Draw a picture to show $\frac{2}{5} \times \frac{4}{5}$.

Ⓒ **24. Persevere** A display in a grocery store has 120 pieces of fruit. Apples make up $\frac{3}{5}$ of the display, and oranges make up $\frac{2}{5}$ of the display. If $\frac{1}{2}$ of the apples are green, how many green apples are there?

   A 24   **C** 48

   B 36   **D** 72

Ⓒ **25. Writing to Explain** Which is greater, $\frac{3}{8} \times \frac{1}{3}$ or $\frac{3}{8} \times \frac{1}{5}$? Explain how you know.

26. Adult horses have about 40 permanent teeth. If people have $\frac{4}{5}$ this number of permanent teeth, how many permanent teeth do people have?

   A 32   **C** 45

   B 40   **D** 50

Common Core

This lesson reinforces concepts and skills required for Topic 9.

Multiplying Mixed Numbers

How can you find the product of mixed numbers?

A small can of tomatoes weighs $7\frac{1}{3}$ ounces.

How much do $4\frac{1}{2}$ cans of tomatoes weigh?

Find $4\frac{1}{2} \times 7\frac{1}{3}$.

$7\frac{1}{3}$ ounces each

half-full

Another Example **How can you use the Distributive Property to multiply a whole number and a mixed number?**

Find $3 \times 4\frac{2}{15}$.

Step 1

Estimate:

$3 \times 4 = 12$

Step 2

Break apart the mixed number; use the Distributive Property:

$3 \times 4\frac{2}{15} = 3 \times (4 + \frac{2}{15})$

$\qquad = (3 \times 4) + (3 \times \frac{2}{15})$

Step 3

Multiply each part and add:

$= 12 + \frac{6}{15}$

$= 12\frac{6}{15}$

The answer, $12\frac{6}{15}$, is close to the estimate, 12, so the answer is reasonable.

Guided Practice*

MATHEMATICAL PRACTICES

Do you know HOW?

In **1** through **8**, find each product. Simplify if possible.

1. $3\frac{1}{12} \times 6$

2. $5\frac{1}{4} \times 1\frac{4}{7}$

3. $2\frac{5}{6} \times 9$

4. $6\frac{2}{3} \times 4\frac{7}{8}$

5. $5\frac{1}{6} \times 3\frac{3}{4}$

6. $5 \times 7\frac{3}{16}$

7. $1\frac{5}{8} \times 3\frac{4}{5}$

8. $4\frac{2}{9} \times 2\frac{1}{3}$

Do you UNDERSTAND?

9. **Communicate** How could you find $3 \times 4\frac{2}{7}$ without using the Distributive Property?

10. One case of $7\frac{1}{3}$-ounce cans of tomatoes contains 25 cans. How many ounces of tomatoes are in one case?

*For another example, see Set D on page 199.

Estimate. Use rounding.

$$4\tfrac{1}{2} \times 7\tfrac{1}{3}$$

$$\downarrow \quad \downarrow$$

$$5 \times 7 = 35$$

So, $4\tfrac{1}{2} \times 7\tfrac{1}{3} \approx 35$.

$$4\tfrac{1}{2} \times 7\tfrac{1}{3}$$ Then multiply. Write each mixed number as an improper fraction.

$$\downarrow \qquad \downarrow$$

$$\overset{3}{\underset{1}{\cancel{\tfrac{9}{2}}}} \times \overset{11}{\underset{1}{\cancel{\tfrac{22}{3}}}}$$ Look for common factors and simplify.

$$\tfrac{3}{1} \times \tfrac{11}{1} = \tfrac{33}{1} = 33$$

The answer is close to the estimate and reasonable.

So, $4\tfrac{1}{2}$ cans of tomatoes weigh 33 ounces.

Independent Practice

In **11** through **18**, find each product. Simplify if possible.

11. $5\tfrac{1}{3} \times 6\tfrac{3}{5}$ **12.** $2\tfrac{5}{8} \times 3\tfrac{4}{9}$ **13.** $7\tfrac{1}{3} \times 4\tfrac{9}{10}$ **14.** $8 \times 3\tfrac{3}{4}$

15. $1\tfrac{3}{8} \times 4\tfrac{5}{6}$ **16.** $5\tfrac{7}{9} \times 3\tfrac{1}{9}$ **17.** $6\tfrac{2}{3} \times 12$ **18.** $7\tfrac{4}{5} \times 2\tfrac{3}{7}$

In **19** through **22**, evaluate each expression for $R = 2\tfrac{1}{4}$.

19. $7\tfrac{1}{2}R$ **20.** $2\tfrac{1}{5}R$ **21.** $3\tfrac{1}{3}R$ **22.** $1\tfrac{2}{3}R$

Problem Solving

MATHEMATICAL PRACTICES

23. Melba's kitchen has tile in the shape of the polygon below. What type of polygon is this?

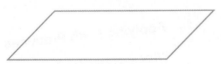

© **24. Model** Juanita's dog weighs $2\tfrac{1}{2}$ times as much as Caleb's dog. Caleb's dog weighs $8\tfrac{3}{4}$ pounds. Solve the equation $w = 8\tfrac{3}{4} \times 2\tfrac{1}{2}$ to find the weight, w, of Juanita's dog.

© **25. Model** Mrs. Damico's bookshelf has a set of 16 books on it. Each book is $1\tfrac{3}{8}$ inches wide. If the books take the full length of the shelf with no space left over, how long is the shelf?

     A $11\tfrac{7}{11}$ inches   **C** 20 inches

     B $17\tfrac{3}{8}$ inches   **D** 22 inches

© **26. Writing to Explain** Explain how to change a mixed number to a fraction.

© **27. Use Tools** Lakenda divided up her garden plot to have $\tfrac{1}{8}$ tomatoes, $\tfrac{1}{4}$ peppers, $\tfrac{1}{6}$ dill, $\tfrac{1}{6}$ basil, and the rest flowers. Draw a diagram of her garden.

Lesson
8-5
Common Core

This lesson reinforces concepts and skills required for Topic 9.

Problem Solving

Multiple-Step Problems

To solve some problems, you first need to answer one or more hidden questions.

How much larger is the area of the family room than the area of the kitchen?

Remember that you can find the area of a rectangular shape by multiplying its length times its width, or $A = \ell w$.

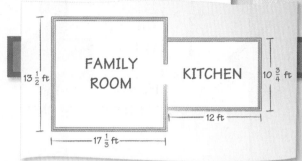

FAMILY ROOM

KITCHEN

$13\frac{1}{2}$ ft

$10\frac{3}{4}$ ft

12 ft

$17\frac{1}{3}$ ft

Guided Practice*

MATHEMATICAL PRACTICES

Do you know HOW?

1. **Persevere** A radio station has a daily vote. On Mondays, Wednesdays, and Fridays, you have $2\frac{2}{3}$ hours to vote. On Tuesdays and Thursdays, you have $1\frac{3}{4}$ hours. How many total hours in a week do you have to submit a vote?

   a What are the hidden questions?

   b Solve the problem.

Do you UNDERSTAND?

2. How can you find the hidden question in a problem?

3. **Write a Problem** Use a real-life situation to write a problem that contains a hidden question or hidden questions.

Independent Practice

MATHEMATICAL PRACTICES

4. **Persevere** Jenny writes $2\frac{2}{3}$ pages a day for a week. Heather writes 4 pages a day for a week. How many more pages does Heather write than Jenny in a week?

   a What are the hidden questions?

   b Solve the problem.

5. Mark has $1\frac{3}{4}$ hours of yardwork each day Monday through Thursday and $3\frac{1}{3}$ hours on Saturday. How many hours of work is this?

6. Baseball tickets cost $12.25 for adults and $8.75 for children under 13. Carlos' father took Carlos and three of his friends to the game. If Carlos and his friends are under 13, what was the total cost for the tickets?

Applying Math Practices

- What am I asked to find?
- What else can I try?
- How are quantities related?
- How can I explain my work?
- How can I use math to model the problem?
- Can I use tools to help?
- Is my work precise?
- Why does this work?
- How can I generalize?

*For another example, see Set E on page199.

What do I know?

The family room is $17\frac{1}{3}$ ft $\times$ $13\frac{1}{2}$ ft.
The kitchen is 12 ft $\times$ $10\frac{3}{4}$ ft.

What am I asked to find?

How much larger is the family room than the kitchen?

Hidden Question 1:
What is the area of the family room?

$A = 17\frac{1}{3} \times 13\frac{1}{2}$

$A = \overset{26}{\underset{1}{\cancel{\frac{52}{3}}}} \times \overset{9}{\underset{1}{\cancel{\frac{27}{2}}}} = 234$

Hidden Question 2:
What is the area of the kitchen?

$A = 12 \times 10\frac{3}{4}$

$A = \overset{3}{\frac{\cancel{12}}{1}} \times \overset{}{\underset{1}{\frac{43}{\cancel{4}}}} = 129$

$$234 - 129 = 105$$

The family room is 105 square feet larger than the kitchen.

In **7** and **8**, identify the hidden questions. Then solve the problem.

7. Francesca has $6.60. Which lunch can she buy? How much will she have left?

8. Eva's college has a choice of two meal plans. Plan A charges a flat fee of $250 per month for 60 meals and $3.25 for every meal over 60. Plan B charges $4.50 per meal with no fee. Which plan would be cheaper for 75 meals?

LUNCH AT THE DELI
Drinks: $1⁲⁵
Sandwich: $5⁵⁰

LUNCH at MANNY'S
Drinks: $2⁰⁰
Burritos: $4⁵⁰

Use the table at the right for **9** and **10**.

9. What is the difference in length between a Lion's Mane jellyfish and a Thimble jellyfish?

10. How many times as long as a Thimble jellyfish is a Lion's Mane jellyfish?

Jellyfish	Length
Thimble jellyfish	1 inch
Lion's Mane jellyfish	7 feet

Data

ⓒ **11. Be Precise** Samantha is measuring the snowfall in a snow gauge for her science project. The first week, she measured $3\frac{3}{4}$ inches of snow. The second week, she measured twice as much snow, and the third week, she measured half as much snow as the first week. It did not snow at all in the fourth week. How much snowfall did Samantha measure for the entire month? Explain.

12. The Golden Eagles are selling shirts to fund their team trip. Jeff, the captain of the team, had 60 shirts printed. Ryan, the co-captain of the team, had a different design printed on $5\frac{1}{3}$ times as many shirts. How many shirts does the Golden Eagles team now have?

A 60

B 300

C 360

D 380

1. An orchard of fruit trees is 6 acres in size. If $\frac{2}{3}$ of the orchard has apple trees, how many acres are planted with apple trees. (8-1)

A 2 acres

B 3 acres

C 4 acres

D 5 acres

2. A parking lot has 85 parking spaces. A parking attendant estimates that about $\frac{1}{3}$ of them are empty. Which is the best estimate of the number of empty spaces? (8-2)

A 20 empty spaces

B 30 empty spaces

C 40 empty spaces

D 42 empty spaces

3. Which of the following expressions is illustrated by the multiplication model pictured below? (8-3)

A $\frac{1}{12} \times \frac{1}{2}$

B $2 \times \frac{1}{2}$

C $\frac{1}{3} \times \frac{1}{2}$

D $\frac{1}{3} \times 2$

4. Identify the hidden question: Tomas's car gets 18 miles per gallon of gas. The gas tank in Tomas's car will hold 15 gallons. Can Tomas make an 800-mile trip on 3 tanks of gasoline? (8-5)

A How far can Tomas's car travel on one tank of gas?

B How long will the trip take?

C How much gasoline is in Tomas's gas tank before the trip?

D What is the price of gasoline?

5. What is the product of $15 \times \frac{2}{5}$? (8-1)

A $15\frac{2}{5}$

B 5

C 6

D 30

6. The student desks in Mrs. Miller's room are $2\frac{1}{4}$ feet wide. If she plans to arrange 4 desks as shown, estimate the approximate width of the 4 desks altogether. (8-2)

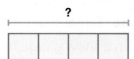

A 8 feet

B 14 feet

C 12 feet

D 15 feet

7. Which of the following can be used to find $\frac{1}{2} \times 6\frac{2}{7}$? (8-4)

A $(\frac{1}{2} + 6) \times (\frac{1}{2} + \frac{2}{7})$

B $(6 + \frac{1}{2}) \times (6 + \frac{2}{7})$

C $(6 \times \frac{1}{2}) + (6 \times \frac{2}{7})$

D $(\frac{1}{2} \times 6) + (\frac{1}{2} \times \frac{2}{7})$

8. The Cougar volleyball team won $\frac{3}{4}$ of their games this year and $\frac{2}{3}$ of their games last year. They play 24 games each year. How many more games did they win this year than last year? (8-5)

A 2 games

B 4 games

C 16 games

D 18 games

9. Ben used $2\frac{1}{3}$ gallons of paint to paint his bedroom. He needs $1\frac{1}{2}$ times as much to paint the living room. How much paint does Ben need to paint the living room? (8-4)

A $2\frac{1}{6}$ gallons

B $3\frac{1}{6}$ gallons

C $3\frac{1}{3}$ gallons

D $3\frac{1}{2}$ gallons

10. What is $\frac{9}{14} \times \frac{7}{10}$? (8-3)

A $\frac{16}{140}$

B $\frac{9}{20}$

C $\frac{9}{10}$

D $\frac{45}{49}$

11. A meatloaf weighs $\frac{7}{8}$ pounds. If $\frac{2}{3}$ of the meatloaf is ground beef, how much is ground beef? (8-3)

A $\frac{9}{24}$ pounds

B $\frac{7}{12}$ pounds

C $\frac{14}{12}$ pounds

D $\frac{14}{11}$ pounds

12. Which of the following uses a compatible whole number to find an estimate of $\frac{3}{4} \times 47$? (8-2)

A $\frac{3}{4} \times 48$

B $\frac{3}{4} \times 42$

C $\frac{3}{4} \times 45$

D $\frac{4}{3} \times 42$

13. What is $\frac{4}{5}$ of 15? (8-1)

A $18\frac{3}{4}$

B 7

C 11

D 12

Set A, pages 186–187

Ⓒ **INTERVENTION**

You can use a model to multiply $6 \times \frac{2}{3}$.

6 is divisible by 3, so divide 6 by 3.

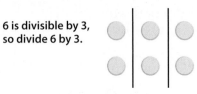

$6 \div 3 = 2$ and $\frac{1}{3} \times 6 = 2$.

$\frac{2}{3} \times 6 = 2(\frac{1}{3} \times 6)$

$\qquad = 2(2)$ or 4.

Remember that if the whole number factor is divisible by the denominator of the fraction factor, you can divide first and then multiply.

1. $\frac{2}{3} \times 9$ 2. $\frac{1}{3} \times 12$

3. $\frac{2}{7} \times 14$ 4. $\frac{2}{5}$ of 20

5. $\frac{1}{20} \times 400$ 6. $\frac{3}{16} \times 48$

7. $\frac{3}{8}$ of 4,000   8. $\frac{1}{20}$ of 10,000

Set B, pages 188–189

Estimate $5\frac{1}{3} \times 4\frac{5}{8}$ using rounding and compatible numbers.

Round to the nearest whole numbers:

$$5\frac{1}{3} \times 4\frac{5}{8}$$
$$\downarrow \quad \downarrow$$
$$5 \times 5 = 25$$

Use compatible numbers:

$$5\frac{1}{3} \times 4\frac{5}{8}$$
$$\downarrow \quad \downarrow$$
$$5 \times 5 = 25$$

Using rounding or compatible numbers sometimes gives the same answer.

Remember that you can use the benchmark fraction $\frac{1}{2}$ as a compatible number for fractions close to $\frac{1}{2}$.

1. $\frac{8}{9} \times \frac{5}{8}$ 2. $24\frac{7}{10} \times 4$

3. $3\frac{5}{6} \times 8\frac{2}{7}$ 4. $27 \times 3\frac{2}{5}$

5. $34\frac{3}{8} \times 12\frac{1}{5}$ 6. $3\frac{11}{12} \times 4\frac{4}{5}$

7. $7\frac{3}{8} \times 3\frac{1}{4}$ 8. $79\frac{3}{4} \times 4\frac{7}{9}$

Set C, pages 190–191

Find $\frac{3}{8} \times \frac{4}{9}$.

Multiply the numerators and denominators.

$$\frac{3}{8} \times \frac{4}{9} = \frac{3 \times 4}{8 \times 9} = \frac{12}{72}$$

Simplify if possible. Divide the numerator and denominator by their GCF. The GCF of 12 and 72 is 12.

$$\frac{12}{72} = \frac{12 \div 12}{72 \div 12} = \frac{1}{6}$$

Remember that you can also simplify before multiplying by using the GCFs of any numerator and any denominator.

1. $\frac{5}{6} \times \frac{3}{5}$ 2. $\frac{2}{7} \times \frac{1}{8}$

3. $\frac{2}{3} \times 45$ 4. $\frac{1}{9} \times \frac{4}{7}$

5. $\frac{3}{4} \times \frac{8}{9}$ 6. $\frac{5}{8} \times 32$

7. $\frac{3}{12} \times 20$ 8. $\frac{1}{3} \times \frac{12}{15}$

Find $5\frac{1}{3} \times 2\frac{7}{8}$.

Write the mixed numbers as improper fractions.

$$5\frac{1}{3} \times 2\frac{7}{8} = \frac{16}{3} \times \frac{23}{8}$$

Look for common factors and simplify.

$$\frac{\overset{2}{\cancel{16}}}{3} \times \frac{23}{\underset{1}{\cancel{8}}}$$

Multiply the numerators and denominators. Then write the improper fraction as a mixed number.

$$\frac{2}{3} \times \frac{23}{1} = \frac{46}{3} = 15\frac{1}{3}$$

Remember that when changing a mixed number to an improper fraction, the denominator does not change.

Find each product. Simplify if possible.

1. $3\frac{1}{5} \times 2\frac{1}{4}$ 2. $4\frac{1}{6} \times 3\frac{3}{5}$

3. $1\frac{3}{8} \times 4\frac{2}{3}$ 4. $5\frac{2}{3} \times 7\frac{1}{2}$

5. $3\frac{1}{6} \times 2\frac{2}{9}$ 6. $6\frac{3}{4} \times 3\frac{3}{7}$

7. $8\frac{1}{4} \times 12$ 8. $1\frac{2}{5} \times 2\frac{1}{4}$

9. $5\frac{2}{5} \times 1\frac{2}{3}$ 10. $4\frac{5}{8} \times 1\frac{7}{9}$

Find and answer hidden questions in multiple-step word problems.

A school sells sweatshirts for $30, T-shirts for $15, and caps for $12. At sports games, the school sells all merchandise for half price. How much money could you save if you bought a sweatshirt, T-shirt, and cap at a sports game?

Hidden Question 1: What is the cost of the items at full price?

You know the regular price of each item.

$30 + 15 + 12 = \$57$

Hidden Question 2: What is the cost of the items at the discounted prices?

$$(30 \times \tfrac{1}{2}) + (15 \times \tfrac{1}{2}) + (12 \times \tfrac{1}{2})$$

$$= 15 + 7.50 + 6 = \$28.50$$

Subtract the totals to find how much you would save by buying the items at a sports game.

$57 - 28.50 = \$28.50$

You could save $28.50.

Remember to find and answer the hidden questions to solve multiple-step problems.

For **1** and **2**, identify the hidden questions, and then solve each problem.

1. A store sells 40 sandwiches on Wednesday and 45 on Thursday. On Friday, it sells as many sandwiches as it sold on Wednesday and Thursday. How many sandwiches were sold from Wednesday to Friday?

2. A DJ for the school dance plans to play dance music for two hours. She has 20 requests for songs, and each song plays for $3\frac{1}{2}$ minutes. If she plays all of the requests, how much time will she have to play other songs?

Dividing Fractions and Mixed Numbers

1 How far can a sloth move in an hour? You will find out in Lesson 9-2.

How much fuel does it take to move the space shuttle from its hangar to the Vehicle Assembly Building? You will find out in Lesson 9-6.

2

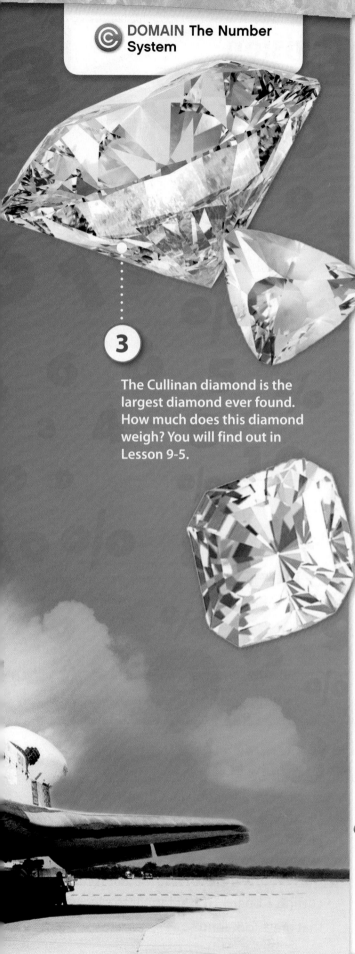

③

The Cullinan diamond is the largest diamond ever found. How much does this diamond weigh? You will find out in Lesson 9-5.

Review What You Know!

Vocabulary

Choose the best term from the box.

- simplest form
- prime number
- Distributive Property

1. When the only common factor of the numerator and denominator of a fraction is 1, then the fraction is in __?__.

2. Use the __?__ to break apart numbers and make it easier to compute products mentally.

3. A(n) __?__ is a whole number greater than 1 having exactly two factors, 1 and itself.

Solving Equations

Solve each equation.

4. $g \div 7 = 45$ 5. $r + 312 = 487$

6. $6m = 252$ 7. $538 = a - 108$

Mixed Numbers

Write each mixed number as an improper fraction.

8. $8\frac{1}{3}$ 9. $5\frac{3}{5}$ 10. $2\frac{5}{8}$

Look for a Pattern

©**11. Writing to Explain** What is the next figure in the series below? Explain the pattern.

ⓒ
**Common
Core**

6.NS.1 Interpret and
compute quotients of
fractions, and solve word
problems involving division
of fractions by fractions,
e.g., by using visual fraction
models and equations to
represent the problem....

Understanding Division of Fractions

How can you model division of fractions?

Mr. Roberts uses pieces of wood that are each $\frac{3}{4}$ of a foot long for a set of shelves he is making. How many pieces of wood can he get from a board that is 3 feet long?

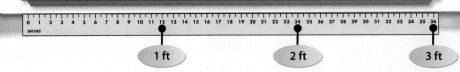

| 1 ft | 2 ft | 3 ft |

Other Examples

Dividing a Fraction by a Whole Number

Find $\frac{1}{2} \div 3$.
Use a picture to show $\frac{1}{2}$.

| **1**
2 | |

Divide $\frac{1}{2}$ into 3 equal parts.
$\frac{1}{2} \div 3$

Each part contains $\frac{1}{6}$ of the whole.
So, $\frac{1}{2} \div 3 = \frac{1}{6}$.

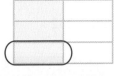

Dividing a Fraction by a Fraction

Find $\frac{3}{4} \div \frac{1}{4}$.

Use a number line to show $\frac{3}{4}$.

$0 \qquad\qquad \frac{3}{4} \quad 1$

Divide $\frac{3}{4}$ into $\frac{1}{4}$ parts. There are 3 parts.

$0 \qquad\qquad \frac{3}{4} \quad 1$

So, $\frac{3}{4} \div \frac{1}{4} = 3$.

Guided Practice*

ⓒ **MATHEMATICAL PRACTICES**

Do you know HOW?

Write a division sentence to represent each.

1.

$0 \qquad 1 \qquad 2 \qquad 3 \qquad 4$

2.
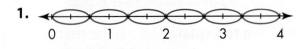

Do you UNDERSTAND?

ⓒ **3. Reason** When you divide a whole number by a fraction less than 1, will the quotient be more or less than the whole number?

4. How many pieces would you get from cutting a board 10 feet long into pieces that are $\frac{2}{3}$ foot long?

 For another example, see Set A on page 218.

One Way

Think How many $\frac{3}{4}$s are in 3?

Use a number line to show 3 feet.

Divide it into $\frac{3}{4}$-foot parts.

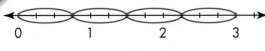

0   1   2   3

So, $3 \div \frac{3}{4} = 4$.

When the divisor is less than 1, the quotient is larger than the dividend.

Another Way

Think of division as repeated subtraction.

Rewrite 3 as an improper fraction, $\frac{12}{4}$.

Then, subtract $\frac{3}{4}$ repeatedly:

$$\begin{array}{r} \frac{12}{4} \\ -\frac{3}{4} \\ \hline \frac{9}{4} \end{array} \qquad \begin{array}{r} \frac{9}{4} \\ -\frac{3}{4} \\ \hline \frac{6}{4} \end{array} \qquad \begin{array}{r} \frac{6}{4} \\ -\frac{3}{4} \\ \hline \frac{3}{4} \end{array} \qquad \begin{array}{r} \frac{3}{4} \\ -\frac{3}{4} \\ \hline 0 \end{array}$$

Mr. Roberts can get 4 pieces.

Independent Practice

Leveled Practice In **5** and **6**, complete each division sentence using the models provided.

5. $6 \div \frac{1}{2} = \blacksquare$

0   1   2   3   4   5   6

6. $\frac{2}{3} \div 3 = \blacksquare$

In **7** through **10**, find each quotient. Simplify if possible.

Tip *Draw a model to help you visualize.*

7. $\frac{6}{7} \div \frac{3}{7}$

8. $\frac{7}{8} \div 3$

9. $8 \div \frac{4}{5}$

10. $\frac{5}{9} \div 10$

Problem Solving

MATHEMATICAL PRACTICES

11. Keiko divided $\frac{3}{8}$ gallon of milk evenly into 5 glasses. Draw a picture to find what fraction of a gallon is in each glass.

© 12. Writing to Explain Without solving, explain how you can compare the quotient of $\frac{6}{7} \div \frac{1}{2}$ to $\frac{6}{7}$.

13. A car trip is 6 hours long. Every $\frac{2}{3}$ of an hour, Brian changes the radio station. Draw a picture to find how many times Brian changes the station during the trip.

© 14. Reason A regular polygon has a perimeter of 8 units. If each side measures $\frac{4}{5}$ unit, how many sides does the polygon have?

15. In a relay race, each runner on a team runs one part of a 1-mile racecourse.

a If each runner runs $\frac{1}{4}$ mile, how many relay runners must be on a team?

b If each runner runs $\frac{1}{3}$ mile, how many runners must be on a team?

© 16. Think About the Structure Which division sentence is shown by this model?

0   1   2   3

A $\frac{3}{8} \div 3$

B $3 \div \frac{3}{8}$

C $8 \div \frac{3}{5}$

D $\frac{3}{5} \div 8$

Lesson
9-2

© Common Core

6.NS.1 Interpret and compute quotients of fractions, and solve word problems involving division of fractions by fractions, e.g., by using visual fraction models and equations to represent the problem....

Dividing a Whole Number by a Fraction

How can you find the quotient of a whole number and a fraction?

Look at the division and multiplication sentences at the right. What is the pattern?

Use the pattern to find the quotient for $4 \div \frac{2}{3}$.

$8 \div \frac{4}{1} = 2$	$8 \times \frac{1}{4} = 2$
$6 \div \frac{2}{1} = 3$	$6 \times \frac{1}{2} = 3$
$5 \div \frac{1}{2} = 10$	$5 \times \frac{2}{1} = 10$
$3 \div \frac{3}{4} = 4$	$3 \times \frac{4}{3} = 4$

Guided Practice*

Do you know HOW?

In **1** through **4**, find the reciprocal of each fraction or whole number.

1. $\frac{3}{5}$

2. $\frac{1}{6}$

3. 9

4. $\frac{7}{4}$

In **5** and **6**, find each quotient. Simplify, if possible.

5. $6 \div \frac{2}{3}$

6. $12 \div \frac{3}{8}$

Do you UNDERSTAND?

7. Is $4 \div \frac{3}{2}$ the same as $4 \div \frac{2}{3}$? Explain.

8. Explain how you would find the reciprocal of a whole number.

© **9. Reason** In the table above, how does the quotient compare to the dividend when the divisor is a fraction less than 1?

Independent Practice

Leveled Practice In **10** through **17**, find the reciprocal of each number.

10. $\frac{3}{10}$

11. 6

12. $\frac{1}{15}$

13. 3

14. $\frac{7}{12}$

15. $\frac{11}{5}$

16. 12

17. $\frac{22}{5}$

Find each quotient. Simplify, if possible.

18. $4 \div \frac{4}{7}$

19. $2 \div \frac{3}{8}$

20. $5 \div \frac{2}{3}$

21. $9 \div \frac{4}{5}$

22. $36 \div \frac{3}{4}$

23. $7 \div \frac{3}{4}$

24. $18 \div \frac{2}{3}$

25. $20 \div \frac{1}{2}$

26. $9 \div \frac{3}{5}$

27. $5 \div \frac{2}{7}$

28. $12 \div \frac{1}{3}$

29. $8 \div \frac{3}{8}$

DIGITAL   Animated Glossary
www.pearsonsuccessnet.com

*For another example, see Set B on page 218.

The pattern in the table shows a rule for dividing by a fraction.

> Dividing by a fraction is the same as multiplying by its reciprocal.

Two numbers whose product is 1 are called reciprocals of each other. If a nonzero number is named as a fraction $\frac{a}{b}$, then its reciprocal can be named $\frac{b}{a}$.

$$\frac{2}{3} \times \frac{3}{2} = 1 \quad \longleftarrow \quad \text{The reciprocal of } \frac{2}{3} \text{ is } \frac{3}{2}.$$

Find $4 \div \frac{2}{3}$.

Rewrite the problem as a multiplication problem. Simplify, then multiply.

$$4 \div \frac{2}{3} = 4 \times \frac{3}{2}$$
$$= \frac{\overset{2}{\cancel{4}}}{1} \times \frac{3}{\cancel{2}_1}$$
$$= \frac{6}{1} = 6$$

$$4 \div \frac{2}{3} = 6$$

Problem Solving

MATHEMATICAL PRACTICES

© **Persevere** Use this information for **30** and **31**.

A tortoise can move 300 ft in $\frac{1}{3}$ h.

A snail can move 40 ft in $\frac{1}{4}$ h.

A sloth can move 50 ft in $\frac{1}{8}$ h.

30. About how far could each animal move in one hour?

31. Which animal would move the farthest in 3 hours traveling at its maximum speed?

© **32. Writing to Explain** A bowl of soup holds 7 ounces. If a spoonful holds $\frac{1}{6}$ ounce, how many spoonfuls are in 3 bowls of soup? Explain.

33. A recording of the current weather conditions lasts $\frac{3}{4}$ minute. How many times could the recording be played in 1 hour?

34. How many $\frac{1}{4}$-pound burgers can Danny make with 12 pounds of ground turkey?

© **35. Use Tools** Draw a picture or number line to show $3 \div \frac{1}{3}$.

36. Valeria bought a 9 ft length of ribbon from which she wants to cut $\frac{2}{3}$-ft pieces. How many $\frac{2}{3}$-ft pieces can she cut?

37. Each health book is $\frac{3}{4}$ inch thick. If Mrs. Menes's bookshelf is 2 feet wide, how many books can she fit on the shelf?

38. In the number 589,745,162, what is the digit in the ten millions place?

   A 5   **B** 8   **C** 9   **D** 7

39. Trey is buying 8 notebooks for $1.25 each. How much money will he need?

Lesson
9-3

Common
Core

6.NS.1 Interpret and
compute quotients of
fractions, and solve word
problems involving division
of fractions by fractions,
e.g., by using visual fraction
models and equations to
represent the problem....

Dividing Fractions

How can you find the quotient of two fractions?

Andrew has $\frac{3}{4}$ of a gallon of lemonade. He wants to pour it into $\frac{1}{6}$-gallon containers. How many containers can he fill?

Choose an Operation Divide to find the number of containers.

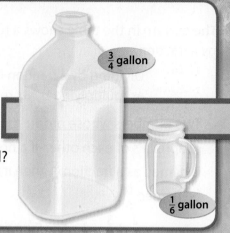

$\frac{3}{4}$ gallon

$\frac{1}{6}$ gallon

Guided Practice*

MATHEMATICAL
PRACTICES

Do you know HOW?

In **1** through **4**, find each quotient. Simplify, if possible.

1. $\frac{3}{4} \div \frac{2}{3}$

2. $\frac{3}{12} \div \frac{1}{8}$

3. $\frac{1}{2} \div \frac{4}{5}$

4. $\frac{7}{10} \div \frac{2}{5}$

Do you UNDERSTAND?

5. **Reason** In the example above, did it change the answer to simplify before multiplying?

6. In the example at the top, how many $\frac{1}{8}$-gallon containers could Andrew fill?

Independent Practice

In **7** through **22**, find each quotient. Simplify, if possible.

7. $\frac{1}{2} \div \frac{1}{2}$

8. $\frac{1}{2} \div \frac{1}{4}$

9. $\frac{7}{8} \div \frac{1}{8}$

10. $\frac{2}{3} \div \frac{3}{4}$

11. $\frac{1}{9} \div \frac{1}{5}$

12. $\frac{2}{7} \div \frac{1}{2}$

13. $\frac{2}{9} \div \frac{4}{5}$

14. $\frac{1}{2} \div \frac{2}{4}$

15. $\frac{3}{8} \div \frac{1}{9}$

16. $\frac{2}{3} \div \frac{1}{4}$

17. $\frac{2}{5} \div \frac{1}{8}$

18. $\frac{5}{6} \div \frac{2}{3}$

19. $\frac{6}{7} \div \frac{1}{3}$

20. $\frac{7}{8} \div \frac{1}{2}$

21. $\frac{12}{14} \div \frac{14}{12}$

22. $\frac{5}{14} \div \frac{4}{7}$

In **23** through **26**, evaluate each expression for $x = \frac{5}{6}$.

23. $x \div \frac{3}{9}$

24. $\frac{10}{13} \div x$

25. $\frac{5}{8} \div x$

26. $x \div \frac{9}{10}$

For another example, see Set B on page 218.

Step 1

Find $\frac{3}{4} \div \frac{1}{6}$.

To divide by a fraction, rewrite the problem as a multiplication problem using the reciprocal of the divisor.

$\frac{6}{1}$ is the reciprocal of $\frac{1}{6}$.

$$\frac{3}{4} \div \frac{1}{6} = \frac{3}{4} \times \frac{6}{1}$$

Step 2

Look for common factors to simplify. Then multiply.

$$\frac{3}{\underset{2}{\cancel{4}}} \times \frac{\cancel{6}^{3}}{1} = \frac{9}{2}$$

$$\frac{9}{2} = 4\frac{1}{2}$$

Andrew can fill 4 containers, plus $\frac{1}{2}$ of an additional container.

Problem Solving

MATHEMATICAL
PRACTICES

27. Tomas tiled $\frac{1}{2}$ of his bathroom floor in blue. He tiled $\frac{2}{3}$ of the remaining bathroom floor in green. He used white tiles for the rest of the bathroom. How much of the bathroom had white tiles? Use the picture to help find your solution.

© 28. Persevere Luis has an 8-cup bag of trail mix to share. If he gives 9 friends $\frac{2}{3}$ of a cup each, how much trail mix does he have left?

29. Which fraction has the greatest value?

A $\frac{7}{12}$ C $\frac{3}{4}$

B $\frac{2}{3}$ D $\frac{7}{9}$

© 30. Model Write an equation for each statement, then solve.

  a One-half of a watermelon was shared among 4 people. How much watermelon did each person get?

  b A recipe for cookies calls for $\frac{1}{4}$ cup of almonds. If Sara has $1\frac{1}{2}$ cups of almonds, how many recipes of cookies can she make?

  c Reena runs a quarter of a mile and then walks one-eighth mile. If she continues this pattern 10 times, how far will she run?

31. A restaurant sells 9 specials for every 6 full-price meals sold. At this rate, how many specials will have been sold when 30 full-price meals have been sold? Make a table to help you find your solution.

© 32. Writing to Explain Write an explanation to a friend telling him or her how to find $\frac{3}{4} \div \frac{2}{3}$.

33. Simplify the following expressions.

  a $2 + (10 - \frac{6}{3})$

  b $5(6 + 3)$

  c $\frac{10}{(25 - 5)}$

Common
Core

6.NS.1 Interpret and
compute quotients of
fractions, and solve word
problems involving division
of fractions by fractions,
e.g., by using visual fraction
models and equations to
represent the problem....

Estimating Quotients

How can you estimate the quotient of mixed numbers?

Lillian and her friends can hike an average of $3\frac{5}{8}$ miles per hour. About how many hours will it take them to hike $15\frac{5}{6}$ miles of the trail?

Estimate the quotient $15\frac{5}{6} \div 3\frac{5}{8}$ to find out.

APPALACHIAN TRAIL

$15\frac{5}{6}$ miles

Other Examples

Estimate $55\frac{1}{3} \div 6\frac{1}{4}$.

Use compatible numbers.

$$55\frac{1}{3} \div 6\frac{1}{4}$$

$$\downarrow \qquad \downarrow$$

$$54 \div 6 = 9$$

$$55\frac{1}{3} \div 6\frac{1}{4} \approx 9$$

Estimate $7\frac{3}{4} \div 1\frac{7}{8}$.

Use rounding.

$$7\frac{3}{4} \div 1\frac{7}{8}$$

$$\downarrow \qquad \downarrow$$

$$8 \div 2 = 4$$

$$7\frac{3}{4} \div 1\frac{7}{8} \approx 4$$

Estimate $26\frac{3}{4} \div 5\frac{1}{4}$.

Use compatible numbers.

$$26\frac{3}{4} \div 5\frac{1}{4}$$

$$\downarrow \qquad \downarrow$$

$$25 \div 5 = 5$$

$$26\frac{3}{4} \div 5\frac{1}{4} \approx 5$$

Guided Practice*

 MATHEMATICAL PRACTICES

Do you know HOW?

In **1** through **4**, estimate the quotient.

1. $35\frac{1}{3} \div 6\frac{2}{3}$

2. $24\frac{5}{8} \div 5\frac{4}{7}$

3. $11\frac{3}{8} \div 3\frac{7}{9}$

4. $26\frac{1}{3} \div 8\frac{3}{4}$

Do you UNDERSTAND?

© **5. Communicate** In the example above, why do you round $7\frac{3}{4}$ to 8? Explain.

© **6. Reason** Estimate the amount of time it would take to hike $20\frac{1}{2}$ miles.

Independent Practice

In **7** through **14**, estimate each quotient.

7. $40\frac{9}{10} \div 20\frac{1}{6}$

8. $35\frac{2}{9} \div 5\frac{8}{9}$

9. $3\frac{7}{8} \div 1\frac{1}{5}$

10. $21\frac{2}{3} \div 6\frac{4}{5}$

11. $13\frac{5}{8} \div 2\frac{1}{3}$

12. $87\frac{4}{7} \div 7\frac{5}{7}$

13. $59\frac{3}{8} \div 11\frac{1}{9}$

14. $18\frac{1}{5} \div 1\frac{5}{9}$

For another example, see Set C on page 218.

One Way

Round to the nearest whole number by comparing the fractions to $\frac{1}{2}$.

$15\frac{5}{6} \div 3\frac{5}{8}$ Both $\frac{5}{6}$ and $\frac{5}{8}$ are greater than $\frac{1}{2}$, so round up to the nearest whole number.

$16 \div 4 = 4$

So, $15\frac{5}{6} \div 3\frac{5}{8} \approx 4$.

It will take Lillian and her friends about 4 hours to finish their hike.

Another Way

Use compatible numbers.

$15\frac{5}{6} \div 3\frac{5}{8}$

$15\frac{5}{6}$ and $3\frac{5}{8}$ are close to the compatible numbers 16 and 4.

$16 \div 4 = 4$

So, $15\frac{5}{6} \div 3\frac{5}{8} \approx 4$.

It will take Lillian and her friends about 4 hours to finish their hike.

In **15** through **22**, estimate each quotient.

15. $32\frac{1}{3} \div 7\frac{2}{3}$

16. $40\frac{1}{4} \div 5\frac{1}{9}$

17. $23\frac{4}{5} \div 11\frac{2}{3}$

18. $49\frac{6}{7} \div 4\frac{2}{3}$

19. $27\frac{2}{3} \div 13\frac{5}{6}$

20. $99\frac{2}{9} \div 4\frac{3}{4}$

21. $74\frac{7}{8} \div 24\frac{2}{5}$

22. $55\frac{2}{3} \div 27\frac{5}{6}$

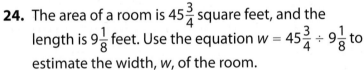

Problem Solving

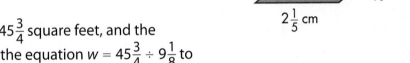

MATHEMATICAL PRACTICES

23. What is the perimeter of the parallelogram at right?

$1\frac{3}{10}$ cm

$2\frac{1}{5}$ cm

24. The area of a room is $45\frac{3}{4}$ square feet, and the length is $9\frac{1}{8}$ feet. Use the equation $w = 45\frac{3}{4} \div 9\frac{1}{8}$ to estimate the width, w, of the room.

25. Alex is driving to his school reunion 30.5 miles away. He stopped for gas 4.3 miles after he started driving. Then he drove 15.2 miles to the first rest stop. How many miles does he have left to drive to his reunion?

26. Use estimation to determine which of the following comparisons is true.

A $13\frac{5}{7} \div 2\frac{1}{3} > 9$ **C** $39\frac{8}{9} \div 3\frac{7}{8} > 9$

B $12\frac{1}{2} \div 4\frac{1}{2} > 6$ **D** $19\frac{4}{5} \div 9\frac{8}{9} > 11$

© **27. Reason** On Monday, John hiked for $24\frac{1}{2}$ miles along the Appalachian Trail. On Tuesday, he covered only $6\frac{3}{4}$ miles. About how many times farther did John hike on Monday than on Tuesday?

© **28. Writing to Explain** Donna has a $25\frac{1}{2}$-foot roll of crepe paper for streamers. Explain how you would estimate the number of $1\frac{3}{4}$-foot streamers Donna can make.

29. Wanda rents a car for 3 days for $18.95 per day and $0.15 per mile. If Wanda traveled 350 miles, what is her total cost, excluding tax?

© **30. Model** Write an equation to show how many quarters are in $10.

Common Core

6.NS.1 Interpret and compute quotients of fractions, and solve word problems involving division of fractions by fractions, e.g., by using visual fraction models and equations to represent the problem....

Dividing Mixed Numbers

How can you find the quotient of mixed numbers?

Damon has $37\frac{1}{2}$ inches of space on his car bumper that he wants to use for bumper stickers. How many short bumper stickers can he fit side by side on his car bumper?

Find $37\frac{1}{2} \div 6\frac{1}{4}$.

Bumper Stickers	Type	Length
DRIVE!	Short	$6\frac{1}{4}$"
MUSIC	Medium	$10\frac{3}{4}$"
basketball	Long	15 "

Guided Practice*

MATHEMATICAL PRACTICES

Do you know HOW?

In **1** through **6**, find each quotient. Simplify, if possible.

 Remember to estimate.

1. $18 \div 3\frac{2}{3}$

2. $4\frac{1}{3} \div 2\frac{4}{5}$

3. $5 \div 6\frac{2}{5}$

4. $6\frac{5}{9} \div 1\frac{7}{9}$

5. $7\frac{2}{3} \div 5\frac{1}{9}$

6. $3\frac{3}{7} \div 5\frac{6}{7}$

Do you UNDERSTAND?

7. Communicate When dividing mixed numbers, why is it important to estimate the quotient first?

8. How many medium bumper stickers could fit on a 76-inch-long bumper?

Independent Practice

Leveled Practice In **9** through **20**, find each quotient. Simplify if possible.

9. $1\frac{3}{8} \div 4\frac{1}{8}$

10. $2\frac{5}{6} \div 6\frac{1}{3}$

11. $3\frac{1}{4} \div 4\frac{2}{7}$

12. $5\frac{1}{2} \div 7\frac{2}{5}$

13. $1 \div 8\frac{5}{9}$

14. $3\frac{5}{6} \div 9\frac{5}{6}$

15. $4\frac{1}{3} \div 3\frac{1}{4}$

16. $8 \div 2\frac{2}{3}$

17. $6\frac{3}{4} \div 1\frac{7}{8}$

18. $2\frac{5}{8} \div 13$

19. $3\frac{6}{7} \div 6\frac{3}{4}$

20. $9\frac{7}{9} \div 8\frac{1}{4}$

In **21** through **28**, evaluate each expression for $n = 2\frac{1}{5}$.

21. $8\frac{1}{2} \div n$

22. $n \div 4$

23. $20\frac{4}{5} \div n$

24. $n \div \frac{5}{8}$

25. $3\frac{4}{5} \div n$

26. $15 \div n$

27. $n \div 2\frac{1}{5}$

28. $n \div 2\frac{4}{9}$

For another example, see Set D on page 219.

Estimate using compatible numbers.

$$37\frac{1}{2} \div 6\frac{1}{4}$$

↓ ↓

$$36 \div 6 = 6$$

So, $37\frac{1}{2} \times 6\frac{1}{4} \approx 6$.

Write each mixed number as an improper fraction.

$$37\frac{1}{2} \div 6\frac{1}{4} = \frac{75}{2} \div \frac{25}{4}$$

$$\frac{75}{2} \times \frac{4}{25}$$ ← Use the reciprocal of $\frac{25}{4}$ to write a multiplication problem.

$$\overset{3}{\underset{1}{\cancel{75}}} \times \overset{2}{\underset{1}{\cancel{4}}} = 6$$

Damon can put 6 short bumper stickers on his car bumper.

Problem Solving

 MATHEMATICAL PRACTICES

Ⓒ **29. Writing to Explain** Explain why $3\frac{7}{8} \div \frac{1}{8}$ is greater than $3\frac{7}{8} \times \frac{1}{8}$.

30. How many $\frac{3}{4}$-ft pieces can you cut from a $6\frac{1}{2}$-ft ribbon?

31. Which number is its own reciprocal? Explain.

32. If $9 \times \frac{x}{6} = 9 \div \frac{x}{6}$, then what does x equal? Explain.

Ⓒ **33. Persevere** Which expression would you use to find how many halves there are in $6\frac{3}{8}$?

A $\frac{1}{2} \times 6\frac{3}{8}$ **C** $\frac{1}{2} \div 6\frac{3}{8}$

B $6\frac{3}{8} \div \frac{1}{2}$ **D** $6\frac{3}{8} \div 2$

34. Evaluate each expression if $T = \frac{2}{3}$.

a $\frac{1}{2}T$ **b** $\frac{8}{9} + T$ **c** $2 \div T$

Ⓒ **35. Reason** Bus 26 takes $2\frac{3}{4}$ hours to complete its route. Estimate how many times Bus 26 can complete its route in 16 hours.

36. The biggest diamond ever found weighed $1\frac{1}{2}$ pounds uncut. If this diamond were cut into 3 equal pieces, how much would each piece weigh?

37. The large room is twice as long as the smaller room.

a How long is the larger room?

b If the length of the smaller room were divided into two equal parts, how long would each part be?

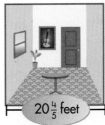
$20\frac{4}{5}$ feet

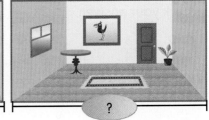
?

© Common Core

6.EE.7 Solve real-world and mathematical problems by writing and solving equations of the form $x + p = q$ and $px = q$ for cases in which p, q and x are all nonnegative rational numbers.

Solving Equations

How can you solve equations involving fractions and mixed numbers?

Melissa split a 6-foot-long strip of fruit leather into two pieces, as shown below. What is the length of the shorter piece of fruit leather?

Use the equation $3\frac{3}{4} + x = 6$ to solve the problem.

$3\frac{3}{4}$ feet

Other Examples

You have learned to solve equations with whole numbers.
Now use what you learned to solve equations with fractions.

Subtraction Equation

Solve: $y - \frac{4}{9} = 5\frac{1}{3}$

$$y - \frac{4}{9} + \frac{4}{9} = 5\frac{1}{3} + \frac{4}{9}$$

$$y = 5\frac{3}{9} + \frac{4}{9}$$

$$y = 5\frac{7}{9}$$

Multiplication Equation

Solve: $\frac{3}{8}n = 15$

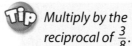 **Tip** *Multiply by the reciprocal of $\frac{3}{8}$.*

$$\frac{3}{8}n = 15$$

$$\left(\frac{8}{3}\right)\frac{3}{8}n = \left(\frac{8}{3}\right)15$$

$$n = \frac{8}{\underset{1}{3}} \times \frac{\overset{5}{15}}{1}$$

$$n = 40$$

Division Equation

Solve: $m \div \frac{2}{5} = 4\frac{3}{4}$

$$m \div \frac{2}{5} = \frac{19}{4}$$

$$m \div \frac{2}{5} \times \frac{2}{5} = \frac{19}{4} \times \frac{2}{5}$$

$$m = \frac{19}{\underset{2}{4}} \times \frac{\overset{1}{2}}{5}$$

$$m = \frac{19}{10}$$

$$m = 1\frac{9}{10}$$

Guided Practice*

© **MATHEMATICAL PRACTICES**

Do you know HOW?

In **1** through **6**, solve each equation and check your answer.

1. $t - \frac{2}{3} = 25\frac{3}{4}$

2. $v + \frac{5}{8} = 9\frac{1}{3}$

3. $\frac{3}{4}x = 27$

4. $y \div \frac{4}{7} = 8\frac{5}{9}$

5. $\frac{7}{9}g = 49$

6. $r - \frac{3}{5} = 15\frac{5}{8}$

Do you UNDERSTAND?

© 7. **Communicate** How did subtracting the mixed number help you solve the problem at the top of the page?

8. Check the answer to each equation in Other Examples.

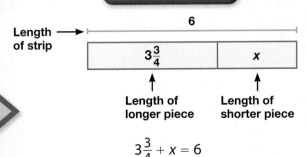

Length of strip →

6

$3\frac{3}{4}$ | x

↑ Length of longer piece   ↑ Length of shorter piece

$3\frac{3}{4} + x = 6$

Use inverse relationships and properties of equality. Subtract $3\frac{3}{4}$ from both sides of the equation to get x alone.

$3\frac{3}{4} + x = 6$

$3\frac{3}{4} + x - 3\frac{3}{4} = 6 - 3\frac{3}{4}$

$x = 2\frac{1}{4}$

The shorter piece is $2\frac{1}{4}$ feet long. Check.

$3\frac{3}{4} + x = 6$

$3\frac{3}{4} + 2\frac{1}{4} = 6$

$6 = 6$

Independent Practice

In **9** through **16**, solve each equation and check your answer.

9. $s \div \frac{1}{6} = 22\frac{2}{3}$

10. $16 = n \div \frac{3}{4}$

11. $3\frac{1}{6} + f = 7\frac{5}{6}$

12. $p - 6 = 2\frac{7}{12}$

13. $7\frac{1}{9} = 2\frac{4}{5} + m$

14. $a + 3\frac{1}{4} = 5\frac{2}{9}$

15. $\frac{5}{6}b = 7\frac{1}{3}$

16. $k - 6\frac{3}{8} = 4\frac{6}{7}$

Problem Solving

MATHEMATICAL PRACTICES

© **17. Writing to Explain** A fraction, f, divided by $\frac{2}{5}$ equals $\frac{7}{8}$. Write an algebraic sentence to show the equation. Then solve the equation and explain how you solved it.

18. The Ramirez family spent several days hiking the Rocky Mountains. Every day they hiked $8\frac{1}{3}$ miles. How many days did they hike if they hiked a total of 50 miles?

© **19. Reason** Is the solution of $b \div \frac{5}{6} = 25$ greater than or less than 25? How can you tell before computing?

© **20. Reason** Choose the expression with the greatest product.

A $3\frac{1}{8} \times \frac{2}{5}$

C $3\frac{1}{8} \times 5\frac{1}{2}$

B $3\frac{1}{8} \times \frac{2}{3}$

D $3\frac{1}{8} \times 5\frac{1}{8}$

© **21. Persevere** How many gallons of fuel does it take to move the space shuttle at the right the 3 miles from its hangar to the Vehicle Assembly Building?

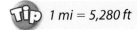

Tip 1 mi = 5,280 ft

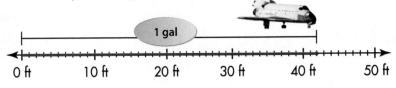

1 gal

0 ft   10 ft   20 ft   30 ft   40 ft   50 ft

Common Core

6.NS.6 Understand a rational number as a point on the number line. Extend number line diagrams and coordinate axes familiar from previous grades to represent points on the line and in the plane with negative number coordinates.

Look for a Pattern

A $12\frac{1}{2}$ mile walk-or-run is being planned. Water stations are to be placed at distance markers using a pattern. What are the distances for the five unmarked signs where water stations will be placed?

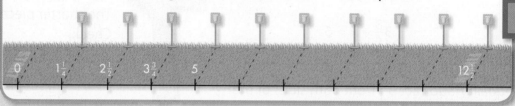

0    $1\frac{1}{4}$ $2\frac{1}{2}$ $3\frac{3}{4}$ 5 $12\frac{1}{2}$

Guided Practice*  MATHEMATICAL PRACTICES

Do you know HOW?

Find the pattern.

1. 0, $\frac{1}{4}$, $\frac{2}{4}$, $\frac{3}{4}$, ▦, ▦, ▦, ▦, $\frac{8}{4}$

2. 0, $\frac{2}{3}$, $\frac{4}{3}$, $\frac{6}{3}$, ▦, ▦, ▦, ▦, $\frac{16}{3}$

3. 2, 6, 18, ▦, ▦, ▦, 1,458

Do you UNDERSTAND?

4. Reasonableness Why should you check two other consecutive points after you find a possible pattern?

5. Write a Problem Write a problem that starts with $5\frac{1}{2}$, uses a pattern three times, and leaves blanks to fill in.

Independent Practice  MATHEMATICAL PRACTICES

Look for Patterns Find the missing numbers. Describe the pattern.

6. $\frac{24}{4}$, $\frac{21}{4}$, $\frac{18}{4}$, $\frac{15}{4}$, ▦, ▦, ▦, ▦, $\frac{0}{4}$

7. 12, $10\frac{1}{2}$, 9, $7\frac{1}{2}$, ▦, ▦, ▦, ▦, 0

8. 100, 94, 88, ▦, ▦, ▦, ▦, 58

9. ▦, ▦, ▦, ▦, 10, $12\frac{1}{2}$, 15, $17\frac{1}{2}$

10. 23, ▦, ▦, ▦, ▦, $21\frac{1}{8}$, $20\frac{3}{4}$, $20\frac{3}{8}$

11. $\frac{9}{2}$, $\frac{9}{4}$, $\frac{9}{8}$, ▦, ▦, ▦, ▦, $\frac{9}{256}$

Applying Math Practices

- What am I asked to find?
- What else can I try?
- How are quantities related?
- How can I explain my work?
- How can I use math to model the problem?
- Can I use tools to help?
- Is my work precise?
- Why does this work?
- How can I generalize?

*For another example, see Set F on page 219.

Look for a pattern. Choose the first 2 markers. How can you mathematically get from the first value to the second?

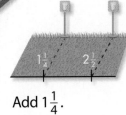

Add $1\frac{1}{4}$.

Check the pattern using other consecutive markers.

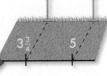

$2\frac{1}{2} + 1\frac{1}{4} = 3\frac{3}{4}$

$3\frac{3}{4} + 1\frac{1}{4} = 5$

The pattern "add $1\frac{1}{4}$" works.

Copy and complete the pattern by adding $1\frac{1}{4}$ mile.

The missing distances are $6\frac{1}{4}$, $7\frac{1}{2}$, $8\frac{3}{4}$, 10, and $11\frac{1}{4}$ miles.

Use the chart at right for **12** through **14**.

$1 \times 8 + 1 = 9$
$12 \times 8 + 2 = 98$
$123 \times 8 + 3 = 987$
$1,234 \times 8 + 4 = 9,876$

12. What is the next equation in the pattern?

13. Use the pattern to find $1,234,567 \times 8 + 7$.

© **14. Writing to Explain** How did you find the answer to Exercise 13 without computing?

© **15. Look for Patterns** Which figure completes this pattern?

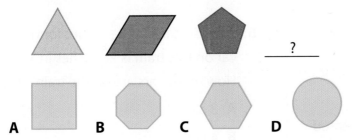

?

A   B   C   D

16. Some pairs of numbers make an interesting pattern when they are squared. $12^2 = 144$, and $21^2 = 441$. Explain whether this pattern is the same for 13^2, 31^2, and 112^2, 211^2.

17. Maya and Carlos are growing crystals for the science fair. They check their crystals' growth at certain times based on a pattern. They began at 1:15. Find the missing times and describe the pattern they used.

1:15, 2:30, 3:45, 5:00, ▨, ▨, ▨, ▨, 11:15

1. Raven is making pillows. Each pillow requires $\frac{3}{5}$ of a yard of fabric. If Raven has 6 yards of fabric, use the model to find $6 \div \frac{3}{5}$, the number of pillows Raven can make. (9-1)

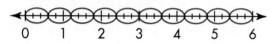

   A 10 pillows

   B 6 pillows

   C 5 pillows

   D 3 pillows

2. What step can be taken to find the solution to the equation shown? (9-6)

   $$\frac{5}{14}x = 20$$

   A Subtract $\frac{5}{14}$ from both sides.

   B Divide both sides by $\frac{14}{5}$.

   C Multiply both sides by $\frac{5}{14}$.

   D Multiply both sides by $\frac{14}{5}$.

3. Which number sentence is represented by the number line? (9-1)

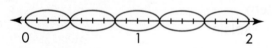

   A $2 \div \frac{4}{10} = 5$

   B $2 \div \frac{1}{10} = \frac{4}{10}$

   C $\frac{4}{10} \div 2 = 5$

   D $5 \div \frac{4}{10} = 2$

4. Which has the same value as $\frac{2}{5} \div \frac{5}{9}$? (9-3)

   A $\frac{5}{2} \times \frac{5}{9}$

   B $\frac{5}{2} \div \frac{5}{9}$

   C $\frac{2}{5} \div \frac{9}{5}$

   D $\frac{2}{5} \times \frac{9}{5}$

5. Holly is displaying a postcard collection on a bulletin board that is $35\frac{3}{4}$ inches wide. If each postcard is $5\frac{7}{8}$ inches in width, about how many postcards can she display in each row? (9-4)

   A about 5 postcards

   B about 6 postcards

   C about 8 postcards

   D about 10 postcards

6. A model train is $15\frac{3}{4}$ inches long. Each car on this train is $2\frac{5}{8}$ inches in length. How many cars are on the train? (9-5)

   A 3 cars

   B 4 cars

   C 5 cars

   D 6 cars

7. Mr. Sanchez is making pancakes. Each batch of pancakes uses $\frac{3}{4}$ cup of milk. If he has 9 cups of milk available, how many batches can he make? (9-2)

   A 3 batches

   B 7 batches

   C 12 batches

   D 27 batches

8. Find $\frac{3}{4} \div \frac{1}{4}$. (9-3)

   A 4

   B 3

   C 2

   D $\frac{3}{16}$

9. How many $\frac{1}{8}$-pint bottles can be filled from a $\frac{3}{4}$-pint bottle of hydrogen peroxide? (9-3)

   A 6

   B 5

   C 4

   D 1

10. Hal is stacking some CD cases on a shelf that is $19\frac{7}{8}$ inches wide. If each stack is $4\frac{11}{16}$ inches wide, estimate how many stacks of cases will fit on the shelf. (9-4)

   A 3 stacks

   B 4 stacks

   C 6 stacks

   D 12 stacks

11. Find $2\frac{1}{6} \div \frac{2}{3}$. (9-5)

   A $1\frac{4}{9}$

   B $2\frac{1}{4}$

   C $3\frac{1}{4}$

   D $6\frac{1}{2}$

12. Solve $t + \frac{1}{4} = 2\frac{7}{12}$. (9-6)

   A $t = 10\frac{1}{3}$

   B $t = 2\frac{1}{3}$

   C $t = 2\frac{5}{6}$

   D $t = \frac{31}{48}$

13. Shasta has 3 lb of wax and uses $\frac{3}{8}$ lb to make one candle. How many candles can she make? (9-2)

   A $\frac{1}{8}$ candle

   B 5 candles

   C 8 candles

   D 9 candles

14. The table shows the weight of a small dog each week since it was born. If the pattern continues, what will be the puppy's weight in week 6? (9-7)

Week	1	2	3	4	5	6
Weight in pounds	$\frac{5}{16}$	$\frac{1}{2}$	$\frac{11}{16}$	$\frac{7}{8}$		

   A $\frac{3}{16}$ pound

   B $1\frac{1}{16}$ pounds

   C $1\frac{1}{4}$ pounds

   D $1\frac{1}{2}$ pounds

Set A, pages 202–203

Find $4 \div \frac{4}{5}$. Use a number line.

Divide 4 into $\frac{4}{5}$ parts.

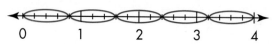

$4 \div \frac{4}{5} = 5$

Remember that when the divisor is less than 1, the quotient is larger than the dividend.

1. $7 \div \frac{1}{2}$ **2.** $6 \div \frac{2}{5}$

3. $2 \div \frac{1}{8}$ **4.** $\frac{8}{9} \div \frac{4}{9}$

5. $\frac{2}{3} \div 2$ **6.** $\frac{3}{4} \div 6$

Set B, pages 204–207

Find $4 \div \frac{8}{13}$.

Dividing by a fraction is the same as multiplying by its reciprocal.

$4 \div \frac{8}{13} = 4 \times \frac{13}{8}$ **Use the reciprocal of the divisor to rewrite the problem.**

$\frac{\cancel{4}^{1}}{1} \times \frac{13}{\cancel{8}^{2}} = \frac{13}{2}$ or $6\frac{1}{2}$ **Look for common factors and simplify.**

Find $\frac{3}{4} \div \frac{5}{8}$.

$\frac{3}{4} \div \frac{5}{8} = \frac{3}{4} \times \frac{8}{5}$ **Rewrite the problem as a multiplication problem.**

$\frac{3}{\cancel{4}^{1}} \times \frac{\cancel{8}^{2}}{5} = \frac{6}{5}$ or $1\frac{1}{5}$ **Simplify. Then, multiply.**

Remember that the product of a number and its reciprocal is 1.

1. $25 \div \frac{4}{9}$ **2.** $12 \div \frac{3}{5}$

3. $8 \div \frac{5}{7}$ **4.** $\frac{7}{8} \div \frac{1}{4}$

5. $\frac{1}{3} \div \frac{3}{5}$ **6.** $\frac{3}{4} \div \frac{1}{3}$

7. $\frac{5}{6} \div \frac{3}{8}$ **8.** $\frac{1}{3} \div \frac{1}{2}$

9. $5 \div \frac{5}{16}$ **10.** $\frac{7}{12} \div \frac{3}{4}$

11. $\frac{8}{9} \div \frac{2}{3}$ **12.** $\frac{2}{7} \div \frac{2}{7}$

Set C, pages 208–209

Estimate $3\frac{1}{5} \div 8\frac{3}{4}$ using rounding or compatible numbers.

$3\frac{1}{5} \div 8\frac{3}{4} \approx 3 \div 9$ **Round to the nearest whole number. $\frac{1}{5} < \frac{1}{2}$ and $\frac{3}{4} > \frac{1}{2}$.**

$3 \div 9 = \frac{3}{9}$ or $\frac{1}{3}$ **$3\frac{1}{5}$ and $8\frac{3}{4}$ round to 3 and 9.**

So, $3\frac{1}{5} \div 8\frac{3}{4} \approx \frac{1}{3}$.

Remember that you can estimate using compatible numbers.

1. $\frac{7}{9} \div 16$ **2.** $24\frac{4}{10} \div 6\frac{1}{3}$

3. $3\frac{5}{6} \div 8\frac{2}{7}$ **4.** $27 \div 3\frac{2}{5}$

5. $36\frac{3}{8} \div 12\frac{2}{5}$ **6.** $3\frac{11}{12} \div 4\frac{4}{5}$

Find $6\frac{1}{2} \div 1\frac{1}{6}$. Estimate. $6\frac{1}{2} \div 1\frac{1}{6} \approx 6$

$6\frac{1}{2} \div 1\frac{1}{6} = \frac{13}{2} \div \frac{7}{6}$ Write the mixed numbers as improper fractions.

$\frac{13}{2} \div \frac{7}{6} = \frac{13}{2} \times \frac{6}{7}$ Then write the problem as a multiplication problem using the reciprocal of the divisor.

$\frac{13}{\cancel{2}} \times \frac{\cancel{6}^{3}}{7} = \frac{39}{7}$ or $5\frac{4}{7}$ Simplify. Then, multiply.

$5\frac{4}{7}$ is close to the estimate of 6.

Remember to estimate before solving the problem so you can check the reasonableness of your answer.

Find each quotient.

1. $6\frac{3}{8} \div 4\frac{1}{4}$ 2. $9 \div 2\frac{2}{7}$

3. $3\frac{3}{5} \div 1\frac{1}{5}$ 4. $5\frac{1}{2} \div 3\frac{3}{8}$

5. $3\frac{2}{5} \div 1\frac{1}{5}$ 6. $12\frac{1}{6} \div 3$

Find $w + 4\frac{1}{3} = 7$.

Subtract $4\frac{1}{3}$ from both sides.

$w + 4\frac{1}{3} - 4\frac{1}{3} = 7 - 4\frac{1}{3}$

$w = 2\frac{2}{3}$

Remember that you can use inverse relationships and properties of equality to solve each equation.

1. $g + 3\frac{5}{8} = 7\frac{1}{4}$

2. $b \div 15 = 8\frac{1}{3}$

3. $\frac{7}{9}y = 49$

If the pattern continues, how tall will the plants be at the end of 5 weeks?

Week	1	2	3	4	5
Plant Growth (in.)	$2\frac{1}{2}$	5	$7\frac{1}{2}$	▢	▢

The plants grew $2\frac{1}{2}$ inches during Week 1.

$2\frac{1}{2} + 2\frac{1}{2} = 5$; $5 + 2\frac{1}{2} = 7\frac{1}{2}$ Check the pattern for Weeks 2 and 3.

$7\frac{1}{2} + 2\frac{1}{2} = 10$; $10 + 2\frac{1}{2} = 12\frac{1}{2}$ Use the pattern to solve the problem.

The plants will be $12\frac{1}{2}$ in. at the end of 5 weeks.

Remember to look for a pattern by finding relationships between numbers, figures, or expressions. Find the missing numbers.

1. $\frac{1}{17}, \frac{3}{17}, \frac{6}{17}, \frac{10}{17}$ ▢

2. $12, 13\frac{1}{3}, 14\frac{2}{3}, 16,$ ▢, ▢

3. $\frac{5}{18}, \frac{4}{18}, \frac{3}{18},$ ▢, ▢

4. $1\frac{1}{2}, 1\frac{1}{4}, 1, \frac{3}{4},$ ▢, ▢

Topic 10

Integers

1 A commercial airplane cruises at about 30,000 feet. Can a bird fly that high? You will find out in Lesson 10-1.

2 Antartica is the coldest and the windiest continent. How much colder can the wind make temperatures feel? You will find out in Lesson 10-4.

3 How deep is an ocean? You will find out in Lesson 10-5.

4 How are stock prices like integers? You will find out in Lesson 10-6.

Review What You Know!

Vocabulary

Choose the best term from the box.

- evaluate
- addend
- sum
- inverse

1. Multiplying and dividing can undo each other; they have a(n) __?__ relationship.

2. In the equation $8 + 7 = 15$, 8 is a(n) __?__ and 15 is the __?__ .

3. When you __?__ an algebraic expression, you substitute a number for the variable.

Order of Operations

Simplify each expression using order of operations.

4. $24 \div (8 - 5)$
5. $4 + 7 \times 2$

6. $9 - 9 + 22$
7. $8 \times 3 \div 6 - 1$

8. $3 + 12 \div 2$
9. $4 + (3 \times 6) - 3$

Evaluating Expressions

Evaluate each expression for $x = 2$ and $x = 8$.

10. $48 \div x$
11. $x \times 0$
12. $1x$

13. $4x \div 2$
14. $x - 2$
15. $x^2 + 1$

16. $x \div x$
17. $100 - x^2$

Properties

18. **Writing to Explain** How can you find 37×9 using the Distributive Property? Explain.

ⓒ
**Common
Core**

6.NS.5 Understand that positive and negative numbers are used together to describe quantities having opposite directions or values. . .; use positive and negative numbers to represent quantities in real-world contexts, explaining the meaning of 0 in each situation. Also **6.NS.6, 6.NS.6.a, 6.NS.6.c, 6.NS.7, 6.NS.7.c**

Understanding Integers

What are integers?

You can compare integers to degrees of temperature measured on a thermometer. When the temperature goes below zero, it is written with a negative sign.

6°C is 6°C warmer than 0°C.

−6°C is 6°C colder than 0°C.

The distance from 0°C is the same.

You have learned how to read the counting numbers. This chart shows how to read negative integers.

Integer	How to Read It
−3	Negative three
−(−3)	The opposite of negative three
|−3|	The absolute value of negative three

Guided Practice*

MATHEMATICAL
PRACTICES

Do you know HOW?

Use the number line below for **1** through **6**. Give the integer that each point represents. Then write its opposite and absolute value.

1. *A* **2.** *B* **3.** *C*

4. *D* **5.** *E* **6.** *F*

Do you UNDERSTAND?

7. What do you know about two different integers that have the same absolute value?

ⓒ **8. Generalize** Which integers do you use for counting?

9. How would you read the number −17?

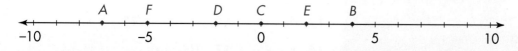

Independent Practice

In **10** through **15**, what is the opposite and absolute value of each integer?

10. 5 **11.** −13 **12.** 22 **13.** −31 **14.** −50 **15.** 66

Animated Glossary
www.pearsonsuccessnet.com

For another example, see Set A on page 256.

A number line can show numbers like on a thermometer. Numbers that are the same distance from 0 are called opposites. −6 and 6 are opposites.

Integers are made up of the counting numbers, their opposites, and zero.

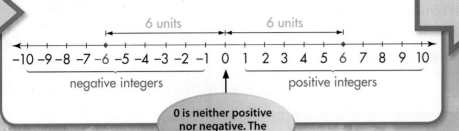

6 units   6 units

−10 −9 −8 −7 −6 −5 −4 −3 −2 −1 0 1 2 3 4 5 6 7 8 9 10

negative integers   positive integers

0 is neither positive nor negative. The opposite of 0 is 0.

The absolute value of an integer is its distance from zero.

Distance is always positive.

The absolute value of 6 is written |6| = 6.

The absolute value of −6 is written |−6| = 6.

Problem Solving

© MATHEMATICAL PRACTICES

16. Which of the following polygons has the greatest perimeter?

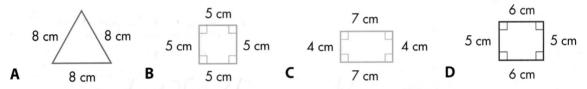

A 8 cm, 8 cm, 8 cm (triangle)

B 5 cm, 5 cm, 5 cm, 5 cm (square)

C 7 cm, 7 cm, 4 cm, 4 cm (rectangle)

D 6 cm, 6 cm, 5 cm, 5 cm (rectangle)

© **17. Writing to Explain** If the opposite of an integer is equal to its absolute value, is the number positive or negative? Explain your answer.

© **18. Be Precise** What is the value of |−14|?

    A the opposite of 14   **C** 14

    B −14   **D** greater than 14

Use the pictures at the right to answer **19** through **21**.

19. About how much higher can a Ruppell's Griffon fly than a migrating bird can fly?

© **20. Reason** Write a negative integer to represent the depth to which a dolphin may dive.

21. Which animal can fly or swim at a greater distance from sea level, a sperm whale or a migrating bird?

Ruppell's Griffons fly up to 37,000 feet.

Mexican free-tailed bats fly up to 10,000 feet.

A migrating bird flies up to 5,000 feet.

A dolphin can swim to 150 feet below sea level.

A sperm whale can swim to 3,000 feet below sea level.

Common
Core

6.NS.7.a Interpret
statements of inequality
as statements about the
relative position of two
numbers on a number
line diagram.…
Also 6.NS.7, 6.NS.7.b

Comparing and Ordering Integers

How can you compare and order integers?

The table shows the low temperatures during a cold week. Find which day had the lowest temperature. Then order the temperatures from least to greatest.

You can use a number line to help.

Day	Temperature
Monday	3°C
Tuesday	−6°C
Wednesday	5°C
Thursday	1°C
Friday	−5°C

Guided Practice*

MATHEMATICAL
PRACTICES

Do you know HOW?

In **1** through **4**, use <, >, or = to compare.

1. 7 ◯ −12

2. −3 ◯ −9

3. −8 ◯ 0

4. |−2| ◯ −2

In **5** through **8**, order the numbers from least to greatest.

5. −6, 5, −7

6. 8, −6, −2

7. −21, |−15|, −12

8. |3|, −3, −19, 11

Do you UNDERSTAND?

© **9. Reason** Is −7 to the right or to the left of −2 on a number line? What does that tell you about their values?

10. From greatest to least, what were the three coldest temperatures in the chart at the top of the page?

11. Which day had the highest temperature?

Independent Practice

In **12** through **19**, use <, >, or = to compare.

 You can draw and use a number line.

12. 5 ◯ −18

13. |−7| ◯ 7

14. 0 ◯ 9

15. 18 ◯ 9

16. −19 ◯ −23

17. 4 ◯ −6

18. |−32| ◯ |7|

19. −1 ◯ 3

In **20** through **28**, order the numbers from least to greatest.

20. −6, 8, −9, 13

21. |−19|, 12, |−21|, −3

22. 17, 14, −10, 4, −2, −4

23. 4.5, −4.66, −5, 7

24. −37, |15|, 11, −3, 8, |−12|

25. 57, −21, 43, −6, 7, 23

26. −6, 1.3, −3.5, 2

27. 2, 0, −8, −11, −5

28. 2.25, −7.5, −7, −3.2

First locate the integers on a number line.

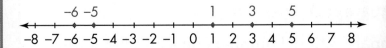

When comparing integers on a number line, the integer that is farther to the left is less.

−6 is farther to the left than −5, so −6 is less. It was colder on Tuesday than on Friday.

You can write this two ways: −6 < −5 or −5 > −6.

Integer values on a number line decrease as you move left and increase as you move right.

The temperature farthest to the left is −6. Tuesday was the coldest day.

Moving left to right, you can write the temperatures from least to greatest: −6, −5, 1, 3, 5

Problem Solving

© **29. Writing to Explain** If $n =$ any integer, explain why $|n| = |-n|$.

30. In miniature golf, the lowest score wins. Scores can be compared to *par*, a number of strokes set for the course.

   a Using the table at right, list the top five finishers in order from first place to fifth place.

   b Which students' scores are opposites?

Player	Par Score
Martha	0 (par)
Madison	−2
Tom	−3
Emma	4
Ben	1
Quincy	−4
Jackson	6

Data

31. Shayla has 4 roses, 7 tulips, and 3 daffodils. Fred has 5 roses, 3 morning-glories, and 3 tulips. Nick has 7 roses and 5 tulips. Who has the most flowers? Who has the least?

32. Cheyenne recorded the temperature three times during the day.

   left for school   −4°F
   lunchtime   2°F
   bedtime   −7°F

   a Order the temperatures from least to greatest.

   b At which of the times was the temperature the coldest?

© **33. Persevere** The variables on this number line represent integers. Order the variables from least to greatest.

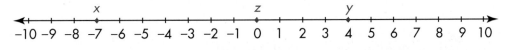

   A x, y, z   **B** y, z, x   **C** x, z, y   **D** y, x, z

6.NS.6.c Find and position integers and other rational numbers on a horizontal or vertical number line diagram; find and position pairs of integers and other rational numbers on a coordinate plane. Also **6.NS.6, 6.NS.7, 6.NS.7.a, 6.NS.7.b**

Rational Numbers on a Number Line

How can you compare rational numbers on a number line?

Any number that can be shown as the quotient of two integers is called a rational number. For any integers a and b ($b \neq 0$), $\frac{a}{b} = a \div b$. Rational numbers can be written in different ways.

Compare $-\frac{4}{3}$ and -1.5.

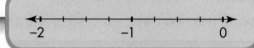

Another Example **How can you order rational numbers on a number line?**

Order $\frac{2}{3}$, 1.75, and -0.75 from least to greatest.

One Way

Use number sense and a number line to order rational numbers:

- -0.75 is a negative number, so it will be farthest to the left.

- $\frac{2}{3}$ is between 0 and 1.

- 1.75 is between 1 and 2.

Place these numbers on a number line.

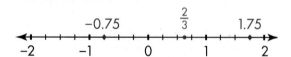

Write the order: -0.75, $\frac{2}{3}$, 1.75

Another Way

Convert the numbers to a common form to order rational numbers.

Use division to convert $\frac{2}{3}$ to a decimal.

$$\frac{2}{3} = 0.\overline{6}$$

- -0.75 is to the left of $0.\overline{6}$.

- $0.\overline{6}$ is to the left of 1.75.

Place these numbers on a number line:

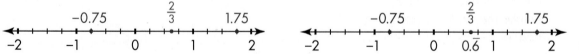

Write the order: -0.75, $\frac{2}{3}$, 1.75

Explain It

1. How can a number line help you to compare rational numbers?

2. Explain how you could use number sense to find the least number among these rational numbers: $1\frac{3}{5}$, -3.2, and 1.5.

One Way

Think of $-\frac{4}{3}$ as a decimal.

$-\frac{4}{3} = -1\frac{1}{3} = -1.\overline{3}$

$$\begin{array}{r} 1.33 \\ 3\overline{)4.00} \\ -3 \\ \hline 10 \\ -9 \\ \hline 10 \\ -9 \\ \hline 1 \end{array}$$

On a number line, $-1.\overline{3}$ is to the right of -1.5.

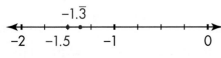

So, $-\frac{4}{3} > -1.5$ or $-1.5 < -\frac{4}{3}$.

Another Way

Think of $-\frac{4}{3}$ and -1.5 as mixed numbers.

$-\frac{4}{3} = -1\frac{1}{3}$

$-1.5 = -1\frac{5}{10} = -1\frac{1}{2}$

On a number line, $-1\frac{1}{3}$ is to the right of $-1\frac{1}{2}$.

So, $-\frac{4}{3} > -1.5$ or $-1.5 < -\frac{4}{3}$.

Guided Practice*

MATHEMATICAL PRACTICES

Do you know HOW?

For **1** through **4**, copy the number line and graph each number.

(number line from −2 to 2)

1. $-\frac{1}{4}$ **2.** -0.4 **3.** 1.3 **4.** $1\frac{1}{5}$

For **5** and **6**, use $<$, $>$, or $=$ to compare.

5. $-\frac{1}{4} \bigcirc -0.4$ **6.** $1.3 \bigcirc 1\frac{1}{5}$

Do you UNDERSTAND?

7. Explain why 8, $\frac{5}{3}$, and -4 are rational numbers.

8. Suppose the Another Example included the number 1.25. Between which two labeled points would 1.25 appear?

© **9.** **Use Tools** Use your number line to order the numbers in Exercises 1 through 4 from least to greatest.

Independent Practice

Leveled Practice In **10** through **19**, use the number line to compare the numbers. Use $<$ or $>$ to compare.

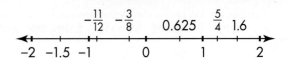

10. $-1.5 \bigcirc -\frac{11}{12}$ **11.** $\frac{5}{4} \bigcirc 1.6$ **12.** $\frac{5}{4} \bigcirc 1$ **13.** $-\frac{11}{12} \bigcirc -\frac{3}{8}$ **14.** $0.625 \bigcirc 0$

15. $1.7 \bigcirc 1\frac{4}{5}$ **16.** $0.1 \bigcirc \frac{1}{12}$ **17.** $-0.5 \bigcirc -\frac{3}{5}$ **18.** $1.625 \bigcirc 1\frac{3}{4}$ **19.** $-1.1 \bigcirc -1\frac{1}{5}$

In **20** through **23**, write the numbers in order from least to greatest.

20. $\frac{4}{5}$, 0.9, $\frac{5}{8}$ **21.** 0.61, $\frac{2}{3}$, $0.\overline{5}$ **22.** 0.7, 0.68, $\frac{5}{8}$ **23.** 4.75, $4\frac{5}{18}$, $\frac{14}{3}$

DIGITAL   Animated Glossary   www.pearsonsuccessnet.com

*For another example, see Set B on page 256.

© 24. Writing to Explain Why is $-1\frac{3}{8}$ a rational number but not an integer?

© 25. Reason Which number is greater: -4.2 or -6.2? Explain.

26. Name three rational numbers that are between 7 and 8.

27. Write a word phrase for $\frac{1}{5}(3x + 4)$.

© 28. Persevere Craig hiked a 2.625 mi trail and a 1.125 mi trail. Aubra hiked a 3.76 mi trail. Who hiked farther? By how much?

29. Order -3.25, $-3\frac{1}{8}$, $-3\frac{3}{4}$, and -3.1 from least to greatest. Did you write all the numbers as fractions or as decimals?

The animals listed in the table live below the ocean's surface. The table shows possible locations of the animals relative to the ocean's surface. Use the table to answer **30** and **31**.

30. Order the anglerfish and eels by their possible locations shown in the table, from deepest to shallowest.

31. Which animal's possible location shown in the table is closest to -0.7 km?

   A Gulper eel

   B Deep sea anglerfish

   C Pacific blackdragon

   D Fanfin anglerfish

Animal	Possible Locations Relative to Ocean's Surface
Bloodbelly comb jelly	-0.8 km
Deep sea anglerfish	$-\frac{2}{3}$ km
Fanfin anglerfish	$-2\frac{1}{4}$ km
Gulper eel	-1.19 km
Pacific blackdragon	$-\frac{3}{10}$ km
Slender snipe eel	-0.6 km

© 32. Reason The diagram to the right shows how sets of numbers are related. Copy the table below. Indicate the sets to which the numbers belong.

Number	Natural	Whole	Integer	Rational
10	Yes	Yes	Yes	Yes
-6				
0				
2.7				
-3.5				

Rational Numbers
numbers that can be expressed as a quotient of 2 integers $\frac{a}{b}$ ($b \neq 0$)

Integers
whole numbers and their opposites

Whole Numbers
zero and natural numbers

Natural Numbers
the set of counting numbers
1, 2, 3, 4, 5, ...

Changing Fractions and Mixed Numbers to Decimal Form

The examples below show two ways you can use your calculator to change fractions and mixed numbers to decimals.

Write $\frac{3}{40}$ in decimal form.

Press: 3 $\div$ 40 **ENTER =**   Display: 0.075

or

Press: 3 **n** 40 **ENTER =** **F↔D**   Display: 0.075

Write $4\frac{19}{20}$ in decimal form.

Press: 4 **+** 19 $\div$ 20 **ENTER =**   Display: 4.950

or

Press: 4 **+** 19 **n** 20 **ENTER =** **F↔D**   Display: 4.950

Practice

Write each fraction or mixed number in decimal form. Try to predict whether the decimal will terminate or repeat before doing each calculation. Remember, your calculator may round decimals to the nearest thousandth.

1. $\frac{7}{8}$

2. $\frac{9}{16}$

3. $\frac{4}{9}$

4. $2\frac{11}{20}$

5. $5\frac{14}{15}$

6. $\frac{31}{40}$

7. $\frac{8}{11}$

8. $16\frac{17}{80}$

9. $\frac{5}{18}$

10. $\frac{37}{200}$

11. $7\frac{19}{30}$

12. $4\frac{31}{33}$

Common Core

7.NS.1.b Understand $p + q$ as the number located a distance $|q|$ from p, in the positive or negative direction depending on whether q is positive or negative. Show that a number and its opposite have a sum of 0 (are additive inverses). Interpret sums of rational numbers by describing real-world contexts. Also **7.NS.1**

Adding Integers

How can you add integers with the same signs?

It was −2°C when Jack left for school at 7:30 A.M. During the next three hours, the temperature decreased three degrees Celsius. What was the temperature at 10:30 A.M. that morning?

Choose an Operation: Add to find the temperature at 10:30. Find −2 + (−3).

Another Example How do you add integers with different signs?

Find −2 + 3.

One Way

Think about walking a number line, walking backward for negative addends and forward for positive addends.

- Start at 0 on the number line, facing the positive integers.

- Walk backward 2 steps for −2 and stop.

- Then walk forward 3 steps for 3. Stop at 1.

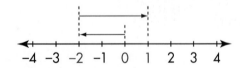

−4 −3 −2 −1 0 1 2 3 4

So, −2 + 3 = 1.

Another Way

Use these **rules for adding integers with different signs**.

- Find the absolute value of each addend. |−2| = 2 and |3| = 3

- Subtract the lesser absolute value from the greater. 3 − 2 = 1

- Give the difference of the absolute values the same sign as the addend with the greater absolute value.

 Think The addend with the greater absolute value is 3. 3 is positive. The sum, 1, is also positive.

So, −2 + 3 = 1.

Explain It

1. Suppose you were finding 2 + (−3) on a number line. Explain the steps.

2. Suppose you were using the rules to find 2 + (−3). What sign would you give the difference of the absolute values?

<table>
<tr><td>

One Way

Think about walking a number line.

- Start at 0 on the number line, facing the positive integers.
- Walk backward 2 steps for –2 and stop.
- Walk backward 3 more steps to add –3.

Stop at –5. So, –2 + (–3) = –5.

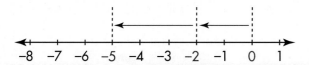

</td><td>

Another Way

Use these **rules for adding integers with the same signs**.

- Find the absolute values of the addends. $|-2| = 2$ and $|-3| = 3$
- Add the absolute values. $2 + 3 = 5$.
- Give the sum the same sign as the addends.

So, $-2 + (-3) = -5$.

</td></tr>
</table>

Guided Practice*

MATHEMATICAL
PRACTICES

Do you know HOW?

Find each sum. Use a number line or the rules for adding integers.

1. $-7 + 4$ **2.** $8 + (-3)$

3. $-5 + 14$ **4.** $18 + 13$

5. $-2 + (-6)$ **6.** $24 + (-7)$

7. $43 + (-19)$ **8.** $-16 + (-12)$

Do you UNDERSTAND?

9. Generalize When is the sum of a positive integer and a negative integer, positive?

10. It was 5°C when Tricia woke up in the morning. The temperature was 7 degrees higher at lunchtime. What was the lunchtime temperature?

Independent Practice

Leveled Practice In **11** and **12**, use the number lines to find the sum.

11. $4 + (-3)$

12. $-2 + 7$

For **13** through **22**, find each sum. *Draw a number line to help you add.*

13. $-25 + (-1)$ **14.** $-23 + (-6)$ **15.** $3 + (-13)$ **16.** $-23 + 8$ **17.** $32 + (-4)$

18. $-7 + 15$ **19.** $6 + (-19)$ **20.** $-3 + (-7)$ **21.** $-4 + (-8)$ **22.** $-8 + 30$

In **23** through **27**, use a number line or the rules for adding integers to find each sum.

23. $3 + (-8)$ **24.** $-9 + 7$ **25.** $-4 + (-8)$ **26.** $-15 + (-23)$ **27.** $19 + (-32)$

In **28** through **32**, evaluate each expression for $b = -18$.

28. $33 + b$ **29.** $b + (-16)$ **30.** $24 + b + (-6)$ **31.** $-11 + |-38| + b$ **32.** $|b| + (-47) + 15$

Problem Solving

MATHEMATICAL
PRACTICES

33. Use the rule to complete the table.

Rule: Add -7

In	3	-19	22	-43	-7
Out					

34. In Antarctica, the temperature often drops below $-40°F$, and the wind speed can exceed 40 miles per hour (mph). A 40-mph wind makes $-40°F$ feel 44°F colder. How cold does $-40°F$ feel when the wind is blowing 40 mph?

35. Bandu lost $4 at the swimming pool. Later that week, he and his sister each earned $10. Does Bandu have less or more money than before he went to the swimming pool?

36. Writing to Explain Describe a situation that the following expression could represent: $17 + (-9)$.

37. Reason If you add an integer and its opposite, what is the sum?

38. Which digit is in the thousandths place? 381,427.659

39. Think About the Structure Which expression has a value of 25?

    A $3 + 4 \times 6 - 2$ **B** $(3 + 4) \times (6 - 2)$ **C** $3 + 4 \times (6 - 2)$ **D** $(3 + 4) \times 6 - 2$

40. Think About the Structure The bus stopped 3 times within the distance of 7 blocks. At the first stop, 2 people got on the bus. At the second stop, 3 people got off. At the third stop, 1 person got off and 4 people got on. Which expression best describes how the number of people on the bus changed?

    A $2 + 3 + (1 + 4)$ **B** $2 + 3 + (-1 + 4)$ **C** $2 + (-3) + (-1 + 4)$ **D** $2 + (-3) + (1 + 4)$

41. Mona went to the library and checked out 5 books. She returned 4 books. Evaluate the expression $5 + (-4)$.

    A 1   **B** -1 **C** $|-4|$ **D** 9

Addition of Integers

Use ⚙ **tools**
Counters
Add $-6 + (-8)$ and $-5 + 9$.

Step 1 Go to the Counters eTool. Let each yellow counter represent positive one and each red counter represent negative one. To show $-6 + (-8)$, show 6 red counters in a row and 8 red counters in another row. ● Click on the red counter and then click in the workspace to show and make the rows. The result is 14 red counters. So, $-6 + (-8) = -14$.

Step 2 🧹 Use the Broom tool to clear the workspace. To show $-5 + 9$, show 5 red counters in one row and 9 yellow counters in a second row. A sum such as $-1 + 1$ or $-5 + 5$ is called a zero pair. The sum of a number and its opposite is always zero and the numbers are called a zero pair. The zero pairs can be removed without changing the sum. ↗ Use the Arrow tool to select 5 red and 5 yellow counters as zero pairs. Remove the zero pairs by using 🖌 the Erase tool. The result is 4 yellow counters. So, $-5 + 9 = 4$.

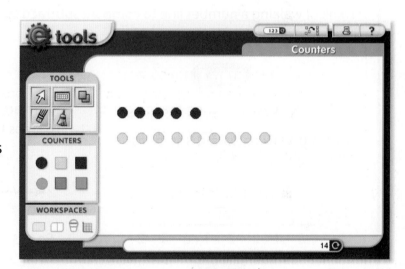

Practice

Find each sum.

1. $-7 + (-5)$ 　　　 2. $-1 + 10$ 　　　 3. $2 + (-8)$

4. $-3 + 11$ 　　　 5. $4 + (-14)$ 　　　 6. $-9 + (-6)$

Common Core

7.NS.1.c Understand subtraction of rational numbers as adding the additive inverse, $p - q = p + (-q)$. Show that the distance between two rational numbers on the number line is the absolute value of their difference, and apply this principle in real-world contexts. Also **7.NS.1**

Subtracting Integers

How can you subtract integers?

Malita is making wind chimes to sell. So far, she has made two. Her first customer liked them so well that she ordered six. How many more does Malita need to make?

Choose an Operation: Subtract to find how many more Malita needs to make. Find $2 - 6$.

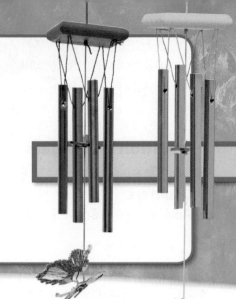

Another Example **What is the rule for subtracting integers?**

Rule: Subtracting an integer is the same as adding its opposite.

Think of walking a number line to compare subtracting an integer to adding its opposite. Find $-3 - 6$.

Step 1

Find $-3 - 6$ by subtracting the integer, 6.

Start at 0. Walk backward 3 steps to -3 and stop.

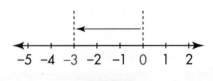

Step 2

Turn around to subtract. Walk forward 6 steps for 6. Stop at -9.

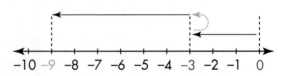

So, $-3 - 6 = -9$.

Step 1

Find $-3 - 6$ by adding the opposite of 6, $-3 + (-6)$.

Start at 0. Walk backward 3 steps to -3 and stop.

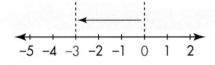

Step 2

Continue to walk backward 6 steps for -6. Stop at -9.

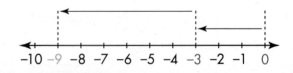

So, $-3 + (-6) = -9$.

Explain It

1. How does the above example show how to subtract integers?

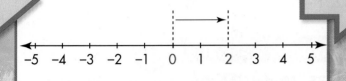

Step 1

Think about walking a number line to help you subtract integers.

Start at 0, facing the positive integers.

Walk forward 2 steps for 2.

Step 2

The subtraction sign means turn around. Then walk forward 6 steps for 6. Stop at −4.

So, 2 − 6 = −4.

Malita still needs to make 4 more wind chimes for her customer.

Guided Practice*

MATHEMATICAL PRACTICES

Do you know HOW?

Find each difference.

 Draw a number line or use the rule for subtracting integers.

1. 5 − 13   **2.** −7 − 4

3. 3 − (−9)   **4.** −11 − (−6)

Evaluate each expression for $n = -5$.

5. $n - 6$ **6.** $-15 - n$

7. $n - (-12)$ **8.** $1 - n$

Do you UNDERSTAND?

9. In the example at the top of the page, how can you tell if 2 − 6 is positive or negative before you compute the answer?

10. Reason Explain why 4 − (−3) = 4 + 3 without solving the equation.

11. Construct Arguments Can the Commutative Property be used to subtract integers? Explain your answer.

Independent Practice

Leveled Practice In **12** through **15**, use a number line like the one below to find each difference.

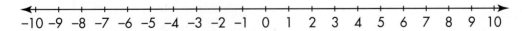

12. 3 − 4   **13.** −7 − 2   **14.** 5 − (−1)   **15.** 5 − 10

In **16** through **25**, use a number line or the rule for subtracting integers to find each difference.

16. −6 − (−8)   **17.** −6 − (−4)   **18.** −11 − 4   **19.** 24 − (−7)   **20.** |−3| − |3|

21. −39 − (−39)   **22.** 14 − |−20| **23.** −7 − (−9)   **24.** −9 − (−6)   **25.** −4 − (−7)

For another example, see Set D on page 257.

Lesson 10-5   **235**

In **26** through **33**, evaluate each expression for $t = -7$.

26. $41 - t$ **27.** $18 - t - (-11)$ **28.** $t - (-25)$ **29.** $|t| - (-39) - 4$

30. $17 - |-29| - t$ **31.** $-10 - t$ **32.** $t - (-4)$ **33.** $9 - t - |-5|$

Problem Solving

MATHEMATICAL PRACTICES

Ⓒ **34. Writing to Explain** Jeremy said that $5 - (-4)$ is the same as $5 + (-4)$. Is he correct? Explain why or why not.

Ⓒ **35. Model** The temperature was 3°C when Maria went to bed. The temperature fell 7°C during the night. Find the temperature when Maria woke up by evaluating $3 - d$ for $d = 7$.

Ⓒ **36. Model** Alfonso was in the elevator of a 45-story building. He went up 24 floors and then went down 30 floors. Which expression shows the difference in number of floors from where he started?

   A $24 - 30$

   B $24 - (-30)$

   C $45 - 30$

   D $45 - (-30)$

37. Cherise plans to build a square fence with sides of 15 feet. If she puts up 10 feet of fencing each day, how many days will it take her to complete the fence?

   A 3 days

   B 6 days

   C 10 days

   D 15 days

Use the table below to answer **38** and **39**.

Tip *Because distance is always positive, think of distances below sea level as absolute values.*

Ⓒ **38. Persevere** How much deeper is the Atlantic Ocean than the Arctic Ocean? Find the difference between the average depths of the Arctic Ocean and the Atlantic Ocean.

Average Depth of Oceans (compared to sea level)	
Atlantic	12,900 feet below
Pacific	14,000 feet below
Arctic	4,300 feet below
Indian	12,800 feet below

39. A scuba diver is diving in the Pacific Ocean. How far is the diver from the average depth of the ocean floor?

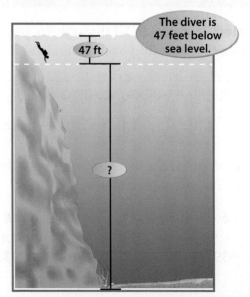

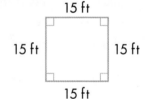

The diver is 47 feet below sea level.

47 ft

?

Mixed Problem Solving

Use the diagram to answer **1** through **3**.

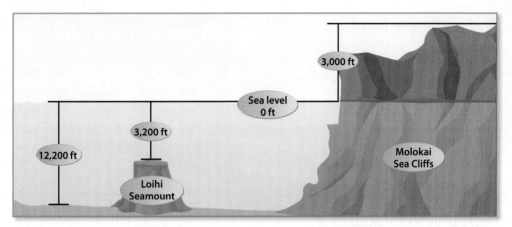

1. What is the difference in elevation between the top of the Molokai Sea Cliffs and the top of the Loihi Seamount?

2. The Loihi Seamount is a volcano located near Hawaii under the surface of the sea. About how tall is the Loihi Seamount?

3. What is the difference in elevation from the top of the Molokai Sea Cliffs to the bottom of the ocean near the Loihi Seamount?

Use the diagram and the diagram above to answer **4** through **7**.

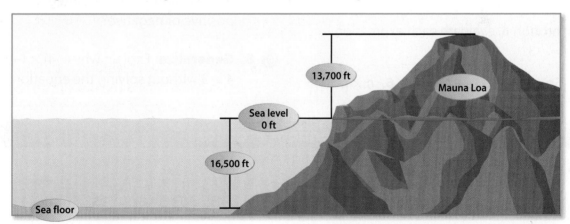

4. What is the difference in elevation from the top of Mauna Loa to the sea floor?

5. What is the difference in elevation between the top of the Molokai Sea Cliffs and the top of Mauna Loa?

6. Mauna Loa depresses the sea floor, resulting in 26,400 more feet added to its height. What is the total height of Mauna Loa?

7. What is the difference in elevation between the top of Mauna Loa and the top of the Loihi Seamount?

Common Core

7.NS.2.a Understand that multiplication is extended from fractions to rational numbers by requiring that operations continue to satisfy the properties of operations, particularly the distributive property, leading to products such as $(-1)(-1) = 1$ and the rules for multiplying signed numbers.... Also **7.NS.2**

Multiplying Integers

How can you identify the sign of the product of two integers?

When multiplying integers, the signs of the factors help you find the sign of their product. For example, find 5×3.

$5 + 5 + 5 = 15$, so $5 \times 3 = 15$.

The product of two positive integers is positive.

Signs of Factors and Products

First Factor		Second Factor		Product
Positive	×	Positive	=	Positive
Positive	×	Negative	=	Negative
Negative	×	Positive	=	Negative
Negative	×	Negative	=	Positive

Rules for Multiplying Integers

The product of two integers with the same sign is positive.

The product of two integers with different signs is negative.

Tip -3×5 can be written $(-3)(5)$.

Guided Practice*

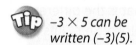

MATHEMATICAL
PRACTICES

Do you know HOW?

In **1** through **3**, find each product.

1. $(3)(-8)$ **2.** $(-9)(-6)$ **3.** $4 \times (-2)$

In **4** through **6**, evaluate each expression for $n = -3$.

4. $5n$ **5.** $-14n$ **6.** $n \times |-31|$

Do you UNDERSTAND?

7. Using the Rules for Multiplying Integers, is the product of two positive integers and a negative integer positive or negative?

 8. Generalize Explain why $(-4) \times (-3) = 4 \times 3$ without solving the equation.

Independent Practice

In **9** through **18**, find the product.

9. $3 \times (-7)$ **10.** $(-8)(6)$ **11.** -9×4 **12.** $15 \times (-8)$ **13.** $(-14)^2$

14. $-1 \times (-27)$ **15.** 4×24 **16.** $(7)(-18)$ **17.** $-5 \times (11)$ **18.** $17 \times (-3)$

In **19** through **28**, use order of operations to evaluate each expression for $a = -2$.

19. $a + 7$ **20.** $a - 6$ **21.** $-5a + (3)(-7)$ **22.** $-2a + 4$ **23.** $-8a$

24. $21 + (-a) + 3$ **25.** $17a$ **26.** $a + 27$ **27.** $a - 14$ **28.** $6a$

Find -3×5 and $5 \times (-3)$.

$-3 \times 5 = (-3) + (-3) + (-3) + (-3) + (-3)$

So, $-3 \times 5 = -15$.

Using the Commutative Property of Multiplication, $5 \times (-3) = -15$, too.

The product of a positive integer and a negative integer is negative.

Find $-5 \times (-3)$.

The products in the table increase by 5.

Continuing the pattern results in 5, 10, 15.

So, $-5 \times (-3) = 15$.

The product of two negative integers is positive.

$-5 \times 3 = -15$
$-5 \times 2 = -10$
$-5 \times 1 = -5$
$-5 \times 0 = 0$
$-5 \times -1 =$
$-5 \times -2 =$
$-5 \times -3 =$

Problem Solving

MATHEMATICAL PRACTICES

© 29. Model The temperature is decreasing 3°F every hour. Which expression shows the change in temperature for h hours?

A $3h$ **B** $3 + h$ **C** $(-3)h$ **D** $h - 3$

30. Decide whether each of the following is negative or positive:

a the product of 2 negative integers and 1 positive integer

b the product of 3 negative integers

© 31. Reason Which shows an expression equal to $8 \times (16 + 7)$?

A $(8 \times 16) + (8 \times 7)$ **C** 8×24

B $8 \times 16 + 7$ **D** $8 \times 7 + 16$

Use the table to answer **32** and **33**.

32. Haru has 30 shares of Red Company stock. How has the value of her stock changed? Find $30 \times (-2)$.

© 33. Writing to Explain Kerry owns 15 shares of Red Company stock and 10 shares of Blue Company stock. Explain which of Kerry's stock values changed more.

Stock Name	Change in Value ($ per share)
Red Company	−2
White Company	1
Blue Company	−3

For **34** and **35**, put numbers in order from least to greatest.

34. 0.324, 0.11, 0.5

35. 1.56, 1.748, 1.009

© Common Core

7.NS.2.b Understand that integers can be divided, provided that the divisor is not zero, and every quotient of integers (with non-zero divisor) is a rational number. If p and q are integers, then $-(p/q) = (-p)/q = p/(-q)$. Interpret quotients of rational numbers by describing real-world contexts. Also 7.NS.2

Dividing Integers

How can you identify the sign of the quotient of two integers?

You know how to use the relationship between multiplication and division to write division facts.

You can also use the relationship between multiplication and division to identify the sign of the quotient of two integers.

Multiplication FACT	Related Division FACT
$3 \times 4 = 12$	$12 \div 3 = 4$
$4 \times 3 = 12$	$12 \div 4 = 3$

Guided Practice*

© MATHEMATICAL PRACTICES

Do you know HOW?

In **1** through **4**, find each quotient.

1. $-54 \div (-6)$ **2.** $-63 \div 7$

3. $35 \div (-5)$ **4.** $-32 \div (-8)$

In **5** through **8**, evaluate each expression for $n = -24$.

5. $n \div (-3)$ **6.** $96 \div n$

7. $\dfrac{-144}{n}$ **8.** $n \div 12$

Do you UNDERSTAND?

© **9. Generalize** How can you tell if the quotient for $-1{,}557 \div 329$ is positive or negative without computing?

10. A hiking club took 2 hours to hike 6 miles down a mountain. Evaluate the expression $-6 \div 2$.

Independent Practice

In **11** through **20**, find each quotient. *Zero does not have a sign.*

11. $21 \div (-7)$ **12.** $-105 \div (-5)$ **13.** $0 \div (-12)$ **14.** $56 \div (-8)$ **15.** $14 \div (-14)$

16. $-52 \div (-26)$ **17.** $144 \div 24$ **18.** $-121 \div 11$ **19.** $120 \div (-1)$ **20.** $150 \div (-15)$

In **21** through **28**, use order of operations to evaluate each expression for $a = -6$.

21. $a \div 2$ **22.** $-48 \div a$ **23.** $126 \div a$ **24.** $25 + (a \div 3)$

25. $0 \div (3a + 27)$ **26.** $36 \div a + 4$ **27.** $a^2 \div 6$ **28.** $(2a - 3) \div 5$

Look for rules for dividing integers in the examples below.

You Know	Related Division Fact	Sign of Quotient
$5 \times 3 = 15$	$15 \div 5 = 3$	⊕
$-5 \times 3 = -15$	$-15 \div (-5) = 3$	⊕
$5 \times (-3) = -15$	$-15 \div 5 = -3$	⊖
$-5 \times (-3) = 15$	$15 \div (-5) = -3$	⊖

The **rules for dividing integers** are similar to the rules for multiplying:

- The quotient of two integers with the same sign is positive.
- The quotient of two integers with different signs is negative.

Problem Solving

MATHEMATICAL PRACTICES

© **29. Persevere** Oleg and Nat went scuba diving and dove to 45 feet below the surface. There are 3 feet in a yard. Evaluate $-45 \div 3$ to find how many yards they dove.

30. The coldest temperature ever recorded in Antarctica was −129°F. The warmest recorded temperature was 59°F. How much warmer is the warmest temperature than the coldest?

© **31. Reason** Mrs. Ortiz is planning a turkey dinner for 20 people. She needs to decide how big a turkey to buy. Each person will eat about 0.62 pounds. Should she buy a 10-, 15-, or 20-pound turkey? Explain.

© **32. Use Tools** Kaden tracked the weather in Anchorage, Alaska, for a week in January.

Day	Lowest Temperature
Monday	−15°F
Tuesday	−8°F
Wednesday	−13°F
Thursday	−13°F
Friday	−14°F
Saturday	−10°F
Sunday	−11°F

© **33. Writing to Explain** Mia solved the problem below. Is Mia's work correct? If not, explain your answer.
$(-9 \div -3) + (-3) = -6$

34. Compute 15×12 mentally by finding the product of twice the first factor and half the second factor.

a What was the coldest temperature for the week?

b What was the warmest temperature?

35. The water level of a lake dropped 15 inches over a period of 5 weeks. At what rate did the water level change per week? Evaluate $-15 \div 5$.

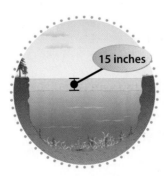
15 inches

Lesson

10-8

Common Core

6.NS.7.d Distinguish comparisons of absolute value from statements about order....
Also 6.NS.6.a, 6.NS.6.b, 6.NS.7, 6.NS.7.c

Absolute Value

How can you use absolute value to order how prices change?

Stock prices rise and fall every day. The table shows the annual change in price for a group of stocks. These changes serve as an important indicator of stock market prices.

During which two years were the stock price changes the greatest?

Year	Price Change (to nearest percent)
2010	11
2009	19
2008	−34
2007	6

Another Example **How can you use absolute value to order from least to greatest?**

The table shows the changes in the number of items answered correctly from a first math test to a second math test for five students.

Order the students based on the least to the greatest change.

Student	Change in Number of Correct Answers
Antoine	4
Lauren	−6
Micah	3
Beth	0
Pat	−5

Find the absolute value of each change.

Antoine: $|4| = 4$
Lauren: $|-6| = 6$
Micah: $|3| = 3$
Beth: $|0| = 0$
Pat: $|-5| = 5$

Order the absolute values from least to greatest.

$|0|, |3|, |4|, |-5|, |-6|$

The order of students from least to greatest change in the number of correct answers is Beth, Micah, Antoine, Pat, and Lauren.

Explain It

1. How do you know that the absolute value of 0 is 0?

2. How would the order change if the students were ordered based on the greatest to the least change?

Remember that the absolute value of a number is its distance from zero on the number line. To find the two years with the greatest change, use absolute value.

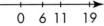

-34   0   6 11   19

2010: $|11| = 11$
2009: $|19| = 19$
2008: $|-34| = 34$
2007: $|6| = 6$

Order the absolute values from greatest to least.

$|-34|, |19|, |11|, |6|$

The change for 2008 was greatest. The negative value means the price dropped by 34%.

The second largest change was for 2009. The positive value means the price increased by 19%.

Guided Practice*

 **MATHEMATICAL PRACTICES**

Do you know HOW?

1. How far away from 0 is $|9|$?

2. How far away from 0 is $|-9|$?

3. Is 5 or -3 farther away from 0? How do you know?

4. Order $|-5|$, 0, $|-7|$, and $|2|$ from *least* to *greatest*.

Do you UNDERSTAND?

© 5. **Writing to Explain** How are the integers -4 and 4 alike? How are they different?

6. Explain how you know that -7 has a greater absolute value than 6.

© 7. **Reason** In 2006, the change in stock price was 16%. This was a greater change than in what years shown in the table?

Independent Practice

For **8** through **10**, use $>$ or $<$ to compare.

8. $|76|$ ▓ $|-36|$

9. $|-55|$ ▓ $|-27|$

10. 41 ▓ $|-42.3|$

For **11** through **13**, order the values from *greatest* to *least*.

11. $|-14|, |-8|, |21|, |3|$

12. $|-99|, |0|, |-62|, |98.05|$

13. $|64|, |-65|, |-67|, |6|$

For **14** through **16**, order the values from *least* to *greatest*.

14. $|6|, |-4|, |-3|, |-18|$

15. $|-1\frac{1}{2}|, |-23|, |-7|, |-9|$

16. $|45|, |-39|, |-14|, |-5|$

 DIGITAL Animated Glossary www.pearsonsuccessnet.com

17. Laura hiked a mountain ridge trail. She climbed a total of 125 ft in the first hour, descended 132 ft the second hour, and descended another 127 ft the third hour. Order the absolute values of her elevation changes from least to greatest.

ⓒ **18. Critique Arguments** Amanda says that the absolute value of 7 is −7 because the distances from 0 to −7 and 0 to 7 are the same. Explain what you know about absolute value that proves she is incorrect.

ⓒ **19. Reason** About how long will it take Tyler to read a 242-page book if he reads at an average rate of 25 pages per hour?

   A about 5 hr

   B about 10 hr

   C about 20 hr

   D about 50 hr

ⓒ **20. Writing to Explain** Cassie started running as part of a fitness program. In the first month, she lost 3 pounds. Write her weight change as an integer and its absolute value. Explain why the absolute value is used to describe her weight loss.

ⓒ **21. Critique Reasoning** Albert and Rebecca toss horseshoes at a stake that is 12 feet away from where they are standing. Whoever is closer to the stake wins. Albert's horseshoe lands 3 feet in front of the stake and Rebecca's lands 2 feet behind the stake. Albert says that −3 is less than 2, so he wins. Explain whether Albert is correct.

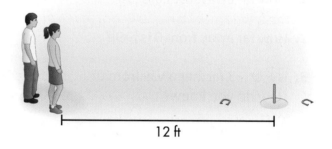

12 ft

For **22** through **24**, use the number line that shows the positions, in feet, of some friends' golf balls relative to the hole, during a miniature golf game.

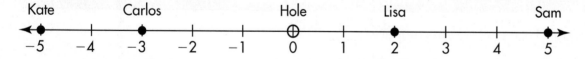

22. Whose golf ball is closest to the hole?

23. Whose golf balls are exactly 5 feet from the hole?

24. What is the distance from Kate's golf ball to Sam's golf ball?

ⓒ **25. Construct Arguments** Describe how the first coordinates of points P and G are alike and how they are different, and what that tells you about their positions relative to the vertical axis.

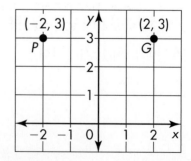

Mixed Problem Solving

Pilots of hot air balloons use different air currents at different elevations to steer the balloons. They make the balloon climb or descend to an elevation with an air current blowing in the direction they want to travel.

The diagram shows the directions of wind at different elevations relative to the balloon's position. Where the balloon appears in the diagram to the left of the right arrow is the original position of the balloon. Use the diagram to answer **1** through **5**.

1. How far will the balloon have to travel to reach the nearest air current that is moving to the left?

2. What is the greatest change in elevation that the balloon will have to travel to reach an air current that is moving to the right?

3. Order the absolute values of the distances from the balloon to right-moving air currents from least to greatest.

4. The balloon climbs to an elevation with an air current taking it to the left. What is the least change from that elevation the balloon would then need to make to be able to change direction and move to the right?

5. The balloon climbs 55 ft from its original position. The pilot then wants to move to an air current moving to the left. Is it closer for the balloon to climb or descend? Explain your answer.

6. A balloon is flying at an elevation of 500 ft. It climbs 17 ft and then descends 22 ft. Is the balloon higher or lower than where it began? Explain how you can use absolute value to find the answer.

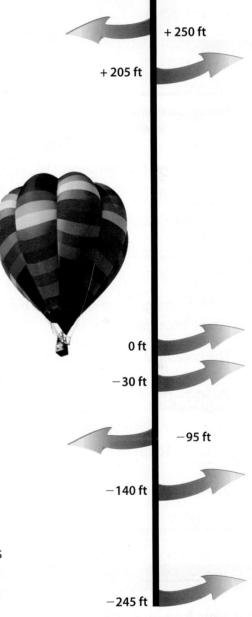

+ 300 ft
+ 250 ft
+ 205 ft
0 ft
−30 ft
−95 ft
−140 ft
−245 ft

Common
Core

6.NS.6.c Find and position
integers and other rational
numbers on a horizontal
or vertical number line
diagram; find and position
pairs of integers and other
rational numbers on a
coordinate plane. Also
6.NS.6, 6.NS.6.b, 6.NS.8

Graphing Points on a Coordinate Plane

Hands-On
grid paper

How can you graph a point on a coordinate plane?

A coordinate plane is a <u>grid containing two number lines that intersect in a right angle at zero</u>. The number lines, called the *x*- and *y*-axes, <u>divide the plane into four</u> quadrants.

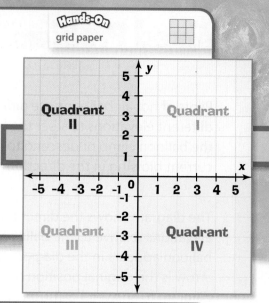

Another Example How can you use a coordinate plane to locate points on a map?

A grid map of Washington, D.C., is shown at the right. Give the coordinates of the Lincoln Memorial.

• Find the Lincoln Memorial on the map.

• Follow the grid line directly to the *x*-axis to find the *x*-coordinate, −5.

• Follow the grid line directly to the *y*-axis to find the *y*-coordinate, −3.

The coordinates of the Lincoln Memorial are (−5, −3).

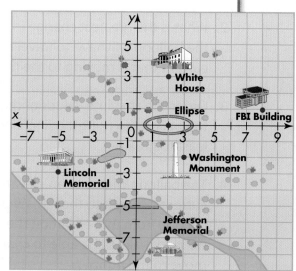

Explain It

1. If a point is to the left of the *y*-axis, what do you know about its *x*-coordinate?

2. What are the coordinates of the Washington Monument?

Guided Practice*

MATHEMATICAL
PRACTICES

Do you know HOW?

For **1** through **3**, draw a coordinate plane. Graph and label the points given.

1. $W(-5, 1)$ **2.** $X(4, 3)$ **3.** $Z(-2, 0)$

Do you UNDERSTAND?

4. In which quadrant does a point lie if its *x*- and *y*-coordinates are negative?

© **5. Communicate** Do (4, 5) and (5, 4) locate the same point? Explain.

An ordered pair (x, y) of numbers <u>gives the coordinates</u> <u>that locate a point relative to each axis</u>. Graph the points Q (2, −3), R (−1, 1), and S (0, 2) on a coordinate plane.

To graph any point P with coordinates (x, y):

- Start at the origin, <u>(0, 0)</u>.
- Use the x-coordinate to move right (if positive) or left (if negative) along the x-axis.
- Then use the y-coordinate of the point to move up (if positive) or down (if negative) following the y-axis.
- Draw a point on the coordinate grid and label the point.

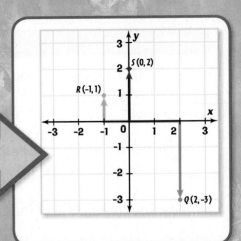

Independent Practice

For **6** through **13**, draw a coordinate grid and label the x- and y-axes between −10 and 10. Graph and label these points on the graph.

6. A (1, −1)

7. B (5, 7)

8. C (−9, 2)

9. D (5, −2)

10. E (−4½, −8)

11. F (1, 3¼)

12. G (−5⅓, 0)

13. H (−4¾, −9½)

For **14** through **21**, give the ordered pair of each point.

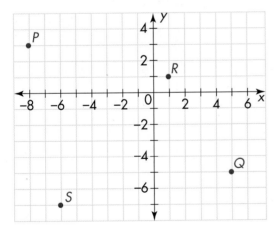

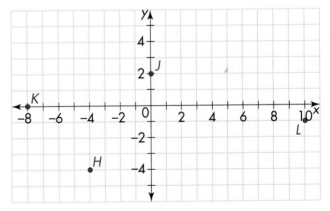

14. P

15. Q

18. H

19. J

16. R

17. S

20. K

21. L

For **22** and **23**, draw a coordinate plane and graph the ordered pairs. Connect the points in order and describe the figure you drew.

22. (−5, 2), (−10, 2), (−10, −3), (−5, −3)

23. (8, −2), (10, −2), (10, 4), (8, 4)

For **24** through **27**, use the map of the town of Descartes at the right. The Market Square is at the origin.

 Use the red dots to locate the coordinates of buildings.

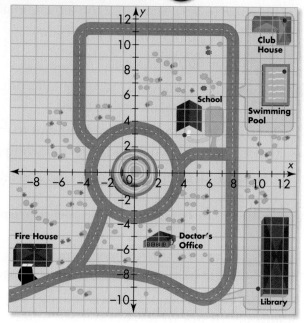

24. Give the coordinates of the Library.

25. What building is located in Quadrant III?

Ⓒ **26.** **Be Precise** $\frac{3}{4}$ of the quadrants have buildings in them. Which quadrants are they?

Ⓒ **27.** **Writing to Explain** If you were at the Market Square and you wanted to get to the Doctor's Office, according to the map, how would you get there?

Draw a coordinate grid like the one at the right, with the *x*- and *y*-axes between −6 and 6. Use the grid for **28** through **30**.

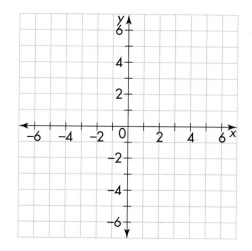

28. Graph and label points $A(-2, 2)$, $B(2, 2)$, $C(2, -2)$, and $D(-2, -2)$. Connect the points to form figure *ABCD*. What figure is formed?

Ⓒ **29.** **Reason** Move point *B* two units up and label the new point *M*. Move point *C* two units up and label the new point *N*. What are the coordinates of point *M* and *N*? What figure does *AMND* form?

30. Multiply the *x*-coordinates of points *A* and *B* by 3 and graph the new points. Label them *R* and *S*. What are the coordinates of points *R* and *S*? What figure does *RSCD* form?

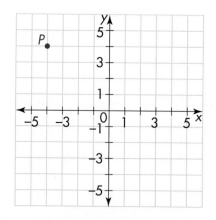

Ⓒ **31.** **Use Structure** Which ordered pair locates point *P* on the coordinate plane on the right?

A $(-4, -4)$ **C** $(4, 3)$

B $(-4, 4)$ **D** $(-3, 4)$

Mixed Problem Solving

Some astronomers use a star map to help them find constellations in the sky. You can use a coordinate grid over the star map to help you locate stars. The section of the sky map at the right shows the Big Dipper. The main stars in the constellation are named with letters from the alphabet.

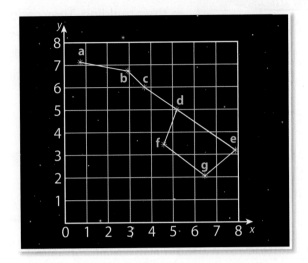

For **1** through **6**, match letters on the map to the coordinate pair.

1. What star is located nearest (3, 7)?

2. What are the nearest coordinates of c?

3. What are the nearest coordinates of e?

4. What star is located nearest (1, 7)?

5. What star is located nearest (5, 5)?

Ⓒ 6. **Writing to Explain** Why would using a coordinate grid help you look at the sky?

Tom stood in his backyard to draw his own sky map. Draw a coordinate grid like the one at the right and mark the positive y-axis as North. Map the following stars, planets, and objects using the coordinate grid.

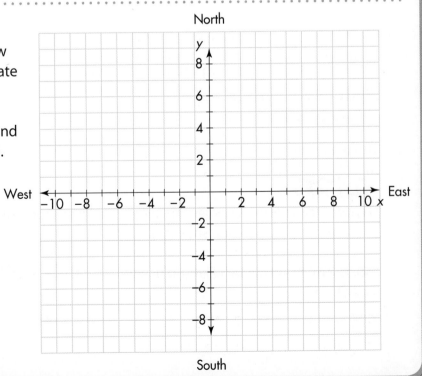

7. Sirius (−7, −6)

8. Betelgeuse (4, 4)

9. North Star (0, 3)

10. Orion (3, 3)

11. Moon (8, −4)

12. Vega (6, 6)

Lesson

10-10

©

Common Core

6.G.3 Draw polygons in the coordinate plane given coordinates for the vertices; use coordinates to find the length of a side joining points with the same first coordinate or the same second coordinate. Apply these techniques in the context of solving real-world and mathematical problems. Also **6.NS.8**

Problem Solving

Use Reasoning

Sanjay and Nathaniel are riding the elevator in their building. They rode up 10 floors, down 16, and up 25. If the elevator ended up on the floor shown in the picture, on which floor did they start?

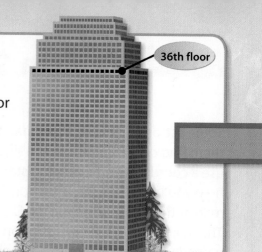

36th floor

Another Example **How can you find the side lengths of a polygon?**

Mike used a coordinate plane to design a patio. He plotted points A(3, 2), B(3, 4), C(7, 4), D(7, 7), E(9, 7) and F(9, 2). The points are the vertices of polygon *ABCDEF*. The line segments that connect the vertices are the sides of polygon *ABCDEF*. The units shown on the grid are in yards. To buy materials to build the patio, he needs to know its perimeter. What is the perimeter of the patio?

To find the length of each side of polygon *ABCDEF*, subtract the endpoint coordinates that are different:

AB: 4 − 2 = 2; *BC*: 7 − 3 = 4; *CD*: 7 − 4 = 3;
DE: 9 − 7 = 2; *EF*: 7 − 2 = 5; *FA*: 9 − 3 = 6

Then add all side lengths to find the perimeter:

AB + *BC* + *CD* + *DE* + *EF* + *FA* =
2 + 4 + 3 + 2 + 5 + 6 = 22.

The perimeter of *ABCDEF* is 22 yards.

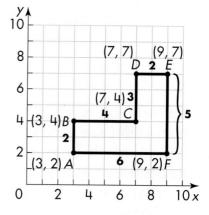

Explain It

1. How can you find the length of a vertical line segment that is part of the polygon shown above?

2. How can you find the length of a horizontal line segment?

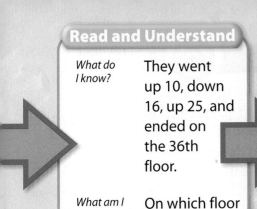

What do I know?	They went up 10, down 16, up 25, and ended on the 36th floor.
What am I being asked to find?	On which floor did they start riding the elevator?

If you know the ending position and each change made, then you can use the inverse of each change to work backward.

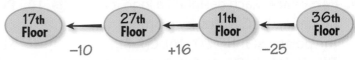

Work backward from the 36th floor.

They started on the 17th floor.

Guided Practice*

MATHEMATICAL PRACTICES

Do you know HOW?

Solve. Check your answer.

1. Gustavo chose a number, added 3 to it, divided the sum by 2, and subtracted 1. The result was 4. What was Gustavo's number?

Do you UNDERSTAND?

2. In the elevator problem, what operation undoes adding 25?

3. **Reason** What is the perimeter of the rectangle *ABCD* with vertices $A(1, 1)$, $B(3, 1)$, $C(3, 6)$, and $D(1, 6)$?

Independent Practice

MATHEMATICAL PRACTICES

Solve. Check your answers.

4. Jessie's mom had a bowl of apples. Liz took three to a picnic, Jessie packed one in her lunch, and Jessie's dad ate one. There were only three left. How many apples were in the bowl to start with?

5. Amy spent $9 at the movies, earned $18 for babysitting, and bought a book for $7. She had $13 left. How much money did she have at the start?

6. **Reason** Nadia draws plans for a rectangular piece of fabric she will cut for a quilt. The vertices are at (1, 2), (1, 4), (5, 4), and (5, 2). How many units long are the shorter sides of the rectangle?

Applying Math Practices

- What am I asked to find?
- What else can I try?
- How are quantities related?
- How can I explain my work?
- How can I use math to model the problem?
- Can I use tools to help?
- Is my work precise?
- Why does this work?
- How can I generalize?

7. Reason Scott, Adrian, and Juan are jumping at the skate park. Scott jumped twice as high as Juan. Adrian jumped 4 ft, which was 2 ft less than Scott. How high did Juan jump?

8. Tyler paid $6.93 for 5.5 pounds of grapes for the class picnic. Find the price per pound of grapes. Write an equation that describes the situation and then solve it.

9. Persevere Zach designed a logo for his band, the C-Notes, by plotting the points: $A(3, 10)$, $B(7, 10)$, $C(7, 8)$, $D(4, 8)$, $E(4, 4)$, $F(7, 4)$, $G(7, 2)$, and $H(3, 2)$. Draw the C-Notes logo on grid paper. Find the perimeter of polygon *ABCDEFGH*.

10. Persevere Allie is saving for new computer equipment that costs $110. She started saving in week one. She saved $26 in week two, spent $14 in week three, and saved $47 in week four. She now has $91. How much did she save during week one?

11. Be Precise Mike has a rain gauge in his backyard. He empties it every night before he goes to bed. There was rain in the gauge when Mike took his first measurement before breakfast. At 10 A.M., Mike measured an increase of 0.3 inch. At lunch, he measured an increase of 0.6 inch. Before dinner, Mike noted an increase of 0.1 inch, and before he emptied it that night there was an increase of 0.4 inch. There was a total of 2.7 inches of rain in the gauge. How much did it rain during the previous night before breakfast?

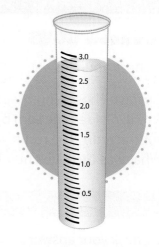

© Think About the Structure

12. Jordan is thinking of a number. If you triple the number, add 9, and divide by 10, you end up with 3. What order of operations would you do to work backward to find the number?

  A addition, multiplication, subtraction

  B multiplication, subtraction, division

  C division, addition, multiplication

  D multiplication, addition, division

13. For softball training, Ursula runs $\frac{1}{4}$ mile, walks $\frac{1}{8}$ mile, and runs $\frac{1}{2}$ mile. She wants to increase her total distance to a whole mile. What expression would you use to find how much more distance she needs to reach her goal?

  A $\frac{1}{4} + \frac{1}{8} + \frac{1}{2} - 1$ **C** $1 + \frac{1}{4} + \frac{1}{8} + \frac{1}{2}$

  B $1 - (\frac{1}{4} + \frac{1}{8} + \frac{1}{2})$ **D** $\frac{1}{4} + \frac{1}{8} + (1 - \frac{1}{2})$

Skills Review Use $<$, $>$, or $=$ to compare.

1. -3 ◯ 4 **2.** -9 ◯ -10

3. 5 ◯ 6 **4.** -5 ◯ -6

Order the following integers from least to greatest.

5. $3, -3, -9, 5$ **6.** $-11, 10, 0, -1$ **7.** $14, -7, 2, -5$

Order the following rational numbers from least to greatest.

8. $\frac{1}{2}, 4, -\frac{3}{2}, -\frac{1}{2}$

9. $-\frac{4}{3}, \frac{3}{4}, \frac{5}{3}, -\frac{3}{4}$

10. $\frac{22}{7}, -\frac{6}{7}, \frac{5}{7}, -\frac{12}{7}$

11. $\frac{5}{19}, -\frac{4}{5}, 0, -\frac{2}{3}$

Find the distance between these points on a number line.

12. -6 and 2 **13.** -7 and 5 **14.** 12 and 19 **15.** -7 and -3

Find the distance between the points on the coordinate plane.

16. $(1, 4)$ and $(1, 8)$ **17.** $(9, 6)$ and $(9, -2)$ **18.** $(0, -5)$ and $(0, 0)$ **19.** $(-3, 6)$ and $(-3, -8)$

Error Search Find each solution that is not correct. Write it correctly and explain the error.

20. $\frac{1}{2} < -2$ **21.** $-3 < 2$ **22.** $-5 > \frac{11}{2}$ **23.** $\frac{2}{3} < \frac{-3}{4}$

Number Sense

Choose the correct answer.

24. The distance between -5 and -17 on a number line is (equal to/greater than/ less than) the sum of their absolute values.

25. The distance between a positive integer and a negative integer on a number line is (equal to/less than/greater than) the sum of their absolute values.

26. The distance between a negative integer and a negative integer on a number line is (always/sometimes/never) the sum of their absolute values.

27. The order of numbers from least to greatest is (always/sometimes/never) the same as the order of their absolute values.

1. Which point on the number line represents −4? (10-1)

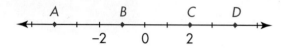

- **A** Point *A*
- **B** Point *B*
- **C** Point *C*
- **D** Point *D*

2. Look at the number line below. Which of the following is the absolute value for the integer located at Point *C*? (10-1)

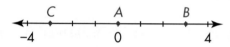

- **A** −3
- **B** 0
- **C** 3
- **D** 4

3. The table shows the resulting golf scores as compared with par after 6 rounds of golf. What is the opposite value of Emma's score? (10-1)

Name	Score
Cassie	−4
Emma	−12
Juanita	6

- **A** −12
- **B** −4
- **C** 4
- **D** 12

4. Which shows the numbers in order from greatest to least? (10-2)

- **A** −5, |−13|, 24, 7
- **B** 24, |−13|, 7, −5
- **C** |−13|, −5, 7, 24
- **D** 24, 7, −5, |−13|

5. In which quadrant would (−4, 4) be graphed? (10-9)

- **A** Quadrant I
- **B** Quadrant II
- **C** Quadrant III
- **D** Quadrant IV

6. Which point represents −1.4 on the number line? (10-3)

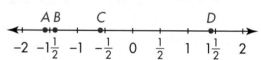

- **A** Point *A*
- **B** Point *B*
- **C** Point *C*
- **D** Point *D*

7. What is the distance between the point at (3, 4) and the point at (3, 13) on a coordinate grid? (10-10)

- **A** 1 unit
- **C** 3 units
- **B** 9 units
- **D** −2 units

8. Which value equals |37|? (10-8)

- **A** −37
- **C** 37
- **B** 0
- **D** 40

9. At the end of a football game, Emilio had a loss of 3 yards, Carson had a loss of 7 yards and Tracy had a loss of 6 yards. Which of the following comparisons is true? (10-2)

A $-3 > -7$

B $-7 > -6$

C $-3 < -7$

D $-3 < -6$

10. Order these absolute values from least to greatest. (10-8)

$|-7|$ $|5|$ $|-4|$ $|6|$ $|-15|$

A $|-15|, |-7|, |-4|, |5|, |6|$

B $|6|, |5|, |-4|, |-7|, |-15|$

C $|-4|, |5|, |6|, |-7|, |-15|$

D $|-7|, |6|, |-4|, |5|, |-15|$

11. The grid map shows the location of some places in Amy's town. What are the coordinates of the library? (10-9)

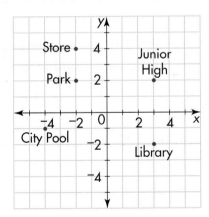

A $(-3, 2)$

B $(-2, 3)$

C $(3, -2)$

D $(2, -3)$

12. Which shows the numbers in order from least to greatest? (10-3)

A $\frac{8}{10}, 0.58, \frac{3}{8}, -1.5$

B $-1.5, \frac{3}{8}, 0.58, \frac{8}{10}$

C $-1.5, 0.58, \frac{3}{8}, \frac{8}{10}$

D $-1.5, \frac{8}{10}, \frac{3}{8}, 0.58$

13. The table gives some elevations, compared to sea level, of places in the United States. Which of the following lists the places in order from the one with the least elevation to the one with the greatest? (10-2)

Place	Elevation
Potomac River	1
New Orleans	-8
Lake Champlain	95
Death Valley	-282

A New Orleans, Death Valley, Potomac River, Lake Champlain

B Death Valley, New Orleans, Potomac River, Lake Champlain

C Death Valley, New Orleans, Lake Champlain, Potomac River

D Potomac River, New Orleans, Lake Champlain, Death Valley

14. Amelia had some money saved before she started saving $2 each week. After 3 weeks, her total savings were $16. How much money had Amelia saved at the beginning of the 3 weeks? (10-10)

A $2

B $8

C $10

D $14

Set A, pages 222–225

For each point on the number line, write the integer, its opposite, and its absolute value.

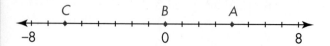

A: 4, −4, 4   B: 0, 0, 0   C: −6, 6, 6

Compare 4 and −6. Which is less?

−6 is farther to the left on the number line than 4, so −6 is less. −6 < 4

Use the number line to help you write 0, 4, and −6 in order from greatest to least.

The order from greatest to least is 4, 0, −6.

Remember that opposites have the same absolute value, which is their distance from zero.

For each point on the number line, write the integer, its opposite, and its absolute value.

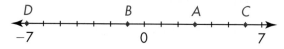

1. A   **2.** B   **3.** C   **4.** D

Use <, >, or = to compare.

5. 7 ◯ −3   **6.** |−23| ◯ 23

7. −50 ◯ −54   **8.** |−4| ◯ 0

Order from *greatest* to *least*.

9. −13, 14, 0, 8, −6, −23

Set B, pages 226–228

Rational numbers are numbers that can be written as a quotient $\frac{a}{b}$, where a and b are integers and b does not equal 0.

Order the numbers −0.1, 0.75, and −$\frac{1}{4}$ from least to greatest by graphing them on a number line.

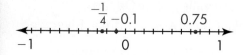

Write the order: −$\frac{1}{4}$, −0.1, 0.75

Compare 0.55 and $\frac{3}{5}$.

Convert $\frac{3}{5}$ to a decimal.

$$5)\overline{3.0}\;\;{}^{0.6}$$

0.6 is to the right of 0.55 on a number line.

So, 0.6 > 0.55 or 0.55 < 0.6.

Remember that all positive decimals, mixed numbers, and fractions have opposites that are located to the left of the zero on the number line.

For **1** through **3**, graph each rational number on the same number line.

1. $\frac{3}{4}$ **2.** −$\frac{2}{5}$ **3.** 0.5

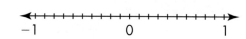

Use <, >, or = to compare.

4. 0.25 ◯ $\frac{1}{4}$ **5.** 1$\frac{5}{8}$ ◯ 1.6

6. 3.65 ◯ 3$\frac{3}{4}$ **7.** −$\frac{2}{3}$ ◯ −$\frac{3}{4}$

Use the rules for adding integers with different signs to find $4 + (-8)$.

Step 1 Find the absolute value of the addends.

$$|4| = 4$$
$$|-8| = 8$$
$$8 - 4 = 4$$

Step 2 Subtract the lesser absolute value.

Step 3 Use the sign of the addend with the greater absolute value.

$$-4$$

So, the sum is -4.

To add integers with the same signs, add the absolute values instead of subtracting and the sum will always have the same sign as both addends.

Remember that you can think about walking a number line to add integers, walking backward for negative addends and forward for positive addends.

Find each sum.

1. $8 + (-7)$ **2.** $-16 + (-2)$

3. $-12 + 4$ **4.** $9 + 29$

5. $1 + (-14)$ **6.** $-5 + (-15)$

7. $15 + (-32)$ **8.** $-11 + (-12)$

9. $-22 + 35$ **10.** $29 + (-17)$

11. $-54 + 4$ **12.** $-27 + (-5)$

Find $7 - (-2)$.

$7 + (-(-2))$ ← Subtracting –2 is like adding the opposite of –2.

$7 + 2$ ← The opposite of –2 is 2.

So, the difference is 9.

Use a number line to find $7 - (-2)$.

Start at 0, facing the positive integers. Walk forward 7 steps for 7.

Since subtracting –2 is like adding 2, walk forward 2 steps for –2. Stop at 9.

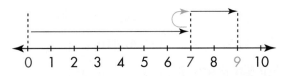

So, $7 - (-2)$ is 9.

Remember that subtracting an integer is the same as adding its opposite. So the rules for adding integers can also help you subtract integers.

Find each difference.

1. $5 - (-9)$ **2.** $-8 - (-6)$

3. $-11 - (-11)$ **4.** $7 - 18$

5. $3 - (-5)$ **6.** $4 - (-13)$

7. $7 - 19$ **8.** $5 - (-4)$

9. $-2 - (-7)$ **10.** $4 - (-4)$

11. $-15 - 15$ **12.** $50 - 57$

 **INTERVENTION**

Find the product $18 \times (-5)$.

Rules for Multiplying Integers

- The product of two integers with the same sign is positive.

- The product of two integers with different signs is negative.

One factor is positive and the other factor is negative, so the product is negative.

$18 \times (-5) = -90$

Remember that the product of two integers with different signs is negative. The product of two integers with the same signs is positive.

Find each product.

1. -12×3 **2.** $-8 \times (-5)$

3. $-4 \times (-41)$ **4.** -18×6

5. $-47 \times (-10)$ **6.** $2 \times (-39)$

7. $-60 \times (-15)$ **8.** $72 \times (-20)$

Find the quotient $-51 \div (-17)$.

Use the relationship between multiplication and division to identify the sign of the quotient.

Both of the integers are negative, so the quotient is positive.

$-51 \div (-17) = 3$

Remember that the quotient of two integers with different signs is negative. The quotient of two integers with the same sign is positive.

Find each quotient.

1. $-32 \div 4$ **2.** $-81 \div (-3)$

3. $121 \div -11$ **4.** $-96 \div (12)$

5. $1{,}500 \div -15$ **6.** $320 \div (-16)$

7. $-525 \div 10$ **8.** $-2.5 \div (-5)$

The absolute value of a number is its distance from 0 on the number line.

Use the number line to compare $|-5|$ to $|-2|$ and order $|3|, |4|, |-2|, |-5|$ from *least* to *greatest*.

-5 -4 -3 -2 -1 0 1 2 3 4 5

$|-5| = 5$

$|-2| = 2$ So, $|-5| > |-2|$

$|3| = 3$ and from least to greatest:

$|4| = 4$ $|-2|, |3|, |4|, |-5|$

Remember number lines can help you compare and order absolute values.

For **1** through **4**, use $<$ or $>$ to compare.

1. $|7| \quad |-9|$ **2.** $|-2| \quad |0|$

3. $|4| \quad |-6|$ **4.** $|10| \quad |-8|$

For **5** through **7**, order the values from least to greatest.

5. $|-3|, |-2|, |10|$

6. $|-7|, |0|, |-5|$

7. $|2|, |-6|, |-8|$

An ordered pair (x, y) of numbers gives the coordinates that locate a point on a coordinate plane.

To graph any point P with coordinates (x, y):

Step 1 Start at the origin, (0, 0).

Step 2 Use the x-coordinate to move right (if positive) or left (if negative) along the x-axis.

Step 3 Then use the y-coordinate of the point to move up (if positive) or down (if negative) following the y-axis.

Step 4 Draw a point on the coordinate grid and label the point.

Remember that the number lines called x- and y-axes divide the coordinate plane into four quadrants.

For **1** through **6**, give the ordered pair for each point.

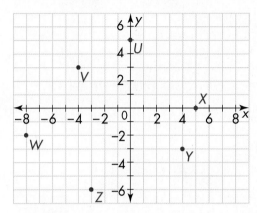

1. U   2. V

3. W   4. X

5. Y   6. Z

Alec's class went to 2 one-act plays. The evening lasted 3 hr, with a 0.25 hr intermission. The second play was 1.25 hr. How long was the first play?

Work backward by subtracting the hours you know from the total time of the evening.

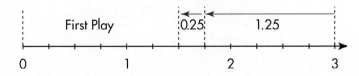

The first play lasted 1.5 hr.

You can work backward when there is an end result after a series of steps, and you are asked to find the information in the first step.

Remember to use reasoning when you solve problems.

1. What is the perimeter of a rectangle with vertices at (6, 2), (9, 2), (9, 9), and (6, 9)?

2. At midnight, Emma's temperature was 99.8 °F, which was 0.4 °F lower than it was at 10 P.M. At 10 P.M., Emma's temperature was 1.1 °F higher than it was at dinner time. What was Emma's temperature at dinner time?

Topic 11

Properties of Two-Dimensional Figures

1 How many lines of symmetry does a sea star have? You will find out in Lesson 11-8.

2 How can you identify some pairs of angles in this geodesic dome? You will find out in Lesson 11-3.

3 What type of triangles does sunlight make on this ancient building in Chichen Itza, Mexico? You will find out in Lesson 11-4.

Review What You Know!

Vocabulary

Choose the best term from the box.

> • perpendicular   • angle
> • congruent

1. Two line segments are __?__ if they are the same length.

2. Two rays that have the same endpoint form a(n) __?__.

3. Two lines that meet to form right angles are called __?__.

Lines and Segments

Identify these pairs of line segments.

4.

5.

6.

7.

Properties

ⓒ **Writing to Explain** Write an answer for each question.

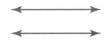

8. How are the two lines above different from perpendicular lines? Explain.

9. Are the two lines above the same length? Explain.

Basic Geometric Ideas

What words can describe two-dimensional figures?

	What You **Show**	What You **Write**
A point is <u>an exact location in space</u>.	• P	P or point P
A line is a <u>straight path of points that goes on forever in two directions</u>.	C D	$\overleftrightarrow{CD}$ or $\overleftrightarrow{DC}$
A ray is <u>part of a line, with one endpoint, extending forever in only one direction</u>.	M N	$\overrightarrow{MN}$

Other Examples

	What You Show	**What You Write**
Intersecting lines <u>pass through the same point</u>.		$\overleftrightarrow{ST}$ intersects $\overleftrightarrow{UV}$
A plane is <u>a flat surface that extends forever in all directions</u>.	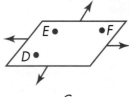	$\square DEF$
Parallel lines are <u>in the same plane</u> but <u>do not ever intersect</u>.		$\overleftrightarrow{CD} \parallel \overleftrightarrow{AB}$
Perpendicular lines are <u>intersecting lines that form a right angle</u>.	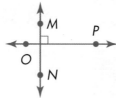	$\overleftrightarrow{MN} \perp \overleftrightarrow{OP}$

Explain It

1. Explain the relationship between parallel lines and a plane.

2. Look around your classroom and identify examples of intersecting line segments, perpendicular line segments, and parallel line segments.

	What You **Show**	What You **Write**
A line segment is <u>part of a line</u> <u>with two endpoints</u>.		$\overline{CD}$ or $\overline{DC}$
<u>Line segments</u> that are the same <u>length</u> are congruent line segments.		$\overline{CD} \cong \overline{EF}$
The midpoint of a line segment is <u>halfway</u> <u>between the two endpoints</u>. It forms two new congruent segments.		*G* or midpoint *G*

Guided Practice*

MATHEMATICAL PRACTICES

Do you know HOW?

Use symbols to identify each figure.

1.

2.

3.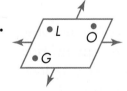

4.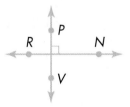

Do you UNDERSTAND?

5. What is formed where two lines intersect?

ⓒ **6. Reason** If $\overline{CD}$ above is 2 inches long, how long is $\overline{EF}$? Explain.

7. In Exercises 1 and 4, why can you say $\overleftrightarrow{AB}$ two ways but $\overrightarrow{NP}$ only one way?

Independent Practice

In **8** though **13**, use symbols to name each figure.

8.

9.

10.

11.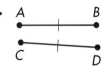

12.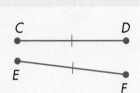

13.
A ——|—— B
C ——|—— D

In **14** and **15**, draw each figure.

14. $\overleftrightarrow{EM} \parallel \overrightarrow{AW}$

15. Point *B* is the midpoint of $\overline{DG}$.

*For another example, see Set A on page 294.

In **16** through **21**, use the diagram to name the figures.

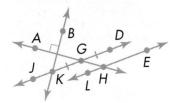

 A small square inside an angle is a sign that the angle is a right angle (the two rays of the angle are perpendicular).

16. two lines that intersect

17. three rays

18. two perpendicular lines

19. three line segments

20. two parallel lines

21. a midpoint

22. First St., Second St., and Third St. intersect Lansing St. and Farmers St. forming 90° angles.

   a Name two streets that are parallel.

   b Name two streets that are perpendicular.

23. **Think About the Structure** Greg earned $935 last month. After he paid his rent, he had $515 left. Which equation would you use to find how much Greg paid as rent?

   A $935 - x = 515$ **C** $x - 515 = 935$

   B $515 - x = 935$ **D** $x - 935 = 515$

24. **Be Precise** Which describes the line segments formed by the mirrors in this periscope?

   A perpendicular   **C** rays

   B intersecting   **D** parallel

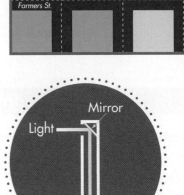

25. If 386 students at Central Middle School are involved in a school sport, how many students are not involved in a school sport?

Central Middle School	
Grade 6	263 students
Grade 7	301 students
Grade 8	278 students

26. **Reason** How many different lines can you draw through one point? How many different lines can you draw through a set of two points?

27. **Writing to Explain** Two bike trails, *AC* and *FH*, are congruent. Trail *AC* is 2.3 miles long and uphill. Which is the longer trail? Explain.

Perpendicular Bisectors

A **perpendicular bisector** is a line that divides a line segment into two equal parts and is perpendicular to the segment. The perpendicular bisector contains the segment's midpoint.

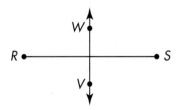

A geometric construction is a step-by-step process to build and draw a geometric shape. To construct the perpendicular bisector of a line segment, use a straightedge and a compass.

Example: To construct the perpendicular bisector of $\overline{AB}$, follow the steps below.

1. Trace $\overline{AB}$.

2. Place your compass center on point A and set the opening more than halfway to point B. Draw a large arc that goes both below and above $\overline{AB}$.

3. With the same compass setting, place the compass center on B and draw another large arc.

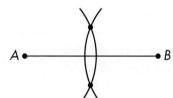

4. Label the points of intersection C and D. Draw $\overleftrightarrow{CD}$. $\overleftrightarrow{CD}$ is the perpendicular bisector of $\overline{AB}$.

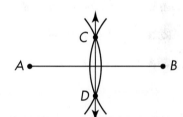

Practice

1. Trace $\overline{MN}$ at right. Construct a perpendicular bisector to $\overline{MN}$.

2. Perpendicular lines cross each other at right angles. In the illustration at the right, $\overleftrightarrow{CD}$ is the perpendicular bisector of $\overline{AB}$. How could you check to see if $\overleftrightarrow{CD}$ is the perpendicular bisector of $\overline{AB}$?

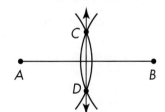

3. Create and color your own geometric construction using a straightedge and a compass. Include at least one perpendicular bisector.

4. Kayla tried to construct a perpendicular bisector. Her results are shown at the right. What do you think she did wrong?

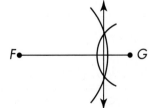

5. Use a compass and straightedge. Draw a line segment and its perpendicular bisector. Place the compass center at the midpoint and draw a circle. Extend the segment and perpendicular bisector so as to intersect the circle at four points. Draw a 4-sided shape connecting the four points. What is this shape?

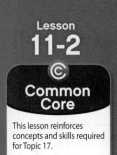

Common Core

This lesson reinforces concepts and skills required for Topic 17.

Measuring and Drawing Angles

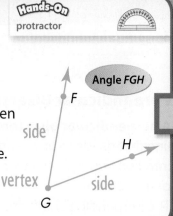

Angle *FGH*

How can you measure angles?

Angle *FGH* is written ∠*FGH*. An angle is formed when <u>two different rays have the same endpoint</u>, called the vertex. The two rays form the sides of the angle.

What is the measure of ∠*FGH*?

You can use a protractor to measure the size of an angle. An angle is measured in degrees (°).

Another Example **What are some different types of angles?**

Angles can be classified by their measures.

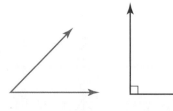

Acute angle: <u>angle between 0° and 90°</u>

Right angle: <u>angle of exactly 90°</u>

Obtuse angle: <u>angle between 90° and 180°</u>

Straight angle: <u>angle of exactly 180°</u>

How can you draw an angle with a given measure?

Draw an obtuse angle with the measure 100°.

Step 1

Draw $\overrightarrow{DW}$ and mark a point *W* on the ray.

D   W

Step 2

Place the protractor's center on endpoint *D* and line up the ray with the 0° mark. Use the same scale to place a point at 100°.

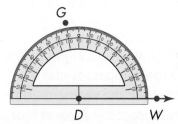

G

D   W

Step 3

Use a straightedge to draw $\overrightarrow{DG}$.

m∠*GDW* = 100°

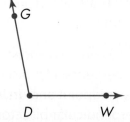

G

D   W

Place the protractor's center on the angle's vertex, G. Then line up the 0° mark on the protractor with one side of the angle.

Find where the other side of the angle crosses the protractor.

Read the angle measure. There are two measures on the protractor. Use the same scale of measures that was used to line up the angle at zero.

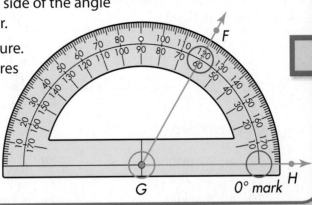

The measure of angle FGH is 60°.

Write:

m∠FGH = 60°

Guided Practice*

MATHEMATICAL PRACTICES

Do you know HOW?

Measure the angle, then classify each angle as acute, right, obtuse, or straight.

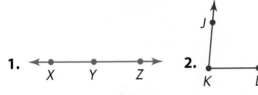

1. X Y Z

2. J K L

Draw the angles. Classify each angle as acute, right, obtuse, or straight.

3. 153° **4.** 30°

Do you UNDERSTAND?

5. Reason Why would obtuse angles always use the larger numbers on a protractor and acute angles always use the smaller numbers?

6. Persevere If $\overrightarrow{GJ}$ is added to endpoint G to make a straight angle JGH in the example at the top of the page, what is the measure of the new ∠JGF?

Independent Practice

In **7** through **12**, measure the angle, then classify each angle as acute, right, obtuse, or straight.

7. V W X

8. S T U

9. A C W

10. G H I

11. 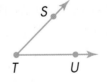 D E F

12.  P Q R

*For another example, see Set B on page 294.

Lesson 11-2 **267**

In **13** through **15**, give the measurement of each angle.
Classify each angle as acute, obtuse, or straight.

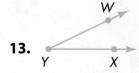

13. Y X W

14. 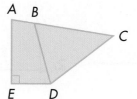 C E V

15. 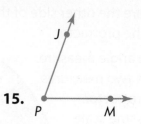 J P M

For **16** through **21**, draw the angles described.

16. a right angle   **17.** an 80° angle   **18.** a 55° angle

19. a 117° angle   **20.** a 22° angle   **21.** a 148° angle

Without using a protractor, draw estimated angles of measures given in **22** through **24**.
Then use a protractor to check your work.

22. 15°   **23.** 83°   **24.** 155°

Use the drawing of Mr. Patel's class garden at the right
for **25** through **27**.

25. Which angle in the garden is a right angle?

26. Which angle in the garden is obtuse?

27. If ∠ABC in the garden is a straight angle, what is
the sum of ∠ABD and ∠CBD?

ⓒ **28. Writing to Explain** Describe how these angles are alike
and different.

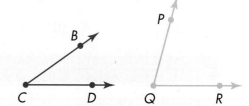

ⓒ **29. Model** A page is separated into x number of columns,
each $2\frac{1}{2}$ inches wide. If the width of the page is 10 inches,
which equation can be used to solve for x?

A $2\frac{1}{2} \times 10 = x$ **C** $2\frac{1}{2}x = 10$

B $10x = 2\frac{1}{2}$ **D** $2\frac{1}{2} \div 10 = x$

ⓒ **30. Reason** Which kind of angle is angle S?

A obtuse   **C** right

B acute   **D** straight

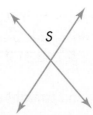

Construct an Angle Bisector

An **angle bisector** is a ray that splits an angle into two congruent angles. The endpoint of the angle bisector is the vertex of the angle.

Tip *When tracing an angle to construct a bisector, extend the rays of the angle. This makes it easier to draw the arcs.*

Example: Trace ∠ABC. Then follow the steps to construct the bisector of ∠ABC.

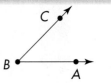

Step 1 Place your compass point on point B and draw an arc intersecting the sides of ∠ABC. Label the points of intersection Q and P.

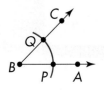

Step 2 Adjust the compass to any setting greater than $\frac{1}{2}$ the length of QP. Place the compass center on Q and draw an arc.

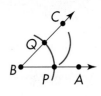

Step 3 With the same compass setting, place the compass point on P and draw another arc. Label the point of intersection R. With a straightedge, draw $\overrightarrow{BR}$. $\overrightarrow{BR}$ is the bisector of ∠ABC.

Practice

Trace ∠QRS at the right.

1. Construct the bisector of ∠QRS. Label the bisector $\overrightarrow{RZ}$.

2. What is the measure of ∠QRZ?

3. Trace ∠LMN. Then construct the bisector $\overrightarrow{MO}$ of ∠LMN.

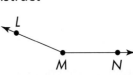

4. Trace ∠DEF. Then construct the bisector $\overrightarrow{EG}$ of ∠DEF.

5. Trace the compass map design at the right. Use what you know about constructing angle bisectors to draw in 45° NE, 135° SE, 225° SW, and 315° NW.

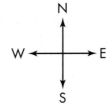

6. How could you use a protractor and straight edge to draw an angle bisector?

Angle Pairs

What are some special pairs of angles?

Look at the scissors. Can you tell by looking at the angle between the blades what the angle between the handles measures?

Vertical angles are <u>a pair of angles that are formed by intersecting lines and have no side in common</u>. The blades and handles of the scissors form vertical angles.

40°

The blades and handles form vertical angles.

Other Examples

Other special pairs of angles:

Adjacent angles are <u>a pair of angles with a common vertex and a common side</u> but no common interior points. For example, ∠EFG and ∠GFH are adjacent angles.

Complementary angles are <u>two angles whose measures add up to 90°</u>. ∠QRS and ∠TUV are complementary angles.

Supplementary angles are <u>two angles whose measures add up to 180°</u>. ∠WXY and ∠ABC are supplementary angles.

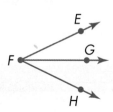

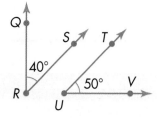

m∠QRS + m∠TUV = 90°

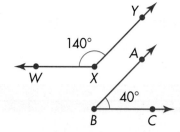

m∠WXY + m∠ABC = 180°

Explain It

1. Why aren't the angles WXY and ABC complementary angles?

2. If ∠QRS and ∠ABC are congruent angles, what kind of angles are ∠QRS and ∠WXY?

Congruent angles <u>have the same measure</u>.
Vertical angles are congruent angles.
∠LPK and ∠MPN are vertical angles.

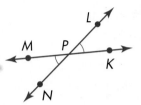

The arcs inside the angles show that they are congruent.

∠LPK is congruent to ∠MPN.
You can write ∠LPK ≅ ∠MPN.

The angle between the blades and the angle between the handles are congruent.

∠LPK ≅ ∠MPN

If m∠LPK = 40°, then m∠MPN = 40°.

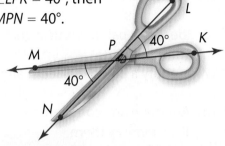

Guided Practice*

MATHEMATICAL
PRACTICES

Do you know HOW?

In **1** through **3**, find the values of the variables.

 Remember that the measure of a straight angle is 180°.

1. x

2. y

3. z

Do you UNDERSTAND?

4. When two lines intersect, how many pairs of vertical angles are formed?

5. Which angle above is supplementary to ∠MPN?

6. Reason Look at the angles formed by the scissors at the top of the page. What are the measures of ∠LPM and ∠KPN?

Independent Practice

In **7** through **10**, find x.

7.

8.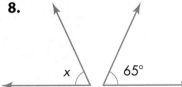

9.

10.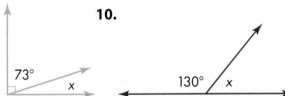

Find the measures of the angles that are complementary to the angles in **11** and **12**.

11. 63°   **12.** 20°

Find the measures of the angles that are supplementary to the angles in **13** and **14**.

13. 63°   **14.** 20°

Animated Glossary
www.pearsonsuccessnet.com

Use the diagram at the right for **15** through **19**.

15. Identify six obtuse angles.

16. Identify a pair of vertical angles.

17. Identify a pair of adjacent angles.

18. Are there any complementary angles in the diagram? If so, identify them.

19. Identify three different pairs of supplementary angles.

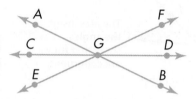

Problem Solving

MATHEMATICAL PRACTICES

Use this map to answer **20** and **21**.

20. What kind of angle does Oak Street make with Elm Street?

21. What kind of angle describes the turn from Pine Street to Ash Street?

ⓒ 22. Writing to Explain Can two acute angles be supplementary? Can two obtuse angles be supplementary? Explain.

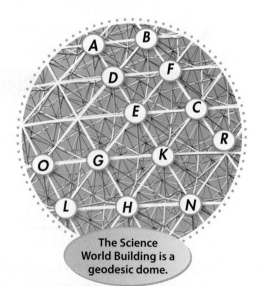

The Science World Building is a geodesic dome.

Use the picture to answer **23** and **24**.

23. Which angles on the dome are vertical angles?

    A ∠ABD and ∠DEF   **C** ∠GHK and ∠LHN

    B ∠DEF and ∠GEK   **D** ∠LHG and ∠GHN

ⓒ 24. Think About the Structure Why are angles *EKH* and *CKN* vertical angles?

    A They are formed by intersecting lines and have a common side.

    B They are formed by intersecting lines and have no common side.

    C They have a common vertex and a common side.

    D They are formed by parallel lines and have no common side.

Supplementary and Complementary Angles

Use tools

Geometry Drawing

Name the measures of two pairs of supplementary angles.

Step 1 Go to the Geometry Drawing eTool. Click on the Draw a line segment tool.

Click in the workspace, drag, and click again to draw line segment *AB*. Click on point *A* and then drag in another direction to create angle *CAB*. Finally, click on point *A* again and drag to point *D* so *D*, *A*, and *B* are all on the same line.

Step 2 Measure the angles.

Click on the distance measurement tool palette. Expand to show the triangle. Click on the Angle Measurement tool. To measure angle *DAC*, click on point *D*, then *A*, and then *C*. See the lower right corner. Measure angle *CAB* similarly. The sum of the measures should be 180 degrees.

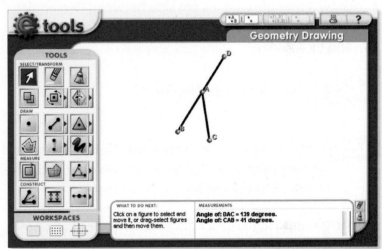

If it isn't, click on the Arrow tool and use it to move point *D* until the sum is 180 degrees, which will mean that *D*, *A*, and *B* are all on the same line. Angles *DAC* and *CAB* are supplementary. Write down their measures.

Step 3 Use the Arrow tool to move point *C* and watch how the measures change.

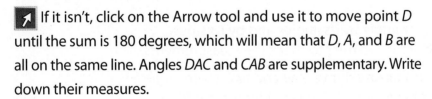
Practice

1. Move point *C* so angle *CAB* is acute. Move point *D* until angle *DAC* plus angle *CAB* is 90 degrees, a right angle. Move point *C* again to find the measure of two pairs of complementary angles. Write down their measures.

Triangles

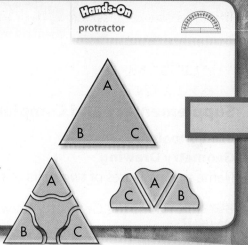

How can you classify triangles?

The angle measures within a triangle are related. The sum of the measures of the three angles of a triangle is 180°.

When the three angles of a triangle are joined together as three adjacent angles, they make a straight angle.

$m\angle A + m\angle B + m\angle C = 180°$

Another Example **How can you draw a triangle from given information?**

Draw a triangle with a 4 cm side between two angles that measure 35° and 55°. Then classify the triangle by its angles and by its sides.

Step 1 Draw a 4 cm line segment.

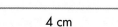
4 cm

Step 2 Use a protractor to draw a 35° angle at one end of the segment and a 55° angle at the other end. Extend the sides of the angles until they meet.

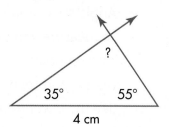

Step 3 Find the missing angle measure. The sum of the measures of the angles of a triangle is 180°.

35 + 55 + ▭ = 180   35 + 55 + 90 = 180

The missing angle measure is 90°.

Step 4 Classify the triangle by its angles and by its sides. Use a protractor and ruler to check the measurements.

The triangle has one right angle and two acute angles, so it is a right triangle. The three sides are different lengths, so it is a scalene triangle. The triangle is a right scalene triangle.

Explain It

1. Explain how to find the missing angle measure.

© 2. **Reason** How would you draw a right isosceles triangle?

Triangles can be classified by their angles.

Acute triangle

<u>All angles are acute angles.</u>

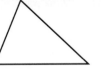

Right triangle

<u>One angle is a right (90°) angle.</u>

Obtuse triangle

<u>One angle is an obtuse angle.</u>

Triangles can be classified by their sides.

Equilateral triangle

<u>All sides are congruent.</u>

Isosceles triangle

<u>At least two sides are congruent.</u>

Scalene triangle

<u>No sides are congruent.</u>

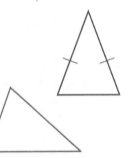

Guided Practice*

MATHEMATICAL **PRACTICES**

Do you know **HOW?**

Find the missing angle measure. Then classify each by its angles and its sides.

 Remember that the three angles of a triangle always add up to 180°.

1.

30°
120°   x

2.
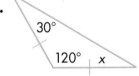
x
60°   60°

Do you **UNDERSTAND?**

© 3. **Reason** How do you know that the two acute angles in a right triangle are complementary?

4. Suppose that a right triangle has a 30° angle. What are the measurements of the other angles?

© 5. **Construct Arguments** Can an isosceles triangle be an obtuse triangle? Explain.

Independent Practice

In **6** through **11**, find the missing angle measures and classify the triangles by their angles and sides.

6.
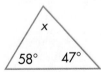
x
58°   47°

7.
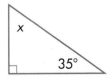
x
35°

8.
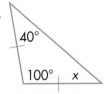
40°
100°   x

9.

x
45°

10.

60°
60°   x

11.
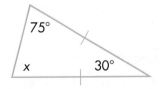
75°
x   30°

Animated Glossary, eTools
www.pearsonsuccessnet.com

*For another example, see Set C on page 295.

Lesson 11-4

275

For **12** through **16**, draw the described triangle. *Start with the angle.*

12. a right isosceles triangle

13. a triangle with two acute angles

14. an obtuse scalene triangle

15. Draw a triangle with a 2-inch side between two 35° angles. Then classify the triangle by its angles and sides.

16. Draw a triangle with a 125° angle between sides of 3 inches and 4 inches.

Problem Solving

MATHEMATICAL
PRACTICES

ⓒ **17. Reason** What type of angle is the largest angle in an equilateral triangle?

ⓒ **18. Writing to Explain** What type of angle is the largest angle in a right triangle? Explain.

19. Haleh earned $108 painting 12 shutters. How much would she earn for painting 15 shutters?

ⓒ **20. Persevere** A triangle has 42° and 29° angles. What is the measure of the third angle? Is it acute, right, or obtuse?

21. The 13-member choir attended a concert. Tickets cost $25 each. The bus ride cost $2.25 per member each way. How much did the choir spend on the trip?

Use the picture to the right to answer **22** and **23**.

22. Isosceles triangles are formed by the light on this pyramid. How would you describe these triangles by their angles?

  A scalene   **C** obtuse

  B acute   **D** right

At 3 P.M. on an equinox, the sun makes triangles of light and shadows on the stairs of El Castillo at Chichen Itza, Mexico.

ⓒ **23. Model** Four stairways, each having 91 steps, extend from the base to the top of El Castillo. Which operation would you use to find how many steps there are in the pyramid?

  A squaring   **C** subtraction

  B multiplication   **D** division

Mixed Problem Solving

Tangrams are ancient Chinese puzzles made up of geometric shapes. All tangrams have the same seven pieces, which fit together to form a square. The objective is to create a design using all seven pieces, called tans. The tans must all be touching, but they may not overlap.

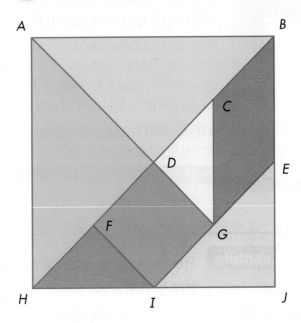

Use the square tangram for **1** through **7**.

1. What shape do the 7 pieces of the tangram make?

2. What shape is determined by points A, D, and H?

3. Identify three pairs of parallel line segments.

4. Identify a pair of perpendicular line segments.

5. What shape is determined by points C, B, E, and G?

6. What shape is formed by points H, B, and J?

7. How many triangles are in the tangram?

On a separate sheet of paper, use the above design to create your own tangram. Using the tans from your tangram, try to make the design at the right, using all seven tans. Make sure none of them overlap. Use the puzzle for **8** through **10**.

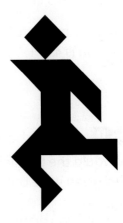

8. Describe the shape the tangram puzzle forms.

9. Make your own tangram puzzle from the pieces. Name your design and describe what shape your design makes.

10. Explain how you created your own shape in Exercise 9.

Common
Core

This lesson reinforces
concepts and skills required
for Topic 17.

Quadrilaterals

Hands-On
protractor

What are the properties of different quadrilaterals?

Any quadrilateral can be divided into two triangles. Because the sum of the measures of the angles of each triangle is 180°, the sum of the measures of the angles of any quadrilateral is 360°.

A trapezoid is <u>a quadrilateral with only one pair of parallel sides</u>.

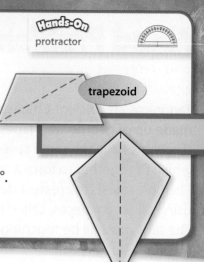

trapezoid

Another Example **How can you draw a quadrilateral from the given information?**

Suppose you want to draw a parallelogram with 5 cm and 2 cm sides. The measures of the opposite angles are 135° and 45°. Using a protractor, follow these steps to draw this parallelogram.

Step 1 Draw a 5 cm line segment.

5 cm

Step 2 Draw a 45° angle at one end of the segment and a 135° angle at the other end. Mark off 2 cm on each side.

Step 3 Connect the two sides with a line segment. Check that the last side measures 5 cm.

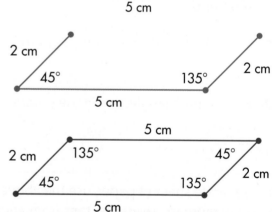

The sum of the measures of the angles of the parallelogram is 45° + 135° + 45° + 135° = 360°.

Explain It

1. How would the parallelogram change if the opposite angles given were both 90°?

2. How could you draw a quadrilateral with congruent sides but no right angles?

A parallelogram is <u>a quadrilateral with both pairs of opposite sides parallel</u>. Opposite sides are congruent, and opposite angles are congruent.

A rhombus is <u>a parallelogram with all sides congruent</u>.

A rectangle is <u>a parallelogram with four right angles</u>.

A square is <u>a rectangle with all sides congruent</u>. A square is also a rhombus.

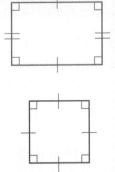

For another example, see Set C on page 295.

Guided Practice*

MATHEMATICAL PRACTICES

Do you know HOW?

Classify each polygon in as many ways as possible. Find the missing angle measurement.

1.
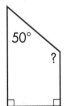
50°
?

2.

120° ?
60° 120°

3.

70°
150°
?

4.
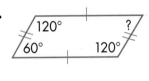
40° 40°
140° ?

Do you UNDERSTAND?

© 5. Be Precise Can all rhombuses be classified as squares? Explain.

6. What is the missing measure of the angle in the diagram? Explain how you found the answer.

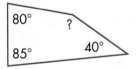
80° ?
85° 40°

Independent Practice

In **7** through **10**, classify each polygon in as many ways as possible.

7.

8.

9.

10.

DIGITAL
Animated Glossary, eTools
www.pearsonsuccessnet.com

For **11** through **13**, three angles of a quadrilateral are given. Find the measure of the fourth angle and classify each quadrilateral according to its angles.

11. 62°, 130°, 110°   **12.** 65°, 115°, 65°   **13.** 90°, 90°, 90°

For **14** and **15**, use the figure at the right to determine whether there is enough information to solve the problem. Solve if possible.

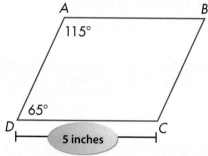

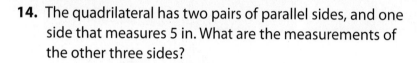

14. The quadrilateral has two pairs of parallel sides, and one side that measures 5 in. What are the measurements of the other three sides?

15. Find the m∠B and m∠C for the figure at the right.

For **16** and **17**, draw quadrilaterals with the given information. Label all side and angle measurements.

16. All four sides of the quadrilateral measure 5 cm. Two of the opposite angles are 130°.

17. A quadrilateral has congruent opposite sides and angles. One side measures 8 cm, and another side measures 2 cm. The top right angle measures 45°.

© **MATHEMATICAL PRACTICES**

© **Model** For **18** and **19**, write each word phrase as an algebraic expression.

18. twice *n* increased by 12

19. *m* squared divided by 3

20. The computer club raised $105.75 for new software. A math program costs $49.50. A reading program costs $65.39. About how much more money does the club need to pay for the software?

21. What quadrilaterals and other polygons can you see in the drawing at the right?

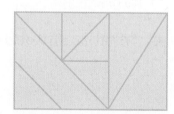

© **22. Construct Arguments** All parallelograms have opposite sides parallel. Are squares and other rectangles parallelograms? Explain.

23. If you divide a square into two congruent triangles, what type of triangles are they?

24. Draw a 5 cm side between a 100° and a 40° angle. Then classify the triangle by its angles and sides.

25. Generalize What is true about every quadrilateral?

    A The angles total 180°.

    B The angles total 360°.

    C There are two sets of congruent sides.

    D There are two sets of congruent angles.

26. What kind of triangle is a yield sign? Classify it in as many ways as possible.

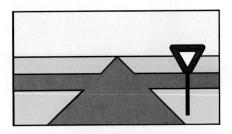

27. Writing to Explain What characteristics help you classify a quadrilateral as a rhombus but not a square? Explain.

28. Persevere A quadrilateral has four congruent sides. One of its angles measures 75°. What are the measures of its other three angles?

29. Think About the Structure Which set of angles could be the measures of angle pairs in a parallelogram?

    A 95°, 120°   **B** 70°, 110°   **C** 25°, 49°   **D** 80°, 90°

30. If you cut off one vertex of a triangle, as shown in the figure, how many sides does the new polygon have? Classify the new polygon in as many ways as possible.

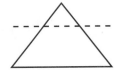

31. In its first week, a new movie had box-office sales of eight million, five hundred sixty-five thousand, four hundred three. Write the number in standard form.

For **32** and **33**, use the table. Tyler's family is planning a trip during a school break. At their destination, some months are rainier than others. They want to go when there is less chance of rain.

Month	Rainfall (inches)
March	3.6
June	1.4
July	0.7
August	1.3
November	2.0
December	6.3

32. Write the rainfall per month in order from least to greatest.

33. Which month would be best for a visit? Explain.

Common Core

7.G.4 Know the formulas for the area and circumference of a circle and use them to solve problems; give an informal derivation of the relationship between the circumference and area of a circle.

Circles

How do you describe circles and parts of circles?

A **circle** is <u>a closed plane figure made up of all points the same distance from a point called the center</u>. A circle is named by its center. Circle *M* is shown below.

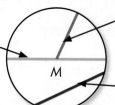

A **radius** (plural, radii) is <u>any line segment that connects the center to a point on the circle</u>.

A **diameter** is <u>any line segment through the center that connects two points on the circle</u>.

A **chord** is <u>any line segment that connects two points on the circle</u>.

Guided Practice*

 MATHEMATICAL PRACTICES

Do you know HOW?

In **1** through **4**, identify the part of each circle shown in red.

1.

2.

3.

4.

Do you UNDERSTAND?

5. If you know the length of the radius of a circle, do you know the length of its diameter? Explain.

© 6. **Reason** A diameter is a special kind of chord that contains the center of the circle. In any given circle, which will be longer, a diameter or some other chord? Explain.

Independent Practice

In **7** through **10**, identify the part of each circle shown in red.

7.

8.

9.

10.

In **11** and **12**, use circle *C* to identify the parts.

11. three central angles

12. two radii

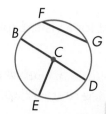

*For another example, see Set D on page 296.

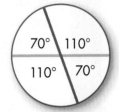

A central angle is <u>an angle whose vertex is the center of the circle</u>. Angle *AMZ* is a central angle.

An arc is <u>part of a circle connecting two points of the circle.</u>

An arc that connects the endpoints of a diameter is a semicircle.

A sector is <u>a region bounded by two radii and an arc.</u>

Two intersecting diameters form 4 adjacent central angles.

The sum of the adjacent central angles of any circle is 360°.

70° | 110°
110° | 70°

Find the measures of all central angles.

13.
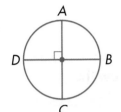

14.
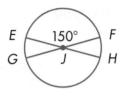

15.
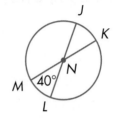

16.
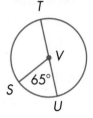

Problem Solving

Ⓒ **17. Model** The algebraic sentence $2x = 34$ describes the diameter of a circle. What part of the circle does *x* stand for?

18. Sylvia bought pencils for $0.13 each. She bought 3 pencils yesterday and 5 pencils today. What was the total cost of the pencils?

Use the picture at the right for **19** and **20**.

Ⓒ **19. Reasonableness** Aristarchus, a circular crater on Earth's moon, is 2.2 miles (3.6 km) deep. What is the radius of this crater?

A 50 mi **B** 80 km **C** 1.1 mi **D** 20 km

25 mi (40 km)

20. Which of the following could be the length of a chord across the crater?

A 30 mi **B** 15 km **C** 80 km **D** 27 mi

Use the circle graph for **21** and **22**.

21. How many other adjacent central angles of the same size make up the shaded part of the graph? Explain.

Ⓒ **22. Writing to Explain** What vocabulary words describe some or all of the area of the missing part? Explain.

60°

Common Core

8.G.2 Understand that a two-dimensional figure is congruent to another if the second can be obtained from the first by a sequence of rotations, reflections, and translations; given two congruent figures, describe a sequence that exhibits the congruence between them. Also **8.G.1**

Transformations and Congruence

What are congruent figures?

Ms. Salujia makes stained-glass windows. She wants to make two triangular windows that are congruent. Congruent figures have the same size and shape.

How can you tell if the two windows are congruent?

Another Example **What are some basic transformations?**

A transformation moves a figure to a new position without changing its size or shape.

A translation moves a figure in a straight direction.

A reflection of a figure gives it a mirror image over a line.

A glide reflection is a translation followed by a reflection.

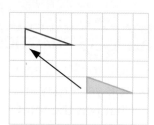

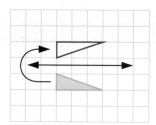

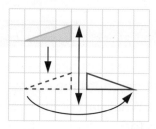

A translation 4 units left and 3 units up

A reflection over a horizontal line.

A glide reflection over a vertical line

A rotation moves a figure about a point.

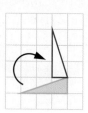

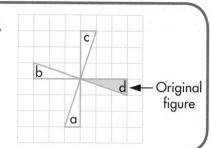

Common rotations, made clockwise:

a. 90° ($\frac{1}{4}$ turn)

b. 180° ($\frac{1}{2}$ turn)

c. 270° ($\frac{3}{4}$ turn)

d. 360° (full turn)

← Original figure

Explain It

1. Compare how a translation and a rotation are similar and different.

Compare the measures of angles and sides.

In congruent polygons:

- Corresponding angles are congruent.
- Corresponding sides are congruent.

Compare the measures of the two windows:

- Corresponding angles are congruent.

  $\angle A \cong \angle L$, $\angle B \cong \angle M$, $\angle C \cong \angle N$

- Corresponding sides are congruent.

  $\overline{AB} \cong \overline{LM}$, $\overline{BC} \cong \overline{MN}$, $\overline{AC} \cong \overline{LN}$

The windows are congruent.

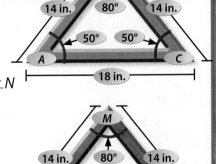

Guided Practice*

MATHEMATICAL PRACTICES

Do you know HOW?

Use the congruent triangles for **1** through **4**.

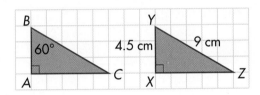

1. Find m $\angle Z$.

2. $AB = \blacksquare$ cm

3. $BC = \blacksquare$ cm

4. Find m $\angle Y$.

Do you UNDERSTAND?

5. When a shape is reflected, is the reflected shape congruent to the original shape? Explain.

6. **Communicate** Explain how you found the measure of $\angle Z$ in Exercise 1.

7. **Be Precise** Are congruent figures similar? Explain.

Independent Practice

In **8** and **9**, tell which transformation each pair shows.

8.

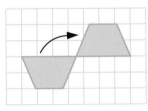

9.

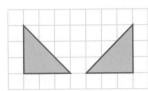

In **10** and **11**, draw the given transformation on grid paper.

10. Rotate 90° counterclockwise about point *P*.

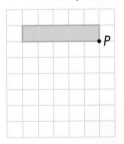

11. Glide 3 units up. Then reflect over the line.

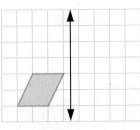

DIGITAL

Animated Glossary
www.pearsonsuccessnet.com

For another example, see Set E on page 296.

In **12** through **15**, use the congruent figures below.

12. Find m∠R.

13. Find m∠S.

14. QR = ☐ cm

15. AB = ☐ cm

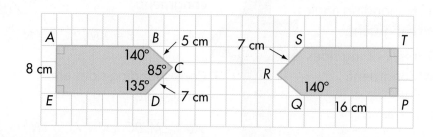

MATHEMATICAL PRACTICES

Ⓒ **16. Writing to Explain** How could you prove that two polygons having the same number of angles are congruent?

Ⓒ **17. Reason** If two circles have congruent diameters, do you think the circles are also congruent? Explain.

18. Use grid paper to draw a figure. Then draw a reflection of that figure over a horizontal line.

Ⓒ **19. Use Tools** Use a protractor to draw a pair of obtuse angles. Label the angle measurements.

20. What kind of transformation is used to make the pattern of congruent figures at the right?

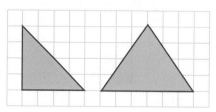

21. Which statement is NOT true about a glide reflection?

 A The original shape is rotated around a point.

 B The shape is reflected across a line.

 C The two shapes are always congruent.

 D The original shape is translated in a straight line.

22. Which pair of shapes is congruent?

A
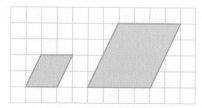

C

B

D
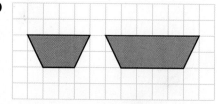

Enrichment

Tessellations

A **tessellation** is a pattern of congruent figures that fills the plane without gaps or overlaps. A parallelogram can tessellate, as shown below. You can alter a parallelogram to make a different shape that tessellates.

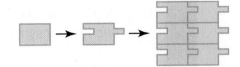

Example: Does the shape below tessellate?

Yes, a rectangle was changed to produce a new shape that tessellates.

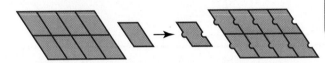

Practice

For **1** through **4**, use each polygon to draw a tessellation.

1. hexagon

2. square

3. right triangle

4. equilateral triangle

For **5** through **8**, determine whether each shape tessellates. If so, trace the figure and draw the tessellation.

5.

6.

7.

8.

Tessellations can also be seen in everyday life and in nature. For **9** through **11**, describe the transformation used to tessellate the shapes.

9.

10.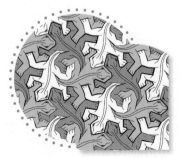

11.

© **Common Core**

8.G.1 Verify experimentally the properties of rotations, reflections, and translations.

Symmetry

What are symmetric figures?

Aria is creating a square mosaic tile design in art class. The art teacher said to create a design that has at least two lines of symmetry.

Does Aria's tile design have at least two lines of symmetry?

Another Example   **What is rotational symmetry?**

When <u>a figure rotates onto itself in less than a full turn</u>, the figure has rotational symmetry. The shapes below have rotational symmetry.

180° (½ turn)   120° (⅓ turn)   90° (¼ turn)   45° (⅛ turn)
rotational symmetry   rotational symmetry   rotational symmetry   rotational symmetry

---

Guided Practice*

MATHEMATICAL PRACTICES

Do you know HOW?

For **1** and **2**, identify the type(s) of symmetry; tell the number of lines of symmetry or smallest turn needed for rotational symmetry.

1.   **2.**

3. How many lines of symmetry, if any, do each of the figures in Another Example have?

Do you UNDERSTAND?

© **4. Persevere** How could you check to see if a paper shape has reflection symmetry?

5. Describe the symmetry of a regular hexagon.

6. Does Aria's mosaic tile design have rotational symmetry? Explain.

Animated Glossary
www.pearsonsuccessnet.com

A figure has reflection symmetry if it can be reflected onto itself. The line of reflection is a line of symmetry. Some figures have more than one line of symmetry.

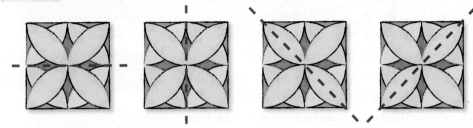

Aria's design has four lines of symmetry. Her design meets her art teacher's directions.

Independent Practice

In **7** through **10**, tell if each figure has reflection symmetry, rotational symmetry, or both. If it has reflection symmetry, how many lines of symmetry are there? If it has rotational symmetry, what is the smallest turn that will rotate the figure onto itself?

7. ❋   8. **H**   9. 🙂   10. ⬣

Problem Solving

MATHEMATICAL PRACTICES

11. Draw a picture of a scalene triangle and its reflection over a vertical line.

© 12. **Reason** Why does a rotation have to be less than 360° to show rotational symmetry?

13. How many times does Caleb have to turn this figure 90° to get it back to its original position?

© 14. **Writing to Explain** How many lines of symmetry does a circle have? Explain.

© 15. **Persevere** Elli wants to draw a figure that has reflection symmetry but not rotation symmetry. What shape might Elli draw?

16. This sea star has 5 arms. How many lines of symmetry does it have?

17. Which shape has exactly 2 lines of symmetry?

A **T**   B **E**   C **N**   D **I**

© Common Core

6.EE.9 Use variables to represent two quantities in a real-world problem that change in relationship to one another; write an equation to express one quantity, thought of as the dependent variable, in terms of the other quantity, thought of as the independent variable. Analyze the relationship between the dependent and independent variables using graphs and tables, and relate these to the equation....

Problem Solving

Make a Table and Look for a Pattern

Polygons with four or more sides can be divided into triangles by connecting vertices. A quadrilateral can be divided into 2 triangles. From a single vertex, how many triangles can a regular polygon with 20 sides be divided into?

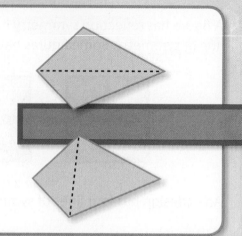

Guided Practice*

© **MATHEMATICAL PRACTICES**

Do you know HOW?

1. Complete the table to show the number of dots needed for the 4th triangle shape in this series.

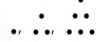

Triangle shape	1st	2nd	3rd	4th
Number of dots	1	3	6	

Do you UNDERSTAND?

2. Explain the pattern for the table in Exercise 1.

© 3. **Communicate** Explain how a table can make it easier to see a pattern.

© 4. **Write a Problem** Write a problem that can be solved by making a table and looking for a pattern.

Independent Practice

© **MATHEMATICAL PRACTICES**

© 5. **Look for Patterns** A diagonal is a line that connects two vertices of a figure that are not already connected by a side. For example, a 5-sided figure can have 5 diagonals. How many diagonals can an 8-sided figure have? Use the simple figures below to help you make a table to solve this problem. State the pattern that you find.

Applying Math Practices

- What am I asked to find?
- What else can I try?
- How are quantities related?
- How can I explain my work?
- How can I use math to model the problem?
- Can I use tools to help?
- Is my work precise?
- Why does this work?
- How can I generalize?

Plan and Solve

Look at some simple figures.

Notice how many sides are in each polygon and how many triangles are formed by connecting a single vertex to other vertices. Make a table and look for a pattern.

Number of sides	4	5	6	7
Number of triangles	2	3	4	5

The pattern is that the number of triangles is 2 less than the number of sides.

From a single vertex, a 20-sided polygon can be divided into 18 triangles.

---

6. A bell is ringing. Each ring lasts 4 seconds. There are 2 seconds between rings. Copy and complete the table for the first 4 rings. Find the pattern to tell how long the ringing lasts if it rings 10 times.

Rings	1	2	3	4
Total time	4 s	10 s	16 s	

© 7. Persevere The three rectangles at right are labeled with their measurements and areas. Create a table to find a pattern for the rectangles. Use the pattern to find the area of a rectangle that is 5 ft × 20 ft.

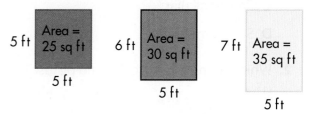

5 ft | Area = 25 sq ft — 5 ft

6 ft | Area = 30 sq ft — 5 ft

7 ft | Area = 35 sq ft — 5 ft

© 8. Persevere These connected triangles form linked sides of three dots each. Use a table to find out how many such triangles you would have to connect to create 20 linked sides of 3 dots each.

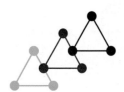

9. What is the pattern for the numbers in the chart on the right? Copy and complete the table.

a	2	3	4	5	10	100
b	6	9	12			

10. XYZ Company is giving a 25¢ discount on the second widget bought and an additional 25¢ discount on each additional widget bought, for up to 5 widgets. Use the pattern in the table to find the total cost of 5 widgets.

Number of widgets	1	2	3	4	5
Total cost	$2.75	$5.25	$7.50	$9.50	

1. The picture shows a diagram of a garden. What is the best description of the relationship between the row of tulips and the row of periwinkles? (11-1)

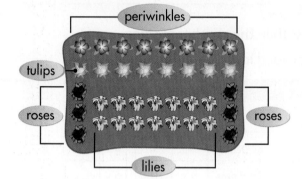

A Intersecting

B Parallel

C Perpendicular

D Supplementary

2. Which triangle is isosceles and obtuse? (11-4)

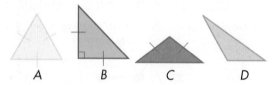

A   B   C   D

A Triangle *A*

B Triangle *B*

C Triangle *C*

D Triangle *D*

3. Travis drew a quadrilateral with opposite sides that were NOT congruent. Which of the following could he have drawn? (11-5)

A Rhombus

B Trapezoid

C Parallelogram

D Rectangle

4. Which of the following angles are acute? (11-2)

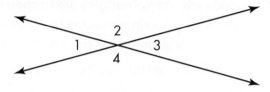

A ∠1 and ∠3

B ∠1 and ∠2

C ∠2 and ∠4

D ∠1, ∠2, ∠3, and ∠4

5. What is the missing angle measure *x*? (11-4)

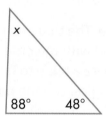

A 44°

B 48°

C 60°

D 68°

6. Which best describes the figure below? (11-1)

A Points *E* and *F*

B $\overleftrightarrow{EF}$

C $\overrightarrow{EF}$

D $\overline{EF}$

7. If you combine the two congruent triangles shown in the figure, which term best describes the new polygon? (11-5)

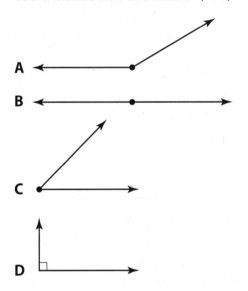

  A Triangle

  B Square

  C Parallelogram

  D Trapezoid

8. Katie drew a 150° angle. Which angle could be the one she drew? (11-2)

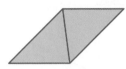

9. Which of the following best describes the edge of a long straight road? (11-1)

  A Point

  B Line

  C Obtuse angle

  D Plane

10. Tiles can be used to frame a square tile pattern of any size as shown in the diagram. How many tiles would be used to frame 25 green tiles arranged in a square? (11-9)

Number of center tiles	1	4	9	16	25
Number of frame tiles	8	12	16		

  A 20

  B 22

  C 24

  D 36

11. Angles are formed when $\overline{AB}$ intersects parallel lines. How many angles do $\overline{AB}$ and 6 parallel lines form? (11-9)

Number of parallel lines	2	3	4	5	6
Number of angles	8	12	16		

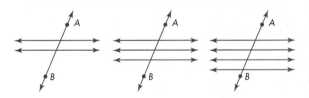

  A 18

  B 20

  C 22

  D 24

Set A, pages 262–264

The terms in the table relate to the figure on the right.

Part	Description	Explanation
$\overrightarrow{GA}$	ray	endpoint at G and extends forever through A
$\overleftrightarrow{AD}$	line	extends forever in both directions
$\overline{GL}$	line segment	part of a line having two endpoints
L	point	midpoint for $\overline{GJ}$
$\overleftrightarrow{FC}$ and $\overleftrightarrow{KN}$	parallel lines	never intersect
$\overleftrightarrow{AD}$ and $\overleftrightarrow{EB}$	perpendicular lines	meet at a right angle
$\overline{GL}$ and $\overline{LJ}$	congruent	are the same length
$\overleftrightarrow{KN}$ and $\overleftrightarrow{BE}$	intersecting lines	pass through the same point, M

Remember that the letters in the diagram below show the location of points, and these points are used to identify rays, lines, line segments, and angles.

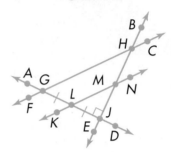

Use the diagram above to answer **1** through **5**.

1. Identify two lines that intersect.

2. Identify two lines that are perpendicular.

3. Identify two lines that are parallel.

4. What is the measure of ∠BJL?

5. If you drew a line through points A and B, how would it relate to $\overleftrightarrow{GH}$?

Set B, pages 266–268, 270–272

The figure below shows a protractor's center placed on the vertex at point K. Use this diagram to complete the exercises.

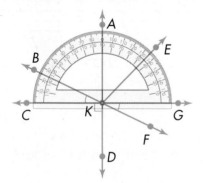

Remember to use the scale on the protractor that lines up an angle side with 0°. Vertical angles are congruent. Adjacent angles share a common vertex and a common side. Adjacent angles do not overlap. The measures of complementary angles total 90°, and the measures of supplementary angles total 180°.

1. Find the measures for ∠GKE and ∠GKB.

2. What are two complementary angles to ∠BKC?

3. Is ∠FKD an acute, right, obtuse, or straight angle?

4. What type of angle is ∠AKF?

5. What angle is adjacent to ∠GKF?

Triangles

Shape	Angles	Sides	Sample
acute triangle	all acute	need not be congruent	
right triangle	one right	need not be congruent	
obtuse triangle	one obtuse	need not be congruent	
equilateral triangle	all congruent	all congruent	
isosceles triangle	at least two congruent	at least two congruent	
scalene triangle	none congruent	none congruent	

Quadrilaterals

Shape	Angles	Sides	Sample
trapezoid	need not be congruent	only one pair parallel	
parallelogram	opposites are congruent	opposites parallel and congruent	
rhombus	opposites are congruent	opposites parallel; all congruent	
rectangle	4 right angles	opposites parallel and congruent	
square	4 right angles	opposites parallel; all congruent	

Remember that the sum of the angles of any triangle is 180°. The sum of the angles of any quadrilateral is 360°. You can use a protractor to draw a triangle or quadrilateral from given information.

Draw the described shapes in **1** through **4**.

1. An obtuse triangle

2. A rhombus with a 55° angle

3. A scalene triangle

4. An equilateral acute triangle

5. What types of triangles do you get if you cut an equilateral triangle in half from a vertex to the opposite side?

6. What types of triangles do you get if you cut a square diagonally?

7. If one angle in a right isosceles triangle is 45°, what are the measures of the other two angles?

8. How are a rhombus and a parallelogram that's not a rhombus alike and different?

9. How are a square and a rhombus that's not a square alike and different?

10. One angle in a parallelogram is 75°. What are the measures of the other three angles?

11. One angle in a trapezoid is 35°. Why can't you use that angle to find the other three angles?

A circle is a closed plane figure made up of all points the same distance from a point called the center. Review these parts of a circle.

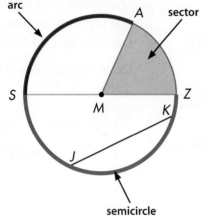

center: *M*
radius: $\overline{MA}$
diameter: $\overline{SZ}$
chord: $\overline{JK}$
central angle: $\angle AMZ$

Remember that the sum of the adjacent central angles of any circle equals 360°.

In **1** and **2**, identify the part of the circle shown in red.

1.

2.

3. What is the length of the diameter of a circle with a 2-inch radius?

4. What are the measures of $\angle CBD$ and $\angle ABC$?

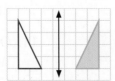

These triangles are congruent. Corresponding sides and angles of congruent polygons are congruent.

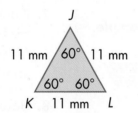

A transformation can be used to move a figure to a new position without changing its size or shape.

A **translation** moves a figure in a straight direction.

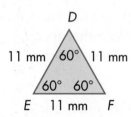

A **reflection** of a figure gives its mirror image over a line.

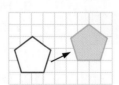

Remember that two figures are congruent if the corresponding sides and angles have the same measures.

1. These quadrilaterals are congruent. Find the measure of $\angle T$, $\overline{TU}$, and $\angle U$.

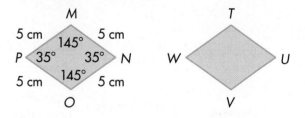

2. Tell whether these figures are related by a translation, a reflection, a glide reflection, or a rotation.

The figure to the right has four lines of reflection symmetry.

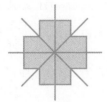

Remember that a figure has reflection symmetry if it can be reflected onto itself.

For **1** and **2**, tell whether each figure has reflection symmetry, rotational symmetry, or both.

The star figure can rotate onto itself in less than a full turn. It has 72° ($\frac{1}{5}$-turn) rotational symmetry.

1.

2.

Figure 1 has 3 rows and 3 columns of squares. For each successive figure, another row and column of squares are added.

Figure 1   **Figure 2**   **Figure 3**

If this pattern continues for 3 more figures, how many squares will be in Figure 6?

Make a table and find the pattern.

Figure	Rows	Columns	Total Squares
1	3	3	9
2	4	4	16
3	5	5	25
4	6	6	36
5	7	7	49
6	8	8	64

There will be 64 squares in Figure 6.

Remember that some problems can be solved by finding a pattern and making a table to extend the pattern.

1. Find the pattern and draw the next three figures.

2. Find the pattern and complete the table.

# of Pounds	Total Cost
2	$3.50
3	$5.25
4	$7.00
5	
6	

Topic 12

Ratios, Rates, and Proportions

1 The *SR-71 Blackbird* is the fastest plane in the world. At top speed, how many miles can it travel in one minute? You will find out in Lesson 12-3.

2 How much water flows over Niagara Falls in one second? You will find out in Lesson 12-1.

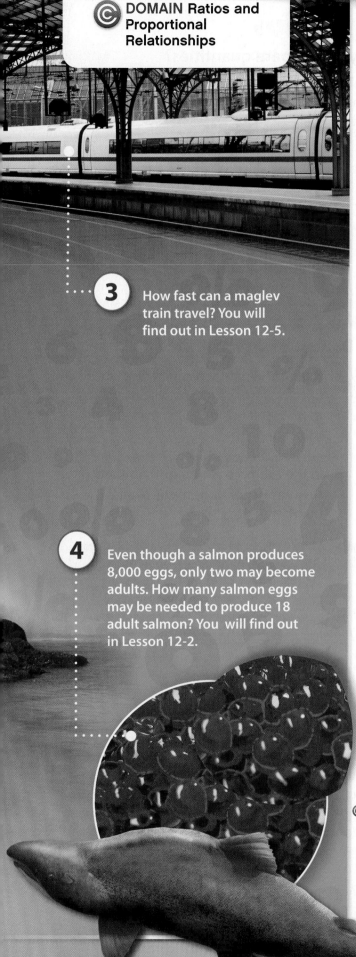

3 How fast can a maglev train travel? You will find out in Lesson 12-5.

4 Even though a salmon produces 8,000 eggs, only two may become adults. How many salmon eggs may be needed to produce 18 adult salmon? You will find out in Lesson 12-2.

Review What You Know!

Vocabulary

Choose the best term from the box.

- fraction
- equivalent fractions
- divisible

1. Fractions that name the same amount are called __?__.

2. A number that can be used to describe a part of a set or a part of a whole is a(n) __?__.

3. A number is __?__ by another number when the quotient is a whole number and the remainder is 0.

Equivalent Fractions

Write two equivalent fractions.

4. $\frac{3}{4}$ **5.** $\frac{7}{8}$ **6.** $\frac{12}{5}$

7. $\frac{1}{2}$ **8.** $\frac{9}{57}$ **9.** $\frac{1}{3}$

Equations

Solve each equation and check your answer.

10. $3n = 24$ **11.** $8c = 0$

12. $y \div 48 = 2$ **13.** $d \div 5 = 7$

Inverse Operations

©**14. Writing to Explain** In the equation $6b = 24$, which operation must you perform to get the variable alone on one side of the equation?

Common
Core

6.RP.1 Understand the
concept of a ratio and use
ratio language to describe a
ratio relationship between
two quantities....

Understanding Ratios

What is a mathematical way to compare quantities?

Tom's Pet Service takes care of cats and dogs.
Currently, there are more dogs than cats.
Compare the number of cats to the
number of dogs. Then compare
the number of cats to the
total number of pets at
Tom's Pet Service.

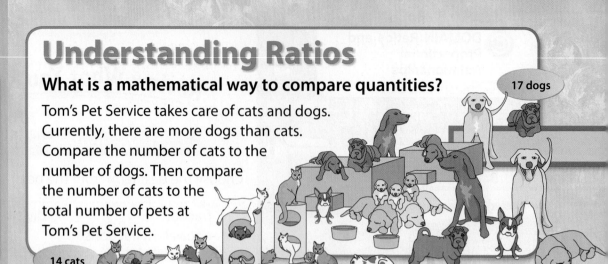

17 dogs

14 cats

Guided Practice*

MATHEMATICAL PRACTICES

Do you know HOW?

A sixth-grade basketball team has 3 centers,
5 forwards, and 6 guards. Write a ratio for
each comparison in three different ways.

1. Forwards to guards

2. Centers to total

3. Centers to guards

Do you UNDERSTAND?

4. **Reason** What are two different types
   of comparisons a ratio can be used
   to make? How is this different from
   a fraction?

5. In the example at the top, compare
   the number of dogs to the total
   number of pets.

Independent Practice

A person's blood type is denoted with the letters A, B,
and O, and the symbols + and −. The blood type A+ is
read as *A positive*. The blood type B− is read as *B negative*.

In **6** through **14**, use the data file to write a ratio
for each comparison in three different ways.

6. O+ donors to A+ donors

7. AB− donors to AB+ donors

8. B+ donors to total donors

9. O− donors to A− donors

10. B− donors to B+ donors

11. O− donors to total donors

12. A+ and B+ donors to
    AB+ donors

13. A− and B− donors to
    AB− donors

14. Which comparison does the ratio $\frac{90}{9}$ represent?

Blood Donors	
Type	**Donors**
A+	45
B+	20
AB+	6
O+	90
A−	21
B−	0
AB−	4
O−	9
Total	195

DIGITAL   Animated Glossary
www.pearsonsuccessnet.com

For another example, see Set A on page 318.

A ratio is <u>a relationship where for every x units of one quantity there are y units of another quantity</u>. A ratio can be written three ways:

x to y,

x:y, or

$\frac{x}{y}$

The <u>quantities</u> x and y <u>in a ratio</u> are called terms.

Use a ratio to compare the number of cats to the number of dogs:

14 to 17,

14:17, or

$\frac{14}{17}$

This ratio compares one part to another part.

Use a ratio to compare the number of cats to the total number of pets:

14 to 31,

14:31, or

$\frac{14}{31}$

This ratio compares one part to the whole.

Problem Solving

MATHEMATICAL
PRACTICES

© 15. Look for Patterns Copy and complete the pattern in the table.

Number of students with pets	1	3	9		81
Total number of students	3	9		81	

16. On average, about 45,000,000 gallons of water flow over the Niagara Falls in 60 seconds. About how much water flows over the Niagara Falls in one second?

© 17. Think About the Structure Martine's quilt is made of 6 red squares and 18 blue squares. Which ratio compares the number of blue squares to the total number of squares in the quilt?

A 6:18 **C** 6:24

B 18:6 **D** 18:24

© 18. Writing to Explain Rita's class has 14 girls and 16 boys. How do the ratios 14:16 and 14:30 describe Rita's class?

© 19. Model Gil has $128 in his savings account. He saves n dollars each week. Write an expression for the amount of money in his account in 10 weeks.

20. A math class surveyed the musical preferences of 42 students. Use their data file to write a ratio for each comparison in three different ways for **a**, **b**, and **c**.

a Students who prefer punk to students who prefer hip-hop

b Students who prefer classic rock to the total number of students surveyed

c Students who prefer rock or classic rock to students who prefer all other types of music

Favorite Music Type	Number of Students
Rock	12
Classic rock	4
Hip-hop	18
Punk	2
Heavy metal	6

Common
Core

6.RP.3 Use ratio and rate reasoning to solve real-world and mathematical problems, e.g., by reasoning about tables of equivalent ratios, tape diagrams, double number line diagrams, or equations.

Equal Ratios and Proportions

How can you find equal ratios?

The ratio of the number of basketball players to the number of baseball players at Grove School is 16 to 48. One way to write the terms of this ratio is $\frac{16}{48}$. You can use what you know about fractions to find equal ratios and to write a ratio in simplest form.

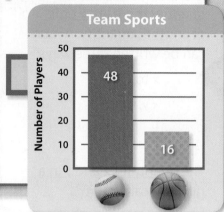

Team Sports

Another Example How can you decide whether two ratios form a proportion?

Use the steps below to decide whether each pair of ratios shown form a proportion.

Ratios to Compare	$\dfrac{7 \text{ laps}}{14 \text{ min}}, \dfrac{12 \text{ laps}}{24 \text{ min}}$	$\dfrac{16 \text{ shots}}{12 \text{ baskets}}, \dfrac{6 \text{ shots}}{4 \text{ baskets}}$
a Compare the units to see if they are the same across the top and bottom.	$\dfrac{\text{Top units}}{\text{Bottom units}} \longrightarrow \dfrac{\text{laps}}{\text{min}}$ The units are the same.	$\dfrac{\text{Top units}}{\text{Bottom units}} \longrightarrow \dfrac{\text{shots}}{\text{baskets}}$ The units are the same.
b Write each ratio in simplest form. Divide by the GCF.	$\dfrac{7 \div 7}{14 \div 7} = \dfrac{1}{2}$ $\dfrac{12 \div 12}{24 \div 12} = \dfrac{1}{2}$	$\dfrac{16 \div 4}{12 \div 4} = \dfrac{4}{3}$ $\dfrac{6 \div 2}{4 \div 2} = \dfrac{3}{2}$
c Compare the simplest forms to see if they are the same.	Both equal $\frac{1}{2}$, so the ratios are proportional.	$\frac{4}{3} \neq \frac{3}{2}$ so the ratios are not proportional.

Explain It

1. What is always true about the simplest forms of two ratios that are proportional?

2. If the ratio of girls to boys in a class is 4 to 5, does that mean there are exactly 4 girls and 5 boys in the class? Explain.

Use multiplication. Multiply both terms by the same nonzero number. For example:

$$\frac{16 \times 3}{48 \times 3} = \frac{48}{144}$$

So, $\frac{16}{48}$, and $\frac{48}{144}$ are equal ratios.

A mathematical statement that two ratios are equal is called a proportion.

So, $\frac{16}{48} = \frac{48}{144}$ is a proportion.

Use division. Divide both terms by the same nonzero number. For example:

$$\frac{16 \div 2}{48 \div 2} = \frac{8}{24}$$

You can divide the terms by their GCF (greatest common factor) to write the ratio in simplest form.

$$\frac{16 \div 16}{48 \div 16} = \frac{1}{3}$$

So, $\frac{16}{48}$, $\frac{8}{24}$, and $\frac{1}{3}$ are all equal ratios.

Guided Practice*

MATHEMATICAL
PRACTICES

Do you know HOW?

In **1** through **3**, write three ratios that are equal to the given ratio.

1. $\frac{12}{21}$ **2.** 1:3   **3.** 6 to 8

Tell if each pair of ratios is proportional.

4. $\frac{3 \text{ hits}}{27 \text{ at bats}}$, $\frac{4 \text{ hits}}{32 \text{ at bats}}$

5. $\frac{7 \text{ hours}}{56 \text{ times}}$, $\frac{3 \text{ hours}}{24 \text{ times}}$

Do you UNDERSTAND?

© **6. Communicate** How can you write a ratio in simplest form?

7. Use the ratios in Another Way above to form a proportion.

© **8. Reason** Do the ratios $\frac{16}{48}$ and $\frac{12}{32}$ form a proportion?

Independent Practice

In **9** through **16**, write three ratios that are equal to the given ratio.

9. $\frac{6}{7}$ **10.** $\frac{4}{5}$ **11.** 13:15   **12.** 4 to 9

13. 5 to 5   **14.** 12:60   **15.** $\frac{25}{15}$ **16.** 1 to 7

Leveled Practice In **17** through **19**, write = if the ratios are proportional. If they are not proportional, write ≠.

17. 1:3 ◯ 3:1   **18.** $\frac{6}{7}$ ◯ $\frac{36}{42}$ **19.** 5 to 8 ◯ 15 to 32

Animated Glossary
www.pearsonsuccessnet.com

In **20** through **22**, tell if each pair of ratios is proportional.

20. $\dfrac{9 \text{ blue}}{17 \text{ red}}$, $\dfrac{36 \text{ blue}}{68 \text{ red}}$ **21.** $\dfrac{20 \text{ balls}}{12 \text{ bats}}$, $\dfrac{15 \text{ balls}}{9 \text{ bats}}$ **22.** $\dfrac{14 \text{ dogs}}{20 \text{ cats}}$, $\dfrac{7 \text{ birds}}{10 \text{ cats}}$

In **23** through **30**, write the ratios in simplest form.

23. $\dfrac{6}{9}$ **24.** 2:30   **25.** 21 to 36   **26.** $\dfrac{8}{64}$

27. 4:20   **28.** $\dfrac{28}{36}$ **29.** 28 to 4   **30.** 16:48

MATHEMATICAL
PRACTICES

31. Use Tools Equal ratios can be found by extending pairs of rows or columns in a multiplication table. Write three equal ratios for $\dfrac{2}{5}$ using the multiplication table.

X	0	1	2	3	4	5	6
0	0	0	0	0	0	0	0
1	0	1	2	3	4	5	6
2	0	2	4	6	8	10	12
3	0	3	6	9	12	15	18
4	0	4	8	12	16	20	24
5	0	5	10	15	20	25	30
6	0	6	12	18	24	30	36

32. Writing to Explain The ratio of the maximum speed of Car A to the maximum speed of Car B is 2:3. Explain whether Car A or Car B is faster.

33. The table to the right shows the time in seconds it takes to burn songs of different lengths on a CD. Write a ratio showing the approximate "length of song in seconds" to "seconds to burn a song."

Length of Song	Seconds to Burn Song
61s	12s
137s	28s
171s	35s
237s	47s
294s	60s

34. Persevere Wildlife officials want to increase the population of wild salmon. Use the information in the picture below to determine which ratio shows how many salmon eggs may be needed to produce 18 adult salmon.

  A 444 eggs to 9 adults

  B 16,000 eggs to 9 adults

  C 72,000 eggs to 18 adults

  D 144,000 eggs to 18 adults

For every 8,000 eggs, only 2 adults may survive.

Mixed Problem Solving

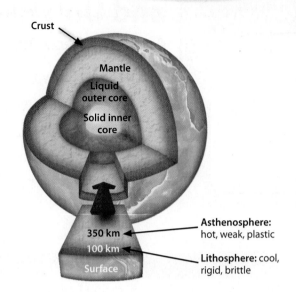

Crust
Mantle
Liquid outer core
Solid inner core
350 km
100 km
Surface

Asthenosphere: hot, weak, plastic

Lithosphere: cool, rigid, brittle

1. What is the ratio of the width of Earth's lithosphere to the width of Earth's asthenosphere shown in the diagram?

2. Earth's diameter is about 12,000 km. The diameter of its inner core is about 2,400 km. The diameter of Planet X is about 6,100 km. If Planet X and Earth are proportional, estimate the diameter of Planet X's inner core.

3. Jupiter's diameter is about 142,900 km. What is the approximate ratio of Earth's diameter to Jupiter's diameter?

4. Because Jupiter's mass is much larger than Earth's mass, gravity is much stronger on Jupiter. The table uses a ratio to approximate what people weigh on Earth compared to what they might weigh on Jupiter.

   a Look for a pattern in the weights. What ratio shows the pattern?

   b What does that ratio mean?

   c Use the ratio you found to determine how much a person weighing 187 lb on Jupiter weighs on Earth.

Data	Weight on Earth	Weight on Jupiter
	70 lb	154 lb
	80 lb	176 lb
	90 lb	198 lb
	100 lb	220 lb
	110 lb	242 lb
	120 lb	264 lb
	130 lb	286 lb

5. One year on Mars equals 1.88 years on Earth. What would your age be if you were born on Mars?

6. The density of ocean water at the surface is about 1,025 kg per 1 m³. Find an equivalent ratio that tells you how much mass of ocean water (in kg) is in 12 m³ of ocean water.

**Common
Core**

6.RP.2 Understand the
concept of a unit rate *a/b*
associated with a ratio *a:b*
with *b* ≠ 0, and use rate
language in the context of
a ratio relationship....

Understanding Rates and Unit Rates

Are there special types of ratios?

A rate is <u>a special type of ratio that compares quantities</u> <u>with unlike units of measure</u>, such as $\frac{150 \text{ miles}}{3 \text{ hours}}$. <u>If the</u> <u>comparison is to 1 unit, the rate is called a</u> unit rate, such as $\frac{50 \text{ miles}}{1 \text{ hour}}$. Find how far the car travels in 1 minute.

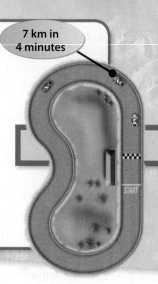

7 km in
4 minutes

Guided Practice*

**MATHEMATICAL
PRACTICES**

Do you know HOW?

Write each as a rate and as a unit rate.

1. 60 km in 12 hours

2. 26 cm in 13 s

3. 230 miles on 10 gallons

4. $12.50 for 5 lb

Do you UNDERSTAND?

© **5. Be Precise** What makes a unit rate different from another rate?

© **6. Communicate** Explain the difference in meaning between these two rates: $\frac{5 \text{ trees}}{1 \text{ chimpanzee}}$ and $\frac{1 \text{ tree}}{5 \text{ chimpanzees}}$.

Independent Practice

In **7** through **18**, write each as a rate and a unit rate.

7. 38 minutes to run 5 laps

8. 36 butterflies on 12 flowers

9. 252 days for 9 full moons

10. 18 eggs laid in 3 days

11. 56 points scored in 8 games

12. 216 apples growing on 9 trees

13. 125 giraffes on 50 hectares

14. 84 mm in 4 seconds

15. 123 miles driven in 3 hours

16. 210 miles in 7 hours

17. 250 calories in 10 crackers

18. 15 countries visited in 12 days

Animated Glossary
www.pearsonsuccessnet.com

For another example, see Set C on page 318.

First, write how fast the car travels as a rate.

7 km in 4 minutes

$$\frac{7 \text{ km}}{4 \text{ min}}$$

To find the unit rate, divide the first term by the second term.

Divide 7 kilometers by 4 minutes.

```
      1.75
 4)7.00
  - 4
    ──
    30
  - 28
    ──
    20
  -  20
     ──
      0
```

To understand why it works, remember that you can divide the terms of any ratio by the same number to find an equal ratio.

$$\frac{7 \div 4}{4 \div 4} = \frac{1.75}{1}$$

The unit rate is $\frac{1.75 \text{ km}}{1 \text{ min}}$.

The car can go 1.75 kilometers in 1 minute.

Problem Solving

MATHEMATICAL PRACTICES

Use the bar graph about the top speeds that different ocean animals can swim for **19** through **21**.

Ⓒ **19. Reason** Give three equivalent rates that describe the top speed of a tuna.

20. At top speeds how much faster can a swordfish swim than a killer whale?

21. Which animal swims at a top speed of about 0.33 mile per minute? Explain how you found your answer.

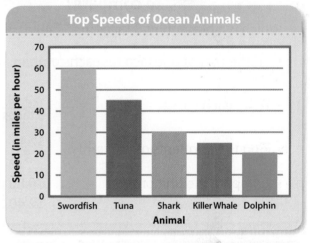

22. The *SR-71 Blackbird* is the fastest plane in the world. It can reach a maximum speed of 2,512 mph. What is its maximum rate of speed in miles per minute?

Ⓒ **23. Think About the Structure** Mischa buys 4 tickets to a soccer game. The total cost before taxes is $90. Which equation would you use to determine the price, *p*, of each ticket?

A $4p = 90$ **C** $4 + p = 90$

B $90p = 4$ **D** $p \div 4 = 90$

Ⓒ **24. Writing to Explain** Make a list of three rates that describe what you do. For example, you could describe how many classes you attend in a day. For each example, explain why it is a rate.

Common
Core

6.RP.3.b Solve unit rate
problems including those
involving unit pricing and
constant speed....

Comparing Rates

How can you use unit rates to compare?

Ethan swam 11 laps in the pool
in 8 minutes. Austin swam 7 laps
in the same pool in 5 minutes.
Which boy swam at a faster rate?

Find the unit rates to compare
who swam faster.

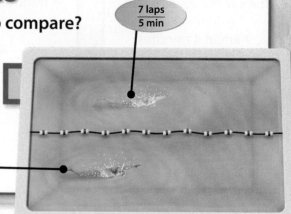

7 laps
5 min

11 laps
8 min

Another Example **How can you use unit prices
to compare?**

Which is a better buy, 3 tacos for $2.40 or 4 tacos for $3.40?

Find the cost of one taco for each comparison:

- Write each cost as a rate.

$$\frac{\$2.40}{3 \text{ tacos}} \qquad \frac{\$3.40}{4 \text{ tacos}}$$

- Find the quotients of the terms.

$$\frac{\$2.40}{3} = \frac{\$0.80}{1} = \$0.80 \qquad \frac{\$3.40}{4} = \frac{\$0.85}{1} = \$0.85$$

- Compare the unit prices.

$0.80 per taco $<$ $0.85 per taco, so 3 tacos for
$2.40 is a better buy.

Guided Practice*

MATHEMATICAL
PRACTICES

Do you know HOW?

Find the unit rates to answer the question.

1. Which has a faster average speed: a car
   that travels 600 feet in 20 seconds or a
   motorcycle that travels 300 feet in
   12 seconds?

   a Write each speed as a rate.

   b Find the unit rate of the car.

   c Find the unit rate of the motorcycle.

   d Compare the unit rates.

Do you UNDERSTAND?

2. How does finding the unit rates allow
   you to compare two rates?

3. **Reason** Why is a unit price a kind of
   unit rate?

4. **Communicate** Explain how to decide
   which is a better buy, an 8-pack of
   pencils on sale for $0.99, or a 10-pack
   of pencils at the regular price of $1.09.

Find Ethan's unit rate.

- Write his rate. $\dfrac{11 \text{ laps}}{8 \text{ minutes}}$

- Divide the first term by the second term.

$$\frac{11}{8} = 1\frac{3}{8} = 1.375$$

- Ethan swam 1.375 laps per minute.

Find Austin's unit rate.

- Write his rate. $\dfrac{7 \text{ laps}}{5 \text{ minutes}}$

- Find the quotient of the terms.

$$\frac{7}{5} = 1\frac{2}{5} = 1.4$$

- Austin swam 1.4 laps per minute.

$1.4 > 1.375$, so Austin swam at a faster rate.

Independent Practice

In **5** through **7**, find each unit rate and determine which rate is greater.

5. 217 miles in 7 hours or 396 miles in 12 hours

6. 12 laps in 8 minutes or 15 laps in 9 minutes

7. 45 strikeouts in 36 innings or 96 strikeouts in 80 innings

In **8** through **10**, determine which is a better buy.

8. 2 books for $15 or 6 books for $45

9. 2 gallons for $5.98 or $\frac{1}{2}$ gallon for $1.69

10. 6 boxes for $3.90 or 24 boxes for $16.80

Problem Solving

MATHEMATICAL PRACTICES

Ⓒ **11. Writing to Explain** How can you find which container is the better value?

$\frac{1}{2}$ gallon for $2.29

1 gallon for $3.99

12. On some days, the temperature quickly changes. On Monday the temperature changed 30°F in 6 hours. On Saturday the temperature changed 44°F in 10 hours. On which day did the temperature change at a quicker rate?

13. Katrina and her friends sent 270 instant messages in the span of 45 minutes. What is the unit rate of the messages they sent?

    A 270 messages: 45 min

    B 60 messages: 1 min

    C 6 messages: 1 min

    D 270 messages: 1 min

14. Estimation The school district requires a 15:1 ratio of students to adults on a field trip. About how many adults will be needed for a field trip with 72 students?

Ⓒ **15. Reason** Amil and Abe rode in a bike-a-thon. Amil rode 15 miles in 55 minutes. Abe rode for 77 minutes. Their rates were proportional. How many miles did Abe ride?

© Common Core

6.EE.9 Use variables to represent two quantities in a real-world problem that change in relationship to one another; write an equation to express one quantity, thought of as the dependent variable, in terms of the other quantity, thought of as the independent variable. Analyze the relationship between the dependent and independent variables using graphs and tables, and relate these to the equation....

Distance, Rate, and Time

How are distance, rate, and time related?

Leilani is flying from Los Angeles to Honolulu. If the flight takes 6 hours and the distance is 2,574 miles, what is the average speed of the airplane?

A formula is <u>a rule that uses symbols to relate quantities.</u> The formula $d = r \times t$ relates distance (d), rate (r), and time (t). Rate in this formula means average speed.

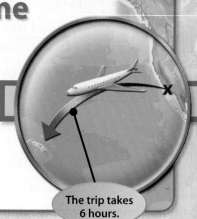

The trip takes 6 hours.

Another Example **How can you use the average speed to find the distance or time?**

Finding Distance

distance = d; rate = 55 mph; time = $\frac{1}{2}$ hr

$$d = r \times t$$

$$d = 55 \times \frac{1}{2}$$

$$d = 27.5$$

The distance is 27.5 miles.

Finding Time

distance = 96 ft; rate = 32 ft per s; time = t

$$d = r \times t$$

$$96 = 32t$$

$$\frac{96}{32} = \frac{32t}{32}$$

$$3 = t$$

The time is 3 seconds.

Explain It

1. In the first example in Another Example, suppose the time had been given as 30 minutes. Why should you convert the 30 minutes to $\frac{1}{2}$ hour before using the formula?

2. How can you use properties of equality and inverse relationships to change the formula $d = r \times t$ to $\frac{d}{r} = t$?

3. How can you use properties of equality and inverse relationships to change the formula $d = r \times t$ to $\frac{d}{t} = r$?

Step 1

Use the formula.

$$d = r \times t$$

Substitute values for the two variables you know. The average speed is the rate.

2,574 miles = $r \times$ 6 hours

Step 2

Use properties of equality and inverse relationships to get the unknown variable alone on one side of the equation:

- Divide both sides by 6 hours.

$$\frac{2,574 \text{ miles}}{6 \text{ hours}} = \frac{r \times 6 \text{ hours}}{6 \text{ hours}}$$

- Simplify each side.

$$\frac{429 \text{ miles}}{1 \text{ hour}} = r$$

The average speed of the plane is 429 miles per hour (mph).

Guided Practice*

MATHEMATICAL PRACTICES

Do you know HOW?

In **1** through **3**, use the following table to find the missing variables.

Trip	time	rate	distance
A	18 hours	r mph	7,794 miles
B	t hours	80 mph	576 miles
C	12 hours	8 mph	d miles

1. Rate of the vehicle in Trip A

2. Time traveled in Trip B

3. Distance traveled in Trip C

Do you UNDERSTAND?

4. Construct Arguments When using a formula to find a missing variable, why is it important to apply the same operation to both sides of the equation?

5. Persevere In the above example, while coming back from Hawaii, the plane enters a jet stream. Traveling in the jet stream shortens the return trip by 1 hour. What is the average rate of the plane during the return trip?

Independent Practice

In **6** through **11**, find the missing variable.

6. distance = 12 mi; time= 2 h;
rate =

7. distance = 568 mi; time= 8 h;
rate =

8. distance = 120 cm; rate = 3 cm per s;
time =

9. rate = 56 mi per day; time = 47 days;
distance =

10. distance = 349 mi; rate = 3 mi per s;
time =

11. time = 12 h; rate = 32 km per h;
distance =

DIGITAL

Animated Glossary
www.pearsonsuccessnet.com

---

*For another example, see Set E on page 319.

12. Writing to Explain Explain how you can find how far a boat has traveled if you know the boat's average rate of speed and the time it has been traveling.

13. Estimation A plane travels at a rate of 470 miles per hour for 6 hours. Use estimation to determine whether the plane has flown more than 3,000 miles.

14. Reason Which rate is faster: a bird traveling at 2 kilometers per hour or an insect traveling at 1,000 meters per hour?

15. Estimation A car traveled from Indianapolis, Indiana, to Miami, Florida, at an average rate of 50 miles an hour. The distance was 1,203 miles. Approximately how much time did the trip take?

A About 12 hours   **C** About 24 hours

B About 22 hours   **D** About 32 hours

16. Marcus took a train to visit his aunt. The train traveled at an average speed of 60 mph. The trip took 45 minutes. How far was the distance traveled?

A 45 miles   **C** 15 miles

B 60 miles   **D** 2,700 miles

17. A leatherback turtle swims at an average rate of 2.5 kilometers per hour.

a At its average rate of speed, how long will it take a leatherback turtle to swim 10 kilometers?

b At its average rate of speed, how far can a leatherback turtle swim in 30 minutes?

In **18** and **19**, determine the time or distance that the maglev train traveled.

18. If the maglev train traveled at 480 kilometers per hour for $\frac{1}{4}$ hour, what distance would the train travel?

19. If the maglev train traveled at 500 kilometers per hour for 10 km, what is the approximate amount of time the train would have traveled?

Because maglev trains use magnets to levitate, they can reach rates of up to 500 kilometers per hour.

Finding Rate, Time, or Distance

Ostriches can run at a top speed of about 40 miles per hour. If an ostrich maintains an average speed of 30 miles per hour, how many minutes would it take the ostrich to run 16 miles?

 Step 1 Use the formula $d = rt$ and substitute for the two variables you know; $d = 16$ miles and $r = 30$ mph.

$$d = rt$$

$$16 = 30t$$

Step 2 Use properties of equality and inverse relationships to get the unknown variable alone on one side of the equation.

$\frac{16}{30} = t$ Press: 16 30 **ENTER =** Display: 0.53333

It would take the ostrich $0.5\overline{3}$ hours to run 16 miles at 30 mph.

$$0.5\overline{3} = t$$

Step 3 Change $0.5\overline{3}$ hours to minutes: 1 hour = 60 minutes.

Press: **×** 60 **ENTER =** Display: 32

It would take the ostrich 32 minutes to run 16 miles at 30 mph.

Practice

1. If an ostrich runs 6 miles in 12 minutes, what is its average speed, in miles per hour?

2. If an ostrich maintains an average speed of 25 miles an hour, how many minutes would it take the ostrich to run 10 miles?

3. An ostrich runs at 40 miles per hour for 10 minutes. How far does it travel?

4. A jet flies 12.5 miles in 4 minutes. What is its average speed in miles per hour?

© **Common Core**

6.RP.2 Understand the concept of a unit rate *a/b* associated with a ratio *a:b* with *b* ≠ 0, and use rate language in the context of a ratio relationship....

Problem Solving

Draw a Picture

Gillian is making jewelry using gold beads and colored beads. The ratio of the number of gold beads to the number of colored beads used in a piece of jewelry is 4:5. What fraction of the beads are colored beads?

Guided Practice*

© **MATHEMATICAL PRACTICES**

Do you know HOW?

Use the picture to solve the problem.

1. Figure A is 3 times as long as Figure B.

   a What is the ratio of the length of Figure A to the length of Figure B?

   b What fraction of the length of Figure A is the length of Figure B?

Do you UNDERSTAND?

© 2. **Communicate** In the example above, how does drawing a picture help solve the problem?

© 3. **Write a Problem** Write a real-world problem that you can solve by drawing a picture.

Independent Practice

© **MATHEMATICAL PRACTICES**

Draw a picture to solve the problem.

4. Tomas and Isaac shared a sum of money in the ratio of 3:5.

   Tomas

   Isaac

   a Express Isaac's share as a fraction of Tomas's share.

   b What fraction of the whole sum of money is Tomas's share?

   c What fraction of the whole sum of money is Issac's share?

Applying Math Practices

- What am I asked to find?
- What else can I try?
- How are quantities related?
- How can I explain my work?
- How can I use math to model the problem?
- Can I use tools to help?
- Is my work precise?
- Why does this work?
- How can I generalize?

Draw a Picture to show the relationship. The ratio of the number of gold beads to the number of colored beads is 4:5.

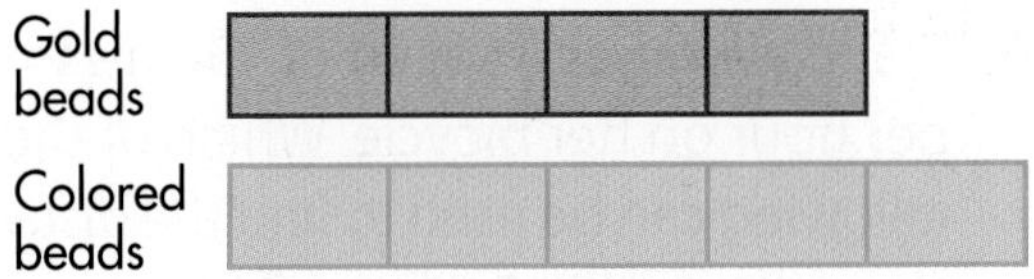

Gold beads

Colored beads

If there were 4 gold beads and 5 colored beads, there would be 9 beads in all. The fraction of colored beads would be $\frac{5}{9}$.

Is your answer reasonable?

Yes, there could be 12 gold and 15 colored beads or 8 gold and 10 colored beads, but the ratio is always 4:5.

$$\frac{12}{15} = \frac{8}{10} = \frac{4}{5}$$

The fraction of colored beads in the jewelry is always $\frac{5}{9}$.

5. **Writing to Explain** Yvette did 30 sit-ups and 18 push-ups. She wrote the ratio 3:5 to compare the number of sit-ups to the number of push-ups. Is this correct? Explain how you know.

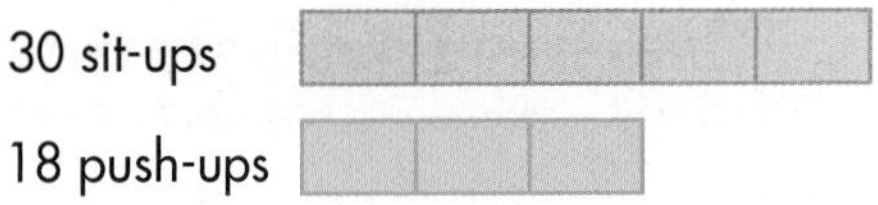

30 sit-ups

18 push-ups

6. Arely is making a necklace of beads. For every 3 silver beads, there is 1 crystal bead and 2 purple beads. If there are 36 beads in the necklace, how many silver, crystal, and purple beads are there?

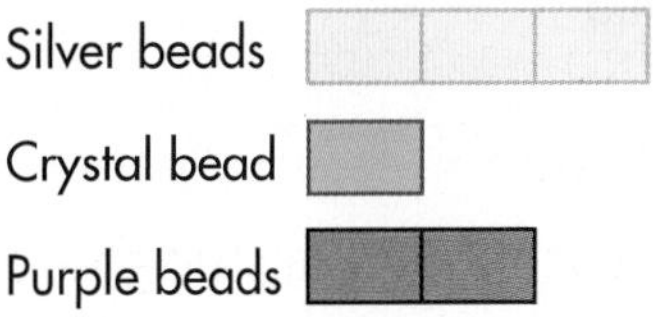

Silver beads

Crystal bead

Purple beads

7. **Use Tools** Hanna wants to take her friends to a movie. If the ticket price is $8, how much will it cost her if 3 or more friends come? Make a table.

8. The picture shows the ratio of Ali's weight to Minghua's weight. What is the ratio of Ali's weight to Minghua's?

Ali

Minghua

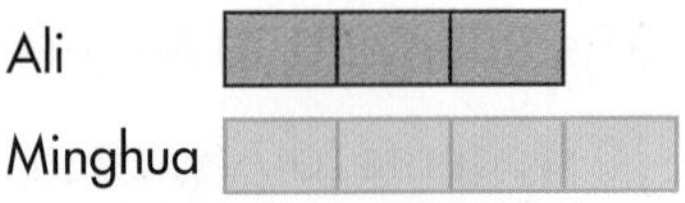

9. Kendall rides his bike at a speed of 15 miles per hour. How far does he ride in 20 minutes? Write an equation.

10. **Use Tools** There are 24 players on a team. Two of every three players were on the team last year. How many players were on the team last year? Draw a picture.

11. **Persevere** A band played 20 songs. They took 3 breaks. After the last break, they played 3 songs. They played twice as many songs after the previous break. They played 5 songs before their first break. How many songs did they play between their first break and their second break?

12. **Think About the Structure** For a 48-ft fence, Horatio used 1 post at the beginning and then 1 post every 6 ft. Which expression will find how many posts he used?

A $(48 - 6) + 1$ C $(48 \div 6) + 1$

B $(48 + 6) + 1$ D $(48 \times 6) + 1$

1. The table shows the party affiliations of Senate members of the 109th Congress. What is the ratio of Republicans to Democrats? (12-1)

Party Affiliation	Number of Senators
Republican	55
Democrat	44
Independent	1

Data

A 4:9

B 5:9

C 4:5

D 5:4

2. A preschool has a student-teacher ratio of 5 to 2. Which of the following ratios is equal to this ratio? (12-2)

A 45 teachers to 18 students

B 45 students to 18 teachers

C 35 students to 10 teachers

D 10 students to 7 teachers

3. In order to make a special color of purple, Sydney mixed 12 pints of red paint and 10 pints of blue. Which of the following is the simplest form of the ratio of red paint to blue paint? (12-2)

A $\frac{6}{11}$

B $\frac{10}{12}$

C $\frac{12}{10}$

D $\frac{6}{5}$

4. Claire averages a speed of 15 miles per hour on her bicycle. Which of the following can be used to find the distance she will travel in 2.5 hours? (12-5)

A $d = \frac{15 \text{ miles}}{1 \text{ hour}} \div 2.5 \text{ hours}$

B $d \times \frac{15 \text{ miles}}{1 \text{ hour}} = 2.5 \text{ hours}$

C $d = \frac{15 \text{ miles}}{1 \text{ hour}} \times 2.5 \text{ hours}$

D $\frac{15 \text{ miles}}{1 \text{ hour}} = d \times 2.5 \text{ hours}$

5. The table shows the results of typing tests administered to 4 job applicants. Which applicant typed the most words per minute? (12-4)

Applicant	Words Typed	Time (in minutes)
Smith	84	2
Johnson	102	3
Ramirez	144	4
Yates	153	3

Data

A Smith

B Johnson

C Ramirez

D Yates

6. Doug caught 10 fish over a period of 4 hours. Which of the following is a unit rate per hour for this situation? (12-3)

A 5 fish per 2 hours

B 2.5 fish per hour

C 4 hours per 10 fish

D 2.5 hours per fish

7. Some elephants drink 350 gallons of water in a week. What step can be used to find the unit rate for water per day? (12-3)

A Divide 7 by 350.

B Multiply 7 by 50.

C Divide 350 by 7.

D Multiply 350 by 7.

8. April can buy a package of 10 folders for $1.20 or a package of 8 folders for $1.12. Which is the better buy? (12-4)

A The 10-pack is cheaper at $0.12 each than the 8-pack at $0.14 each.

B The 8-pack is cheaper at $0.12 each than the 10-pack at $0.14 each.

C The 10-pack is cheaper at $0.12 each than the 8-pack at $0.15 each.

D The 8-pack is cheaper at $0.12 each than the 10-pack at $0.15 each.

9. The table shows the number of units that are rented and owned in a building. What is the ratio of the rented units to the total number of units in the building? (12-1)

Type of Occupancy	Number of Units
Rented	24
Owned	52

A 6 to 19

B 6 to 13

C 19 to 6

D 13 to 6

10. Which number makes the two ratios form a proportion? (12-2)

$$\frac{6}{9} = \frac{\blacksquare}{36}$$

A 3

B 10

C 15

D 24

11. An accountant wrote 52 checks in 4 days. Which of the following is the rate for this situation? (12-3)

A $\frac{52 \text{ days}}{\text{check}}$

B $\frac{52 \text{ checks}}{4 \text{ days}}$

C $\frac{26 \text{ checks}}{\text{day}}$

D $\frac{52 \text{ checks}}{\text{day}}$

12. An animal shelter has a ratio of cats to dogs that is 9:7. What fraction of these animals are dogs? (12-6)

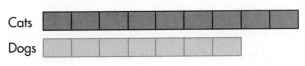

Cats
Dogs

A $\frac{7}{16}$

B $\frac{9}{16}$

C $\frac{7}{9}$

D $\frac{16}{7}$

Set A, pages 300–301

Write a ratio comparing the number of rectangles to the number of circles in three ways.

There are 4 rectangles and 3 circles.

4 to 3	4:3	$\frac{4}{3}$

Remember that a ratio compares two quantities and it can be written in three ways.

Write a ratio for each comparison in three ways.

1. green figures to purple figures

2. rectangles to diamonds

3. purple figures to all figures

Set B, pages 302–304

Find two ratios equal to $\frac{21}{126}$.

One Way

Multiply.

$$\frac{21 \times 2}{126 \times 2} = \frac{42}{252}$$

Another Way

Divide.

$$\frac{21 \div 3}{126 \div 3} = \frac{7}{42}$$

Write the ratio $\frac{64}{88}$ in simplest form.

Divide both terms by the GCF of 64 and 88, which is 8.

$$\frac{64}{88} = \frac{64 \div 8}{88 \div 8} = \frac{8}{11}$$

Remember that to find equal ratios, you must multiply or divide both terms by the same value.

Give two ratios that are equal to each.

1. $\frac{5}{12}$ 2. 14:32

3. 3 to 4   4. $\frac{7}{8}$

Write each ratio in simplest form.

5. 30 to 42   6. $\frac{56}{72}$

Set C, pages 306–307

Write 20 meters in 4 minutes as a rate and as a unit rate.

Think of the expression "20 meters in 4 minutes" as a rate, a special type of ratio that compares quantities with unlike units of measure.

$$\frac{20 \text{ meters}}{4 \text{ min}}$$

To find the unit rate, divide the first term by the second term.

$20 \div 4 = 5$ The unit rate is 5 meters per minute.

Remember that a unit rate is a comparison to 1 unit.

Write each example as a unit rate.

1. 78 miles on 3 gallons

2. 18 laps in 6 minutes

3. 48 sandwiches for 16 people

4. 49 houses in 7 blocks

5. 500 pounds of fish caught in 2 days

On Pet Day, Meg's turtle crawled 30 feet in 6 minutes, and Pat's turtle crawled 25 feet in 5 minutes. Whose turtle crawled at a faster rate?

Find each unit rate and determine which rate is greater.

Write each rate: $\dfrac{30 \text{ ft}}{6 \text{ min}}, \dfrac{25 \text{ ft}}{5 \text{ min}}$

Find each unit rate: $\dfrac{5 \text{ ft}}{1 \text{ min}}, \dfrac{5 \text{ ft}}{1 \text{ min}}$

Both turtles crawled at the same rate.

Remember that converting rates to unit rates or unit prices makes them easy to compare.

Find each unit rate to answer the question.

1. Which is the better buy?
   $5.00 for 4 mangoes
   $6.00 for 5 mangoes

2. Who earned more each month?
   Atif: $84 over 3 months
   Jafar: $100 over 4 months

Julia flies a plane at a rate of 390 miles per hour. How far will she fly in 3.5 hours?

Use the formula $d = r \times t$ to relate distance (*d*), rate (*r*), and time (*t*). You can substitute values for any two variables you know and use properties of equality and inverse relationships to find the unknown variable.

$d = 390 \text{ miles per hour} \times 3.5 \text{ hours}$

$\quad = 1,365 \text{ miles}$

Remember that rate is the average speed.

In **1** through **3**, copy and complete the table.

Race	Rate	Distance	Time
1	56 mph	4,480 mi	▢ h
2	70 mph	▢ mi	9 h
3	▢ mph	111 mi	2 h

Haley is making a beaded bracelet. The ratio of turquoise beads to crystal beads is 6:4. What fraction of the beads are crystal beads?

Draw a picture to show the relationship. The ratio of turquoise beads to crystal beads is 6:4.

Turquoise beads
Crystal beads

If there are 6 turquoise beads and 4 crystal beads in a bracelet, there would be 10 beads in all. The fraction of crystal beads is $\dfrac{4}{10} = \dfrac{2}{5}$.

Remember to look back and check the question that was asked.

Draw a picture to solve each problem.

1. A wall is made up of green tiles and yellow tiles. If $\dfrac{1}{3}$ of the tiles are green, what is the ratio of green tiles to yellow tiles?

2. Raevan jogs two blocks and walks one block intervals for 12 blocks. How many blocks did she jog?

Solving Proportions

1 The Chinese calendar has years named after animals. Which animal represents the year you were born? You will find out in Lesson 13-4.

2 What is the ratio of Indonesian islands to languages spoken in Indonesia? You will find out in Lesson 13-4.

3 This is the Empire State Building in New York. How can you find the scale to make models and drawings of something this tall? You will find out in Lesson 13-6.

4 Cheetahs can run very fast. How can proportions help you find out about how far a cheetah can run per minute? You will find out in Lesson 13-2.

Review What You Know!

Vocabulary

Choose the best term from the box.

> • common factor   • ratio
> • unit rate

1. A __?__ is a ratio in which one of the terms is 1 unit.

2. A __?__ is used to compare unlike quantities.

3. A factor that is the same for two or more numbers is a __?__.

Simplifying Fractions

Simplify each fraction.

4. $\dfrac{12}{18}$ 5. $\dfrac{21}{36}$ 6. $\dfrac{55}{11}$

Multiplication and Division

Find each product.

7. 9×13 8. 7×15

Find each quotient.

9. $134 \div 5$ 10. $434 \div 2$

Ratios and Proportions

© **Writing to Explain** Write an answer for each question.

11. If *rate* × *time* = *distance*, what equation expresses time?

12. What is the difference between a ratio and a proportion?

Common Core

6.RP.3 Use ratio and rate reasoning to solve real-world and mathematical problems, e.g., by reasoning about tables of equivalent ratios, tape diagrams, double number line diagrams, or equations. Also **6.RP.3.a**

Using Ratio Tables

How can you use ratio tables to solve a proportion?

For every 7 cans of tennis balls sold at a sports store, 3 tennis rackets are sold. At this rate, how many cans of tennis balls would be sold if 15 tennis rackets were sold?

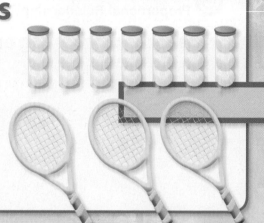

Guided Practice*

MATHEMATICAL PRACTICES

Do you know HOW?

1. To make plaster, Kevin mixes 3 cups of water with 4 pounds of plaster powder. Complete this ratio table. How much water will he mix with 20 pounds of powder?

Cups of water	3	▪	▪	▪	▪
Pounds of powder	4	8	12	▪	▪

2. Writing to Explain How would you find the number of cups of water Kevin would mix with 40 pounds of powder?

Do you UNDERSTAND?

3. In the example above, what equivalent ratio would you use to find how many tennis rackets would be sold if a total of 49 cans of tennis balls were sold?

4. Use Tools Suppose 2 out of 3 campers on the trip were boys. How many of the 15 campers were boys? Make a ratio table to show how you solved this proportion.

$$\frac{2 \text{ boys}}{3 \text{ campers}} = \frac{n \text{ boys}}{15 \text{ campers}}$$

Independent Practice

The local radio station schedules 2 minutes of news for every 20 minutes of music. Complete the ratio table. Then use the table for **5** through **7**.

5. What is the ratio of minutes of music to minutes of news?

6. If there were only one minute of news, how many minutes of music would there be? Write a proportion.

7. How many minutes of news would the disc jockey have to play for every 60 minutes of music?

Minutes of music	20	30	40	50	60
Minutes of news	2	3	▪	▪	▪

Write a proportion. Use x for the number of cans of tennis balls that would be sold if 15 rackets were sold.

$$\frac{7 \text{ cans}}{3 \text{ rackets}} = \frac{x}{15 \text{ rackets}}$$

Make a ratio table to solve the proportion. Find ratios equivalent to $\frac{7}{3}$. Multiply both terms of the ratio by 2, 3, 4, and so on, until you find 15 tennis rackets sold.

Total cans sold	7	14	21	28	
Total rackets sold	3	6	9	12	15

$$\frac{7}{3} = \frac{35}{15}$$

If 15 rackets were sold, then 35 cans of tennis balls would be sold.

In **8** through **13**, answer the question and draw a ratio table to show how you solved each proportion.

8. $\dfrac{3 \text{ yellow balls}}{7 \text{ green balls}} = \dfrac{\text{ yellow balls}}{21 \text{ green balls}}$

9. $\dfrac{\$200}{8 \text{ hours}} = \dfrac{\$50}{\text{ hours}}$

10. $\dfrac{110 \text{ mi}}{2 \text{ h}} = \dfrac{\text{ mi}}{6 \text{ h}}$

11. $\dfrac{2 \text{ girls}}{3 \text{ boys}} = \dfrac{\text{ girls}}{24 \text{ boys}}$

12. $\dfrac{6 \text{ ft}}{\text{ sec}} = \dfrac{180 \text{ ft}}{60 \text{ sec}}$

13. $\dfrac{\$3}{2 \text{ oz}} = \dfrac{\text{ }}{16 \text{ oz}}$

Problem Solving

MATHEMATICAL
PRACTICES

14. Alberta found that 6 cars passed her house in 5 minutes. At this rate, how many cars would you expect to pass her house in 2 hours?

ⓒ 15. Writing to Explain Explain the difference between tables that show data and a ratio table.

16. Anya rode 4 miles on her bicycle in 20 minutes. At this rate, how long will it take her to ride 24 miles?

17. Carol needs $\frac{1}{3}$ yard of ribbon for each bow she makes. If she has $5\frac{1}{2}$ yards of ribbon, how many complete bows can she make?

ⓒ 18. Reason Lauren drove her car 240 miles on 10 gallons of gasoline. At this rate, about how many gallons will she use on a 1,200 mile trip?

    A 2,400 gallons

    B 120 gallons

    C 50 gallons

    D 24 gallons

19. Ramon read 12 pages in 20 minutes. At this rate, how many pages can he read in 30 minutes?

ⓒ 20. Model Giyo wants to divide her $10\frac{1}{2}$-foot by $7\frac{1}{4}$-foot garden into 3 sections. What is the area of each section? Find $10\frac{1}{2} \times 7\frac{1}{4} \div 3$.

Common
Core

6.RP.3.b Solve unit rate
problems including those
involving unit pricing and
constant speed....
Also 6.RP.2

Using Unit Rates

How can you use a unit rate to solve a proportion?

A bicycle tour group travels 320 miles in 5 days. How far
could they travel in 8 days if they maintained the same
average speed?

Find a unit rate to
solve the problem.

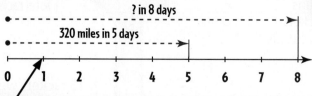

? miles in 1 day

Guided Practice*

MATHEMATICAL
PRACTICES

Do you know HOW?

In **1** and **2**, compute the unit rate.

1. Another bicycle tour group travels
245 miles in 5 days. How far do they
travel in 1 day, if they traveled the
same amount each day?

2. A construction crew can spread 2 tons
of gravel in 90 minutes. How long does
it take them to spread 1 ton?

Do you UNDERSTAND?

Use the information in the example above
to answer **3** and **4**.

3. **Reasonableness** How do you know
that 512 miles in 8 days is a reasonable
answer?

4. Write another proportion to represent
the situation in the example above.
What is the solution to your new
proportion?

Independent Practice

Leveled Practice In **5** through **12**, find the unit rate.

5. $\dfrac{320 \text{ mi}}{16 \text{ gal}}$

6. $\dfrac{75 \text{ cm}}{3 \text{ h}}$

7. $\dfrac{150 \text{ snacks}}{50 \text{ students}}$

8. $\dfrac{54 \text{ songs}}{3 \text{ h}}$

9. $\dfrac{60 \text{ min}}{20 \text{ calls}}$

10. $\dfrac{33 \text{ books}}{11 \text{ weeks}}$

11. $\dfrac{1,275 \text{ ants}}{5 \text{ anthills}}$

12. $\dfrac{\$60}{5 \text{ days}}$

In **13** through **18**, use unit rates to solve the proportions.
Estimate to check reasonableness.

13. $\dfrac{2 \text{ in.}}{1 \text{ yr}} = \dfrac{x \text{ in.}}{13 \text{ yr}}$

14. $\dfrac{8 \text{ h}}{1 \text{ day}} = \dfrac{56 \text{ h}}{x \text{ days}}$

15. $\dfrac{x \text{ sales}}{1 \text{ h}} = \dfrac{45 \text{ sales}}{5 \text{ h}}$

16. $\dfrac{39 \text{ chairs}}{1 \text{ row}} = \dfrac{x \text{ chairs}}{6 \text{ rows}}$

17. $\dfrac{3 \text{ hikes}}{1 \text{ week}} = \dfrac{48 \text{ hikes}}{x \text{ weeks}}$

18. $\dfrac{3 \text{ strikeouts}}{1 \text{ inning}} = \dfrac{x \text{ strikeouts}}{3 \text{ innings}}$

For another example, see Set B on page 340.

Step 1

Find the unit rate.

The group traveled 320 miles in 5 days. The unit rate tells how many average miles they traveled per day.

　　Divide 320 by 5.　　　$320 \div 5 = 64$

The unit rate is $\frac{64}{1}$. The group traveled an average of 64 miles a day.

Step 2

Use the unit rate to find how far the group could travel in 8 days.

　　　　1 unit = 64 mi

　　　　Multiply 64 mi by 8.

　　　　$8 \times 64 = 512$

The group could travel 512 miles in 8 days.

Problem Solving

MATHEMATICAL
PRACTICES

19. Elephants can charge at speeds of 0.7 kilometers a minute. Use a proportion to find this speed in kilometers per hour.

20. A cheetah can chase after its prey at about 110 kilometers per hour. Use a proportion to calculate about how many kilometers a cheetah could run in 1 minute.

Tip *Use the number of minutes in an hour to help you find a unit rate.*

21. Reason If a machine takes 1 minute to fill 6 cartons of eggs, about how long will it take to fill 418 cartons?

22. Writing to Explain How are the ratios 4 laps : 1 h and 32 laps : 8 h alike and how are they different?

Use the table for **23** through **25**.

23. What is Martha's unit rate?

24. What is Allison's unit rate?

Data		Number of Laps	Time
	Martha	20	82 min
	Allison	16	64 min

25. About how many hours would it take Martha to run 44 laps?

26. Think About the Structure Suppose the unit rate for people passing through a turnstile is 7 people per minute. How would you express the number of people passing through the turnstile in 5.5 minutes?

　　A Use multiplication, and then division.

　　B Use multiplication, and then round.

　　C The problem cannot be answered.

　　D Change the unit rate so the answer is a whole number.

Common Core

6.RP.3 Use ratio and rate reasoning to solve real-world and mathematical problems, e.g., by reasoning about tables of equivalent ratios, tape diagrams, double number line diagrams, or equations.

Applying Ratios

How can a diagram help you solve a ratio problem?

The ratio of footballs to soccer balls at a sporting goods store is 5 to 3. If the store has 100 footballs in stock, how many soccer balls does the store have in stock?

Another Example **How can a double number line diagram be used to solve a problem involving ratios?**

Kate can run 2 miles in 23 minutes. At this rate, how long will it take her to run 10 miles? Draw a double number line diagram showing Kate's distance and time. Count by 2s along the line for distance until you get to 10 miles. Count by 23s along the line for time, using the same-size spaces.

It will take Kate 115 minutes to run 10 miles.

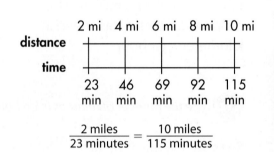

$$\frac{2 \text{ miles}}{23 \text{ minutes}} = \frac{10 \text{ miles}}{115 \text{ minutes}}$$

Guided Practice*

MATHEMATICAL
PRACTICES

Do you know HOW?

Draw a diagram to solve each problem.

1. Tye is making some trail mix based on a recipe that combines 2 cups of nuts with 3 cups of granola. If Tye has 6 cups of nuts, how many cups of granola should he use?

2. Angela is helping her father paint a fence. She can paint 3 sections of the fence in 25 minutes. How many minutes will it take Angela to paint 12 sections of this fence?

Do you UNDERSTAND?

3. **Writing to Explain** Andre can read 10 pages of his history book in 1 hour. Explain which type of diagram he should use to help him find how long it would take to read 4 pages.

4. This diagram shows the ratio of sports card collectors to toy collectors in a club as being 2 to 5. If there are 8 card collectors in the club, how can you find the number of toy collectors in the club?

*For another example, see Set C on page 340.

Model the relationship. The ratio of the number of footballs to the number of soccer balls is 5:3.

Footballs

Soccer balls

You can use the same diagram and equal ratios to find the number of soccer balls the store has in stock.

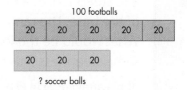

100 footballs

| 20 | 20 | 20 | 20 | 20 |

| 20 | 20 | 20 |

? soccer balls

$$\frac{5 \text{ footballs}}{3 \text{ soccer balls}} = \frac{100 \text{ footballs}}{60 \text{ soccer balls}}.$$

There are $3 \times 20 = 60$ soccer balls.
The sporting goods store has 60 soccer balls.

Independent Practice

For **5** through **8**, draw a diagram to solve the problem.

5. A cashier sells 7 DVDs for every 3 CDs she sells. How many CDs does the cashier sell if she sells 35 DVDs?

6. Anne's family drove 165 miles in 3 hours. At this speed, how long would it take them to drive 825 miles?

7. Jeremy made 4 out of every 5 free throws he attempted last season. If he had 35 free-throw attempts during the season, how many free throws did Jeremy make?

8. There are 4 adult chaperones for every 15 students who attend a school field trip. How many adults are there if there are 135 students attending the field trip?

Problem Solving

© **MATHEMATICAL PRACTICES**

© **9. Reason** The ratio of adult dogs to puppies at a park on Monday was 3:2. There were 12 puppies there that day. Tuesday, 15 adult dogs were at the park. How many adult dogs were at the park on Monday? What is the difference between the number of adult dogs at the park on Monday and Tuesday?

© **10. Persevere** Your respiration rate measures the number of breaths you take per minute. Reggie counted 48 breaths in 3 minutes and Joan counted 34 breaths in 2 minutes. Convert each rate to a unit rate. Who had the higher respiration rate? How many breaths per minute higher was their rate?

11. Of the students taking a foreign language class, 8 students take Spanish for every 5 students who take French. If there are 72 students taking Spanish, how many students are taking French?

  A 40   **C** 54

  B 45   **D** 63

© **12. Model** Copy and complete the diagram. Chen can ride his bike 3 miles in 15 minutes. At this rate, how long will it take him to ride 18 miles?

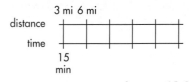

distance

3 mi 6 mi

time

15 min

Common Core

6.RP.3 Use ratio and rate reasoning to solve real-world and mathematical problems, e.g., by reasoning about tables of equivalent ratios, tape diagrams, double number line diagrams, or equations.

Problem Solving

Writing to Explain

The steepness of a ramp is the ratio of the height to the length of the base. The ramp at the right has a steepness of 3:4. What would be the length of another ramp with the same steepness if the height were 9 feet?

Jim's answer: 9 is 6 more than 3. If I add 6 to 4, the sum is 10. The new length is 10 feet.

Is Jim's answer correct? Explain.

$h = 3$ ft

$b = 4$ ft

Guided Practice*

 MATHEMATICAL **PRACTICES**

Do you know HOW?

Explain your solution. Show your work.

1. In the example at the top, explain how you could use a proportion to solve the problem.

2. Tom uses a ratio of 2 cups of broth to 1 cup of vegetables to make his famous soup. If he uses 4 cups of vegetables, how many cups of broth does he need?

Do you UNDERSTAND?

3. **Use Tools** In the example above, how does the picture help in writing the explanation?

4. **Write a Problem** Write a problem that includes a picture to use to help solve the problem. Then solve the problem.

Independent Practice

 MATHEMATICAL **PRACTICES**

Explain your solution. Show your work.

5. **Reason** Jackie goes for a 1-mile run every morning. Today she ran the mile in less time than she did yesterday. On which day did she run faster?

6. Bob earns $5 each day delivering newspapers. He saves $3 and spends the rest. If he saved $27 in a month, how much money did he spend?

7. **Communicate** Ursula's car travels 160 miles on 4 gallons of gas. How far will the car travel on 3 gallons of gas? Explain.

Applying Math Practices

- What am I asked to find?
- What else can I try?
- How are quantities related?
- How can I explain my work?
- How can I use math to model the problem?
- Can I use tools to help?
- Is my work precise?
- Why does this work?
- How can I generalize?

For another example, see Set D on page 341.

Show the information you know.

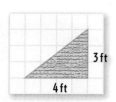

Use words, pictures, numbers, and symbols to write good math explanations.

Build a bigger ramp using the smaller ramp several times.

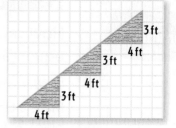

Height: 3 + 3 + 3 = 9

Length of the base: 4 + 4 + 4 = 12

The ratio 9:12 is equal to 3:4. The correct length of the new ramp is 12 feet.

Jim's answer is not correct.

---

8. Dionne read 40 pages in 20 minutes. How many pages did she read per minute?

© 9. Communicate The Picnic Basket sells 60 soups for every 96 sandwiches. At this rate, how many soups will be sold for every 32 sandwiches? Explain.

© 10. Persevere A truck driver started the year making $0.35 per mile. Halfway through the year, she received a raise and began earning $0.43 per mile. She drove 48,000 miles the first 6 months and 45,000 miles the second 6 months. How much did she earn for the year?

11. The Chinese calendar has years named after animals. The animals are named in this order: Rat, Ox, Tiger, Rabbit, Dragon, Snake, Horse, Sheep, Monkey, Rooster, Dog, and Pig. If 2012 is the Year of the Dragon, how would you find the name of the year you were born? What is the name of the year you were born?

12. Indonesia has more than 13,000 islands, and over 250 languages are spoken there. What is the ratio of islands to languages spoken? Reduce your answer.

© 13. Model October 31 is National Knock-Knock Joke Day. To honor the day, Annika wants to give 3 different knock-knock jokes to each friend. Make a table that shows how many jokes she will need to collect for 1 to 5 friends. Write an expression that describes the relationship.

14. Children in the United States go to school about 180 days per year. Children in Japan go to school about 240 days per year. Which ratio describes the correct relationship of U.S. school days to Japanese school days?

A 240:180   **B** 3:4   **C** 4:3   **D** 12:9

Common
Core

6.RP.3.a Make tables of
equivalent ratios relating
quantities with whole-
number measurements,
find missing values in the
tables, and plot the pairs of
values on the coordinate
plane. Use tables to
compare ratios.

Ratios and Graphs

How can you use tables and graphs to represent equal ratios?

Ellen is shopping for supplies at Jake's Party Store.

Make a table to show how much Ellen will spend to buy 3, 6, 9, or 12 balloons. Then plot the pairs of values in a coordinate graph and use the graph to find how much Ellen would spend if she wanted to buy 18 balloons.

Jake's Party
Store
Balloons 3 for $2
Hats 5 for $3
Streamers 4 for $1

Another Example **How can you use tables and graphs to compare ratios?**

Ricardo bought 100 key chains for $15. Sam bought 200 key chains for $28. Complete the table to show who will pay less for 400 key chains, and how much less.

Number of Key Chains	100	200	300	400
Ricardo's Cost				
Sam's Cost				

Write a ratio to show each person's cost. Then find equal ratios to complete the table.

Ricardo

$$\frac{100 \text{ key chains}}{15 \text{ dollars}} = \frac{100}{15} = \frac{200}{30} = \frac{300}{45} = \frac{400}{60}$$

Sam

$$\frac{200 \text{ key chains}}{28 \text{ dollars}} = \frac{100}{14} = \frac{200}{28} = \frac{300}{42} = \frac{400}{56}$$

Comparing Costs

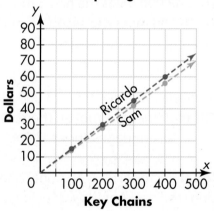

Plot the pairs of values for Sam and Ricardo on the coordinate plane. Connect the points for each person with a dashed line. You can see that as the costs increase, the lines become farther apart.

Compare the costs: $60 − $56 = $4.

Sam will pay $4 less.

Explain It

1. Describe how the graphs of Ricardo's and Sam's costs are the same and how they are different.

The ratio $\frac{3 \text{ balloons}}{\$2}$ represents the cost of the balloons. Find equal ratios for 6, 9, and 12 balloons. Make a table using the equal ratios.

Number of Balloons	3	6	9	12
Cost ($)	2	4	6	8

Ellen can buy 3 balloons for $2, 6 balloons for $4, 9 balloons for $6, and 12 balloons for $8.

Plot the pairs of values on the coordinate plane for each ratio, x to y. Connect the points with a dashed line and extend the line to find the cost of 18 balloons.

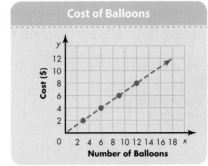

Cost of Balloons

Ellen would spend $12 to buy 18 balloons.

Guided Practice*

Do you know HOW?

1. Complete the table to show equal ratios for $\frac{3}{8}$.

3	6	9	12	15
8				

2. Complete the table to show equal ratios for 5 to 4, and make a graph of the pairs of values.

5				
4	12	24	36	40

Do you UNDERSTAND?

© 3. Writing to Explain What does a graph of equal ratios show you that a table of the same ratios does not?

© 4. Use Structure Explain how you can graph the pairs of values in this table. How can you tell from your graph how much money 25 hats will cost?

Number of Hats	5	10	15	20
Cost ($)	3	6	9	12

Independent Practice

For **5** through **8**, complete the table to show equal ratios, and make a graph of the pairs of values.

5.

2				
3	6	9	12	15

6.

4	8	16	24	32
7				

7.

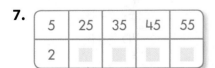

5	25	35	45	55
2				

8.

9				
12	8	4	24	48

---

9. A bakery uses a bread recipe that calls for 4 cups of white flour for every 3 cups of whole-wheat flour. Complete the table to show how many cups of whole-wheat flour are needed to mix with 20 cups of white flour. Make a graph of the pairs of values.

Cups of White Flour	4	8	12	16	20
Cups of Whole-Wheat Flour					

Problem Solving

MATHEMATICAL PRACTICES

10. A can of 3 tennis balls costs $5. Complete the table to show how many tennis balls Carlos can buy for $20.

Number of Tennis Balls				
Cost ($)	5	10	15	20

11. Use Tools Kallie is making bouquets of flowers. She puts 4 carnations, 2 sunflowers, and 3 lilies in each bouquet. If Kallie uses a total of 72 flowers, how many of each type of flower does she use? Hint: Draw a picture.

12. Reason Jeff walked $\frac{1}{2}$ of a mile. Fred walked $\frac{11}{12}$ of a mile. Who walked farther? How many miles farther?

13. Model The temperature dropped 17° to 53°F. Write an equation to find the temperature before it dropped.

14. Communicate Ishwar can read 5 pages in 15 minutes. Anne can read 15 pages in 1 hour. Explain how you could use a table or graph to find how much longer it would take Anne to read a 300-page book than Ishwar.

15. Jacob and Jordan are getting ready for track season. Jacob did 39 sit-ups in 30 seconds. Jordan did 59 sit-ups in 50 seconds. Find the unit rate for each. Who did more sit-ups per second?

16. Model The soccer team charged $8 per car during a fund-raising carwash. The team received an additional $45 in donations during the carwash. Which expression shows the total amount of money the team raised if it washed c cars?

A $80c$

B $8c + 45$

C $45c + 8$

D $c(45 + 8)$

17. The floor area of a 120-square-foot van is separated into 3 sections. The first section will take up $\frac{1}{2}$ of the floor area. The second section will contain boxes and will take up $\frac{3}{8}$ of the floor area. What is the area of the third section that will be used for yard equipment?

A 15 ft²

B 30 ft²

C 45 ft²

D 60 ft²

Ratios of Areas of Rectangles

Use 🔧 **tools**

Geometry Drawing

The area of a rectangle can be found by multiplying its length times its width. Draw rectangles that measure 2 × 4, 2 × 5, and 2 × 6. Compare the area of each rectangle to its length and make a table of the ratios.

Step 1 Draw the rectangles.

Go to the Geometry Drawing eTool. ⬚ Click on the Geoboard workspace icon. 🔺 Then click on the Polygon tool icon. Click on one dot on the geoboard, drag straight down 2 units, then click again. Drag right 4 units and click again. Complete rectangle *ABCD*.

Use the same process to draw a 2 × 5 rectangle *EFGH* and a 2 × 6 rectangle *IJKL*.

Step 2 Measure the areas.

⬚ Click on the icon for measuring the area of a figure. Then click on any side of rectangle *ABCD*. The Measurements window should show that the area of rectangle *ABCD* is 8 square units.

Use the same process to find the areas of rectangles *EFGH* and *IJKL*.

Step 3 Make a table of ratios to compare side length and area of the rectangles you drew.

Copy and complete the table to compare side length and area of other rectangles that could be drawn.

Length (units)	4	5	6	8	10
Area (square units)	8				

Practice

Use the broom tool to clear the workspace. Draw each set of rectangles and find each rectangle's area. Then complete the table to compare side length and area.

1. Rectangle *ABCD*: 4 units by 3 units
Rectangle *EFGH*: 4 units by 5 units
Rectangle *IJKL*: 4 units by 7 units

Length	3	5	7	9	11
Area					

2. Rectangle *ABCD*: 4 units by 3 units
Rectangle *EFGH*: 6 units by 3 units
Rectangle *IJKL*: 8 units by 3 units

Length	4	6	8	10	20
Area					

Ⓒ

Common Core

7.G.1 Solve problems involving scale drawings of geometric figures, including computing actual lengths and areas from a scale drawing and reproducing a scale drawing at a different scale.

Maps and Scale Drawings

What is a scale drawing?

For the school yearbook, Mikayla needs to reduce a photo to fit a spot that is 2 inches high.

How wide would the yearbook photo be if the smaller photo was the same scale as the original photo?

2 in.

10 in.

8 in.

Another Example   How can you use the scale on a map?

What You Think

A map is also a scale drawing.

The scale on the map is 1 inch = 112 miles.

On the map, the distance from Brandonsville to New Patterson is 2 inches. What is the actual distance?

Use a proportion to find the actual distance.

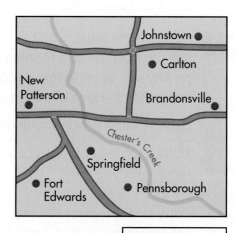

Scale 1 in. = 112 mi

What You Write

Let d be the actual distance between Brandonsville and New Patterson.

$$\frac{1 \text{ inch}}{112 \text{ miles}} = \frac{2 \text{ inches}}{d \text{ miles}}$$ ← map distance
 ← actual distance

$$\frac{1 \text{ inch} \times 2}{112 \text{ miles} \times 2} = \frac{2 \text{ inches}}{214 \text{ miles}}$$ Solve.

$$d = 224$$

The actual distance from Brandonsville to New Patterson is 224 miles.

Explain It

1. Estimate. About how many miles does $3\frac{1}{8}$ inches represent on the map?

2. If the map were enlarged, is it reasonable to assume that the scale would remain the same? Explain.

In a scale drawing, <u>the dimensions of an object are reduced or enlarged by the same ratio or scale</u>.

The dimensions of the scale drawing and the original figure are proportional. They are similar figures.

To find the scale, compare the heights of the figures.

The scale is 10 in. : 2 in.

Write and solve a proportion to find the width of the reduced photo. Use y for the reduced width.

Height   Width

$$\frac{10 \text{ in.}}{2 \text{ in.}} = \frac{8 \text{ in.}}{y \text{ in.}}$$ ← actual measurements
                                                          ← reduced measurements

$$10y = 16$$

$$y = 1.6$$

The width of the yearbook photo will be 1.6 in.

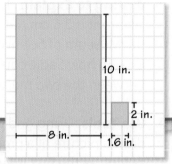

MATHEMATICAL
PRACTICES

Do you know HOW?

Determine the actual distance based on the scale.

1. If the scale on a map is 1 cm: 15 km, how many km would 6.5 cm represent?

2. If the map scale is 1 in. : 550 mi, what is the actual distance if the map distance is 7 in.?

Do you UNDERSTAND?

© 3. **Persevere** If the height of a photo in the yearbook above is 4 in., what strategy would you use to find the width? What is the width?

© 4. **Write a Problem** Write a real-world problem using the following information: a map has a scale of 1 inch: 2 miles.

Use the scale drawing to answer **5** through **7**.

5. Caleb walked from his house to the water park. What was the actual distance he walked?

6. It took Caleb 30 minutes to walk from his house to the water park. If he walks at the same pace, how long will it take him to walk from the water park to the theater?

7. If Caleb walked from his house to the theater, from the theater to the water park, and from the water park to his house, what would be the total actual distance he walked?

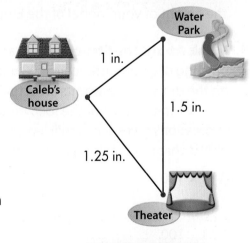

Scale: 0.5 inch = 1 mile

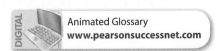

Animated Glossary
www.pearsonsuccessnet.com

For another example, see Set F on page 341.

Lesson 13-6 **335**

8. Rectangles *A* and *B* are proportional figures. Find the height of rectangle *B*.

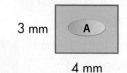

3 mm

4 mm

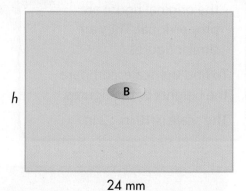

h

B

24 mm

9. **Writing to Explain** The scale on a map of Chicago's lakefront is 2.5 cm = 4 km. Both the Field Museum and the Museum of Science and Industry are on the map. Explain how Sadie could calculate the actual distance between the two museums.

10. **Use Tools** Using grid paper, draw a pencil. Then draw a picture of a proportional pencil that is twice as long as the first pencil. Include a scale on your drawing.

Use the formula $d = r \times t$ to solve **11** and **12**.

11. **Persevere** Jorge drives at a rate of 30 miles per hour. How long will it take him to drive 150 miles?

12. Ileana runs at a rate of 6 miles per hour. If she ran for 7 hours last week, how many miles did she run?

13. If the actual distance between Charlotte, North Carolina and Charleston, South Carolina is about 200 miles, what would be the distance on a map with a scale of 0.5 inch = 50 miles?

14. The Empire State Building in New York is about 1,450 feet tall. Suppose you used the scale 1 in. = 50 ft to make a model of the Empire State Building. Use a proportion to find the height of your model of the Empire State Building.

15. **Think About the Structure** On a scale drawing of a computer chip, 100 mm on the drawing represents an actual size of 1 mm. Which of the following expressions gives the actual length of an object that is 3 mm long in the drawing?

   A 3×100

   B $3 - 100$

   C $3 \div 100$

   D $100 \div 3$

16. **Think About the Structure** A recipe that feeds 2 people calls for 4 tomatoes, 2 onions, and 5 oz of cheese. What operation will help you change the recipe to feed 6 people?

   A Add 3 to each item.

   B Multiply each item by 3.

   C Divide each item by 3.

   D Multiply each item by itself.

Mixed Problem Solving

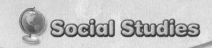

The Great Pyramid of Giza, Egypt, is one of the seven wonders of the ancient world. It was built more than 4,000 years ago and remained the tallest building in the world until the 20th century. Use proportions and similar figures in **1** through **6**.

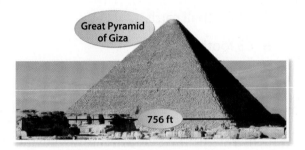

Great Pyramid of Giza

756 ft

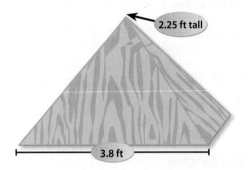

2.25 ft tall

3.8 ft

1. A model proportional to the Great Pyramid is shown above. Use the dimensions of the model to find the height of the Great Pyramid. Round your answer to the nearest whole number.

2. The pyramid at Menkaure, Egypt, was 215 ft tall, and its base was 345.5 ft wide. If a model proportional to the pyramid at Menkaure is 4.3 ft tall, what is the width of the base of the model? Round your answer to the nearest tenth.

3. The illustration below shows one side of the Great Pyramid and a triangle that is similar. Find the measure of $\angle D$.

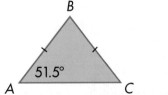
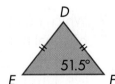

B

51.5°

A   C

D

51.5°

E   F

4. Solve using the strategy: Write an equation. The base of the Great Pyramid is made of large limestone blocks. The top figure in the drawing below shows the length and width of one block. The lower figure is proportional to the pyramid block. What is the height, x, of the pyramid's base block?

5. The base of the Great Pyramid is a square with an area of 571,536 ft². If one of the sides of a similar figure is 5 cm, what is the area of this figure?

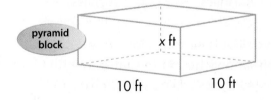

pyramid block

x ft

10 ft   10 ft

6. Write a problem that compares the dimensions of the Great Pyramid with those of another square pyramid.

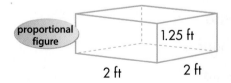

proportional figure

1.25 ft

2 ft   2 ft

1. The ratio of width to height is 4 to 3. What is the width if the height is 18 inches? (13-1)

Width inches	4	8	12	16		
Height inches	3	6	9	12	15	18

A 21 inches

B 23 inches

C 24 inches

D 26 inches

2. In one hour, 32 cars pass through a particular intersection. At the same rate, how long would it take for 96 cars to pass through the intersection? (13-2)

A 2 hours

B 3 hours

C 8 hours

D 16 hours

3. Nick flew 1,560 miles in 3 hours on his airline flight. How far did Nick fly in 1 hour? Compute the unit rate. (13-2)

A $\dfrac{780 \text{ miles}}{1 \text{ hour}}$ C $\dfrac{580 \text{ miles}}{1 \text{ hour}}$

B $\dfrac{760 \text{ miles}}{1 \text{ hour}}$ D $\dfrac{520 \text{ miles}}{1 \text{ hour}}$

4. A deli sells 44 soups for every 60 sandwiches. At this rate, how many soups will be sold for every 15 sandwiches? (13-4)

A 9 soups

B 10 soups

C 11 soups

D 12 soups

5. Max has 4 baseball cards for every 3 football cards in his collection. If he has 72 baseball cards, how many football cards does Max have? (13-3)

A 54 football cards

B 63 football cards

C 65 football cards

D 72 football cards

6. A shower uses 5 gallons of water each minute. Which of the following can be used to find x, the number of gallons of water used during an 8-minute shower? (13-2)

A $\dfrac{5 \text{ gal}}{1 \text{ min}} = \dfrac{x \text{ gal}}{8 \text{ min}}$

B $\dfrac{5 \text{ gal}}{1 \text{ min}} = \dfrac{8 \text{ min}}{x \text{ gal}}$

C $\dfrac{5 \text{ gal}}{x \text{ min}} = \dfrac{1 \text{ gal}}{8 \text{ min}}$

D $\dfrac{5 \text{ gal}}{8 \text{ min}} = \dfrac{x \text{ gal}}{1 \text{ min}}$

7. Which number is missing from the table of equal ratios? (13-5)

5	10	25	40	65
4	8	20		52

A 24

B 28

C 32

D 36

8. There are 7 campers for every 2 counselors at summer camp. How many counselors are there if there are 84 campers? (13-3)

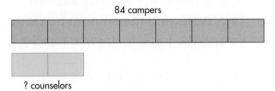

84 campers

? counselors

A 12 counselors

B 24 counselors

C 28 counselors

D 30 counselors

9. The table shows the relationship between gallons and quarts. What is the missing value in the table? (13-1)

Gallons	2	4	6		10
Quarts	8	16	24	32	40

A 4

B 8

C 16

D 20

10. Claudio is fertilizing his lawn. Four pounds of fertilizer are to be applied to every 1,000 square feet of lawn. How many pounds should Claudio apply if his lawn is 8,750 square feet? (13-2)

A 2.2 pounds

B 32 pounds

C 35 pounds

D 70 pounds

11. CDs are on sale at 4 for $38. Which explains correctly how much 6 CDs cost? (13-4)

A Divide $38 by 4 to get a unit price of $9.50. Then multiply 6 by $9.50 to get $63.

B Divide $38 by 6 to get a unit price of $6.33. Then multiply 4 by $6.33 to get $25.33.

C Divide $38 by 4 to get a unit price of $9.50. Then multiply 6 by $9.50 to get $57.

D Divide 4 by 6. Then multiply that quotient by $38 to get $25.

12. Which ratio could be graphed on the same dashed line as shown in the graph below? (13-5)

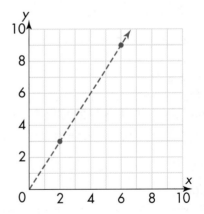

A $\frac{1}{2}$

B $\frac{3}{8}$

C $\frac{2}{6}$

D $\frac{4}{6}$

Set A, pages 322–323

About 1,024 MB (megabytes) are equal to 1 GB (gigabyte). About how many songs could a 1 GB (gigabyte) music player hold?

File size	256 MB	512 MB	1 GB
Songs	60 songs	120 songs	

Find a ratio equivalent to $\frac{512}{120}$. Multiply both terms by 2.

$$\frac{512 \times 2}{120 \times 2} = \frac{1,024}{\mathbf{240}}$$

$$x = 240$$

A 1 GB music player can hold about 240 songs.

Remember that the values in a ratio table are proportional.

The ratio table below shows the relationship between the amount Toby earns and the amount he saves. Extend the table to answer **1** and **2**.

Earnings	$10	$20	$30
Savings	$7	$14	$21

1. How much would Toby save if he earned $40?

2. If Toby saved $35, how much did he earn?

Set B, pages 324–325

If a car travels 240 miles in 5 hours, how many miles will it travel in 1 hour?

Find the unit rate.

$$240 \div 5 = 48 = \frac{48}{1}$$

The car will travel 48 miles in 1 hour.

Remember to make sure your proportion contains equivalent units.

Solve each proportion using the unit rate given.

1. $\frac{17 \text{ applicants}}{1 \text{ week}} = \frac{x \text{ applicants}}{14 \text{ weeks}}$

2. $\frac{\$12.29}{1 \text{ ticket}} = \frac{x}{4 \text{ tickets}}$

Set C, pages 326–327

Use diagrams to solve ratio problems. Model the ratio of 6 men to 4 women.

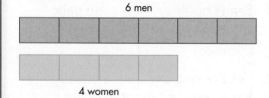
6 men

4 women

Remember that you can also use reasoning to solve ratio problems.

1. The ratio of men to women at a small wedding is 6:4. If there are 16 women at the wedding, how many men are there?

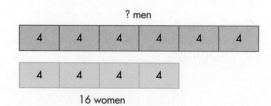
? men

| 4 | 4 | 4 | 4 | 4 | 4 |

| 4 | 4 | 4 | 4 |

16 women

Brand A shampoo is $7.68 for a 24 oz bottle. Brand B shampoo is $12.60 for 36 oz. Which is a better buy?

Compare the unit price for each shampoo.

$7.68 for 24 oz ➞ unit price is $0.32 per oz

$12.60 for 36 oz ➞ unit price is $0.35 per oz

The 24 oz bottle is a better buy.

Remember that you can use words, pictures, numbers, symbols, graphs, tables, diagrams, and models to explain your reasoning.

1. Which is the better buy, 2 boxes of Hearty Bran cereal at $4.86 or 4 boxes for $10? Explain.

You can graph values from a ratio table on a coordinate grid.

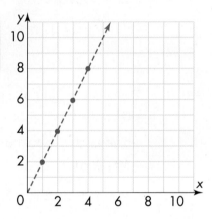

1	2	3	4
2	4	6	8

Plot each pair of values. Connect the points with a dashed line.

Remember to use a dashed line when graphing values.

1. Complete the table to show equivalent ratios for $\frac{4}{7}$. Graph the set of values on a coordinate grid.

4	8	12	16	20
7				

The scale on a map is 1 inch: 240 miles. If two cities are 5 inches apart, what is the actual distance in miles?

Write a proportion to find the data.

$$\frac{1 \text{ inch}}{240 \text{ miles}} = \frac{5 \text{ inches}}{x \text{ miles}}$$

$$\frac{1 \times 5}{240 \times 5} = \frac{5}{1,200}$$

$$x = 1,200$$

The map distance between the two cities is 5 inches, so the actual distance between the two cities is 1,200 miles.

Remember that maps and scale drawings are reduced or enlarged by the same ratio.

1. The map scale is 1 in. : 5 mi. If the map distance between Sean's home and the state park is 3 inches, what is the actual distance?

2. The drawing of the new school has a scale of 1 in. : 8 ft. In the drawing, the school is 6 inches tall. What is the actual height of the school?

Topic 14 Understanding Percent

1 Many chemical elements can be found in Earth's atmosphere. What percent is nitrogen? You will find out in Lesson 14-2.

2 The *Queen Mary 2* is the largest cruise ship in the world. How does the length of the *Queen Mary 2* compare in size to the height of the Washington Monument? You will find out in Lesson 14-3.

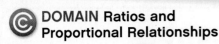

DOMAIN Ratios and Proportional Relationships

3 Easton the Great won Best in Show in 60% of his shows. In how many shows was Easton entered? You will find out in Lesson 14-1.

4 What percent of an adult's weight is water? You will find out in Lesson 14-5.

Review What You Know!

Vocabulary

Choose the best term from the box.

- proportion
- fraction
- ratio
- decimal

1. A __?__ can be written as x to y, $x : y$, or $\frac{x}{y}$.

2. A __?__ is a mathematical statement that two ratios are equal.

3. A number with one or more numbers to the right of the decimal point is a __?__.

4. A number that can be used to describe a part of a whole is a __?__.

Proportions

Solve each proportion.

5. $\dfrac{60 \text{ mi}}{1 \text{ h}} = \dfrac{x \text{ mi}}{5 \text{ h}}$

6. $\dfrac{8 \text{ h}}{2 \text{ days}} = \dfrac{x \text{ h}}{7 \text{ days}}$

7. $\dfrac{12 \text{ ft}}{2 \text{ sec}} = \dfrac{x \text{ ft}}{11 \text{ sec}}$

8. $\dfrac{68 \text{ beats}}{1 \text{ min}} = \dfrac{x \text{ beats}}{10 \text{ min}}$

Decimal Computation

Simplify.

9. 679.53×100

10. $4.75 \times 1{,}000$

11. $12{,}359 \div 1{,}000$

12. $4 \div 100$

13. $1 \div 1{,}000$

14. 0.25×0.1

Decimals and Fractions

© 15. **Writing to Explain** Explain how to convert $\frac{3}{8}$ to a decimal.

© Common Core

6.RP.3 Use ratio and rate reasoning to solve real-world and mathematical problems, e.g., by reasoning about tables of equivalent ratios, tape diagrams, double number line diagrams, or equations.

Understanding Percent

What is a percent?

A percent is <u>a special kind of ratio in which the first term is compared to 100</u>. The percent is the number of hundredths that represents the part of the whole.

What percent of people prefer Bright White Toothpaste?

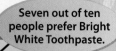

Seven out of ten people prefer Bright White Toothpaste.

Another Example **How do percents relate to the whole?**

Each line segment below represents 100%, but the line segments are different lengths. Points A, B, and E are the same distance from zero on each line segment. Use a proportion to find what percent or part of each line segment points A, B, and E represent. The length from zero to each point is relative to the length of each line segment.

Point A	Point B	Point E
$\dfrac{1}{2} = \dfrac{A}{100}$	$\dfrac{1}{4} = \dfrac{B}{100}$	$\dfrac{1}{5} = \dfrac{E}{100}$
$100 = 2A$	$100 = 4B$	$100 = 5E$
$50 = A$	$25 = B$	$20 = E$
Point A = 50%	Point B = 25%	Point E = 20%

```
0%         A        100%
←+————————•—————————→
 0         1"        2"
```

```
0%      B        C        D        100%
←+——————•————————•————————•——————————→
 0      1"       2"       3"       4"
```

```
0%      E        F        G        H       100%
←+——————•————————•————————•————————•——————→
 0      1"       2"       3"       4"       5"
```

Explain It

1. Use mental math to find the percents associated with the points C, D, F, G, and H.

One Way

Use a grid to model the percent.

$$\frac{7}{10} = \frac{70}{100} = 70\%$$

Another Way

Use number lines to model the percent.

$$\frac{7}{10} = \frac{70}{100} = 70\%$$

Another Way

Use a proportion to find the percent.

$$\frac{7}{10} = \frac{x}{100}$$

$$700 = 10x$$

$$70 = x$$

70% of people prefer Bright White Toothpaste.

Guided Practice*

MATHEMATICAL PRACTICES

Do you know HOW?

In **1** through **3**, write the percent of each figure that is shaded.

1.

2.

3.

Do you UNDERSTAND?

© **4. Be Precise** What is the whole to which a percent is compared?

© **5. Generalize** Why are tenths, fifths, and fourths easy to convert to percents?

6. Suppose that 4 out of 5 people prefer Bright White Toothpaste. What percent of people prefer that toothpaste?

Independent Practice

In **7** through **13**, write the percent of each figure that is shaded.

7.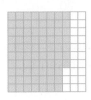

8.

9.

10.

11.

12.

13.

*For another example, see Set A on page 366.

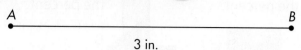
Use line segment $\overline{AB}$ to find the answers to **14** and **15**.

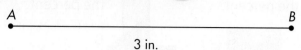

A ———————————————————— B

3 in.

14. If line segment $\overline{AB}$ represents 50%, what is the length of a line segment that is 100%?

15. If line segment $\overline{AB}$ is 300%, what is the length of a line segment that is 100%?

16. Persevere Draw a picture or use a proportion to find each percent.

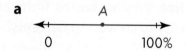

a $\frac{3}{4}$ **b** $\frac{4}{5}$ **c** $\frac{13}{20}$

17. Suppose that a diamond weighs 0.0182 carat. What is that number in expanded form?

18. Writing to Explain Is 25% always the same amount? Explain your answer and provide examples.

19. Easton won Best in Show in 60% of the shows he entered. In how many shows was Easton entered if he won Best in Show 15 times last year?

20. Estimation Each line segment below represents 100%. Estimate the percents that points *A*, *B*, and *C* represent.

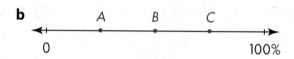

a
A
0   100%

b
A   B   C
0   100%

21. Sixteen lizards have white stripes on their tails. The ratio of lizards with white tail stripes to those with yellow tail stripes is 1:2. How many lizards have yellow tail stripes?

22. Think About the Structure Fifty runners started the race. Nineteen runners finished in under 30 minutes. Which of the following proportions shows how to find what percent 19 is of 50?

A $\frac{19}{50} = \frac{x}{100}$ **B** $\frac{19}{100} = \frac{x}{50}$ **C** $\frac{19}{x} = \frac{50}{100}$ **D** $\frac{50}{19} = \frac{x}{100}$

23. Model One side of a school building has 10 windows. Four windows have the blinds down. Which model represents the percent of windows with the blinds down?

A

B

C

D

Mixed Problem Solving

The After School Center took a survey of its members to find out which types of music are most popular among boys and girls. They displayed the data in two circle graphs. Use the graphs to answer the questions.

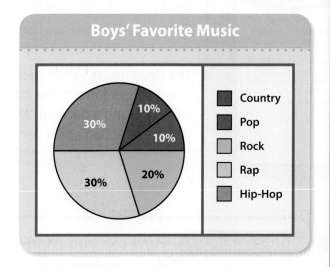

Boys' Favorite Music

- Country
- Pop
- Rock
- Rap
- Hip-Hop

1. What percentage of boys like hip-hop the most?

2. Which type of music do girls like most?

3. Which two types of music do the boys like the most?

4. Which type of music was chosen by $\frac{1}{5}$ of the boys?

5. Which type of music did $\frac{1}{4}$ of the girls choose as their favorite?

6. Twenty girls were surveyed. Which type of music did three girls choose? (Hint: Use a proportion.)

7. Twenty boys were surveyed. Which two types of music were chosen by 2 boys each?

8. Which type of music do the girls like least?

9. If fifteen boys chose hip-hop as their favorite, how many boys were surveyed?

10. If fourteen girls chose pop music, how many girls were surveyed?

11. If 200 boys were surveyed, which type of music did 60 boys choose?

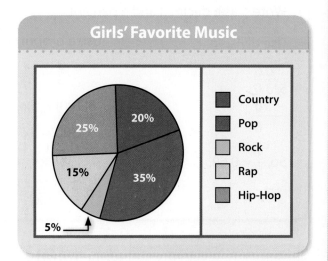

Girls' Favorite Music

- Country
- Pop
- Rock
- Rap
- Hip-Hop

Common
Core

6.RP.3 Use ratio and rate reasoning to solve real-world and mathematical problems, e.g., by reasoning about tables of equivalent ratios, tape diagrams, double number line diagrams, or equations.

Fractions, Decimals, and Percents

How are fractions, decimals, and percents related to one another?

Fractions, decimals, and percents are three ways to show portions of a whole.

The circle graph shows each part in a different form. Write 30% as a fraction and a decimal. Write 0.10 as a fraction and a percent.

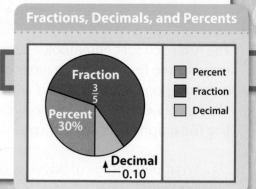

Fractions, Decimals, and Percents

- Percent
- Fraction
- Decimal

Another Example How can you change a fraction to a decimal and percent?

Write $\frac{3}{5}$ as a decimal and a percent.

Use division.

$$5\overline{)3.0} = 0.6$$
$$-30$$
$$0$$

So, $\frac{3}{5} = 0.60$.

Use a proportion.

$$\frac{3}{5} = \frac{x}{100}$$

$$3(100) = 5x$$

$$300 = 5x$$

$$60 = x$$

So, $\frac{3}{5} = \frac{60}{100} = 60\%$.

Guided Practice*

MATHEMATICAL
PRACTICES

Do you know HOW?

In **1** through **6**, write each number in two other ways.

1. 27%   **2.** 0.91   **3.** $\frac{6}{100}$

4. 0.465   **5.** 49%   **6.** $\frac{5}{8}$

Do you UNDERSTAND?

© **7. Reason** Why are you able to change between fractions, decimals, and percents?

© **8. Communicate** How is the decimal point moved when changing from a decimal to a percent?

Independent Practice

In **9** through **11**, express the value in two other ways.

9. 0.25   **10.** $\frac{2}{2}$ **11.** 7%

For another example, see Set B on page 366.

A percent compares a number to 100, so you can write 30% as a fraction and a decimal.

$$30\% = \frac{30}{100}$$

Simplify the fraction:

$$\frac{30 \div 10}{100 \div 10} = \frac{3}{10}$$

30% can also be written as $\frac{3}{10}$ or 0.30.

Use decimal place value to write the decimal 0.10 as a fraction and a percent.

Fraction:

$$0.10 = \frac{10}{100} = \frac{1}{10}$$

Percent:

$$0.10 = \frac{10}{100} = 10\%$$

0.10 can also be written as $\frac{1}{10}$ or 10%.

In **12** through **20**, express the value in two other ways.

12. 38%

13. $\frac{7}{8}$

14. 0.04

15. $\frac{1}{3}$

16. 65%

17. 0.46

18. 29%

19. 0.01

20. $\frac{5}{12}$

Problem Solving

MATHEMATICAL
PRACTICES

21. Many chemical elements can be found in Earth's atmosphere. Use the circle graph to answer the following questions.

   a What fraction of Earth's atmosphere is made up of nitrogen?

   b What part of Earth's atmosphere is made up of oxygen? Write the part as a decimal.

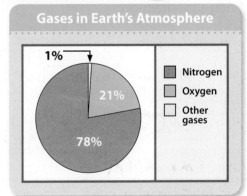

Gases in Earth's Atmosphere

1%

21%

78%

Nitrogen
Oxygen
Other gases

22. Estimation Mrs. Nellon's class sold 18 rolls of wrapping paper. Altogether, the school sold 82 rolls. About what percent of the sales came from Mrs. Nellon's class?

© **23. Writing to Explain** Explain how you would use mental math to express $\frac{16}{25}$ as a percent.

© **24. Persevere** Choose the answer that shows the following values in order from least to greatest: $\frac{1}{3}$, 0.25, 16%.

   A $\frac{1}{3}$, 0.25, 16%   **C** 16%, 0.25, $\frac{1}{3}$

   B 0.25, 16%, $\frac{1}{3}$ **D** 16%, $\frac{1}{3}$, 0.25

25. In a stock market game, Sergio bought 150 shares of stock at a price of $\frac{5}{8}$ a game dollar per share. How much game money did 150 shares cost?

©
Common
Core

6.RP.3.c Find a percent
of a quantity as a rate per
100 (e.g., 30% of a quantity
means $\frac{30}{100}$ times the
quantity); solve problems
involving finding the
whole, given a part and
the percent.

Percents Greater Than 100 and Less Than 1

How can you express percents greater than 100?

Jan and Kim built model cars for a science project. Kim's car traveled 140% as far as Jan's car. How can you write 140% as a fraction and as a decimal?

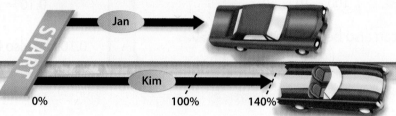

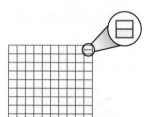

0%   100%   140%

Another Example   **How can you express percents less than 1?**

Write $\frac{1}{2}$% as a fraction and as a decimal.

Use what you know about the relationships among fractions, decimals, and percents.

Change to a fraction.

$\frac{1}{2}\% = 0.5\%$ ⬅ decimal form of $\frac{1}{2}$% ➡ $\frac{1}{2}\% = 0.5\%$

$0.5\% = \frac{0.5}{100}$ ⬅ fraction as part of 100 ➡ $0.5\% = \frac{0.5}{100}$

$\frac{0.5}{100} = \frac{5}{1,000}$ ⬅ multiplied by $\frac{10}{10}$ ➡ $\frac{0.5}{100} = \frac{5}{1,000}$

$= \frac{1}{200}$ equivalent forms $= 0.005$

Change to a decimal.

Guided Practice*

© **MATHEMATICAL PRACTICES**

Do you know HOW?

In **1** through **4**, write each percent as a fraction and as a decimal. Write fractions in simplest form.

1. 150%   **2.** 0.2%

3. 325%   **4.** $\frac{3}{10}$%

Do you UNDERSTAND?

© **5. Reason** Why is 140% greater than 1?

© **6. Communicate** Explain the difference between $\frac{1}{2}$ and $\frac{1}{2}$%.

7. Why was $\frac{0.5}{100}$ multiplied by $\frac{10}{10}$?

For another example, see Set C on page 367.

A percent compares a number to 100. The distance Jan's car traveled represents the whole or 100%.

```
        0                    1
        |————————————————————|————————|
       0%                  100%    140%
```

Kim's car traveled 140% as far. Expressed as a fraction, a percent greater than 100 will always be an improper fraction.

$$140\% = \frac{140}{100} = \frac{7}{5}$$

Similarly, percents greater than 100% will always have a decimal value greater than 1.

$$140\% = \frac{140}{100} = 1.40 = 1.4$$

So, $140\% = \frac{7}{5} = 1.4$.

Independent Practice

In **8** through **19,** write each percent as a fraction and as a decimal. Write fractions in simplest form.

8. 28%

9. 322%

10. 54%

11. 210%

12. 72%

13. 555%

14. 90%

15. 300%

16. 0.75%

17. 160%

18. 120%

19. $\frac{1}{5}$%

Problem Solving

MATHEMATICAL
PRACTICES

20. Use the information about the *Queen Mary 2* to answer the following questions.

   a How do you express 200% as a fraction and a decimal?

   b Three-quarters of the staterooms on the *Queen Mary 2* have balconies. How would you express this number as a fraction, a decimal, and a percent?

The *Queen Mary 2* is more than 200% longer than the Washington Monument is high.

Washington Monument

© **21. Writing to Explain** Nathan set his computer to print at 50% of the 8.5 in. × 11 in. page he normally uses. Ahmad thinks a document 50% its size will look huge. Is Ahmad correct about Nathan's printed report? Explain.

© **22. Persevere** Which is NOT equivalent to the others?

   A 0.56%   **B** 0.056   **C** 0.0056   **D** $\frac{0.56}{100}$

Common Core

6.RP.3 Use ratio and rate reasoning to solve real-world and mathematical problems, e.g., by reasoning about tables of equivalent ratios, tape diagrams, double number line diagrams, or equations.

Estimating Percent

How can you use fractions to estimate percents?

This graph shows the eye colors among students at Lake Mark School. You can use fraction equivalents and compatible numbers to estimate the percent of a number.

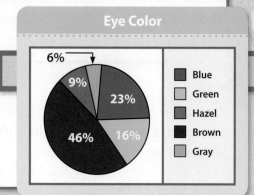

Eye Color

6%
9%
23%
46%
16%

■ Blue
□ Green
■ Hazel
■ Brown
□ Gray

Use these benchmark percents and their fraction equivalents to help you estimate.

Percent	10%	20%	25%	$33\frac{1}{3}$%	50%	$66\frac{2}{3}$%	75%
Fraction	$\frac{1}{10}$	$\frac{1}{5}$	$\frac{1}{4}$	$\frac{1}{3}$	$\frac{1}{2}$	$\frac{2}{3}$	$\frac{3}{4}$

Guided Practice*

 MATHEMATICAL PRACTICES

Do you know HOW?

In **1** and **2**, estimate the percent of each number.

Tip *Use benchmark fractions and compatible numbers.*

1. 47% of 77; 47% ≈ 50% and 77 ≈ 80
So, 50% of 80 = ▢.

2. 18% of 48; 18% ≈ 20 and 48 ≈ 50
So, 20% of 50 = ▢.

Do you UNDERSTAND?

3. Communicate Explain how to estimate 32% of 212.

4. In the graph at the top, suppose that there are 195 students in the fifth grade. How can you estimate the number of fifth graders who have hazel eyes?

Independent Practice

In **5** through **16**, estimate the percent of each number.

5. 74% of 63

6. 18% of 96

7. 47% of 183

8. 8% of 576

9. 34% of 55

10. 27% of 284

11. 67% of 866

12. 4% of 802

13. 47% of 78

14. 33% of 238

15. 65% of 89

16. 6% of 489

For another example, see Set D on page 367.

Mr. Weinstein's class has 28 students. Use the graph to estimate how many students in his class have brown eyes.

Think 46% ≈ 50% and 50% = $\frac{1}{2}$

So, 46% of 28 ≈ $\frac{1}{2}$ of 28.

$$\frac{1}{2} \times 28 = 14$$

About 14 students in Mr. Weinstein's class have brown eyes.

The total number of fifth-grade students is 118. Use the graph to estimate how many fifth-grade students have blue eyes.

Think 23% ≈ 25% and 118 ≈ 120

25% = $\frac{1}{4}$. So, 23% of 118 ≈ $\frac{1}{4}$ of 120.

$$\frac{1}{4} \times 120 = 30$$

About 30 fifth-grade students have blue eyes.

Problem Solving

MATHEMATICAL
PRACTICES

17. **Reason** If 10% of 60 is 6, what is 5% of 60? Explain how you found your answer.

18. Granola bars cost 24 cents each. Estimate how much money Heather needs to buy 19 granola bars.

19. Use estimation to complete the following sentences:

   a 49% of ▢ is about 8.

   b 26% of ▢ is about 20.

   c 198% of ▢ is about 99.

20. **Writing to Explain** A winter jacket is marked down 50% from $80. A sign says to take an additional 50% off the sale price. Does that mean the jacket is free? Explain.

21. Explain how you use prime factors to find the GCF of 45 and 75.

22. Estimate to find x if 25% of x is about 30.

23. Roland has 180 coins in his collection. Approximately 67% of the coins are quarters. About how many quarters does he have?

24. There are about 300 million residents in the U.S. If 36% of them live in the South, estimate how many live in this area of the U.S.

25. **Think About the Structure** Vanessa scored 78% on a test with 120 questions on it. Which benchmark fraction could you use to best **estimate** the number of questions that Vanessa answered correctly?

   A $\frac{1}{2}$ **B** $\frac{3}{4}$ **C** $\frac{2}{3}$ **D** $\frac{78}{100}$

26. **Generalize** What do the decimal forms of $\frac{2}{3}$, $\frac{1}{6}$, and $\frac{2}{9}$ have in common?

Common Core

6.RP.3.c Find a percent of a quantity as a rate per 100 (e.g., 30% of a quantity means $\frac{30}{100}$ times the quantity); solve problems involving finding the whole, given a part and the percent.

Finding the Percent of a Number

How can you calculate percentages?

The fourth, fifth, and sixth graders at Green Oaks School are taking a field trip to the museum. The circle graph shows what percent of the students are in each grade. Of the 575 students attending the field trip, how many are sixth graders?

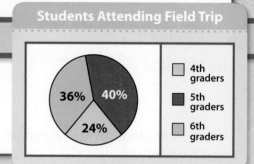

Students Attending Field Trip

36% 40% 24%

☐ 4th graders
■ 5th graders
☐ 6th graders

Another Example How can you find what percent one number is of another number?

Kevin had $180 in savings. He used his savings to buy a new bicycle that cost $108. What percent of his total savings did the bicycle cost?

Estimate.

```
0            ?        100%
●────────────●──────────●
0           108        180
```

Think of compatible numbers to 180.
$108 \approx 120$

$$\frac{108}{180} \approx \frac{120}{180} = \frac{12}{18} = \frac{2}{3}$$

$$\frac{2}{3} = 66\frac{2}{3}\%$$

My estimate is $66\frac{2}{3}\%$.

Write a proportion. $\frac{part}{whole} = \frac{percent\ value}{100}$

Let p = the percent value.

$$\frac{108}{180} = \frac{p}{100}$$

$$10{,}800 = 180p$$

$$60 = p$$

60% is close to $66\frac{2}{3}\%$. The bicycle cost 60% of Kevin's savings.

How can you use a calculator to find the percent of a number?

Find 24% of 47.

Enter: 24   47 **ENTER =**   Display: `11.28`

Or use the decimal form of the percent.

Enter: 0.24 47 **ENTER =**   Display: `11.28`

Estimate.

Think $36\% \approx 33\frac{1}{3}\% = \frac{1}{3}$ and $575 \approx 600$.

So, 36% of 575 is about $\frac{1}{3}$ of 600.

$\frac{1}{3} \times 600 = 200$

About 200 sixth graders are attending.

Write a decimal to find 36% of 575.

$$36\% = 0.36$$
$$0.36 \times 575 = 207$$

207 is close to 200. The answer is reasonable.

Write a proportion.

$$\frac{part}{whole} = \frac{percent\ value}{100}$$

Let x = unknown part.

$$\frac{x}{575} = \frac{36}{100}$$
$$100x = 20,700$$
$$x = 207$$

207 sixth graders are attending the field trip.

Guided Practice*

Do you know HOW?

In **1** and **2**, estimate and then find the percent of each number.

1. 26% of 50   **2.** 47% of 300

In **3** and **4**, write what percent the first number is of the second number.

3. 18 of 62   **4.** 14 of 42

Do you UNDERSTAND?

5. Be Precise In math, what operation does the word "of" mean?

6. In the example at the top, how could you use a decimal to find the number of 4th graders attending the field trip?

7. Use Tools In Another Example, how could you use a calculator to find what percent 108 is of 180?

Independent Practice

Leveled Practice In **8** through **13**, estimate the percent of each number.

 Convert the percent to a benchmark fraction and use compatible numbers.

8. 52% of 38

$52\% \approx \quad \%$

$38 \approx \quad$

9. 47% of 79

$47\% \approx \quad \%$

$79 \approx \quad$

10. 23% of 117

$23\% \approx \quad \%$

$117 \approx \quad$

11. 18% of 74

$18\% \approx \quad \%$

$74 \approx \quad$

12. 72% of 98

$72\% \approx \quad \%$

$98 \approx \quad$

13. 8% of 832

$8\% \approx \quad \%$

$832 \approx \quad$

In **14** through **21**, find the percent of each number.

14. 2.5% of 16   **15.** 24% of 17   **16.** 42% of 12   **17.** 5.2% of 12

18. 125% of 80   **19.** 52% of 117   **20.** 250% of 20   **21.** 38% of 1,500

In **22** through **29**, write what percent the first number is of the second number.

22. 32 of 72   **23.** 9 of 45   **24.** 85 of 65   **25.** 63 of 70

26. 20 of 33   **27.** 48 of 64   **28.** 16 of 16   **29.** 10 of 7.5

MATHEMATICAL
PRACTICES

30. A medium artichoke contains about 2 g of dietary fiber. It also contains about 12% of the recommended dietary fiber an average adult should eat each day. About how many artichokes would an average adult have to eat to get the recommended amount of dietary fiber?

31. A medium artichoke contains 5% of the recommended amount of potassium an average adult should have each day. How many grams of potassium should the average adult have each day?

A medium artichoke contains about 0.17 g of potassium.

32. **Think About the Structure** Liam is walking 15 miles in a walkathon. His goal is to raise $214. He has already raised $97. Which of the following equations could be used to determine what percent of his goal he has reached so far?

A $97x = \dfrac{214}{100}$ **B** $\dfrac{97}{214} = \dfrac{x}{100}$ **C** $\dfrac{214}{97} = \dfrac{x}{100}$ **D** $97 \times 214 = 100x$

33. **Writing to Explain** An art museum received a collection of 92 African American paintings. The museum can display 40 of the paintings on the first floor. Explain how you could find the percent of paintings displayed on the first floor.

34. **Persevere** In a 135-pound adult, about 94 pounds of the adult's weight is water. What percent of the weight is water, rounded to the nearest whole percent?

35. There are 5,280 feet in a mile. If a cloud is 5.3 miles above the ground, about how many feet above the ground is it?

36. Which of the following is a good **estimate** for 24% of 1,224?

A 300   **B** 293.76   **C** 50   **D** 28,000

Solving Percent Problems

Use a calculator.

Travis bought a puppy that normally sells for $125. The pet store had a sale with all animals 15% off the original prices. What was the sale price of the puppy?

One Way

Find 15% of 125 or 0.15 × 125.

Press: 0.15 [×] 125 [ENTER =]

Display: *18.75*

The discount is $18.75.
Subtract 125 − 18.75.

Press: 125 [−] 18.75 [ENTER =]

Display: *106.25*

Another Way

Find what percent the sale price is of the original price. 15% from 100%.

Press: 100 [−] 15 [ENTER =]

Display: *85*

Find 85% of 125 or 0.85 × 125.

Press: 0.85 [×] 125 [ENTER =]

Display: *106.25*

The sale price of the puppy was $106.25.

Practice

1. In addition to the $106.25, Travis had to pay 4.5% sales tax. How much was the sales tax to the nearest penny? How much did Travis pay for the puppy in all?

2. At El Tapatio, Josie spent $5.75 for the burritos and Miranda spent $6.25 for the fajitas. How much were their meals together? If tax is 5%, how much tax did they pay? How much did they spend for their meals, with tax? If they left a 20% tip on the total check (not including tax), how much tip did they leave? How much did they spend in all, including taxes and tip?

3. Tracy bought a jar of peanut butter that was 50% off. She had a coupon for an additional 10% off. How much did Tracy pay if the peanut butter originally cost $3.69?

Common Core

6.RP.3.c Find a percent of a quantity as a rate per 100 (e.g., 30% of a quantity means $\frac{30}{100}$ times the quantity); solve problems involving finding the whole, given a part and the percent.

Applying Percents: Finding the Whole

How can you find the whole, given a part and the percent?

Bree scored 90% correct on her last math test. She scored 135 points on this test. How many possible points were on the test?

90% of what number is 135?

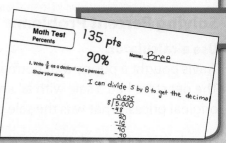

Math Test
Percents

135 pts

90%

Name: Bree

1. Write $\frac{5}{8}$ as a decimal and a percent. Show your work.

I can divide 5 by 8 to get the decimal

$$8\overline{)5.000}$$
0.625
-48
20
-16
40
-40

Another Example How can you find the whole, given a part and a percent that is greater than 100?

200% of what number is 40?

One Way

Use models.

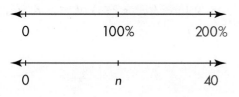

0   100%   200%

0   n   40

 Think The number lines show *2 times*.

200 is 2 times 100.

 Think 40 is *2 times* what number?

40 is 2 times 20, so $n = 20$.

200% of 20 is 40.

Another Way

Write a proportion.

$$\frac{200}{100} = \frac{40}{n}$$

Use equal ratios: $\frac{200}{100} = \frac{2}{1}$.

$$\frac{2}{1} = \frac{40}{n}$$

Think What number times 2 is 40?

$$\frac{2 \times 20}{1 \times 20} = \frac{40}{20}, \text{ so } n = 20.$$

200% of 20 is 40.

Explain It

1. Use the reasoning from above. 300% of what number is 60?
   Draw a number line or write a proportion to solve.

Use number lines to model the relationship among the percent, the part, and the whole you are trying to find.

Let p = the number of possible points on the test.

0   90% 100%

0   135 p

The relationship can be written as a proportion.

$$\frac{90}{100} = \frac{135}{p}$$

Use the proportion to find the whole. Find the common factor.

$$\frac{90}{100} = \frac{135}{p}$$

 90 times what number is 135?

$135 \div 90 = 1.5$

The common factor is 1.5.

Multiply 100×1.5 to find p.

$p = 150$

There were 150 possible points on Bree's math test.

Guided Practice*

MATHEMATICAL
PRACTICES

Do you know HOW?

1. 40% of what number is 80?

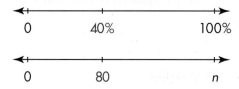

0   40%   100%

0   80 n

2. 50% of what number is 60?

Do you UNDERSTAND?

Ⓒ **3. Be Precise** Tony ran in 6 races, or 10% of the events. Do the 6 races represent the part, the percent, or the whole?

Ⓒ **4. Persevere** Explain the difference between what x and y represent in the problems "20 is 35% of x" and "y is 35% of 20."

Independent Practice

In **5** through **8**, use the number lines and write a proportion to solve for n.

5. 70% of what number is 35?

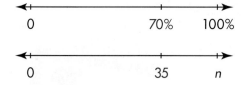

0   70%   100%

0   35 n

6. 300% of what number is 75?

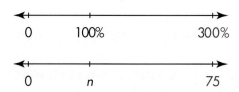

0   100%   300%

0   n 75

7. 44% of what number is 11?

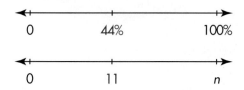

0   44%   100%

0   11 n

8. 200% of what number is 6?

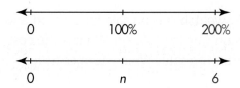

0   100%   200%

0   n 6

*For another example, see Set F on page 369.

For **9** through **14**, find each whole.

9. 25% of what number is 2?

10. 150% of what number is 48?

11. 100% of what number is 6?

12. 50% of what number is 15?

13. 300% of what number is 51?

14. 200% of what number is 42?

Problem Solving

MATHEMATICAL
PRACTICES

15. Reason Fifteen wrestlers arrived early to practice. This was 60% of the team. How many players were on the team?

16. Reason One inch, or 20% of the sand has been poured for a new playground. How deep will the sand be when the job is finished?

17. Reasonableness A runner ran 4 miles. Is it reasonable to say he ran $33\frac{1}{3}$% of a race if the total length of the race is 18 miles? Explain.

18. Sixteen pizzas were eaten at a party. This is 40% of the pizzas that were ordered. How many pizzas were ordered for the party?

19. Use Structure 80% of what number is 80? 60% of what number is 60? 127% of what number is 127? Describe the pattern you found after you solved each of these problems.

20. Writing to Explain Of the players on a bowling team, $\frac{7}{10}$ or 7 won trophies. Explain how you can find the number of players on the team.

21. Members of the school band sold $1,800 worth of fruit. This was 60% of their fundraising goal. How much was their goal?

A $3,500   **B** $3,000   **C** $2,500   **D** $2,000

For **22** and **23**, use the store information.

22. Lea bought a pair of jeans that were on sale for 25% off the regular price. She also bought 3 T-shirts at the regular price. What was Lea's total cost before taxes for these items?

Jeans: $35
T-Shirts: $12.99
Sweat Shirts: $20.50
Shorts: $17.50

23. A sweatshirt is on sale for 30% off and a pair of shorts is on sale for 15% off. What is the cost of each item after the sale? Which item costs less to buy?

Algebra Connections

Equations with Percents

Remember to use fraction or decimal equivalents to solve equations using percents. Then get the variable alone by using operations that have inverse relationships.

Adding w undoes subtracting w.

Subtracting x undoes adding x.

Multiplying by y undoes dividing by y.

Dividing by z undoes multiplying by z.

> **Example:** 20% of w is 3.5.
>
> Write an equation and solve:
>
> $$20\% \times w = 3.5$$
> $$0.20w = 3.5$$
> $$0.20w \div 0.20 = 3.5 \div 0.20$$
> $$w = 17.5$$
>
> To check, substitute 17.5 for w.
>
> $$0.20w = 3.5$$
> $$0.20\,(17.5) = 3.5$$
> $$3.5 = 3.5 \quad \text{It checks.}$$

Solve and check.

1. $20\% \times 45 = m$ **2.** $60\% \times g = 3$ **3.** $t \times 40\% = 120$ **4.** $(j\% \times 60) - 5 = 25$

5. 22% of $m = 55$ **6.** 15% of R is \$3.15   **7.** 16% of C is \$12   **8.** 35% of D is 26.25

9. 50% of $3h$ is 30   **10.** 25% of S is $\frac{1}{8}$ **11.** $66\frac{2}{3}\%$ of n is 8

12. 60% more than B is 1,200   **13.** 20% less than c is 32   **14.** 10% more than z is 22

15. $33\frac{1}{3}\%$ more than p is 16   **16.** 100% more than k is 110   **17.** 80% less than q is 16

· ·

18. Marni wants to give a 15% tip for her \$18 haircut. Find the amount of tip Marni should give. Write an equation.

19. 80% of Greg's class went on the field trip with 4 chaperones. If a total of 28 students and chaperones went, how many students are in Greg's class? Write an equation to solve the problem.

20. Nigel increased his book collection in the first month by 10%, to 55 books. Then he increased his collection by 20% in the second month. How many books were in his collection before the increase in the first month? How many books did he have at the end of the two months?

Problem Solving

Reasonableness

The original price of a bicycle was $150. The
bike went on sale for 10% off the original price.
The bike didn't sell, and the sale price was raised
by 10%. What is the final price of the bicycle?

It was calculated that the final price is $150.

After you solve a problem, look back and
check the answer.

New!
$150
10% OFF

Guided Practice*

MATHEMATICAL
PRACTICES

Do you know HOW?

Look back and check. Tell if the answer
given is reasonable. Explain.

1. Reasonableness David wants to buy
a sweater for his mother. The original
price of the sweater was $65. The store
is having a sale in which all sweaters
are 20% off. What is the sale price of
the sweater?
Answer: The sale price is $52.

Do you UNDERSTAND?

2. In the problem above, what is the
final price of the bicycle? Explain.

3. Write a Problem Write a problem
about the sale price of a pair of shoes.
Then give an answer for someone to
look back and check.

Independent Practice

MATHEMATICAL
PRACTICES

Look back and check. Tell if the answer given is
reasonable. Explain.

4. Reasonableness The sale price on a
bicycle is $80. A sign on the bike reads,
"Reduced 25% off the original price." How
much was the original price of the bicycle?
Answer: The original price of the bike
was $60.

5. In Exercise 4, what was the original price of
the bicycle?

Applying Math Practices

- What am I asked to find?
- What else can I try?
- How are quantities related?
- How can I explain my work?
- How can I use math to model the problem?
- Can I use tools to help?
- Is my work precise?
- Why does this work?
- How can I generalize?

Look Back and Check

Is the answer reasonable?

10% of $150 is $15. The sale price is $150 – $15 = $135.

For the final price to be $150, I need to add $15 to $135. But 10% of $135 is not $15. So, $150 is not a reasonable answer for the final price of the bicycle.

Look Back and Check

Did I answer the right question?

The question asks for the final price of the bicycle.

The correct question was answered, but the number part of the answer was not correct.

6. The sixth graders at Mahone Middle School are raising money for a new flowerbed in front of the school. For every $10 raised by the students, a local business owner will match 50%. If the students raise $139, is it reasonable that they will have $240 after the money is matched?

7. **Persevere** Of 30 students, $\frac{2}{3}$ are girls. Exactly 25% of the girls in the class wear glasses. How many girls wear glasses? Is 10 girls a reasonable answer?

8. A family-size box of laundry detergent is 72 oz. The regular-size box is 25% smaller. Both boxes of detergent cost 5 cents per ounce. Is $2.70 a reasonable price for the regular-size box?

9. Raul has 50 blocks. Of these blocks, 40% are red and 60% are blue. Among the red blocks, 20% are cube-shaped. How many red blocks are cube-shaped? Check your answer.

10. **Think About the Structure** Anita has gymnastics practice at 6:00 P.M. She needs to finish dinner at least 1 hour before practice, and it takes her about $\frac{1}{2}$ hour to eat dinner. If it takes Anita's parents about 45 minutes to make dinner, what is a reasonable time for them to start making dinner? What do you need to do to solve this problem?

Make dinner	Eat dinner	Finish dinner	Practice
▢ P.M.	▢ P.M.	▢ P.M.	6:00 P.M.
+ 45 min	$+ \frac{1}{2}$ h	+ 1 h	

1. What percent of the line segment is shaded? (14-1)

A 8%

B 18%

C 20%

D 80%

2. What is 0.4% written as a decimal? (14-3)

A 0.0004

B 0.004

C 0.04

D 0.4

3. Most U.S. households spend about 5% of their income on entertainment. Which of the following is equal to 5%? (14-2)

A $\frac{1}{20}$

B $\frac{1}{5}$

C $\frac{5}{10}$

D $\frac{1}{2}$

4. The population of Gilbert, Arizona, increased 275% from 1990 to 2000. Which of the following is equal to 275%? (14-3)

A 275

B $27\frac{1}{2}$

C $2\frac{3}{4}$

D $\frac{11}{40}$

5. A study found that 9% of dog owners brush their dog's teeth. Of 578 dog owners, about how many would be expected to brush their dog's teeth? (14-4)

A 60 **C** 100

B 80 **D** 300

6. Paula weeded 40% of her garden in 8 minutes. How many minutes will it take her to weed all of her garden? (14-6)

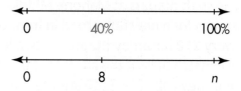

A 16 minutes **C** 20 minutes

B 18 minutes **D** 24 minutes

7. The circle graph shows the distribution of children at an elementary school. If there are 205 children in the school, about how many are in the 5th grade? (14-4)

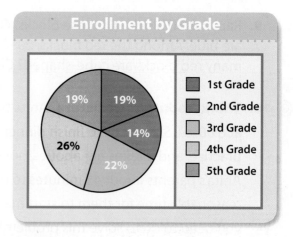

A 20 **C** 50

B 40 **D** 100

8. All but 5 state capitals have an interstate highway serving them. What percent of 50 is 5? (14-5)

   A 1%

   B 5%

   C 10%

   D 20%

9. What percent of the grid is shaded? (14-1)

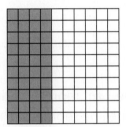

   A 20%

   B 40%

   C 50%

   D 250%

10. Which of the following can be used to find 65% of 28? (14-5)

   A $\dfrac{n}{28} = \dfrac{65}{100}$

   B $\dfrac{n}{28} = \dfrac{100}{65}$

   C $\dfrac{n}{100} = \dfrac{28}{65}$

   D $\dfrac{28}{n} = \dfrac{65}{100}$

11. If 20% of a number is 30, what is 50% of the number? (14-5)

   A 150

   B 100

   C 90

   D 75

12. What is $\dfrac{7}{25}$ written as a percent? (14-2)

   A 70%

   B 28%

   C 7%

   D 2.8%

13. What is the total amount if the percent is 16% and the part is 48? (14-6)

   A 214

   B 224

   C 280

   D 300

14. About 25% of the students at a college are freshmen. Of those, about 50% are women. Does that mean that 75% of the students at the college are freshman women? (14-7)

   A No, because only $\dfrac{1}{4}$ of the students are freshmen; so 75%, or $\dfrac{3}{4}$, could not be freshman women.

   B No, because 50% – 25% is only 25%. Therefore, about 25% are freshman women.

   C Yes, because 25% + 50% = 75%.

   D Yes, because 25% × 50% = 75%.

15. Jill walked 6 blocks. This was 25% of her walk. How far was Jill's walk? (14-6)

   A 14 blocks

   B 30 blocks

   C 12 blocks

   D 24 blocks

Set A, pages 344–346

This figure has 54 out of 100, or $\frac{54}{100}$ parts shaded. So, 54% of the figure is shaded.

Use a proportion to find what percent each of the points *Q* and *R* represent in relation to the line segment on which they are located.

Point Q:

$$\frac{2}{4} = \frac{Q}{100}$$

$$200 = 4Q$$

$$50 = Q$$

Point *Q* = 50%

Point R:

$$\frac{3}{4} = \frac{R}{100}$$

$$300 = 4R$$

$$75 = R$$

Point *R* = 75%

Remember that *percent* means "of a hundred."

Find the percent shaded in each diagram.

1.   **2.**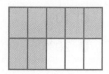

3.

Find the percent represented by each point on the line segment. The line segment represents 100%.

4.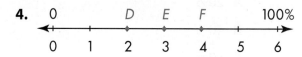

Set B, pages 348–349

Write 37% as a fraction and a decimal.

To find the fraction:

37% means 37 "of a hundred," or $\frac{37}{100}$.

To find the decimal:

$\frac{37}{100}$ can be read as "37 divided by 100."

To divide by 100, move the decimal point 2 places to the left.

37% = 0.37

Remember that you can also set up a proportion to change a fraction to a percent.

Write each value in two other ways.

1. 0.16   **2.** $\frac{63}{100}$

3. 27%   **4.** $\frac{7}{8}$

5. 0.55   **6.** 7%

7. 42%   **8.** $\frac{3}{5}$

9. 0.125   **10.** $\frac{47}{100}$

11. $\frac{3}{8}$ **12.** $33\frac{1}{3}\%$

13. 1   **14.** $\frac{2}{5}$

Percents Greater Than 100

Express the shaded area in 3 ways.

Fraction as part of 100: $\frac{221}{100}$ or $2\frac{21}{100}$

Percent: $\frac{221}{100} = 221\%$

Decimal: $\frac{221}{100} = 2.21$

Percents Smaller Than 1

Express the shaded area of the circled part in 3 ways.

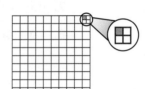

Fractions as part of 100: $\frac{0.25}{100}$

Percent: $\frac{0.25}{100} = 0.25\%$

Decimal: $\frac{0.25}{100} = 0.0025$

Remember that percents less than 1% are less than $\frac{1}{100}$, and that percents greater than 100% are more than one whole.

Express each as a fraction, a decimal, and a percent.

1.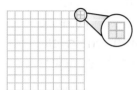

2.

Write each as a percent.

3. 0.0025   **4.** $2\frac{1}{2}$

5. $\frac{7}{5}$ **6.** 0.0033

7. $\frac{8}{3}$ **8.** $\frac{1}{200}$

9. 0.00125   **10.** $\frac{12}{5}$

You can use benchmark fractions and compatible numbers to estimate percents.

Find 24% of 83.

$24\% \approx 25\% = \frac{1}{4}$ and $83 \approx 80$

So, 24% of 83 $\approx \frac{1}{4}$ of 80.

$\frac{1}{4} \times 80 = 20$

24% of 83 is about 20.

Remember that it is easy to multiply a fraction and a number when the denominator of the fraction is a factor of the number.

Estimate the following values.

1. 22% of 96   **2.** 38% of 58

3. 47% of 88   **4.** 33% of 99

5. 12% of 358   **6.** 55% of 138

7. 68% of 72   **8.** 6% of 501

Set E, pages 354–356

Find 16% of 73.

Write a Decimal

Change the percent to a decimal and multiply.

$$16\% = 0.16$$

$$0.16 \times 73 = 11.68$$

16% of 73 is 11.68

Write a Proportion

Write a proportion:

$$\frac{part}{whole} = \frac{percent\ value}{100}$$

Let p equal part.

$$\frac{p}{73} = \frac{16}{100}$$

$$100p = 1,168$$

$$p = 11.68$$

16% of 73 is 11.68.

Use a Calculator

Find 54% of 80.

Enter: 0.54 [×] 80 [ENTER =]

Display: 43.2

or

Enter: 54 [%] [×] 80 [ENTER =]

Display: 43.2

54% of 80 is 43.2.

Remember that you can write a proportion to find the percent of a number.

$$\frac{Part}{Whole} = \frac{Percent\ Value}{100}$$

Find each value.

1. 9% of 124

2. 43% of 82

3. 90% of 40

4. 120% of 45

5. 0.5% of 150

6. 1% of 13

7. 45% of 55

8. 10% of 75

Tell what percent the first number is of the second number.

9. 3 of 20

10. 50 of 22

11. 24 of 30

12. 63 of 90

13. 52 of 30

14. 78 of 94

15. 65 of 73

16. 32 of 12

17. 8 of 20

18. 35 of 7

A number line model can be used to help you find the whole when you know a part and the percent.

Greg read 120 pages of a book on ecosystems for his science class. This is 30% of the number of pages of a novel he read for his literature class. How many pages did Greg read for his literature class?

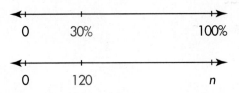

From the number lines you can write a proportion to help you find the value of *n*. Think about the relationship between 30 and 120 in the proportion.

$$\frac{30}{100} \times \frac{4}{4} = \frac{120}{400}$$

$$n = 400 \text{ pages}$$

Greg read 400 pages of a book he read for his literature class.

Remember to write a proportion to solve for the missing whole. You can use the numbers from the number line model you drew.

1. Trina spent 9 minutes studying her spelling words for the week. This is 18% of the time she spent studying for her math test. How many minutes did Trina study for her math test?

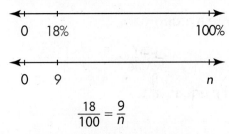

$$\frac{18}{100} = \frac{9}{n}$$

For **2** through **4**, find each whole. You may use a number line model and proportion.

2. 40% of what number is 10?

3. 80% of what number is 120?

4. 200% of what number is 28?

The scuba equipment Carey wants was originally $180 and is on sale for 20% off. Carey calculated the sale price is $36.

Is Carey's answer reasonable?

Look Back and Check

20% of $180 is $36

The discount is $36.

The sale price is $180 − $36 = $144.

Carey's estimate is not reasonable because the sales price should not be less than half the original price.

Remember to look back and check to make sure your answer is reasonable and that you answered the right question.

Look back and check. Tell if the answer given is reasonable.

1. Ben is in charge of calculating the tip. The bill is $46.82. He wants to leave a 15% tip. He calculated that the tip should be about $7.00. Is Ben's answer reasonable?

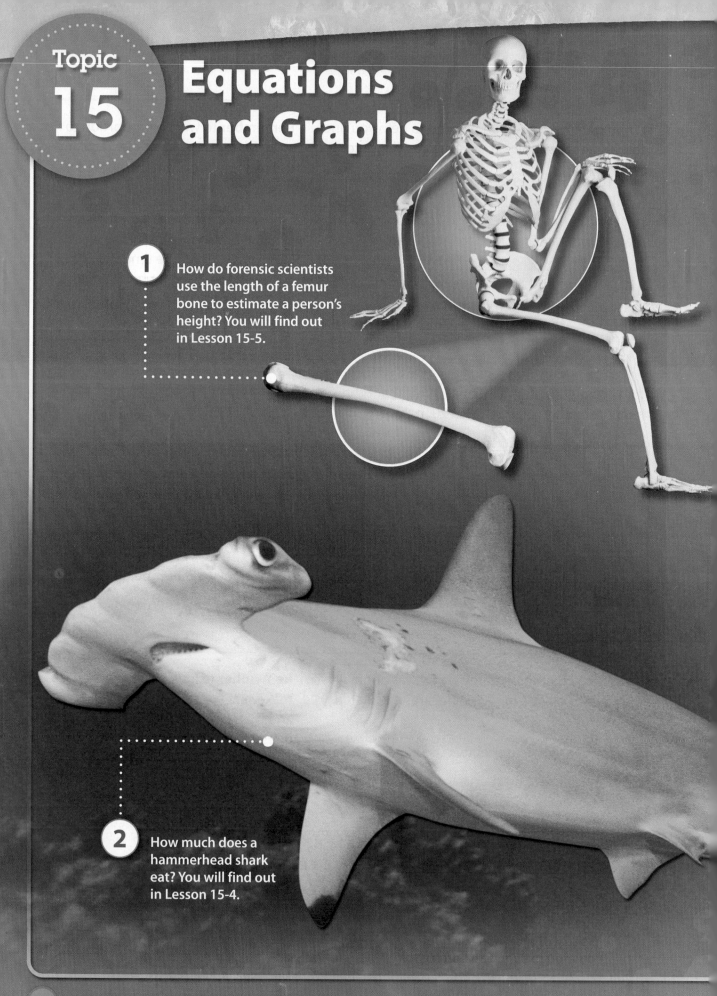

Topic 15

Equations and Graphs

1 How do forensic scientists use the length of a femur bone to estimate a person's height? You will find out in Lesson 15-5.

2 How much does a hammerhead shark eat? You will find out in Lesson 15-4.

Review What You Know!

Vocabulary

Choose the best term from the box.

- variable
- data
- solution

1. A ___?___ is a value of the variable that makes an equation true.

2. A ___?___ is a quantity that can change, often represented by a letter.

3. Information that is gathered is ___?___.

Using Variables

Calculate y for the given value of x.

4. $y = 13x$, $x = 3$ **5.** $y = 10x$, $x = 0$

6. $y = 7x + 7$, $x = 5$ **7.** $y = 4x - 5$, $x = 14$

Understanding Rates

For each of the following, convert the rates given into unit rates.

8. 3 gallons of juice per 20 children

9. 63 strokes per 18 holes of golf

Writing Equations

© **10. Writing to Explain** For every inch of necklace Ting is making, she uses 5 beads. If B equals the number of beads, and L equals the length of the necklace, write an equation that shows the relationship. Then explain how to solve this equation for B if the necklace is 24 inches long.

3

These tiles form an interesting design. How can you use an equation to express a pattern in a row of tiles? You will find out in Lesson 15-3.

4

How much does one of the most expensive teddy bears in the world cost? You will find out in Lesson 15-2.

7.EE.4.a Use variables to represent quantities in a real-world or mathematical problem, and construct simple equations and inequalities to solve problems by reasoning about the quantities.
a. Solve word problems leading to equations of the form $px + q = r$ and $p(x + q) = r$, where p, q, and r are specific rational numbers. Solve equations of these forms fluently…

Equations with More Than One Operation

What steps can you use to solve some equations?

The hiking club has hiked 5 miles of the trail shown. How many miles must they hike each hour to finish the trail in 4 hours? Let x equal the number of miles to hike each hour.

APPALACHIAN TRAIL

17 MI.

miles left to hike	+	miles already hiked	=	total number of miles
$4x$	+	5	=	17

Another Example **What inverse relationships and properties can you use?**

Charles rented rock-climbing equipment for $20 per day. The store refunded $15 when he returned the equipment in good condition. After the refund, Charles spent $65 in all. For how many days did Charles rent the equipment? Let d represent the number of days Charles rented the equipment.

total rental fee	−	refund	=	amount Charles paid
$20d$	−	15	=	65

Step 1

First undo the subtraction using the Addition Property of Equality.

$$20d - 15 = 65$$
$$20d - 15 + 15 = 65 + 15$$
$$20d = 80$$

Step 2

Then undo the multiplication using the Division Property of Equality.

$$20d = 80$$
$$\frac{20d}{20} = \frac{80}{20}$$
$$d = 4$$

Step 3

Check.

$$20d - 15 = 65$$
$$20(4) - 15 = 65$$
$$80 - 15 = 65$$
$$65 = 65$$

It checks.

Charles rented the rock climbing equipment for 4 days.

Explain It

1. In the example above, how many steps did it take to solve the equation for d?

2. In the example above, what simpler equation do you have after adding 15 to both sides of the equation?

Step 1

When an equation has more than one operation, first undo addition or subtraction.

$$4x + 5 = 17$$

Subtract 5 from both sides.

$$4x + 5 - 5 = 17 - 5$$
$$4x = 12$$

Step 2

Then undo multiplication or division.

$$4x = 12$$

Divide both sides by 4.

$$\frac{4x}{4} = \frac{12}{4}$$
$$x = 3$$

They must hike 3 miles each hour.

Step 3

Check.

$$4x + 5 = 17$$
$$4(3) + 5 = 17$$
$$12 + 5 = 17$$
$$17 = 17$$

It checks.

Guided Practice*

Do you know HOW?

Copy and solve by filling in the blanks.

1. $\frac{x}{4} - 5 = 19$

$\frac{x}{4} - 5 + \boxed{} = 19 + \boxed{}$

$\frac{x}{4} = \boxed{}$

$\frac{x}{4} \times \boxed{} = 24 \times \boxed{}$

$x = \boxed{}$

Do you UNDERSTAND?

© **2. Use Structure** In the example at the top, why do you subtract 5 from both sides of the equation?

3. Suppose the hiking club members in the example had to complete their hike in 3 hours. How many miles would they have to hike each hour?

Independent Practice

Leveled Practice For **4** through **7**, tell which operation you would undo first and which operation you would undo next.

4. $15t - 15 = 45$

5. $62 = 3c + 8$

6. $25 = 5q - 50$

7. $\frac{d}{30} + 1 = 4$

For **8** through **19**, solve each equation and check your answer.

8. $\frac{x}{7} - 3 = 4$

9. $5b - 7 = 13$

10. $\frac{s}{4} + 3 = 9$

11. $24 + 12n = 60$

12. $12 + 5y = 92$

13. $11n - 1 = 10$

14. $81 = 45 + \frac{r}{5}$

15. $\frac{m}{11} - 8 = 12$

16. $25 = 11g + 3$

17. $18 = \frac{z}{3} + 3$

18. $2m + 5 = 6$

19. $n + 2.5 = 6.5$

Ⓒ **20. Model** Janine's family bought 5 box lunches and some bottled water for their hike. The bottled water cost $4. The total cost of the water and lunches was $19. How much did each box lunch cost? Let x represent the cost of a box lunch. Use the equation $5x + 4 = 19$ to solve.

Ⓒ **21. Model** Alejandro bought 4 T-shirts to give to his friends. After using a $10-off coupon, he paid $18 for the shirts. How much did each shirt cost? Let s represent the cost of each shirt. Use the equation $4s - 10 = 18$ to solve.

Ⓒ **22. Writing to Explain** Marty solved the equation below. Is Marty's solution correct? Why or why not?

Marty's work: $\frac{x}{3} - 5 = 6$
$$3(\tfrac{x}{3}) - 5 = 3(6)$$
$$x - 5 = 18$$
$$x - 5 + 5 = 18 + 5$$
$$x = 23$$

Ⓒ **23. Think About the Structure** After you add 3 to both sides of the equation $27 = \frac{m}{6} - 3$, what should you do next?

A Multiply both sides by 6.

B Divide both sides by 6.

C Add 6 to both sides.

D Subtract 6 from both sides.

Ⓒ **24. Think About the Structure** After you subtract 3 from both sides of the equation $42x + 3 = 87$, which operation should you *use* next to undo the multiplication?

A addition

B subtraction

C multiplication

D division

Ⓒ **25. Think About the Structure** Which operation would you *undo* first to solve the equation $12n + 23 = 83$?

A addition

B multiplication

C division

D subtraction

Ⓒ **26. Reasonableness** Without solving, how can you tell that $x = 7$ is not a solution of $3x + 10 = 20$?

27. The month of April has 30 days. Corey's iguana eats $2\frac{1}{2}$ ounces of peas a day. How many ounces of peas will Corey's iguana eat during the month of April?

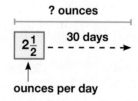

28. Vladimir exercises for at least 30 minutes each evening. One evening he jogged for $\frac{3}{4}$ hour and biked for $\frac{1}{8}$ hour. How much time did Vladimir spend that evening on his two exercises?

Algebra Connections

Equation Sense: Estimate the Solution to the Equation

Remember that you can estimate the solution to an equation by using number sense and rounding.

Use number sense and rounding to estimate a solution for each equation. For **1** through **12**, estimate the value of the variable in each equation.

1. $x + 56 = 93$

2. $x - 34 = 121$

3. $254 = 75 + x$

4. $24 - J = 5$

5. $62 + k = 108$

6. $f - 81 = 38$

7. $y + 78 = 91$

8. $96 - b = 26$

9. $15a = 120$

10. $\frac{180}{t} = 45$

11. $7r = 112$

12. $\frac{h}{6} = 18$

Example: Find $x + 12 = -37$.

Use number sense and rounding to estimate the solution to the equation.

$x + 12 = -37$ ← **Will x be negative or positive?**

Think *negative + positive = negative for this equation.*

So, x is negative.

Then, use rounding to estimate the solution. Round 12 to 10 and -37 to -40.

$x + 10 = -40$ ← **What number added to 10 equals -40?**

$-50 + 10 = -40$

So, $x \approx -50$.

For **13** through **16**, solve each problem.

13. Estimate the value of one-third of 1,612 feet.

14. Ronna is estimating the amount of a 15% tip for a $20.36 bill. Her friend Suri said that $2 is a good estimate. Do you agree? Explain.

15. Why would you use estimation to solve an equation?

16. Rob charges $0.01 per square yard to mow a lawn. He estimates that each of his steps is about a yard. Before he gave Mrs. Rodriguez an estimate to mow her lawn, he paced the width of the yard in 33 steps and the length of her yard in 68 steps. What would be a good cost estimate for Rob to give to Mrs. Rodriguez? Estimate the area of the yard and then estimate the cost. Explain.

© Common Core

6.EE.9 Use variables to represent two quantities in a real-world problem that change in relationship to one another; write an equation to express one quantity, thought of as the dependent variable, in terms of the other quantity, thought of as the independent variable. Analyze the relationship between the dependent and independent variables using graphs and tables, and relate these to the equation....

Patterns and Equations

How can you find a pattern to write and solve an equation?

The table shows the cost of weekend tickets to the Slide and Splash Water Park. Find a pattern between the number of tickets, n, and the cost, c, of the tickets. How much would 6 tickets cost?

Write a rule and an equation that tells a pattern.

Number, n	Cost, c
3	$16.50
4	$22.00
5	$27.50
6	▩

Guided Practice*

MATHEMATICAL PRACTICES

Do you know HOW?

1. The table shows Brenda's age, b, when Talia, t, is age 7, 9, and 10. Write a rule and an equation that describes a pattern. Then find Brenda's age when Talia is 12.

Talia's age, t	Brenda's age, b
7	2
9	4
10	5
12	▩

Do you UNDERSTAND?

© 2. **Look for Patterns** How can you find a pattern in a table to write a rule and an equation that describes a pattern?

3. In the example at the top, how much will 12 tickets cost?

© 4. **Writing to Explain** What should be done if the pattern does not check for other values in the table?

Independent Practice

Leveled Practice In **5** through **8**, write a rule and an equation to fit a pattern in each table.

5.

x	1	2	3	4	5
y	33	34	35	36	37

6.

m	0	1	2	3	4
n	0	3	6	9	12

7.

a	0	3	6	9	12
b	14	17	20	23	26

8.

x	0	6	12	18	24
y	0	1	2	3	4

*For another example, see Set B on page 395.

Find the price of one ticket, p, when 3 tickets cost $16.50.

$$3p = \$16.50$$
$$\frac{3p}{3} = \frac{\$16.50}{3}$$
$$p = \$5.50$$

One ticket costs $5.50. Check the cost for 4 and 5 tickets.

$$4 \times \$5.50 = \$22.00$$
$$5 \times \$5.50 = \$27.50$$

$5.50 checks for 4 and 5 tickets.

State the rule:

The total cost, c, is $5.50 times the number of tickets, n.

Write an equation:

$$c = \$5.50 \times n, \text{ or } c = 5.5n$$

Find the cost of 6 tickets:

$$c = 5.5(6)$$
$$c = 33$$

The cost of 6 tickets is $33.00.

Write a rule and an equation to fit a pattern in each table for **9** and **10**. Then use the rule to complete the table.

9.

u	0	1	2	3	4
v	25	24	23		

10.

x	0	9	18	27	36
y	0	1	2		

Problem Solving

MATHEMATICAL
PRACTICES

11. To celebrate their 125th anniversary, a company in Germany produced 125 very expensive teddy bears. The bears, known as the "125 Karat Teddy Bears," are made of mohair, silk, and gold thread and have diamonds and sapphires for eyes.

The chart at the right shows the approximate cost of different numbers of these bears. Based on the pattern, how much does one bear cost?

Cost of "125 Karat Teddy Bears"	
Number, n	Cost, c
4	$188,000
7	$329,000
11	$517,000
15	$705,000

© **12. Writing to Explain** Explain how you can find a pattern in the chart showing the cost of "125 Karat Teddy Bears." Use the pattern to write a rule and an equation.

© **Think About the Structure** For **13** and **14**, which equation best describes the pattern in each table?

13.

r	2	4	6	8	10	12
s	0	2	4	6	8	10

A $s = r \div 2$ **C** $s = 2r$

B $s = r - 2$ **D** $s = r$

14.

x	0	$\frac{1}{2}$	1	$1\frac{1}{2}$	2	$2\frac{1}{2}$
y	0	1	2	3	4	5

A $y = x \div 2$ **C** $y = 2x$

B $y = x$ **D** $y = 3x$

Common Core

7.EE.4.a Use variables to represent quantities in a real-world or mathematical problem, and construct simple equations and inequalities to solve problems by reasoning about the quantities.
a. Solve word problems leading to equations of the form $px + q = r$ and $p(x + q) = r$, where p, q, and r are specific rational numbers. Solve equations of these forms fluently...

More Patterns and Equations

How can you use patterns to solve an equation that has more than one operation?

Ethan owes his mother $75. He is repaying her $5 each week. How much will Ethan still owe after 12 weeks?

| Week 1 | Week 2 | Week 3 | Week 4 | Week 5 | Week 6 | Week 7 |

Guided Practice*

MATHEMATICAL
PRACTICES

Do you know HOW?

In **1**, use the equation given to complete the table.

1. $y = 2x - 7$

x	4	5	6	7	8
y	1	3	5	▢	▢

2. State the rule for the pattern in the table in words.

Do you UNDERSTAND?

3. In the example at the top, look for a pattern. What happens to the value of y when the value of x is increased by 1?

Ⓒ **4. Reason** Find the value for y when $x = 10$. What does this mean in relation to the example?

Independent Practice

Leveled Practice In **5** and **6**, use the pattern and equation to complete each table.

5. $t = 5d + 5$

d	0	1	2	3	4
t	5	10	15	▢	▢

6. $y = \frac{1}{2}x - 1$

x	2	4	6	8	10
y	0	1	2	▢	▢

In **7** and **8**, use the equation to complete each table.

7. $y = 2x + 1$

x	0	1	2	3
y	1	3	▢	▢

8. $p = q + 4$

q	4	8	12	16
p	8	▢	▢	▢

*For another example, see Set C on page 395.

Make a table to show the amount Ethan still owed after 0, 1, 2, and 7 weeks.

Week, x	Amount still owed, y
0	$75
1	$70
2	$65
7	$40

Use the pattern to write an equation.

Let x = the number of weeks

Let y = the amount still owed

Amount still owed		Loan amount		Amount paid after x weeks
y	$=$	$75	$-$	$5x$

Find how much Ethan will still owe after 12 weeks.

$y = 75 - 5x$

$y = 75 - 5(12)$

$y = 75 - 60$

$y = 15$

Ethan will still owe $15 after 12 weeks.

In **9** and **10**, use the equation to complete each table.

9. $b = \dfrac{a}{2} - 2$

a	17	14	11	8	5
b	▪	▪	▪	▪	▪

10. $y = 3x + 10$

x	2	4	6	8	10
y	▪	▪	▪	▪	▪

Problem Solving

MATHEMATICAL PRACTICES

ⓒ 11. Think About the Structure Which equation describes this pattern?

x	1	2	3	4
y	2	8	14	20

A $y = 4x - 2$ **C** $y = x + 2$

B $y = \dfrac{1}{6}x + 4$ **D** $y = 6x - 4$

12. A parking garage charges $2.50 for parking up to 1 hour and $1.25 for each additional hour. If a car is parked for h hours, what is the parking charge? How much would it cost to park 6 hours? Use the equation $c = \$2.50 + \$1.25 (h - 1)$ to make a table for 2, 3, 4, 5, and 6 hours.

13. Elizabeth is using 1-inch square tiles to decorate a wall. Use the equation $p = 2t + 2$ to make a table to show the perimeter, p, of t tiles in a single row when t is 1, 2, 3, and 6.

ⓒ 14. Writing to Explain Explain the rule for the pattern given by the equation $p = 2t + 2$ in Exercise 13.

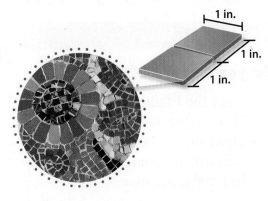

Lesson
15-4

Common
Core

6.EE.9 Use variables to represent two quantities in a real-world problem that change in relationship to one another; write an equation to express one quantity, thought of as the dependent variable, in terms of the other quantity, thought of as the independent variable. Analyze the relationship between the dependent and independent variables using graphs and tables, and relate these to the equation....

Graphing Equations

Hands-On
grid paper

How can you graph a linear equation?

The booster club members are making school pompoms. Their supplies cost $4, and they plan to sell the pompoms for $1 apiece.

Let x = the number of pompoms sold.
Let y = the profit.

Graph the equation $y = x - 4$ to show the relationship between x and y.

Each pompom sells for $1.

Another Example **When does the graph of a linear equation go through the origin?**

Make a T-table and graph of $y = 4x$.

Step 1

Make a T-table, using at least three x-values.

$y = 4x$	
x	y
0	0
1	4
2	8

$4(0) = 0$
$4(1) = 4$
$4(2) = 8$

Step 2

Graph each ordered pair. Draw a line through the points and extend the line in both directions. The line shows all the values that make the equation true.

The graph of a linear equation will go through the origin if the equation is $y = ax$, where a can be any nonzero number.

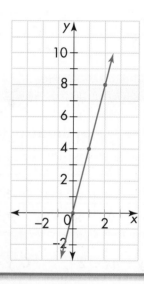

Guided Practice*

MATHEMATICAL
PRACTICES

Do you know HOW?

1. Copy the T-table and fill in the values using the equation $y = 3x$. Draw a coordinate plane and graph the equation.

$y = 3x$	
x	y
-2	-6
0	▦
2	▦

Do you UNDERSTAND?

2. **Generalize** In the Another Example, what is true about the x-value and y-value of any point on the line of the graph?

3. In the example at the top, explain why points with negative x-values do not relate to the problem.

DIGITAL Animated Glossary, eTools
www.pearsonsuccessnet.com

Make a T-table for $y = x - 4$.

x	y
0	−4
2	−2
6	2

Always choose at least three x-values; then find the corresponding y-values.

Graph each ordered pair in the T-table on a coordinate plane.

Use a straight edge to draw a line through the points.

<u>Since the graph of $y = x - 4$ is a straight line, the equation is</u> a linear equation.

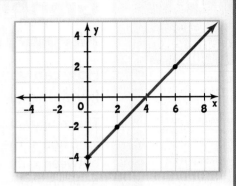

Independent Practice

In **4** through **11**, make a T-table using the values 2, 4, and 6 for x. Draw a coordinate plane and graph the equations.

4. $y = x$ **5.** $y = 3 + x$ **6.** $y = x + 8$ **7.** $y = x - 2$

8. $y = 2x$ **9.** $y = x + 1$ **10.** $y = x + 7$ **11.** $y = \frac{x}{2}$

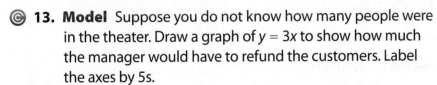

Problem Solving

MATHEMATICAL
PRACTICES

During a movie matinee, the film broke, so the manager refunded the ticket price to everyone attending.

12. If the manager had to refund $33.00, how many people were at the theater?

Movie Price Board

Data

Adults	$5.50
Children & Seniors	$5.00
Matinees: All Ages	$3.00

Ⓒ **13.** **Model** Suppose you do not know how many people were in the theater. Draw a graph of $y = 3x$ to show how much the manager would have to refund the customers. Label the axes by 5s.

Ⓒ **14.** **Use Structure** Which equation was used to make the graph on the right?

A $y = 4x$ **C** $y = 2x$

B $y = \frac{x}{2}$ **D** $y = x + 2$

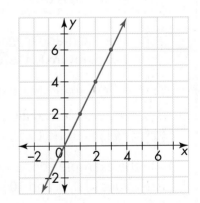

15. A hammerhead shark may eat about 4% of its body weight in food each day. If one shark eats about 7.5 pounds of food a day, make a T-table of $y = 7.5x$ to show how many pounds of food this shark eats in x days. Use x-values of 0, 6, and 8.

Step-Up Lesson
15-5

ⓒ
Common Core

7.EE.4.a Use variables to represent quantities in a real-world or mathematical problem, and construct simple equations and inequalities to solve problems by reasoning about the quantities. **a.** Solve word problems leading to equations of the form $px + q = r$ and $p(x + q) = r$, where p, q, and r are specific rational numbers. Solve equations of these forms fluently…

Graphing Equations with More Than One Operation

Hands-On grid paper

How can you graph a linear relationship involving two operations?

The temperature was 6°C and increased 2°C each hour for 6 hours. The equation $y = 6 + 2x$ shows the relationship between x, the number of hours, and y, the temperature. After how many hours was the temperature 10°C?

Another Example **How can you use a linear relationship to convert measures of temperature?**

Most of the world uses the Celsius temperature scale. The equation $F = 1.8C + 32$ shows the relationship between degrees in Celsius (the independent variable C) and degrees in Fahrenheit (the dependent variable F). Graph the equation to analyze the relationship between the dependent and independent variables. Use the graph to estimate what 15° Celsius is in degrees Fahrenheit.

Step 1 $F = 1.8C + 32$

Make a T-table for $C = 0$, 5, and 10.

°C	0	5	10
°F	32	41	50

Tip The independent variable is one of two variables in a relationship. Any value can be used for the independent variable. The value that is used determines the value of the other variable, the dependent variable.

Step 2 Graph the ordered pairs. Draw a line showing all the values for which the equation is true.

Step 3 Use the graph to estimate the Fahrenheit temperature for 15°C.

15°C equals about 59°F.

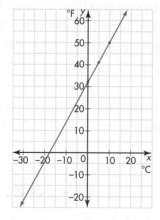

Explain It

1. In the example above, why do you think the C-values of 0, 5, and 10 were used?

2. How can you convert 25°C to degrees Fahrenheit? Convert 25°C to degrees Fahrenheit.

Step 1

Make a T-table for $y = 6 + 2x$.

x	y
0	6
2	10
4	14

Step 2

Graph each ordered pair on a coordinate plane. Draw a line through the points.

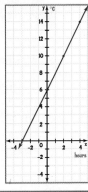

Step 3

Use the graph to find the point with a y-value of 10.

Point (2, 10) is on the graph of $y = 6 + 2x$.

The temperature was 10°C after 2 hours.

Guided Practice*

MATHEMATICAL
PRACTICES

Do you know HOW?

1. Copy and complete the T-table below for $y = 5x - 1$. Then graph the equation.

x	y
0	−1
1	▨
2	▨

$y = 5x - 1$
← $y = 5(0) - 1$
$y = 0 - 1$
$y = -1$

Do you UNDERSTAND?

© 2. **Communicate** Is the equation $y = 5x - 1$ a linear equation? Explain.

3. At what point does the equation $y = 5x - 1$ cross the y-axis?

4. Is the point (1, 4) a solution of $y = 5x - 1$? Explain.

Independent Practice

Leveled Practice Copy and complete the T-tables for each of the equations below. Then graph each equation.

5. $y = 3x + 1$

x	y
0	1
1	▨
2	▨

6. $y = 2x + 3$

x	y
−1	1
0	▨
1	▨

7. $y = 3 - 2x$

x	y
−1	5
0	▨
1	▨

For **8** through **11**, make a T-table and graph each equation.

8. $y = 4x + 5$ 9. $y = 2x - 2$ 10. $y = x + 10$ 11. $y = 2x - 1$

DIGITAL
Animated Glossary, eTools
www.pearsonsuccessnet.com

For another example, see Set E on page 396.

A zookeeper uses the chart at right to figure out how much food to put in the pens of different herbivores. The zookeeper adds a fixed amount of extra food per pen.

For **12** through **14**, use the equation given to make a T-table and draw a graph in the first quadrant showing the relationship between the amount of food and number of animals. Let x = the number of animals, and let y = the total amount of food.

Data	animal	feed per animal (lb)	extra feed per pen (lb)
	deer	2.5	3
	sheep	4	3
	goats	1	5
	antelope	1.5	3
	elk	7	3

12. antelope $y = 1.5x + 3$ **13.** deer $y = 2.5x + 3$ **14.** sheep $y = 4x + 3$

Use the graphs made in 12 through 14 to answer **15** and **16**.

15. If there are 2 antelope in a pen, how much feed should the zookeeper give them?

 16. Writing to Explain The zookeeper brings 15 pounds of food to the sheep pen. How can you determine how many animals there are?

 17. Think About the Structure Which equation is shown in the graph at right?

A $y = 0.5x + 3$ **C** $y = 3x + 3$

B $y = 3x - 7$ **D** $y = -3x + 3$

18. Which of the following ordered pairs is found on the line $y = 5 + 6x$?

A $(1, -1)$ **B** $(0, 6)$ **C** $(5, 6)$ **D** $(1, 11)$

 19. Persevere At what point does the line $y = 6x + 7$ cross the y-axis?

A $(0, -7)$ **B** $(0, 7)$ **C** $(-8, 7)$ **D** $(15, 0)$

20. Terry received 44 points out of a possible 50 points on the math test. What was his score as a percent?

 21. Model Forensic scientists can use the length of the thighbone or femur in centimeters to help estimate the height of a skeleton. One equation they may use is $h = 2.6f + 65$, where h represents height and f represents the length of the femur in centimeters. About how tall was this person?

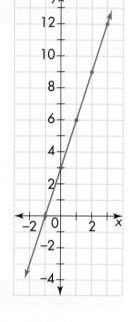

femur = 37 cm

Graphing Equations

Use 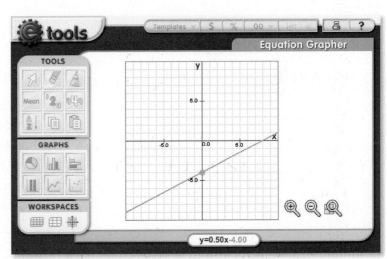 tools
Spreadsheet/Data/Grapher

Graph $y = x + 5$, $y = 3x$, and $y = \frac{1}{2}x - 4$.
Compare each graph to $y = x$.

Step 1 Go to the Spreadsheet/Data/Grapher eTool. Click on the Equation Grapher workspace icon.

The graph of $y = x$ is shown. Note that $y = x$ is the same as $y = 1.00x + 0.00$. Click on the dot and drag the line up until the equation shows $y = 1.00x + 5.00$. So $y = x + 5$ is up 5 units from $y = x$.

Step 2 Move the line back to $y = 1.00x + 0.00$. Choose another place on the line and drag until the equation shows $y = 3.00x + 0.00$. Notice how the equation goes through the points $(0, 0)$ and $(3, 1)$. From $(0, 0)$ you can find another point by going up 3 units and right 1 unit.

Step 3 Since $\frac{1}{2} = 0.5$, move the line until the equation shows $y = 0.50x - 4.00$. Notice, from $(0, -4)$ you go up 1 unit and right 2 units to get to another point.

Practice

Predict what each graph will look like and then graph to check.

1. $y = x + 7$

2. $y = x - 6$

3. $y = 2x$

4. $y = \frac{1}{3}x$

5. $y = 4x$

6. $y = 3x - 1$

7. $y = 2x - 5$

8. $y = \frac{1}{4}x + 2$

Lesson
15-6

©
Common
Core

6.EE.8 Write an inequality
of the form $x > c$ or $x < c$
to represent a constraint
or condition in a real-world
or mathematical problem.
Recognize that inequalities
of the form $x > c$ or $x < c$
have infinitely many
solutions; represent
solutions of such
inequalities on number
line diagrams. Also 6.EE.5

Understanding Inequalities

How can you solve an inequality?

An inequality uses $>$, $<$, $\geq$, or $\leq$ to compare two expressions.

One solution to the inequality $x > 5$ is $x = 7$ because $7 > 5$. Inequalities have more than one solution. Graph all of the solutions of $x > 5$.

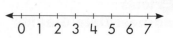

0 1 2 3 4 5 6 7

Another Example **How can you determine if a given value is a solution for an inequality?**

The table at the right shows the length of the longest jump for each of four track athletes at Howard High School. In order to qualify for the conference meet, an athlete must jump at least 18 ft. If the inequality $j \geq 18$ describes the length of a jump that qualifies, which of the students will qualify?

Howard High School Long Jump Results	
Amir	$22\frac{1}{3}$ ft
Jake	16 ft
Tyrell	$18\frac{1}{4}$ ft
Ryan	$20\frac{1}{2}$ ft

One Way

Substitute each of the values for j:

$22\frac{1}{3} \geq 18$; so, $22\frac{1}{3}$ is a solution.

Since $16 < 18$, 16 is NOT a solution.

$18\frac{1}{4} \geq 18$; so, $18\frac{1}{4}$ is a solution.

$20\frac{1}{2} \geq 18$; so, $20\frac{1}{2}$ is a solution.

Since $22\frac{1}{3}$ ft, $18\frac{1}{4}$ ft, and $20\frac{1}{2}$ ft are all solutions to the inequality $j \geq 18$, Amir, Tyrell, and Ryan will qualify.

Another Way

Graph the inequality on a number line.

Draw a number line. Include several numbers that are greater and less than the number in the inequality. Since $j \geq 18$, draw a closed circle at 18 and a thick line from the closed circle to the right with an arrow.

15 16 17 18 19 20 21 22 23

Since $22\frac{1}{3}$, $18\frac{1}{4}$, and $20\frac{1}{2}$ are all located on the shaded portion of the number line, they are solutions. Amir, Tyrell, and Ryan will qualify.

Step 1

To graph $x > 5$, draw an open circle at 5 on a number line.

0 1 2 3 4 5 6 7 8 9 10

The open circle shows that 5 is not a solution.

Step 2

Find several solutions and color those on a number line.

0 1 2 3 4 5 6 7 8 9 10

7 and 9 are solutions because $7 > 5$ and $9 > 5$.

Step 3

Start at the open circle and color over the solutions you found. Draw an arrow to show that the solutions go on forever.

0 1 2 3 4 5 6 7 8 9 10

Guided Practice*

MATHEMATICAL PRACTICES

Do you know HOW?

For **1** and **2**, write the inequality that each graph represents.

1. $z \bigcirc \blacksquare$

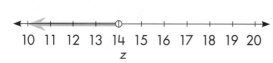

10 11 12 13 14 15 16 17 18 19 20
z

2. $c \bigcirc \blacksquare$

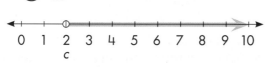

0 1 2 3 4 5 6 7 8 9 10
c

Do you UNDERSTAND?

3. Explain why 7 is a solution to $x > 5$.

4. Explain why 2 is **NOT** a solution to $x > 5$.

5. **Use Tools** How does the number line above imply that 5.1 and 50 are solutions to $x > 5$?

6. **Communicate** In Another Example, suppose a fifth student jumped $19\frac{1}{4}$ ft. Explain how you can determine if $19\frac{1}{4}$ is a solution to $j \geq 18$.

Independent Practice

For **7** through **10**, write the inequality that each graph represents.

7.

5 6 7 8 9 10 11 12 13 14 15
x

8.

0 1 2 3 4 5 6 7 8 9 10
f

9.

0 1 2 3 4 5 6 7 8 9 10
y

10.

0 1 2 3 4 5 6 7 8 9 10
b

For **11** through **15**, name three solutions to each inequality, and graph all the solutions on a number line.

11. $y < 3$ **12.** $c \geq 5$ **13.** $m > 22$ **14.** $z \leq 11$ **15.** $h > 8$

16. Writing to Explain For the inequality $g \geq 6$, Patty said 5, 6, and 8.5 are solutions. Is she correct? Explain and show a graph of the solutions.

17. An airline allows passengers to bring one piece of carry-on luggage. The carry-on has to weigh less than 20 pounds. Use the inequality $c < 20$ to find three possible weights of carry-on luggage.

18. A square has 4 right angles and 4 congruent sides. If one side is 9 inches, what is its perimeter and area?

19. Evaluate the expression $y(3x + 23)$ for $x = 3.1$ and $y = 2.4$.

20. Use Tools The number line to the right shows the inequality $x > 7$. Is 7.1 a solution? Is 7.01 a solution? Explain how you can tell.

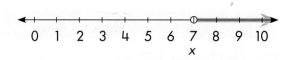

21. Death Valley is the hottest place in the United States. The highest temperature recorded there was 134°F. The lowest temperature recorded was 15°F. Name 3 possible temperatures that fall between these temperatures recorded in Death Valley.

22. Reason What number below would NOT be a solution to the inequality $v > 12$?

A 12   C 12.1

B 15   D 13.11

23. Reason Adam is training for a race. For every 3 minutes he runs, he walks for 4 minutes. Yesterday, he ran for 27 minutes. How many minutes did he walk?

24. The maximum load in a freight elevator is 1,500 lbs. Use the variable w to represent the weight in the elevator. Write an inequality to describe the allowable weights in the elevator.

25. Model You go to your favorite diner and have $5 to spend.

  a Write an inequality that describes the amount of money d you can spend at the diner.

  b At the right is a portion of the menu from the diner. Which, if any, of the items on the menu are solutions to the inequality you wrote in part **a**? Graph the solution.

Mr. T's Diner	
Turkey Sandwich	$3.99
Tuna Sandwich with Fruit	$5.45
Italian Beef Sandwich	$4.75
Slice of Cheese Pizza	$2.25
Grilled Chicken Sandwich	$6.00

Enrichment

Solving Inequalities

An inequality is a mathematical sentence that contains $>$, $<$, $\geq$, or $\leq$. You know that any value that makes an inequality true is a solution. To solve inequalities, use inverse relationships and the following rules describing properties of inequalities.

> You may add or subtract any positive or negative number to both sides of an inequality without changing the inequality.

	Add	Subtract
You know:	$3 < 7$	$3 < 7$
So:	$3 + 2 < 7 + 2$	$3 - 2 < 7 - 2$
Check:	$5 < 9$	$1 < 5$

> You may multiply or divide both sides of an inequality by any **positive** number without changing the inequality.

	Multiply	Divide
You know:	$6 < 8$	$6 < 8$
So:	$6 \times 2 < 8 \times 2$	$6 \div 2 < 8 \div 2$
Check:	$12 < 16$	$3 < 4$

Example: Solve $2x - 6 < 2$. Then graph the solution.

1. Add 6 to both sides.

$$2x - 6 + 6 < 2 + 6$$
$$2x < 8$$

2. Divide both sides by 2.

$$2x \div 2 < 8 \div 2$$
$$x < 4$$

3. Graph the solution on a number line.

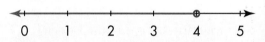

Because x is not equal to 4 and x is also less than 4, the arrow points to the left. The open circle means that 4 is *not* a solution.

Use a point on the graph to check the solution, such as $x = 3$.

$$(2 \times 3) - 6 < 2$$
$$6 - 6 < 2$$
$$0 < 2 \quad \text{The inequality is true, so 3 is a solution.}$$

Practice

Solve **1** through **6** for x. Then graph each solution.

1. $3x - 7 < 2$

2. $2x - 5 \geq x - 3$

3. $4 + 5x \geq 2x + 13$

4. $(x \times 3) - 8 < 4$

5. $\frac{x}{5} - 4 > 1$

6. $4x - 9 < 23$

7. a What inequality is shown at the right?

b Solve the inequality for x.

Lesson
15-7

Common Core

6.EE.5 Understand solving an equation or inequality as a process of answering a question: which values from a specified set, if any, make the equation or inequality true? Use substitution to determine whether a given number in a specified set makes an equation or inequality true.

Problem Solving

Act It Out and Use Reasoning

Ernie is packing 6 boxes and 6 bags of food for hurricane disaster relief.

The food distribution rules are:

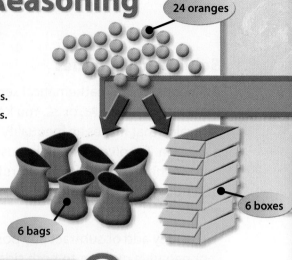

24 oranges

1. Each bag must have the same number of oranges.
2. Each box must have the same number of oranges.
3. Each bag or box must have at least 1 orange.

How many different ways can Ernie pack the oranges?

6 bags

6 boxes

Guided Practice*

MATHEMATICAL PRACTICES

Do you know HOW?

For **1**, make a table and use counters to solve.

1. Geri has two fish tanks and 20 fish. She wants each tank to contain an even number of fish. How many different ways can Geri arrange the fish in the tanks?

Tank 1				
Tank 2				

Do you UNDERSTAND?

 2. Generalize In the hurricane relief example above, how do you know when you have found all of the possible solutions?

3. Write a Problem Write a real-world problem that you can solve by using logical reasoning and acting it out.

Independent Practice

MATHEMATICAL PRACTICES

In **4** and **5**, act out the problem and use reasoning to solve.

 4. Persevere Ramon has 20 gift cards to give to his mom, dad, and twin sisters. He wants to give each of them at least 1 card, and he wants to give each sister the same number and each parent the same number. How many different ways can he give out the cards?

Make a table to show your reasoning. Show all the possible combinations that reach this goal.

5. Eileen is giving 12 of her old toys to 2 different charities. She wants to give a minimum of 2 toys to each charity. How many different ways are possible for Ellen to distribute the toys?

Applying Math Practices

- What am I asked to find?
- What else can I try?
- How are quantities related?
- How can I explain my work?
- How can I use math to model the problem?
- Can I use tools to help?
- Is my work precise?
- Why does this work?
- How can I generalize?

Make a table to show the possibilities.

Oranges per Bag		
Oranges per Box		

Think If there is 1 orange in each bag, is it possible to put the remaining oranges evenly in 6 boxes?

Use 24 counters to find all possibilities.

Oranges per Bag	1	2	3
Oranges per Box	3	2	1

There are 3 different ways Ernie can pack the oranges.

In **6** through **14**, solve each problem.

6. Model Parker jogged 2 more miles than half the distance that Mackie jogged. The equation $P = \frac{M}{2} + 2$ shows the relationship. Make a table and a graph that show the relationship.

7. Sari washes cars. She charges $7 per minivan and $4 per car. She earned $41 last weekend. How many vehicles of each type did she wash?

8. Model Write an equation for the area of a rectangle that is three times as long as it is wide. Use only one variable.

9. Be Precise The water in the birdbath is frozen today. Is the outside temperature 20°F or 20°C? Explain.

10. Of the 56 members in the Drama Club, 25% had speaking roles in the new play. How many members had speaking roles?

11. Jolie wants to score a total of 225 points on three tests. She has a 73 and a 70. What score must she get on the third test?

12. Tanya needs 19 bottles of juice for the field trip. The store sells the bottles of juice in packs of 6. If she already has 1 bottle of juice, complete the table to find how many packs she should buy.

Packs of Juice			
Total Number of Bottles			

13. Writing to Explain Ross bought classic comic books for $10 each. When the price increased to $17 per book, he sold all of his comic books except one. His profit was $49. How many comic books did Ross buy? Explain how you found the answer.

14. Sara needs a total of 90 points to get an A in class. She already has 6 points. If each book report is worth 7 points, what is the least number of book reports Sara can do and still get her A?

84 points

7	- - - - ➤	7

? Number of book reports

A 12   **B** 13   **C** 15   **D** 16

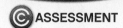
1. Which point is on the graph of the equation $y = 4 - x$? (15-4)

   A (1, 3)

   B (0, 0)

   C (2, 6)

   D (5, 1)

2. Which equation can be used to describe the pattern in the table? (15-2)

a	5	6	7	8	9
b	0	1	2	3	4

   A $b + a = 5$

   B $b = a + 5$

   C $b = a - 5$

   D $a = b - 5$

3. Which of the following equations can be used to graph the line shown? (15-4)

   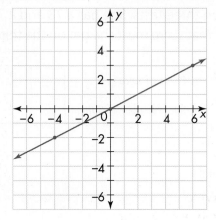

   A $y = 2x$

   B $y = x \div 2$

   C $y = x + 2$

   D $y = x - 2$

4. Jorge has 16 quarters to spend on arcade games. He only wants to play pinball and the racing game. If each game takes 2 quarters to play and he plays both games at least one time, how many different combinations of times can Jorge play the two games? (15-7)

   A 16 combinations of times

   B 8 combinations of times

   C 7 combinations of times

   D 6 combinations of times

5. April pays a dog-walking service $30 each week to walk her dog. Which of the tables below could represent how many dollars, d, April spends on dog-walking in w weeks? (15-2)

   A
w	1	2	3	4	5
d	31	32	33	34	45

   B
w	1	2	3	4	5
d	30	60	90	120	150

   C
w	1	2	3	4	5
d	30	33	36	39	42

   D
w	1	2	3	4	5
d	30	35	40	45	50

6. Tables at a banquet hall seat 6 or 10 people. Monti can use any combination of tables to arrange seating for 60 people. Any table he uses must be filled. How many combinations of tables are possible? (15-7)

A 2

B 3

C 6

D 10

7. Which graph represents the solutions of the inequality $p \geq 10$? (15-6)

A

```
 5  6  7  8  9  10 11 12 13 14 15
                  p
```

B
```
 5  6  7  8  9  10 11 12 13 14 15
                  p
```

C
```
 5  6  7  8  9  10 11 12 13 14 15
                  p
```

D
```
 5  6  7  8  9  10 11 12 13 14 15
                  p
```

8. Which point is on the graph of the equation $y = 2x$? (15-4)

A (3, 6)

B (3, 1)

C (6, 3)

D (1, 3)

9. The table shows the number of cups of coffee that can be made from coffee beans. Which equation describes the pattern in the table? (15-2)

Pounds of beans, p	1	2	3	4
Cups of coffee, c	32	64	96	128

A $c = p - 31$

B $c = p + 31$

C $p = 32c$

D $c = 32p$

10. Which equation can be used to graph the line shown? (15-4)

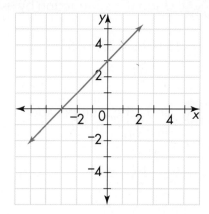

A $y = -3x$

B $y = 3x$

C $y = x - 3$

D $y = x + 3$

11. Which inequality does the graph represent? (15-6)

```
 0    1    2    3    4    5
```

A $x < 5$

B $x \leq 5$

C $x \geq 2$

D $x > 2$

Set A, pages 372–374

Use inverse relationships to undo the operations in an equation. Multiplication undoes division. Addition undoes subtraction.

When solving equations with more than one operation, undo addition and subtraction first. Then undo multiplication and division next.

Georgia owes $15 dollars to her brother. She earns $6 an hour babysitting. How many hours does she have to baby-sit to have $27 after she repays her brother?

Solve the equation and check the answer.

$$6x - 15 = 27$$

Step 1 Undo the subtraction by using addition.

$$6x - 15 + 15 = 27 + 15$$
$$6x = 42$$

Step 2 Undo the multiplication by using division.

$$\frac{6x}{6} = \frac{42}{6}$$
$$x = 7$$

Georgia needs to baby-sit 7 hours to have $27 after repaying her brother.

Check.

$$6x - 15 = 27$$
$$6(7) - 15 = 27$$
$$42 - 15 = 27$$
$$27 = 27$$

It checks.

Remember to keep the equation balanced when undoing operations. When you perform an operation on one side of an equation, you must perform the same operation on the other side of the equation.

Tell which operation you would undo first and which operation you would undo next to solve.

1. $8H + 2 = 18$

2. $5 + 3J = 26$

3. $\frac{m}{3} - 5 = 35$

4. $\frac{s}{4} + 2 = 26$

5. $\frac{C}{9} - 3 = 0$

6. $4 + 11d = 48$

Solve each equation and check your answer.

7. $4k - 8 = 16$

8. $5p - 4 = 26$

9. $\frac{t}{9} + 80 = 81$

10. $9 + 2w = 33$

11. $\frac{s}{2} - 13 = 3$

12. $11d + 1 = 100$

13. $5r + 2 = 42$

14. $6 + 9C = 33$

15. $12F - 15 = 81$

16. $\frac{W}{6} + 7 = 29$

Find the rule that shows the pattern. Then use the rule to complete the table.

x	3	4	6	7	8
y	12	16	24		

Step 1 Find the rule.

What operation and relation can be used to get:

- From 3 to get 12
- From 4 to get to 16
- From 6 to get to 24?

Rule: The y-value is 4 times the x-value.

Equation: $y = 4x$.

Step 2 Evaluate the rule for $x = 7$ and $x = 8$.

$y = 4(7) = 28$

$y = 4(8) = 32$

Remember that you can use multiplication, division, addition, or subtraction to find the rule.

Find a rule and use the rule to write an equation to fit the pattern in each table. Then complete the table.

1.

x	0	2	10	16	20
y	0	1	5		

2.

x	0	5	7	10	15
y	5	10	12		

3.

x	8	10	12	15	20
y	0	2	4		

Alex has $10 saved. He earns $8 per week doing household chores. If he saves half of his earnings each week, how many weeks will it take him to save enough money to buy a $30 game?

Make a table to show Alex's total savings each week. Use the table and the equation $s = 10 + \frac{8}{2}(w)$ to answer the question.

w	1	2	3	4	5	6
s	14	18	22	26	30	34

Alex will have enough money to buy a $30 game from his savings after 5 weeks.

Remember to substitute a value for one of the variables in the equation to complete the table.

Use the equation to copy and complete each table.

1. $y = 2x - 2$

x	1	2	3	4	5
y	0	2	4		

2. $y = 6x + 1$

x	1	2	3	4	5
y					

Set D, pages 380–381

© **INTERVENTION**

Draw a graph of the equation $y = x + 1$.

Step 1 Make a T-table. Always include at least 3 x-values.

x	y
0	1
2	3
3	4

Step 2 Graph each ordered pair on a coordinate plane. Then draw a line through the points. Extend the line to show more values that make the equation true.

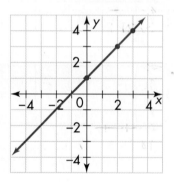

Remember that ordered pairs that make an equation true can be used to graph the equation.

Copy the coordinate plane below and use it to graph **1** and **2**.

1. $y = x + 3$ **2.** $y = 3x$

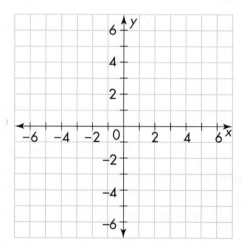

Set E, pages 382–384

The temperature on the mountain was 15°F. During the day it increased 2°F each hour. How many hours will it take for the temperature to rise to 32°F? Graph the equation $T = 2H + 15$ to find out.

Step 1 Make a T-table. List at least three values for H.

H	T
0	15
5	25
10	35

Step 2 Graph each ordered pair and draw a line through the points.

Step 3 Use the graph to find the point with a T-value of 32. It will take $8\frac{1}{2}$ hours for the temperature to rise to 32°.

Remember to include at least three x-values in your T-table.

Make a T-table and graph each equation.

1. $y = 6 + 3x$ **2.** $y = 2x + 1$

3. $y = 10 - x$ **4.** $y = 4x + 4$

5. $y = x$

6. At what value does the graph of the equation $y = 6 + 3x$ cross the y-axis?

7. Does the graph of $y = 2x - 2$ pass through the origin?

8. Does the ordered pair (7, 6) lie on the line $y = 2x - 8$?

Name three solutions for $r < 15$, and graph the inequality on a number line.

Draw a number line with an open circle at 15.

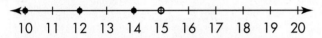

On the number line, r can be any number less than 15. Find three solutions and mark those on a number line.

Start at the open circle and color over the solutions you found. Draw an arrow to show that all numbers less than 15 are solutions.

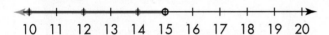

Graph $x \geq 5$ on a number line. Think of the solutions. Since the inequality is greater than or equal to 5, the graph needs to include 5 as part of the solution.

Draw a number line with a closed circle at 5. Draw an arrow to show that all numbers greater than and equal to 5 are solutions.

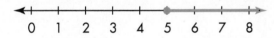

Remember you use an open circle to show that the number under the circle is not a solution. You use a closed circle to show that a number is part of the solution.

Write the inequality that each graph represents.

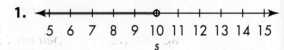

1.
```
5  6  7  8  9  10 11 12 13 14 15
              s
```

2.
```
0  1  2  3  4  5  6  7  8  9  10
              m
```

3.
```
20 21 22 23 24 25 26 27 28 29 30
              j
```

4.
```
10  11  12  13  14  15  16  17  18
        t
```

5.
```
14 15 16 17 18 19 20 21 22 23
              p
```

Graph each inequality on a number line.

6. $y < 12$　　　　**7.** $x > 3$

8. $t \geq 20$　　　　**9.** $s \leq 6$

Linda has 12 puppets that she keeps in two different boxes. She wants to keep a non-zero multiple of 3 puppets in each box. In how many ways can she store all of the puppets in the two different boxes?

Make a table to show the possibilities. Then use 12 counters to find all of the possibilities.

Box 1	3	6	9
Box 2	9	6	3

There are 3 ways to store the puppets.

Remember, acting out a problem can help you use logical reasoning to find a solution.

1. Maria has 10 goldfish that she keeps in two different aquariums. She always keeps a prime number of goldfish in each aquarium.

In how many ways can she divide up the goldfish among the two different aquariums?

Measurement

1 How fast did the winning wheelchair athlete complete the New York marathon? You will find out in Lesson 16-5.

2 How fast is the fastest pickup truck? You will find out in Lesson 16-4.

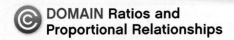
Review What You Know!

Vocabulary

Choose the best terms from the box.

- length
- weight
- capacity
- mass

1. The __?__ of an object can be measured in inches and centimeters.

2. The __?__ of an object can be measured in pints and liters.

3. The __?__ of an object can be measured in pounds, and the __?__ of an object can be measured in kilograms.

Units of Measurement

What is the best unit of measurement for each? Choose inch, foot, yard, ounce, pound, ton, cup, quart, or gallon.

4. length of a soccer field

5. height of a person

6. weight of a newborn kitten

7. weight of a truck trailer

8. gasoline

9. serving of trail mix

Number Sense

©Writing to Explain Write an answer for each question.

10. Explain how to find the value of a number with an exponent.

11. Explain why the value 1,000,000 is written as 10^6.

3 How can you make green slime? You will find out in Lesson 16-1.

4 How can you find the length of a dinosaur bone in millimeters? You will find out in Lesson 16-2.

Lesson
16-1

Common
Core

6.RP.3.d Use ratio
reasoning to convert
measurement units;
manipulate and transform
units appropriately when
multiplying or dividing
quantities.

Converting Customary Measures

How can you change between units of customary measurement?

The sidewalk in front of a store is 54 feet long and 4.5 feet wide. What is the length of the sidewalk in yards? What is the width of the sidewalk in inches?

A table of customary units can help you convert from one unit of measurement to another.

Customary Units of **Length**

foot (ft)	1 ft = 12 in.
yard (yd)	1 yd = 3 ft
	1 yd = 36 in.
mile (mi)	1 (mi) = 5, 280 ft
	1 (mi) = 1, 760 yd

Another Example How can you convert units of weight and capacity using ratios?

56 oz = ☐ lb ⟵ An ounce is smaller than a pound, so divide.

$$\frac{1 \text{ lb}}{16 \text{ oz}} = \frac{\text{☐ lb}}{56 \text{ oz}}$$

```
     3.5
16)56.0
   −48
     80
   −80
      0
```

56 oz = 3.5 lb

Data

Customary Units of Weight

pound (lb)	1 lb = 16 ounces (oz)
ton (T)	1T = 2,000 lb

Capacity is <u>the volume of a container measured in liquid units</u>.

2 gal = ☐ pt ⟵ A gallon is larger than a pint, so multiply.

First, find the number of pints in a gallon.

1 gal = 4 qt and 4 × 2 pt = 8 pt

1 gal = 8 pt

Next, find the number of pints in 2 gallons.

$$\frac{1 \text{ gal}}{8 \text{ pt}} = \frac{2 \text{ gal}}{\text{☐ pt}}$$

8 pt × 2 = 16 pt

2 gal = 16 pt

Data

Customary Units of Capacity

cup (c)	1 c = 8 fluid ounces (fl oz)
pint (pt)	1 pt = 2 c
quart (qt)	1 qt = 2 pt
gallon (gal)	1 gal = 4 qt

Explain It

1. If you were changing tons to pounds, which operation would you use?

54 ft =   yards
To change from smaller units to larger units, divide.

1 ft   2 ft   3 ft

Think 3 feet = 1 yard

54 ÷ 3 = 18

54 ft = 18 yd

The sidewalk is 18 yards long.

4.5 ft =   inches
To change from larger units to smaller units, multiply.

12 inches = 1 foot

4.5 × 12 = 54

4.5 ft = 54 in.

The sidewalk is 54 in. wide.

Guided Practice*

MATHEMATICAL **PRACTICES**

Do you know HOW?

In **1** through **4**, copy and complete.

1. 3 gal =   qt

2. 36 in. =   ft

3. 2 mi =   ft

4. 5 pt =   c

Do you UNDERSTAND?

5. When do you divide to convert units?

© **6. Be Precise** Using the information about capacity in the Another Example, find how many cups are in 2 gallons.

Independent Practice

Copy and complete.

Tip *You may need to solve a simpler problem in order to convert some amounts.*

7. 4 yd =   ft

8. 32 oz =   lb

9. 2 pt =   c

10. 4 qt =   gal

11. 2,000 lb =   T

12. 450 in. =   yd

13. 4 pt =   qt

14. 6,000 lb =   T

15. 21 pt =   c

16. 6 pt =   qt

17. 96 in. =   ft

18. 2 qt =   fl oz

19. 16 c =   pt

20. 9 T =   lb

21. 1.5 mi =   ft

22. 2,640 yd =   mi

23. 4 lb =   oz

24. 360 ft =   yd

25. How many one-cup servings are in 1 gallon?

26. How many inches are in $6\frac{1}{2}$ ft?

27. How many ounces are in 2 lb 8 oz?

DIGITAL

Animated Glossary
www.pearsonsuccessnet.com

*For another example, see Set A on page 422.

Lesson 16-1

28. The note card shows one recipe for green slime. To make 2 recipes of slime for a class project, Cheryl needs 2 pints of water. She has 3 cups of water. Is this enough water for 2 recipes?

© **29. Writing to Explain** Len needs to run at least 3 miles a day to get ready for a cross-country race. One lap of the school track is 400 yards. If Len runs 10 laps a day will he cover at least 3 miles? Explain.

Green Slime Recipe

- 1 pint water
- 1/2 cup cornstarch
- Green food coloring

Add hot water to cornstarch and stir constantly. Then add green food coloring, and stir. Allow the slime to cool to room temperature. This makes a messy slime that goes from liquid to solid. Make sure to play with it on a plastic covered surface. Always have adult supervision when using hot water.

30. Suppose that a space shuttle weighs 4.5 million pounds at liftoff. What is the space shuttle's weight in tons?

© **31. Generalize** How is converting units from cups to pints similar to converting units from ounces to pounds?

32. A door is $3\frac{1}{2}$ feet wide. How many inches are in $3\frac{1}{2}$ feet?

   A 36 inches   **C** 40 inches

   B 38 inches   **D** 42 inches

33. The pilot of an airplane announced the plane was at a cruising altitude of $6\frac{1}{2}$ miles. How many feet is this?

© **34. Reason** Bill is making smoothies for his friends. If 4 ounces of fruit is needed for each smoothie, how many pounds of fruit does he need to make 10 smoothies?

35. Chrissy is buying a yard of felt for an art project. Two stores at the right have the felt she needs. Which felt is a better buy?

Artistic Supplies $1.25/ft

Craft Center $3/yd

© **36. Think About the Stucture** To convert from feet to inches, which operation do you perform?

   A Addition   **C** Multiplication

   B Subtraction   **D** Division

© **37. Think About the Stucture** To convert from pints to gallons, which operation do you perform?

   A Addition   **C** Multiplication

   B Subtraction   **D** Division

Mixed Problem Solving

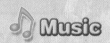

The values of musical notes can be written as fractions. Each note is twice as long as the one below it in the table. For instance, a half note equals 2 quarter notes.

Use this table for **1** through **3**.

Musical Note	Standard Symbol
Whole note	𝅝
Half note	𝅗𝅥
Quarter note	𝅘𝅥
Eighth note	𝅘𝅥𝅮
Sixteenth note	𝅘𝅥𝅯
Thirty-Second note	𝅘𝅥𝅰

1. If you convert a whole note to half notes, how many half notes will you have?

2. If you convert a quarter note to sixteenth notes, how many sixteenth notes will you have?

3. If you convert a sixteenth note to thirty-second notes, how many thirty-second notes will you have?

In music, rests are an important part of the rhythm. A rest has the same value as its corresponding note. For instance, a whole rest has the same value as a whole note.

Like notes, each rest is twice as long as the one below it in the table. For instance, a whole rest equals 2 half rests.

Use this table for **4** through **6**.

Musical Rest	Standard Symbol
Whole rest	▬
Half rest	▬
Quarter rest	𝄽
Eighth rest	𝄾
Sixteenth rest	𝄿
Thirty-Second rest	𝅀

4. What type of rest has the same value as a sixteenth note?

5. If you convert a quarter rest to eighth rests, how many eighth rests will you have?

6. If you convert a quarter rest to sixteenth rests, how many sixteenth rests will you have?

7. If a quarter note has 1 beat, what is the value of the rests in the 2nd measure of the music to the right?

2nd measure

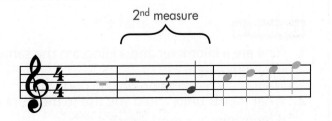

Lesson

16-2

Common Core

6.RP.3.d Use ratio reasoning to convert measurement units; manipulate and transform units appropriately when multiplying or dividing quantities.

Converting Metric Measures

How can you change between metric units of measurement?

The metric system, like our number system, is based on powers of 10.

The **meter** (m) is <u>the basic unit of length</u>, the **gram** (g) is <u>the basic unit of mass</u>, and the **liter** (L) is <u>the basic unit of capacity</u>.

Other Examples

 Multiply to change from larger units to smaller units. Divide to change from smaller units to larger units.

Converting Units of Length:

1,800 m = ▮ km

$\dfrac{1 \text{ km}}{1{,}000 \text{ m}} = \dfrac{▮ \text{ km}}{1{,}800 \text{ m}}$

1,800 ÷ 1,000 = 1.800 = 1.8

1,800 m = 1.8 km

4.5 m = ▮ cm

$\dfrac{1 \text{ m}}{100 \text{ cm}} = \dfrac{4.5 \text{ m}}{▮ \text{ cm}}$

4.5 × 100 = 450

4.5 m = 450 cm

Converting Units of Capacity:

750 mL = ▮ L

$\dfrac{1 \text{ L}}{1{,}000 \text{ mL}} = \dfrac{▮ \text{ L}}{750 \text{ mL}}$

750 ÷ 1,000 = 0.75

750 mL = 0.75 L

2 kg = ▮ g

$\dfrac{1 \text{ kg}}{1{,}000 \text{ g}} = \dfrac{2 \text{ kg}}{▮ \text{ g}}$

2 × 1,000 = 2,000

2 kg = 2,000 g

Explain It

1. How are a kilometer and a kilogram the same? How are they different?

2. What metric units could you use to measure the dimensions of a model car?

The metric system uses prefixes to describe amounts that are larger or smaller than the basic units. For example, kilo- means 1,000; centi- means $\frac{1}{100}$; and milli- means $\frac{1}{1,000}$.

To change from one unit to another, multiply or divide by a power of 10.

	÷10	÷10	÷10	÷10	÷10	÷10
milli-	centi-	deci-	unit	deka-	hecto-	kilo-
mm	cm	dm	meter (m)	dam	hm	km
mg	cg	dg	gram (g)	dag	hg	kg
mL	cL	dL	liter (L)	daL	hL	kL
	×10	×10	×10	×10	×10	×10

Guided Practice*

MATHEMATICAL
PRACTICES

Do you know HOW?

For **1** through **3**, name the most appropriate metric unit for each measurement.

1. the mass of a dollar bill

2. the capacity of a pitcher of water

3. the height of a house

For **4** and **5**, copy and complete.

4. 50 mL = ☐ L

5. 7 m = ☐ cm

Do you UNDERSTAND?

6. When converting from kilograms to grams, by what number do you multiply or divide?

7. **Construct Arguments** Which do you think is easier, converting customary measures or converting metric measures?

8. **Reason** Which is greater, 250 m or 0.25 km?

Independent Practice

Copy and complete.

9. 4 m = ☐ cm   10. 2 L = ☐ mL   11. 2 kg = ☐ g   12. 800 mL = ☐ L

13. 2.1 L = ☐ mL   14. 3 km = ☐ m   15. 300 g = ☐ kg   16. 800 mm = ☐ cm

17. 20.2 L = ☐ mL   18. 6 g = ☐ kg   19. 8 mm = ☐ cm   20. 9 mL = ☐ L

21. 486 cm = ☐ m   22. 3.02 m = ☐ cm   23. 90.25 kg = ☐ g   24. 40,280 cm = ☐ m

Animated Glossary
www.pearsonsuccessnet.com

25. Tara is the editor of the school newspaper. She tries to devote about $\frac{1}{2}$ of the paper to news, $\frac{1}{3}$ to pictures, and the remainder to advertising. About how much of the paper is devoted to news and pictures?

27. Reason Jess is competing in a 20 km bike race. He has just passed the 17,000 m marker. How many meters does he have left?

28. Reasonableness The largest breed of rabbit is the White Flemish Giant, which can weigh up to 8 kilograms. In a report, Rebecca said this kind of rabbit weighed about 800 grams. Is this reasonable?

30. The south rim of the Grand Canyon is about 2,072 m above sea level. About how many kilometers is this? Round to the nearest tenth.

32. Is an adult golden retriever more likely to have a mass of 28 grams or 28 kilograms?

34. How many quarters have the same value as a ten-dollar bill?

26. Writing to Explain About how many millimeters long is this dinosaur bone? Explain how you calculated your answer.

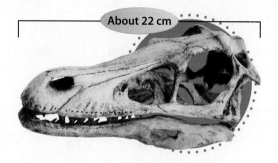
About 22 cm

29. Gordon went to the bank with his penny jar. The bank put the pennies through a change machine and gave him $10.50. How many pennies were in the jar?

31. Reasonableness To measure the mass of a bowling ball, would you use grams or kilograms? Why?

33. What power of 10 lets you convert kilograms to grams?

35. Think About the Structure To convert from millimeters to centimeters, which operation do you need to perform?

    A Addition   **C** Multiplication

    B Subtraction   **D** Division

36. Think About the Structure To convert from kilograms to grams, which operation do you need to perform?

    A Addition   **C** Multiplication

    B Subtraction   **D** Division

Mixed Problem Solving

The Persistence of Memory, by Salvador Dali, and *Water Lilies*, by Claude Monet, are two famous oil-on-canvas paintings.

For **1** through **3**, use the data in the chart about the size of the canvas for each painting.

Painting Title	Length (meters)	Height (meters)
The Persistence of Memory	0.33	0.241
Water Lilies	5.966	1.98

1. What is the length and height of *The Persistence of Memory* in centimeters?

2. What is the length and height of *Water Lilies* in centimeters?

3. The height of *Water Lilies* is about how many times the height of *The Persistence of Memory*?

4. Claude Monet was born in France in 1840. He is a founder of a style of art called *Impressionism*. He often painted outdoor scenes, using bold colors but not a lot of detail. Salvador Dali was born in Spain in 1904. He is a founder of a style of art called *Surrealism*. His paintings were often based on dreams. How many years apart were these two artists born?

Use the data table to the right for **5** through **7**.

Hedi went to a local park to draw. She drew a scale drawing of a slide, a tree, and a bench in one area of the park.

Object	Actual height (cm)	Drawn height (cm)
Slide	180 cm	15 cm
Tree	360 cm	
Bench		$3\frac{1}{3}$ cm

5. The data table gives the actual height of the slide and the height that Hedi made it on her drawing. What fraction of the object's size did Hedi make her drawing?

6. Use the scale you found in Exercise 5 to find the missing values in the table.

7. What is the actual height of each object in meters?

Common Core

This lesson reinforces concepts and skills required for Topic 18.

Units of Measure and Precision

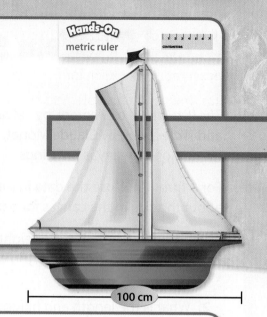

Hands-On
metric ruler

Which metric measurement is the most precise?

Don and Stacy are building a model boat that is 100 cm long. They need to measure accurately. Which measurement is more precise, centimeters or millimeters?

|⊢————— 100 cm —————⊣|

Another Example ## Which customary measurement is the most precise?

The pencil at the right measures about 4 inches. What is its length to the nearest whole, half, quarter, eighth, and sixteenth of an inch? Which of these measurements is the most precise?

INCHES

CENTIMETERS

Measure the length to the nearest units and record your findings.

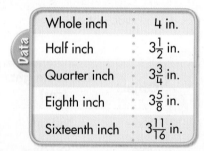

Data		
Whole inch	4 in.
Half inch	$3\frac{1}{2}$ in.
Quarter inch	$3\frac{3}{4}$ in.
Eighth inch	$3\frac{5}{8}$ in.
Sixteenth inch	$3\frac{11}{16}$ in.

As with metric measurements, the smaller the customary units used for measuring, the more precise the measurement. A sixteenth of an inch is the smallest unit used for inches.

$3\frac{11}{16}$ is the most precise measurement.

Explain It

1. How do you measure the pencil to the nearest quarter inch?

2. Which measurement is more precise, sixteenth inch or millimeter? Explain.

All measurements are approximations. Don measured the model plank below to the nearest centimeter. It measured about 5 cm long.

Stacy measured the plank to the nearest millimeter. It measured about 52 mm long.

A millimeter is a smaller unit than a centimeter.

CENTIMETERS
1 2 3 4 5 6 7 8 9 10

The smaller the units used for measuring, the more precise the measurement.

52 mm is more precise than 5 cm.

Don and Stacy should measure the pieces of the boat in millimeters.

Guided Practice*

MATHEMATICAL
PRACTICES

Do you know HOW?

For **1** and **2**, measure each segment to the nearest eighth inch and nearest centimeter.

1. ├───────┤

2. ├──────────────┤

For **3** and **4**, measure each segment to the nearest sixteenth inch and nearest millimeter.

3. ├──────────┤

4. ├─────┤

Do you UNDERSTAND?

5. How do you know which unit of measurement is more precise?

© **6. Writing to Explain** Manuel and Ava each measured the perimeter of the garden. Their measurements were 6 yards and 17 feet. Which measurement is more precise?

Independent Practice

For **7** through **12**, measure each segment to the nearest eighth inch and nearest centimeter.

7. ├──────┤

8. ├──────────────┤

9. ├────────────────────┤

10. ├──────────┤

11. ├──────────────┤

12. ├──────────────────┤

eTools
www.pearsonsuccessnet.com
DIGITAL

For **13** through **16**, measure each segment to the nearest sixteenth inch and nearest millimeter.

13. ├───────┤

14. ├────────────┤

15. ├─────────────────────┤

16. ├───────────────────────┤

For each pair of measurements in **17** through **28**, tell which measurement is more precise.

17. 12 cm or 123 mm

18. 634 mm or 63 cm

19. 21 mm or 2 cm

20. 3 m or 302 cm

21. 6.1 m or 612 mm

22. 1,100 mm or 1 m

23. 4 ft or 1 yd

24. 3 L or 3,100 mL

25. 850 g or 1 kg

26. $2\frac{1}{2}$ ft or 28 in.

27. 4 yd or 13 ft

28. 1.5 mi or 7,600 ft

MATHEMATICAL **PRACTICES**

© **29. Critique Arguments** Wendy measured a shoelace and said it was 1 foot long. Bill measured the same shoelace and said it was 12 inches long. Even though 12 inches = 1 foot, explain why Bill's measurement is more precise.

© **30. Persevere** Kristen wants to rent a bicycle. The table at the right shows how much two shops charge to rent bicycles. Which bicycle shop would be less expensive if Kristen rents a bicycle for 5 hours?

Data

Rental Cost		
Bicycle Shop	Cost for 1st Hour	Each Additional Hour
Cycle Pro Shop	$10	$6
Bev's Bicycles	$12	$5

© **31. Be Precise** Three students measured the height of the door to the classroom. The measurements were 7 feet, 2 yards, and 6 feet 10 inches. Which of these measurements is the most precise?

32. The height of Mt. Everest is 8,848 m. Express this height in kilometers.

© **33. Be Precise** Suppose you want to measure the length of a small paper clip. Which unit would you use to get the most precise measurement?

A Meters

C Inches

B Millimeters

D Centimeters

Exact Answer or Estimate

Some problems require exact answers, while others need only an estimate. How can you tell if an exact answer or an estimate is needed to answer a word problem?

Phrases, such as "about how many," "more than," or "less than," mean that an estimate may give you enough information to answer the problem. If an estimate is all that is needed, you can often estimate using mental math.

If the problem asks, "What is the total?," "how many," or "how much," calculate the exact amount.

Example: Susan wants to put a wallpaper border in the hallway. The hallway is a rectangle with a length of 9 feet and a width of $4\frac{1}{3}$ feet. If one roll of wallpaper border is 16 feet long, will 2 rolls be enough for Susan to complete the hallway?

Step 1   What do you know?

The dimensions of the hall are 9 feet by $4\frac{1}{3}$ feet and one roll is 16 feet.

Step 2   What are you trying to find?

Whether 2 rolls of wallpaper border are enough to complete the hallway An estimate is all that is needed; 2 rolls are enough.

Practice

Tell whether an exact answer or an estimate is needed. Then solve.
For **1** through **3**, use the information on the map.

1. How much greater is the length of the forest preserve than the width?

2. If Jack can walk $\frac{1}{2}$ mile every 10 minutes, would he be able to walk from the cabin to the ranger's station in less than 20 minutes?

3. Jack takes a daily walk from his cabin to the ranger station, to the lake, then along the lake and back to his cabin. How far will he have walked in three days?

Forest Preserve

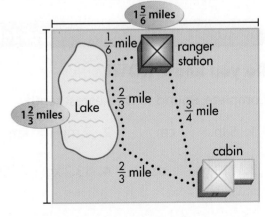

4. Mara is making three recipes that each require milk. One recipe calls for $\frac{5}{6}$ cup of milk, another calls for $\frac{2}{3}$ cup, and the third requires $1\frac{1}{3}$ cup. How much milk will Mara need?

5. A truck is built to haul up to 2 tons of cargo. If the truck is loaded with 54 barrels, and each barrel weighs 190 pounds, is the truck over or under its limit?

Lesson
16-4

©

Common Core

6.RP.3.d Use ratio reasoning to convert measurement units; manipulate and transform units appropriately when multiplying or dividing quantities.

Relating Customary and Metric Measures

How can you convert between measurement systems?

Tim is building a scarecrow to keep birds out of his garden. The directions use metric units and suggest that the scarecrow be at least 2 meters tall. Rounded to the nearest tenth, how many inches is 2 meters?

2 meters tall

Other Examples

Converting Customary Units and Metric Units for Weight/Mass and Capacity

12 kg ≈ ▢ lb	5 gal ≈ ▢ L	3 qt ≈ ▢ L
1 kg ≈ 2.2 lb	1 gal ≈ 3.79 L	1 L ≈ 1.06 qt
Multiply.	Multiply.	Divide.
$12 \times 2.2 = 26.4$	$5 \times 3.79 = 18.95$	$3 \div 1.06 = 2.83$
12 kg ≈ 26.4 lb	Round to the nearest tenth. 5 gal ≈ 19.0 L	Round to the nearest tenth. 3 qt ≈ 2.8 L

Guided Practice*

© **MATHEMATICAL PRACTICES**

Do you know HOW?

Complete. Round to the nearest tenth.

1. 5 in. = ▢ cm　　**2.** 2 mi ≈ ▢ km

3. 113 g ≈ ▢ oz　　**4.** 13.2 kg ≈ ▢ lb

Do you UNDERSTAND?

© **5. Reason** When converting centimeters to inches, do you multiply or divide by 2.54?

© **6. Use Structure** How would you find the number of liters in 1 pint?

Independent Practice

Copy and complete. Round to the nearest tenth.

7. 9.1 qt ≈ ▢ L　　**8.** 1.0 gal ≈ ▢ L　　**9.** 2 in. = ▢ cm　　**10.** 4 gal ≈ ▢ L

The table shows the relationships between customary and metric measurements. Only the equivalent for inches and centimeters is exact. All other equivalents are approximate.

Customary and Metric Unit Equivalents		
Length	**Weight/Mass**	**Capacity**
1 in. = 2.54 cm	1 oz ≈ 28.35 g	1 L ≈ 1.06 qt
1 m ≈ 39.37 in.	1 kg ≈ 2.2 lb	1 gal ≈ 3.79 L
1 mi ≈ 1.61 km	1 metric ton (t) ≈ 1.102 T	

Use 1 m ≈ 39.37 in.

To change from a larger unit to a smaller unit, multiply.

2m ≈ ▢ in.

2 × 39.37 = 78.74

Round to the nearest tenth.

2 meters is about 78.7 inches.

Copy and complete. Round to the nearest tenth.

11. 5 km ≈ ▢ mi

12. 85 g ≈ ▢ oz

13. 196 in. ≈ ▢ m

14. 10 L ≈ ▢ qt

15. 5.5 t ≈ ▢ T

16. 50 lb ≈ ▢ kg

17. 25 in. ≈ ▢ cm

18. 30.2 kg ≈ ▢ lb

19. 51.6 gal ≈ ▢ L

20. 10 oz ≈ ▢ g

21. 3 pt ≈ ▢ L

22. 3.5 m ≈ ▢ in.

Problem Solving

Ⓒ MATHEMATICAL PRACTICES

Ⓒ **23. Persevere** Suppose that 1 British pound (£) has a value of $1.80. In London, a magazine costs £ 2. In Chicago, the same magazine costs $3.50. In which city is the magazine cheaper?

24. Temperature can be measured in degrees Fahrenheit (F) and in degrees Celsius (C). Use this formula to convert 50° Fahrenheit to Celsius:
$9 \times C = (F - 32) \times 5$

Ⓒ **25. Writing to Explain** Francesca wants to convert 1 meter to feet. Use what you know about customary measures to explain how she could do this.

Ⓒ **26. Reason** How could you use estimation to convert 15 oz into grams?

27. The fastest production-model pickup truck reached a top speed of 154.587 miles per hour. How fast did this truck travel in kilometers per hour?

Mount McKinley is approximately 20,320 ft high.

28. How high is Mount McKinley in meters? Round to the nearest whole number.

Ⓒ **29. Think About the Structure** To convert pounds to kilograms, which operation do you need to perform?

   A Addition   **C** Multiplication

   B Subtraction   **D** Division

Common Core

6.RP.3.d Use ratio reasoning to convert measurement units; manipulate and transform units appropriately when multiplying or dividing quantities.

Elapsed Time

How can you find how much time passes between two events?

Yul biked along a part of the Lewis and Clark Trail. He started at 8:05 A.M. and finished biking at 1:25 P.M. How long did Yul bike?

The difference in time between 8:05 A.M. and 1:25 P.M. is the elapsed time.

Start | Lewis and Clark TRAIL | End

8:05 AM   1:25 PM

Another Example **How can renaming help you find elapsed time?**

Find the elapsed time from
4:25:55 P.M. to 6:15:20 P.M.

$$
\begin{array}{l}
6 \text{ h } 15 \text{ min } 20 \text{ s} \longrightarrow 5 \text{ h } 74 \text{ min } 80 \text{ s} \\
- 4 \text{ h } 25 \text{ min } 55 \text{ s} \longrightarrow - 4 \text{ h } 25 \text{ min } 55 \text{ s} \\
\hline
\phantom{- 4 \text{ h } 25 \text{ min }} 1 \text{ h } 49 \text{ min } 25 \text{ s}
\end{array}
$$

Think Since 15 min < 25 min and 20 s < 55 s, I need to rename to subtract.
1 h = 60 min and 1 min = 60 s

Elapsed Time: 1 h 49 min 25 s

How do you find the starting time or ending time using elapsed time?

End Time: 11:20 A.M.
Elapsed Time: 3 h 40 min

Subtract the elapsed time from the ending time to find the start time.

$$
\begin{array}{l}
11 \text{ h } 20 \text{ min } \longrightarrow 10 \text{ h } 80 \text{ min} \\
- 3 \text{ h } 40 \text{ min } \longrightarrow - 3 \text{ h } 40 \text{ min} \\
\hline
\phantom{- 3 \text{ h }} 7 \text{ h } 40 \text{ min}
\end{array}
$$

Start Time: 7:40 A.M.

Start Time: 6:20 P.M.
Elapsed Time: 6 h 15 min

Add the elapsed time to the starting time to find the end time.

$$
\begin{array}{l}
6 \text{ h } 20 \text{ min} \\
+ 6 \text{ h } 15 \text{ min} \\
\hline
12 \text{ h } 35 \text{ min}
\end{array}
$$

End Time: 12:35 A.M. ← 12 midnight is 12:00 A.M.

Explain It

1. When adding or subtracting units of time, when do you need to rename?

One Way

Break the elapsed time into parts.

12 h 00 min

− 8 h 05 min

3 h 55 min ← Elapsed time before noon

+ 1 h 25 min ← Elapsed time from noon to 1:25 P.M.

4 h 80 min

or

5 h 20 min ← Total elapsed time

Yul biked for 5 hours 20 minutes.

Another Way

Use mental math to find the elapsed time. Count forward from the starting time for each unit.

Count the number of hours from 8:05 A.M. to 1:25 P.M.: 5 hours.

Count the number of minutes from 1:05 to 1:25 20 minutes.

Yul biked for 5 hours 20 minutes.

Guided Practice*

MATHEMATICAL
PRACTICES

Do you know HOW?

In **1** through **3**, find each elapsed time.

1. 6:02 P.M. to 9:17 P.M.

2. 2:13 A.M. to 10:09 P.M.

3. 10:09 P.M. to 2:13 A.M.

In **4** and **5**, add or subtract.

4. 1 h 13 min 42 s
  + 20 min 29 s

5. 1 h 13 min 42 s
  − 20 min 29 s

Do you UNDERSTAND?

6. Generalize When should you break a problem into parts to find elapsed time?

7. Writing to Explain In the example at the top, if Yul started at 8:30 A.M., how would you use mental math to find the elapsed time?

8. If Yul made a stop 2 hours 35 minutes after starting the ride, what time did he stop?

Independent Practice

For **9** through **14**, find each elapsed time.

9. 3:05 P.M. to 9:27 P.M.

10. 4:11 A.M. to 8:09 A.M.

11. 4:15 P.M. to 6:33 P.M.

12. 1:39 P.M. to 7:17 P.M.

13. 9:29 A.M. to 2:14 P.M.

14. 9:05 A.M. to 9:05 P.M.

In **15** through **20**, find each starting time or ending time.

15. Start Time: 3:24 A.M.
Elapsed Time: 7 h 4 min

16. End Time: 7:48 P.M
Elapsed Time: 5 h 5 min

17. Start Time: 11:21 P.M.
Elapsed Time: 8 h 6 min

18. End Time: 12:16 P.M.
Elapsed Time: 3 h 5 min

19. Start Time: 5:18 P.M.
Elapsed Time: 5 h 50 min

20. End Time: 10:39 P.M.
Elapsed Time: 8 h 45 min

For **21** through **26**, add or subtract.

21.   29 min 17 s
        +   7 min 21 s
        ▢

22.   14 h 4 min 14 s
        − 6 h 24 min
        ▢

23.   3 h 24 min 49 s
        + 2 h 36 min 13 s
        ▢

24.   1 h 15 min 42 s
        −   20 min 29 s
        ▢

25.   6 h 18 min 32 s
        +   56 min 39 s
        ▢

26.   5 h 39 min 44 s
        − 2 h 42 min 51 s
        ▢

Problem Solving

MATHEMATICAL
PRACTICES

27. Jill is preparing Thanksgiving dinner. She wants the turkey to be done by 5:30 P.M. The turkey will take approximately 3 hours 20 minutes to cook. What is the latest time that she should put the turkey into the oven?

28. It took Mark a total of 4 hours 40 minutes to clean the garage and cut the grass. If it took 1 hour 45 minutes to cut the grass, how long did it take him to clean the garage?

ⓒ **29. Model** A homing pigeon flew a distance of 120 miles in 4 days. If it flew x miles in the first 3 days, write an expression to tell how many miles it flew on the last day.

30. Every morning Tyler jogs 2.85 kilometers. Every evening before dinner he jogs 1.5 kilometers. How many kilometers does he jog each week?

31. In a recent year, the winner in the wheelchair race of the New York Marathon finished in 1:31:11 (1 hour, 31 minutes, 11 seconds). In the following year, the winning wheelchair athlete's time was 1:29:22. How much faster was the winning time in the following year?

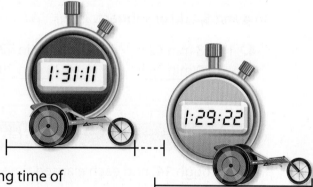

ⓒ **32. Writing to Explain** Explain how to find the ending time of a concert that begins at 8:05 P.M. and lasts 2 hours 14 minutes.

ⓒ **33. Persevere** Ross had been driving for 3 hours 15 minutes. He arrived at his destination at 11:40 A.M. What time did he leave?

  A 8:55 A.M.   **C** 2:55 P.M.

  B 8:25 A.M.   **D** 8:40 P.M.

34. Which number is a composite number?

  A 13   **C** 57

  B 7   **D** 29

Temperature Conversion

Temperatures in degrees Fahrenheit (°F), or in degrees Celsius (°C), can be measured with a thermometer. To convert between Fahrenheit and Celsius temperature scales, use the following equations.

Conversion Formulas

Celsius (C) to Fahrenheit (F)

$$F = \frac{9}{5}C + 32$$

Fahrenheit (F) to Celsius (C)

$$C = \left(\frac{5}{9}\right)(F - 32)$$

Temperatures should be to the nearest whole degree.

Example:
Pure water boils at 100°C. What is 100°C in degrees Fahrenheit?

Step 1 Choose the correct conversion formula.

Use $F = \frac{9}{5}C + 32$.

Step 2 Substitute the value of the temperature you know and solve.

$$F = \left(\frac{9}{5}\right)(100) + 32$$

$$F = 180 + 32$$

$$F = 212$$

Pure water boils at 212°F.

Practice

For **1** through **8**, find each temperature in degrees Fahrenheit to the nearest whole degree.

1. 25°C   **2.** 10°C   **3.** 45°C   **4.** 0°C

5. 16°C   **6.** 29°C   **7.** −2°C   **8.** −25°C

For **9** through **16**, find each temperature in degrees Celsius to the nearest whole degree.

9. 65°F   **10.** 85°F   **11.** 63°F   **12.** 72°F

13. 45°F   **14.** 102°F   **15.** 6°F   **16.** 5°F

17. African violets grow best in a temperature warmer than 60°F and cooler than 80°F. Will they grow well if they are kept in an area that is 30°C? Explain.

18. If the temperature is 5°C, is 15°F or 45°F a better estimate for the temperature? Explain.

Lesson
16-6

Common Core

6.RP.3.d Use ratio reasoning to convert measurement units; manipulate and transform units appropriately when multiplying or dividing quantities.

Problem Solving

Use Reasoning

Jane's game has three sizes of jumps: small, medium, and large. How can you find the size of the small, medium, and large jumps?

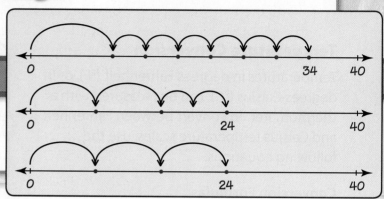

Guided Practice*

 MATHEMATICAL PRACTICES

Do you know HOW?

1. If Jane takes two large jumps, how many small jumps will it take her to reach 40?

2. Jane is on 11 and wants to get as close as she can to 40 in the fewest jumps possible without going over. How many jumps can she take?

Do you UNDERSTAND?

3. **Reason** If there are 2 small jumps in a medium jump, which operation should you use to convert from small jumps to medium jumps?

4. **Write a Problem** Use the jump diagram above to create and solve a problem.

Independent Practice

 MATHEMATICAL PRACTICES

A fruit market sells fruit based on equivalent amounts. Use the table for **5** through **7**.

Equivalent Amounts
12 apples = 1 watermelon
10 grapes = 1 kiwi
3 kiwis = 1 apple
2 cantaloupes = 1 watermelon

Data

Applying Math Practices

- What am I asked to find?
- What else can I try?
- How are quantities related?
- How can I explain my work?
- How can I use math to model the problem?
- Can I use tools to help?
- Is my work precise?
- Why does this work?
- How can I generalize?

5. How many kiwis are equivalent to 5 apples?

6. How many apples are equivalent to 1 cantaloupe?

7. How many grapes are equivalent to 1 watermelon?

*For another example, see Set F on page 423.

Plan and Solve

Use reasoning to make conclusions and find the size of each jump.

Begin with medium jumps.
3 medium jumps end at 24.

$3 \times \boxed{} = 24$

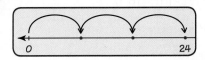

$3 \times 8 = 24$

So, a medium jump is 8 units.

Use the size of the medium jumps to find the size of a small jump. Since 2 medium jumps is 16, $24 - 16 = 8$.

$2 \times \boxed{} = 8$

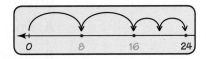

$2 \times 4 = 8$

So, a small jump is 4 units.

Use the size of the small jumps to find a large jump. 6 small jumps of 4 units each make 24.

$34 - 24 = \boxed{}$

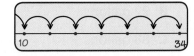

$34 - 24 = 10$

So, a large jump is 10 units.

---

8. **Think About the Structure** Rebecca runs 12 laps on a track. There are 400 meters per lap. What is the best first step to find how many yards she ran?

   A Find the total number of meters.

   B Find the total number of yards.

   C Find the number of yards in a meter.

   D Find the number of meters in a kilometer.

9. **Think About the Structure** What operation would you use to convert Pacific Standard Time to Eastern Standard Time?

   A Addition　　C Multiplication

   B Subtraction　　D Division

10. If the Moon orbits Earth once in about a month, about how many times does the Moon orbit Earth in five years?

11. **Persevere** Katie, Brian, Jessica, Callie, and Dave are all wearing different-colored shirts (red, blue, green, white, and orange). Katie and Brian never wear primary colors. The boys are not wearing white. None of the girls are wearing green. Only Dave is wearing a color that has the letter O in it. Callie is not wearing red. Find the color of shirt that each person is wearing.

Use Tools Use the clocks for **12** and **13**.

12. If it is 4:00 A.M. in Tokyo, what time is it in London?

13. New York is five hours behind London. If it is 2:00 P.M. in New York, what time is it in Tokyo?

14. When it is 10:00 A.M. in Los Angeles, it is 1:00 P.M. in New York. If it is 3:00 A.M. in New York, what time is it in Los Angeles?

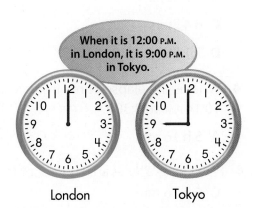

When it is 12:00 P.M. in London, it is 9:00 P.M. in Tokyo.

London　　Tokyo

1. If Mrs. Banks made 44 quarts of jelly, how many gallons did she make? (16-1)

   A 11 gallons

   B 22 gallons

   C 88 gallons

   D 176 gallons

2. How many milliliters are in the container shown? (16-2)

   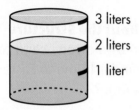

   3 liters
   2 liters
   1 liter

   A 2 milliliters

   B 20 milliliters

   C 200 milliliters

   D 2,000 milliliters

3. An average adult has about 6 quarts of blood in his or her body. How many liters are equal to 6 quarts? Use 1 L ≈ 1.06 qt to convert. Round to the nearest tenth. (16-4)

   A 4.9 liters

   B 5.7 liters

   C 6.4 liters

   D 7.1 liters

4. What is the elapsed time from 10:14 P.M. to 3:30 A.M.? (16-5)

   A 5 h 16 min

   B 5 h 26 min

   C 6 h 16 min

   D 6 h 44 min

5. The Willamette meteorite found near Portland, Oregon, weighs 14 tons. How many pounds does the meteorite weigh? (16-1)

   A 7 pounds

   B 28 pounds

   C 7,000 pounds

   D 28,000 pounds

6. Debbie's pet bird has a mass of 125 grams. How many kilograms is the mass of the bird? (16-2)

   A 0.125 kilograms

   B 1.25 kilograms

   C 1,250 kilograms

   D 125,000 kilograms

7. The table shows some of the world's tallest towers. How many inches high is the Milad Tower? Use 1 m ≈ 39.37 in. to convert. Round to the nearest tenth. (16-4)

Tower	Height in Meters
Canadian National Tower, Toronto	553
Ostankino Tower, Moscow	537
Oriental Pearl Tower, Shanghai	468
Milad Tower, Tehran	435

   A 11 inches

   B 17,126.0 inches

   C 5,708.7 inches

   D 43,500 inches

8. A football game started at 11:50 A.M. and lasted for 3 hours and 48 minutes. At what time did the football game end? (16-5)

A 4:02 P.M.

B 3:38 P.M.

C 2:38 P.M.

D 3:02 A.M.

9. Which of the following measurements is the most precise? (16-3)

A 1 meter

B 125 centimeters

C 1,253 millimeters

D 1.2 meters

10. Which step can be taken to convert 6 inches to centimeters? (16-4)

A Multiply 6 by 2.54.

B Divide 6 by 2.54.

C Multiply $\frac{1}{2}$ by 2.54.

D Divide $\frac{1}{2}$ by 2.54.

11. The table shows the relationship among the points for markers in a game. How many purple markers are equal to a green marker? (16-6)

5 red = 1 green
15 purple = 1 yellow
10 yellow = 1 red

A 50

B 75

C 150

D 750

12. The deepest lake in the world is Lake Baikal in Siberia, Russia. It is a natural lake that is 5,712 feet deep. Which step can be taken to find the depth of the lake in yards? (16-1)

A Divide 5,712 feet by 12.

B Multiply 5,712 feet by 12.

C Divide 5,712 feet by 3.

D Multiply 5,712 feet by 3.

13. Mount Everest is 8,850 meters tall. How many kilometers high is Mount Everest? (16-2)

A 0.885 kilometers

B 8.85 kilometers

C 88.5 kilometers

D 88,850 kilometers

14. A designer measured the width of a window to the nearest whole, quarter, eighth, and sixteenth of an inch. The measurements are shown in the table. Which measurement is the most precise? (16-3)

Unit	Width
Whole inch	36 in.
Quarter inch	$35\frac{3}{4}$ in.
Eighth inch	$35\frac{7}{8}$ in.
Sixteenth inch	$35\frac{13}{16}$ in.

A Whole inch

B Quarter inch

C Eighth inch

D Sixteenth inch

Reteaching

Set A, pages 400–402

How many feet is 5 miles?

	Data	
foot (ft)	1 ft = 12 in.	
yard (yd)	1 yd = 3 ft 1 yd = 36 in.	
mile (mi)	1 mi = 5,280 ft 1 mi = 1,760 yd	

1 mi = 5,280 ft

5 × 5,280 = 26,400

> To change from larger units to smaller units, multiply.

5 mi = 26,400 ft

Remember to divide when changing from smaller units to larger units.

Copy and complete.

1. 1 mi = ___ ft
2. 36 in. = ___ yd
3. 3 yd = ___ ft
4. 3,520 yd = ___ mi
5. 2 yd = ___ in.
6. 264 ft = ___ yd
7. Tony's bedroom is 12 feet long. How many yards long is his bedroom?

Set B, pages 404–406

How many meters is 7.01 km?

	Name	Abbreviation	Number of Base Units
Length	**kilo**meter	km	1,000
	meter	m	1
	centimeter	cm	$\frac{1}{100}$
	millimeter	mm	$\frac{1}{1,000}$

1,000 m = 1 km; 7.01 km, × 1,000 = 7,010 m

Remember that to convert within the metric system, you always multiply or divide by a power of 10.

Copy and complete.

1. 5 km = ___ m
2. 900 cm = ___ m
3. 83 mm = ___ cm
4. 3.7 m = ___ mm
5. Jessie wants to swim 1.5 km. How many meters is this?

Set C, pages 408–410

Measure the paper clip to the nearest sixteenth inch and nearest millimeter.

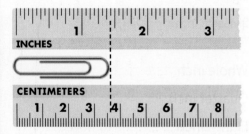

Nearest sixteenth inch: $1\frac{7}{16}$ inches

Nearest millimeter: 36 millimeters

Remember to line up the zero mark of your ruler with one end of the object being measured. The smaller the units used for measuring, the more precise the measurement.

Measure each segment to the nearest sixteenth inch and nearest millimeter.

1. ⊢————————⊣

2. ⊢——————————————⊣

Round to the nearest tenth. 5 km ≈ ▢ mi

Customary and Metric Unit Equivalents		
Length	Weight/Mass	Capacity
1 in. = 2.54 cm	1 oz. ≈ 28.35 g	1 L ≈ 1.06 qt
1 m ≈ 39.37 in.	1 kg ≈ 2.2 lb	1 gal ≈ 3.79 L
1 mi ≈ 1.61 km	1 metric ton (t) ≈ 1.102 T	

Data

1 mi ≈ 1.61 km

To change from a smaller unit to a larger unit, divide.

5 ÷ 1.61 = 3.106

5 km ≈ 3.11 mi

Remember to use the table to tell how to change between customary and metric units.

Round to the nearest tenth.

1. 2 in. ≈ ▢ cm   2. 5 mi ≈ ▢ km

3. 3 oz ≈ ▢ g   4. 7 lb ≈ ▢ kg

5. 10 L ≈ ▢ qt   6. 5.5 t ≈ ▢ T

7. Frank's cat weighs 8 pounds. How many kilograms is this?

8. A marathon is 26.2 miles. How many kilometers is this?

Find the elapsed time from 8:20 A.M. to 11:12 A.M.

Subtract the starting time from the ending time.

$$\begin{array}{rcl} 11 \text{ h } 12 \text{ min} & \rightarrow & 10 \text{ h } 72 \text{ min} \\ - \ 8 \text{ h } 20 \text{ min} & \rightarrow & - \ 8 \text{ h } 20 \text{ min} \\ \hline \text{Elasped time} & \rightarrow & 2 \text{ h } 52 \text{ min} \end{array}$$

Remember to break the problem into parts when the elapsed time extends past noon or midnight.

1. 1:43 P.M. to 6:21 P.M.

2. 7:13 A.M. to 10:42 A.M.

3. 10:15 A.M. to 3:02 P.M.

What is the size of the small and large jumps? Use reasoning to find the size of each jump.

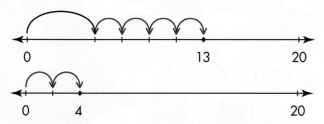

Two small jumps end at 4: 2 × ▢ = 4.
Since 2 × 2 = 4, a small jump must be 2.
Use the size of the small jumps to find the size of the large jump: ▢ + (4 × 2) = 13.
The large jump must be 5: 5 + 8 = 13.

Large jump: 5 units   Small jump: 2 units

Remember that you can use reasoning to solve some problems.

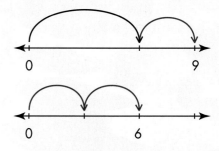

1. Use the number lines to find the sizes of the large and small jumps.

Topic 17

Perimeter and Area

1 What is the area covered by this giant lily pad? You will find out in Lesson 17-5.

2 Look at the shapes in these origami figures. How can you find the area of them? You will find out in Lesson 17-3.

Review What You Know!

Vocabulary

Choose the best term from the box.

- polygon
- parallelogram
- perpendicular

1. A triangle is an example of a __?__, but a circle is not.

2. __?__ lines form a right angle.

3. A __?__ has opposite sides that are parallel and the same length.

Evaluating Expressions

Find the value of each expression when $\ell = 7$ and $w = 9$.

4. $\ell \times w$

5. $\ell + \ell + w + w$

6. $2\ell + 2w$

7. $w \times \ell$

Multiplying Decimals

Find each answer.

8. 3.14×12

9. 45.8×5^2

10. 35×12.8

11. 64.9×5.8

Geometry

© **Writing to Explain** Write an answer for each question.

12. Why is a circle not considered a polygon?

13. How is a parallelogram like a rectangle?

14. How is a parallelogram different from a rectangle?

3 How can you find the circumferences of Saturn's rings? You will find out in Lesson 17-4.

4 How much area is needed to create a living chessboard? You will find out in Lesson 17-2.

© Common Core

6.EE.2.c Evaluate expressions at specific values of their variables. Include expressions that arise from formulas used in real-world problems. Perform arithmetic operations, including those involving whole-number exponents, in the conventional order when there are no parentheses to specify a particular order.... Also **6.EE.7**

Perimeter

How can you find the distance around a polygon?

<u>The distance around a polygon</u> is called the perimeter of a polygon.

The perimeter (P) of a polygon is the sum of the lengths of its sides.

For the figure at the right:
$P = 4 + 4 + 5 + 6 + 8$. Its perimeter is 27 cm.

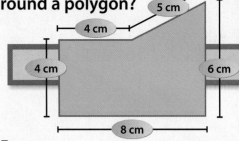

Another Example How can you find the perimeter of a polygon that has unknown sides?

Find the perimeter of the figure.

The length of side x is 17 inches because it equals the sum of the lengths of two parallel sides, 13 in. and 4 in.

The length of side y is 3 inches because it equals the difference between the lengths labeled 9 in. and 6 in.

The lengths of all the sides are known. So, the perimeter can be found.

$$P = 17 + 6 + 4 + 3 + 13 + 9 = 52$$

The perimeter is 52 inches.

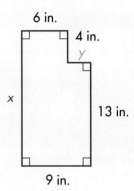

Explain It

1. Diane extended two sides to make a rectangle. Explain what she did and how it helps to find the measures of x and y.

2. Write a formula for finding the perimeter of an equilateral triangle. Let s equal the length of one side.

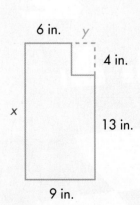

Perimeter of a Square

Since a square has 4 sides (s) that have equal lengths, you can use the formula $P = 4s$.

7.6 cm

$P = 4s$
$P = 4(7.6)$
$P = 30.4$

4s means 4 × s

The perimeter of the square is 30.4 cm.

Perimeter of a Rectangle

Since a rectangle has two equal lengths (ℓ) and two equal widths (w), you can use the formula $P = 2\ell + 2w$.

7 in.

21 in.

$P = 2\ell + 2w$
$P = 2(21) + 2(7)$
$P = 42 + 14$
$P = 56$

The perimeter of the rectangle is 56 in.

Guided Practice*

© **MATHEMATICAL PRACTICES**

Do you know HOW?

In **1** through **4**, find the perimeter of each shape.

1. square with 5-inch sides

2. rectangle with length 12 cm and width 8 cm

3.

23 mm

4.
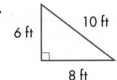
6 ft   10 ft
8 ft

Do you UNDERSTAND?

© **5. Reason** If you do not remember the formula for finding the perimeter of a rectangle, how could you find its perimeter?

6. A carpenter is putting wood molding around a room that is 10 feet by 10 feet. How many feet of molding does he need?

Independent Practice

In **7** through **14**, find the perimeter of each shape.

Tip *A regular polygon has sides of equal length.*

7. regular hexagon, sides 5 in. long

8. rectangular rug, 5 ft long, 3 ft wide

9. equilateral triangle, sides 12 in.

10. octagonal stop sign, sides 12 in.

11. plywood piece, 3 ft wide, 4 ft long

12. rectangular room, 20 m long, 9 m wide

13. square tile, side 30 cm long

14. regular decagon, sides 8 mm long

DIGITAL Animated Glossary www.pearsonsuccessnet.com

In **15** through **17**, find the perimeter.

15. 8 m

16. 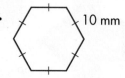 10 mm

17.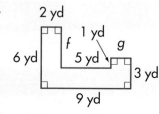
22 in.
5 in.
7 in.
5 in.

In **18** through **20**, find the length of each unknown side, and then find the perimeter.

18.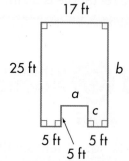
17 ft
25 ft
b
a
c
5 ft   5 ft
5 ft

19.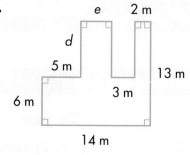
e   2 m
d
5 m
6 m
3 m
13 m
14 m

20.
2 yd
1 yd
f   g
6 yd   5 yd
9 yd
3 yd

Problem Solving

MATHEMATICAL
PRACTICES

21. Greta bought 3 lb 4 oz of peanuts and shared 1 lb 12 oz with the class. What is the weight of the remaining peanuts?

22. Model The perimeter of a regular octagon is 26 ft. What is the length of each side?

23. Writing to Explain Name two units that could be used to measure perimeter and two that could not be used. Explain the difference.

24. Manuel wanted some film for a field trip. Film costs $4.50 a roll. How much will 5 rolls cost?

25. Reasonableness Fort Ross was built by Russian settlers in 1812 as a farming and trading outpost. Approximately, what was the total length of the fort's walls?

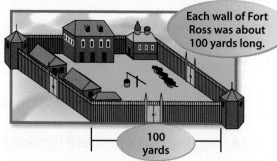
Each wall of Fort Ross was about 100 yards long.
100 yards

A About 100 yards   **C** About 400 yards

B About 200 yards   **D** About 10,000 yards

26. Persevere Jack and Rina are putting a wallpaper border around the walls of a game room. A floor plan of the game room is shown below. If the border comes in 15-foot rolls, about how many rolls will they need?

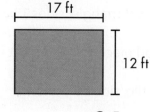
17 ft
12 ft

A 2   **C** 5

B 4   **D** 58

Algebra Connections

Perimeters of Similar Figures

Remember that when polygons are similar, their corresponding sides are proportional.

Rectangles **A** and **B** shown below are similar figures.

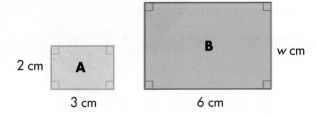

2 cm

3 cm

6 cm

For **1**, the parallelograms are similar. Use what you know about similar figures to solve for x; then find the perimeter of Parallelogram **N**.

1.

10 in.

5 in.

8 in.

x in.

For **2** and **3**, write and solve a proportion to find the missing values for the similar figures shown.

2.

6 m

B

y

1 m

1 m A

3.

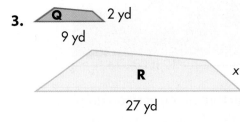

Q   2 yd

9 yd

R x

27 yd

For **4** and **5**, use the figure at the right.

4. Write and solve an equation for the perimeter of Polygon **P**.

5. If a shape similar to Polygon **P** has a perimeter of 64 cm, what would the length of each side be? Explain how you found your answer.

P   4 cm

Common
Core

6.EE.2.c Evaluate expressions at specific values of their variables. Include expressions that arise from formulas used in real-world problems. Perform arithmetic operations, including those involving whole-number exponents, in the conventional order when there are no parentheses to specify a particular order.... Also **6.EE.7, 6.G.1**

Area of Rectangles and Irregular Figures

How can you measure the area of a rectangle?

The area of a figure is <u>the amount of surface it covers</u>. Tessa is covering a bulletin board with fabric. The board is 4 feet high and 5 feet long. How much fabric does she need?

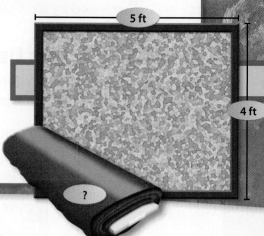

5 ft

4 ft

?

Another Example How can you measure the area of an irregular figure?

Richard is helping his father put sod in a portion of the yard. The yard is rectangular, 12 feet long and 8 feet wide, with a 5-foot-by-5-foot flower garden in one corner. How much sod will they need?

One Way

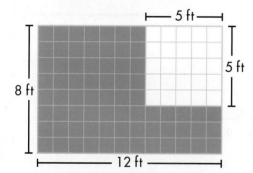

Draw a picture of the yard on graph paper. Let each square represent 1 square foot of sod. Count the squares in the picture, excluding the squares for the garden.

They will need 71 square feet of sod.

Another Way

Use a formula to find the total area of the yard and subtract the area of the garden.

Area of the yard:

$A = \ell \times w = 12 \times 8 = 96$

Area of the garden:

$A = \ell \times w = 5 \times 5 = 25$

Area to be sodded:

$A = 96 - 25 = 71$

They will need 71 ft² of sod.

Explain It

1. Look at the picture above. How could you use a formula to calculate the amount of sod needed without finding the area of the garden?

One Way

Draw a picture on graph paper. Then count the squares covered by the drawing.

There are 20 squares.

$A = 20 \text{ ft}^2$

"ft²" is read "square feet."

Tessa needs 20 square feet of fabric.

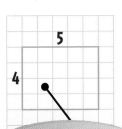

Area is always given in square units. A square foot, for example, is one foot high and one foot wide.

Another Way

Use a formula. The formula for finding the area of a rectangle is $A = \ell \times w$.

$A = \ell \times w$ ← **Think** ℓ is the length and w is the width.

$A = 5 \times 4$

$A = 20 \text{ ft}^2$

Tessa needs 20 square feet of fabric.

Other Examples

Use the formula for the area of a rectangle to find an unknown measurement when you know the area and the length of one side. Find the length, ℓ, of the rectangle.

$A = 120 \text{ cm}^2$ 8 cm ℓ

$$A = \ell \times w$$
$$120 = \ell \times 8$$
$$120 \div 8 = \ell \times 8 \div 8$$
$$15 = \ell$$

The length of the rectangle is 15 cm.

Guided Practice*

MATHEMATICAL PRACTICES

Do you know HOW?

Find the area of the figures in **1** and **2**.

1.

11 cm

15 cm

2.

10 in.

8 in.

20 in.

6 in.

3. Find the missing length.

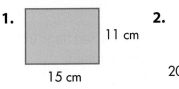

7 ft $A = 175 \text{ ft}^2$

ℓ

Do you UNDERSTAND?

4. Find the area and perimeter of a square measuring 4 inches on each side. Compare the answers. What is the same? What is different?

ⓒ **5. Communicate** In the example at the top, suppose Tessa used 24 ft² of fabric to cover a bulletin board that is 3 ft wide. How long is the bulletin board? Explain how you found the answer.

Animated Glossary
www.pearsonsuccessnet.com

In **6** through **11**, find the area of each figure.

6.
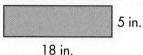
5 in.
18 in.

7.
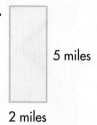
5 miles
2 miles

8.
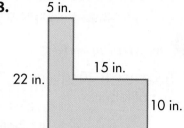
5 in.
15 in.
22 in.
10 in.

9.
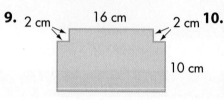
2 cm   16 cm   2 cm
10 cm

10.
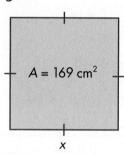
5 cm
15 cm
6 cm
15 cm

11.
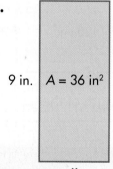
26 ft
15 ft
5 ft→
3 ft   4 ft

In **12** through **14**, find the missing lengths.

12.
$A = 7.7 \text{ ft}^2$ y
3.5 ft

13.
$A = 169 \text{ cm}^2$
x

14.
9 in. $A = 36 \text{ in}^2$
x

MATHEMATICAL
PRACTICES

ⓒ **15. Persevere** Tito is painting a wall that measures 8 ft by 16 ft. There is a window that is 5 ft by 4 ft in the wall. What is the area that Tito will paint?

16. Flags can come in many sizes. Copy the chart below and fill in the areas for the rectangular flags. Then use your completed chart for **17** through **19**.

Flag Size	Flag Area
4 in. × 6 in.	
12 in. × 18 in.	
2 ft × 3 ft	
3 ft × 5 ft	
4 ft × 6 ft	

17. Are all of the different-sized flags in the chart similar figures? Explain.

ⓒ **18. Reason** Which flag is larger, the one with an area of 216 in² or the one with an area of 6 ft²?

ⓒ **19. Writing to Explain** The 4 ft × 6 ft flag has a solid red rectangular area that covers $\frac{1}{3}$ of the flag. What could be the dimensions of this red area? Explain.

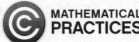
© 20. Be Precise Can the distance from your house to your school be measured in square miles? Explain.

© 21. Persevere Marcy rode her bike around a $\frac{1}{4}$-mile track 16 times in 30 minutes. What was her speed in miles per hour?

22. Janelle purchased a bathing suit on sale for $25.00, with sales tax of 6%. What was the total cost for her suit?

© 23. Model Suppose the length of a side of a square is s. Write a formula to find the area of a square.

© 24. Construct Arguments If you know the perimeter of a rectangle and the length of one side, can you calculate the width? Explain.

25. Marcus wants to put a $6\frac{1}{2}$-foot bookcase against a $12\frac{1}{4}$-foot long wall. If he centers the bookcase, how far will it be from each end of the wall?

26. Hayley wants to plant ivy in her back yard in a shady part that is 24 feet long and 6 feet wide. Ivy to cover 1 square foot will cost $2.50. How much will it cost to plant enough ivy to cover the shaded area?

27. Mr. Scott's workroom is a rectangle that measures 25 feet by 27 feet. His new woodworking equipment will take up an area of 300 ft². Will the new equipment fit into the workroom?

© 28. Reason On a chessboard, the squares alternate betweeen light and dark. Which best describes the area of the light squares?

   A Half as much as the dark squares

   B Twice as much as the dark squares

   C Equal to the dark squares

   D One-fourth less than the dark squares

29. Suppose that a square on a living chessboard measures 4 ft × 4 ft. How much area does the whole board cover?

   A 72 ft²

   B 256 ft²

   C 512 ft²

   D 1,024 ft²

4 ft   4 ft

A living chess board has 64 squares.

Lesson
17-3

©
Common Core

6.EE.2.c Evaluate expressions at specific values of their variables. Include expressions that arise from formulas used in real-world problems. Perform arithmetic operations, including those involving whole-number exponents, in the conventional order when there are no parentheses to specify a particular order.... Also 6.EE.7, 6.G.1

Area of Parallelograms and Triangles

How can you use the formula for the area of a rectangle to find the area of a parallelogram?

Look at the parallelogram below. If you move the triangle to the opposite side, you form a rectangle with the same area as the parallelogram.

Another Example How can you use the formula for the area of a parallelogram to find the area of a triangle?

Since two congruent triangles can form a parallelogram, the area of one triangle must be half the area of the parallelogram that has the same base and height.

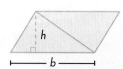 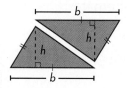 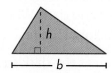

Area of a Parallelogram

$$A = bh$$

Area of a Triangle

$$A = \frac{1}{2} bh$$

 Tip *Remember to write area in square units (units²).*

Explain It

1. A rectangle and a parallelogram have the same base and height. How are their areas related?

2. A parallelogram and a triangle have the same base and height. How are their areas related?

The base of the parallelogram (b) equals the length of the rectangle (ℓ).

The height of the parallelogram (h), which is perpendicular to the base, equals the width of the rectangle (w).

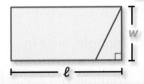

The area of the parallelogram equals the area of the rectangle.

Area of a Rectangle → $A = ℓ \times w$

Area of a Parallelogram → $A = b \times h$

$A = bh$

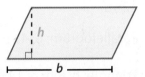

Other Examples

Find the area of the parallelogram.

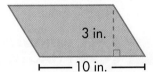

$A = b \times h$

$A = 10 \times 3$

$A = 30$

The area of the parallelogram is 30 in².

Find the area of the triangle.

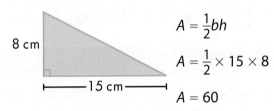

$A = \frac{1}{2}bh$

$A = \frac{1}{2} \times 15 \times 8$

$A = 60$

The area of the triangle is 60 cm².

Guided Practice*

MATHEMATICAL PRACTICES

Do you know HOW?

Use a formula to find the area of each parallelogram or triangle.

1.
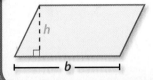
21.5 in.
20 in.

2.
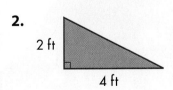
2 ft
4 ft

3. Triangle: b: 14 cm; h: 23 cm

4. Parallelogram: b: 27 ft; h: 32 ft

Do you UNDERSTAND?

© 5. **Writing to Explain** If you cut a parallelogram into 2 triangles, will the triangles be congruent? How does the area of one triangle compare to the area of the original parallelogram? Explain.

6. The base of a parallelogram is 8 meters, and its height is 5 meters. Two congruent triangles can form this parallelogram. What is the area of one of these triangles?

© 7. **Critique Reasoning** A parallelogram is 5 yards long and 9 feet high. Lori said that the area is 45 square feet. Is she correct? Explain why or why not.

Find the area of each parallelogram or triangle.

8.
6 yd

2 yd

9.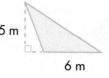
5 m

6 m

10.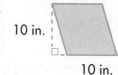
10 in.

10 in.

11.
14 cm

31 cm

12. Parallelogram: *b*: 42 m; *h*: 33 m

13. Triangle: *b*: 32 in.; *h*: 2 yd

14. Triangle: *b*: 8 ft; *h*: 14 ft

15. Triangle: *b*: 12 ft; *h*: 6 in.

16. Parallelogram: *b*: 22 in.; *h*: 22 in.

17. Parallelogram: *b*: 30 cm; *h*: 10 mm

18. Triangle: *b*: 5 yd; *h*: 3 yd

19. Parallelogram: *b*: 24 in.; *h*: 2 ft

20. Triangle: *b*: 32 cm; *h*: 2 m

21. Estimate the area of a triangle with a base of 19.64 cm and a height of 30.23 cm.

22. Parallelogram: *b*: 8 ft; *h*: 2 yd

Problem Solving

MATHEMATICAL PRACTICES

23. Reason If you know both the area and height of a triangle, how can you find the base?

24. Generalize When can the leg of an isosceles triangle be used as the height of the triangle?

25. Fawzia wanted to make an origami fish for each of her 22 classmates. It takes 30 minutes to make one fish. How long will it take Fawzia to make all the fish?

A 320 minutes   **C** 600 minutes

B 11 hours   **D** 660 hours

26. Reason Ms. Lopez drew parallelogram *M* with *h* = 6 in. and *b* = 6 in., and parallelogram *N* with *h* = 4 in. and *b* = 8 in. Which parallelogram has the greater area, *M* or *N*?

Use the origami figure for **27** and **28**.

27. What is the area in square centimeters of the triangle outlined on the figure?

28. What is the area of the parallelogram outlined on the figure?

A 4.44 cm²

B 10.44 cm²

C 9.44 cm²

D Need more information

b = 3 cm
h = 1.76 cm

b = 4 cm
h = 2.36 cm

Enrichment

Area of Trapezoids

A trapezoid is a quadrilateral that has only one pair of opposite sides that are parallel. These parallel sides are called bases. They are labeled b_1 and b_2.

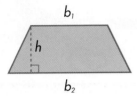

If a congruent trapezoid is joined with the trapezoid as shown, the two figures form a parallelogram. The area of a parallelogram is $A = bh$.

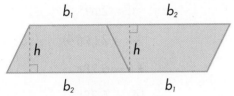

The base of this parallelogram is $b_1 + b_2$.

Half the area of this parallelogram is the area of one trapezoid. So, the formula for the area of a trapezoid is $A = \frac{1}{2}h(b_1 + b_2)$.

Example:

Find the area of the trapezoid.

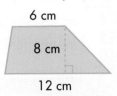

Tip *Area should be expressed in square units.*

$$A = \frac{1}{2}h(b_1 + b_2)$$

$$A = \frac{1}{2} \times 8(6 + 12)$$

$$= \frac{1}{2} \times 8(18)$$

$$= \frac{1}{2} \times 144$$

$$= 72$$

The area of the trapezoid is 72 cm².

Practice

For **1** through **4**, find the area of each trapezoid.

1.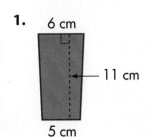

2.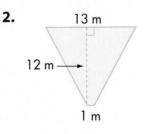

3.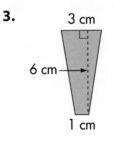

4.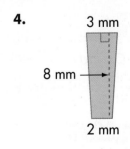

For **5** and **6**, find the missing measurement for each trapezoid.

5. Base b_1 = 5 ft   Base b_2 = ▨

   Height h = 17 ft   Area = 255 ft²

6. Base b_1 = 9 cm   Base b_2 = 13 cm

   Height h = ▨   Area = 88 cm²

Ⓒ
Common Core

7.G.4 Know the formulas for the area and circumference of a circle and use them to solve problems; give an informal derivation of the relationship between the circumference and area of a circle.

Circumference

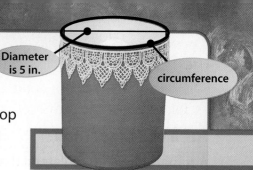

Diameter is 5 in.

circumference

How can you find circumference?

Anna is going to glue some lace around the top edge of a lampshade whose circular opening has a diameter of 5 in. and a radius of 2.5 in. How much lace does she need?

Use a formula to find the circumference of the lampshade.

Circumference (*C*) is <u>the distance around a circle</u>.

Another Example # How can you find the diameter or radius if you know the circumference of a circle?

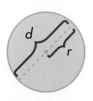

C = 14 in.

d = ▢

r = ▢

Substitute the value of *C* and π. Solve the equation for *d*.

$$C = \pi d$$

$$14 = 3.14d$$

$$\frac{14}{3.14} = \frac{3.14d}{3.14}$$

$$4.46 = d$$

The diameter is approximately 4.46 inches.

Substitute the value of *C* and π. Solve the equation for *r*.

$$C = 2\pi r$$

$$14 = 2(3.14)r$$

$$14 = 6.28r$$

$$\frac{14}{6.28} = \frac{6.28r}{6.28}$$

$$2.23 = r$$

The radius is approximately 2.23 inches.

How can you find circumference using a calculator?

14.5 cm

Press: [π] [×] 14.5 [ENTER =]

C = π*d*   Display: ⁤45.55309

The circumference is about 45.55 cm.

Explain It

1. Explain when you would use $\frac{22}{7}$ for π instead of 3.14.

2. How would you find the radius of a circle whose circumference is 10 cm?

Use the formula, $C = \pi d$.

C is the circumference of the circle and d is the diameter. The Greek letter π (read pi) represents the ratio of the circumference to the diameter for every circle.

π is approximately 3.14, or $\frac{22}{7}$. The digits do not repeat and never end. All calculations involving π are approximations.

$C = \pi d$

In the book, equal signs are used for calculations involving π.

$C = (3.14)(5)$

$C = 15.70$

Anna needs about 16 inches of lace.

Use the formula, $C = 2\pi r$.

Since the diameter of a circle is twice the radius, 2r can be used to replace d in the formula.

$C = 2\pi r$

$C = 2(3.14)(2.5)$

$C = 15.70$

The answer is the same. Anna needs about 16 inches of lace.

Guided Practice*

MATHEMATICAL PRACTICES

Do you know HOW?

Use the diameter or radius shown for each circle to find its circumference. Use 3.14 or $\frac{22}{7}$ for π.

1. 14 in.

2. 5 m

Do you UNDERSTAND?

3. **Be Precise** What variables are used in the formula $C = 2\pi r$?

4. **Reason** In the problem above, how would you estimate the circumference?

Independent Practice

In **5** through **8**, find the circumference. Use 3.14 for π.

5. 28 ft

6. 6 km

7. 35 in.

8. 25 cm

Find the missing measurement. Use 3.14 for π. Round to the nearest hundredth.

9. $r = 21$ ft
$C = $

10. $d = 9$ yd
$C = $

11. $C = 35$ mm
$r = $

12. $C = 32$ m
$d = $

13. $d = 21$ in.
$C = $

14. $r = $
$C = 9$ mm

15. $d = $
$r = 15$ in.
$C = $

16. $d = $
$r = $
$C = 109.9$ cm

Animated Glossary
www.pearsonsuccessnet.com
DIGITAL

For **17** through **20**, find each circumference using 3.14 for π.
Then find each circumference using $\pi = \frac{22}{7}$.

17.
84 cm

18.
14 ft

19.
63 in.

20.
17.5 m

Problem Solving

Ⓒ **MATHEMATICAL PRACTICES**

21. If a clock face has a radius of 5.5 centimeters, what is the circumference of the clock face?

Ⓒ **23. Writing to Explain** Explain how finding the circumference using both 3.14 and $\frac{22}{7}$ can help you check an answer.

Ⓒ **24. Reason** The minute hand of a clock is 4.2 inches long. Does the point of the hand move more or less than 24 inches in one hour?

Ⓒ **25. Be Precise** The number π to four decimal places is 3.1416. How do you read this number?

22. How is this graph incorrect?

This table shows the diameter and circumference for some of Saturn's rings. Use the information for **26** and **27**.

26. Estimation Explain how you can estimate the diameter of Ring G.

Ring	Diameter	Circumference
C	184,000 km	
B	235,000 km	737,900 km
A	273,600 km	859,104 km
G		1,091,464 km

27. What is the circumference of Ring C?

A about 860,000 km

B about 254,000 km

C about 577,760 km

D about 225,000 km

Ⓒ **28. Think About the Structure** If the circumference of a circle is known, how would you find the missing diameter?

A Multiply the circumference by 2π.

B Divide the circumference by π.

C Multiply the circumference by $\frac{\pi}{2}$.

D Divide the circumference by 2π.

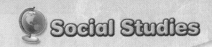
Mixed Problem Solving

The earliest known use of a wheel was in Mesopotamia in 3500 B.C. It was used as a tool to help people make pots and dishes out of clay. Wheels made it possible to turn pots and dishes as they were made.

Use this potter's wheel for **1** through **3**.

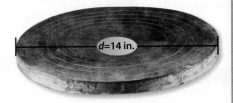
d=14 in.

1. Suppose you wanted to make a circular dish with a circumference of 50 in. Would it fit on this potter's wheel?

2. Would a circular pot with a diameter of 11 inches fit on the wheel? How can you tell without doing a calculation?

3. Why would a circular dish that has a radius of 13 inches not fit on the wheel in the picture?

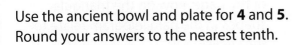

Use the ancient bowl and plate for **4** and **5**.
Round your answers to the nearest tenth.

r=7.85 cm

4. This ancient bowl and plate were made by hand before the potter's wheel was invented. What is the circumference of the ancient bowl?

d=12.5 cm

5. What is the circumference of the plate?

Cylinder seals were often used in Mesopotamia as a way for people to initial clay tablets. As the seal was rolled along a piece of clay, the pictures on the cylinder pressed into the clay.

6. The diameter of a cylinder seal is 2.5 cm. What is the circumference?

7. How is the length of the marking made by one complete rotation of the seal related to the circumference of the cylinder seal?

8. Approximately how many complete rotations of the cylinder were needed to create an image that was 25 cm long?

Area of a Circle

How do you find the area of a circle?

A circular garden has a radius of 21 feet. What is the area of the garden?

Rearrange the sections of a circle to approximate a parallelogram. The area of a parallelogram, $A = bh$, may be used to find the formula for the area of a circle.

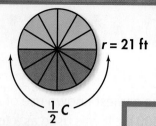

$r = 21$ ft

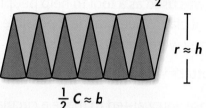

$\frac{1}{2}C$

$r \approx h$

$\frac{1}{2}C \approx b$

Guided Practice*

© MATHEMATICAL PRACTICES

Do you know HOW?

Find the area of each circle to the nearest whole number. Use 3.14 or $\frac{22}{7}$ for π.

1.

10 yd

2.

35 m

3. $d = 54$ in.

4. $r = 10$ mi

Do you UNDERSTAND?

© **5. Reason** In the comparison at the top of the page, how do the triangular shapes in the parallelogram relate to the circle?

6. Find the area of the garden above using 3.14 for π. Why is the value of the area slightly different than the values calculated using $\frac{22}{7}$ or the calculator?

Independent Practice

For **7** through **10**, find the area of each circle to the nearest whole number. Use 3.14 or $\frac{22}{7}$ for π.

7.

16 cm

8.

12 km

9.

7 ft

10.

32 yd

Find the missing measurements for each figure. Round to the nearest whole number. Use 3.14 or $\frac{22}{7}$ for π.

11. $d = 8$ in.
$r = \blacksquare$
$C = \blacksquare$
$A = \blacksquare$

12. $d = \blacksquare$
$r = 32$ mm
$C = \blacksquare$
$A = \blacksquare$

13. $d = \blacksquare$
$r = \blacksquare$
$C = 371$ mm
$A = \blacksquare$

14. $d = \blacksquare$
$r = \blacksquare$
$C = \blacksquare$
$A = 113$ sq in.

For another example, see Set C on page 451.

Find the formula for area of a circle.

$A = b \times h$	Area of a parallelogram
$A = \frac{1}{2}C \times r$	Equivalent measures
$A = \frac{1}{2}(2\pi r) \times r$	$C = 2\pi r$
$A = \pi r \times r$	Simplified
$A = \pi r^2$	Area of a circle

Use the formula for a circle to find the area of the garden.

$A = \pi r^2$ ← Use $\frac{22}{7}$ for π.

$A = \frac{22}{7}(21)(21)$

$A = 1,386 \text{ ft}^2$

Use a calculator to find the area.

Press: 21 2

Display:

Problem Solving

MATHEMATICAL PRACTICES

15. Find the approximate area and circumference of each coin. Round your answer to the nearest whole number.

  a Dime

  b Nickel

  c Quarter

24.26 mm   17.91 mm   21.21 mm

16. Communicate When you use both 3.14 and $\frac{22}{7}$ for π, why don't you get exactly the same answer?

17. Writing to Explain Explain how to find the area of a semicircle with a radius of 5 feet.

18. A small radio station broadcasts in all directions to a distance of 40 miles. About how many square miles are in the station's broadcast area?

  A About 1,256 sq mi

  B About 2,512 sq mi

  C About 5,024 sq mi

  D About 20,096 sq mi

19. Persevere Giant lily pads found in Brazil can have a diameter of 4 feet. What is the area of the top of the lily pad?

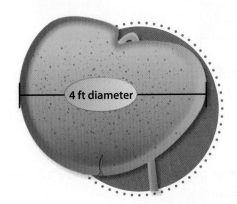

4 ft diameter

20. A dartboard has a radius of 25 cm. What is the area of the board at which you would throw darts?

Lesson
17-6

Common
Core

6.G.4 Represent three-dimensional figures using nets made up of rectangles and triangles, and use the nets to find the surface area of these figures. Apply these techniques in the context of solving real-world and mathematical problems.

Problem Solving

Use Objects

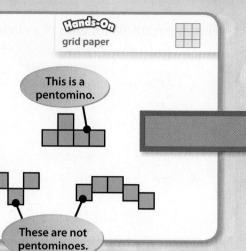

Hands-On
grid paper

A pentomino is an arrangement of 5 identical squares, each having a common side with at least one other square. There are 12 possible pentominoes.

Find a pentomino that can be folded along the lines to make an open-top box.

This is a pentomino.

These are not pentominoes.

Guided Practice*

MATHEMATICAL
PRACTICES

Do you know HOW?

1. Which figure is a pentomino?

A

C

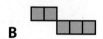

B

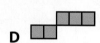

D

2. Can Pentomino P fold into an open-top box?

Do you UNDERSTAND?

3. Besides T, find two more pentominoes that can be folded to create an open-top box.

4. **Write a Problem** Write a problem that you can solve by using objects.

Independent Practice

MATHEMATICAL
PRACTICES

Fit two pentominoes together to create the shapes for **5** and **6**.

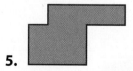

5.

6.

7. **Model** Suppose each square in a pentomino is a table that seats one person on a side. Draw a table arrangement (a pentomino) that can seat 12 people.

8. Arrange pentominoes U, F, and P to create a rectangle.

Applying Math Practices

- What am I asked to find?
- What else can I try?
- How are quantities related?
- How can I explain my work?
- How can I use math to model the problem?
- Can I use tools to help?
- Is my work precise?
- Why does this work?
- How can I generalize?

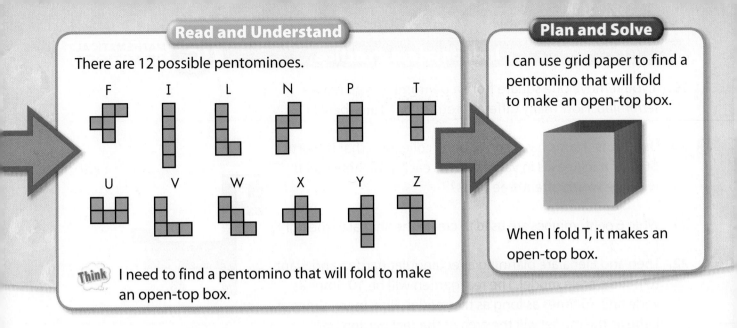

There are 12 possible pentominoes.

F   I   L   N   P   T

U   V   W   X   Y   Z

Think I need to find a pentomino that will fold to make an open-top box.

I can use grid paper to find a pentomino that will fold to make an open-top box.

When I fold T, it makes an open-top box.

© **9. Be Precise** If 1 square in a pentomino is equal to 1 unit, how many square units are there in a pentomino?

10. If you combine two pentominoes, how many square units is the figure that they form?

11. Use pentominoes to create a rectangle with 20 square units.

12. Use pentominoes to create a rectangle with 15 square units.

© **13. Persevere** If you used all 12 pentominoes to create a figure, how many square units would the figure have?

14. Use pentominoes to create a rectangle with 20 square units that is different from the rectangle you created for Exercise 11.

15. How many square units are in this figure using 5 pentominoes?

16. Use exactly 4 pentominoes to create this shape.

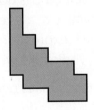

17. How many square units are in this figure using 4 pentominoes?

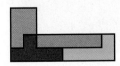

© **18. Construct Arguments** Can you make this shape with exactly 2 pentominoes? Explain.

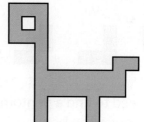

19. If you remove one square from a pentomino, you have a *tetromino*. How many different tetrominoes are there?

© **20. Use Tools** Harris has a comic book collection that is worth $600. If it increases in value by 10% each year, how much will it be worth after three years?

21. What 6 pentominoes are used to create the animal to the right?

22. Theo and Elena are planning a rectangular garden and want to build a scale model. The real garden will be 10 times as wide and 10 times as long as the model. How many times as large as the model will the area of the real garden be?

23. It is possible to form a 3 × 20 rectangle with all 12 pentominoes. Here is a start, using 8 of the pentominoes. Can you add the last 4 pentominoes to complete the rectangle?

24. Which pentomino has the greatest perimeter? Which has the least?

© **25. Writing to Explain** Kyle says that for a rectangle, the larger the perimeter is, the larger the area will be. Is he right? If not, explain why he is wrong.

© **Think About the Structure**

26. The Outdoor Club is going on a 6-mile hike. They hike at a rate of 3 miles per hour. Which expression will find how long the whole hike will take?

A 6 miles × 3 miles per hour

B $\dfrac{6 \text{ miles}}{3 \text{ miles per hour}}$

C $\dfrac{3 \text{ miles per hour}}{6 \text{ miles}}$

D (2 miles × 3 miles per hour) + (4 miles × 2 miles per hour)

27. Juli is planning a bulletin board by making a model. She wants a square with a side of p units inside a square with a side of 8 units. Which expression will find the area of the shaded dark blue region?

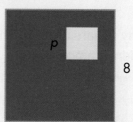

A $64 + 4p$ **C** $64 - p^2$

B $64 - 2p$ **D** $64 + p^2$

Circumference and Area of a Circle

Use ⚙ **tools**
Geometry Drawing
A sprinkler for watering a lawn sprays water 6 feet from the sprinkler head. What is the circumference of the circle the sprinkler waters? What is the area of the lawn the sprinkler waters?

Step 1 Go to the Geometry Drawing eTool. ⚠ On the Draw tool palette, click on the button next to the triangle polygon to expand this tool palette. ⊙ Click on the Circle tool. Click near the center of the workspace to set the center of the circle. Then click on another point.

Step 2 ⇄ Click on the Distance Measurement tool. Click on point *A*, the center of the circle. Then click on point *B* on the circle. The distance between points *A* and *B* (the radius) should appear in the lower right corner of the workspace. ↗ Click on the Arrow tool icon. Then click on point *B* and drag until the radius is close to 6 units. If the circle does not fit in the workspace, use the Arrow tool to drag the center to the middle until it does fit.

Step 3 ▢ Click on the Perimeter Measurement tool and then on the circle.

⬠ Click on the Area Measurement tool and then on the circle. Are the measures that appear reasonable? A formula for circumference of a circle is $C = \pi(2r)$, so the circumference should be a little more than $3 \times 2 \times 6 = 36$ units. The formula for the area of a circle is $A = \pi r^2$, so the area should be a little more than $3 \times 6^2 = 108$ square units. Use the eTool to answer the questions in the problem above.

Practice

Find the circumference and area of a circle with each radius.

1. *r* = 5 units   **2.** *r* = 3 units   **3.** *r* = 4.5 units   **4.** *r* = 1 unit

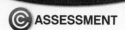

1. Caroline is framing a rectangular picture that measures 8 inches by 10 inches. Which of the following can be used to find the perimeter of the picture? (17-1)

A $P = 2(8) \times 2(10)$

B $P = 2(8) + 2(10)$

C $P = 2(8) - 2(10)$

D $P = 8 \times 10$

2. Two figures are arranged as shown. Which of the following can be used to find the area of the yellow figure? (17-2)

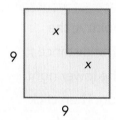

A $9^2 - x^2$

B $(9 - x)^2$

C $2(9) + 2(9 - x)$

D $9^2 + x^2$

3. What is the perimeter of the figure shown? (17-1)

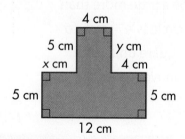

A 35 cm

B 40 cm

C 44 cm

D 120 cm

4. Which equation can be used to find A, the area of the parallelogram shown, in square meters? (17-3)

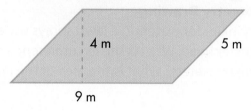

A $A = 5 \times 9$

B $A = 4 \times 9$

C $A = \frac{1}{2} \times 5 \times 9$

D $A = \frac{1}{2} \times 4 \times 9$

5. What is the area of the rectangular garden shown? (17-2)

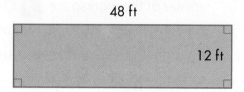

A 56 square feet

B 120 square feet

C 480 square feet

D 576 square feet

6. What is the area of a square flower bed if one side has a length of 8 feet? (17-2)

A 16 square feet

B 24 square feet

C 32 square feet

D 64 square feet

7. What is the area of the parallelogram shown below? (17-3)

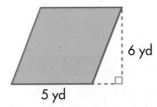

6 yd

5 yd

A 22 square yards

B 30 square yards

C 35 square yards

D 36 square yards

8. What is the area of a triangle with a base of 7 feet and a height of 13 feet? (17-3)

A 91 square feet

B 45.5 square feet

C 45 square feet

D 44.5 square feet

9. What is the area of the figure shown? (17-2)

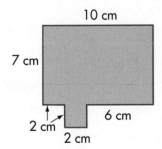

10 cm

7 cm

6 cm

2 cm

2 cm

A 74 square centimeters

B 78 square centimeters

C 90 square centimeters

D 108 square centimeters

10. If the perimeter of the rectangle shown is 18 millimeters, which equation can be used to find n? (17-1)

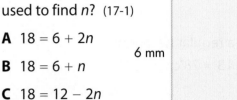

n mm

6 mm

A $18 = 6 + 2n$

B $18 = 6 + n$

C $18 = 12 - 2n$

D $18 = 12 + 2n$

11. Mr. Aufleger is painting the gable of his house which is triangular shaped. If the base of the triangle is 16 feet and the height is 6 feet, what is the area of the gable? (17-3)

A 24 square feet

B 44 square feet

C 48 square feet

D 96 square feet

12. If each square of a pentomino represents a table that seats one person on each side, which of the following will NOT seat 12 people? (17-6)

A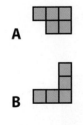

B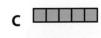

C

D

Set A, pages 426–428

Find the perimeter of the shapes below.

The perimeter is the distance around a polygon.

For a regular hexagon:
$6 \times 13 = 78$ cm

13 cm

For a parallelogram:
$(2 \times 20) + (2 \times 12) = 64$ in.

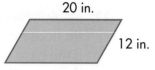

20 in.

12 in.

For an irregular polygon:
$5 + 3 + 1 + 10 + 6 +$
$4 + 10 + 17 = 56$ yd

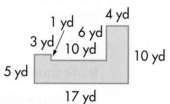

1 yd   4 yd
6 yd
3 yd   10 yd
10 yd
5 yd

17 yd

Remember that you can use what you know about geometric shapes to find unknown sides.

Find the perimeter.

1.

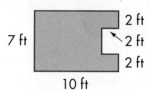

2 ft
7 ft   2 ft
2 ft
10 ft

2.

5 in.

3. A rhombus with side lengths of 14 cm

4. A rectangle with width 8 in. and length 2 in.

Set B, pages 430–436

Use these formulas to find the area of each figure.

Rectangles: $A = \ell \times w$

Parallelograms: $A = b \times h$

Triangles: $A = \frac{1}{2} b \times h$

$A = \ell \times w$
$A = 18 \times 12$
$A = 216$ m²

12 m

18 m

$A = b \times h$
$A = 12 \times 8$
$A = 96$ ft²

8 ft

12 ft

$A = \frac{1}{2} b \times h$

$A = \frac{1}{2} (26) \times 20$

$A = 260$ cm²

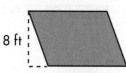
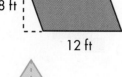

20 cm

26 cm

Remember that areas are measured in square units.

Find the area.

1.

9 m

4 m

2.

5 yd

2 yd

3.

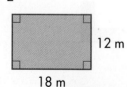

22 mm

4.

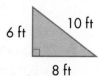

10 ft
6 ft
8 ft

5. If the square in Exercise 3 were divided diagonally into two triangles, what would be the heights of the triangles?

Use a formula to find the circumference and area. Use both 3.14 and $\frac{22}{7}$ for π.

Circumference

$C = \pi d$ or $C = 2\pi r$

Since the radius is shown, use the second formula.

$C = 2 \times 4 \times 3.14 = 25.12$ ft

$C = 2 \times 4 \times \frac{22}{7} = 25\frac{1}{7}$ ft

4 ft

Area

$A = \pi r^2$

$A = 3.14 \times 4 \times 4 = 50.24$ ft²

$A = \frac{22}{7} \times 4 \times 4 = 50\frac{2}{7}$ ft²

Remember that the units for area are square units.

Find the missing measurements. Use 3.14 or $\frac{22}{7}$. Round to the nearest whole number.

1. d =

r = 5 m

C =

A =

5 m

2. d = 3 in.

r =

C =

A =

3 in.

A pentomino is a shape made of 5 squares. Each square in a pentomino shares at least one side with another square.

 Pentomino

The figure above is made up of 5 squares. Each square shares at least one side with another square. This figure is a pentomino.

 Not a pentomino

The figure above is made up of 5 squares, but each square does not share at least one side with another square. This figure is not a pentomino.

Remember that a pentomino has an area of 5 square units.

1. Which of these figures is <u>not</u> a pentomino?

A

C

B

D

2. How many pentominoes would make this figure?

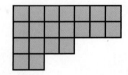

3. Can this shape be made using exactly 3 pentominoes? Explain.

Volume and Surface Area

1

This Ice Hotel is built entirely out of ice and snow. What is the volume of the blocks that are used to build this temporary hotel? You will find out in Lesson 18-3.

DOMAIN Geometry

2 How can you find the volume of a gold bar whose dimensions are not in whole units? You will find out in Lesson 18-4.

3 How could you classify the shape of the Hubble Telescope? You will find out in Lesson 18-1.

Review What You Know!

Vocabulary

Choose the best term from the box.

- area
- vertex
- perimeter

1. The surface of a figure covers the figure's __?__.

2. The distance around the outside of a polygon is its __?__.

3. The point where two rays that form an angle meet is a __?__.

Area

Find the area of each figure.

4. A rectangle with dimensions 4 ft × 7 ft

5. A triangle with a base 14 in. long and a height of 9 in.

6. A square with a side 3 m long

Operations

Multiply or divide.

7. 16 × 6   8. 3 × 42   9. 216 ÷ 3

10. 364 ÷ 14   11. 4.75 × 2.5   12. 128 ÷ 4

Formulas

© **Writing to Explain** Write an answer for the question.

13. How is finding the area of a triangle different from finding the area of a rectangle?

Common Core

6.G.4 Represent three-dimensional figures using nets made up of rectangles and triangles, and use the nets to find the surface area of these figures. Apply these techniques in the context of solving real-world and mathematical problems.

Solid Figures

How are polyhedrons classified?

A polyhedron is a <u>three-dimensional figure made of flat polygon-shaped surfaces</u> called faces. The <u>line segment where two faces intersect</u> is called an edge. The <u>point where several edges meet</u> is called a vertex.

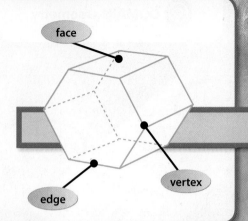

face

edge

vertex

Another Example | **How are three-dimensional figures with curved surfaces classified?**

Some three-dimensional figures are not polyhedrons.

Cylinder	**Sphere**	**Cone**
A cylinder <u>has two circular bases that are parallel and congruent.</u>	A sphere <u>has no base. Every point on a sphere is the same distance from the center.</u>	A cone <u>has one circular base. The points on this circle are joined to one point outside the base.</u>

Explain It

1. Why is a cylinder NOT a polyhedron?

2. What is the shape of the face of a cylinder that connects to the two bases?

3. How are a cylinder, a sphere, and a cone alike and different?

Prisms

Rectangular prism **Pentagonal prism** **Triangular prism**

A prism is <u>a polyhedron with two congruent, parallel, polygon-shaped bases</u>. A prism is named by the shape of its bases. The other faces are parallelograms.

Pyramids

Triangular pyramid **Rectangular pyramid** **Hexagonal pyramid**

A pyramid is <u>a polyhedron that has one base</u>. A pyramid is named by the shape of its base. Triangular faces join the edges of the base to a point outside the base, which is called a vertex.

Another Example **How can you identify a solid from its net?**

A net is <u>a plane figure pattern which, when folded, makes a solid</u>.

Think about unfolding a box to make a net for a rectangular prism.

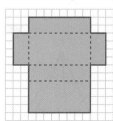

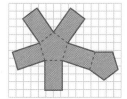

The net shows 2 congruent pentagonal bases and 5 rectangular sides, so it represents a pentagonal prism.

The net shows a triangular base and 3 triangular faces, so it represents a triangular pyramid.

The net shows a rectangle and 2 circular faces that appear to be parallel and congruent, so it represents a cylinder.

Explain It

1. What solid figures are represented by the two nets shown below?

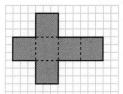
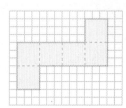

Animated Glossary
www.pearsonsuccessnet.com

Guided Practice*

Do you know HOW?

Classify each polyhedron. Name all faces (including bases), edges, and vertices.

1.

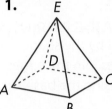

2.

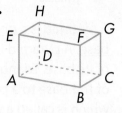

Do you UNDERSTAND?

3. Be Precise Explain the difference between a vertex and an edge.

4. Be Precise Explain the difference between a pyramid and a prism.

5. What would you look for if you were classifying polyhedrons?

Independent Practice

For **6** through **8**, classify each polyhedron. Name all vertices, edges, faces, and bases.

6.

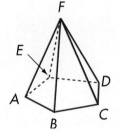

7.

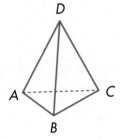

8.

For **9** through **12**, classify each figure.

9.

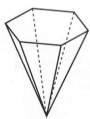

10.

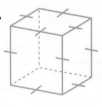

11.

12.

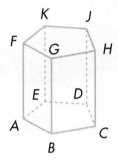

For **13** through **15**, identify each solid from its net.

13.

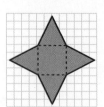

14.

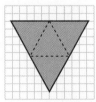

15.

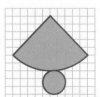

Use the information in the chart for **16** through **18**.

16. Mrs. Stanford wants to buy supplies for the classroom. She would like to purchase 2 dozen pencils, 4 dozen pieces of paper, 24 pens, and 17 folders. What is her total cost?

Data		Price for 1	Price for 5	Price for 1 dozen
	Pencils	$0.10	$0.45	$0.80
	Pens	$0.25	$1.00	$2.25
	Paper	$0.05	$0.20	$0.50
	Folder	$0.50	$2.00	$5.00

17. What is the least amount of money a student could spend to buy 21 pencils?

A $1.35 **B** $1.65 **C** $1.90 **D** $2.10

18. Suzette wants to buy 15 folders. Find the price if she buys them individually, in groups of 5, or as a dozen with 3 singles. Which way does she save the most money?

Use the table at right for **19** through **22**.

19. The Swiss mathematician Leonhard Euler (OY-ler) and the French mathematician Rene Descartes (dā KART) both discovered a pattern in the numbers of edges, vertices, and faces of polyhedrons. Complete the table to look for a pattern.

Polyhedron	Faces (F)	Vertices (V)	F + V	Edges (E)
Trianglar Pyramid				
Cube				
Pentagonal Prism				

© 20. **Look for Patterns** Describe any pattern you see in the table that relates the number of edges to the number of faces and vertices.

© 21. **Model** Write a formula to describe your pattern. Does the pattern work for a hexagonal prism?

© 22. **Writing to Explain** If a rectangular prism has 12 edges and 6 faces, how could you use a formula to find the number of vertices the figure has?

23. The Hubble Telescope was launched in 1990. Classify the shape of the Hubble Telescope. How many bases does this shape have?

© 24. **Writing to Explain** Why are the faces on a pyramid triangular, regardless of the shape of its base?

© 25. **Persevere** An octagonal pyramid has 9 faces and 9 vertices. How many edges does it have?

A 9 **B** 16 **C** 18 **D** 20

ⓒ
Common
Core

6.G.4 Represent three-dimensional figures using nets made up of rectangles and triangles, and use the nets to find the surface area of these figures. Apply these techniques in the context of solving real-world and mathematical problems.

Surface Area

How can you find the surface area of a polyhedron?

Cornelius wants to cover a shoe box with decorative paper to make a storage box for his photos. How much paper will he need to cover the box?

Find the surface area (*SA*) of the shoe box.

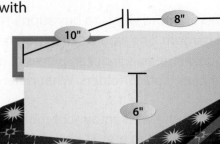

(**Another Example**) **How do you find the surface area of a triangular prism and a square pyramid?**

Triangular prism

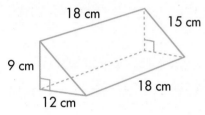

$SA = 2 \times$ (area of base) + (area of rectangular faces)

$= 2(\frac{1}{2} \times 9 \times 12) + (12 \times 18) + (9 \times 18) + (15 \times 18)$

$= 108 + 216 + 162 + 270 = 756$

The surface area is 756 cm².

Square pyramid

$SA =$ (area of base) + (number of triangular faces) $\times$ (area of a triangular face)

$= (3 \times 3) + 4(\frac{1}{2} \times 3 \times 5)$

$= 9 + 4(7.5) = 39$

The surface area is 39 in.²

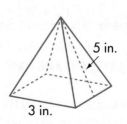 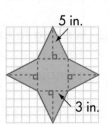

Explain It

1. Name a difference between finding the surface area of a triangular prism and the surface area of a square pyramid.

2. Why do you need to add the different areas of the bases and faces together to find the surface area of a triangular prism?

Draw a net of the shoe box or rectangular prism and find the area of each face.

Then add the areas to find the surface area of the box.

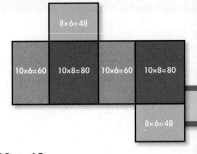

8×6=48

10×6=60 10×8=80 10×6=60 10×8=80

8×6=48

$SA = 60 + 80 + 60 + 80 + 48 + 48$

$SA = 376$ in²

Cornelius needs 376 square inches of paper to cover the box.

Use a formula to find the total surface area of the shoe box.

Notice how the opposite pairs of sides of the shoe box have the same area.

$SA = 2(\ell w) + 2(wh) + 2(\ell h)$

$SA = 2(80) + 2(48) + 2(60)$

$SA = 376$ in²

Cornelius needs 376 square inches of paper to cover the box.

Guided Practice*

MATHEMATICAL
PRACTICES

Do you know HOW?

1. The candle shown is shaped like a cube. Draw a net for the candle.

←2 in.→

   a What is true about all of the faces of a cube?

   b Find the surface area of the candle.

2. Use a formula to find the surface area of this rectangular prism.

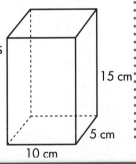

15 cm

5 cm

10 cm

Do you UNDERSTAND?

Ⓒ 3. **Model** Use your work in Exercise 1 to write a formula for the surface area of a cube. Let *s* equal the length of each side.

Ⓒ 4. **Construct Arguments** If the candle in Exercise 1 were cut in half vertically, would each piece have a surface area that is equal to half of the original surface area? Explain.

5. When finding the surface area of a square pyramid, why do you multiply the area of a triangular face by 4?

Independent Practice

6. What is the shape of the base of a square pyramid? Draw the net of this figure.

7. Use a formula to find the surface area of the rectanglular prism shown.

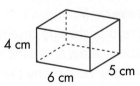

4 cm

6 cm   5 cm

8. If each side of the base of the square pyramid is 8 inches and the height of each triangular face is 10 inches, what is the surface area of the square pyramid?

For **9** through **11**, find the surface area of each figure.

9.

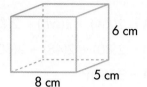

6 cm

8 cm   5 cm

10.

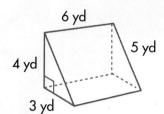

6 yd

5 yd

4 yd

3 yd

11.

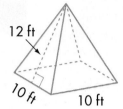

12 ft

10 ft   10 ft

MATHEMATICAL PRACTICES

12. Persevere Mr. and Mrs. Hernandez have a pool in their backyard with a length of 32 feet and a width of 16 feet. They want to purchase a cover for the pool. If the cover needs to be 2 feet longer and 2 feet wider than the pool, what will be the perimeter of the cover?

13. What is the area of Mr. and Mrs. Hernandez's pool cover?

14. Fred listened to the weather report in the afternoon. The meteorologist said that the temperature had risen 25°F from the early morning temperature of 12°F. What was the afternoon temperature?

A 47°F   **B** 37°F   **C** 27°F   **D** 12°F

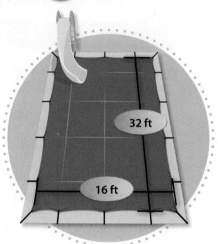

32 ft

16 ft

15. Mia wants to use brown paper to cover a ballot box for the student council election. The box is 18 inches long, 15 inches wide, and 12 inches tall. How many square inches of paper will Mia need?

The table shows the dimensions of three colors of tiles. Use the table for **16** through **19**.

16. Fill in the area of each color tile.

17. Persevere Miriam wants to tile the surface of a rectangular storage case that is 24 inches long, 16 inches wide, and 8 inches tall. If she uses all green tiles, how many tiles will she need?

Color	Tile Size	Area
Black	4 in. × 4 in.	
Red	2 in. × 2 in.	
Green	8 in. × 8 in.	

18. If Miriam uses all black tiles, how many tiles will she need?

19. Reason How many red tiles together have the same total area as 6 green tiles together?

A 24   **B** 96   **C** 16   **D** 32

Algebra Connections

Is It a Function?

A function is a special relationship in which there is only one *y*-value for each *x*-value.

Tell whether each set of ordered pairs is a function.

1.

x	−4	−2	0	3
y	4	6	8	11

2.

x	−1	0	−1	0
y	2	3	−2	−3

3.

x	2	2	2	2
y	−1	1	−4	4

Example:

Think *x*-values −2, −1, and 2 only have one *y*-value.

Function

x	−2	−1	2
y	0	1	4

The *x*-value −2 has more than one *y*-value.

Not a function

x	−2	−1	−2
y	−4	−2	4

4.

x	−3	−2	2	4
y	−2	1	13	19

. . . .

For **5** and **6**, copy and complete the tables to solve the problems.

5. Jess is going bowling with his friends. He is making a table showing how much they will pay for the games. Find the missing values in the table and write a rule that fits the pattern.

6. Janice is planning a trip. She is making a table to show how many miles she can travel. Complete the table and write a rule that fits the pattern.

Data

Games	Price
1	$0.75
2	
3	$2.25
4	
5	$3.75
6	

Data

Gallons of Gas	Miles
1	28
4	112
5.5	154
6.5	
7	
8.5	
10	

. . . .

7. The drama club is going to see a play. If the club has $110 for the trip and tickets cost $13.50 each, how many members can attend the play? Make a function table to find the group cost for 1 to 10 members.

Lesson
18-3

Ⓒ
Common
Core

6.G.2 Find the volume of a right rectangular prism with fractional edge lengths by packing it with unit cubes of the appropriate unit fraction edge lengths, and show that the volume is the same as would be found by multiplying the edge lengths of the prism. Apply the formulas $V = \ell wh$ and $V = bh$ to find volumes...in the context of solving real-world and mathematical problems.

Volume of Rectangular Prisms

How can you determine the volume of a rectangular prism?

Volume is <u>the number of cubic units needed to fill a solid figure</u>. To find the volume (V) of a rectangular prism, multiply the area of the base (B) by the height (h) of the figure. Use the formula $V = B \times h$.

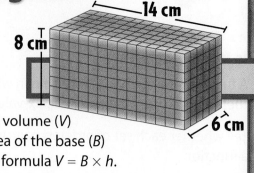

14 cm

8 cm

6 cm

Guided Practice*

Ⓒ MATHEMATICAL
PRACTICES

Do you know HOW?

Find the volume of each rectangular prism.

1. 3 in.
3 in.   3 in.

2. 3 m
6 m   2 m

3. 7 cm
2 cm   1 cm

4. 5 ft
3 ft   2 ft

Do you UNDERSTAND?

Ⓒ 5. **Communicate** If you know the area of the base and the volume of a rectangular prism, how can you find the height?

Ⓒ 6. **Reason** If you turned the rectangular prism from the example above on one side, how would your formula change? Would the volume change?

6 cm

14 cm

8 cm

Independent Practice

Leveled Practice In **7** through **10**, find the volume of each rectangular prism.

7. 4 in.
3 in.   2 in.

$V = B \times h$
$V = 6 \text{ in}^2 \times$ ▢
$V =$ ▢

8. 3 m
7 m   2 m

$V = B \times h$

9. 6 ft
3 ft   2 ft

10. 7 cm
7 cm   7 cm

*For another example, see Set C on page 473.

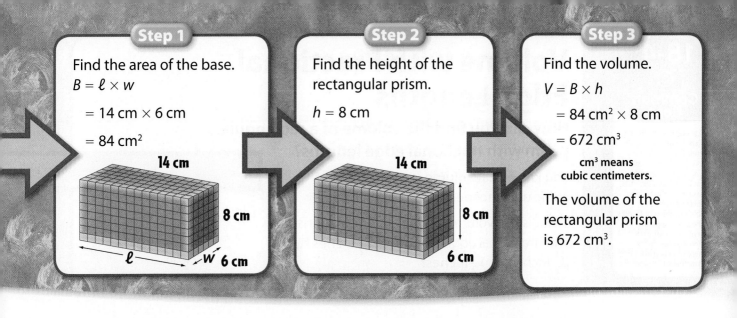

Step 1

Find the area of the base.
$B = \ell \times w$

$= 14 \text{ cm} \times 6 \text{ cm}$

$= 84 \text{ cm}^2$

14 cm

8 cm

ℓ — w 6 cm

Step 2

Find the height of the rectangular prism.

$h = 8 \text{ cm}$

14 cm

8 cm

6 cm

Step 3

Find the volume.
$V = B \times h$

$= 84 \text{ cm}^2 \times 8 \text{ cm}$

$= 672 \text{ cm}^3$

cm³ means cubic centimeters.

The volume of the rectangular prism is 672 cm³.

In **11** through **13**, find the missing value for each rectangular prism.

11. Volume: 56 in³
Length: 4 in.
Width: 7 in.
Height: ▓

12. Volume: 144 ft³
Length: ▓
Width: 9 ft
Height: 4 ft

13. Volume: 240 ft³
Length: 8 ft
Width: ▓
Height: 6 ft

Problem Solving

 MATHEMATICAL PRACTICES

ⓒ **14. Be Precise** How many cubic inches are in one cubic foot?

15. Would 150 cm³ of sand fit inside a 4 cm × 3 cm × 10 cm rectangular prism?

ⓒ **16. Writing to Explain** Why can the formula for the volume of a rectangular prism also be written as $V = \ell \times w \times h$?

ⓒ **17. Think About the Structure** Which of these equations gives the volume of a cube?

A $V = 16 \times 4$ **C** $V = 9 \times 4$

B $V = 8 \times 2$ **D** $V = 12 \times 6$

18. Suppose the blocks of ice used to build the rooms of the Ice Hotel are 4 ft × 4 ft × 5 ft. What is the volume of a block of ice?

ⓒ **19. Construct Arguments** Consider a rectangular prism that measures 3 cm × 2 cm × 6 cm.

a Will the actual volume of the rectangular prism change if you measure the sides in inches rather than centimeters? Explain.

b Does the numerical volume change if you measure the sides in inches? Explain.

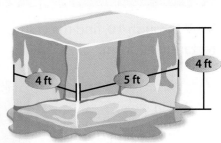
4 ft 5 ft 4 ft

6.G.2 Find the volume of a right rectangular prism with fractional edge lengths by packing it with unit cubes of the appropriate unit fraction edge lengths, and show that the volume is the same as would be found by multiplying the edge lengths of the prism. Apply the formulas $V = \ell wh$ and $V = bh$ to find volumes...in the context of solving real-world and mathematical problems.

Volume with Fractional Edge Lengths

How can you find the volume of a rectangular prism with fractional edge lengths?

You know that volume is the number of cubic units needed to fill a solid figure.

What is the volume of this rectangular prism with fractional edge lengths of $2\frac{1}{2}$ inches by $2\frac{1}{2}$ inches by $1\frac{1}{2}$ inches?

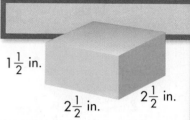

$1\frac{1}{2}$ in.

$2\frac{1}{2}$ in.

$2\frac{1}{2}$ in.

Guided Practice*

MATHEMATICAL
PRACTICES

Do you know HOW?

For **1** and **2**, tell how many of each size cube can fill a 1-inch cube.

1. Edge $= \frac{1}{3}$ inch   **2.** Edge $= \frac{1}{4}$ inch

For **3** and **4**, find the volume of each rectangular prism.

3.

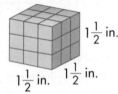

$1\frac{1}{2}$ in.

$1\frac{1}{2}$ in. $1\frac{1}{2}$ in.

4.

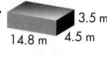

3.5 m

14.8 m   4.5 m

Do you UNDERSTAND?

ⓒ **5. Writing to Explain** How is finding the volume of a rectangular prism with fractional edge lengths similar to finding the volume of a rectangular prism with whole-number edge lengths?

ⓒ **6. Model** Show how to use the formula $V = B \times h$ to find the volume of a rectangular prism with a base that measures $2\frac{1}{2}$ in. by $2\frac{1}{2}$ in. and with a height of $1\frac{1}{2}$ in.

Independent Practice

For **7** through **10**, find the volume of each rectangular prism.

7.

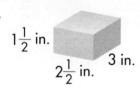

$1\frac{1}{2}$ in.

3 in.

$2\frac{1}{2}$ in.

8.

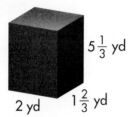

$5\frac{1}{3}$ yd

2 yd $1\frac{2}{3}$ yd

9.

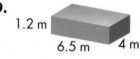

1.2 m

6.5 m   4 m

10.

2.4 m

0.7 m   0.9 m

Look at a cube with an edge length of $\frac{1}{2}$-inch. Eight of these cubes will fill a cube with an edge length of 1 inch.

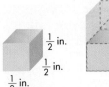

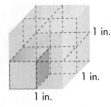

$\frac{1}{2}$ in.
$\frac{1}{2}$ in.
$\frac{1}{2}$ in.
1 in.
1 in.
1 in.

The volume of a cube with edge length 1 inch = 1 in³, so the volume of the smaller cube is 1 in³ ÷ 8 = $\frac{1}{8}$ in³.

Find the number of $\frac{1}{2}$-inch cubes that will fill the rectangular prism.

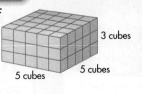

3 cubes
5 cubes
5 cubes

The prism can be filled with 5 × 5 × 3 = 75 cubes. The volume of the rectangular prism is 75 cubes × $\frac{1}{8}$ in³ per cube = $9\frac{3}{8}$ in³.

You can also use the formula for finding the volume of a rectangular prism:

$$V = \ell \times w \times h = 2\frac{1}{2} \times 2\frac{1}{2} \times 1\frac{1}{2} = 9\frac{3}{8} \text{ in}^3.$$

For **11** through **13**, find the missing value for each rectangular prism.

11. Volume: $74\frac{3}{8}$ in³
Base: $8\frac{3}{4}$ in²
Height:

12. Volume: 84 yd³
Length:
Width: $2\frac{2}{3}$ yd
Height: $4\frac{2}{3}$ yd

13. Volume: 357.075 m³
Length: 11.5 m
Width:
Height: 4.5 m

Problem Solving

MATHEMATICAL
PRACTICES

For **14** and **15**, use the information in the table.

14. Reasonableness Which box can hold cubes that have $\frac{1}{2}$-inch edges with no gaps between the cubes? Explain how you decided.

	Length	Width	Height
Box A	$7\frac{1}{2}$ in.	2 in.	$11\frac{1}{2}$ in.
Box B	9 in.	$2\frac{1}{4}$ in.	$8\frac{1}{2}$ in.

15. Persevere How much greater is the volume of the box with the greater volume than the volume of the box with the lesser volume?

16. A gold bar is similar in shape to a rectangular prism. A standard mint bar is approximately 7 in. × $3\frac{5}{8}$ in. × $1\frac{3}{4}$ in. What is the volume of the gold bar?

For **17** and **18**, use the drawing of the rectangular prism at the right.

17. How many $\frac{1}{4}$-inch cubes will fill the prism?

18. What is the volume of the prism?

A $7\frac{7}{8}$ in³

C 14 in³

B $12\frac{1}{2}$ in³

D $17\frac{1}{2}$ in³

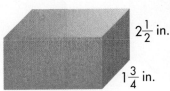

$2\frac{1}{2}$ in.
$1\frac{3}{4}$ in.
4 in.

Lesson
18-5

©
Common Core

6.G.4 Represent three-dimensional figures using nets made up of rectangles and triangles, and use the nets to find the surface area of these figures. Apply these techniques in the context of solving real-world and mathematical problems.

Problem Solving

Use Objects and Reasoning

Figure A has a volume of 2 cubic centimeters (cm³). It has a surface area of 10 square centimeters (cm²).

Find the volume and surface area of Figure B.

Then use cubes to make a figure with a volume of 4 cm³ and a surface area of 18 cm².

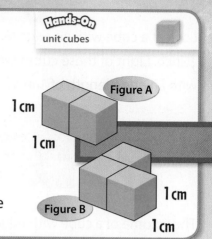

Hands-On
unit cubes

Figure A

1 cm

1 cm

Figure B

1 cm

1 cm

Guided Practice*

© **MATHEMATICAL PRACTICES**

Do you know HOW?

1.

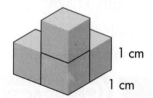

1 cm

1 cm

a What is the volume of this solid?

b What is the surface area of this solid?

Do you UNDERSTAND?

2. How can using cubes help you answer questions about volume and surface area?

© **3. Write a Problem** Arrange 5 cubes, each measuring 1 centimeter on each edge, to form a solid figure. Draw the solid. Write questions about the volume and surface area for a partner to answer. Include the answer.

Independent Practice

© **MATHEMATICAL PRACTICES**

Find the volume and surface area of each solid.

4.

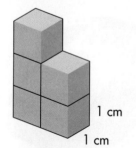

1 cm

1 cm

1 cm

5.

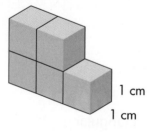

1 cm

1 cm

6.

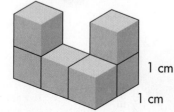

1 cm

1 cm

7.

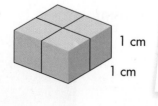

1 cm

1 cm

Applying Math Practices

• What am I asked to find?
• What else can I try?
• How are quantities related?
• How can I explain my work?
• How can I use math to model the problem?
• Can I use tools to help?
• Is my work precise?
• Why does this work?
• How can I generalize?

Count the cubes to find the volume.

I see 3 cubes. None are hidden.

The volume is 3 cm³.

Count all the outside faces of the cubes in the figure to find the surface area.

I see 7 faces, and 7 more faces on the bottom and the back of the figure are hidden.

7 faces are hidden

The surface area is 14 cm².

Use centimeter cubes to make a figure with 4 cubes that has 18 outside faces.

Think I counted the number of cubes to find the volume and the outside faces to find the surface area.

It has a volume of 4 cm³ and a surface area of 18 cm².

For **8** through **11**, use centimeter cubes to make a shape with the given volume and surface area. Draw your answers.

8. Matt used centimeter cubes to make a solid that had a volume of 5 cubic centimeters and a surface area of 22 square centimeters. What might his solid have looked like?

9. April and Julie each made differently shaped solids with a volume of 4 cubic centimeters and a surface area of 18 square centimeters or less. What might their 2 solids have looked like?

10. Sebastian made a solid shape with a volume of 6 cubic centimeters and a surface area greater than 21 square centimeters. What might his solid have looked like?

11. Alberto made a solid shape with a volume of 8 cubic centimeters and a surface area of 28 square centimeters. What might his solid have looked like?

Use the solid shape to the right for **12** and **13**. Draw your answers.

© **12. Use Tools** Use 7 centimeter cube blocks to make a different shape with the same surface area.

© **13. Use Tools** Use centimeter cube blocks to make a shape that has the same volume as the illustration but a smaller surface area.

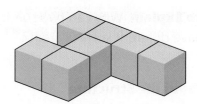

eTools
www.pearsonsuccessnet.com

14. You can use a formula to find the surface area of a tower of centimeter cube blocks.

   a Using your blocks, make a stack x blocks tall. Fill in the table with the surface area of your tower.

Blocks, x	2	3	5	7	10
Surface area, y					

   b Find a pattern and make a conjecture. Look at your table. What pattern do you see? Write an equation for the pattern.

   c Test your conjecture. Substitute the value 6 for x in the formula. What is the value of y? Build a tower 6 blocks tall. Count the faces to determine the surface area. Is your conjecture correct?

© 15. **Reason** How does the sum of the volume of 4 individual cubes compare to the volume of a stack of 4 cubes?

For **16** and **17**, use centimeter cube blocks to help draw your pictures.

© 16. **Use Tools** Draw a cube that has twice the length, width, and height of the 1 cm cube. What is the volume and surface area of the new solid?

© 17. **Use Tools** Draw a cube that has triple the length, width, and height of the 1 cm cube. What is the volume and surface area of the new solid?

volume = 1 cubic centimeter
surface area = 6 square centimeters

© 18. **Writing to Explain** Why can two solids with the same volume have different surface areas?

© **Think About the Structure**

19. Which expression shows how to find the total surface area of 4 individual 1 cm blocks? The blocks are not touching each other.

   A 4(4)

   B 4(1) + 2

   C 4(4) + 2

   D 4 × (4 + 2)

20. How can you find the surface area of the figure on the right?

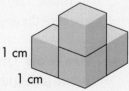

1 cm
1 cm

   A Count the number of faces.

   B Count the number of cubes.

   C Count the number of cubes and subtract by 2.

   D Count the number of cubes and multiply by 6.

Classify each figure. Identify whether or not the figure is a polyhedron.

1.

2.

3.

4.

For **5** through **7**, complete the following table.

	Number of Faces	Number of Vertices	Number of Edges
5.	▢	▢	▢
6.	▢	▢	▢
7.	▢	▢	▢

For **8** through **10**, find the volume of each figure.

8. 6 cm, 6 cm, 6 cm

9. 2 ft, 2 ft, 8 ft

10. 8 ft, $4\frac{1}{2}$ ft, 2 ft

Error Search Determine if the volume is correct. If the volume is incorrect, write it correctly and explain the error.

11.
length: 3 cm
width: 3 cm
height: 3 cm
volume: 9 cm³

12.
length: 12 in.
width: 3 in.
height: 15 in.
volume: 540 in³

13.
length: 10.5 cm
width: 10.5 cm
height: 10.5 cm
volume: 1,000 cm³

14.
length: $3\frac{1}{2}$ in.
width: 2 in.
height: $5\frac{1}{2}$ in.
volume: $38\frac{1}{2}$ in³

Number Sense

Write whether each statement is true or false. Explain your answer.

15. A cube and a rectangular prism with half the width, twice the length, and the same height as the cube will have equal volumes.

16. The volume of an 8 cm cube will be less than 100 cm³.

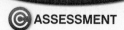

1. Which of the following can be used to find the volume of a rectangular prism whose base area is 15 square inches and height is 4 inches? (18-3)

   A $V = 15 + 4$

   B $V = 15 \times 4 \times 4$

   C $V = 15 \times 4$

   D $V = \pi \times 15 \times 4$

2. What is the surface area of the triangular prism shown? (18-2)

   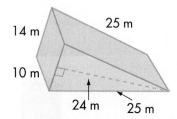

   A 558 m²

   B 976 m²

   C 1,680 m²

   D 1,750 m²

3. A rectangular prism has a volume of 400 cubic feet. The length and width of the base are 5 feet and 10 feet. Which equation can be used to find h, the height of the prism, in feet? (18-3)

   A $400 = 50h$

   B $400 = 30h$

   C $400 = 25h$

   D $400 = 15h$

4. A speaker is shown below. How many faces does it have? (18-1)

   A 4

   B 6

   C 8

   D 12

5. Which shows how to find the volume of this rectangular prism by filling it with $\frac{1}{2}$-inch cubes? (18-4)

   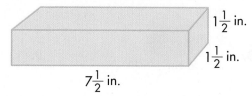

   $1\frac{1}{2}$ in.

   $1\frac{1}{2}$ in.

   $7\frac{1}{2}$ in.

   A $15 \times 3 \times 3 = 135; \ 135 \times \frac{1}{2} = 67\frac{1}{2}$ in³

   B $15 \times 3 \times 3 = 135; \ 135 \times \frac{1}{8} = 16\frac{7}{8}$ in³

   C $7\frac{1}{2} + 1\frac{1}{2} + 1\frac{1}{2} = 10\frac{1}{2}; \ 10\frac{1}{2} \times \frac{1}{2} = 5\frac{1}{4}$ in³

   D $22\frac{1}{2} \times 4\frac{1}{2} \times 4\frac{1}{2} = 455\frac{5}{8}; \ 455\frac{5}{8} \times \frac{1}{8}$
   $= 56\frac{7}{8}$ in³

6. What is the volume of the play oven shown? (18-3)

   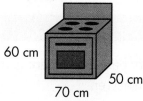

   60 cm

   50 cm

   70 cm

   A 3,500 cm³

   B 4,200 cm³

   C 7,200 cm³

   D 210,000 cm³

7. Find the missing measure of the height of the rectangular prism. (18-4)

Volume: 383.04 m³
Length: 10.5 m
Width: 7.6 m
Height:

A 3.9 m

B 4.8 m

C 5.1 m

D 5.8 m

8. A rectangular box has a length equal to 12 inches, a width equal to 4 inches, and a height equal to 2 inches. Which of the following expressions can be used to find the surface area of the box? (18-2)

A 2(48) + 2(8) + 2(24)

B 2(48) × 2(8) × 2(24)

C 48 + 8 + 24

D 48 × 8 × 24

9. Some shipping boxes are stacked as shown. If the face of each box is a square and each box represents one cubic unit, what is the surface area of the figure formed by the shipping boxes? (18-5)

A 14 square units

B 17 square units

C 18 square units

D 24 square units

10. What is the volume of this rectangular prism? (18-4)

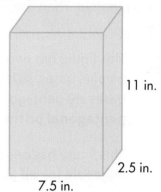

11 in.

2.5 in.

7.5 in.

A 165 in³

B 192.5 in³

C 206.25 in³

D 215.75 in³

11. Which of the following does NOT represent a polyhedron? (18-1)

A

B

C

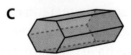

D

12. Which of the following best describes the shape of a baseball? (18-1)

A cylinder

B cone

C prism

D sphere

Set A, pages 454–457

To classify a polyhedron, first determine whether it is a prism or a pyramid. Then use the shape of its base to name it.

This figure has two congruent parallel bases, so it is a prism. The bases are pentagons, so it is a **pentagonal prism**.

This figure has one base, and the edges are joined at a point outside the base, so it is a pyramid. The base is a square and the faces are triangles, so it is a **square pyramid**.

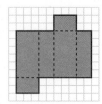

A **net** shows what a polyhedron would look like "unfolded," with all surfaces on the plane. This is a net of a rectangular prism.

Remember that not all solids are polyhedrons. Cylinders, spheres, and cones have curved surfaces and are not polyhedrons.

Identify each solid figure in **1** through **3**, and state whether the solid figure is a polyhedron.

1.   2.   3.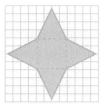

4. What figure can be made from this net?

Set B, pages 458–460

To find the total surface area (*SA*) of a polyhedron, add the areas of each face. Find the *SA* of the rectangular prism below.

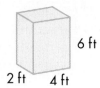

6 ft
2 ft   4 ft

All faces are rectangles. The opposite faces of a rectangular prism have the same area. The prism has a length (ℓ) of 4 feet, a width (*w*) of 2 feet, and a height (*h*) of 6 feet.

The formula for the area of a rectangle is $\ell \times w$.

$$SA = 2(\ell \times w) + 2(w \times h) + 2(\ell \times h)$$
$$= 2(4 \times 2) + 2(2 \times 6) + 2(4 \times 6)$$
$$= 2(8) + 2(12) + 2(24)$$
$$= 16 + 24 + 48$$
$$= 88 \text{ ft}^2$$

The surface area of the rectangular prism is 88 ft².

Remember that surface area is always measured in square units, such as in², ft², and m².

Find the surface area of each solid.

1. 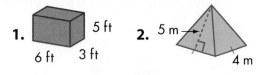 5 ft
6 ft   3 ft

2. 5 m
4 m

3. Use the net to find the surface area of the triangular prism.

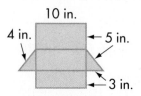
10 in.
4 in.   5 in.
3 in.

To find the volume (*V*) of a rectangular prism, multiply the area of the base (*B*) by the height (*h*) of the figure:

Volume (*V*) = area of base × height = $B \times h$

Since the area of the base of a rectangular prism is the length (*ℓ*) multiplied by the width (*w*) you also can use the formula:

Volume (*V*) = length × width × height = $\ell \times w \times h$

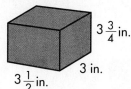

Volume of a rectangular prism:

$B = \ell \times w = 4 \text{ ft} \times 6 \text{ ft} = 24 \text{ ft}^2$

$V = 24 \text{ ft}^2 \times 2 \text{ ft} = 48 \text{ ft}^3$

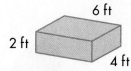

Volume of a rectangular prism with fractional edge lengths:

$V = \ell \times w \times h$

$= 3\frac{1}{2} \text{ in.} \times 3 \text{ in.} \times 3\frac{3}{4} \text{ in.}$

$= 39\frac{3}{8} \text{ in}^3$

Remember that volume is always measured in cubic units, such as in^3, ft^3, and m^3.

Find the volume of each solid.

1.

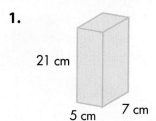

21 cm 5 cm 7 cm

2.

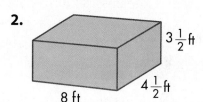

$3\frac{1}{2}$ ft $4\frac{1}{2}$ ft 8 ft

3.

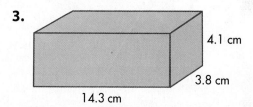

4.1 cm 3.8 cm 14.3 cm

You can use objects and reasoning to find patterns and solve problems.

The blocks in the figure are 1-centimeter cubes. Find the volume and surface area of the figure.

Shared surface
1 cm
1 cm 1 cm

Volume

1 cube is 1 cubic centimeter

2 cubes are 2 cubic centimeters

Surface Area

Area of 1 face: 1 square centimeter

Faces on 1 cube: 6

Shared faces on 2 cubes together: 2

Number of faces you can see: 10

Area of 2 cubes together: 10 square centimeters

Remember that figures made up of the same number of one-unit cubes (same volume) may have different surface areas. When finding the surface area of figures made of the same kind of cubes, do not count surfaces that face each other.

Find the volume and surface area of each figure below. The figures are made of 1-centimeter cubes.

1.

2.

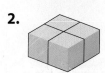

Data and Graphs

1

The Guadalupe Peak is the tallest peak in Texas. How does the height of this peak compare to others in Texas? You will find out in Lesson 19-3

2

What is the median speed of pitches thrown in a middle school baseball game? You will find out in Lesson 19-6.

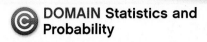
3 On warm days, many people love to go swimming. What is the most common age of swimmers at a public pool? You will find out in Lesson 19-5.

Review What You Know!

Vocabulary

Choose the best terms from the box.

- interval
- data
- percent
- ratio

1. __?__ are the values represented by graphs.

2. One-quarter can also be named as 25 __?__.

3. A(n) ____ is the distance between values along the side or bottom of a graph.

Naming Graphs

Name the types of graphs below.

4.
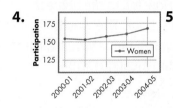

5.
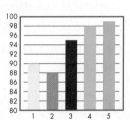

Summarizing Data

A data set includes the numbers 6, 12, 2, 6, and 3.

6. What is the least value?

7. What is the greatest value?

8. What number is repeated?

Displaying Data

©**9. Writing to Explain** How can you display the data set 4, 6, 3, 7, 9, 12, 3, 3, 7, 9 using a line plot? Explain.

Common Core

6.SP.1 Recognize a statistical question as one that anticipates variability in the data related to the question and accounts for it in the answers.... Also **6.SP.5.b**

Statistical Questions

What is a statistical question?

Mr. Borden wants to ask his class a question that will give several different answers. Which question could he ask?

- *What is the area of one sheet of notebook paper?*

- *How many sheets of paper do you use each week?*

Another Example **How do you interpret statistical questions?**

You can display variations in data in different ways. A dot plot is like a line plot, except that each data value is shown as a dot above a number line.

The dot plot shows the responses to another statistical question–*How far, to the nearest mile, do you live from school?* The way the data appears in the graph helps you interpret the answers to the statistical question.

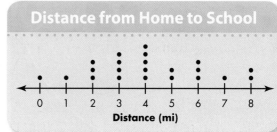

Distance from Home to School

Distance (mi)

Explain It

1. What information does the dot plot show?

Guided Practice*

MATHEMATICAL PRACTICES

Do you know HOW?

For **1** through **4**, tell whether or not each question is statistical.

1. How many siblings do students in your class have?

2. In which month is your birthday?

3. How many states are in the United States?

4. How tall are the students in Grade 6?

Do you UNDERSTAND?

5. **Writing to Explain** Write a statistical question that involves movies your classmates saw last month. Then describe how to display the data.

6. Look at the bar graph at the top of page 477. How many students use 30 or more sheets of paper each week?

Animated Glossary
www.pearsonsuccessnet.com

For another example, see Set A on page 504.

The question Mr. Borden should ask is, *How many sheets of paper do you use each week?*

This is a statistical question, or a question that anticipates there will be different answers in the data.

Mr. Borden can display the various answers in the data using a bar graph.

The bar graph shows the information collected by Mr. Borden.

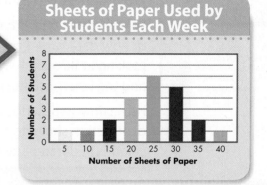

Independent Practice

For **7** through **10**, give a statistical question that could be used to gather data on each topic.

7. Numbers of pets classmates own

8. Heights of different plants growing

9. Weights of pumpkins for sale

10. Visitors' ages at a park on a Saturday

11. Kim asked her class, *How many other states have you visited*? She got the following responses: 0, 1, 2, 1, 2, 0, 3, 1, 0, 5, 5, 1, 3, 1, 0, 2, 4, 1, 3, 0. Make a dot plot to display the data.

12. The data below are the responses to *What is your favorite color*? Make a bar graph to display the information.

green	blue	blue	red	green
green	yellow	blue	green	red

Problem Solving

 MATHEMATICAL PRACTICES

Ⓒ **13. Use Tools** Tony asked his class, *To the nearest 10 minutes, how many minutes did you spend on homework last night?* How many students studied for 30 minutes or more?

A 5 students   **C** 11 students

B 8 students   **D** 13 students

Time Spent on Homework

(dot plot with axis labeled 0, 10, 20, 30, 40, 50, 60, Time (min))

Ⓒ **14. Reason** Explain why the question, *What is our school mascot?* is not a statistical question, and change the question to make it statistical.

Ⓒ **15. Critique Reasoning** Jo says *How do you get to school each morning?* is not a statistical question because each student who answers it can give only one answer. Do you agree with Jo? Explain.

Common
Core

6.SP.2 Understand that
a set of data collected to
answer a statistical question
has a distribution which can
be described by its center,
spread, and overall shape.

Looking at Data Sets

How can you describe a data distribution?

We can describe a data distribution, or how data values are arranged, by looking at its overall shape, its center, and the least and greatest values.

How can you describe this data distribution showing the number of calories in different fast-food burgers?

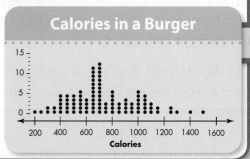

Calories in a Burger

Guided Practice*

MATHEMATICAL
PRACTICES

Do you know HOW?

The dot plot shows the duration in minutes of an eruption of the Old Faithful geyser in Yellowstone National Park.

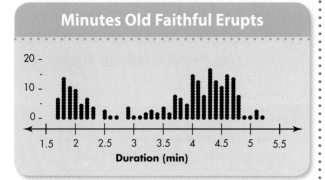

Minutes Old Faithful Erupts

1. Where are there groupings of data?

Do you UNDERSTAND?

© 2. **Construct Arguments** Using the graph of the eruption duration of the Old Faithful geyser, where do you think the center of the data is? Explain how you found your answer.

© 3. **Writing to Explain** Is there any data point on the eruption duration dot plot that is an outlier? Explain.

4. Is the shape of the data symmetric or spread to one side?

5. What is the least value of the data? What is the greatest value of the data?

Independent Practice

For **6** through **8** use the line plot at the right.

6. What is the least temperature? Greatest temperature?

7. About where is the center of the data?

8. Are the any outliers? How do you know?

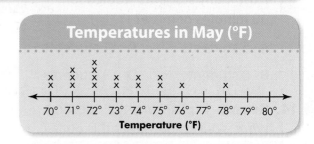

Temperatures in May (°F)

DIGITAL

Animated Glossary
www.pearsonsuccessnet.com

*For another example, see Set B on page 504.

The data distribution can be described as–

- Spread out to the right
- Least value = 200
- Greatest value = 1,500
- Center is about 700.
- Overall shape is not symmetric.
- Grouped between 400 and 1,200.
- Some gaps in the data

A dot for a large, 2,000-calorie burger is added to the data.

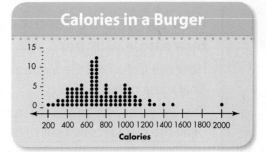

The differences in this data distribution can be described as–

- Spread out more to the right
- The greatest value, 2,000, is an <u>outlier</u>, or <u>an extreme value with few data points located near it</u>.

Problem Solving

MATHEMATICAL
PRACTICES

A number cube is tossed 50 times with the results shown in the table. Use the table at the right for **9** and **10**.

Result	Number of Times Tossed
1	11
2	12
3	7
4	4
5	8
6	8

© **9. Use Tools** Make a dot plot for the data and describe the shape of the data distribution.

© **10. Writing to Explain** Are the results what you would expect? Explain.

11. Shelley is making tomato soup. A 1-pint can of tomato juice costs $0.90. A 1-quart can of tomato juice costs $1.65. Which is the better buy for one quart of juice? How much money will she save?

12. What is the volume of the rectangular prism shown on the right?

A 9 cm³   **C** 16 cm³

B 15 cm³   **D** 20 cm³

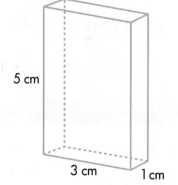

5 cm

3 cm   1 cm

© **13. Reason** How do you know that any value for y will be a solution to the inequality $y + 3.9 > y$?

© **14. Model** Write an inequality using subtraction and the variable x so that solutions to the inequality include $x = 3, 5, 7,$ and 9.

© **15. Critique Reasoning** Alberto studied the distribution of two sets of data. He found that both sets had the same greatest value and the same center. Alberto says that this does not mean the data distributions are the same. Is he correct? Explain.

Lesson
19-3

Common Core

6.SP.3 Recognize that a measure of center for a numerical data set summarizes all of its values with a single number, while a measure of variation describes how its values vary with a single number. Also **6.SP.5.c**

Mean

How can data be described by a single number?

How can Carla find the average final score of five bowlers?

The <u>mean</u>, or average, is <u>the sum of all the numbers in a set of data divided by the number of numbers in the set.</u>

9	10	FINAL SCORE
86 ⁷ ²	95 ⁶ ³ −	95
80 ⁴ ²	87 ⁷ ⁰ −	87
77 ⁵ ¹	84 ⁴ ³ −	84
74 ² ⁴	81 ⁵ ² −	81
75 ³ ³	83 ⁶ ² −	83

Guided Practice*

Do you know HOW?

In **1** through **7**, find the mean for each set of data.

1. 5, 4, 4, 9, 8

2. 19, 55, 34, 16

3. 101, 105, 103

4. 8, 2, 11, 6, 8

5. 85, 70, 84, 91, 88, 92

6. 205, 204, 398, 405, 894, 102

7. 28, 32, 36, 40, 42, 57, 58, 59

Do you UNDERSTAND?

8. Another team had 6 bowlers. Would the mean automatically decrease as the number of bowlers increases?

9. Reason In the example above, how could the mean be raised to 90?

10. Writing to Explain Dave said that the mean of 1, 2, 3, 4, and 5 is 8. How do you know this is incorrect without finding the mean?

Independent Practice

In **11** through **22**, find the mean for each set of data.

11. 2, 5, 4, 5

12. 5, 4, 6, 9, 11

13. 6, 17, 12, 11, 4, 6, 7

14. 89, 98, 101

15. 17, 30, 45, 46, 27

16. 13, 16, 19, 21, 26

17. 35, 45, 70

18. 40, 41, 54, 55, 66, 79, 43

19. 164, 198, 301

20. 7.6, 6.2, 6.0, 7.8, 7.4

21. 11, 8.3, 9.0, 3.7

22. 129; 8,002; 1,003; 866

Animated Glossary
www.pearsonsuccessnet.com

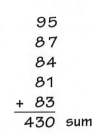

Add the final scores in the set of data.

$$
\begin{array}{r}
95 \\
87 \\
84 \\
81 \\
+\ 83 \\
\hline
430 \ \text{sum}
\end{array}
$$

Divide the <u>sum</u> by the <u>number of numbers in the set</u>.

$$430 \div 5 = 86$$

$$
\begin{array}{r}
86 \\
5\overline{)430} \\
-\ 40 \\
\hline
30 \\
-\ 30 \\
\hline
0
\end{array}
$$

The average, or mean, score for the 5 bowlers is 86.

Problem Solving

MATHEMATICAL
PRACTICES

Meredith recorded her score for each game of miniature golf she played. Use her scorecard for **23** through **25**.

23. What was Meredith's mean golf score?

24. If Meredith had scored a 50 for the eighth game, how much would her mean score change?

Miniature Golf Scores								
Game	1	2	3	4	5	6	7	8
Score	52	56	49	51	54	52	60	58

Ⓒ 25. Persevere In miniature golf, the lower the score is, the better the game. Meredith wants to find the mean golf score of her four best games. What is this mean score?

26. Which can be modeled by light beaming from a lighthouse?

    A Point   **C** Ray

    B Plane   **D** Segment

27. Scientists have recorded the lengths of different species of hammerhead sharks. The lengths that have been recorded are 20 ft, 14 ft, 11 ft, and 7 ft. What is the mean length of the hammerhead shark?

    A 12.5 ft   **C** 17 ft

    B 13 ft   **D** 52 ft

Ⓒ 29. Reason A data set consisting of 3 numbers has a mean of 24. If two of the numbers are 23 and 25, what is the third number?

28. Estimation What is the approximate mean height of the 7 tallest peaks in Texas listed below?

Peaks in Texas	Height in Feet
Guadalupe Peak	8,749
Bush Mountain	8,631
Shumard Peak	8,615
Bartlett Peak	8,508
Mount Livermore	8,378
Hunter Peak	8,368
El Capitan	8,085

© **Common Core**

6.SP.5.c Summarize numerical data sets in relation to their context, such as by giving quantitative measures of center (median and/or mean) and variability (interquartile range and/or mean absolute deviation), as well as describing any overall pattern and any striking deviations from the overall pattern with reference to the context in which the data were gathered.

Median, Mode, and Range

How can data be described by one number?

Trey listed, in order, the playing times for the best-selling CD of each music type.

How can he describe the data with one number?

CD Playing Times	
Minutes	**Music Type**
59	Popular
61	Country
63	Blues
63	Sound track
64	Gospel
67	Jazz
72	Classical

Guided Practice*

© **MATHEMATICAL PRACTICES**

Do you know HOW?

In **1** through **3**, identify the median, mode, and range for each set of data.

1. 5, 7, 5, 4, 6, 3, 5

2. 21, 21, 23, 32, 43

3. 13, 14, 14, 16, 17, 19

 Tip *For an even number of values, the median is the number halfway between the two middle values.*

Do you UNDERSTAND?

4. What operation is used to find the range?

© **5. Reason** In the example at the top, how would the median and mode change if the playing time for the Blues CD changed to 61 minutes?

6. What would the range of playing times be if the 72-minute CD were removed from the list?

Independent Practice

In **7** through **9**, use the table at the right.

7. What are the median, mode, and range for the data?

8. What would happen to the range if the temperature were 82°F on Monday?

9. If the data for Friday were removed from the table, what would the median, mode, and range be?

5-day Weather Forecast	
Day	**Temperature**
Monday	80°F
Tuesday	80°F
Wednesday	82°F
Thursday	84°F
Friday	78°F

DIGITAL Animated Glossary
www.pearsonsuccessnet.com

For another example, see Set C on page 505.

Find the median.

List the data from least to greatest.
59, 61, 63, **63**, 64, 67, 72

Identify the median, or the middle data value in an odd numbered, ordered set of data.

The median of the number of minutes of playing time is 63.

Find the mode.

59, 61, **63, 63**, 64, 67, 72

Identify the mode, or the data value that occurs most often in the data set.

The mode of the number of minutes of playing time is 63.

Find the range.

59, 61, 63, 63, 64, 67, **72**

Identify the range, or the difference between the greatest and least values.

72 − 59 = 13

The range of the number of minutes of playing time is 13.

Problem Solving

MATHEMATICAL PRACTICES

10. Ricardo kept a record of the 7 hottest days of the summer. Use the list below to find the median, mode, and range of the temperatures.

   98°F   102°F   100°F   99°F
   103°F   98°F   101°F

© 11. **Reasonableness** How can you tell the difference between the net for a triangular prism and the net for a triangular pyramid?

© 12. **Reason** For each statistical measure (mean, median, mode, and range) tell whether that number is always, sometimes, or never one of the numbers in the data set.

© 13. **Think About the Structure** One side of a rectangular garden is 13 feet and the other side is 3 feet. Which expression shows how to find the perimeter?

   A $(2 \times 13) + (2 \times 3)$ **C** $2 \times 13 \times 3$

   B 13×3 **D** $3 + 13$

For **14** through **17**, use the table.

14. What was the median number of visitors to the Statue of Liberty from May to September in 2005?

15. What is the range of the data?

16. How many months had over 500,000 visitors?

© 17. **Writing to Explain** Why do you suppose there had been many fewer visitors in September, than in July or August?

Visitors to the Statue of Liberty, 2005	
Month	**Visitors**
May	430,235
June	492,078
July	589,166
August	542,292
September	367,441

© Common Core

6.SP.5.a Summarize numerical data sets in relation to their context, such as by reporting the number of observations. Also 6.SP.4

Frequency Tables and Histograms

How can you make and use a frequency table?

Mr. Maxwell timed the cross country team in a 2-mile run. How can he represent the data? Make a frequency table <u>to show the number of times a data value or range of values occurs in the data set.</u>

Times	
16:45	17:14
14:25	14:02
18:40	16:52
16:03	15:18
15:12	17:49
17:35	23:10
19:15	17:55

Another Example **How can you make and use a histogram?**

A histogram is <u>a graph that uses bars to show the frequency of equal ranges or groups of data</u>. Use the frequency table above to make a histogram displaying the cross-country team times.

Step 1 Title your graph.

Step 2 Use the frequency of the data to choose the scale for the vertical axis.

Step 3 List the time intervals along the horizontal axis.

Step 4 Graph the data by drawing a bar for each interval.

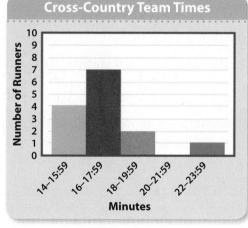

Most of the running times cluster between 14 and 18 minutes. There is a gap in the data between 20 and 22 minutes. The running time between 22 and 24 minutes may be considered an outlier, a data point that has a value much greater or much less than the other points in a data set.

Explain It

1. What does the tallest bar of the histogram represent?

2. How many running times were less than 18 minutes? How do you know?

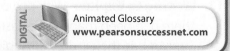

DIGITAL

Animated Glossary
www.pearsonsuccessnet.com

Step 1	Step 2	Step 3
Choose a range that contains all of the data and divide that range into equal intervals or groups.	Mark the data in the frequency table using a tally mark for each data value in the range.	Count the tally marks and record the frequency.

Running Times	Tally	Frequency
14:00–15:59	IIII	4
16:00–17:59	HHT II	7
18:00–19:59	II	2
20:00–21:59		0
22:00–23:59	I	1

Guided Practice*

MATHEMATICAL PRACTICES

Do you know HOW?

A toy-store owner asked the age of each child who came into his store one day. The ages of the children were 12, 8, 3, 5, 5, 10, 13, 11, 7, 6, 9, 6, 10, 12, 7, 6.

1. What is the range of ages?

2. Complete the frequency table below for the children shopping at the toy store.

Age Range	Tallies	Frequency
3–5		
6–8		
9–11		
12–14		

Do you UNDERSTAND?

3. Use the information from the frequency table in Exercise 2 to copy and complete the histogram.

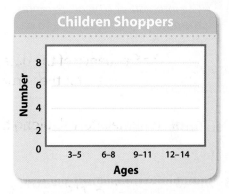

4. Construct Arguments If you wanted to know how many 8-year-olds shopped at the toy store, would this histogram help you? Explain.

Independent Practice

Use the information on the right for **5** and **6**.

5. How long do the largest group of students spend reading each vacation day?

    A 0–10 minutes   **C** 21–30 minutes

    B 11–20 minutes   **D** 31–40 minutes

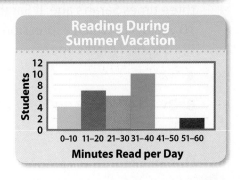

6. Which interval of minutes represents a gap in the data?

For another example, see Set D on page 505.

Walter tracked the average daily temperature for two weeks. When he finished, he made a frequency table of his data. Use the table for **7** and **8**.

Average Daily Temperatures		
Temp(°F)	Tally	Frequency
36–40	I	1
41–45	IIII	4
46–50	HHT II	7
51–55		0
56–60		0
61–65	II	2

7. What size of interval did Walter choose to group the daily temperatures?

8. Which interval of temperatures contains outliers? Explain.

Problem Solving

MATHEMATICAL
PRACTICES

Use the data at the right for **9** through **13**.

ⓒ **9.** **Model** Make a frequency table to represent the data about the ages of swimmers.

> **Tip** *Use intervals of 10 years to represent the data: 1–10, 11–20, and so on.*

Ages of Swimmers at Public Pool			
12	74	13	20
12	7	19	11
9	7	10	12
6	10	21	24

10. Use your frequency table to represent the data as a histogram.

ⓒ **11.** **Use Tools** Where do most of the data cluster?

    A 0–20   **C** 41–60

    B 21–40   **D** Above 61

ⓒ **12.** **Use Tools** Where are the gaps in the data?

ⓒ **13.** **Writing to Explain** Does the data have an outlier? Explain.

ⓒ **14.** **Persevere** Matt's age is 14 less than three times Sarah's age. If Sarah is 10 years old, which expression can be used to find Matt's age?

    A $14 - 3x$

    B $3x - 14$

    C $3(x - 14)$

    D $14x - 3$

ⓒ **15.** **Think About the Structure** Which type of graph would be best to display the percentages of sixth-grade students' favorite sports?

    A Line graph

    B Histogram

    C Bar graph

    D Circle graph

Algebra Connections

Comparing Line Graphs

Remember that a line graph often represents data collected over time. The double-line graph, below on the right, compares the rates of two boats. Use what you know about rates to describe the trends and compare their speeds.

Use the graph to answer **1** through **4**.

1. What is the unit rate of speed of the ski boat? At this rate, how far will it travel in 6 hours?

2. How much farther does the ski boat travel than the houseboat travels in 2 hours?

3. Let x = the number of times faster the ski boat travels than the houseboat travels. Solve $30 = 10x$.

4. Based on the trends shown, is it reasonable to predict that the ski boat will always travel farther than the houseboat in the same amount of time?

Example: What is the speed, as a unit rate, of the houseboat in the double-line graph below? If the houseboat continues at this speed, how far will it travel in 6 hours?

The speed is the distance that the houseboat travels in 1 hour. It travels 10 miles per hour (mph).

$$\frac{10 \text{ mi}}{1 \text{ hr}} = \frac{x}{6 \text{ hrs}}$$
$$\frac{10}{1} = \frac{x}{6}$$
$$x = 60 \text{ mi}$$

The houseboat can travel 60 miles in 6 hours.

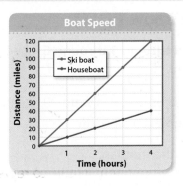

Use the data in the line graphs for **5** and **6**.

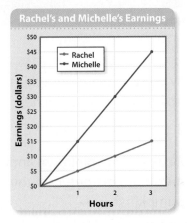

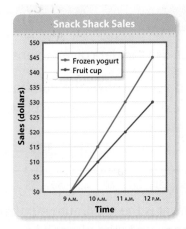

5. Rachel and Michelle work at a different rate per hour. How much will each of them earn in 5 hours? Describe the trend you see in their earnings.

6. The Snack Shack tracked the sales for frozen yogurt and fruit cups for each hour of the morning. Compare the sales of each snack. Predict how much the sales will be at 3 P.M.

Lesson
19-6

Common
Core

6.SP.4 Display numerical data in plots on a number line, including dot plots, histograms, and box plots.

Box Plots

How can you draw a box plot?

A box plot <u>shows a distribution of data values on a number line.</u> Quartiles are <u>values that divide a data set into four equal parts</u>.

Helen wants to make a box plot to show the lengths of the 15 fish she caught.

Length of Fish (in.)		
7	9	10
7	13	13
10	15	15
18	11	13
22	14	17

Guided Practice*

MATHEMATICAL
PRACTICES

Do you know HOW?

Use Structure In **1** through **6**, use the data below.

Sarah's scores on tests were 79, 75, 82, 90, 73, 82, 78, 85, and 78.

1. Find the median.

2. Find the first quartile.

3. Find the third quartile.

Do you UNDERSTAND?

4. **Generalize** What would be a good scale to use for a number line that will include Sarah's scores?

5. **Reason** What values are included inside the box of a box plot?

6. Draw a box plot that shows the distribution of Sarah's test scores.

Independent Practice

In **7** and **8**, use the data given to answer the related questions.

7. The box plot shows the number of home runs a major league player hit in 9 seasons.

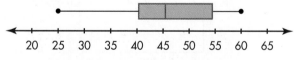

20 25 30 35 40 45 50 55 60 65

   a What is the maximum number of home runs the player hit for the seasons shown?

   b What is the minimum number of home runs the player hit?

   c What is the first quartile?

   d What is the third quartile?

8. Harry grew 12 giant pumpkins. Below are their diameters, in inches.

42, 38, 25, 47, 44, 43, 38, 39, 55, 52, 53, 55

   a What are the minimum and maximum diameters of the pumpkins?

   b What is the median?

   c What is the first quartile?

   d What is the third quartile?

Animated Glossary
www.pearsonsuccessnet.com

DIGITAL

For another example, see Set E on page 506.

- Find the median, minimum, and maximum values.

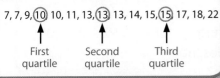

7, 7, 9, 10, 10, 11, 13, 13, 13, 14, 15, 15, 17, 18, 22

↑ minimum   ↑ median   ↑ maximum

- Find the median for each half.

7, 7, 9, 10, 10, 11, 13, 13, 13, 14, 15, 15, 17, 18, 22

↑ First quartile   ↑ Second quartile   ↑ Third quartile

- Draw the box plot. Show a number line with an appropriate scale, a box between the first and third quartiles, and a vertical segment that shows the median.
- Draw segments that extend from the box to the minimum and to the maximum values.

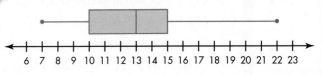

For **9** and **10**, make a box plot using the data provided.

9. The sprint times in seconds of students who tried out for the track team:

44, 40, 40, 42, 49, 43, 41, 47, 54, 48, 42, 52, 48

10. Test scores students earned on their science tests:

73, 78, 66, 61, 85, 90, 99, 76, 64, 70, 72, 72, 93, 81

Problem Solving

MATHEMATICAL PRACTICES

11. Which box plot shows the data in the following set?

12, 11, 9, 18, 10, 11, 7, 16, 14, 11, 6

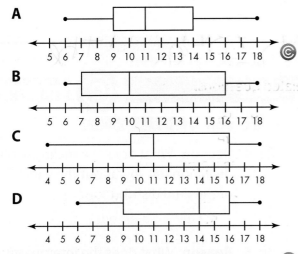

12. The temperature forecast for Topeka for the next 8 days showed the following daily highs in °F: 29, 31, 24, 26, 29, 35, 27, 32. Use a box plot to find between what two temperatures the first quartile falls.

© **13. Persevere** Coach Henderson clocked the speed in miles per hour of pitches thrown during the first inning of a middle school game:

45.3, 47, 48.1, 51.3, 55.8, 61.1, 48.5, 60.7, 49

a Draw a box plot of the pitch speeds.

b Identify the median and the first and third quartiles.

© **14. Reason** The price, per share of a stock, over 9 days, rounded to the nearest dollar, was as follows:

$16, $17, $16, $16, $18, $18, $21, $22, $19

Use a box plot. How many dollars greater per share was the third quartile than the first quartile?

© **15. Generalize** Alana made the box plot below to represent classroom attendance last month. Without seeing the values, what generalization can you make about whether attendance was mostly high or low last month? Explain.

© Common Core

6.SP.5.c Summarize numerical data sets in relation to their context, such as by giving quantitative measures of center (median and/or mean) and variability (interquartile range and/or mean absolute deviation), as well as describing any overall pattern and any striking deviations from the overall pattern with reference to the context in which the data were gathered. Also 6.SP.3

Measures of Variability

How can variability of data be described with one number?

The center of the data for Ann's math quiz scores can be described using a single number.

Median = 88 Mean = 86

Variability describes the spread and clustering of data in a set. How can a single number describe how much Ann's scores vary from the mean?

Ann's Math Quiz Scores (%)	
82	99
76	73
92	90
88	88

Another Example **How can you describe variability based on a median?**

Another measure of variability is the interquartile range (IQR). This is the difference between the third quartile and the first quartile. Since half of the data values lie in this interval, it is easy to see the IQR using a box plot.

The dot plot shows Ann's quiz scores for science. The interquartile range is $82 - 79 = 3$.

Science Quiz Scores (%)

So, half of Ann's science quiz scores were within an interval of 3 points.

Guided Practice*

© **MATHEMATICAL PRACTICES**

Do you know HOW?

Use the following data set for these questions: 4, 5, 5, 6, 7, 8, 8, 10, 10

1. Find the sum of the absolute deviations from the mean.

2. Find the mean absolute deviation.

3. Find the interquartile range.

Do you UNDERSTAND?

© 4. **Reason** What does the mean absolute deviation tell you about the variability of the data distribution?

© 5. **Reason** What does the interquartile range tell you about the variability of the data distribution?

Animated Glossary
www.pearsonsuccessnet.com

*For another example, see Set E on page 506.

Absolute deviation is <u>the distance between each data value and the mean</u>. You can find the absolute deviation from the mean by computing the absolute value of the difference between these numbers.

Score	Absolute Deviation
73	$\lvert 86 - 73 \rvert = 13$
76	$\lvert 86 - 76 \rvert = 10$
82	$\lvert 86 - 82 \rvert = 4$
88	$\lvert 88 - 86 \rvert = 2$
88	$\lvert 88 - 86 \rvert = 2$
90	$\lvert 90 - 86 \rvert = 4$
92	$\lvert 92 - 86 \rvert = 6$
99	$\lvert 99 - 86 \rvert = 13$

Find the mean absolute deviation, <u>the mean of the absolute deviations of a set of data</u>. Add the absolute deviations and divide by the number of data values in the set.

$$\frac{13 + 10 + 4 + 2 + 2 + 4 + 6 + 13}{8}$$

$$= \frac{54}{8} = 6.75 \qquad \text{number of scores}$$

Generally, Ann's quiz scores varied 6.75 points from the mean.

Independent Practice

For **6** through **11**, use the data set shown in the table.

6. What is the mean for the data set?

7. Give the absolute deviation from the mean for these values from the set:

   a 5   **b** 12   **c** 7

Miles Biked		
5	9	11
10	8	6
7	12	4

8. How would you find the mean absolute deviation for the data set?

9. What is the mean absolute deviation for the data set?

10. How would you find the interquartile range for the data set?

11. What is the interquartile range for the data set?

For **12** through **18**, use the data set shown in the table.

12. The data show low temperatures in °F for an 8-day period in January of a particular year in Chicago. What was the mean temperature for this period?

Low Temperatures (°F)			
11	17	20	16
19	16	15	22

13. What is the absolute deviation from the mean on the day when the temperature was 19°F?

14. Find the absolute deviation for each of the other temperatures. Which absolute deviation is farthest from the mean?

15. What is the mean absolute deviation?

16. What is the median temperature?

17. What was the first quartile? What is the third quartile?

18. Ken said the interquartile range for the temperatures was 11. Dina said it was 4. Which student was right? Explain.

19. Persevere Robert and his 8 friends were in a golf tournament. The table at the right shows the number of strokes that Robert and his friends had during the first round of the tournament. Create a box plot for the data. Then give the IQR.

Golf Scores

69	72	74
71	73	69
70	76	74

20. Use Tools Santos collected the following amounts for a school fund raiser on different days:

$18, $27, $33, $19, $41, $23, $29, $20

Find the mean of the amounts Santos collected. Then create a table showing the absolute deviations from the mean.

21. Writing to Explain Last year, Lorraine's average weekly paycheck was $400. This year her earnings vary each week. She wants to know how much 6 of her weekly paychecks vary from last year's average. What steps would Lorraine need to take to find the mean absolute deviation for her data?

22. Be Precise Juan's last eight math quiz scores were 78, 87, 85, 82, 92, 77, 99, and 88. What are the first and third quartiles for the scores in this data set? What is the interquartile range?

23. Reason Examine the data distributions:

2, 2, 3, 3, 4, 5, 7, 8, 11

2, 2, 3, 3, 3, 7, 8, 8, 9

Choose a measure of variability to describe each data set. Describe which is more variable.

For **24** and **25**, use the box plot below.

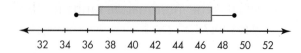

32 34 36 38 40 42 44 46 48 50 52

24. What is the IQR of the data?

A 5   **C** 14

B 10   **D** 37

25. Think of a question whose data could look like this box plot.

26. You are considering buying a new bike. The regular price for the Cyclone is $424.00. The bike shop is offering 25% off the regular price and will take another $15 off if you buy the bike this weekend. What will the bike cost after these discounts?

27. On opening night, 40% of the total number of people who went to a play, thought it was excellent. The rest thought it was either average or poor. If 60 people thought it was excellent, how many people went to the play?

Algebra Connections

Number Sequences

Remember that a numerical pattern is a sequence of numbers that occurs in some predictable way. Numerical patterns can be based on one or more operations.

For **1** through **6**, find a pattern and the next three numbers in each sequence, using that pattern.

> **Example:** Find a pattern and the next three numbers in the sequence 2, 3, 6, 7, 14, 15, 30, …
>
> **Think** $2 + 1 = 3, 3 \times 2 = 6, 6 + 1 = 7,$
> $7 \times 2 = 14, 14 + 1 = 15, 15 \times 2 = 30.$
>
> The pattern is add 1, multiply by 2. The next three numbers are 31, 62, 63.

1. 7, 15, 23, 31, 39, …

2. 50, 44, 38, 32, 26, …

3. 12, 22, 20, 30, 28, 38, 36, …

4. 65, 60, 63, 58, 61, 56, 59, …

5. 2, 4, 8, 16, 32, …

6. 3, 7, 15, 31, …

7. 1, 3, 6, 10, …
What is the 8th number in this pattern?

8. 75, 72, 69, 66, …
What is the 7th number in this pattern?

9. 1, 4, 9, 16, …
What is the nth number in this pattern?

10. The table shows the population for Green Mountain for 5 years. If this pattern in population growth continues, what will the population be in 2010?

Year	Population
2001	3,356
2002	3,399
2003	3,442
2004	3,485
2005	3,528

11. The table shows Jamie's savings account balances. If he continues his pattern of spending and saving, how much money will Jamie have in his bank on March 15?

Date	Amount
March 1	$15.00
March 2	$13.50
March 3	$18.50
March 4	$17.00
March 5	$22.00

12. Justyne sets her alarm clock for 5:45 A.M. on school days. Hitting "snooze" lets her sleep 3 more minutes before the alarm rings again. Today, Justyne hit "snooze" 4 times. What time did she finally wake up?

13. A train into the city stops 7 times. When the train starts, there are 35 passengers on board. At the first stop, 10 new passengers get on board. At the next stop, 6 passengers get off. This pattern continues all the way into the city. How many passengers are on the train when it arrives in the city?

Lesson
19-8

Common
Core

6.SP.5.d Summarize
numerical data sets in
relation to their context,
such as by relating the
choice of measures of center
and variability to the shape
of the data distribution and
the context in which the
data were gathered.
Also 6.SP.5

Appropriate Use of Statistical Measures

Which measure of center is most useful to describe a given situation?

Gary says he usually gets 98 on his weekly quiz. Does his statement accurately describe his overall performance? Justify your answer using measures of center.

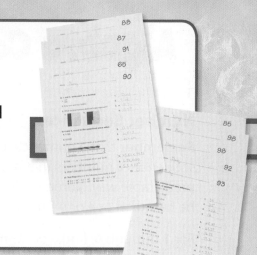

Other Examples

When describing the variability of a given situation, it is helpful to know which measure of variability to use.

Use the Interquartile Range

Use the interquartile range when the *median* is the appropriate measure of center.

In the example above involving Gary's quiz scores, the median is the appropriate measure of center, so it is better to use the IQR.

To find the IQR of Gary's quiz scores:
third quartile − first quartile = 93 − 87 = 6.

Half of Gary's quiz scores are between 87 and 93. This accurately describes the cluster of his scores.

Quiz Scores		
Gary		**Yoshi**
65		80
85		80
87		82
88		82
90		84
91		84
92		86
93		86
98		88
98		88

Use the Mean Absolute Deviation

Use the mean absolute deviation when the *mean* is the appropriate measure of center.

Since Yoshi's quiz scores are close together and symmetric, it makes sense to use the mean, 84, as the appropriate measure of center.

To find the mean absolute deviation of Yoshi's quiz scores:

$4 + 4 + 2 + 2 + 0 + 0 + 2 + 2 + 4 + 4 = 24$

$24 \div 10 = 2.4.$

Yoshi's quiz score is typically within 2.4 points of her mean score of 84.

Step 1

You can organize Gary's scores using a dot plot. Find the mean, median, mode, and outliers.

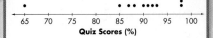

Quiz Scores (%)

Mean: 88.7; median: 90.5; mode: 98; 65 is an outlier.

Step 2

Look for clusters, gaps, and outliers to help you reason what the measures of center tell you about Gary's scores.

- The mode, 98, makes his typical score seem better than it really is.

- The mean, 88.7, is affected by the outlier. It makes his typical score seem lower than it really is.

- The median, 90.5, is in the middle of the cluster of his typical scores.

Step 3

Draw conclusions: Gary's statement is misleading.

The median, 90.5, best describes his performance.

It includes the outlier and falls within the cluster of his typical scores.

Guided Practice*

MATHEMATICAL PRACTICES

Do you know HOW?

Suppose that 5 different stores sell a quart of milk for one of the following prices:

$1.50, $1.55, $1.80, $1.70, $1.50

1. What is the median, mode, and mean?

2. Which measure of center best describes the data set? Why?

3. What is the mean absolute deviation of the data set rounded to the nearest cent?

Do you UNDERSTAND?

4. Should you use mean or median to describe the age of a typical sixth grader? What measure of variability?

5. In the example at the top, suppose the data set had only 3 values: 30, 98, and 90. Is the median the best measure of center for this data set? Explain.

6. **Reason** What does the mean absolute deviation you found in Exercise 3 tell you about the variability of the data set?

Independent Practice

For **7** through **12**, use the data in the chart.

7. Make a dot plot to organize the data set.

8. What are the mean, median, and mode of the data set?

9. Identify any outliers.

10. Which measure of center best describes the data set? Why?

11. What is the mean absolute deviation of the scores? Explain what this value tells you about the variability of the data set.

12. If a score of 30 is added to the data set, which measure of center would best describe the new set?

9 Game Scores		
50	60	100
65	50	55
65	70	50

Data

*For another example, see Set F on page 506.

The table shows the measures of center based on 5 data points in a set. Use the table for **13** through **17**.

	Mean	Median	Mode
Data	14,000	13,000	12,500

13. What is the middle number of the data set?

14. Which number occurs at least twice?

15. Why must the other two numbers in the data set be greater than 13,000?

16. What is a possible data set for these measures?

17. Which measure of center best describes the data set you wrote in Exercise 16? Why?

Problem Solving

MATHEMATICAL
PRACTICES

© **18. Model** A data set containing 3 values has a median of 100 and a mean of 120. It has no mode. If x and y are the two values other than the median, which equation best represents their value?

   A $(x + y) = 120$

   B $(x + y + 100) = 120$

   C $(x + y) = 120 + 100$

   D $(x + y + 100) \div 3 = 120$

© **19. Reason** Last month an automobile dealership sold 3,116 vehicles. Of these, 455 were trucks. Approximately what percent of the vehicles sold last month were trucks?

   A approximately 0.15%

   B approximately 4.55%

   C approximately 15%

   D approximately 455%

© **20. Writing to Explain** A data set contains the following values: 0, 1, 3, 5, 18.

   a What is the outlier in this data set?

   b Does the outlier affect the interquartile range? Does the outlier affect the mean absolute deviation? Explain your reasoning.

© **21. Be Precise** The table at the right shows 2 students' scores for their last 9 games bowled.

For the next meet, the coach needs to choose his top bowler. If the coach bases his decision on one of the following criteria, which player should he choose? In your answers, back up your decisions using measures of center and measures of variability.

   a Player with the best average.

   b Player who is most consistent.

Madison High School Bowling Team Individual Game Results	
Jessie	Sam
151	186
145	187
181	192
235	195
196	194
211	157
204	192
221	162
185	200

Mean, Median, Mode, and Range

Use **e tools**

Spreadsheet/Data/Grapher eTool

The heights in inches of the 12 members of the sixth-grade boys' basketball team at Jefferson Middle School are listed below. Find the mean, median, mode, and range of the data.

70, 60, 63, 65, 62, 61, 65, 64, 68, 65, 59, 62

Step 1 Go to the Spreadsheet/Data/Grapher eTool. Type the data in a column. Use the arrow tool to select the data. Click on the mean icon. The mean is 63.67. Click OK.

Step 2 Click on the median icon. The median is 63.5. Click OK.

Step 3 Click on the mode icon. The mode is 65. Click OK.

Step 4 Click on the sort data icon. The greatest number in the data is 70 and the least is 59. In column B, type = 70 − 59 and press Enter. The range is 11.

Practice

Find the mean, median, mode, and range of each set of data.

1. Heights in inches of the members of the girls' basketball team:
   60, 63, 56, 64, 63, 65, 62, 62, 59, 62

2. Points Tammy scored in each game:
   5, 4, 0, 2, 8, 4, 5, 1

3. Points scored by the team in each game:
   39, 53, 44, 36, 38, 39, 49, 51

Lesson
19-9

Common
Core

6.SP.5.c Summarize
numerical data sets in
relation to their context,
such as by giving
quantitative measures of
center (median and/or
mean) and variability
(interquartile range or mean
absolute deviation), as well
as describing any overall
pattern… with reference
to the context in which the
data were gathered.
Also 6.SP.5, 6.SP.5.a,
6.SP.5.b, 6.SP.5.d

Summarizing Data Distributions

How can a data set be summarized?

The fat content, in grams, was measured for one slice
($\frac{1}{6}$ pizza) of 24 different 12-inch pizzas. What
observations can be made about the fat content of
24 different slices of pizza?

? g fat

11 g	16 g	14 g	15 g	13 g	13 g	20 g	13 g
6 g	12 g	9 g	10 g	9 g	8 g	19 g	9 g
8 g	13 g	11 g	11 g	10 g	10 g	20 g	10 g

Guided Practice*

MATHEMATICAL
PRACTICES

Do you know HOW?

To measure the length of a shadow, five
different students used a measuring tape
marked in inches. Use the measurements
the students found for Exercises **1** through **6**.

38 in. $38\frac{1}{2}$ in. $37\frac{3}{4}$ in. 38 in. $38\frac{1}{4}$ in.

1. Find the mean and the median of the
   measurements.

2. Draw a box plot of the data.

3. Find the interquartile range.

Do you UNDERSTAND?

4. **Writing to Explain** Make a
   generalization about the data
   distribution of the shadow
   measurements.

5. **Critique Reasoning** A sixth student
   measured the length of the same
   shadow using a ruler and got 3 feet.
   Why is this result different?

6. If a seventh measurement of 30 inches
   is made of the same shadow, would it
   be preferable to use the mean or the
   median to describe the center of the
   new data?

Independent Practice

In **7** through **10**, use the data about home runs from the table below.

Number of Home Runs Hit by Players on My Team								
Player Number	1	2	3	4	5	6	7	8	9
Home Runs	23	9	12	22	7	11	9	10	9

7. Find the mean and the median.

8. Draw a box plot of the data.

9. Find the interquartile range.

10. Which would be the preferable measure
    of center, median or mean? Explain.

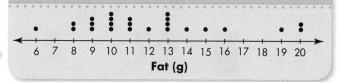

Fat Content of One Slice of Different 12-inch Pizzas

Fat (g)

The typical slice of pizza has a fat content of about 11 grams.

Half of the slices have fat content within an interval of 4 grams, between 9.5 and 13.5 grams of fat.

- Spread out to the right, not symmetric
- Small sample
  Use the median (11) to describe the center.
  Use the IQR (13.5 − 9.5 = 4) to describe the variability.

Problem Solving

MATHEMATICAL PRACTICES

For **11** through **13** use the data in the table below.

Rob conducted a salary survey of 10 adults. He recorded his data in the table below.

Adult	1	2	3	4	5	6	7	8	9	10
Salary	$35,000	$46,000	$38,000	$34,000	$52,000	$99,000	$64,000	$435,000	$22,000	$88,000

11. Make a box plot for the data. What are the median, first quartile, third quartile, and the interquartile range?

12. Make a dot plot of the data. Look at the shape of the distribution in the plot you made and describe it.

13. Writing to Explain Which would be the preferable measure of center, median or mean? Explain.

14. A data set includes 2, 7, 4, 6, 5, 7, 2, 3, 16, 3. What is the least value? The greatest value? Are there any outliers?

15. Five friends run a race and get the following times: Brad, 15 sec.; Tanya, 22 sec.; Amanda, 16 sec.; Autumn, 12 sec.; Kristen, 14 sec. Whose time is the median time for the race?

    A Tanya   **C** Amanda

    B Kristen   **D** Brad

16. Communicate Jill is taking a survey of some of her classmates to find the number of hours they spend studying per night. She asked 5 people. Her data are as follows: 0, 1, 5, 6, and 6. Which would be the preferable measure of center, median or mean? Explain.

17. Reason How do you know that any value of x will be a solution to the inequality $x + 1.6 > x$?

18. Model Write an inequality using addition and the variable y so that solutions to the inequality include $y = 0, 1, 2,$ and 3.

©
**Common
Core**

6.SP.3 Recognize that
a measure of center for
a numerical data set
summarizes all of its
values with a single
number, while a measure
of variation describes how
its values vary with a single
number.

Problem Solving

Try, Check, and Revise

A store sells 5 different kinds of milk
in gallon jugs. The mean price of a
gallon of milk is $3.29. No two prices
are the same. List 5 possible prices
for the gallons of milk. Make sure
that each price is a reasonable
price for a gallon of milk.

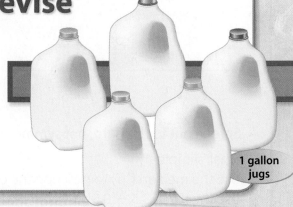

1 gallon
jugs

Guided Practice*

MATHEMATICAL
PRACTICES

Do you know **HOW?**

In **1** through **3**, find possible prices for
4 kinds of yogurt sold at a store.

1. What are 4 possible prices, if the
   mean price is $0.73?

2. What are 4 possible prices, if the
   median price is $0.75?

3. What are 4 possible prices, if the
   mode for the prices is $0.80?

Do you **UNDERSTAND?**

4. In the example above, what are
   5 possible prices for a gallon of milk
   if the median price is $3.29? if the
   mode is $3.29?

© 5. **Generalize** If 5 prices for a gallon
   of milk are *V*, *W*, *X*, *Y*, and *Z*, write an
   equation for the mean, $3.29.

Independent Practice

MATHEMATICAL
PRACTICES

Solve.

© 6. **Reason** An electronics store sells 3 kinds of printers.
   The mean price of a printer at the store is $150.
   What are possible prices for the 3 printers
   the store sells?

7. A bike shop sells 4 kinds of mountain bikes.
   The mean price of the bikes is $320, and the
   median price of the bikes is $325. What are
   possible prices for the 4 kinds of mountain bikes?

8. An office supply store sells 3 brands of paper.
   The mode and mean prices are both $2.29.
   What are possible prices for the 3 brands?

Applying Math Practices

- What am I asked to find?
- What else can I try?
- How are quantities related?
- How can I explain my work?
- How can I use math to model the
  problem?
- Can I use tools to help?
- Is my work precise?
- Why does this work?
- How can I generalize?

Use reasoning. Find 5 possible prices having a mean of $3.29.

Try these possible prices: $2.89, $2.99, $3.09, $3.29, $3.49

Check to see if the mean is equal to $3.29.

2.89 + 2.99 + 3.09 + 3.29 + 3.49 = 15.75

15.75 ÷ 5 = $3.15

The mean is too low, so you need to use higher prices.

Revise the prices using what you know. The mean was 14 cents too low.

Try adding 14 cents to each price: $3.03, $3.13, $3.23, $3.43, $3.63

Check to see if the mean equals $3.29.

3.03 + 3.13 + 3.23 + 3.43 + 3.63 = 16.45

16.45 ÷ 5 = $3.29

5 possible prices for the milk are $3.03, $3.13, $3.23, $3.43, and $3.63.

A table at a yard sale has 7 miscellaneous items for sale. For **9** through **11**, find possible prices for the items.

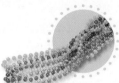
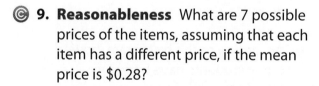

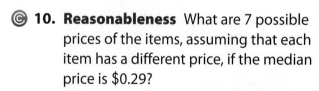

9. Reasonableness What are 7 possible prices of the items, assuming that each item has a different price, if the mean price is $0.28?

10. Reasonableness What are 7 possible prices of the items, assuming that each item has a different price, if the median price is $0.29?

11. What are 7 possible prices of the items, assuming that some of the items have the same price, if the mode of the prices is $0.27?

12. The mode of a set of 5 numbers is 57. What are 5 possible numbers in the set if the other numbers are less than the mode?

13. Be Precise The mean of a set of 5 positive numbers is 29. The median is 28. The mode is 33. What are 5 possible numbers?

14. The mean of a set of 3 numbers is 39. One of the numbers is 35. What are possible values of the 2 other numbers, assuming that all 3 numbers are different?

15. The scores on Briana's first 4 science exams gave her an average (mean) of 88. What are 4 possible scores she might have received?

16. Look for Patterns The mode of a set of 5 temperatures is positive and the median is negative. What are 5 possible temperatures of the data set?

1. The data below show amounts Kelly made babysitting each week for 7 weeks.

$16, $28, $28, $32, $21, $16, $35

Which of the following box plots shows the data? (19-6)

A

B

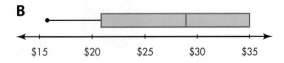

C

D

2. The years of experience for a group of dentists are listed below. Which measure of center best describes the data set? (19-8)

8, 6, 10, 7, 4, 4, 10, 35, 1, 5

A Mode

B Mean

C Median

D Outlier

3. According to the dot plot of the number of pets owned by sixth graders, which is the center of this data set? (19-2)

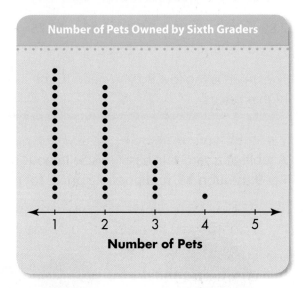

A 1 pet

B 2 pets

C 3 pets

D 4 pets

4. According to the histogram, how many students have between 8 and 15 absences? (19-5)

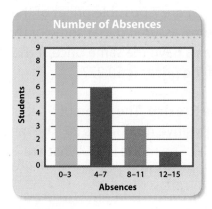

A 1 student

B 3 students

C 4 students

D 5 students

5. The mean price of a textbook is $82 and the range of prices is $16. What are possible prices for the textbook? (19-10)

  A $82, $82, $82, $82, $98

  B $90, $90, $74, $74, $74

  C $82, $82, $88, $76, $82

  D $82, $84, $90, $80, $74

6. Which of the following questions is a statistical question that could be asked to a group of students? (19-1)

  A How many different combinations of outfits can be made using 3 pairs of pants and 2 shirts?

  B What color is the shirt you are wearing?

  C What colors are the school's team uniforms?

  D How many tables are in the cafeteria?

7. How do you know this dot plot displays the answers to a statistical question? (19-1)

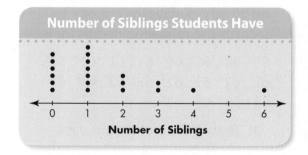

  A Various data are shown in the display.

  B Each data is the same number.

  C There is an outlier in the data.

  D Students were all asked the same question.

8. The ages of the people in a golf club are listed below. What is the mean age of the members? (19-3)

58, 62, 55, 61, 64

  A 61 years

  B 60 years

  C 59 years

  D 58 years

9. The eight home rooms in the school had the following distribution of students

28, 32, 33, 27, 30, 30, 29, 23

What is the mean absolute deviation for this data set? (19-7)

  A 2

  B 2.125

  C 2.25

  D 2.365

10. What is the interquartile range of data in the box plot below? (19-9)

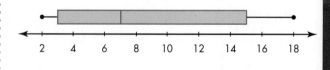

  A 12   **C** 7

  B 8   **D** 4

11. The ages of the girls in the dance recital are listed below. What are the median and mode of the ages? (19-4)

7, 6, 8, 6, 8, 7, 8, 7, 8, 6

  A 7, 6   **C** 6, 8

  B 7, 8   **D** 8, 8

Set A, pages 476–477

Ramon asked this question to his classmates, "How much time, to the nearest hour, do you spend online each week?"

His question anticipated a variety of answers from his classmates, so it is a statistical question.

Ramon surveyed his classmates and made this dot plot to display the answers. A dot plot displays numerical data. You can also tell from the data displayed, that Ramon's question is statistical.

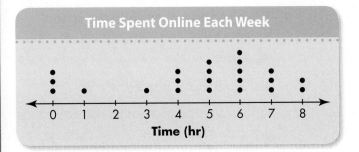

Remember that statistical questions anticipate that there will be different answers in the data.

For **1** through **3**, tell whether or not each question is statistical.

1. How many stations are there in a subway system?

2. How would passengers of a subway system rate the quality of service on a scale of 1 to 10?

3. How many passengers travel on each of the Green, Blue, Red, and Orange Lines of the subway system each day?

Set B, pages 478–479

We can describe a data distribution, or how data values are arranged, by looking at its overall shape, its center, and the least and greatest values.

The dot plot below shows 20 temperatures in °F taken during the month of September.

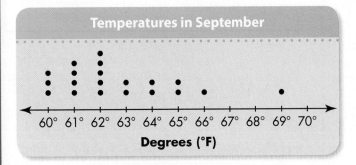

The data can be described as–

- Spread out to the right
- Least value: 60°F
- Greatest value: 69°F
- Center is about 62°F.

Remember that if the data is symmetric, both sides of the data from the mean will look the same.

Liam measures the temperatures on 20 school days in October. He records the following results in °F:

55°, 60°, 60°, 60°, 61°, 61°, 61°, 61°, 62°, 62°, 62°, 62°, 62°, 62°, 62°, 63°, 63°, 63°, 64°, 65°

1. Draw a dot plot for this data.

2. What is the greatest temperature in October? The least temperature?

3. Is the data symmetric or spread out to one side?

4. About where is the center of the data?

Find the mean, median, mode, and range of the following set of data.

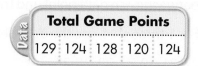

Total Game Points

129 124 128 120 124

The mean is the sum of all the data in a set divided by the total number of data values in the set. The mean is 125.

$$(129 + 124 + 128 + 120 + 124) \div 5 = 125$$

The median is the middle number in a data set that is arranged in numerical order.

120, 124, 124, 128, 129

The mode is the number that occurs most often. The mode is 124.

120, 124, 124, 128, 129

The range is the difference between the greatest number and least number in the data set.

$$129 - 120 = 9$$

Remember to order the data values from least to greatest before you begin. The mean, median, and mode are measures of center. A data set can have more than one mode or no mode. The range describes how spread out the data is.

For **1** through **5** find the mean, median, mode, and range of each data set.

1. 2, 5, 5

2. 11, 13, 11, 13

3. 27, 26, 25, 24

4. 100, 200, 500, 300, 500

5. 1.4, 1.3, 1.1, 1.4, 1.9, 1.8, 1.7, 1.4

6. Make up a data set of five numbers that have the same mean, median, and mode.

At a summer camp, the ages of the campers are listed below.

12, 14, 12, 14, 10, 11, 15, 13, 13, 11, 12, 12, 7, 14, 12

The data can be organized in a frequency table.

Divide the range of data into equal intervals and mark the frequency of the data using tally marks.

Ages of Campers	6–8	9–11	12–14	15–17
Tally	I	III	‖‖‖ ‖‖‖	I
Frequency	1	3	10	1

Remember that a histogram is a graph that uses bars to show the frequency of equal ranges or groups of data. It shows the shape of the data.

1. Represent the data in the frequency table on the left in a histogram.

2. Use your histogram in Exercise 1 to identify any clusters, gaps or outliers.

INTERVENTION

At 20 mph, seven top-selling cars have stopping distances of:

60 ft, 75 ft, 45 ft, 55 ft, 70 ft, 40 ft, and 65 ft.

To find the first quartile, order the numbers from least to greatest, find the median value, and then find the median of the numbers to the left of the median. Do the same for the third quartile by finding the median of the second half of numbers.

40 (45) 55 (60) 65 (70) 75

1ˢᵗ quartile Median 3ʳᵈ quartile

- The IQR = third quartile − first quartile: 70 − 45 = 25.
- Make a box plot. Show the minimum and maximum values, the median, and the first and third quartiles.

Stopping Distances of Top Selling Cars

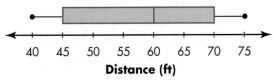

40   45   50   55   60   65   70   75
Distance (ft)

Remember that absolute deviation is the absolute value of the difference between each data point and the mean.

For **1** through **4**, use the data below.

27, 31, 30, 33, 29, 25, 28

1. Order the original data set from least to greatest and make a box plot.

2. What is the IQR?

3. What is the mean? What is absolute deviation from the mean for each data point?

4. What is the mean absolute deviation of the data?

Which measure of center and measure of variability best describe the data set?

Games Sold Each Week						
81	90	85	86	82	55	90

Find the mean, median, and mode of the number of games sold each week.

Mean: 81.3, Median: 85, and Mode: 90

Since most of the data clusters between 81 and 86, the mean is the best measure of center.

- Use the interquartile range when the median is the most appropriate measure of center. The IQR for this data set is 9.

- Use the mean absolute deviation when the mean is the most appropriate measure of center. The mean absolute deviation for this data set is 7.6.

Remember to use the IQR when the median is more appropriate and the mean absolute deviation when the mean is more appropriate.

For **1** through **3**, use the data below.

Home Runs Hit			
40	29	36	27
40	42	58	60

1. Find the mean, median, and mode of the number of home runs hit by 8 sluggers.

2. Which measure of center and measure of variability best describe the data set?

3. Does the data set contain any outliers? Explain.

You can summarize a data set by using mean or median for a measure of center, and by using a dot or box plot to find the shape of the data.

Make a box plot to show the data distribution for the rainfall in March over seven years.

3 in., 9 in., 14 in., 17 in., 19 in., 21 in., 24 in.

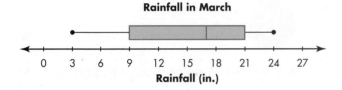

Rainfall in March

The typical rainfall in March is around 17 inches. Half of the March rainfall totals are between 9 and 21 inches.

The range of the March rainfalls is 21 inches.

Remember that you should use words and numbers that best describe the data set.

Dana listed all the fish (in inches) she caught this summer at the lake:

10 in., 12 in., 12 in., 13 in., 13 in., 14 in., 14 in., 15 in., 15 in., 16 in., 17 in., 18 in., 19 in., 20 in., 25 in.

1. Is the mean or the median more affected by the outlier, 25 inches?

2. What is the shape of the data?

3. Would a box plot or a dot plot better display this data? Draw both and compare.

4. Write two generalizations about the fish Dana caught. Use information from the plots you drew.

Four people on an elevator have a mean weight of 115 pounds. No one weighs the same. What are 4 possible weights for the people?

Try: 103, 108, 114, 123

Check: $\dfrac{(103 + 108 + 114 + 123)}{4} = 112$

Revise:

Try adding 3 pounds to each weight.

4 possible weights for the people are 106, 111, 117, and 126.

$$\dfrac{(106 + 111 + 117 + 126)}{4} = 115$$

Remember, it may take many repetitions of Try, Check, and Revise to solve a problem.

1. Four friends drank a pitcher of lemonade. No person drank the same amount. If the mean amount the 4 friends drank is 2.5 cups, what are 4 possible amounts the four friends drank?

2. If the mode for the amount 4 friends drank is 2 cups and the mean amount is 2.5 cups, what are 4 possible amounts?

Glossary

A

absolute deviation The distance between each data point and the mean.

absolute value The distance that an integer is from zero on the number line.

acute angle An angle with a measure between 0° and 90°.

acute triangle A triangle with three acute angles.

adjacent angles A pair of angles with a common vertex and a common side but no common interior points. *Example:* ∠RSP and ∠PST

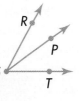

algebraic expression A mathematical phrase that has at least one variable and one operation. *Example:* $10 \times n$ or $10n$

angle Two rays with the same endpoint.

angle bisector A ray that divides an angle into two adjacent angles that are congruent.

arc A part of a circle connecting two points on the circle. *Example:*

area The number of square units needed to cover a surface or figure.

associative properties Properties that state the way in which addends or factors are grouped does not affect the sum or product.

average The sum of the values in a data set divided by the number of data values in the set. Also called the *mean*.

axis (*pl.* axes) Either of two lines drawn perpendicular to each other in a graph.

B

bar graph A graph that uses bars to show and compare data.

base (in geometry) A designated side of a polygon to which the height is drawn perpendicular; one of the two parallel and congruent faces on a prism; a particular flat surface of a solid, such as a cylinder or cone.

base (in numeration) A number multiplied by itself the number of times shown by an exponent. *Example:* $4 \times 4 \times 4 = 4^3$, where 4 is the base.

benchmark fraction Common fractions used for estimating, such as $\frac{1}{4}, \frac{1}{3}, \frac{1}{2}, \frac{2}{3}$, and $\frac{3}{4}$.

box plot A diagram that shows a distribution of data values on a number line.

break apart Using the Distributive Property to compute mentally.

C

capacity The volume of a container measured in liquid units.

categorical data Data that is grouped by some common property.

Celsius (°C) A metric unit for measuring temperature.

center (in geometry) The interior point from which all points of a circle are equally distant.

center (in statistics) The part of a data set where the middle values are concentrated.

centi- Prefix meaning $\frac{1}{100}$.

central angle An angle with its vertex at the center of a circle. *Example:*

chord A line segment with both endpoints on a circle.

circle A closed plane figure with all points the same distance from a given point called the center.

circle graph A graph that represents a total divided into parts.

circumference The distance around a circle.

cluster An interval with a greater frequency compared to the rest of the data set.

coefficient The number that is multiplied by a variable in an algebraic expression. *Example:* For $6x + 5$, the coefficient is 6.

common denominator A denominator that is the same in two or more fractions.

common factor A factor that is the same for two or more numbers.

common multiple A multiple that is the same for two or more numbers.

commutative properties The properties that state the order of addends or the order of factors does not affect the sum or product.

compatible numbers Numbers that are easy to compute mentally.

compensation Choosing numbers close to the numbers in a problem, and then adjusting the answer to compensate for the numbers chosen.

complementary angles Two angles with measures that add up to 90°.

composite number A natural number greater than one that has more than two factors.

cone A three-dimensional figure that has one circular base. The points on this circle are joined to one point outside the base.

congruent angles Angles having the same measure.

congruent figures Figures that have the same size and shape.

congruent line segments Line segments that are the same length.

conjecture A generalization that you think is true.

construction A geometric drawing that uses a limited set of tools, usually a compass and a straightedge.

coordinate plane A two-dimensional system in which a location is described by its distances from two perpendicular number lines called the *x*-axis and the *y*-axis.

cubic unit A unit measuring volume, consisting of a cube with edges one unit long.

cylinder A three-dimensional figure that has two circular bases which are parallel and congruent. *Example:*

data Information that is gathered.

data distribution How data values are arranged.

decagon A polygon with ten sides.

decimal A number with one or more digits to the right of the decimal point.

degree (°) A unit for measuring angles or temperatures.

denominator The number below the fraction bar in a fraction; the total number of equal parts in all.

dependent variable One of two variables in a relationship whose value is determined by the value used for the other variable, the independent variable.

diagonal A line segment that connects two vertices of a polygon and is not a side. *Example:*

diameter A line segment that passes through the center of a circle and has both endpoints on the circle. *Example:*

discount The amount by which the regular price of an item is reduced.

Distributive Property Multiplying a sum by a number produces the same result as multiplying each addend by the number and adding the products.
Example: $2 \times (3 + 4) = (2 \times 3) + (2 \times 4)$

dividend The number being divided by another number. *Example:* In $12 \div 3$, 12 is the dividend.

divisible A number is divisible by another number if its quotient is a whole number and the remainder is zero.

divisor The number used to divide another number. *Example:* In $12 \div 3$, 3 is the divisor.

dot plot A display of data values where each data value is shown as a dot above a number line.

edge The line segment where two faces of a polyhedron meet.

elapsed time Total amount of time that passes from the beginning time to the ending time.

equation A mathematical sentence stating that two expressions are equal.

equilateral triangle A triangle with three sides of the same length.

equivalent fractions Fractions that name the same amount.

estimate To find a number that is close to an exact answer.

evaluate To find a value that an algebraic expression names by replacing a variable with a given value. *Example:* Evaluate $2n + 5$ when $n = 3$; $2(3) + 5 = 11$.

expanded form A number written as the sum of the place values of its digits.

expanded form using exponents A number written in expanded form with the place values written in exponential form. *Example:* $3{,}246 = (3 \times 10^3) + (2 \times 10^2) + (4 \times 10^1) + (6 \times 10^0)$

exponent The number that tells how many times the base is being multiplied by itself. *Example:* $8^3 = 8 \times 8 \times 8$, where 3 is the exponent and 8 is the base.

exponential form A way of writing repeated multiplication of a number using exponents. *Example:* 2^5

expression A mathematical phrase containing variables or constants and operations. *Example:* $12 - x$

face A flat surface of a polyhedron.

factor A number that divides another number without a remainder.

Fahrenheit (°F) A standard unit for measuring temperature.

formula A rule that uses symbols to relate two or more quantities.

fraction A number that can be used to describe a part of a whole, a part of a set, a location on a number line, or a division of whole numbers.

frequency table A table which shows the number of times a data value or range of values occurs in a data set.

gap An interval with a lesser frequency compared to the rest of the data set.

glide reflection The change in the position of a figure that moves it by a translation followed by a reflection.

gram (g) Metric unit of mass.

greatest common factor (GCF) The largest number that is a factor of two or more numbers.

height The segment from a vertex perpendicular to the line containing the opposite side; the perpendicular distance between the bases of a solid.

heptagon A polygon with seven sides.

hexagon A polygon with six sides.

histogram A graph that uses bars to show the frequency of equal ranges or groups of data.

identity properties The properties that state the sum of any number and zero is that number and the product of any number and one is that number.

improper fraction A fraction in which the numerator is greater than or equal to its denominator.

independent variable One of two variables in a relationship. Any value can be used for the independent variable. The value that is used determines the value of the other variable, the dependent variable.

inequality A statement that contains > (greater than), < (less than), ≥ (greater than or equal to), or ≤ (less than or equal to) to compare two expressions.

input/output table A table of related values.

integers The counting numbers, their opposites, and zero.

interquartile range (IQR) A measure of variability that is the difference between the third quartile and the first quartile.

intersecting lines Lines that have exactly one point in common. *Example:*

interval A range of numbers used to represent data.

inverse relationships Relationships between operations that "undo" each other, such as addition and subtraction, or multiplication and division (except multiplication or division by 0).

isosceles triangle A triangle with at least two congruent sides.

kilo- Prefix meaning 1,000.

least common denominator (LCD) The least common multiple of the denominators of two or more fractions. *Example:* 12 is the LCD of $\frac{1}{4}$ and $\frac{1}{6}$.

least common multiple (LCM) The least number, other than zero, that is a multiple of two or more numbers.

like denominators Denominators in two or more fractions that are the same.

line A straight path of points that goes on forever in two directions.

line of symmetry A line on which a figure can be folded into two congruent parts.

line plot A display of data values where each data value is shown as a mark above a number line.

line segment Part of a line that has two endpoints.

linear equation An equation whose graph is a straight line.

liter (L) Metric unit of capacity.

mass Measure of the amount of matter of an object.

maximum The greatest data value in a data set.

mean The sum of the values in a data set divided by the number of values in the set. Also called the *average*.

mean absolute deviation The mean of the absolute deviations of a set of data.

measure of center A single number that summarizes the center of a data set. *Example:* mean

measure of variability A single number that summarizes the variability of a data set. *Example:* interquartile range

median The middle data value in a data set.

meter (m) Metric unit of length.

metric system (of measurement) A system using decimals and powers of 10 to measure length, mass, and capacity.

midpoint The point that divides a segment into two segments of equal length.

milli- Prefix meaning $\frac{1}{1000}$.

minimum The least data value in a data set.

mixed number A number that combines a whole number and a fraction.

mode The data value that occurs most often in a data set.

multiple The product of a number and a whole number greater than zero.

net A plane figure pattern which, when folded, makes a solid.

nonagon A polygon with nine sides.

numerator The number above the fraction bar in a fraction; the number of objects or equal parts being considered.

numerical data Data where each value is a number.

obtuse angle An angle with a measure between 90° and 180°.

obtuse triangle A triangle with an obtuse angle.

octagon A polygon with eight sides.

opposites The integer on the opposite side of zero from a given number, but at the same distance from zero. *Example:* 7 and −7 are opposites.

order of operations A set of rules mathematicians use to determine the order in which operations are performed.

ordered pair A pair of numbers (x, y) used to locate a point on a coordinate plane.

origin The point (0, 0), where the x- and y-axes of a coordinate plane intersect.

outlier An extreme value with few data points located near it.

parallel lines Lines in the same plane that do not intersect.

parallelogram A quadrilateral with both pairs of opposite sides parallel.

pentagon A polygon with five sides.

percent A ratio where the first term is compared to 100.

perimeter Distance around a figure.

perpendicular bisector A line, ray, or segment that intersects a segment at its midpoint and is perpendicular to it. *Example:*

perpendicular lines Intersecting lines that form right angles.

pi (π) The ratio of the circumference of a circle to its diameter. Pi is approximately 3.14 or $\frac{22}{7}$.

plane A flat surface that extends forever in all directions.

point An exact location in space.

polygon A closed plane figure made up of three or more line segments.

polyhedron A three-dimensional figure made of flat surfaces that are polygons.

power The number of times a base number is multiplied by itself.

prime factorization The set of primes whose product is a given composite. *Example:* $60 = 2^2 \times 3 \times 5$

prime number A whole number greater than 1 with exactly two factors, 1 and itself.

prism A polyhedron with two congruent and parallel polygon-shaped faces. *Examples:*

proper fraction A fraction less than 1; its numerator is less than its denominator.

properties of equality Properties that state performing the same operation to both sides of an equation keeps the equation balanced.

proportion A statement that two ratios are equal.

pyramid A polyhedron whose base can be any polygon and whose faces are triangles. *Examples:*

quadrant One of the four regions into which the x- and y-axes divide the coordinate plane. The axes are not parts of the quadrant.

quadrilateral A polygon with four sides.

quartiles Values that divide a data set into four equal parts.

quotient The answer in a division problem. *Example:* In $45 \div 9 = 5$, 5 is the quotient.

radius Any line segment that connects the center of the circle to a point on the circle. *Example:*

range The difference between the greatest and least numbers in a data set.

rate A ratio that compares two quantities with different units of measure.

ratio A relationship where for every *x* units of one quantity there are *y* units of another quantity.

rational number Any number that can be written as a quotient $\frac{a}{b}$, where *a* and *b* are integers and $b \neq 0$.

ray Part of a line with one endpoint, extending forever in only one direction.

reciprocals Two numbers whose product is one. *Example:* The reciprocal of $\frac{3}{4}$ is $\frac{4}{3}$ because $\frac{3}{4} \times \frac{4}{3} = 1$.

rectangle A parallelogram with four right angles.

reflection The change in the position of a figure that gives a mirror image over a line.

reflection symmetry Property of a figure that can be reflected onto itself.

regular polygon A polygon that has sides of equal length and angles of equal measure.

repeating decimal A decimal in which a digit or digits repeat endlessly.

rhombus A parallelogram with all four sides congruent.

right angle An angle which measures 90°.

right triangle A triangle with one right angle.

rotation The change in the position of a figure that moved it around a point.

rotational symmetry Property of a figure that rotates onto itself in less than a full turn.

round To give an approximation for a number to the nearest one, ten, hundred, thousand, or other place value.

scale The ratio of the measurements in a drawing to the actual measurements of the object.

scale drawing A drawing made so that distances in the drawing are proportional to actual distances.

scalene triangle A triangle with no congruent sides.

sector A region bounded by two radii and an arc. *Example:*

semicircle An arc that connects the endpoints of a diameter.

side A segment used to form a polygon; a ray used to form an angle.

simplest form A fraction for which the greatest common factor of the numerator and denominator is 1.

sphere A three-dimensional figure such that every point is the same distance from the center. *Example:*

square A rectangle with all sides congruent.

squared When a number has been multiplied by itself.
Example: 5 squared = 5^2 = 5 × 5 = 25

statistical question A question which anticipates that there will be different answers in the data.

straight angle An angle which measures 180°.

substitution The replacement of the variable of an expression with a number.

supplementary angles Two angles with measures that add up to 180°.

surface area (SA) The sum of the areas of each face of a polyhedron.

symmetric data Data which is distributed evenly on both sides of the center.

T-table A table of x- and y-values used to graph an equation.

terminating decimal A decimal with a finite number of digits.
Example: 0.375

terms The quantities x and y in a ratio.

transformation A move such as a translation, reflection, or rotation that moves a figure to a new position without changing its size or shape.

translation The change in the position of a figure that moves it up, down, or sideways in a straight direction.

trapezoid A quadrilateral with only one pair of opposite sides parallel.

tree diagram A diagram used to find the prime factorization of a composite number.

triangle A polygon with three sides.

trillions A place value or period of place values for numbers greater than billions.

unit rate A rate in which the comparison is to one unit. *Example:* 25 feet per second

unlike denominators Denominators in two or more fractions that are different.

variability A measure of how a data set is spread, and what clusters and gaps the data set has.

variable A quantity that changes or varies, often represented with a letter.

vertex (in an angle) The common endpoint of two rays that form an angle.

vertex (in a polygon) The point of intersection of two sides of a polygon.

vertex (in a polyhedron) The point of intersection of the edges of a polyhedron.

vertical angles A pair of angles formed by intersecting lines, the angles have no side in common. Vertical angles are congruent. *Example:*

volume The number of cubic units needed to fill a solid figure.

x-axis The horizontal line on a coordinate plane.

x-coordinate The first number in an ordered pair that tells the position left or right of the *y*-axis.

y-axis The vertical line on a coordinate plane.

y-coordinate The second number in an ordered pair that tells the position above or below the *x*-axis.

Illustrations
326, 330, 476 Rob Schuster.

Photographs
Every effort has been made to secure permission and provide appropriate credit for photographic material. The publisher deeply regrets any omission and pledges to correct errors called to its attention in subsequent editions.

Unless otherwise acknowledged, all photographs are the property of Pearson Education, Inc.

Photo locators denoted as follows: Top (T), Center (C), Bottom (B), Left (L), Right (R), Background (Bkgd)

Cover
Luciana Navarro Powell

2 (Bkgrd) Digital Vision/Thinkstock, (T) Nick Galante/PMRF/NASA; **3** (TL) Vaclav Janousek/Fotolia; **6** (CR) Vaclav Janousek/Fotolia; **9** (BC) Nick Galante/PMRF/NASA, (BL) scoutingstock/Fotolia; **20** (TR) Comstock Images/Thinkstock; **30** (Bkgrd) Caleb Foster/Fotolia, (BL) Fotographix/Fotolia; **31** (TL) Digital Vision/Thinkstock, (BL) Lightvision/Fotolia; **44** (BR) Caleb Foster/Fotolia; **60** (T) 2010 /Photos to Go/Photolibrary, (BL) Getty Images/Thinkstock, (BR) Jupiter Images; **61** (BL) jupiterimages/Thinkstock; **68** (CR) Jupiter Images; **94** (Bkgrd) Getty Images/Ablestock/Thinkstock; **95** (TL) Comstock Images/Thinkstock; **100** (CR) Getty Images/Ablestock/Thinkstock; **118** (TR) Getty Images, (L) Tom Brakefield/Thinkstock; **119** (BL) Beboy/Fotolia, (TL) Joseph Dudash/Fotolia; **135** (TR) Getty Images; **142** (TL) 2010 / Photos to Go/Photolibrary, (B) Clément Bille/Fotolia, (Bkgrd) Medioimages/Photodisc/Thinkstock; **143** (R) 2011/Photos to Go/Photolibrary; **146** mendogyal/Fotolia; **149** (BC) 2010 /Photos to Go/Photolibrary; **160** (Bkgrd) Comstock/Thinkstock, (L) Elena Moiseeva/Fotolia, (TR) John Gourlay/Fotolia; **161** (TL) seraphic06/Fotolia; **184** (TL, Bkgrd) Getty Images/Jupiterimages/Thinkstock; **185** (L) Getty Images; **200** (TL) hotshotsworldwide/Fotolia, (Bkgrd) NASA; **201** (CL) Fotolia, Igor Kaliuzhnyi/Fotolia; **205** (CR) hotshotsworldwide/Fotolia, (CL, C) Jupiter Images; **213** (BR) NASA/Thinkstock; **220** (Bkgrd) Comstock Images/Jupiter Images, (TL) Goinyk Volodymyr/Fotolia, (TR) Nicola_G/Fotolia; **221** (TL) Karen Struthers/Fotolia; **223** (BR) ©Royalty-Free/Corbis, (CR) 2010 /Photos to Go/Photolibrary, (CR) Nicola_G/Fotolia, (BR) Sebastian French/Fotolia; **245** (CR) Getty Images/Ablestock/Thinkstock; **249** (TR) mihail1981/Fotolia; **260** (TL) Stockbyte/Thinkstock, (BL) 2010/Photos to Go/Photolibrary, (Bkgrd) Creatas /Jupiter Images, (CL) Getty Images/Jupiterimages/Thinkstock; **276** (BR) 2010/Photos to Go/Photolibrary; **283** (BR) NASA/ESA/HST Moon Team/NASA; **287** (BC) Fandorina Liza/Fotolia, (BR) Joe Gough/Fotolia, (BL) Richard Blaker/Fotolia; **289** (B) Stockbyte/Thinkstock; **298** (Bkgrd) Getty Images, (TR) Jose Gil/Fotolia; **299** (BL) 2010/Photos to Go/Photolibrary, (TL) Dmitry Nikolaev, (BL) radarreklama/Fotolia; **304** (BR) radarreklama/Fotolia; **312** (BR) Dmitry Nikolaev; **320** (Bkgrd) Getty Images/Thinkstock, (TR) Liquidlibrary/Thinkstock, (CL) Photos to Go/Photolibrary; **321** (TR) PhotoDisc/Thinkstock; **337** (TL) Julia Chernikova/Fotolia; **342** (Bkgrd) Colette/Fotolia, (TR) Getty Imagesimages/Thinkstock; **343** (BL) EastWest Imaging, (TL) Jupiter Images; **351** (BR) Colette/Fotolia, (BR) Jeffrey Kraker/Fotolia; **356** (CR) Tom Brakefield/Thinkstock; **370** Stockbyte/Getty Images, (B) Comstock/Thinkstock; **371** (BL) Getty Images/Thinkstock, (TL) Goran Bogicevic/Fotolia; **379** (BR) Goran Bogicevic/Fotolia; **384** (CR) Stockbyte/Getty Images; **398** (B) Christopher Dodge, (TR) dbvirago/Fotolia; **399** (BL) Getty Images/Hamera Technologies/Thinkstock; **406** (TR) Getty Images/Hamera Technologies/Thinkstock; **424** (B) ©Tomas Kopecny/Alamy, (TR) Getty Images, (L) Getty Images/Jupiterimages/Thinkstock; **425** (TL) Digital Vision/Thinkstock; **433** (BR) ©Tomas Kopecny/Alamy; **436** (BR) Getty Images; **441** (CR) Getty Images/Hamera Technologies/Thinkstock, (CR) Vladimir Wrangel/Fotolia; **442** (BC) Getty Images, (BR) Getty Images/Hamera Technologies/Thinkstock, (BL) Image Source/Getty Images; **452** (BL) ©Brian Hagiwara/Jupiter Images, (C) Marco Regalia/Fotolia; **453** (TL) Getty Images, (BL) NASA; **457** (BR) NASA; **465** (BR) Getty Images; **474** (TL) Caitlin Mirra/Shutterstock, (B) Photos to Go/Photolibrary; **475** (L) Photos/Thinkstock; **498** (T) Africa Studio/Shutterstock.

Index

A

Absolute deviation, 491

Absolute value, 223, 242–244

Act It Out strategy, 390–391

Acute angles, 266–267

Acute triangles, 275

Addend, 221

Addition
Addition Property of Equality, 96, 372
associative properties, 35, 42
commutative properties, 34, 42
decimals and, 64–65
estimation and, 62–63, 170–171
fractions, 162–163, 166–168
identity properties, 35
integers, 230–232, 233
mixed numbers, 172–173
solving equations and, 98–100, 105

Addition Property of Equality, 96, 372

Adjacent angles, 270, 283

Algebra Connections
Comparing Line Graphs, 487
Completing Tables, 131
Equation Sense: Estimate the Solution, 375
Equations with Fractions, 169
Equations with Percents, 361
Is It a Function?, 461
Perimeters of Similar Figures, 429
Number Sequences, 493
Solution Pairs, 13
True or False?, 73
What's the Rule?, 153

Algebraic expressions, 31, 33
describing patterns and, 48–49
evaluating, 46–47
variables in, 73
writing, 32–33

Angle bisectors, 269

Angle pairs, 270–272

Angles, 261
angle bisectors, 269
angle pairs, 270–272
central angles, 283
measuring and drawing angles, 266–268
right angles, 266–268
supplementary and complementary angles, 270–273
triangles, 274–276

Arcs, 269, 283

Area, 430, 453
of circles, 442–443, 447
of irregular figures, 430–433
of parallelograms, 434–436
of rectangles, 333, 430–433
surface area, 458–460
of trapezoids, 437
of triangles, 434–436

Array, 119

Art, 277, 407

Assessment
Review What You Know!, 3, 31, 61, 95, 119, 143, 161, 185, 201, 221, 261, 299, 321, 343, 371, 399, 425, 453, 475
Stop and Practice, 53, 87, 113, 253, 469
Topic Tests, 26–27, 54–55, 88–89, 114–115, 138–139, 156–157, 180–181, 196–197, 216–217, 254–255, 292–293, 316–317, 338–339, 364–365, 392–393, 420–421, 448–449, 470–471, 502–503

Associative properties
addition, 35, 42
multiplication, 35, 42

Associative Property of Addition, 35

Associative Property of Multiplication, 35

Averages, 475, 480–481

Axis (pl. axes)
x-axis, 246
y-axis, 246

B

Balance, equations and, 96–97, 98–100

Bar diagrams, 327

Bar graphs, 477, 484–486

Bases, 11
cones, 454
cylinders, 454
exponential forms and, 11
parallelograms, 434–435
prisms, 455
pyramids, 455

Benchmark fractions, 352–355

Box plots, 488–489, 498

Brackets, evaluating expressions, 80–81

Breaking apart, mental math and, 41, 42–43

Faces, 454–456

Factors, 119, 120–122
  Greatest Common Factor (GCF), 126–127, 161, 185
  prime, 124–125

Factor trees, 124, 126, 164

Feet, 400–401

Formulas, 310
  area, 430–433, 434–436
  circumference, 438–440
  distance, rate, and time, 310–311, 313
  perimeter, 426–427
  volume, 462–463, 464–465

Fractional edge lengths, 464–465

Fractions, 119, 128–130, 143, 299, 343
  addition, 162–163, 166–168
  and decimals, 146–147, 185
  decimals and percent, 348–349
  decimal forms of, 150–152, 229
  division, 144–145, 202–203, 204–205, 206–207
  equations with, 169
  equivalent fractions, 132–133, 143, 161
  estimating products, 188–189
  improper fractions, 148–149
  multiplication, 186–187, 190–191
  proper fractions, 149
  simplest form of, 134–135, 143
  simplifying fractions, 143, 321
  solving equations, 212–213
  subtraction, 162–163, 166–168

Fraction strips, 132

Frequency tables, 484–486

Functions, 461

Gallons, 400–401

Geometry, 425
  angle bisectors, 269
  angle pairs, 270–272
  area of circles, 442–443
  area of parallelograms and triangles, 434–436
  area of rectangles and irregular figures, 430–433
  area of trapezoids, 437
  basic geometric ideas, 262–264
  circles, 282–283
  circumference, 438–440
  congruence, 284–286
  measuring and drawing angles, 266–268
  perimeter, 426–428, 429
  perpendicular bisectors, 265
  polygons, 290–291
  quadrilaterals, 278–281
  supplementary and complementary angles, 270–273
  symmetry, 288–289
  tangrams, 277
  tessellations, 287
  transformations, 284–286
  triangles, 274–276

Geometry Drawing, 273, 333, 447

Glide reflection, 284

Going Digital. *See* Digital Resources.

Grams, 404

Graphs and graphing
  bar graphs, 475, 477, 484–486
  box plots, 488–489, 498
  circle graphs, 348, 352, 354
  dot plots, 476–477, 478–479, 499
  equations, 380–385
  histograms, 484–486
  line graphs, 475, 487

points of a coordinate plane, 246–248
ratios and, 330–332

Greatest Common Factor (GCF), 126–127, 135, 161, 185

Hands-On
  fraction strips, 132
  grid paper, 444
  metric rulers, 408
  protractors, 266–267, 278
  unit cubes, 466–467

Histograms, 484–486

Identity properties
  addition, 35
  multiplication, 35

Identity Property of Addition, 35

Identity Property of Multiplication, 35

Improper fractions, 148–149, 161

Independent variables, 382

Inequalities, 82–83, 386–388, 389

Input/output tables, 48–49

Integers, 222–223
  absolute value, 223
  addition, 230–232, 233
  comparing and ordering, 224–225
  division, 240–241
  multiplication, 238–239, 240–241
  subtraction, 234–236